Praise for

STATISTICS With R
Solving Problems Using Real-World Data
Jenine K. Harris

"A UNIQUE introduction to statistics using characters in a storyline who are themselves learning how to solve REAL CASE STUDIES using the R programming language. The first statistics textbook of its kind!"

—Patrick Bolger
Department of Psychology
Texas A&M University

"*Statistics With R* is easily the MOST ACCESSIBLE and almost FUN introduction to statistics and R that I have read. Even the most hesitant student is likely to embrace the material with this text."

—David A. M. Peterson
Department of Political Science
Iowa State University

"This is an ENTERTAINING and UNORTHODOX text that explains statistical concepts in a way that engages students and rewards them for achievements. As useful to instructors as it is to their students."

—Matthew Phillips
Department of Criminal Justice
University of North Carolina at Charlotte

"This text makes the R statistics software accessible to all students by providing EXCELLENT EXAMPLES and step-by-step processes. The student gains mastery over statistical analysis that can be applied to the real world."

—Mary A. Moore
Department of Healthcare Administration
Colorado State University

"This is a WONDERFUL, INNOVATIVE statistics text that integrates R coding into learning about quantitative methods. The HIGHLY ENGAGING lessons walk students through each stage of the analytical process and teach students how to perform a statistical analysis, including the presentation of results in graphical form, using code."

—Jennifer Bachner
Center for Advanced Governmental Studies
Johns Hopkins University

Statistics With R

Statistics With R

Solving Problems Using Real-World Data

Jenine K. Harris
Washington University in St. Louis

Los Angeles | London | New Delhi
Singapore | Washington DC | Melbourne

FOR INFORMATION:

SAGE Publications, Inc.

2455 Teller Road

Thousand Oaks, California 91320

E-mail: order@sagepub.com

SAGE Publications Ltd.

1 Oliver's Yard

55 City Road

London EC1Y 1SP

United Kingdom

SAGE Publications India Pvt. Ltd.

B 1/l 1 Mohan Cooperative Industrial Area

Mathura Road, New Delhi 110 044

India

SAGE Publications Asia-Pacific Pte. Ltd.

18 Cross Street #10-10/11/12

China Square Central

Singapore 048423

Printed in Canada

Library of Congress Cataloging-in-Publication Data

Names: Harris, Jenine K., author.

Title: Statistics with R : solving problems using real-world data / Jenine K. Harris.

Description: Los Angeles : SAGE, [2021] | Includes bibliographical references and index.

Identifiers: LCCN 2019034537 | ISBN 9781506388151 (paperback ; alk. paper) | ISBN 9781506388137 (epub) | ISBN 9781506388144 (epub) | ISBN 9781506388168 (pdf)

Subjects: LCSH: Social sciences—Statistical methods—Data processing. | Social sciences—Statistical methods. | R (Computer program language)

Classification: LCC HA32 .H37 2021 | DDC 519.50285/5133—dc23

LC record available at https://lccn.loc.gov/2019034537

Acquisitions Editor: Helen Salmon

Editorial Assistant: Megan O'Heffernan

Content Development Editor: Chelsea Neve

Production Editor: Laureen Gleason

Copy Editor: Liann Lech

Typesetter: C&M Digitals (P) Ltd.

Proofreader: Scott Oney

Indexer: Beth Nauman-Montana

Cover Designer: Rose Storey

Marketing Manager: Shari Countryman

This book is printed on acid-free paper.

20 21 22 23 24 10 9 8 7 6 5 4 3 2 1

/// BRIEF CONTENTS

/// DETAILED CONTENTS

1 The goals of this book

The main goal of this book is to prepare students and other readers for the messy and exciting reality of working with data. As data on many aspects of life accumulate at unprecedented rates, there is an increasing need for people who can clean, manage, and analyze information. Secondarily, the book aims to encourage women and other underrepresented groups to consider data science careers. Representation of women has decreased in computer science and math fields since 2006, and gaps persist in data science fields by race and ethnicity, limiting the perspectives contributing to the growth of this field. Finally, this book aims to improve the quality of social science through the promotion of reproducible research practices. Science has been increasingly under scrutiny for use of questionable research practices, some of which can be overcome through well-formatted and documented code for data importing, cleaning, and analysis.

To reach all three of these goals, I employed several strategies, such as a narrative writing style, diversity in the main and supporting characters, a focus on social problems, use of publicly available data and open-source R statistical software, and demonstrations of reproducible research practices.

2 The audience for the book

This book was written with first-year statistics courses in the social sciences in mind. Often, these courses start with descriptive statistics and probability theory and continue through general and generalized linear modeling. Others who may find this book useful include people working with data who are interested in learning R for the first time, learning more R, or reinforcing and improving their statistical skills. General readers interested in data science might find this book to be an accessible introduction to one of the primary software packages and many of the foundational concepts used in data science.

3 The features of the book

3.1 A NARRATIVE APPROACH

The book includes an underlying storyline about three characters working together to learn statistics and R: Nancy, Kiara, and Leslie. Nancy and Kiara are data scientists, and Leslie is a student. The first chapter describes their initial meeting at an R-Ladies community event where they discuss the benefits and challenges of using R and decide to work together to learn R and statistics. The remaining chapters each start in a different setting with a conversation between the three introducing the statistical method of the chapter and the social problem they will address while learning the method. The use of narrative serves at least two purposes. The first purpose is to provide an accessible and relatable way to introduce statistical topics that are often perceived as some combination of difficult and boring. Students start by reading a casual conversation among friends that gently transitions into more technical concerns. The second purpose is to show women in the roles of experts and learners of coding and statistics. Through dialogue, character development, and images, I portray scenarios of women collaborating to learn and apply data management and analysis skills to important social issues.

Each of the three main characters has expertise or interest in a different aspect of learning and applying R code and statistical concepts. Their expertise and interests are highlighted in three different types of boxed features that appear throughout the chapters:

- **Nancy's Fancy Code:** Nancy is interested in writing code and has expertise in more advanced or quirky R coding, which she shares with the other characters in this feature.

- **Kiara's Reproducibility Resource:** Kiara is interested in improving data science by ensuring her work and the work of her colleagues is reproducible through the use of good coding practice; she shares tips for improving reproducibility in this feature.

- **Leslie's Stats Stuff:** Leslie has interest and expertise in statistical theory and adds detail to their discussions through her explanations of statistical concepts in this feature.

3.2 A FOCUS ON SOCIAL PROBLEMS

Each chapter of the book focuses on a different problem from a social science or related field using publicly available data sources. One reason the social sciences are so interesting is because they help us understand and advocate for the world—the one we live in and the one we want to create. I've tried to choose compelling topics, including several with moral dilemmas that are in the news and in students' lives. Most readers should be able to find at least some of the chapters intriguing and relevant. This approach contrasts with textbooks that focus exclusively or predominantly on statistical theory, use simulated data, or choose data sources specifically to avoid controversial topics.

The topics for the chapters are as follows:

- Chapter 1: Marijuana legalization policy

- Chapter 2: Cancer screening for transgender patients

- Chapter 3: Gun deaths, gun use, gun manufacturing, and funding for gun research

- Chapter 4: Opioid deaths, opioid policy, and opioid treatment facilities

- Chapter 5: Perceptions about voter registration and mandatory voting

- Chapter 6: Blood pressure

- Chapter 7: Time spent using technology

- Chapter 8: Global access to clean water, sanitation, and education

- Chapter 9: Distance to needle exchanges

- Chapter 10: The digital divide and library use

- Chapter 11: Representation of women in data science careers

3.3 USE OF PUBLICLY AVAILABLE DATA SETS

Each chapter uses one or more publicly available data sets, and most chapters include instructions for importing the data directly into R from the original online location to encourage the use of reproducible research practices.

Many textbooks in statistics use simulated data or data that have been pre-cleaned. This book takes a different approach in order to provide the audience experience with data situations they are likely to encounter outside of the learning environment. Simulated and pre-cleaned data sources have advantages, including being useful for clearly demonstrating what it means to meet assumptions for statistical models or fail assumptions in specific ways. However, use of pre-cleaned data can set unrealistic expectations of how most data actually look outside the classroom. Likewise, simulated data can reinforce the stereotype that learning and using statistics are not only difficult but also disconnected from the real world. My book tries to overcome these challenges by using real data that address compelling social problems.

Admittedly, there are challenges to my approach. It is decidedly more difficult to demonstrate some concepts and to meet statistical model assumptions with real-world data. That's life. The challenges with this approach mimic the challenges of data science. Moreover, readers will be introduced to strategies for thinking like a data scientist to identify and deal with common obstacles.

The data sets used are as follows:

- 2016 General Social Survey (Chapter 1)

- 2014 Behavioral Risk Factor Surveillance Survey (Chapter 2)

- 2016 Federal Bureau of Investigation homicide data table (Chapter 3)

- 2011–2012 National Health and Nutrition Examination Survey (Chapter 3)

- 2017 Kaiser Family Foundation state opioid policy data (Chapter 4)

- 2017 American Foundation for AIDS Research distance to substance use treatment facility data (Chapter 4)

- 2017 Pew Research Center voting perceptions data (Chapter 5)

- 2015–2016 National Health and Nutrition Examination Survey (Chapter 6)

- 2018 General Social Survey (Chapter 7)

- 2015 World Health Organization data on access to water and sanitation (Chapter 8)

- 2015 United Nations Educational, Scientific, and Cultural Organization data on education (Chapter 8)

- 2017 American Foundation for AIDS Research distance to needle exchange data (Chapter 9)

- 2016 Pew Research Center library use data (Chapter 10)

- 2017 National Science Foundation Scientists and Engineers Statistical Data System (Chapter 11)

3.4 USE OF R STATISTICAL SOFTWARE

R is a coding language used to conduct statistical analyses and to create visual displays of data. The options available in R for analysis and graphing are competitive with, and in some cases surpass, the Statistical Package for the Social Sciences (SPSS) and Statistical Analysis System (SAS) software packages. However, R statistical software is free and open source. Anyone can contribute a "package" to R and, if it is accepted to the Comprehensive R Archive Network (CRAN) (https://cran.r-project.org/

submit.html), it becomes available for all R users worldwide to access and use. As of July 2019, there are approximately 15,000 user-contributed packages available on the CRAN, with most packages being designed to conduct some specific type of analysis. The use of R has been growing and, by some metrics, has caught up to or surpassed SPSS and SAS when it comes to data-related jobs (Muenchen, 2019). Because R is free, it allows people and organizations with fewer resources to access and use a high-quality data science tool (Krishnaswamy & Marinova, 2012; Sullivan, 2011). Consequently, the software is more egalitarian and inclusive, creating opportunities for collaborations and contributions to emerge from less privileged nations and individuals.

Among the unique qualities of R is the community that has formed around its use. On any given day, the #rstats hashtag on Twitter includes several hundred tweets from people making suggestions, asking questions, and posting R memes and jokes. The R community is also highly focused on diversity. For example, groups like R-Ladies Global support and encourage underrepresented voices in R (Daish, Frick, LeDell, de Queiroz, & Vitolo, 2019).

3.5 INCLUSION OF DIVERSE CHARACTERS, AUTHORS, AND ARTWORK

The book emphasizes diversity and inclusion in several ways. First, to address the underrepresentation of women in math and computer science fields, the underlying story features three women. In addition, the final chapter of the book examines data related to job type, job satisfaction, and sex, with a focus on computer science and math. The chapter portrays the student character coming to terms with data on employment and job satisfaction as she ponders a data science career. Third, when relevant and available, I cited women and authors from countries underrepresented in the statistical literature. Specifically, when two equally citable sources supporting the same concept were available, I opted for the underrepresented authors as determined by a commonsense reading of names and affiliations and, in some cases, searching for and reading of online profiles. Finally, the main and supporting characters in the artwork included throughout the text include diverse representation of race, ethnicity, and sex. If women and students of color can literally "see" themselves in the characters, they may find data jobs more appealing and feasible (Herrmann et al., 2016; Johnson, 2011).

3.6 EMPHASIS ON REPRODUCIBLE RESEARCH PRACTICES

Science is increasingly under scrutiny for the use of questionable research practices that threaten the quality of the evidence underlying decisions that impact lives (Banks, Rogelberg, Woznyj, Landis, & Rupp, 2016; Steen, Casadevall, & Fang, 2013). Among the many strategies that could improve the quality of the science is the use of reproducible practices during data management and analysis that allow other scientists to reproduce the work (Harris et al., 2019; Harris, Wondmeneh, Zhao, & Leider, 2019). This text suggests and demonstrates choices that contribute to reproducibility when importing, cleaning, managing, and analyzing data. Reproducibility is mentioned throughout the text by one of the characters, and most chapters have a resource box that offers one or more strategies for ensuring that data management and analysis tasks are performed in a reproducible way. For example, one of the sections in the first chapter describes and demonstrates how to pick a consistent and clear way to name and format constants, variables, and functions. This strategy results in code that is more readable for humans, which improves code comprehension and facilitates the reuse of code to verify results with the same data or new data.

4 Book website

The book website at **edge.sagepub.com/harris1e** includes the following resources:

INSTRUCTOR TEACHING SITE: edge.sagepub.com/harris1e

SAGE edge for instructors supports your teaching by making it easy to integrate quality content and create a rich learning environment for students with

- A **password-protected site** for complete and protected access to all text-specific instructor resources;

- **Test banks** that provide a diverse range of ready-to-use options that save you time—you can also easily edit any question and/or insert your own personalized questions;

- **Tutorial videos** produced exclusively for this text that demonstrate **how to use R** to conduct key statistical tests using real-world data;

- **Editable, chapter-specific PowerPoint® slides** that offer complete flexibility for creating a multimedia presentation for your course;

- **Downloadable Coder (beginner/intermediate) and Hacker (advanced) exercises** from the book that can be used as homework or labs—students can take the **multiple choice pre-test questions** electronically first to check their level;

- **Downloadable data files and R code available** for use with the book and exercises;

- **Solutions** to selected in-text exercises;

- **Instructor Ideas for Gamification** compiled by the author, offered for those who want to gamify their course; and

- **Full-color figures** from the book available for download.

STUDENT STUDY SITE: edge.sagepub.com/harris1e

SAGE edge for students enhances learning, it's easy to use, and it offers

- An **open-access site** that makes it easy for students to maximize their study time, anywhere, anytime;

- **Tutorial videos** produced exclusively for this text that demonstrate **how to use R** to conduct key statistical tests using real-world data;

- **Downloadable Coder (beginner/intermediate) and Hacker (advanced) exercises** from the book—students can take the **multiple choice pre-test questions** electronically first to check their level; and

- **Downloadable data files and R code available** for use with the book and exercises.

5 Acknowledgments

Many people helped in major and minor and in obvious and subtle ways throughout the development of this text. Leanne Waugh read well over half of the book, found typos, and identified places where an explanation or the storyline was incomplete or unclear. Amy Sklansky suggested major improvements to the narrative and chapter openings and taught me the difference between writing a story and writing stage directions. Shelly Cooper read several chapters and offered suggestions for fixing and improving the code, including suggesting a useful figure that is a combination of a boxplot, a violin plot, and a scatterplot (check it out in Chapter 9). Scott Harris used his expert copyediting skills to help me with grammar, punctuation, and an unusual amount of repeated words, even for me me. Bobbi Carothers offered helpful suggestions on very early drafts of the first few chapters, providing a more solid foundation for the rest of the work. Leslie Hinyard answered too many text messages to count. Chelsea West, Chris Prener, Angelique Zeringue, Sarah Van Alsten, Bryan Newman, Alexis Duncan, Kristen Ruckdashel, Joe Steensma, Kim Johnson, Robert Singer, Paaige Turner, Doug Luke, Ellen Mrazek, and some people I do not know on Twitter also gave helpful opinions and suggestions. Thank you all!

At SAGE, Helen Salmon and Chelsea Neve were the epitome of patience, enthusiasm, and professionalism. The reviewers in the following list had great ideas and enthusiastic suggestions that improved the work immensely:

Jennifer Bachner, *Johns Hopkins University*

Matthew C. Bell, *Santa Clara University*

Patrick Bolger, *Texas A&M University*

William J. Bosl, *University of San Francisco*

Joseph Nathan Cohen, *City University of New York–Queens College*

Daniel Conroy-Beam, *University of California, Santa Barbara*

Gabriel I. Cook, *Claremont McKenna College*

James J. Cortright, *University of Wisconsin–River Falls*

Jacqueline S. Craven, *Delta State University*

Todd Daniel, *Missouri State University*

Michael Erickson, *Hawaii Pacific University*

Marte Fallshore, *Central Washington University*

Sylvain Fiset, *Université de Moncton, Edmundston*

Jonathan S. Hack, *Harvard Law School*

Johannes Karreth, *Ursinus College*

George Kikuchi, *California State University, Fresno*

Brandon LeBeau, *University of Iowa*

Michael S. Lynch, *University of Georgia*

Michael E. J. Masson, *University of Victoria*

Avery McIntosh, *Boston University*

Matthew R. Miles, *Brigham Young University, Idaho*

Maura J. Mills, *University of Alabama*

Mary Moore, *Colorado State University–Global*

Derek Mueller, *Carleton University*

David A. M. Peterson, *Iowa State University*

Matthew D. Phillips, *UNC Charlotte*

Darrin L. Rogers, *State University of New York at Fredonia*

Samantha Seals, *University of West Florida*

Yi Shao, *Oklahoma City University*

Ches Thurber, *Northern Illinois University*

Drew Tyre, *University of Nebraska–Lincoln*

Mary Beth Zeni, *Ursuline College*

The artists, Rob Schuster and Rose Storey, did an excellent job producing graphics that fit with the story and goals of the work. My thanks to Hadley Wickham for permission to include one of his tweets as a figure, and to Hao Zhu and Matt Dowle for permission to include their `kableExtra` and `data .table` hex stickers, respectively, in the cover art. Thank you to the data teams at the General Social Survey; the National Health and Nutrition Examination Survey; the World Health Organization; the United Nations Educational, Scientific and Cultural Organization; the Federal Bureau of Investigation; the Pew Research Center; the Kaiser Family Foundation; the Foundation for AIDS Research; and the National Science Foundation. Special thanks go to Dr. David Stark and Dr. Nigam Shaw, who answered my emails, sent me a spreadsheet of the data from their 2017 article (Stark & Shah, 2017), and sent the GitHub location of the data and R code for the paper that was the inspiration for Chapter 3 (https://github.com/davidestark/gun-violence-research/).

Finally, all the hard work in the world would not have resulted in much had I not had the great fortune of having a math-teaching mom with an unfathomably big heart; too many smart, fun, and supportive friends to count (you know who you are, or, if you don't, you'll be receiving a text to confirm!); and a spouse who is an inspiration and true partner.

Jenine K. Harris earned her doctorate in public health studies and biostatistics from Saint Louis University School of Public Health in 2008. Currently, she teaches biostatistics courses as an Associate Professor in the Brown School public health program at Washington University in St. Louis. In 2013, she authored *An Introduction to Exponential Random Graph Modeling*, which was published in Sage's Quantitative Applications in the Social Sciences series and is accompanied by the `ergmharris` R package available on the Comprehensive R Archive Network (CRAN). She is an author on more than 80 peer-reviewed publications, and developed and published the `odds.n.ends` R package available on the CRAN. She is the leader of R-Ladies St. Louis, which she co-founded with Chelsea West in 2017 (@rladiesstl). R-Ladies St. Louis is a local chapter of R-Ladies Global (@rladiesglobal), an organization devoted to promoting gender diversity in the R community. Her recent research interests focus on improving the quality of research in public health by using reproducible research practices throughout the research process.

1

PREPARING DATA FOR ANALYSIS AND VISUALIZATION IN R

The R-Team and
the Pot Policy Problem

1.1 Choosing and learning R

Leslie walked past her adviser's office and stopped. She backed up to read a flyer hanging on the wall. The flyer announced a new local chapter of *R-Ladies* (see Box 1.1). Yes! she thought. She'd been wanting to learn R the entire year.

1.1 R-Ladies

R-Ladies is a global group with chapters in cities around the world. The mission of R-Ladies is to increase gender diversity in the R community. To learn more, visit the R-Ladies Global website at https://rladies.org/ and the R-Ladies Global Twitter feed, @RLadiesGlobal.

Leslie arrived at the R-Ladies event early. "Hi, I'm Leslie," she told the first woman she met.

"Hey! Great to meet you. I'm Nancy," answered the woman as they shook hands.

"And I'm Kiara, one of Nancy's friends," said another woman, half-hugging Nancy as she reached out to shake Leslie's hand. "Can we guess you're here to learn more about R?"

Leslie nodded.

"You've come to the right place," said Nancy. "But let's introduce ourselves first. I'm an experienced data scientist working for a biotech startup, and I love to code."

"You might call me a data management guru," Kiara said. "I just gave notice at my job with a large online retailer because I'm starting a job with the Federal Reserve next month."

Leslie asked Kiara and Nancy about their experience with R. "What do you like about R compared to other traditional statistics software options I've been learning in my degree program?"

Nancy thought for a minute and answered, "Three main reasons: cost, contributors, and community."

First, Nancy explained, "The cost of R can't be beat. R is free, while licenses for other statistics software can cost hundreds of dollars for individuals and many thousands for businesses. While large, successful businesses and universities can often afford these licenses, the cost can be an insurmountable burden for small businesses, nonprofits, students, teachers, and researchers."

Kiara added, "The cost of the tools used in data science can be a social justice issue [Krishnaswamy & Marinova, 2012; Sullivan, 2011]. With R, students, researchers, and professionals in settings with limited resources have just as much access as an executive in a fancy high-rise in the middle of downtown San Francisco."

The second thing that Nancy loved about R was the contributors. She explained, "R is not only free but it is also *open source*. Anyone can contribute to it!"

Leslie looked confused. Nancy explained that anyone can write a *package* in the R language and contribute the package to a repository that is accessible online. Packages are small pieces of software that are often developed to do one specific thing or a set of related things.

SAGE edge™

Visit **edge.sagepub.com/harris1e** to watch an R tutorial

Kiara offered, "A package I use a lot is called `tidyverse`. The **tidyverse** package includes functions that are useful for common data management tasks like recoding variables. By using code that someone else has written and made available, I don't have to write long programs from scratch to do the typical things I do on a regular basis."

Leslie asked, "OK, but how is it possible for everyone to have access to software written by anyone in the world?"

Kiara explained that people write packages like **tidyverse** and submit them to the Comprehensive R Archive Network, also known as CRAN. After volunteers and resources from the nonprofit R Foundation (https://www.r-project.org/foundation/) review them, they decide whether to reject or accept new packages. New packages are added to the CRAN (CRAN Repository Policy, n.d.) for everyone to access.

Leslie nodded. Then Kiara pulled up the *contributed packages* website and showed Leslie the more than 14,000 packages available on the *CRAN* (https://cran.r-project.org/submit.html). Leslie was still a little confused about the idea of a package.

Kiara said, "Think of a package as a computer program that you open when you want to do a specific thing. For example, if you wanted to create a slide show, you might open the Microsoft PowerPoint program. But if you wanted to do a data management or analysis task, you would use packages in R. Unlike PowerPoint, however, anyone in the world can write a package and contribute it to the CRAN for anyone in the world to use."

Nancy had saved the best for last: the R community. She explained, "The R community is inclusive and active online, and R community groups like R-Ladies Global [Daish et al., 2019] specifically support voices that are underrepresented in the R community and in data science. Plus, R users love to share their new projects and help one another."

Kiara agreed enthusiastically. "I look at (and post to) the #rstats hashtag often on Twitter and keep learning great new features of R and R packages."

Kiara shared two more benefits of using R. The first was great graphics. She explained that R is extraordinary for its ability to create high-quality visualizations of data. "The code is extremely flexible, allowing users to customize graphics in nearly any way they can imagine," she said. The second benefit was that R is a great tool for conducting analyses that are *reproducible* by someone else. She noted that the R community is actively building and supporting new packages and other tools that support reproducible workflows.

Nancy mentioned that reproducibility has become an important part of science as the scientific community addressed the problem of poor and unethical scientific practices exposed in published research (Steen et al., 2013) (see Box 1.2).

"This all sounds great," said Leslie. "What's the catch?"

Nancy and Kiara looked at each other for a minute and smiled.

"OK," Kiara said. "I admit there are a few things that are challenging about R, but they are related to the reasons that R is great." The first challenge, she explained, is that the contributors to R can be anyone from anywhere. With such a broad range of people creating packages for R, the packages end up following different formats or rules. This means that learning R can be tricky sometimes when a function or package does not work the way other, similar packages do.

Nancy agreed and said, "Also, since R is open source, there is no company behind the product that will provide technical support. But there is a very active community of R users, which means that solutions to problems can often be solved relatively quickly with a tweet, email, or question posted to a message board."

1.2 Kiara's reproducibility resource: Reproducible research

The scientific standard for building evidence is replication, which is repeating scientific studies from the beginning and comparing results to see if you get the same thing. While replication is ideal, it can be very time-consuming and expensive. One alternative to replication is reproducibility. Reproducing a study is reanalyzing existing data to determine if you get the same results. Reproducibility requires, at a minimum, accessible data and clear instructions for data management and analysis (Harris et al., 2019).

Science is currently facing a reproducibility crisis. Recent research has found that

- 20% to 80% of papers published in a sample of journals included an unclear or unknown sample size (Gosselin, n.d.),

- up to 40% of papers per journal in a sample of journals included unclear or unknown statistical tests (Gosselin, n.d.),

- approximately 6% of p-values were reported incorrectly in a sample of psychology papers (Nuijten, Hartgerink, Assen, Epskamp, & Wicherts, 2015),

- 11% of p-values were incorrect in a sample of medical papers (García-Berthou & Alcaraz, 2004),

- just 21% of 67 drug studies and 40% to 60% of 100 psychological studies were successfully replicated (Anderson et al., 2016; Open Science Collaboration, 2015; Prinz, Schlange, & Asadullah, 2011), and

- 61% of economics papers were replicated (Camerer et al., 2016).

As you make your way through this text, you will find tips on how to format the code you write to manage and analyze your data. Writing, formatting, and annotating your code clearly can increase reproducibility.

Leslie was intrigued. She wanted to learn more about R. Kiara and Nancy had enjoyed the conversation, too.

"Why don't we form our own small group to teach Leslie about R and learn collaboratively?" Kiara said.

"Let's do it!" said Nancy. She had been watching a lot of 1980s TV lately, so she suggested that they call themselves the "R-Team." "We'll be like the 80s show, the *A-Team*." Then she sang some of the theme song, "If you have a problem, if no one else can help . . ."

"I think we get the idea," said Kiara, laughing.

"I don't know that show," Leslie said, smiling. "But I'm all for joining the R-Team!"

1.2 Learning R with publicly available data

Before the evening ended, Kiara recommended that they use publicly available data to learn strategies and tools that would be useful in the real world. Who wants to use fake data? Real data may be messier, but they are more fun and applicable. Nancy agreed. Since she was especially interested in data about current issues in the news, she suggested that they begin by working with data on marijuana policy. She pointed out that several states had legalized medicinal and recreational marijuana in the past few years and that she'd recently come across legalization questions in a large national publicly available data set called the *General Social Survey* (National Opinion Research Center, 2019) that is available online from the National Opinion Research Center (NORC) at the University of Chicago.

Nancy suggested that the first day of R should be focused on getting used to R and preparing data for analysis. The R-Team agreed that they would work on preparing data for analysis and would use marijuana legalization data to practice the skills. Kiara put together a list of things to achieve in their first meeting.

1.3 Achievements to unlock

- Achievement 1: Observations and variables
- Achievement 2: Using reproducible research practices
- Achievement 3: Understanding and changing data types
- Achievement 4: Entering or loading data into R
- Achievement 5: Identifying and treating missing values
- Achievement 6: Building a basic bar chart

1.4 The tricky weed problem

1.4.1 MARIJUANA LEGALIZATION

When Leslie showed up for the first meeting of the R-Team, Kiara offered her coffee and bagels. Leslie was enjoying learning R already! To start the meeting, Nancy shared some marijuana legalization research. She told them she had learned that California had become the first state to legalize medical marijuana in 1996 ("Timeline of Cannabis Laws," n.d.). She had also learned that marijuana use remained illegal under federal law, but that 29 states and the District of Columbia had legalized marijuana at the state level for medical or recreational use or both by 2017. With new ballot measures at the state level being introduced and passed by voters on a regular basis, as of 2017 there appeared to be momentum for a nationwide shift toward legalization.

Nancy refilled her coffee and continued. She said that in 2017, Jeff Sessions was appointed as attorney general of the United States. Sessions did not support legalization and regularly expressed interest in prosecuting medical marijuana providers. Despite this difficult climate, in 2018, Michigan voters approved a ballot measure to legalize recreational cannabis, and voters in Missouri, Oklahoma, and Utah passed ballot measures legalizing medical marijuana. In 2018, Vermont became the first to legalize recreational marijuana via the state legislature (Wilson, 2018).

In 2019, Sessions was replaced as attorney general by William Barr, who testified that he would not pursue marijuana companies that complied with state laws and stated that he was supportive of expanding marijuana manufacturing for scientific research (Angell, 2019). However, Barr did not indicate his support, or lack of support, for additional legalization. With the existing federal policy and the unstable legal environment, it is unclear what will happen next for marijuana policy.

Nancy explained that, with the exception of Vermont, policy changes had primarily happened through successful ballot initiatives. She suggested that learning more about support among voters for legalization could help understand what is likely to happen next. Leslie and Kiara agreed.

Kiara looked up the General Social Survey, or GSS. She explained to Leslie that the GSS is a large survey of U.S. residents conducted each year since 1972, with all of the data available for public use. The GSS Data Explorer (https://gssdataexplorer.norc.org) allows people to create a free account and browse the data that have been collected in the surveys, which have changed over time. In several years, including 2018, the GSS survey included a question asking the survey participants whether they support marijuana legalization. Kiara used the Data Explorer to select the marijuana legalization question and a question about age.

Leslie asked her why she selected age. Kiara explained that, since marijuana legalization had been primarily up to voters so far, the success of ballot initiatives in the future will depend on the support of people of voting age. If younger people are more supportive, this suggests that over time, the electorate will become more supportive as the old electorate decreases. Leslie found that to be logical, although a little morbid.

Kiara was also interested in how the marijuana legalization and age questions were worded in the GSS and what the response options were. She saw that the GSS question was worded as follows:

> Do you think the use of marijuana should be legal or not?

Below the question, the different response options were listed: legal, not legal, don't know, no answer, not applicable.

Kiara found the age variable and noticed that the actual question was not shown and just listed as "RESPONDENT'S AGE." The variable is recorded as whole numbers ranging from 18 to 88. At the bottom of the web page about the age variable, the GSS Data Explorer showed that age was recorded as "89 OR OLDER" for anyone 89 years old or older.

Nancy was eager to put her love of coding to work. She imported the GSS data and created a graph about marijuana legalization to get them started (Figure 1.1).

Leslie examined the graph. She saw that the x-axis across the bottom was labeled with the marijuana question and the two response categories. She noticed that the y-axis was the percentage who responded. The bar with the Yes label went up to just past 60 on the y-axis, indicating that just over 60% of people support legalization. The bar labeled No stopped just under 40, so just under 40% do not think marijuana should be legal.

Although marijuana legalization appeared to have a lot of support from this first graph, Leslie thought it might not be that simple. Policy change depended on *who* supports marijuana legalization. Are the supporters voters? Do they live in states that have not yet passed legalization policy or in the states that have already legalized it? In addition to answering these important questions, one thing that might provide a little more information about the future is to examine support by the age of the supporter. If supporters tend to be older voters, then enthusiasm for legalization may weaken as the population ages. If supporters are younger voters, then enthusiasm for legalization may strengthen as the population ages. Nancy

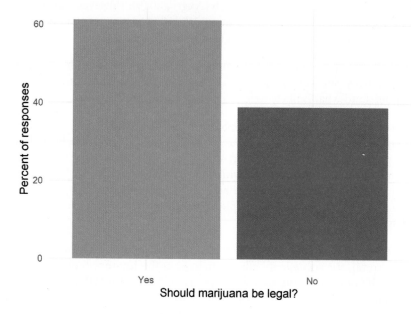

was delighted at a second chance (already) to jump right in and write some additional code so that the graph included age groups as well (Figure 1.2).

The R-Team could see a pretty clear pattern in the graph. The x-axis now showed the age groups, while the y-axis showed the percentage of people. The bar colors represent Yes and No. Leslie saw that the percentage of people supporting legalization looked three times larger than the percentage who did not

FIGURE 1.2 Support for marijuana legalization by age group among participants in the 2016 General Social Survey

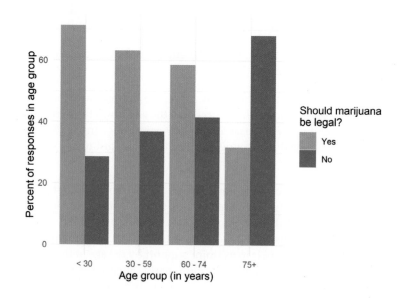

1.3 Kiara's reproducibility resource: Installing R and RStudio

To follow along with this text, install R and RStudio. R can be downloaded from The Comprehensive R Archive Network (https://cran.r-project.org). Once R has been installed, then install RStudio (https://www.rstudio.com). RStudio is an interactive development environment, which in this case makes R much easier to use.

Open RStudio (not R) and make sure that everything has installed correctly. There should be a window open on the left-hand side of the RStudio screen that says "Console" in small bold print in the top left corner. RStudio automatically finds R and runs it for you within this console window.

Check to see if R is working properly by typing in the following code (shown in shading) at the R > prompt in the console on the left. Press Enter after typing each line of code to get the results shown on the lines that begin with ##:

```
2+2
## [1] 4
(4+6)/2
## [1] 5
10^2
## [1] 100
a <- 3
a
## [1] 3
```

support in the youngest age group. In the oldest age group, those who do not support legalization are a much larger group. Leslie noted that, as those in the younger categories age, it appeared that support would continue to rise and marijuana legalization ballot initiatives would continue to be supported in future elections.

Kiara explained to Leslie that visual representations of data like Figures 1.1 and 1.2 could be powerful tools for understanding and communicating with data. Although the two graphs may look simple, there is a lot going on behind the scenes. For the remainder of the R-Team meeting, they would focus on how to prepare data for analysis and visualization in R. Preparing data for analysis is *data management*, so Kiara explained she would be the primary guide (with help from Nancy, who loves to code).

Kiara told Leslie that she would use R and RStudio for examples and that she highly recommended Leslie follow along with R and RStudio on her own computer. To make sure that Leslie could follow along, Kiara wrote instructions for installing R and RStudio on a computer (see Box 1.3).

1.5 Achievement 1: Observations and variables

1.5.1 DEFINING OBSERVATIONS AND VARIABLES

Before Kiara began data management tasks, she thought a few vocabulary terms would be useful to discuss. Kiara explained that data scientists were usually interested in the characteristics and behaviors of humans and organizations. To understand these things, scientists often measured and recorded information about people or organizations. For example, a data scientist working on political science might be interested in understanding whether income is related to voting. To get this information, she could ask a group of people whether they voted in the most recent election and what they earned in income in the most recent year. In this case, each person is an *observation*, and there are two variables, income and voting behavior.

Leslie thought she understood, so she summarized that people being measured are observations and the various pieces of information about each person are *variables*. Kiara nodded in agreement and emphasized that observations and variables were key concepts in data science, so it is worth taking a few more minutes to think about. Kiara thought a visual representation of observations and variables might be useful. She explained that, in a typical data set, observations are the rows and variables are the columns. For the example of voting and income, a data set might look like this:

```
  income voted
1  34000   yes
2 123000    no
3  21500    no
```

In this very small data set, there are three observations (the rows) and two variables (the columns). The first observation is a person with an income of $34,000 who answered "yes" for voted. The second observation is a person with an income of $123,000 who answered "no" for voted. The third observation is a person with an income of $21,500 who responded "no" for voted. The two variables are income and voted.

1.5.2 ENTERING AND STORING VARIABLES IN R

Now that she had introduced the basic idea for observations and variables, Kiara transitioned into talking about R. She explained that R stores information as *objects*, and then data analysis and data management are performed on these stored objects. Before an object can be used in data management or analysis in R, it has to be stored in the R environment.

Information is stored as objects in R by *assigning* the information a name, which can be a single letter or some combination of letters and numbers that will serve as the name of the object. Assigning an object to a name is done by using an arrow like this: <-. The arrow separates the name of the object on the left from the object itself on the right, like this: name <- object. An object can be as simple as one letter or number, or as complex as several data sets combined.

Since this was their first task in R, Kiara had Leslie try storing the value of 29—for the number of states with legal medical marijuana—in an object called states by typing the following at the R prompt (>) in the Console pane of the RStudio window. Leslie had read about the panes in an email from Kiara earlier (see Box 1.4) and typed the following at the > prompt:

```
states <- 29
```

1.4 Kiara's reproducibility resource: RStudio is a pane

When opening RStudio for the first time, you will notice it is divided into sections. Each of these sections is a **pane** in the RStudio window. The default panes are the Console (left), Environment & History (top right), and Files & Plots & Connections & Packages & Help & Viewer (bottom right). The panes you will use the most throughout this text are the Source pane, which opens when a new R script file is opened through the File menu, Console, Environment & History, Help, and Plots.

- **Source**: Allows you to write R code
- **Console**: Shows the results of running code
- **Environment**: Shows what objects you currently have open and available in R
- **History**: Keeps a running list of the code you have used so far
- **Help**: Provides information on functions and packages you are using
- **Plots**: Shows graphs you create

If you would like to choose and organize your visible panes, click on the View menu and choose Panes to see all of the available options.

When Leslie tried typing the code and pressing Enter, she noticed that running the `states <- 29` code did not seem to result in anything actually happening in the Console window. Kiara explained that when she pressed Enter, the object was stored and there is no result to display. Specifically, R is storing the number 29 as an object called `states` for Leslie to use in her work. While nothing happened in the Console, something did happen. Kiara explained that the `states` object is now stored under the Environment tab in the top right pane of the RStudio window. Looking at the tab, Leslie noticed that the window shows `states` and its value of 29 under a heading titled Values (Figure 1.3).

Leslie saw that there was a *History* tab next to the *Environment* tab in the upper right pane. She clicked on the History tab and was surprised to see `states <- 29`. Kiara explained that this tab holds all of the code run since the History pane was last cleared. Nancy admitted this was one of her favorite parts of R; you can double-click on any of the code shown in the History pane and R will send the code to the Console, ready to run again. There was no need to type anything twice!

FIGURE 1.3 Environment window in RStudio showing the newly created `states` variable and its value

Leslie had clearly missed some things in Kiara's email and wanted to review it again to learn more about the panes, but for now she was excited to try double-clicking on the `states <- 29` code in the History pane. As soon as she did, the code was sent to the Console. Leslie was delighted! This seemed like a great feature. To see the value of the `states` object created in the Console pane, Kiara had Leslie type the name of the object, `states`, at the R > prompt and press Enter. In shaded sections throughout this text, the rows starting "##" show the output that will appear after running the R code just above it.

```
states
## [1] 29
```

Now the value of `states` appears!

To demonstrate using the `states` object in a mathematical expression, Kiara told Leslie to type the expression `2 + states` at the R > prompt and press Enter.

```
2 + states
## [1] 31
```

Leslie noted that 31 is printed in the Console. This is the value of `2 + 29`. Before they continued, Kiara wanted to explain a few vocabulary terms to Leslie. When Leslie entered code and then hit Enter, the result displayed on the screen is the *output*. For example, the 31 printed after running the code above is output.

1.5.3 ACHIEVEMENT 1: CHECK YOUR UNDERSTANDING

Assign your age in years to an object with your name. Add 5 to the object and press Enter to see how old you will be in 5 years.

1.6 Achievement 2: Using reproducible research practices

Before getting too far into coding, Kiara wanted Leslie to be thinking about how to choose things like object names so that they are useful not only right now but in the future for anyone (including the original author) who relies on the R code. Kiara had learned this lesson well in her many years of coding.

1.6.1 USING COMMENTS TO ORGANIZE AND EXPLAIN CODE

For example, the meaning of the code above—`states <- 29`, `states`, and `2 + states`—may seem obvious right now while they are new, but in a few weeks, it might be less clear why `states` has a value of 29 and what this object means. One way to keep track of the purpose of code is to write short explanations in the code while coding. For this to work, the code needs to be written in the *Source* pane, which is opened by creating a new *Script file*. To create a new Script file, Kiara told Leslie to go to the File menu in the upper left corner of RStudio and choose "New File" from the choices. Then, from the New File menu, choose "R Script." Nancy suggested using the shortcut command of Control-Shift-n. Leslie tried the shortcut, and a fourth pane opened in the upper left side of the RStudio window with a new blank file that said "Untitled1" in a tab at the top. This is a Script file in the Source pane that can be used for writing code.

Kiara paused here to give Leslie more information about the difference between writing R code in the Console versus writing R code in a Script file. She explained that the difference is mostly about being able to edit and save code; code written in the Console at the > prompt is executed immediately and cannot be edited or saved (e.g., like an instant message). Leslie suggested that the History pane saves the code. Kiara confirmed that this is true and that the history can even be saved as a file using the save icon in the history tab. However, she explained that code saved from the history tab is not usually well formatted and cannot be edited or formatted before saving, so this code will usually be pretty messy and not too useful.

A Script file, however, is a text file similar to something written in the Notepad text editor on a Windows computer or the TextEdit text editor on a Mac computer. A Script file can be edited, saved, and shared just like any text file. When Script files of R code are saved, they have the .R file extension.

Kiara opened a new Script file and showed Leslie how to include information about the code by typing comments that explain what the code is for, like this:

```
# create an object with the number of states with
# legal medical marijuana in 2017
states <- 29

# print the value of the states object
states

# determine how many states there would be if 2
# more passed this policy
2 + states
```

Each line of code is preceded by a short statement of its purpose. These statements are called comments, and the practice of adding comments to code is called *commenting* or *annotation*. The practice of commenting or annotating is one of the most important habits to develop in R or in any programming language.

In R, comments are denoted by a hashtag #, which notifies R that the text following the # on the same line is a comment and not something to be computed or stored. Comments are not necessary for code to run, but are important for describing and remembering what the code does. Annotation is a *best practice* of coding. When writing and annotating code, keep two goals in mind.

- Write clear code that does not need a lot of comments.
- Include useful comments where needed so that anyone (including yourself in the future) can run and understand your code.

Kiara explained that clear R code with useful annotation will help Leslie's work be *reproducible*, which is one of the most important characteristics of good data science. Kiara had collected some information about reproducible research for Leslie (see Box 1.2).

Before moving on, Leslie tried writing the code and comments above in the Script file she had open in the Source pane (see Box 1.4). She finished writing the code but then was not sure how to run the code to check her work. Kiara explained that the code can be run in several ways. One way is to highlight all the code at once and click on Run at the top right corner of the Source pane. To run one line of code at a time, highlighting the line of code or putting the cursor anywhere in the line of code and clicking Run also works. The keyboard shortcut for Run is Control-Enter (or Command-Enter on a Mac), so putting the cursor on a line of code and pressing Control-Enter will run the code on that line (Figure 1.4).

Leslie highlighted all of the code and clicked on Run at the top of the Source pane. In the Console window, she saw the code and the output from the code shown in Figure 1.5.

FIGURE 1.4 Source pane in RStudio showing R code and comments

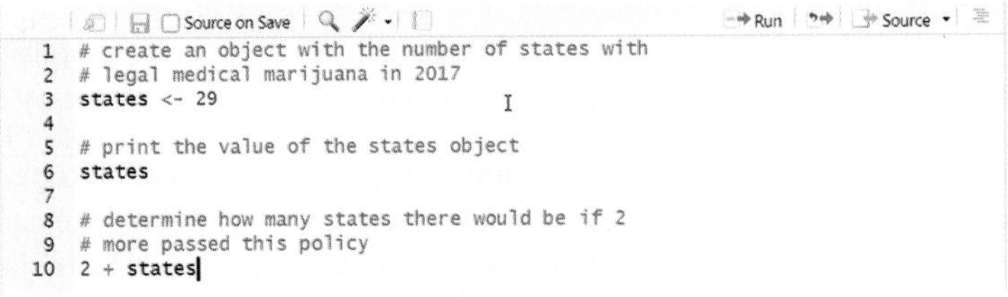

```
 1  # create an object with the number of states with
 2  # legal medical marijuana in 2017
 3  states <- 29                          I
 4
 5  # print the value of the states object
 6  states
 7
 8  # determine how many states there would be if 2
 9  # more passed this policy
10  2 + states
```

FIGURE 1.5 Console pane in RStudio showing R code, comments, and results

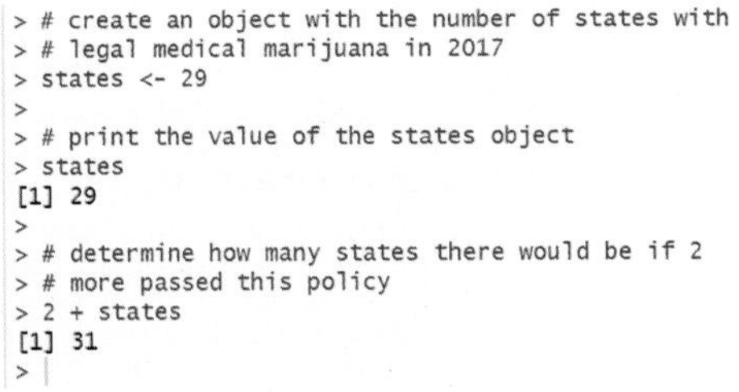

```
> # create an object with the number of states with
> # legal medical marijuana in 2017
> states <- 29
>
> # print the value of the states object
> states
[1] 29
>
> # determine how many states there would be if 2
> # more passed this policy
> 2 + states
[1] 31
>
```

1.6.2 INCLUDING A PROLOG TO INTRODUCE A SCRIPT FILE

Before moving on to more statistics and R code, Kiara wanted Leslie to add one more thing to her code, a *prolog*. She explained that a prolog is a set of comments at the top of a code file that provides information about what is in the file. Including a prolog is another best practice for coding. A prolog can have many features, including the following:

- Project name
- Project purpose
- Name(s) of data set(s) used in the project
- Location(s) of data set(s) used in the project
- Code author name (you!)
- Date code created
- Date last time code was edited

Kiara gave Leslie two examples, one formal and one informal. The formal prolog might be set apart from the code by a barrier of hashtags, like this:

```
# PROLOG    ################################################################

# PROJECT: NAME OF PROJECT HERE #

# PURPOSE: MAJOR POINT(S) OF WHAT I AM DOING WITH THE DATA HERE #

# DIR:     list directory(-ies) for files here #

# DATA:    list data set file names/availability here, e.g., #

#          filename.correctextension #

#          somewebaddress.com #

# AUTHOR:  AUTHOR NAME(S) #
```

```
# CREATED: MONTH dd, YEAR #
# LATEST:  MONTH dd, YEAR ############################################
# NOTES:   indent all additional lines under each heading, #
#          & use the hashmark bookends that appear #
#          KEEP PURPOSE, AUTHOR, CREATED & LATEST ENTRIES IN UPPER CASE, #
#          with appropriate case for DIR & DATA, lower case for notes #
#          If multiple lines become too much, #
#          simplify and write code book and readme. #
#          HINT #1: Decide what a long prolog is. #
#          HINT #2: copy & paste this into new script & replace text. #

# PROLOG          ##################################################
```

An informal prolog might just include the following elements:

```
####################################
# Project name
# Project purpose
# Code author name
# Date last edited
# Location of data used
####################################
```

Kiara had Leslie write a prolog at the top of her code file in the Source pane. Leslie's code in the Source pane now looked like this:

```
##########################################
# Project: R-Team meeting one
# Purpose: Code examples for meeting one
# Author: Leslie
# Edit date: April 19, 2019
# No external data files used
##########################################

# create an object with the number of states with
# legal medical marijuana in 2017
states <- 29

# print the value of the states object
states

# determine how many states there would be if 2
# more passed this policy
2 + states
```

Before continuing, Kiara suggested Leslie save her Script using the Save icon at the top left side of the Source pane or through the File menu.

Leslie saved it as analysis.R on her desktop and looked up just in time to see Kiara cringe. When saving a file, Kiara explained, include information in the file name that is a reminder of what is contained in the file. For example, a file name with date_project_author will make identifying the most recent file created for a project easier. In this case, Leslie might save the file as 171130_chap1_leslie.R for the date of November 30, 2017. Kiara mentioned that putting the year first and then the month and the day is a good idea to avoid problems with reading the date since not all countries use the same order in common practice.

Leslie resaved her file with a better name.

1.6.3 NAMING OBJECTS

In addition to annotating code, using a prolog, and including useful information in a file name, Kiara suggested to Leslie that she name objects so they are easy to understand. It is much easier to guess what might be in an object called `states` than what might be in an object called `var123`. Kiara remembered when she used to use generic names for her variables and was asked to revise a table for an important report that she had finished a few months earlier. It took her *hours* to figure out what she meant in the code when all the variables were named things like `x1` and `x2`.

Kiara mentioned that, in addition to choosing meaningful names, some letters and words are already used by R and will cause some confusion if used as object names. For example, the uppercase letters `T` and `F` are used in the code as shorthand for `TRUE` and `FALSE`, so they are not useful as object names. When possible, use words and abbreviations that are not common mathematical terms.

1.6.3.1 NAMING CONSTANTS

Kiara explained that there are recommended methods for naming objects in R that depend on the type of object ("Google's R Style Guide," n.d.). There are several types of objects in R. The `states` object is a *constant* because it is a single numeric value. The recommended format for constants is starting with a "k" and then using *camel case*. Camel case is capitalizing the first letter of each word in the object name, with the exception of the first word (the capital letters kind of look like camel humps 🐪). Leslie thought she understood and wanted to correct the naming of the `states` object. Kiara said she could make an entirely new object from scratch, like this:

```
# make a new object with well-formatted name
kStates <- 29
```

Or, she could assign the existing `states` object to a new name, like this:

```
# assign the existing states object a new name
kStates <- states
```

Leslie noticed that this uses the same format with the `<-` as assigning the value of 29 to `states`. Kiara explained that this arrow assigns whatever is on the right side of the arrow to the object name on the left. In this case, the `states` object is assigned to the `kStates` object name. Leslie noticed that `states` and `kStates` are now both listed in the environment. This was unnecessary since they both hold the same information. Kiara showed her how to remove an object using the `rm()` function.

```
# remove the states object
rm(states)
```

This looked different from what they had been doing so far since it included a function, `rm()`, and the name of an object (`states`). Kiara said that this format is common in R, having some instruction or function for R and a set of parentheses like `function()`. Then, inside the parentheses is typically the name of one or more objects to apply the function to, so `function(object)` is a common thing to see when using R. The information inside the parentheses is called an ***argument***, so the `states` object is the argument entered into the `rm()` function. Sometimes, R functions will need one argument to work, and sometimes they will require multiple arguments. Arguments do not all have to be objects; some are just additional instructions for R about how the functions should work. Leslie was a little confused by this, but Kiara said it would become more clear as they learned more functions. Kiara wanted to mention one last thing before the next topic. She explained that it is common for R users to call `rm()` and other functions "commands" instead of "functions," and these two words tend to be used interchangeably by many R users.

1.6.3.2 NAMING VARIABLES

Another type of object is a variable. Variables are measures of some characteristic for each observation in a data set. For example, `income` and `voted` are both variables. Variable objects are named using ***dot case*** or camel case. Dot case puts a dot between words in a variable name while camel case capitalizes each word in the variable name (except the first word 🐫). For example, if Leslie measured the number of medical marijuana prescriptions filled by each cancer patient in a data set during a year, she could use dot case and call the variable `filled.script.month` or use camel case and call it `filledScriptMonth`. Kiara mentioned that dot case and camel case are frequently used, and there are other variable naming conventions used by some R users (see Box 1.5).

1.6.3.3 NAMING FUNCTIONS

Functions are objects that perform a series of R commands to do something in particular. They are usually written when someone has to do the same thing multiple times and wants to make the process more

1.5 Kiara's reproducibility resource: Naming variables

Using useful names for variables in code will improve clarity. For example, a variable named `bloodPressure` probably contains blood pressure information, while a variable named `var123` could be anything. A couple of widely used practices for naming variables are as follows:

- Use nouns for variable names like `age`, `income`, or `religion`.
- Use dot case or camel case to separate words in multiple-word variable names.
  - `blood.pressure` uses dot case with a period separating words
  - `bloodPressure` is camel case with capital letters starting each word, except for the first word

efficient. Kiara explained that writing functions is a more advanced skill that they would cover later. For now, she just wanted to give the naming format for a function, which is camel case with the first letter capitalized (this is also called "upper camel case" or "*Pascal case*"). For example, a function that multiplies everything in a data set by 2 might be called `MultiplyByTwo` or something similar.

Kiara explained to Leslie that when she first starts to code, she should develop a coding style and begin using a consistent way of annotating code and one of the recommended ways of naming things. Kiara preferred dot case for variable names and using underscores for file names. Leslie agreed. Nancy thought one more thing was worth mentioning while they were talking about writing clear code. Lines of code can get far too long to read without annoying side scrolling, especially on small laptop screens. The recommended limit for the length of a line of code is 80 characters, but shorter is even better. Leslie wrote this down to make sure she remembered this new detail later when she was writing more complicated code.

1.6.4 ACHIEVEMENT 2: CHECK YOUR UNDERSTANDING

Open a new Script file (or modify the existing file if you have been following along) and create a prolog. Make a constant named `kIllegalNum` and assign it the value of 21. Subtract 2 from the `kIllegalNum` object and check the output to find the value.

1.7 Achievement 3: Understanding and changing data types

Kiara explained to Leslie that objects like `kStates` are interpreted by R as one of several *data types*. To see what data type `kStates` is, Kiara demonstrated the `class()` function, like this:

```
# identify data type for states object
class(x = kStates)
## [1] "numeric"
```

1.7.1 NUMERIC DATA TYPE

In the case of the `kStates` object, R prints the data type *numeric* from the `class()` function. The numeric data type is the default that R assigns to constants and variables that contain only numbers. The numeric data type can hold whole numbers and numbers with decimal places, so it is the most appropriate data type for variables measured along a continuum, or *continuous* variables. For example, both height and temperature can be measured along a continuum and would usually be a numeric data type in R.

To practice, Leslie created a constant that contains the ounces of medical marijuana legally available to purchase per person in Rhode Island, then used `class()` to identify the data type. As she wrote, she annotated the code.

```
# assign Rhode Island limit for medical marijuana
# in ounces per person
kOuncesRhode <- 2.5

# identify the data type for kOuncesRhode
class(x = kOuncesRhode)
## [1] "numeric"
```

1.7.2 INTEGER DATA TYPE

The *integer* data type is similar to numeric but contains only whole numbers. There are true integers that can only be measured in whole numbers, like the number of cars parked in a lot. There are also things that could be numeric but are measured as integers, like measuring age as *age in years*. When a whole number is assigned to a variable name in R, the default type is numeric. To change the variable type to integer, use the R function `as.integer()`. The `as.integer()` function can also be used to truncate numbers with decimal places. Note that truncation is not the same as rounding! Truncation cuts off everything after the decimal place. For example, truncating the value 8.9 would leave 8. Rounding goes up or down to the nearest whole number, so 8.9 would round to 9.

Kiara explained to Leslie that the default integer type is not always the best type for the data and had her explore the integer data type.

```
# assign the value of 4 to a constant called kTestInteger
# make sure it is an integer
kTestInteger <- as.integer(x = 4)

# use class() to determine the data type of kTestInteger
class(x = kTestInteger)
## [1] "integer"

# use as.integer() to truncate the constant kOuncesRhode
as.integer(x = kOuncesRhode)
## [1] 2

# multiply the kTestInteger and kOuncesRhode constants
kTestInteger * kOuncesRhode
## [1] 10

# multiply kTestInteger and integer kOuncesRhode constants
kTestInteger * as.integer(x = kOuncesRhode)
## [1] 8

# type the object name to see what is currently saved
# in the object
kOuncesRhode
## [1] 2.5
```

1.7.3 LOGICAL DATA TYPE

The *logical* data type contains the values of TRUE and FALSE. The values of TRUE and FALSE can be assigned to a logical constant, like this:

```
# create the constant
kTestLogical <- TRUE
```

```
# print the value of the constant
kTestLogical
## [1] TRUE

# check the constant data type
class(x = kTestLogical)
## [1] "logical"
```

Logical constants can also be created as the result of some expression, such as the following:

```
# store the result of 6 > 8 in a constant called kSixEight
kSixEight <- 6 > 8

# print kSixEight
kSixEight
## [1] FALSE

# determine the data type of kSixEight
class(x = kSixEight)
## [1] "logical"
```

Because 6 is not greater than 8, the expression 6 > 8 is FALSE, which is assigned to the kSixEight constant.

1.7.4 CHARACTER DATA TYPE

The *character* data type contains letters, words, or numbers that cannot logically be included in calculations (e.g., a zip code). They are always wrapped in either single or double quotation marks (e.g., 'hello' or "world"). Kiara had Leslie try creating a few character constants.

```
# make constants
kFirstName <- "Corina"
kLastName <- "Hughes"

# check the data type
class(x = kFirstName)
## [1] "character"

# create a zip code constant
# check the data type
kZipCode <- "97405"
class(x = kZipCode)
## [1] "character"
```

Leslie was confused as to why the zip code class was character when it is clearly an integer. Kiara reminded her that putting things in quote marks signifies to R that it is a character data type.

1.7.5 FACTOR DATA TYPE

In addition to the data types above, the *factor* data type is used for constants and variables that are made up of data elements that fall into categories. Variables measured in categories are *categorical*.

Examples of categorical variables can include variables like religion, marital status, age group, and so on. There are two types of categorical variables: *ordinal* and *nominal*. Ordinal variables contain categories that have some logical order. For example, categories of age can logically be put in order from younger to older: 18–25, 26–39, 40–59, 60+. Nominal variables have categories that have no logical order. Religious affiliation and marital status are examples of nominal variable types because there is no logical order to these characteristics (e.g., Methodist is not inherently greater or less than Catholic).

1.7.6 ACHIEVEMENT 3: CHECK YOUR UNDERSTANDING

Check the data type for the `kIllegalNum` constant created in the Check Your Understanding exercise for Achievement 1.

1.8 Achievement 4: Entering or loading data into R

Usually, when social scientists collect information to answer a question, they collect more than one number or word since collecting only one would be extremely inefficient. As a result, there are groups of data elements to be stored together. There are many ways to enter and store information like this. One commonly used object type is a *vector*. A vector is a set of data elements saved as the same type (numeric, logical, etc.). Each entry in a vector is called a *member* or *component* of the vector. Vectors are commonly used to store variables.

1.8.1 CREATING VECTORS FOR DIFFERENT DATA TYPES

The format for creating a vector uses the `c()` function for concatenate. The parentheses are filled with the member of the vector separated by commas. If the members of the vector are meant to be saved as character-type variables, use single or double quotes around each member. Kiara demonstrated creating and printing character, numeric, and logical vectors:

```
# creates character vector char.vector
char.vector <- c('Oregon', 'Vermont', 'Maine')
# prints vector char.vector
char.vector

## [1] "Oregon" "Vermont" "Maine"

# creates numeric vector nums.1.to.4
nums.1.to.4 <- c(1, 2, 3, 4)
# prints vector nums.1.to.4
nums.1.to.4

## [1] 1 2 3 4

# creates logical vector logic.vector
logic.vector <- c(TRUE, FALSE, FALSE, TRUE)
```

```
# prints vector logic.vector
logic.vector

## [1] TRUE FALSE FALSE TRUE
```

Kiara mentioned that she had added a space after each comma when creating the vectors, and that this was one of the good coding practices Leslie should use. While the space is not necessary for the code to work, it does make it easier to read. Leslie wondered why some of the code is a different color. Specifically, she saw the code after a hashtag is a different color from other code. Nancy explained that these are the comments. They can appear alone on a line, or they can be at the end of a line of regular code.

Nancy chimed in with her favorite thing, a coding trick. This one is for creating new objects and printing them at the same time by adding parentheses around the code that creates the object.

```
# create and print vectors
( char.vector <- c('Oregon', 'Vermont', 'Maine') )
## [1] "Oregon" "Vermont" "Maine"
( nums.1.to.4 <- c(1, 2, 3, 4) )
## [1] 1 2 3 4
( logic.vector <- c(TRUE, FALSE, FALSE, TRUE) )
## [1]  TRUE FALSE FALSE TRUE
```

The next thing Kiara covered is how vectors can be combined, added to, subtracted from, subsetted, and other operations. She used the nums.1.to.4 vector to show examples of each of these with comments that explain what is happening with each line of code.

```
# add 3 to each element in the nums.1.to.4 vector
nums.1.to.4 + 3
## [1] 4 5 6 7

# add 1 to the 1st element of nums.1.to.4, 2 to the 2nd element, etc
nums.1.to.4 + c(1, 2, 3, 4)
## [1] 2 4 6 8

# multiply each element of nums.1.to.4 by 5
nums.1.to.4 * 5
## [1] 5 10 15 20

# subtract 1 from each element and then divide by 5
(nums.1.to.4 - 1) / 5
## [1] 0.0 0.2 0.4 0.6

# make a subset of the vector including numbers > 2
nums.1.to.4[nums.1.to.4 > 2]
## [1] 3 4
```

As she read the code, Leslie kept reminding herself that the dots in the middle of the variable names are not decimal points, but are there to separate parts of the variable names, which use dot case.

So far, the results of these operations are just printed in the Console; they are nowhere to be found in the Environment pane. Leslie asked how to keep the results. Kiara explained that the results could be assigned to a new vector object using the assignment arrow, like this:

```
# add 3 to number vector and save
# as new vector
( nums.1.to.4.plus.3 <- nums.1.to.4 + 3 )
## [1] 4 5 6 7

# divide vector by 10 and save
# as new vector
( nums.1.to.4.div.10 <- nums.1.to.4 / 10 )
## [1] 0.1 0.2 0.3 0.4
```

The results show the original vector with 3 added to each value and the result of that addition divided by 10. The results print in the Console and also are saved and can be found in the Environment pane.

Kiara explained that it is possible to do multiple computations on a single vector.

```
# add 3 and divide by 10 for each vector member
( nums.1.to.4.new <- (nums.1.to.4 + 3) / 10 )
## [1] 0.4 0.5 0.6 0.7
```

1.8.2 CREATING A MATRIX TO STORE DATA IN ROWS AND COLUMNS

In addition to the vector format, Kiara explained that R also uses the *matrix* format to store information. A matrix is information, or data elements, stored in a rectangular format with rows and columns. Coders can perform operations on matrices, or more than one matrix, as with vectors.

The R function for producing a matrix is, surprisingly, matrix(). This function takes arguments to enter the data, data =, and to specify the number of rows, nrow =, and columns, ncol =. Kiara explained that the most confusing part of matrix() is the byrow = argument, which tells R whether to fill the data into the matrix by filling across first (fill row 1, then fill row 2, etc.) or by filling down first (fill column 1 first, then fill column 2, etc.). In this case, Kiara chose byrow = TRUE so the data fill across first. For the columns to fill first, she would have to use byrow = FALSE instead.

```
# create and print a matrix
( policies <- matrix(data = c(1, 2, 3, 4, 5, 6),    #data in the matrix
                     nrow = 2,                       # number of rows
                     ncol = 3,                       # number of columns
                     byrow = TRUE) )                 # fill the matrix by rows
##      [,1] [,2] [,3]
## [1,]   1    2    3
## [2,]   4    5    6
```

Say the matrix includes the number of states with policies legalizing medical, recreational, and both types of marijuana that were in effect in 2013 and 2014. Leslie asked about naming the rows and columns so she can remember what they are. Kiara started to explain when Nancy jumped in to demonstrate by writing the code, which uses dimnames() to assign names to rows and columns. As Nancy typed the code, Kiara explained that the names are entered in vectors inside a list, with the first vector being the row names and the second vector being the column names. In this case, the row names were c("2013", "2014") for the two years of data and the column names were c("medical", "recreational", "both") for the three types of policy.

```
# add names to the rows and columns of the matrix
dimnames(x = policies) <- list(
  c("2013", "2014"),                          # row names
  c("medical", "recreational", "both")        # column names
)

# print the policies matrix
policies
##        medical recreational both
## 2013         1            2    3
## 2014         4            5    6
```

Now Leslie could find specific data elements in her matrix, such as the number of states with legal medical marijuana policies in 2014.

Leslie was still trying to remember all the data types and asked what would happen if she had a vector of the types of policies that had passed instead of the number of policies per year. Would this be a factor data type?

```
# vector of policy types
policy.2013.and.2014 <- c('medical', 'medical', 'both', 'recreational',
                          'medical', 'both', 'both')

# data type
class(x = policy.2013.and.2014)
## [1] "character"
```

Leslie thought this would be a factor data type since the policy type is a categorical variable, but R assigned the character type to her vector. Kiara explained that she could use the as.factor() function to change the variable type to factor instead.

```
# change the data type to factor
policy.2013.and.2014 <- as.factor(x = policy.2013.and.2014)

# check the data type
class(x = policy.2013.and.2014)
## [1] "factor"
```

1.8.3 CREATING A DATA FRAME

Similar to a matrix format, the *data frame* format has rows and columns of data. In the data frame format, rows are observations and columns are variables. Data frames are often entered outside of R into a spreadsheet or other type of file and then imported into R for analysis. However, R users can also make their own data frame using vectors or matrices. For example, if Kiara looked up five states, the year they made medical marijuana legal, and the limit per person in ounces for possession of medical marijuana, she could enter these data into three vectors and combine them into a data frame using the `data.frame()` function, like this:

```
# state, year enacted, personal oz limit medical marijuana
# create vectors
state <- c('Alaska', 'Arizona', 'Arkansas', 'California', 'Colorado')
year.legal <- c('1998', '2010', '2016', '1996', '2000')
ounce.lim <- c(1, 2.5, 3, 8, 2)

# combine vectors into a data frame
# name the data frame pot.legal
pot.legal <- data.frame(state, year.legal, ounce.lim)
```

Just like in the `matrix()` function, the `data.frame()` function reads in multiple arguments. The `data.frame()` function has three arguments: `state`, `year.legal`, and `ounce.lim`. This time, all of the arguments are objects, but that will not always be the case. In fact, arguments can even be functions with their own arguments!

After entering and running these code lines, Kiara suggested that Leslie check the Environment pane, where she should now see a new entry called `pot.legal`. To the right of the label `pot.legal`, Leslie saw "5 obs. of 3 variables" indicating she had entered five observations and three variables. The blue and white circle with a triangle in it to the left of `pot.legal` allowed Leslie to expand this entry to see more information about what is contained in the `pot.legal` object, like Figure 1.6.

Leslie noticed in the Environment window that the `state` variable in the `pot.legal` data frame was assigned the variable type of factor, which is incorrect. Names of states are unique and not categories in this data set. Leslie wanted to change the name variable to a character variable using the `as.character()` function.

Because the state variable is now part of a data frame object, Kiara explained to Leslie that she would have to identify both the data frame and the variable in order to change it. To demonstrate, Kiara

FIGURE 1.6 Environment window in RStudio showing the newly created data frame

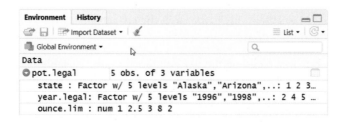

entered the name of the data frame first, a `$` to separate the data frame name, and the variable name, like this:

```
# change state variable from pot.legal data frame
# to a character variable
pot.legal$state <- as.character(x = pot.legal$state)

# check the variable type
class(x = pot.legal$state)
## [1] "character"
```

Now that Leslie had a data frame, there were many options open for data management and analysis. For example, she could examine basic information about the variables in her data by using the `summary()` function. The `summary()` function requires at least one argument that identifies the object that should be summarized, like this:

```
# summarize the data frame
summary(object = pot.legal)
##     state            year.legal     ounce.lim
##   Length:5           1996:1       Min.   :1.0
##   Class :character   1998:1       1st Qu.:2.0
##   Mode  :character   2000:1       Median :2.5
##                      2010:1       Mean   :3.3
##                      2016:1       3rd Qu.:3.0
##                                   Max.   :8.0
```

This output looked a little confusing to Leslie, so Kiara explained what she was seeing. The top row contains the names of the three variables in the `pot.legal` data frame. Below each variable is some information about that variable. What is shown there depends on the data type of the variable. The `state` variable is a character variable, so the information below `state` shows how many observations there were for this variable in the `Length:5` row. The next row shows the class of the `state` variable with `Class :character` and the `mode` or most common value of the variable. Leslie was curious about this use of mode since she had learned it before as a measure of *central tendency*; Kiara explained that mode is one of the descriptive statistics they would talk about next time they met.

The next column of information is for the `year.legal` variable, which is a factor variable. This entry shows each of the categories of the factor and how many observations are in that category. For example, 1996 is one of the categories of the factor, and there is one observation for 1996. Likewise, 2016 is one of the categories of the factor, and there is one observation in this category. Kiara mentioned that this output shows up to six rows of information for each variable in a data frame, and many variables will have more than six categories. When this is the case, the six categories with the most observations in them will be shown in the output of `summary()`.

Finally, the `ounce.lim` column, based on the `ounce.lim` numeric variable, shows `Min. :1.0`, which indicates that the minimum value of this variable is 1. This column also shows `Max. :8.0` for the maximum value of 8 and a few other *descriptive statistics* that Kiara assured Leslie the R-Team would discuss more the next time they meet.

1.8.4 IMPORTING DATA FRAMES FROM OUTSIDE SOURCES

Kiara mentioned that, while typing data directly into R is possible and sometimes necessary, most of the time analysts like Leslie will open data from an outside source. R is unique among statistical software packages because it has the capability of importing and opening data files saved in most formats. Some formats open directly in the base version of R. Other data formats require the use of an *R package*, which Kiara reminded Leslie is a special program written to do something specific in R.

To know what format a data file is saved in, examine the file extension. Common file extensions for data files are as follows:

- **.csv**: comma separated values
- **.txt**: text file
- **.xls** or **.xlsx**: Excel file
- *.sav*: *SPSS* file
- **.sasb7dat**: SAS file
- **.xpt**: SAS transfer file
- **.dta**: Stata file

1.8.5 IMPORTING A COMMA SEPARATED VALUES (CSV) FILE

Kiara added that, in addition to knowing which kind of file a data file is, Leslie would need to know the location of the file. R can open files saved locally on a computer, in an accessible shared location, or directly from the Internet. The file Nancy analyzed at the beginning of the day was saved in csv format online. There are several possible ways to read in this type of file; the most straightforward way is with the `read.csv()` function; however, Kiara warned that this function may sometimes result in misreading of variable names or row names and to look out for that.

While the GSS data can be read into R directly from the GSS website, Kiara had experienced this and knew that it could be frustrating. Since this was Leslie's first time importing data into R from an external source, Kiara decided they should try a more straightforward example. She saved two of the variables from the GSS data Nancy imported for Figure 1.1 and made the data file available at **edge.sagepub .com/harris1e** with the file name **legal_weed_age_GSS2016_ch1.csv**.

Kiara explained to Leslie that it might work best to make a data folder inside the folder where she is keeping her code and save the downloaded data there. Once Leslie created the folder and saved the data, Kiara explained that the `read.csv()` function could be used to import the data from that folder location, like this:

```
# read the GSS 2016 data
gss.2016 <- read.csv(file = "[data folder location]/data/legal_weed_age_
GSS2016_ch1.csv")

# examine the contents of the file
summary(object = gss.2016)
##       ï..grass        age
##   DK    : 110    57    :  70
##   IAP   : 911    58    :  67
```

```
##   LEGAL    :1126    52        :  65
##   NOT LEGAL: 717    53        :  60
##   NA's     :   3    27        :  58
##                     (Other):2537
##                     NA's    :  10
```

The summary() function output shows two column headings, i..grass and age. Kiara pointed out the strange i..grass heading should probably just be grass, and this is an example of what can happen with read.csv(). These two column headings are the two variables in the data set. Under each of these headings are two more columns separated by colons. The column before the colon lists the values that are present in the variable. The column after the colon lists the number of times the value is present in the variable. The information under the i..grass column heading shows that DK is one of the values of the i..grass variable, and this value occurs 110 times.

Kiara advised Leslie that the fread() function in the *data.table* package or the read_csv() function in the **tidyverse** package might be more useful for opening csv files saved from online sources. To install a package, go to the Tools menu in RStudio and select Install Packages.... Type "data.table" or the name of whichever package should be installed in the dialog box that opens. For other ways to install packages, see Box 1.6.

1.6 Nancy's fancy code: Working with R packages

The basic R functions included with R can do a lot, but not everything. Additional functions are included in packages developed by researchers and others around the world and contributed to the R open-source platform. We will use many of these packages throughout this text. One that was used to create the plots above was *ggplot2*, which is available as a standalone package or as part of the **tidyverse** package. To use a package, it first has to be installed. There are at least two ways to install an R package. One is to use the Tools menu and select Install Packages . . . and choose or type the exact name of the package you want to install.

The second way is to use the R install.packages() function, like this:

```
install.packages(pkgs = "tidyverse")
```

Using Install Packages . . . from the Tools menu may work best because installing a package is a *one-time* task, so writing code is not very efficient.

To use **ggplot2** after **tidyverse** is installed, it has to be opened. Unlike installing, every time a package is used, it must be opened first. This is similar to other software programs. For example, Microsoft Word is installed once but opened every time it is used. Use the library() function to open an R package.

```
library(package = "tidyverse")
```

Once a package is open, all of its functions are available. Run the code below to make Figure 1.7 from one of the data sets built into R. The USArrests data set includes information on assaults, murder, rape, and percentage of the population living in urban areas for all 50 states. Note that the code may seem confusing now since the **ggplot2** functions are complicated, but code to make great graphs will be explored and repeated throughout the upcoming meetings.

```
# pipe the data set into ggplot (Figure 1.7)
# in the aesthetics provide the variable names for the x and y axes
# choose a geom for graph type
# add axis labels with labs
# choose a theme for the overall graph look
USArrests %>%
  ggplot(aes(x = UrbanPop, y = Assault)) +
  geom_point() +
  labs(x = "Percent of state population living in urban areas",
       y = "Number of reported assaults per 100,000 annually") +
theme_minimal()
```

FIGURE 1.7 Urban population and assaults at the state level from USArrests built-in R data source

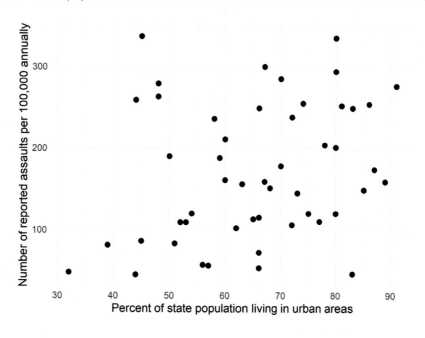

Once a package is installed, Kiara explained, there are two ways Leslie could use it. If she wanted to use more than one or two functions from the package, she could open it with the `library()` function. In this case, `library(package = "data.table")` opens the **data.table** package for use. Once the package is open, Leslie could use the functions defined in the package. Also useful, explained Kiara, is the documentation for each package that shows all the functions available ("Available CRAN Packages," n.d.; Dowle & Srinivasan, 2019).

Using `library(package = )` is the common practice for opening and using packages most of the time in R. Once the package is opened using `library(package = )`, it stays open until R is closed. When using a function from a package one time, it is not necessary to open the package and leave it open. Instead, there is another way to open a package temporarily just to use a particular function. To temporarily open a package in order to use a function from the package, add the package name before the function name and separate with two colons, like this: `package.name::function()`.

At Kiara's suggestion, Leslie installed **data.table** and used the temporary way with the `::` to open the **data.table** package and used the fast and friendly file finagler `fread()` function from the package to open the GSS data file. She then used the summary function to see what was in the file.

```
# bring in GSS 2016 data
gss.2016 <- data.table::fread(input = "[data folder location]/data/legal_
weed_age_GSS2016_ch1.csv")

# examine the contents of the file
summary(object = gss.2016)
##     grass              age
## Length:2867        Length:2867
## Class :character   Class :character
## Mode  :character   Mode  :character
```

Leslie noticed that the variable names now look better, but both the variables now seem to be character variables, so they might have to use `as.factor()` and `as.numeric()` to fix the data types before using these variables.

Before they continued, Kiara wanted to mention another important benefit of the `::` way of opening a package for use. Occasionally, two different packages can have a function with the same name. If two packages containing function names that are the same are opened at the same time in an R file, there will be a *namespace* conflict where R cannot decide which function to use. One example is the function `summarize()`, which is included as part of the *dplyr* package and the *Hmisc* package. When both packages are open, using the `summarize()` function results in an error. Kiara explained that the **dplyr** package is loaded with the **tidyverse**. To demonstrate the error, she installed and opened **tidyverse** and **Hmisc**.

```
# load Hmisc and tidyverse
library(package = "tidyverse")
library(package = "Hmisc")
```

Kiara typed the `summarize()` function to try to get the length of the `age` variable from the `gss.2016` data frame. Kiara noted that this code is more complicated than what they had looked at so far, and they will go through the formatting soon, but for now, this is just to demonstrate how the use of the `summarize()` function results in a conflict when both **dplyr** and **Hmisc** are open.

```
# use the summarize function
gss.2016 %>%
  summarize(length.age = length(x = age))
```

The result of running her code is the error message in Figure 1.8.

FIGURE 1.8 Namespace error with `summarize()` function

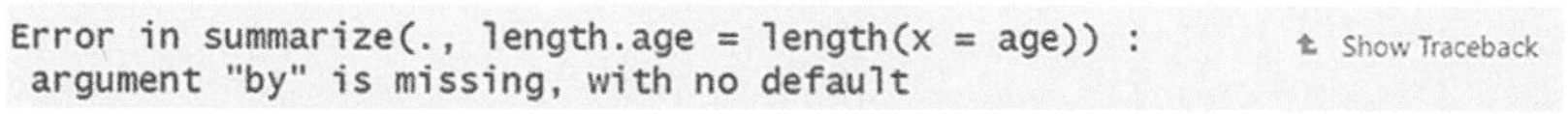

```
Error in summarize(., length.age = length(x = age)) :
 argument "by" is missing, with no default        ⟲ Show Traceback
```

Kiara mentioned that this was relatively rare, but it was a good thing to keep in mind when a function does not run. Leslie asked what could be done at this point. Kiara said there are a couple of ways to check to see if a namespace conflict is occurring. The first is to use the `conflicts()` function.

```
# check for conflicts
conflicts()
##  [1] "%>%"            "%>%"            "src"            "summarize"
##  [5] "%>%"            "discard"        "col_factor"     "%>%"
##  [9] "add_row"        "as_data_frame"  "as_tibble"      "data_frame"
## [13] "data_frame_"    "frame_data"     "glimpse"        "lst"
## [17] "lst_"           "tbl_sum"        "tibble"         "tribble"
## [21] "trunc_mat"      "type_sum"       "alpha"          "enexpr"
## [25] "enexprs"        "enquo"          "enquos"         "ensym"
## [29] "ensyms"         "expr"           "quo"            "quo_name"
## [33] "quos"           "sym"            "syms"           "vars"
## [37] "between"        "first"          "last"           "transpose"
## [41] "filter"         "lag"            "body<-"         "format.pval"
## [45] "intersect"      "kronecker"      "Position"       "setdiff"
## [49] "setequal"       "union"          "units"
```

Among the conflicts, Leslie saw the `summarize()` function. Kiara said the easiest thing to do to address the conflict is to use the `::` and specify which package to get the `summarize()` function from. To use the `summarize()` function from **dplyr**, the code would look like this:

```
# use summarize from dplyr
gss.2016 %>%
  dplyr::summarize(length.age = length(x = age))
##    length.age
## 1       2867
```

The function now works to find the length of the `age` variable. Another way to check and see if a function is in conflict after an error message is to use the `environment()` function and check which package is the source for the `summarize()` function. Kiara wrote the code to do this:

```
# check source package for summarize
environment(fun = summarize)
## <environment: namespace:Hmisc>
```

The output shows that the namespace for `summarize()` is the **Hmisc** package instead of the **dplyr** package. Use of the `::` works to fix this, but another strategy would be to detach the **Hmisc** package before running `summarize()`, like this:

```
# detach Hmisc
detach(name = package:Hmisc)

# try summarize
gss.2016 %>%
  summarize(length.age = length(x = age))
##    length.age
## 1        2867
```

This works too! If the package is not needed again, this method of addressing the namespace conflict will avoid additional conflicts in the document.

1.8.6 CLEANING DATA TYPES IN AN IMPORTED FILE

After that long detour, Kiara went back to the task at hand. She noted for Leslie that, while the variable names look good after loading with `fread()`, both of the variables were the character data type. Leslie knew that most data sets have a codebook that lists all the variables and how they were measured. This information would help her to identify what data types are appropriate for variables and other information about the data. She checked the codebook for the GSS (National Opinion Research Center, 2019) that was saved as **gss_codebook.pdf** at **edge.sagepub.com/harris1e** to determine what data types these variables are. On page 304 of the codebook, it shows the measurement of the variable `grass`, which has five possible responses:

- Do you think the use of marijuana should be made legal or not?
  - Should
  - Should not
  - Don't know
  - No answer
  - Not applicable

Leslie remembered that variables with categories are categorical and should be factor type variables in R.

Leslie tried to find the `age` variable in the codebook, but the codebook is difficult to use because it is too long. Kiara suggested Leslie look on the GSS Data Explorer website for more information about the `age` variable and how it is measured. Leslie found and reviewed the `age` variable in the Data Explorer, and it appears to be measured in years up to age 88, and then "89 OR OLDER" represents people who are 89 years old or older.

Kiara suggested Leslie use the `head()` function to get a sense of the data. This function shows the first six observations.

```
# first six observations in the gss.2016 data frame
head(x = gss.2016)
##           grass age
## 1:          IAP 47
## 2:        LEGAL 61
## 3: NOT LEGAL 72
## 4:          IAP 43
## 5:        LEGAL 55
## 6:        LEGAL 53
```

After she viewed the six observations, Leslie determined `grass` should be a factor and `age` should be numeric. Kiara agreed, but before Leslie wrote the code, Nancy added that since "89 OR OLDER" is not saved as just a number, trying to force the `age` variable with "89 OR OLDER" in it into a numeric variable would result in an error. She suggested that before converting `age` into a numeric variable, they should first *recode* anyone who has a value of "89 OR OLDER" to instead have a value of "89." Nancy explained that this will ensure that `age` can be treated as a numeric variable. Kiara warned that they will need to be careful in how they use and report this recoded `age` variable since it would be inaccurate to say that every person with the original "89 OR OLDER" label was actually 89 years old. However, Nancy reminded Kiara that they were going to look at age categories like she did for Figure 1.2 and that changing the "89 OR OLDER" people to have an age of 89 would be OK for making a categorical age variable. Their plan was to change the `grass` variable to a factor and recode the `age` variable before changing it to either numeric or integer. When it is unclear whether to choose between numeric and integer data types, numeric is more flexible.

Leslie started with converting `grass` into a factor. Because she was *not* changing the contents of the variables, she kept the same variable names. To do this, she used the arrow to keep the same name for the variable with the new assigned type . Kiara pointed out the data frame name and variable name on the left of the assignment arrow `<-` are exactly the same as on the right. When new information is assigned to an existing variable, it overwrites whatever was saved in that variable.

```
# change grass variable to a factor
gss.2016$grass <- as.factor(x = gss.2016$grass)
```

For the trickier bit of recoding `age`, Nancy took over.

```
# recode the 89 OR OLDER category to 89
gss.2016$age[gss.2016$age == "89 OR OLDER"] <- "89"
```

Nancy explained that this line of code can be read as follows: "In the `age` variable of the `gss.2016` data frame, find any observation that is equal to '89 OR OLDER' and assign those particular observations to be the character '89.'" Kiara reassured Leslie that even though this particular line of code is tricky, it would be covered in more detail later and Leslie would surely get the hang of it.

Leslie went back and tried to integrate what she had learned.

```
# bring in GSS 2016 data
gss.2016 <- data.table::fread(input = "[data folder location]/data/legal_
weed_age_GSS2016_ch1.csv")

# change the variable type for the grass variable
gss.2016$grass <- as.factor(x = gss.2016$grass)

# recode "89 OR OLDER" into just "89"
gss.2016$age[gss.2016$age == "89 OR OLDER"] <- "89"

# change the variable type for the age variable
gss.2016$age <- as.numeric(x = gss.2016$age)

# examine the variable types and summary to
# check the work
class(x = gss.2016$grass)
## [1] "factor"
class(x = gss.2016$age)
## [1] "numeric"
summary(object = gss.2016)
##        grass             age
## DK         : 110   Min.   :18.00
## IAP        : 911   1st Qu.:34.00
## LEGAL      :1126   Median :49.00
## NOT LEGAL: 717     Mean   :49.16
## NA's       :   3   3rd Qu.:62.00
##                    Max.   :89.00
##                    NA's   :10
```

Leslie used `class()` and `summary()` to check and confirm that the variables were now the correct type.

1.8.7 ACHIEVEMENT 4: CHECK YOUR UNDERSTANDING

Use `fread()` to open the GSS 2016 data set. Look in the Environment pane to find the number of observations and the number and types of variables in the data frame.

1.9 Achievement 5: Identifying and treating missing values

In addition to making sure the variables used are an appropriate type, Kiara explained that it was also important to make sure that missing values were treated appropriately by R. In R, missing values are recorded as *NA*, which stands for *not available*. Researchers code missing values in many different ways when collecting and storing data. Some of the more common ways to denote missing values are the following:

- blank
- 777, −777, 888, −888, 999, −999, or something similar
- a single period
- −1
- NULL

Other responses, such as "Don't know" or "Inapplicable," may sometimes be treated as missing or as response categories depending on what is most appropriate given the characteristics of the data and the analysis goals.

1.9.1 RECODING MISSING VALUES TO NA

In the summary of the GSS data, the `grass` variable has five possible values: DK (don't know), IAP (inapplicable), LEGAL, NOT LEGAL, and NA (not available). The DK, IAP, and NA could all be considered missing values. However, R treats only NA as missing. Before conducting any analyses, the DK and IAP values could be converted to NA to be treated as missing in any analyses. That is, the `grass` variable could be recoded so that these values are all NA. Note that NA is a reserved "word" in R. In order to use NA, both letters must be uppercase (Na or na does not work), and there can be no quotation marks (R will treat "NA" as a character rather than a true missing value).

There are many ways to recode variables in R. Leslie already saw one way, using Nancy's bit of code for the `age` variable. Kiara's favorite way uses the data management package **tidyverse** (https://www .rdocumentation.org/packages/tidyverse/). Kiara closed her laptop to show Leslie one of her laptop stickers. It shows the **tidyverse** logo in a hexagon. Kiara explained that R users advertise the packages they use and like with hexagonal laptop stickers. It is not unusual, she said, to see a laptop covered in stickers like the one in Figure 1.9.

FIGURE 1.9 **tidyverse** hex laptop sticker

Source: RStudio.

Since Leslie had installed and opened **tidyverse**, they could start on data management. Kiara mentioned that if a package is not installed before using `library()` to open it, the library function will show an error.

Kiara showed Leslie the pipe feature, `%>%`, that is available in the **tidyverse** package and useful for data management and other tasks. The `%>%` works to send or *pipe* information through a function or set of functions. In this case, Kiara said, they would pipe the `gss.2016` data set into a `mutate()` function that can be used to recode values. The `mutate()` function takes the name of the variable to recode and then information on how to recode it. Kiara thought it might just be best to show Leslie the code and walk through it.

```
# start over by bringing in the data again
gss.2016 <- data.table::fread(input = "[data folder location]/data/legal_
weed_age_GSS2016_ch1.csv")

# use tidyverse pipe to change DK to NA
gss.2016.cleaned <- gss.2016 %>%
  mutate(grass = as.factor(x = grass)) %>%
  mutate(grass = na_if(x = grass, y = "DK"))

# check the summary, there should be 110 + 3 in the NA category
summary(object = gss.2016.cleaned)
##           grass            age
##   DK        :    0   Length:2867
##   IAP       :  911   Class :character
##   LEGAL     : 1126   Mode  :character
##   NOT LEGAL :  717
##   NA's      :  113
```

Kiara walked Leslie through the data management code. First is the `gss.2016.cleaned <-`, which indicates that whatever happens on the right-hand side of the `<-` will be assigned to the `gss.2016.cleaned` object name. The first thing after the arrow is `gss.2016 %>%`, which indicates that the `gss.2016` data are being piped into whatever comes on the next line; in this case, it is being piped into the `mutate()` function. The `mutate()` function on the next line uses the `na_if()` function to make the `grass` variable equal to `NA` if the `grass` variable is currently coded as `DK`.

Leslie was a little confused but tried to summarize what the code did. First she asked Kiara why they now have a new name for the data with `gss.2016.cleaned`. Kiara explained that it is good practice to keep the original data unchanged in case you need to go back to it later. Then Leslie said she believed the function was changing the `DK` values in the `grass` variable to `NA`, which is R shorthand for missing. Kiara said that was correct and it was completely fine to be confused. She admitted it just took a while to get used to the way R works and the way different structures like the `%>%` work. Kiara thought maybe adding the `IAP` recoding to the code might be useful for reinforcing the ideas. She added to her code to replace `IAP` with `NA`.

```
# use tidyverse pipe to change DK and IAP to NA
gss.2016.cleaned <- gss.2016 %>%
  mutate(grass = as.factor(x = grass)) %>%
  mutate(grass = na_if(x = grass, y = "DK")) %>%
  mutate(grass = na_if(x = grass, y = "IAP"))

# check the summary, there should now be 110 + 911 + 3 in the NA category
summary(object = gss.2016.cleaned)
##       grass             age
## DK        :   0    Length:2867
## IAP       :   0    Class :character
## LEGAL     :1126    Mode  :character
## NOT LEGAL : 717
## NA's      :1024
```

That worked!

Leslie found the summary information accurate, with zero observations coded as DK or IAP. However, the DK and IAP category labels were still listed even though there are no observations with these coded values. Kiara explained that R will keep all the different levels of a factor during a recode, so Leslie would need to remove unused categories with a droplevels() function if she no longer needed them. Leslie wanted to try this herself and added a line of code to Kiara's code.

```
# use tidyverse pipe to change DK and IAP to NA
gss.2016.cleaned <- gss.2016 %>%
  mutate(grass = as.factor(x = grass)) %>%
  mutate(grass = na_if(x = grass, y = "DK")) %>%
  mutate(grass = na_if(x = grass, y = "IAP")) %>%
  mutate(grass = droplevels(x = grass))

# check the summary
summary(object = gss.2016.cleaned)
##       grass             age
## LEGAL     :1126    Length:2867
## NOT LEGAL : 717    Class :character
## NA's      :1024    Mode  :character
```

Leslie was pretty excited that she had figured it out! She asked Kiara if she could do the change of data type for the grass and age variables in the same set of functions as the recoding of NA values. Kiara thought this was a great idea and suggested that they do one more recoding task and combine the recoding of `age` and `grass` functions so they would have everything all together. Nancy explained that this means a slightly different way of recoding the "89 OR OLDER" observations using `mutate()`. Leslie was excited to see this! It worked well to have all the data management together in one place.

In addition to adding the `age` and `grass` recoding, the final function to add was to create the age categories shown in Figure 1.2. The `age` variable currently holds the age in years rather than age categories. The graph Kiara made at the beginning showed age in four categories:

- 18–29
- 30–59
- 60–74
- 75+

Kiara suggested naming the categorical `age` variable `age.cat`. She clarified that this is not referring to the age of actual cats, but instead is for the categories of ages. Nancy rolled her eyes at this joke attempt. Kiara was unfazed and showed Leslie the function `cut()`, which can be used to divide a continuous variable into categories by cutting it into pieces and adding a label to each piece. Leslie added `as.numeric()` and `as.factor()` to the `mutate()` functions in the set of data management tasks and then asked Kiara for help with the `cut()` function. Kiara explained that `cut` takes a variable like `age` as the first argument, so it would look like `cut(x = age,`.

The second thing to add after the variable name is a vector made up of the **breaks**. Breaks specify the lower and upper limit of each category of values. The first entry is the lowest value of the first category, the second entry is the highest value of the first category, the third entry is the highest value of the second category, and so on. The function now looks like `cut(x = age, breaks = c(-Inf, 29, 59, 74, Inf),`. Leslie noticed that the first and last values in the vector are `-Inf` and `Inf`. She guessed that these are negative infinity and positive infinity. Kiara confirmed that this was correct and let Leslie know that this was for convenience rather than looking up the smallest and largest values. It also makes the code more flexible in case there is a new data point with a smaller or larger value.

The final thing to add is a vector made up of the **labels** for the categories, with each label inside quote marks, like this: `labels = c("< 30", "30 - 59", "60 - 74", "75+" )`. The final `cut()` function would include these three things. Leslie gave it a try.

```
# use tidyverse to change data types and recode
gss.2016.cleaned <- gss.2016 %>%
  mutate(age = recode(.x = age, "89 OR OLDER" = "89")) %>%
  mutate(age = as.numeric(x = age)) %>%
  mutate(grass = as.factor(x = grass)) %>%
  mutate(grass = na_if(x = grass, y = "DK")) %>%
  mutate(grass = na_if(x = grass, y = "IAP")) %>%
  mutate(grass = droplevels(x = grass)) %>%
  mutate(age.cat = cut(x = age,
                  breaks = c(-Inf, 29, 59, 74, Inf),
                  labels = c("< 30", "30 - 59", "60 - 74", "75+" )))
summary(object = gss.2016.cleaned)
```

```
##       grass           age            age.cat
##  LEGAL      :1126   Min.   :18.00   < 30    : 481
##  NOT LEGAL: 717    1st Qu.:34.00   30 - 59:1517
##  NA's       :1024   Median :49.00   60 - 74: 598
##                     Mean   :49.16   75+     : 261
##                     3rd Qu.:62.00   NA's    :  10
##                     Max.   :89.00
##                     NA's   :10
```

Kiara thought they were ready to try the last task for the day, making a bar chart. First, though, she asked Leslie to practice putting all her code together and adding a prolog. She suggested Leslie make one change, which is to rename the data `gss.2106.cleaned` after all the data management and cleaning. This way she would have both the original `gss.2016` and the cleaned version of the data if she needed both.

```
########################################################
# Project: First R-team meeting
# Purpose: Clean GSS 2016 data
# Author: Leslie
# Edit date: April 20, 2019
# Data: GSS 2016 subset of age and marijuana use variables
########################################################

# bring in GSS 2016 data from the web and examine it
library(package = "data.table")
gss.2016 <- fread(file = "[data folder location]/data/legal_weed_age_
GSS2016_ch1.csv")

# use tidyverse to clean the data
library(package = "tidyverse")
gss.2016.cleaned <- gss.2016 %>%
  mutate(age = recode(.x = age, "89 OR OLDER" = "89")) %>%
  mutate(age = as.numeric(x = age)) %>%
  mutate(grass = as.factor(x = grass)) %>%
  mutate(grass = na_if(x = grass, y = "DK")) %>%
  mutate(grass = na_if(x = grass, y = "IAP")) %>%
  mutate(grass = droplevels(x = grass)) %>%
  mutate(age.cat = cut(x = age,
                  breaks = c(-Inf, 29, 59, 74, Inf),
                  labels = c("< 30", "30 - 59", "60 - 74", "75+" )))
```

```
# check the summary
summary(object = gss.2016.cleaned)
##        grass             age          age.cat
##   LEGAL     :1126  Min.   :18.00   < 30   : 481
##   NOT LEGAL: 717  1st Qu.:34.00   30 - 59:1517
##   NA's      :1024  Median :49.00   60 - 74: 598
##                    Mean   :49.16   75+    : 261
##                    3rd Qu.:62.00   NA's   : 10
##                    Max.   :89.00
##                    NA's   :10
```

1.9.2 ACHIEVEMENT 5: CHECK YOUR UNDERSTANDING

Describe what `mutate()`, `na_if()`, and `%>%` did in the final code Leslie wrote.

1.10 Achievement 6: Building a basic bar chart

Leslie was now ready to finish up a *very* long first day of R by creating the graph from the beginning of their meeting. Kiara introduced her to an R package called **ggplot2** to create this graph. The "gg" in **ggplot2** stands for the "grammar of graphics." The **ggplot2** package (https://www.rdocumentation.org/packages/ggplot2/) is part of the **tidyverse**, so it did not need to be installed or opened separately, and creating the graph would use some of the **tidyverse** skills from the data management. Before Kiara showed Leslie how to make the first graph, she examined it one more time (Figure 1.10).

FIGURE 1.10 Support for marijuana legalization among participants in the 2016 General Social Survey

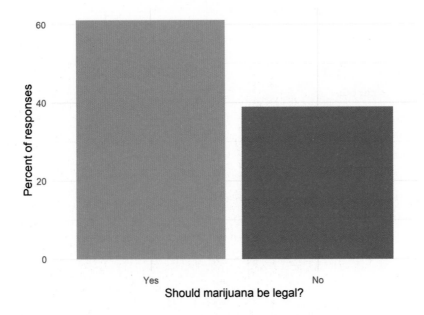

Kiara pointed out some of the important features of the graph:

- Both axes have titles.

- The *y*-axis is a percentage.

- The *x*-axis is labeled as Yes and No.

- It includes an overall title.

- The background for the graph is white with a light gray grid.

- The Yes bar is green, and the No bar is purple.

With Kiara's help, Leslie started with a basic plot using the `ggplot()` function. Kiara advised her to store the graph in a new object with a new name. Leslie chose `legalize.bar`. Kiara said to follow a similar structure to the data management from earlier. She started by piping the `gss.2016.cleaned` data frame. Kiara said the data would be piped into the `ggplot()` function this time. The `ggplot()` function needs to know which variable(s) from `gss.2016.cleaned` will be placed on the axes. In the *grammar of graphics*, this information is considered *aesthetics* and is included in the `aes()` function within the `ggplot()` function. There is only one variable for this graph, the `grass` variable, which is on the *x*-axis. Kiara helped Leslie write the code. After the basics of the graph were included in the `ggplot()` function, the graph type was added in a new *layer*.

Kiara explained that graphs built with `ggplot()` are built in layers. The first layer starts with `ggplot()` and contains the basic information about the data that are being graphed and which variables are included. The next layer typically gives the graph type, or *geometry* in the grammar of graphics language, and starts with `geom_` followed by one of the available types. In this case, Leslie was looking for a bar chart, so `geom_bar()` is the geometry for this graph. Leslie started to write this by adding a `%>%` after the line with `ggplot()` on it, but Kiara stopped her. The `geom_bar()` is not a separate new function, but is a layer of the plot and so is added with a + instead of a `%>%`. Leslie typed the code to create Figure 1.11.

FIGURE 1.11 Support for marijuana legalization among participants in the 2016 General Social Survey

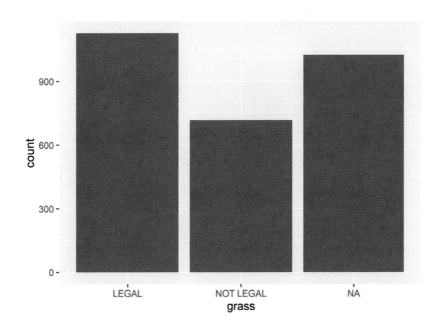

```
# make a bar chart for grass variable (Figure 1.11)
legalize.bar <- gss.2016.cleaned %>%
  ggplot(aes(x = grass)) +
  geom_bar()

# show the chart
legalize.bar
```

Leslie was happy it worked, even though it looked wrong. Kiara was happy, too—this was a great result for a first use of ggplot(). One of the first things Leslie noticed was that there were three bars instead of two. The missing values are shown as a bar in the graph. In some cases, Leslie might be interested in including the missing values as a bar, but for this graph she was interested in comparing the Yes and No values and wanted to drop the NA bar from the graphic.

1.10.1 OMITTING NA FROM A GRAPH

Kiara explained that there are many ways to remove the NA bar from the graph, but one of the easiest is adding drop_na() to the code. In this case, the NA should be dropped from the grass variable. To drop the NA values before the graph, Kiara suggested Leslie add drop_na() above ggplot() in the code. Leslie gave it a try, creating Figure 1.12.

```
# make a bar chart for grass variable (Figure 1.12)
legalize.bar <- gss.2016.cleaned %>%
  drop_na(grass) %>%
  ggplot(aes(x = grass)) +
  geom_bar()
# show the chart
legalize.bar
```

FIGURE 1.12 Support for marijuana legalization among participants in the 2016 General Social Survey

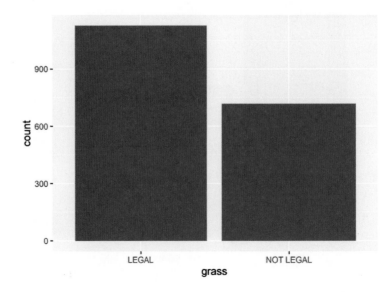

1.10.2 WORKING WITH COLOR IN A BAR CHART

Well, that was easy! Leslie thought. She wanted to work on the look of the graph next. She noticed that there was a light gray background instead of white and that the bars were dark gray instead of green and purple. Kiara introduced Leslie to the concept of `fill =`. To fill the bars with color based on a category of the `grass` variable, the aesthetic needs to have `fill =` specified. Leslie looked at Kiara with a blank stare. Kiara reached over to Leslie's keyboard and added `fill = grass` to the aesthetic so that the bars would each be filled with a different color for each category of the `grass` variable (Figure 1.13).

```
# make a bar chart for grass variable (Figure 1.13)
legalize.bar <- gss.2016.cleaned %>%
  drop_na(grass) %>%
  ggplot(aes(x = grass, fill = grass)) +
  geom_bar()

# show the chart
legalize.bar
```

Leslie wasn't sure that was any closer to correct since the colors weren't right and there was now a legend to the right of the graph that was redundant with the *x*-axis. Kiara told her not to worry, they could fix both of these things with a single added layer. The `scale_fill_manual()` layer allows the selection of colors for whatever argument is included in `fill =`, and it also has a `guide =` option to specify whether

---

FIGURE 1.13 Support for marijuana legalization among participants in the 2016 General Social Survey.

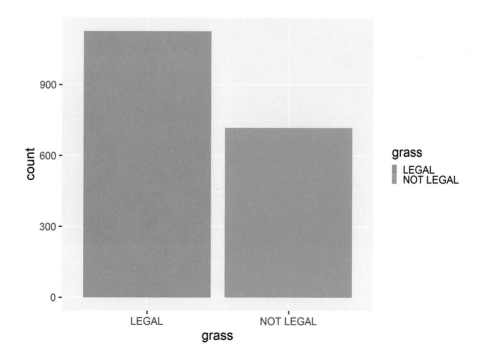

or not the legend appears. Kiara added the `scale_fill_manual()` function with the options for Leslie (Figure 1.14).

```r
# make a bar chart for grass variable (Figure 1.14)
legalize.bar <- gss.2016.cleaned %>%
  drop_na(grass) %>%
  ggplot(aes(x = grass, fill = grass)) +
  geom_bar() +
  scale_fill_manual(values = c("#78A678", "#7463AC"),
                    guide = FALSE)

# show the chart
legalize.bar
```

It was starting to look good, thought Leslie. Still, she wondered about the meaning of the values `78A678` and `7463AC`. Kiara said those are **RGB** (red-green-blue) codes that specify colors. She told Leslie that the Color Brewer 2.0 website (http://colorbrewer2.org) is a great place to find RGB codes for colors that work well for different sorts of graphs, are color-blind safe, and work with printing or copying. The names of colors can also be used; for example, after replacing the codes with the words "green" and "purple," the graph will look like Figure 1.15.

FIGURE 1.14 Support for marijuana legalization among participants in the 2016 General Social Survey

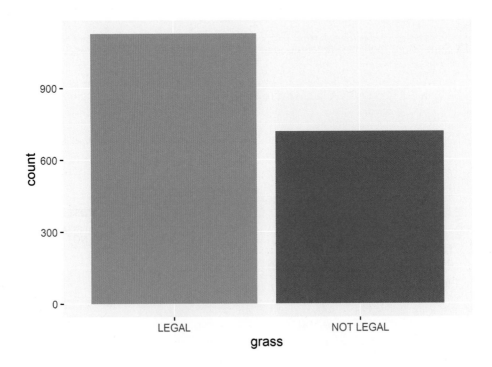

FIGURE 1.15 Support for marijuana legalization among participants in the 2016 General Social Survey

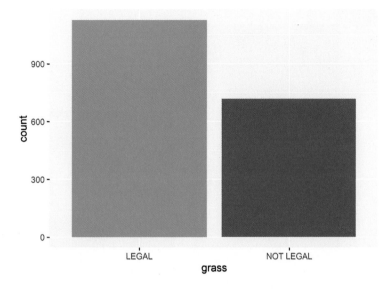

```
# make a bar chart for grass variable (Figure 1.15)
legalize.bar <- gss.2016.cleaned %>%
  drop_na(grass) %>%
  ggplot(aes(x = grass, fill = grass)) +
  geom_bar() +
  scale_fill_manual(values = c("green", "purple"),
                    guide = FALSE)

# show the chart
legalize.bar
```

Yikes! Leslie thought the RGB codes were much better and changed the code back to show the original green and purple. The rest of the R-Team agreed, and Nancy mentioned that besides RGB codes, there are also R color palettes that mimic the color schemes in scientific journals and from shows like *Star Trek* and *Game of Thrones* (Xiao & Li, 2019).

Leslie decided that next she would like to remove the gray background and add the labels to the *x*-axis and *y*-axis. Kiara let her know that the background is part of a theme and that there are many themes to choose from (Wickham, n.d.). The theme that Nancy used in the original graphs was the *minimal* theme, which uses minimal color so that printing the graph requires less ink. This sounded great to Leslie. Kiara said this theme can be applied by adding another layer using theme_minimal(). She said another layer for the labels can be added using the labs() function with text entered for x = and y =. Nancy was starting to get bored and really wanted to help with the coding, so she asked Leslie if she could take over and let Leslie direct her. Leslie agreed and directed her to add the theme and the labels. Nancy added the theme layer and the labels layer and ran the code for Figure 1.16.

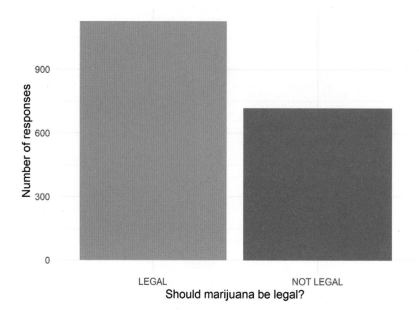

```
# make a bar chart for grass variable (Figure 1.16)
legalize.bar <- gss.2016.cleaned %>%
  drop_na(grass) %>%
  ggplot(aes(x = grass, fill = grass)) +
  geom_bar() +
  scale_fill_manual(values = c("#78A678", '#7463AC'),
                    guide = FALSE) +
  theme_minimal() +
  labs(x = "Should marijuana be legal?",
       y = "Number of responses")

# show the chart
legalize.bar
```

This looked great but Leslie was starting to get tired of this graph and the code was really complicated. Nancy was so fast at the coding, which looked confusing to Leslie. Leslie started to think that she was in over her head.

Kiara reassured her that everyone felt this way when they started to learn ggplot(). Like many things, ggplot() and R will make more sense with practice and time. Kiara encouraged her to make the last two changes that were needed. First, the y-axis should be a percentage. Second, the labels on the x-axis should be Yes and No.

1.10.3 USING SPECIAL VARIABLES IN GRAPHS

To get the y-axis to show percentage rather than count, the y-axis uses *special variables* with double periods around them. Special variables are statistics computed from a data set; the *count* special variable counts the number of observations in the data set. Nancy saw that Leslie was tired and thought that now was her opportunity to do some more coding. She slid the laptop away from Leslie and added the special variables to the aesthetics using ..count.. to represent the *frequency* of a category, or how often it occurred, and sum(..count..) to represent the sum of all the frequencies. She multiplied by 100 to get a percentage in Figure 1.17.

```
# make a bar chart for grass variable (Figure 1.17)
legalize.bar <- gss.2016.cleaned %>%
  drop_na(grass) %>%
  ggplot(aes(x = grass,
             y = 100 * (..count..) / sum(..count..),
             fill = grass)) +
  geom_bar() +
  theme_minimal() +
  scale_fill_manual(values = c("#78A678", '#7463AC'),
                    guide = FALSE) +
    labs(x = "Should marijuana be legal?",
         y = "Percent of responses")

# show the chart
legalize.bar
```

The last thing to do was to recode the levels of the grass variable to be Yes and No. Kiara nodded at Nancy and Nancy added the final code needed with mutate() and recode_factor() to create Figure 1.18. Leslie thought the mutate() with recode_factor() looked complicated, and Nancy assured her they would practice it many times in their next few meetings.

FIGURE 1.17 Support for marijuana legalization among participants in the 2016 General Social Survey

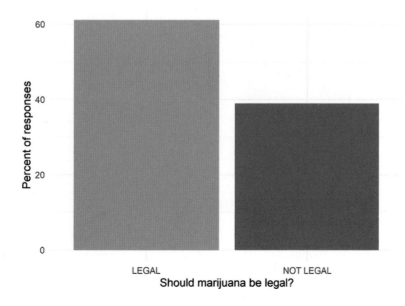

```
# make a bar chart for grass variable (Figure 1.18)
legalize.bar <- gss.2016.cleaned %>%
  drop_na(grass) %>%
  mutate(grass = recode_factor(.x = grass,
                               `LEGAL` = "Yes",
                               `NOT LEGAL` = "No")) %>%
  ggplot(aes(x = grass,
             y = 100 * (..count..) / sum(..count..),
             fill = grass)) +
  geom_bar() +

  theme_minimal() +
  scale_fill_manual(values = c("#78A678", '#7463AC'),
                    guide = FALSE) +
  labs(x = "Should marijuana be legal?",
       y = "Percent of responses")

# show the chart
legalize.bar
```

Kiara wanted to show Leslie one more trick to add the `age.cat` variable into the graphic, but she realized Leslie had had about enough `ggplot()`. Kiara told Nancy what she wanted, and Nancy wrote the code with Leslie looking over her shoulder. She changed the *x*-axis variable in the aesthetics to be `x = age.cat`, removed the `guide = FALSE` from the `scale_fill_manual()` layer, changed the *x*-axis label, and added `position = 'dodge'` in the `geom_bar()` layer. The code `position = 'dodge'` makes the bars for Yes and No in each age category show side by side (Figure 1.19).

FIGURE 1.18 Support for marijuana legalization among participants in the 2016 General Social Survey

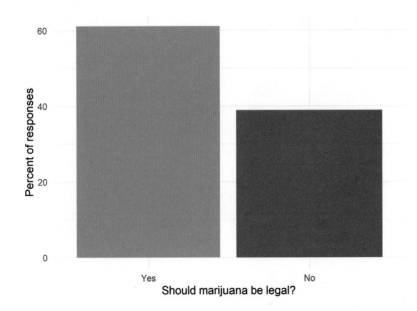

```
# adding dodge to show bars side by side (Figure 1.19)
legalize.bar <- gss.2016.cleaned %>%
  drop_na(grass) %>%
  drop_na(age) %>%
  mutate(grass = recode_factor(.x = grass,
                               `LEGAL` = "Yes",
                               `NOT LEGAL` = "No")) %>%
  ggplot(aes(x = age.cat,
             y = 100*(..count..)/sum(..count..),
             fill = grass)) +
  geom_bar(position = 'dodge') +
  theme_minimal() +
  scale_fill_manual(values = c("#78A678", '#7463AC'),
                    name = "Should marijuana\nbe legal?") +
  labs(x = "Age category",
       y = "Percent of total responses")
legalize.bar
```

Finally, the full graph appeared. Leslie was overwhelmed by what seemed to be hundreds of layers in `ggplot()` to create a single graph. Kiara and Nancy both reassured her that this is complicated coding and she will start to understand it more as she practices. They planned to do a whole day about graphs soon, but they wanted her to see the power of R early on. Leslie noticed that while the general pattern was the same, Figure 1.19 showed different percentages than Figure 1.2. Nancy explained that the bars in Figure 1.19 added up to 100% total, whereas the bars in Figure 1.2 added up to 100% in each age

FIGURE 1.19 Support for marijuana legalization among participants in the 2016 General Social Survey

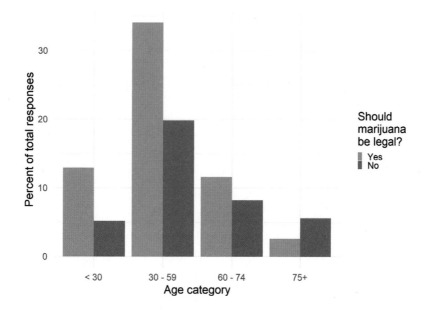

group. She said that this required the use of some additional R coding tricks that they would get to in their next two meetings. Leslie was curious about the code, so Nancy showed her as a preview, but suggested they wait to discuss all the new functions until next time. Leslie agreed that this was a good idea, given all the R ideas swimming around in her head already.

```
# code to create Figure 1.2
legalize.bar <- gss.2016.cleaned %>%
  drop_na(grass) %>%
  drop_na(age) %>%
  mutate(grass = recode_factor(.x = grass,
                               `LEGAL` = "Yes",
                               `NOT LEGAL` = "No")) %>%
  group_by(grass, age.cat) %>%
  count() %>%
  group_by(age.cat) %>%
  mutate(perc.grass = 100*n/sum(n)) %>%
  ggplot(aes(x = age.cat, fill = grass,
             y = perc.grass)) +
  geom_col(position = 'dodge') +
  theme_minimal() +
  scale_fill_manual(values = c("#78A678", '#7463AC'),
                    name = "Should marijuana\nbe legal?") +
  labs(x = "Age group (in years)",
       y = "Percent of responses in age group")
legalize.bar
```

The R-Team learned a little more about marijuana policy during their introduction to R day. They found that more people support legalizing marijuana than do not support it. They also found that support for legalization is higher in younger age categories, so support is likely to increase as those who are currently in the younger categories get older over time. Leslie mentioned that this seems important for state-level policymakers to consider. Even if legalization does not have enough support currently, this may change over time, and state government officials might start paying attention to the challenges and benefits realized by those states that have already adopted legal marijuana policies.

1.10.4 ACHIEVEMENT 6: CHECK YOUR UNDERSTANDING

Think about the number of missing values for grass (*after* DK and IAP were converted to NAs) and age. Run the summary function to confirm. If 1,836 of the 2,867 observations had values for both grass and age, 10 observations were missing age, and 1,024 observations were missing grass, then how many observations were missing values for both?

Now try some visual changes to the graph. Change the No bar to the official R-Ladies purple color 88398a and change the Yes bar to the color gray40. Change the theme to another theme of your choice by selecting from the **ggplot2** themes available online (see Wickham, n.d.).

1.11.1 Achievements
unlocked in this chapter: Recap

Congratulations! Like Leslie, you've learned and practiced a lot in this chapter.

1.11.1.1 Achievement 1 recap:
Observations and variables

R is a coding language in which information is stored as objects that can then be used in calculations and other procedures. Information is assigned to an object using the <–, which puts the information on the right of the arrow into an object name included to the left of the arrow. To print the object in R, type its name and use one of the methods for running code.

Data are stored in many formats, including vectors for single variables and matrix and data frame formats for rows and columns. In data frames, rows typically hold observations (e.g., people, organizations), while columns typically hold variables (e.g., age, revenue).

1.11.1.2 Achievement 2 recap:
Using reproducible research practices

It is important to think about how to write and organize R code so it is useful not only right now but in the future for anyone (including the original author) to use. Some of the practices to start with are using comments to explain code, limiting lines of code to 80 characters, naming variables with logical names and consistent formatting, naming files with useful human and machine readable information, and including a prolog in each code file.

1.11.1.3 Achievement 3 recap:
Understanding and changing data types

Most statistics are appropriate for only certain types of data. R has several data types, with the more commonly used ones being numeric, integer, factor, character, and logical. The `class` function can be used to check a data type, and the appropriate `as` function (e.g., `as.factor()`) can be used to change data types.

1.11.1.4 Achievement 4 recap:
Entering or loading data into R

R is unique in its ability to load data from most file formats. Depending on what file type the data are saved as, a different R function can be used. For example, `read.csv()` will read in a data file saved in the comma separated values (csv) format.

1.11.1.5 Achievement 5 recap:
Identifying and treating missing values

In addition to making sure the variables used are an appropriate type, it is also important to make sure that missing values are treated appropriately by R. In R, missing values are recorded as `NA`, which stands for *not available*. Researchers code missing values in many different ways when collecting and storing data. Some of the more common ways to denote missing values are blank, 777, -777, 888, -888, 999, -999, a single period, -1, and `NULL`. Other responses, such as "Don't know" or "Inapplicable," may sometimes be treated as missing or treated as response categories depending on what is most appropriate given the characteristics of the data and the analysis goals. There are many ways to recode these values to be `NA` instead.

1.11.1.6 Achievement 6 recap:
Building a basic bar chart

One of the biggest advantages to using R is the ability to make custom graphics. The **ggplot2**, or grammar of graphics, package is useful for making many types of graphs, including bar charts. The `ggplot()` function takes the name of the data frame object and the name of the variable within the data frame that you would like to graph. Layers following the initial function are used to change the look of the graph and refine its elements.

1.11.2 Chapter exercises

The coder and hacker exercises are an opportunity to apply the skills from this chapter to a new scenario or a new data set. The coder edition evaluates the application of the concepts and code learned in this R-Team meeting to scenarios similar to those in the meeting. The hacker edition evaluates the use of the concepts and code from this R-Team meeting in new scenarios, often going a step beyond what was explicitly explained.

The coder edition might be best for those who found some or all of the Check Your Understanding activities to be challenging, or if you needed review before picking the correct responses to the multiple-choice questions. The hacker edition might be best if the Check Your Understanding activities were not too challenging and the multiple-choice questions were a breeze.

The multiple-choice questions and materials for the exercises are online at **edge.sagepub.com/harris1e**.

Q1: Which R data type is most appropriate for a categorical variable?

   a. Numeric

   b. Factor

   c. Integer

   d. Character

Q2: Which of the following opens `ggplot2`?

   a. `install.packages("ggplot2")`

   b. `library(package = "ggplot2")`

   c. `summary(object = ggplot2)`

   d. `open(x = ggplot2)`

Q3: The block of text at the top of a code file that introduces the project is called

   a. library.

   b. summary.

   c. prolog.

   d. pane.

Q4: In a data frame containing information on the age and height of 100 people, the people are the _____ and age and height are the _____.

   a. observations, variables

   b. variables, observations

   c. data, factors

   d. factors, data

Q5: The results of running R code show in which pane?

   a. Source

   b. Environment

   c. History

   d. Console

1.11.2.1 Chapter exercises: Coder edition

Use the National Health and Nutrition Examination Survey (NHANES) data to examine marijuana use in the United States. Spend a few minutes looking through the NHANES website (https://www.cdc.gov/nchs/nhanes/index.htm) before you begin, including finding the online codebook for the

2013–2014 data. Complete the following tasks to explore whether age is related to marijuana use in the United States.

1) Open the 2013–2014 NHANES data file saved as nhanes_2013_ch1.csv with the book materials at **edge.sagepub.com/harris1e** (Achievement 4).

2) Examine the data types for `DUQ200`, `RIDAGEYR`, and `RIAGENDR`, and fix data types if needed based on the NHANES codebook (Achievement 3).

3) Based on the online NHANES codebook, code missing values appropriately for `DUQ200`, `RIDAGEYR`, and `RIAGENDR` (Achievement 5).

4) Create a bar chart showing the percentage of NHANES participants answering yes and no to marijuana use (Achievement 6).

5) Recode `age` into a new variable called `age.cat` with 4 categories: 18–29, 30–39, 40–49, 50–59 (Achievement 5).

6) Create a bar chart of marijuana use by age group (Achievement 6).

7) Add a prolog and comments to your code (Achievement 2).

8) Following the R code in your code file, use comments to describe what you found. Given what you found and the information in the chapter, what do you predict will happen with marijuana legalization in the next 10 years? Discuss how the omission of older people from the marijuana use question for NHANES influenced your prediction. Write your prediction and discussion in comments at the end of your code file (Achievement 2).

1.11.2.2 Chapter exercises: Hacker edition

Read the coder instructions and complete #1–#5 from the coder edition. Then do the following:

6) Create a bar chart of marijuana use by age group and sex with side-by-side bars (Achievement 6).

7) Add a prolog and comments to your code (Achievement 2).

8) Following the R code in your code file, use comments to describe what you found in no more than a few sentences. Given what you found and the information in the chapter, what do you predict will happen with marijuana legalization in the next 10 years? Discuss how

the omission of older people from the marijuana use question for NHANES influenced your prediction. Write your prediction and discussion in comments at the end of your code file (Achievement 2).

1.11.2.3 Instructor note

Solutions to exercises can be found on the website for this book, along with ideas for gamification for those who want to take it further.

Visit **edge.sagepub.com/harris1e** to download the data sets, complete the chapter exercises, and watch R tutorial videos.

COMPUTING AND REPORTING DESCRIPTIVE STATISTICS

The R-Team and the Troubling Transgender Health Care Problem

Leslie was excited for the second meeting of the R-Team. She met Kiara and Nancy at a local café for lunch.

Nancy said, "Today, I thought we would discuss descriptive statistics." Consistent with the name, she explained, descriptive statistics are statistics that describe whatever is being studied, like people or organizations. Descriptive statistics are important since they provide information about the characteristics of the observations in a data set and provide context for interpretation of the results from complex statistical tests. Descriptive statistics may also be used to help choose the correct statistical test to use to answer your questions.

"Sounds good," Leslie said. Then she shared the rest of her fries with the team. After getting used to the R environment and preparing data for analysis with the pot policy problem, Leslie had her own idea to propose. "So I was listening to a podcast about the issue of transgender health and how transgender patients are treated in a system that has traditionally focused on two sexes, and I wondered if we might tackle that with R?"

"Totally," said Kiara.

"Right after I finish my sandwich," Nancy said.

Kiara chuckled and said, "After that, let's develop a list of R achievements to improve Leslie's R skills while we work together on understanding transgender health care."

2.1 Achievements to unlock

- Achievement 1: Understanding variable types and data types
- Achievement 2: Choosing and conducting descriptive analyses for categorical (factor) variables
- Achievement 3: Choosing and conducting descriptive analyses for continuous (numeric) variables
- Achievement 4: Developing clear tables for reporting descriptive statistics

2.2 The transgender health care problem

Before coming to meet with Nancy and Kiara, Leslie had done some reading on the problem, including a recent paper on mammography that demonstrated some of the challenges for transgender people in the current system. Over lunch, she summarized what she'd found.

First, Leslie wanted to clarify the definition of transgender to make sure they were all on the same page. Leslie told them she thought the term *sex* referred to biology and the term *gender* referred to identity. Nancy agreed with the definition of sex, but had heard broader definitions of gender that included biological, psychosocial, and cultural factors along with identity (Mayer et al., 2008). She looked up the World Health Organization's definition for gender:

Gender refers to the socially constructed characteristics of women and men—such as norms, roles and relationships of and between groups of women and men. It varies from society to society and can be changed. While most people are born either male or female, they are taught appropriate norms and behaviours—including how they should interact with others of the same or opposite sex within households, communities and work places. (World Health Organization [WHO], 2019)

Note: In shaded sections throughout this text, the rows starting "##" show the output that will appear after running the R code just above it.

Leslie was glad they looked this up because it was much clearer than her initial description. She went on to explain that *transgender* people are people whose *biological sex* is not consistent with their *gender* (Mayer et al., 2008). She quoted an article from 2008 that she thought had a definition that might be helpful: "Transgender is an inclusive term to describe people who have gender identities, expressions, or behaviors not traditionally associated with their birth sex" (Mayer et al., 2008, p. 990).

The paper Leslie read gave a few examples of transgender, including a person who is biologically female but identifies as a man, a person who is biologically male but identifies as a woman, or someone who feels like both genders or neither gender (Mayer et al., 2008). Nancy looked at the Centers for Disease Control and Prevention (CDC) website, which explained that gender identity is the gender a person identifies as, and gender expression is the gender a person outwardly shows (CDC, n.d.). When describing individuals, typically the person's chosen identity is included. So, a person who is biologically female but identifies as a man would be described as a "transgender man." Kiara said that was consistent with what she'd experienced when she learned that her second cousin was transgender. For a while, it had been difficult to remember to refer to her cousin, who had previously been *she*, as *he*. Leslie and Nancy nodded. Sensing they were ready to proceed, Leslie gave some background on health and health care for transgender people.

Transgender people face serious physical and mental health disparities (Safer et al., 2016), often related to discrimination (Bradford, Reisner, Honnold, & Xavier, 2013). Among the most prevalent and concerning disparities are extremely high rates of HIV and other sexually transmitted infections, poor mental health, and high rates of substance use and abuse. For example, transgender women have a 19.1% prevalence of HIV worldwide (Baral et al., 2013), while reproductive-aged adults have an HIV prevalence of 0.4%. A survey of transgender adults in the United States found that 44.1% have clinical depression, 33.2% have anxiety, and 27.5% have somatization symptoms (i.e., physical symptoms stemming from depression, anxiety, or another psychiatric condition; Lombardi, 2010). Attempted suicide rates range from 32% to 50% of transgender people worldwide, with higher rates among younger age groups (Virupaksha, Muralidhar, & Ramakrishna, 2016).

In 2001, an Institute of Medicine report found that 35.5% of transgender adults are current smokers; this is more than twice the percentage of cisgender (i.e., people whose gender identity matches their biological sex) adults (14.9% smoking rate) (Institute of Medicine, 2001). Transgender adults also have higher rates of alcohol and substance abuse (Benotsch et al., 2013; Santos et al., 2014) and of overweight and obesity (Boehmer, Bowen, & Bauer, 2007). Exacerbating these health disparities are limitations on access to health care (Meyer, Brown, Herman, Reisner, & Bockting, 2017) and limitations of the health care system to effectively address the unique health needs of transgender people (Daniel & Butkus, 2015; Reisner et al., 2016).

Given the high smoking rate, substance and alcohol use, and the prevalence of overweight and obesity, it is important that transgender people are adequately screened for cancer and other health conditions. Leslie found conflicting evidence about screening for transgender people. A 2015 study that examined medical charts from 2012–2013 found that transgender adults had 47% lower odds of breast cancer screening than cisgender adults (Bazzi, Whorms, King, & Potter, 2015). However, a different study published in 2017 and based on 2014 survey data reported that transgender and nontransgender adults have comparable rates of mammography screening (Narayan, Lebron-Zapata, & Morris, 2017). Nancy suggested maybe the rate is increasing over time, but Kiara thought the data were not collected far enough apart for that to be the case. She thought the survey data, which were a representative sample of U.S. residents from the Behavioral Risk Factor Surveillance System (BRFSS) survey, in the 2017 study likely measured people with different characteristics from the people in the 2015 study, which reviewed charts from people seeking care at an urban clinic.

Leslie looked up the BRFSS (https://www.cdc.gov/brfss/index.html) and found that it is a large national survey conducted by the CDC in the United States by phone every year. The 2017 mammogram paper was based on data from participants who responded to the 2014 BRFSS survey. The 2014 BRFSS was administered by states and had 464,664 participants. The BRFSS sampling process was designed so that the sample would represent the U.S. population as much as possible. The survey included questions about characteristics like age, sex, and income, along with questions about health behaviors and outcomes.

In 2014, 19 states and Guam included a question on the BRFSS about transgender transition status, with choices of male to female (MtF), female to male (FtM), or non-conforming. The entire sample from the 19 states and Guam contained 151,456 people. Of the 151,456 participants, the study authors identified 222 survey participants who reported they were transgender, were 40–74 years old (the age range when mammograms are recommended), and were asked about having a mammogram (Narayan, Lebron-Zapata, & Morris, 2017). The mammogram question was only asked of those who described themselves as being female sex.

Leslie shared the first table of statistics, published as Table 1 in Narayan et al. (2017), with Kiara and Nancy.

Kiara explained that, prior to examining statistical relationships among variables, published studies in academic journals usually present descriptive statistics like the ones in Table 2.1. She added that descriptive statistics are often displayed in the first table in a published article or report and are therefore sometimes referred to as the *Table 1* statistics or, even more commonly, as the *descriptives*. She also pointed out that, in this case, all the descriptives in the transgender health paper were percentages

TABLE 2.1 Reproduced Table 1, "Transgender Survey Participant Demographics," from Narayan et al. (2017)

Survey participant demographics (*n* = 220)	Percent
Transition status	
Male to female	35.0
Female to male	50.9
Gender non-conforming	14.1
Age category	
40–44	12.2
45–49	12.2
50–54	14.4
55–59	19.8
60–64	19.8
65–69	10.8
70–74	10.8
Race/ethnicity	
White	68.5
Black	14.0
Native American	1.8
Asian/Pacific Islander	2.7
Other	13.1

(Continued)

TABLE 2.1 (Continued)

Survey participant demographics (*n* = 220)	Percent
Income category	
Less than $15,000	20.7
$15,000 to less than $25,000	19.8
$25,000 to less than $35,000	8.6
$35,000 to less than $50,000	11.7
$50,000 or more	29.3
Don't know/not sure/missing	9.9
Education category	
Did not graduate high school	10.8
Graduated high school	38.7
Attended college/technical school	30.6
Graduated from college/technical school	19.8
Health insurance?	
Yes	89.2

showing the percent of people in each category. She explained that percentages were computed for this table because of the types of variables the researchers examined. Now that they had some background and an idea of the topic and data they were working with, Nancy and Kiara were ready to get started.

2.3 Data, codebook, and R packages for learning about descriptive statistics

Before they examined the data, Kiara made a list of all the data, documentation, and R packages needed for learning descriptive statistics.

- Two options for accessing the data*
  - Download the clean data file **transgender_hc_ch2.csv** from **edge.sagepub.com/harris1e**
  - Follow the instructions in Box 2.1 to download and clean the data directly from the Internet
- Two options for accessing the codebook
  - Download **brfss_2014_codebook.pdf** from **edge.sagepub.com/harris1e**
  - Download the codebook from the Behavioral Risk Factor Surveillance Survey website (https://www.cdc.gov/brfss/index.html)

*While many internet data sources are stable, some will be periodically updated or corrected. Use of updated data sources may result in slightly different results when following along with the examples in the text.

- Install R packages if not already installed
  - **`tidyverse,`** by Hadley Wickham (https://www.rdocumentation.org/packages/tidyverse/)
  - *`haven`*, by Hadley Wickham (https://www.rdocumentation.org/packages/haven/)
  - *`Hmisc`*, by Frank E. Harrell Jr. (https://www.rdocumentation.org/packages/Hmisc/)
  - *`descr`*, by Jakson Alves de Aquino (https://www.rdocumentation.org/packages/descr/)
  - *`tableone`* (Yoshida, n.d.)
  - *`kableExtra`*, by Hao Zhu (https://www.rdocumentation.org/packages/kableExtra/)
  - *`semTools`*, by Terry Jorgensen (https://www.rdocumentation.org/packages/semTools/)
  - *`qualvar`*, by Joel Gombin (https://cran.r-project.org/web/packages/qualvar/index.html)
  - *`labelled`*, by Joseph Larmarange (https://www.rdocumentation.org/packages/labelled/)
  - *`knitr`*, by Yihui Xie (https://www.rdocumentation.org/packages/knitr/)

2.4 Achievement 1: Understanding variable types and data types

2.4.1 DATA TYPES FOR CATEGORICAL VARIABLES

In Section 1.7, Kiara introduced Leslie to several data types, including factor, numeric, integer, and character. Arguably, the two data types most commonly used in social science research are factor and numeric. Kiara reminded Leslie that the factor data type is used for information that is measured or coded in categories, or categorical variables. Leslie remembered from the previous meeting that there were two types of categorical variables, nominal and ordinal.

Nominal categorical variables are variables measured in categories that do not have any logical order, like marital status, religion, sex, and race. Ordinal categorical variables have categories with a logical order. One way Leslie liked to remember this was to notice that ordinal and order both start with *o-r-d*, so ordinal variables have an order. For example, income can be measured in categories such as <$10,000, $10,000–$24,999, $25,000–$99,999, and $100,000+. These categories have a logical order from the lowest income group to the highest income group.

One common ordinal way of measuring things is the use of a *Likert scale*. Likert scales have categories that go in a logical order from *least to most* or *most to least*. For example, Leslie suggested that measuring agreement with the statement "R is awesome" could use a Likert scale with the following options: *strongly agree, somewhat agree, neutral, somewhat disagree, strongly disagree.* Leslie explained that often people refer to the number of categories as the *points* in a Likert scale. The agreement scale from *strongly agree* to *strongly disagree* is a 5-point Likert scale because there are five options along the scale.

2.4.2 DATA TYPES FOR CONTINUOUS VARIABLES

On the other hand, explained Kiara, the numeric data type in R is used for continuous variables. Leslie confirmed that continuous variables are the variables that can take *any* value along some continuum, hence continuous. Just like *o-r-d* is in order and ordinal, *c-o-n* is in continuum and continuous, which can be a good way to remember this variable type. Examples of continuous variables include age, height, weight, distance, blood pressure, temperature, and so on.

Kiara explained that the numeric data type is also often used for variables that do not technically qualify as continuous but are measured along some sort of a continuum. Age in years would be one example since it falls along a continuum from 0 years old to over 100. However, by specifying age *in years,* the values for this variable cannot be any value between 0 and over 100, but instead are limited to the whole numbers in this range. Likewise, the number of cars in a parking lot, or the number of coins in a piggy bank, would be numeric but not truly continuous. If the variable is a whole number, the integer data type could also be used, but it has more limitations for analysis than does the numeric data type in R.

Leslie knew that each different type of variable required a different approach for analysis. Before getting into any complex statistical modeling, she remembered that descriptive statistics are key for understanding who or what is in the data set and often help in choosing an appropriate statistical test.

2.4.3 ACHIEVEMENT 1: CHECK YOUR UNDERSTANDING

Identify the most appropriate data type for the following variables:

- Number of healthy days per month
- Marital status
- Religious affiliation
- Smoking status
- Number of alcoholic beverages per week

2.5 Achievement 2: Choosing and conducting descriptive analyses for categorical (factor) variables

Since the table from the paper (Table 2.1) shows all categorical variables, the R-Team started there. Leslie knew that the two most commonly used and reported descriptive statistics for categorical (or factor) data types are frequencies and percentages. For a categorical variable, frequencies are the number of observations—often people or organizations—that fall into a given category. Percentages are the proportion of all observations that fall into a given category.

2.5.1 COMPUTING FREQUENCIES AND FREQUENCY DISTRIBUTIONS

Leslie also remembered that a *frequency distribution* shows the number of observations in each category for a factor or categorical variable. She suggested that they could use a frequency distribution to examine how many observations there were for each transgender transition category in the BRFSS data set from the mammogram paper.

Before getting started, the team looked through the 2014 BRFSS codebook together, which they found on the CDC BRFSS website (CDC, 2015). They found the transgender transition status information on page 83 of the codebook. The frequency distribution shown in the codebook indicated 363 MtF transgender, 212 FtM transgender, 116 gender non-conforming, 150,765 not transgender, 1,138 don't know/not sure, 1,468 refused, and 310,602 not asked or missing (Figure 2.1).

Kiara suggested that Leslie re-create this frequency distribution in R by first opening the BRFSS data file and then using an R function for frequencies. On the BRFSS website (https://www.cdc.gov/brfss/index .html), the data file is available in *xpt* or *ASCII* format. The xpt is a file format used by SAS statistical software; Kiara explained that one of the great features of R is that it can open most data sets from most software packages. This is one of the features of R that makes it easier to do reproducible work. She said R can open the xpt file type by using the **haven** package that is part of the **tidyverse** in R. For now, Kiara said she had already downloaded, opened, and cleaned the data, so they did not need to do all of

Do you consider yourself to be transgender?

Module:	16.2	Sexual Orientation and Gender Identity	**Type:**	Num
Column:	583		**SAS Variable Name:**	TRNSGNDR
Prologue:				

Description: Do you consider yourself to be transgender?   (If yes, ask "Do you consider yourself to be male-to-female, female-to-male, or gender non-conforming?")

Value	Value Label	Frequency	Percentage	Weighted Percentage
1	Yes, Transgender, male-to-female	363	0.24	0.27
2	Yes, Transgender, female to male	212	0.14	0.16
3	Yes, Transgender, gender nonconforming	116	0.08	0.09
4	No	150,765	97.86	97.63
7	Don't know/Not Sure	1,138	0.74	0.85
9	Refused	1,468	0.95	1.00
BLANK	Not asked or Missing	310,602		

2.1 Kiara's reproducibility resource: Bringing data in directly from the Internet

The more that can be done in R with documented and organized code, the more reproducible analyses will be. If the entire process of importing, managing, analyzing, and reporting results can all be together in a single document, the opportunity for errors is greatly decreased.

The BRFSS data set can be found on the CDC website in a zipped SAS transport file with the file extension of xpt. It is possible to bring data directly into R from websites. One of the ways to do this is with the **haven** package. The process is not straightforward like the `read.csv()` function or other importing functions are. The **haven** package cannot unzip and import an xpt file directly from the Internet, so the file has to be imported into a temporary location on a local computer and then read using `read_xpt()` from **haven**. Kiara wrote out the steps for downloading, importing, and exporting the data from a zipped xpt file online. Note that the `download.file()` function will take several minutes to run on most personal computers.

```
# open the haven package to read an xpt
library(package = "haven")

# create a temporary file to store the zipped file
# before you open it
temp <- tempfile(fileext = ".zip")
```

(Continued)

(Continued)

```
# use download.file to put the zipped file in the temp file
# this will take a couple of minutes depending on computer speed
download.file(url = "http://www.cdc.gov/brfss/annual_data/2014/files/
LLCP2014XPT.zip", destfile = temp)

# unzip it and read it
brfss.2014 <- read_xpt(file = temp)

# open tidyverse to select variables
library(package = "tidyverse")

# select variables for analysis
# use ` around variable names starting with underscores
transgender_hc_ch2 <- brfss.2014 %>%
  select(TRNSGNDR, `_AGEG5YR`, `_RACE`, `_INCOMG`, `_EDUCAG`,
      HLTHPLN1, HADMAM, `_AGE80`, PHYSHLTH)

# export the data set to a csv file in a local folder called data
write.csv(x = transgender_hc_ch2,
        file = "[data folder location]/data/transgender_hc_ch2.csv",
        row.names = FALSE)
```

that. Leslie was interested in understanding how she did this, so Kiara shared with Leslie the code she used to download the data so that she could review it later (Box 2.1).

After importing the data, Kiara exported a *csv* (comma separated values) file with the variables needed to re-create the table. Nancy reminded Leslie of the `read.csv()` function to import the data from their previous meeting. Leslie wrote a line of code, being sure to use the object naming recommendations she'd learned during the data preparation day. She entered the location where the **transgender_hc_ch2.csv** data file was saved between the quote marks after `file =` in the `read.csv()` function.

```
# read the 2014 BRFSS data
brfss.trans.2014 <- read.csv(file = "[data folder location]/data/
transgender_hc_ch2.csv")
```

Leslie highlighted the code and used the Run button to import the data. The data appeared in the Environment tab in the top right pane of RStudio. The entry in the Environment tab was under the Data heading and was called `brfss.trans.2014` (the name given to the object). Next to the data frame name, Leslie saw that there were 464,664 observations and nine variables in the data frame.

This indicates that the data set contains 464,664 observations, or 464,664 people in this case. This was consistent with the codebook, so Leslie was assured that these were the data she was looking for.

Leslie used `summary()` to learn more about the data before starting to compute other statistics.

```
# examine the data
summary(object = brfss.trans.2014)
##      TRNSGNDR          X_AGEG5YR           X_RACE           X_INCOMG
##  Min.   :1.00      Min.   : 1.000     Min.   : 1.000     Min.   :1.000
##  1st Qu.:4.00      1st Qu.: 5.000     1st Qu.: 1.000     1st Qu.:3.000
##  Median :4.00      Median : 8.000     Median : 1.000     Median :5.000
##  Mean   :4.06      Mean   : 7.822     Mean   : 1.992     Mean   :4.481
##  3rd Qu.:4.00      3rd Qu.:10.000     3rd Qu.: 1.000     3rd Qu.:5.000
##  Max.   :9.00      Max.   :14.000     Max.   : 9.000     Max.   :9.000
##  NA's   :310602                       NA's   :94
##     X_EDUCAG          HLTHPLN1           HADMAM            X_AGE80
##  Min.   :1.000     Min.   :1.000     Min.   : 1.00     Min.   :18.00
##  1st Qu.:2.000     1st Qu.:1.000     1st Qu.: 1.00     1st Qu.:44.00
##  Median :3.000     Median :1.000     Median : 1.00     Median :58.00
##  Mean   :2.966     Mean   :1.108     Mean   : 1.22     Mean   :55.49
##  3rd Qu.:4.000     3rd Qu.:1.000     3rd Qu.: 1.00     3rd Qu.:69.00
##  Max.   :9.000     Max.   :9.000     Max.   : 9.00     Max.   :80.00
##                                      NA's   :208322
##     PHYSHLTH
##  Min.   : 1.0
##  1st Qu.:20.0
##  Median :88.0
##  Mean   :61.2
##  3rd Qu.:88.0
##  Max.   :99.0
##  NA's   : 4
```

Leslie thought it was good to see the variable names and some information about each variable before she started on the frequency tables. She slid her laptop over to Nancy, who looked ready to code.

2.5.2 MAKING A BASIC TABLE OF FREQUENCIES AND PERCENTAGES

Nancy started by showing Leslie an easy way to get a frequency distribution in R, which is to use `table()`. Using `table()` results in a plain table listing each value of a variable and the number of observations that have that value. The `table()` function takes the name of the data frame followed by $ and then the name of the variable for the table (e.g., data$variable). The data frame was called `brfss.trans.2014`, and the variable was called TRNSGNDR, so Nancy wrote `table(brfss.trans.2014$TRNSGNDR)` and used a keyboard shortcut to run the line of code.

```
# frequency distribution for transgender
# participants in the 2014 BRFSS
table(brfss.trans.2014$TRNSGNDR)
##
##      1      2      3      4      7      9
##    363    212    116 150765   1138   1468
```

The output showed a set of numbers with the top row representing the categories and the bottom row giving the number of observations in each category. The number of observations in each category is the *frequency*. The frequencies in this simple table matched the frequencies in the 2014 BRFSS codebook. For example, the first category of MtF—where MtF stands for Male to Female—shows 363 in the codebook and 363 in the table from Nancy's code.

While the numbers were correct, Nancy suggested that this table was poorly formatted, and there was no way to know what any of the numbers meant without more information. She explained that a table should include several features to make the contents of the table clear, such as the following:

- A main title indicating what is in the table, including
  ○ the overall sample size
  ○ key pieces of information that describe the data such as the year of data collection and the data source
- Clear column and row labels that have
  ○ logical row and column names
  ○ a clear indication of what the data are, such as means or frequencies
  ○ row and column sample sizes when they are different from overall sample sizes

2.5.3 DATA MANAGEMENT

In order to make a clear frequency table, Nancy advised Leslie to use some of the tools from their first meeting along with some new tools. The first thing to do might be to add labels to the TRNSGNDR variable so that it is clear which categories the frequencies represent. Leslie reminded herself that labels are the words that describe each category of a categorical- or factor-type variable. Before she could add labels, Leslie needed to know the data type of the TRNSGNDR variable. She started by examining the data type of the variable with the class() function. To get the class of TRNSGNDR, Leslie added brfss.trans.2014$TRNSGNDR to the class() function.

```
# check data type for TRNSGNDR variable
class(x = brfss.trans.2014$TRNSGNDR)
## [1] "integer"
```

The class was *integer*, which was not what Leslie was expecting. Leslie knew that this variable had categories and so should be the factor data type in R (Section 1.7). She started her data management by changing the data type of TRNSGNDR to a factor using the **tidyverse** package with the mutate() function and as.factor(). She gave the data a new name of brfss.2014.cleaned so that she had the original data and the cleaned data in separate objects.

```
# open tidyverse for data management
library(package = "tidyverse")

# change variable from integer to factor
brfss.2014.cleaned <- brfss.trans.2014 %>%
  mutate(TRNSGNDR = as.factor(TRNSGNDR))

# check data type again
class(x = brfss.2014.cleaned$TRNSGNDR)
## [1] "factor"
```

Now Leslie wanted to add the category labels to the variable. She decided to add this onto the data management code she had already started. Nancy said this sounded great, and that the `recode_factor()` they used in the data preparation activities could work to recode *and* to change the variable to a factor. She suggested Leslie could save a line of code and just use `recode_factor()` with `mutate()` instead of using `as.factor()` and then `recode_factor()`. Leslie looked skeptical but went ahead and found the category names in the codebook (https://www.cdc.gov/brfss/annual_data/2014/pdf/CODEBOOK14_LLCP.pdf).

- 1 = Male to female
- 2 = Female to male
- 3 = Gender non-conforming
- 4 = Not transgender
- 7 = Not sure
- 9 = Refused
- NA

While Leslie was distracted with the codebook, Nancy seized her chance to do some of the coding. She slid the laptop over and changed the `mutate()` code to use `recode_factor()` with the category labels. When she was done, she shared her work with Leslie. Nancy showed Leslie that `recode_factor()` requires the original value of the variable on the left side of the = and that the original values are enclosed in backticks (`` `value` ``) because the values are considered *names* rather than numbers. In R, names are labels given to a category or a variable or another object. Names that begin with a number are enclosed in backticks (or quote marks) in order to be recognized by R as a name and not a number.

```
# cleaning the TRNSGNDR variable
brfss.2014.cleaned <- brfss.trans.2014 %>%
  mutate(TRNSGNDR = recode_factor(.x = TRNSGNDR,
                          `1` = 'Male to female',
                          `2` = 'Female to male',
                          `3` = 'Gender non-conforming',
                          `4` = 'Not transgender',
                          `7` = 'Not sure',
                          `9` = 'Refused'))
```

Leslie wondered aloud how she would ever be able to remember the rule about putting numbers in backticks for `recode_factor()`. Nancy said that some code is easy to remember for her, especially if she uses it a lot, but otherwise she uses the help documentation and the Internet almost every day she is coding. She reminded Leslie that the help documentation is easy to use directly from RStudio and can be found under one of the tabs in the bottom right pane. She showed Leslie how to type "recode_factor" in the search box at the top of the help pane, and the documentation for `recode_factor()` appears in the pane. She also shared that Leslie can type a single "?" and then the name of the function into the Console (`?recode_factor`) and press Return or Enter, and the help page will appear under the Help tab in the lower right pane.

While she had the help documentation open, Nancy showed Leslie one feature of the help documentation, which is that the package for a function shows at the top left of the help documentation (Figure 2.2). In this case, the documentation lists *{dplyr}* in the top left, so `recode_factor()` is in the **dplyr** package. Occasionally, Kiara said, she remembers some function to use but not the package it comes from, so the help documentation can be useful for that as well as for how to use a function.

Once they were done looking at the help pane, Nancy suggested Leslie rerun `table()` from above. Leslie used the trick of opening the History tab and double-clicking on the `table(brfss.2014 .cleaned$TRNSGNDR)` code to send it to the Console. She pressed Enter to run the code from there.

```
# table of transgender status frequencies
table(brfss.2014.cleaned$TRNSGNDR)
##
##         Male to female      Female to male Gender non-conforming
##                    363                 212                   116
##         Not transgender            Not sure               Refused
##                 150765                1138                  1468
```

Nancy wanted to give a quick caution about factor variable recoding. Since factors are particularly useful for social scientists, it is worthwhile to understand a bit more about how R treats factors because they can

---

FIGURE 2.2 Screenshot of recode help documentation

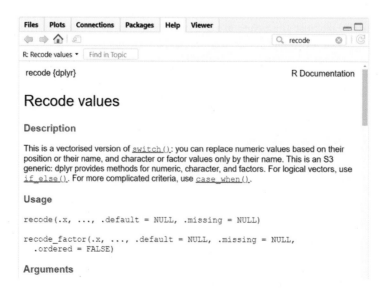

sometimes be tricky. She explained that each category of a factor is called a level in R and that these levels can be plain numbers or have labels, which is what they had added with recode_factor() for TRNSGNDR. She explained that the levels() function can be used to know what the categories are for a factor variable.

The tricky part is that R will treat each unique value of a factor as a different level. So for a vector saved as a factor that looks like height <- c("short", "tall", "Short", "tll"), R would consider it to have four levels: short, tall, Short, and tll. Leslie looked confused because the first and third observations should be part of the same category. Nancy said that short and Short are different categories because the first letter is capitalized in one and not the other. The same thing is true with tall and tll—spelling matters! So in order to get a factor with two levels, it would need to look like height <- c("short", "tall", "short", "tall"). Nancy suggested that Leslie could check the levels of a factor using levels() to see if the levels need to be cleaned up.

For now, the table looked better, but it still needed some work on the formatting before it was ready to share with others. Leslie started thinking about the summary() function from their last session and wondered if that might be a good way to get frequencies for more than one variable at a time. Nancy thought this was an interesting idea and they tried using summary().

```
# use summary for frequencies
summary(object = brfss.2014.cleaned)
##                     TRNSGNDR        X_AGEG5YR         X_RACE
##   Male to female       :   363    Min.   : 1.000   Min.   : 1.000
##   Female to male       :   212    1st Qu.: 5.000   1st Qu.: 1.000
##   Gender non-conforming:   116    Median : 8.000   Median : 1.000
##   Not transgender      :150765    Mean   : 7.822   Mean   : 1.992
##   Not sure             :  1138    3rd Qu.:10.000   3rd Qu.: 1.000
##   Refused              :  1468    Max.   :14.000   Max.   : 9.000
##   NA's                 :310602                     NA's   :94
##     X_INCOMG         X_EDUCAG         HLTHPLN1          HADMAM
##   Min.   :1.000    Min.   :1.000    Min.   :1.000    Min.   :1.00
##   1st Qu.:3.000    1st Qu.:2.000    1st Qu.:1.000    1st Qu.:1.00
##   Median :5.000    Median :3.000    Median :1.000    Median :1.00
##   Mean   :4.481    Mean   :2.966    Mean   :1.108    Mean   :1.22
##   3rd Qu.:5.000    3rd Qu.:4.000    3rd Qu.:1.000    3rd Qu.:1.00
##   Max.   :9.000    Max.   :9.000    Max.   :9.000    Max.   :9.00
##                                                      NA's   :208322
##     X_AGE80         PHYSHLTH
##   Min.   :18.00    Min.   : 1.0
##   1st Qu.:44.00    1st Qu.:20.0
##   Median :58.00    Median :88.0
##   Mean   :55.49    Mean   :61.2
##   3rd Qu.:69.00    3rd Qu.:88.0
##   Max.   :80.00    Max.   :99.0
##                    NA's   :4
```

They reviewed the results and decided that summary() was really similar to table(), and the format does not look even close to what they want for the formatted table. Leslie wondered if there was any other code like summary() that summarized all the variables at once. Nancy said she has used describe() from the **Hmisc** package. Leslie recalled that a package must be installed once, but after it's installed there are two ways to access the functions that come from the package. The first way is to load the entire package using library(package = "Hmisc") or using the :: structure. Since they just wanted to test out describe(), Leslie tried using ::.

```
# trying describe for descriptive statistics
Hmisc::describe(x = brfss.2014.cleaned)
## brfss.2014.cleaned
##
##  9  Variables      464664   Observations
## --------------------------------------------------------------------
## TRNSGNDR
##          n   missing distinct
##     154062    310602        6
##
## Male to female (363, 0.002), Female to male (212, 0.001), Gender
## non-conforming (116, 0.001), Not transgender (150765, 0.979), Not sure
## (1138, 0.007), Refused (1468, 0.010)
## --------------------------------------------------------------------
## X_AGEG5YR
##          n   missing distinct      Info      Mean       Gmd       .05       .10
##     464664         0        14     0.993     7.822     3.952         1         3
##        .25       .50       .75       .90       .95
##          5         8        10        12        13
##
## Value            1     2     3     4     5     6     7     8     9    10
## Frequency    24198 19891 23662 25444 28597 32686 43366 49432 52620 50680
## Proportion   0.052 0.043 0.051 0.055 0.062 0.070 0.093 0.106 0.113 0.109
##
## Value           11    12    13    14
## Frequency    40160 29310 38840  5778
## Proportion   0.086 0.063 0.084 0.012
## --------------------------------------------------------------------
## X_RACE
##          n   missing distinct      Info      Mean       Gmd
##     464570        94         9     0.546     1.992     1.687
##
## Value            1     2     3     4     5     6     7     8     9
```

```
## Frequency  356808   35062    7076    9314     1711    2109    8824   35838   7828
## Proportion   0.768   0.075   0.015a   0.020    0.004   0.005   0.019   0.077   0.017
## -----------------------------------------------------------------------------
## X_INCOMG
##           n  missing  distinct      Info      Mean       Gmd
##      464664        0         6     0.932     4.481     2.522
##
## Value          1        2        3        4        5        9
## Frequency  44142    68042    44315    57418   179351    71396
## Proportion 0.095    0.146    0.095    0.124    0.386    0.154
## -----------------------------------------------------------------------------
## X_EDUCAG
##           n  missing  distinct      Info      Mean       Gmd
##      464664        0         5     0.911     2.966     1.153
##
## Value          1        2        3        4        9
## Frequency  37003   131325   125635   166972     3729
## Proportion 0.080    0.283    0.270    0.359    0.008
## -----------------------------------------------------------------------------
## HLTHPLN1
##           n  missing  distinct      Info      Mean       Gmd
##      464664        0         4     0.233     1.108    0.2022
##
## Value          1        2        7        9
## Frequency 425198    37642      934      890
## Proportion 0.915    0.081    0.002    0.002
## -----------------------------------------------------------------------------
## HADMAM
##           n  missing  distinct      Info      Mean       Gmd
##      256342   208322         4     0.483     1.215    0.3488
##
## Value          1        2        7        9
## Frequency 204705    51067      253      317
## Proportion 0.799    0.199    0.001    0.001
## -----------------------------------------------------------------------------
## X_AGE80
##           n  missing  distinct      Info      Mean       Gmd       .05       .10
##      464664        0        63     0.999     55.49     19.22     24 30
##       .25      .50       .75       .90       .95
```

```
##       44        58         69        78        80
##
## lowest : 18 19 20 21 22, highest: 76 77 78 79 80
## ----------------------------------------------------------------
## PHYSHLTH
##          n  missing distinct      Info      Mean       Gmd      .05      .10
##     464660        4       33     0.752      61.2     36.37        2        3
##        .25      .50      .75       .90       .95
##         20       88       88        88        88
##
## lowest :  1  2  3  4  5, highest: 29 30 77 88 99
## ----------------------------------------------------------------
```

They looked through the output from describe() and saw that proportions were included, which is something that was not in the summary() output. However, there was a lot of output to read through to find specific information. Kiara mentioned that she prefers to use functions with output that is more targeted to what she is interested in, so she just uses summary() and describe() to get a sense of the data or to confirm that her data management tasks have worked, but uses other options once she is ready to create tables or other displays of data. Leslie thought this was a good strategy, although she was curious about alternatives from other packages.

Nancy said that the **descr** (short for descriptives) package has a good option for a basic table of frequencies and percentages with the freq() function. Nancy also knew that a graph was automatically printed with the freq() output and the graph is not useful at this point, so she showed Leslie how she uses the plot = FALSE option with freq() to stop the graph from printing with the output. Since she just wanted the one function from **descr**, Nancy used the :: format to access the freq() function.

```
# use freq from the descr package to make a table of frequencies and percents
# suppress the bar plot that automatically prints
descr::freq(x = brfss.2014.cleaned$TRNSGNDR, plot = FALSE)
## brfss.2014.cleaned$TRNSGNDR
##                       Frequency    Percent Valid Percent
## Male to female             363    0.07812       0.23562
## Female to male             212    0.04562       0.13761
## Gender non-conforming      116    0.02496       0.07529
## Not transgender         150765   32.44603      97.85995
## Not sure                  1138    0.24491       0.73866
## Refused                   1468    0.31593       0.95286
## NA's                    310602   66.84443
## Total                   464664  100.00000     100.00000
```

Leslie noticed that there were two columns in the output that show percentages. She reviewed the columns and found that the Percent column includes the missing data (NA) in the calculation of the percentage of observations in each category. The Valid Percent column removes the NA values and calculates the percentage of observations that falls into each category *excluding the observations missing values on this variable.*

Since they were already using the **tidyverse** package, Nancy suggested they try using it for this instead of opening a new package. She wrote some alternate code to show Leslie how she might create this table.

```
# use tidyverse to make table of frequency and percent
brfss.2014.cleaned %>%
  group_by(TRNSGNDR) %>%
  summarize(freq.trans = n()) %>%
  mutate(perc.trans = 100 * (freq.trans / sum(freq.trans)))
## # A tibble: 7 x 3
##    TRNSGNDR              freq.trans perc.trans
##    <fct>                      <int>      <dbl>
## 1 Male to female               363     0.0781
## 2 Female to male               212     0.0456
## 3 Gender non-conforming        116     0.0250
## 4 Not transgender           150765    32.4
## 5 Not sure                    1138     0.245
## 6 Refused                     1468     0.316
## 7 <NA>                      310602    66.8
```

Leslie was not impressed. She thought this looked like a lot more code to get the same information they got from `freq()`. Nancy agreed that the code was more complicated to get the same table. She explained that sometimes it was worth the time to use the more complicated code in order to keep a consistent style or to be able to use the code again later. Leslie nodded but remained skeptical. Kiara pointed out that this is an example of how you can do the same thing in a number of different ways in R. Often, there is no single correct way.

Nancy noted that both the `freq()` and **tidyverse** tables included the information needed for reporting, but they were still not formatted in a way that could be directly incorporated into a report or other document. Leslie suggested that they copy these results into a word-processing program and format the table there.

Kiara cringed at this suggestion. Copying from statistical output into another document is where many errors occur in scientific reporting (Harris et al., 2019) and is a major reason why some research results are not reproducible. It is more efficient and accurate to create a formatted table in R and use it without transcribing or changing the contents. Nancy suggested there were two great options for creating reproducible tables directly in R using the **tableone** and **kableExtra** packages. Kiara promised to explain how to make pretty tables later, but for now the R-Team agreed to use the **tidyverse** to make their table.

Before they moved on to numeric variables, Leslie wanted to make sure she understood how to report and interpret the descriptive statistics for factor variables. She wrote a few sentences to share with Nancy and Kiara.

The 2014 BRFSS had a total of 464,664 participants. Of these, 310,602 (66.8%) were not asked or were otherwise missing a response to the transgender status question. A few participants refused to answer ($n = 1,468$; 0.32%), and a small number were unsure of their status ($n = 1,138$; 0.24%). Most reported being not transgender ($n = 150,765$; 32.4%), 116 were gender non-conforming (0.03%), 212 were female to male (0.05%), and 363 were male to female (0.08%).

Nancy and Kiara agreed that this was good for reporting frequencies and percentages. Leslie thought it might be more useful to just include the *valid* percentages for people who responded to the question. Without a word, Nancy used [] to omit the NA from TRNSGNDR to calculate the valid percentages.

```
# use tidyverse to make table of frequency and percent
brfss.2014.cleaned %>%
  group_by(TRNSGNDR) %>%
  summarize(freq.trans = n()) %>%
  mutate(perc.trans = 100 * (freq.trans / sum(freq.trans))) %>%
  mutate(valid.perc = 100 * (freq.trans / (sum(freq.trans[na.omit(object =
TRNSGNDR)]))))
## # A tibble: 7 x 4
##     TRNSGNDR              freq.trans perc.trans valid.perc
##     <fct>                 <int>      <dbl>      <dbl>
## 1 Male to female            363      0.0781     0.236
## 2 Female to male            212      0.0456     0.138
## 3 Gender non-conforming     116      0.0250     0.0753
## 4 Not transgender        150765     32.4       97.9
## 5 Not sure                 1138      0.245      0.739
## 6 Refused                  1468      0.316      0.953
## 7 <NA>                   310602     66.8       202
```

Nancy said to just ignore the <NA> valid.perc for now; it is a tricky data management problem to delete this value to have a perfect table. Leslie understood and updated her sentences to share with Nancy and Kiara.

The 2014 BRFSS had a total of 464,664 participants. Of these, 310,602 (66.8%) were not asked or were otherwise missing a response to the transgender status question. Of the 33.2% who responded, some refused to answer ($n = 1,468$; 0.95%), and a small number were unsure of their status ($n = 1,138$, 0.74%). Most reported being not transgender ($n = 150,765$; 97.9%), 116 were gender non-conforming (0.08%), 212 were female to male (0.14%), and 363 were male to female (0.24%).

Leslie felt much better about this interpretation. Her R-Team friends agreed.

2.5.4 ACHIEVEMENT 2: CHECK YOUR UNDERSTANDING

Use one of the methods shown to create a table of the frequencies for the HADMAM variable, which indicates whether or not each survey participant had a mammogram. Review the question and response options in the codebook and recode to ensure that the correct category labels show up in the table before you begin.

2.6 Achievement 3: Choosing and conducting descriptive analyses for continuous (numeric) variables

2.6.1 WHY FREQUENCY DISTRIBUTIONS DO NOT WORK FOR NUMERIC VARIABLES

Now that they had a good table of descriptive statistics for a factor variable, Nancy and Leslie switched to numeric variables. Numeric variables are measured on a continuum and can be truly continuous or just close to continuous. Leslie knew these types of variables were not well described using frequency distributions. For example, a frequency table of the age variable (X_AGE80) looked like this:

```
# table with frequencies from the age variable
table(brfss.2014.cleaned$X_AGE80)
##
##     18     19     20     21     22     23     24     25     26     27     28     29
##   3447   3209   3147   3470   3470   3632   3825   3982   3723   3943   4191   4054
##     30     31     32     33     34     35     36     37     38     39     40     41
##   4719   4169   4988   4888   4925   5373   5033   5109   5152   4891   5897   4672
##     42     43     44     45     46     47     48     49     50     51     52     53
##   6029   6215   6091   6463   6252   6963   6994   7019   8925   7571   9060   9015
##     54     55     56     57     58     59     60     61     62     63     64     65
##   9268   9876   9546  10346  10052  10293  11651  10310  11842  10955  10683  11513
##     66     67     68     69     70     71     72     73     74     75     76     77
##  10704  11583   9129   8092   9305   8388   8239   7381   6850   6844   6048   5845
##     78     79     80
##   5552   5021  38842
```

Nancy agreed that this display of age data provides very little useful information and pointed out that there are descriptive statistics to examine numeric variables directly. Leslie knew all about these statistics, which include measures of the central tendency and *spread* of the values for a numeric variable.

2.6.2 DEFINING AND CALCULATING CENTRAL TENDENCY

Leslie remembered from her statistics courses that central tendency was a measure of the center, or typical value, of a variable and that there were three measures of central tendency: mean, median, and mode.

- The *mean* is the sum of the values divided by the number of values.

- The *median* is the middle value (or the mean of the two middle values if there is an even number of observations).

- The *mode* is the most common value or values.

2.6.2.1 USING THE MEAN

The most well-understood and widely used measure of central tendency is the mean. Leslie knew that the mean is calculated by adding up all the values of a variable and dividing by the number of values. She wrote out Equation (2.1).

$$m_x = \frac{\sum_{i=1}^{n} x_i}{n} \tag{2.1}$$

Nancy was not as interested in the statistical theory, and Leslie saw her eyes glaze over as soon as she saw Equation (2.1), but Leslie explained anyway. She said that the *numerator* (top of the fraction) is the sum (Σ) of all the values of x from the first value ($i = 1$) to the last value (n) divided by the number of values (n). Leslie remembered that, to use the mean, a variable should be *normally distributed*, or have values that resemble a bell curve when graphed. Nancy saw an opportunity and quickly coded a graph of a normal distribution to show Leslie (Figure 2.3). Leslie was impressed and confirmed that this is how a variable should be distributed in order to use the mean.

Nancy decided to show off a little and added the bell-shaped normal curve to the normal distribution graph (Figure 2.4).

Leslie recognized that the underlying graph in Figures 2.3 and 2.4 is a *histogram*, which shows the values of a variable along the horizontal *x-axis* and some kind of probability (or sometimes the frequency) of each value of the variable along the vertical *y-axis*. That was all Leslie could remember about this graph, and Kiara assured her that they would talk more about histograms in detail at their next meeting. For now, they would just remember that *normality* is signified by the shape of the graph.

Leslie remembered that, for a variable with a distribution that is normal, or near normal, the mean value would be a good representation of the middle of the data. But if the data look *skewed*, with some very large values on the right (**right** or *positively skewed*) or left (**left** or *negatively skewed*), the median would be more appropriate. Nancy got her coding fingers ready and made a couple of skewed histograms as examples (Figure 2.5).

FIGURE 2.3 The shape of the distribution for a normally distributed variable

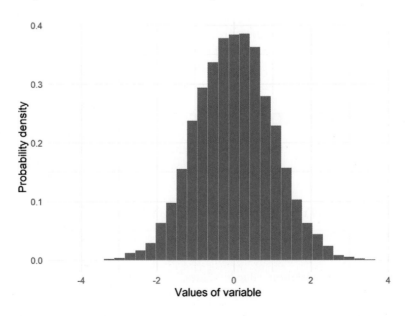

FIGURE 2.4 Normally distributed variable with normal curve

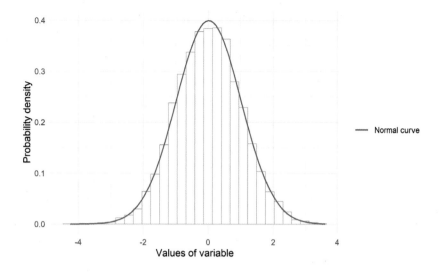

FIGURE 2.5 Examples of skewed distributions

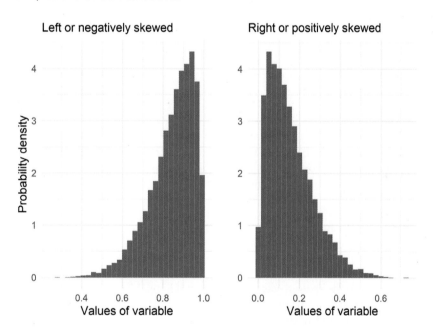

Leslie explained that the reason the mean is not a good representation of skewed data is that adding together a set of values that includes a few very large or very small values like those on the far left of a *left-skewed* distribution or the far right of a *right-skewed* distribution will result in a large or small total value in the numerator of Equation (2.1), and therefore the mean will be a large or small value relative to the actual middle of the data.

That is, she said, the mean is influenced by the very large or very small values and is therefore not representative of a typical value or the middle of the data; instead, the mean of a skewed variable is larger or smaller than the actual middle values in the data. Nancy remembered one example of this that is often used is income. Say you collected the incomes of five of your friends and billionaire Bill Gates. Your friends made the following annual salaries in U.S. dollars: $25,000, $62,000, $41,000, $96,000, and $41,000. Adding these five values together and dividing by five would result in a mean salary among your friends of $53,000. Given the salaries listed, this seems like a reasonable value that accurately represents a typical salary of your friends.

While she explained this to Leslie, Nancy introduced the `mean()` function.

```
# create salaries vector and find its mean
salaries <- c(25000, 62000, 41000, 96000, 41000)
mean(x = salaries)
## [1] 53000
```

However, Nancy explained, if Bill Gates just happened to be a friend of yours, you would include his estimated $11.5 billion annual earnings by adding it to the existing `salaries` vector. Adding a value to a vector can be done by concatenating the existing values with the new values in a new vector using `c()`, like this:

```
# add Bill Gates
salaries.gates <- c(salaries, 11500000000)

# find the mean of the vector with gates
mean(x = salaries.gates)
## [1] 1916710833
```

Now it appears that your friends make a mean salary of $1,916,710,833. While technically this may be true if Bill Gates is among your friends, it is not a good representation of a typical salary for one of the friends. In the case of skewed data, the median is a better choice.

Leslie looked away for a minute, and when she looked back, the code magician (Nancy) had coded a normal distribution with the mean represented by a line in the middle of the distribution (Figure 2.6). Visually, the mean for a normally distributed variable would be in the middle like the vertical line in Nancy's fancy distribution.

Nancy also added means to the skewed-variables graphic (Figure 2.7). This demonstrated that the mean was not in the middle, but instead was toward the longer *tail* of data. The tails of a distribution are the values to the far right and far left in the distribution. Often, there are fewer values in these parts of the distribution, so they taper off and look like a tail.

2.6.2.2 USING THE MEDIAN

Leslie reminded everyone that the median is the middle number when numbers are in order from smallest to largest. When there are an even number of numbers, the median is the mean of the middle two numbers. Nancy typed some quick code to show that, in the examples above, the median for the friend groups with and without Bill Gates would be as follows:

FIGURE 2.6 Normally distributed variable with mean

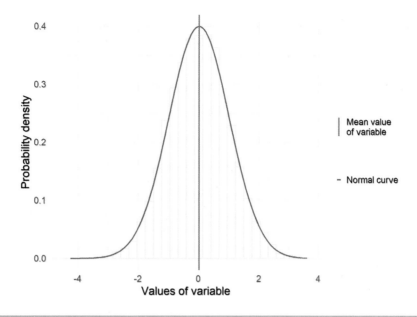

FIGURE 2.7 Examples of skewed distributions showing mean values

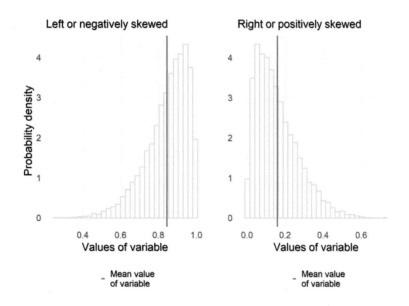

```
# median salary without Bill Gates
median(x = salaries)
## [1] 41000
# median salary with Bill Gates
median(x = salaries.gates)
## [1] 51500
```

While Leslie noticed that the median increased with the addition of Bill Gates to her friend group, the result was still a reasonable representation of the middle of the salaries of this group of friends, unlike the mean of $1,916,710,833.

Leslie went on to explain that in a perfect normal distribution, the median would be exactly the same as the mean. In skewed distributions, the median will not be the same as the mean. For a variable that is left skewed, the median will usually be to the right of the mean (von Hippel, 2005). For a variable that is right skewed, the median will usually be to the left of the mean. Nancy was not paying close attention but realized she could write some code to show the mean and the median on the skewed distribution to demonstrate Leslie's point (Figure 2.8).

In this case, the median is not too far from the mean. Leslie was curious about how different from normal a distribution has to be before people use the median instead of the mean. From the examples so far, she thought that median salary was a more accurate representation of the middle of the `gates.salaries` vector than the mean of `gates.salaries`. However, for the two skewed distribution histogram examples in Figure 2.8, the median and mean are very close to each other, and since the mean seems like a more widely used and understood measure, might it be a better choice?

She looked through her statistics materials and found that one way some people make this decision is to calculate a measure of skewness. *Skewness* is a measure of the extent to which a distribution is skewed. There are a few variations on the formula, but she found one that is commonly used (von Hippel, 2005). She showed Nancy and Kiara Equation (2.2).

$$skewness_x = \frac{1}{n}\sum_{i=1}^{n}\left(\frac{x_i - m_x}{s_x}\right)^3$$

(2.2)

In Equation (2.2), n is the sample size, x_i is each observation of x, m_x is the sample mean of x, and s_x is the sample standard deviation of x. Leslie reviewed the equation slowly. The first thing she found to note is that the mean of x, m_x, is subtracted from each observation x_i. These differences between the mean and

---

FIGURE 2.8 Examples of skewed distributions with means and medians

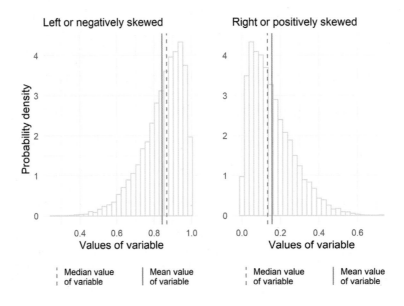

each observed value are called *deviation scores*. Each deviation score is divided by the standard deviation, *s*, and the result is cubed. Finally, sum the cubed values and divide by the number of cubed values (which is taking the mean) to get the skewness of *x*. The resulting value is usually *negative* when the skew is to the left and usually *positive* when the skew is toward the right. Because skewness is strongly impacted by the sample size with $\frac{1}{n}$ in Equation (2.2), the value of skew that is considered *too skewed* differs depending on sample size.

Leslie found this helpful and asked Nancy if there was a way to compute skewness in R. Nancy said the **semTools** package has skew() to compute this value and a few related values. She typed in the code and tried skew() for the salary vector with Bill Gates and for the two variables used to create the skewed histograms in Figure 2.8, left.skewed for the left-skewed histogram and right.skewed for the right-skewed histogram. Leslie did not have the data Nancy used for these variables, so she could only follow along with the skew() calculation for the salaries.gates object.

```
# skewness of salaries variable
semTools::skew(object = salaries.gates)
##   skew (g1)          se          z          p
## 2.44948974 1.00000000 2.44948974 0.01430588

# skewness of Figure 2.8 left-skewed distribution variable
semTools::skew(object = left.skewed)
##    skew (g1)          se           z           p
##  -1.0739316   0.0244949 -43.8430756   0.0000000

# skewness of Figure 2.8 right-skewed distribution variable
semTools::skew(object = right.skewed)
##    skew (g1)         se          z          p
##   1.0454195  0.0244949 42.6790709  0.0000000
```

Leslie was expecting a single number, but instead each skew() calculation contained four values. She looked in the help documentation and found that the first value is the skewness and the second value is the *se*, or the *standard error* of the skew. Leslie remembered that the standard error is often used to quantify how much variation there is in data, but she decided to leave that for later. The third number, *z*, is the value of the skew divided by its *se*. She determined from some of the readings she had in her statistics materials that *z* is the number useful for determining if the level of skew is too much for the variable to be treated as normally distributed (Kim, 2013). If the sample size is small ($n < 50$), *z* values outside the –2 to 2 range are a problem. If the sample size is between 50 and 300, *z* values outside the –3.29 to 3.29 range are a problem. For large samples ($n > 300$), using a visual is recommended over the statistics, but generally *z* values outside the range of –7 to 7 can be considered problematic.

Leslie looked back at the *se*, *z*, and *p* statistics in the output and decided that gaining a deep understanding of these statistics was a little too much for what they were doing in this meeting. She decided to focus on gaining a little more foundation in descriptive statistics and sampling instead. For now, she relied on graphs and the general rules. Since the *z* for the skewness of salaries.gates is greater than 2 ($z = 2.45$) and the sample size is small, the data have a skew problem. This makes sense given the huge Bill Gates salary included in these data. The *z* statistics for the data underlying the left.skewed and right.skewed distributions in Figure 2.8 were much larger in magnitude and far beyond the threshold for problematic, which made sense to Leslie since those distributions were clearly not normal.

2.6.2.3 USING THE MODE

Finally, the mode is the most common value in a data set. Leslie suggested that the mode is not widely used in the research she had read, but it was still good to know that it existed as an option. She did recall that, for numeric variables, the mode can be used along with the mean and median as an additional indicator of a normal distribution. In a perfect normal distribution, the mean, median, and mode are all exactly the same.

Nancy explained that, unfortunately, perhaps because it is rarely used, there is no mode function. Instead, she showed Leslie how to use `sort()` with `table()` to sort a table from highest to lowest (decreasing order) or lowest to highest (increasing order). Nancy walked Leslie through computing the mode in R. Start with a table, `table(salaries)`, which will show the frequencies of each value in the data.

```
# table showing salaries frequencies
table(salaries)
## salaries
## 25000 41000 62000 96000
##     1     2     1     1
```

There is one salary of $25,000, two salaries of $41,000, and so on. With data this simple, it would be easy to stop here and notice that $41,000 is the mode. However, most data sets will be much larger, and it will be more efficient to have a set of R functions to use. Nancy put the table in order from largest frequency to smallest frequency using `sort()` with `decreasing = TRUE`.

```
# table showing salaries frequencies
sort(x = table(salaries), decreasing = TRUE)
## salaries
## 41000 25000 62000 96000
##     2     1     1     1
```

This orders the table starting with the salary with the highest frequency, or the most common salary. This salary is the mode. To just have R print the salary (not its frequency), use `names()`, which will print the salary category names shown in the top row of the table.

```
# table showing salaries frequencies
names(x = sort(x = table(salaries), decreasing = TRUE))
## [1] "41000" "25000" "62000" "96000"
```

Finally, to just print the first category name, use the square brackets, `[ ]`. In R, the square brackets are used to grab a particular location (sometimes called an "index"). For example, the `salaries` vector has 5 observations: 25000, 62000, 41000, 96000, 41000. To get the 4th observation of `salaries`, you can type `salaries[4]`, which is 96000. Here, to get the first category name, use the same bit of code, and add a `[1]` to the end.

```
# no mode function so find the mode using a table
# and sort values in decreasing order
# so the most common value comes first
names(x = sort(x = table(salaries), decreasing = TRUE))[1]
## [1] "41000"
```

All together, the three measures can be computed for the `salaries` vector.

```
# mean, median, and mode of salaries
mean(x = salaries)
## [1] 53000
median(x = salaries)
## [1] 41000
names(x = sort(x = table(salaries), decreasing = TRUE))[1]
## [1] "41000"
```

The mean is $53,000, and the median and mode are both $41,000. So the mean, median, and mode were not exactly the same, and Leslie concluded that the data are not *perfectly* normally distributed.

The mode is sometimes used to identify the most common (or typical) category of a factor variable. For example, in the tables above, the mode of the `TRNSGNDR` variable is "Not transgender," with more than 150,000 observations in that category.

2.6.3 MESSY DATA AND COMPUTING MEASURES OF CENTRAL TENDENCY

Using these functions with variables from a data frame like `brfss.2014.cleaned` is similar. Nancy wanted to show Leslie how to create a histogram and compute the mean, median, and mode for the `PHYSHLTH` variable from the 2014 BRFSS data set. `PHYSHLTH` is the number of physically unhealthy days a survey participant has had in the last 30 days. On page 11 of the BRFSS codebook, the values of `77` and `99` are `Don't know/ Not sure` and `Refused`, so they could be coded as missing before examining the variable. It also looks like `88` is `None` for the number of unhealthy days and should be coded as zero. Leslie copied and pasted her data management code from earlier. Nancy was eager to keep coding and slid the laptop over to type in the new code for changing `77` and `99` to `NA`. She also recoded `88` in `PHYSHLTH` to be `0`, which was a little complicated.

```
# pipe in the original data frame
# recode the TRNSGNDR factor so it's easy to read
# recode 77, 88, 99 on PHYSHLTH
brfss.2014.cleaned <- brfss.trans.2014 %>%
  mutate(TRNSGNDR = recode_factor(.x = TRNSGNDR,
                                   `1` = 'Male to female',
                                   `2` = 'Female to male',
```

```
                                  `3` = 'Gender non-conforming',
                                  `4` = 'Not transgender',
                                  `7` = 'Not sure',
                                  `9` = 'Refused')) %>%
  mutate(PHYSHLTH = na_if(x = PHYSHLTH, y = 77)) %>%
  mutate(PHYSHLTH = na_if(x = PHYSHLTH, y = 99)) %>%
  mutate(PHYSHLTH = as.numeric(recode(.x = PHYSHLTH, `88` = 0L)))
```

Once Nancy had completed and run the code, she checked the recoding of PHYSHLTH.

```
# examine PHYSHLTH to check data management
summary(object = brfss.2014.cleaned$PHYSHLTH)
##   Min. 1st Qu.  Median   Mean 3rd Qu.   Max.   NA's
##  0.000   0.000   0.000  4.224   3.000 30.000  10303
```

The maximum number of unhealthy days shown in the output for summary() was 30, so the recoding worked as planned. Nancy showed Leslie how to make a histogram from the cleaned data. The code was similar to what they used at the end of the data preparation meeting, but the geom_, or geometry, layer this time is geom_histogram() to make a histogram (Figure 2.9).

```
# make a histogram
brfss.2014.cleaned %>%
  ggplot(aes(x = PHYSHLTH)) +
  geom_histogram()
```

FIGURE 2.9 Distribution of the PHYSHLTH variable

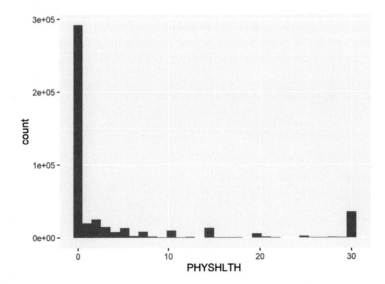

The histogram showed most people have between 0 and 10 unhealthy days per 30 days. Leslie wanted to take a turn coding and wrote the code for the measures of central tendency for the PHYSHLTH variable.

```
# get mean, median, mode
mean(x = brfss.2014.cleaned$PHYSHLTH)
## [1] NA
median(x = brfss.2014.cleaned$PHYSHLTH)
## [1] NA
names(x = sort(x = table(brfss.2014.cleaned$PHYSHLTH), decreasing = TRUE))[1]
## [1] "0"
```

Well, that didn't work very well! The mode looks like 0 unhealthy days. The mean and the median show NA. Nancy explained that the mean() and median() functions require removal of NA values. They worked for the salaries vector because there were no NA values. To fix this, she needed to include a second argument that tells the mean() function how to treat missing data. She added the option na.rm = TRUE, where na stands for NA and rm stands for "remove."

```
# get mean, median, mode
mean(x = brfss.2014.cleaned$PHYSHLTH, na.rm = TRUE)
## [1] 4.224106
median(x = brfss.2014.cleaned$PHYSHLTH, na.rm = TRUE)
## [1] 0
names(x = sort(table(brfss.2014.cleaned$PHYSHLTH), decreasing = TRUE))[1]
## [1] "0"
```

Leslie admitted at this point that she was concerned that she would never be able to remember all the arguments and rules for the different functions. Kiara reassured her that she does *not* need to memorize them! First, Kiara explained, Leslie can always check the help documentation. The help documentation will list what a function does, the arguments it can take, and what the output of the function means, and there are often examples at the bottom of the help documentation that show how to use the function.

Additionally, Kiara showed Leslie how to use tab completion to make her life easier. Kiara told Leslie to start typing the letters "me" in the Console and then hit her laptop's Tab key. Leslie noticed that a lot of different functions starting with "me" appear, and that mean() was first! Since mean() was first and highlighted, Kiara told Leslie to press the Enter or Return key on her laptop keyboard. Leslie was relieved that she didn't need to type out the rest of the word "mean" *and* that the parentheses automatically appeared!

Kiara told Leslie to hit the Tab key once again. The first argument x appeared, and a brief description of that argument. Here, x is the variable that you want to get the mean of. Leslie pressed Enter and the x = argument appeared in her code and was ready to be filled in with brfss.2014.cleaned$PHYSHLTH. Leslie started typing the letters "brf" and hit Tab. Sure enough, she saw the name of the data frame she needed and highlighted before she pressed Enter and added the $. After she added $, the same thing happened when she started to type the PHYSHLTH variable name. Kiara explained that arguments within a function are separated by commas. She suggested Leslie type a comma after PHYSHLTH and press Tab. Leslie saw the na.rm argument appear! It was like magic. Leslie finished the line of code using the Tab-complete trick and was relieved that she didn't have to remember or type so much.

Kiara suggested that **tidyverse** code might be clearer to get the central tendency measures since the name of the data frame would not have to be included in all three functions. To pipe the data frame into the central tendency functions, use `summarize()`. Nancy mentioned that some code uses British spellings, but the American spellings usually work, too. For example, in **tidyverse**, `summarize()` is the same as `summarise()`.

```
# get mean, median, mode
brfss.2014.cleaned %>%
  summarize(mean.days = mean(x = PHYSHLTH,
                             na.rm = TRUE),
            med.days = median(x = PHYSHLTH,
                              na.rm = TRUE),
            mode.days = names(x = sort(table(PHYSHLTH),
                                       decreasing = TRUE))[1])
##    mean.days med.days mode.days
## 1   4.224106        0         0
```

So the mean number of unhealthy days per month is 4.22 and the median and mode are 0. This makes sense given the right skew of the histogram. The people with 30 poor health days are making the mean value higher than the median. A few very large (or very small) values relative to the rest of the data can make a big difference for a mean.

Leslie wanted to calculate the skewness to see what it is for a variable that looks this skewed. Based on what she learned above, she expected the z for skewness of PHYSHLTH to be a positive number and greater than 7. She wrote and ran the code.

```
# skewness for PHYSHLTH
semTools::skew(object = brfss.2014.cleaned$PHYSHLTH)
##      skew (g1)           se             z            p
## 2.209078e+00 3.633918e-03 6.079054e+02 0.000000e+00
```

Leslie noticed that the results were shown using *scientific notation*. While she was familiar with scientific notation, which is useful for printing large numbers in small spaces, she knew it is not well-understood by most audiences. Kiara said they would see more of it later (Box 3.2), but for now, they should just remember that the 2.209078e+00, 3.633918e−03, 6.079054e+02, and 0.000000e+00 were shorthand ways of writing 2.209078×10^0, 3.633918×10^{-3}, 6.079054×10^2, and 0.000000×10^0. Kiara suggested that they think of the +00, −03, and +02 as the direction and how many places to move the decimal point. So, +00 is move the decimal point 0 places to the right, −03 is move the decimal point 3 places to the left, and +02 is move the decimal point 2 places to the right.

Since 2.209078×10^0 is just 2.209078 after moving the decimal point 0 places (or after recognizing that anything raised to the power of zero is 1, so $10^0 = 1$), PHYSHLTH has a skewness of 2.209078. After moving the decimal point 2 places to the right, z is 607.9054, which is much higher than 7. The graph showed a clear right skew, so there is plenty of evidence that this variable is not normally distributed.

2.6.4 DEFINING AND CALCULATING SPREAD

In addition to using central tendency to characterize a variable, Leslie remembered that reporting a corresponding measure of how spread out the values are around the central value is also important to understanding numeric variables. Each measure of central tendency has one or more corresponding measures of spread.

- Mean: use *variance* or *standard deviation* to measure spread
- Median: use *range* or *interquartile range* (IQR) to measure spread
- Mode: use an *index of qualitative variation* to measure spread

2.6.4.1 SPREAD TO REPORT WITH THE MEAN

The variance is the average of the squared differences between each value of a variable and the mean of the variable. Leslie showed Nancy the formula from an old statistics textbook, and Nancy wrote Equation (2.3) so they could review how it worked.

$$s_x^2 = \frac{\sum_{i=1}^n (x_i - m_x)^2}{n-1} \tag{2.3}$$

Leslie saw that the s_x^2 is the variance of x, the Σ symbol is sum, the x_i is each individual value of x, the m_x is the mean of x, and n is the sample size. The variance is the sum of the squared differences between each value of x and the mean of x (or the sum of squared deviation scores) divided by the sample size minus 1. "Fun fact," said Nancy, "the $n - 1$ in the formula is called the Bessel correction."

"I'm not sure how that's fun," Leslie said, smiling, "but OK."

Nancy showed her that, in R, the `var()` function finds the variance.

```
# variance of unhealthy days
var(x = brfss.2014.cleaned$PHYSHLTH, na.rm = TRUE)
## [1] 77.00419
```

After looking it up in her statistics textbook and online, Leslie determined there was no direct interpretation of the variance. It is a general measure of how much variation there is in the values of a variable. She found that a more useful measure of spread is the standard deviation, which is the square root of the variance. She shared Equation (2.4) showing the standard deviation of x, or s_x.

$$s_x = \sqrt{\frac{\sum_{i=1}^n (x_i - m_x)^2}{n-1}} \tag{2.4}$$

Nancy continued her coding and added the variance and standard deviation to the **tidyverse** descriptive statistics code they had been accumulating.

```
# get mean, median, mode, and spread
brfss.2014.cleaned %>%
```

```
summarize(mean.days = mean(x = PHYSHLTH, na.rm = TRUE),
          sd.days = sd(x = PHYSHLTH, na.rm = TRUE),
          var.days = var(x = PHYSHLTH, na.rm = TRUE),
          med.days = median(x = PHYSHLTH, na.rm = TRUE),
          mode.days = names(x = sort(x = table(PHYSHLTH),
                                     decreasing = TRUE))[1])
##   mean.days sd.days var.days med.days mode.days
## 1  4.224106 8.775203 77.00419        0         0
```

Leslie remembered that the standard deviation was sometimes interpreted as the average amount an observation differs from the mean. After walking through Equation (2.4) one more time, Leslie concluded that this is conceptually close and a good way to think about it, but not 100% accurate. Regardless, she found that the standard deviation was the best measure of spread to report with means. Nancy thought a visual representation might help and added lines to the normal distribution graph showing how far away one standard deviation is from the mean in the histogram in Figure 2.10.

The R-Team noticed that most of the observations of the variable were between the standard deviation lines. Most observations are within one standard deviation away from the mean. This reminded Kiara of a picture she took in Brussels at an R conference there in 2017 (Figure 2.11).

Leslie had a feeling that there was something else they needed to look at before they were done discussing normal distributions. Kiara suggested that maybe she was remembering *kurtosis*. Kiara explained that kurtosis measures how many observations are in the tails of a distribution. She said that some distributions look bell-shaped, but have a lot of observations in the tails (platykurtic) or very few observations in the tails (leptokurtic) (Westfall, 2004). Leslie asked Kiara whether she was remembering correctly that *platykurtic* distributions are more *flat* (as in a *platy*pus has a flat beak) and *leptokurtic*

FIGURE 2.10 Normally distributed variable showing mean plus and minus one standard deviation

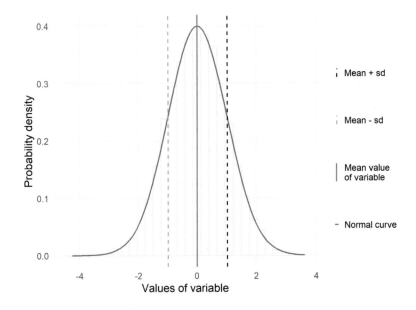

FIGURE 2.11 Street sign from Brussels, Belgium (2017)

Source: Jenine K. Harris.

distributions are more *pointy*. Kiara said this is a common way of describing the shapes of these distributions, but that, technically, kurtosis measures whether there are many or few observations in the tails of the distribution (Westfall, 2004).

Nancy saw an opening for more coding and made Figure 2.12 with histograms that had problems with kurtosis so the team could get an idea of what they are looking for.

From her data management work, Kiara learned that platykurtic and leptokurtic deviations from normality do not necessarily influence the mean, since it will still be a good representation of the middle of the data *if the distribution is symmetrical and not skewed*. However, platykurtic and leptokurtic distributions will have smaller and larger values of variance and standard deviation, respectively, compared to a normal distribution. The variance and standard deviation are not only used to quantify spread, but also used in many of the common statistical tests.

Leslie found the formula for kurtosis (Westfall, 2004) and showed Equation (2.5) to the team.

$$kurtosis_x = \frac{1}{n}\sum_{i=1}^{n}\left(\frac{x_i - m_x}{s_x}\right)^4 \tag{2.5}$$

Leslie read that, in Equation (2.5), n is the sample size, s_x is the standard deviation of x, x_i is each value of x, and m_x is the mean of x. The $\sum_{i=1}^{n}$ symbol indicates the values from the first value of x ($i = 1$) to

FIGURE 2.12 Examples of different-shaped distributions with means of 55

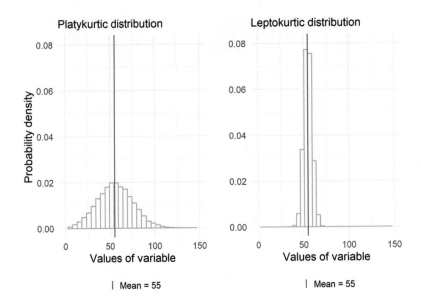

the last value of x ($i = n$) should be summed. A normal distribution will have a kurtosis value of 3; distributions with kurtosis = 3 are described as ***mesokurtic***. If kurtosis is above or below 3, there is excess kurtosis. Values of kurtosis above 3 indicate the distribution is *leptokurtic*, with fewer observations in the tails than a normal distribution (the fewer observations in the tails often give a distribution a pointy look). Values of kurtosis below 3 indicate the distribution is *platykurtic*, with more observations in the tails than a normal distribution would have given the mean, standard deviation, and sample size.

Leslie looked at the **semTools** package documentation and found `kurtosis()` to compute the kurtosis and a few related values. The `kurtosis()` function subtracts 3 from the kurtosis, so positive values will indicate a leptokurtic distribution and negative will indicate a platykurtic distribution. The same cutoff values from skew also apply for the z for small, medium, and large sample sizes in kurtosis. Leslie tried it for the two variables used in the leptokurtic and platykurtic graph above, saved as `var1` in `lepto.plot` and `platy.plot` respectively.

```
# kurtosis of Figure 2.12 leptokurtic distribution variable
semTools::kurtosis(object = lepto.plot$var1)
## Excess Kur (g2)            se              z              p
##      0.05206405    0.04898979     1.06275295     0.28789400

# kurtosis of Figure 2.12 platykurtic distribution variable
semTools::kurtosis(object = platy.plot$var1)
## Excess Kur (g2)            se              z              p
##     -0.04920369    0.04898979    -1.00436604     0.31520221
```

The values of z for the two variables used in the example graphs are relatively small and so are not problematic regardless of sample size, so using statistics that rely on a normal distribution seems OK. Kiara mentioned that they would learn some additional statistical tests later that are useful for identifying non-normal distributions. Often, values of kurtosis and skewness will be reported with these statistical tests as additional information describing the nature of the non-normality (DeCarlo, 1997), rather than as the only piece of information on which to base a decision about normality.

2.6.4.2 SPREAD TO REPORT WITH THE MEDIAN

When distributions are not normally distributed, the median is often a better choice than the mean. For medians, however, the variance and standard deviation will not work to report the spread. Just like the very large values influence the mean, they also influence the standard deviation since the mean is part of the standard deviation formula. The R-Team found two options for reporting spread for non-normal variables. First, the range is the span between the largest and smallest values of a variable. Nancy added the ranges to the skewed distributions (Figure 2.13).

The range does not seem too informative on these graphs, Leslie noted, because it marks the very highest and very lowest values for a variable, but there is no indication of how the observations are spread out between these values. In order to get exact values, Nancy demonstrated by computing the range for the PHYSHLTH variable.

```
# range of days of physical health
range(brfss.2014.cleaned$PHYSHLTH, na.rm = TRUE)
## [1]  0 30
```

Leslie noticed that they *finally* had values that were easy to interpret: The range of unhealthy days in a month is 0 to 30. For the PHYSHLTH variable, the ends of the range are the highest and lowest possible values of the variable. The range does not provide any indication of how the data are distributed across the possible values. For example, maybe there is one person who has 30 days of poor physical health and everyone else is between 0 and 10. Or, maybe half the people have 0 and half the people have 30 and no people have anything in between. Leslie thought another option would be better for understanding spread.

FIGURE 2.13 Examples of skewed distributions with medians and range boundaries

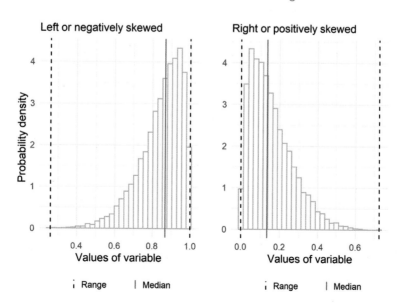

FIGURE 2.14 Examples of skewed distributions with medians and IQR boundaries

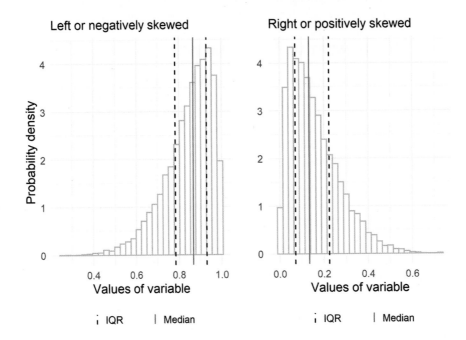

Leslie looked up the interquartile range, or IQR, and found that it might be more appropriate for these data, or for data that are highly skewed. The IQR is the difference between the first and third quartiles. A quartile is one-quarter of the data, so the difference between the first and third quartiles would be the boundaries around the middle 50% of the data. Nancy plotted the IQR on the skewed distributions (Figure 2.14).

This was more useful to Leslie. To find the IQR of PHYSHLTH, Nancy used IQR() and added it to the **tidyverse** descriptive statistics list.

```
# get descriptive statistics for PHYSHLTH
brfss.2014.cleaned %>%
  summarize(mean.days = mean(x = PHYSHLTH, na.rm = TRUE),
            sd.days = sd(x = PHYSHLTH, na.rm = TRUE),
            var.days = var(x = PHYSHLTH, na.rm = TRUE),
            med.days = median(x = PHYSHLTH, na.rm = TRUE),
            iqr.days = IQR(x = PHYSHLTH, na.rm = TRUE),
            mode.days = names(x = sort(x = table(PHYSHLTH),
                                       decreasing = TRUE))[1])
##    mean.days  sd.days var.days med.days iqr.days mode.days
## 1  4.224106 8.775203 77.00419        0        3         0
```

Leslie noticed that they had typed na.rm = TRUE for all but one of the statistics in the summarize() code. She asked Nancy if there was some way to remove NA to make the code less repetitive. Nancy was delighted that Leslie was starting to think about the format of her code. She reminded Leslie that there was a way to omit NA values using drop_na() with the name of the variable of interest, like this:

```
# get descriptive statistics for PHYSHLTH
brfss.2014.cleaned %>%
  drop_na(PHYSHLTH) %>%
  summarize(mean.days = mean(x = PHYSHLTH),
            sd.days = sd(x = PHYSHLTH),
            var.days = var(x = PHYSHLTH),
            med.days = median(x = PHYSHLTH),
            iqr.days = IQR(x = PHYSHLTH),
            mode.days = names(x = sort(x = table(PHYSHLTH),
                                decreasing = TRUE))[1])
##   mean.days  sd.days var.days med.days iqr.days mode.days
## 1  4.224106 8.775203 77.00419        0        3         0
```

Leslie examined the statistics so far. She noted that the IQR value makes sense; there is a 3-day difference between the first and third quartiles for unhealthy days. She remembered she had usually seen the IQR reported without much interpretation, like this: IQR = 3.

Leslie would rather see the upper and lower bounds of the IQR. Nancy said there was no way to do this in the `IQR()` function, but the `quantile()` function could be used to find the bounds around the middle 50%, which are the IQR boundaries.

```
# interquartile range of unhealthy days
quantile(x = brfss.2014.cleaned$PHYSHLTH, na.rm = TRUE)
##   0%  25%  50%  75% 100%
##    0    0    0    3   30
```

The middle 50% of the data is between the 25% and 75% quantiles. Leslie could now report the bounds around the middle 50% of unhealthy days, 0 to 3. Fifty percent of observations (people) in this data set have between 0 and 3 physically unhealthy days per month. Nancy added the median and IQR boundaries to the PHYSHLTH plot with new layers and did a little formatting so they are easier to see (Figure 2.15).

Leslie noticed that the lower boundary of the IQR is the same as the median in the graph. Kiara said this was due to so many values being zero and this being the lowest possible value of the variable. Leslie was curious about the graph code, but Nancy said it had some complex features and suggested they save it for next time when they are working on graphs.

2.6.4.3 SPREAD TO REPORT WITH THE MODE

Leslie remembered that spread is not often reported for categorical variables. Leslie and Kiara discussed what the idea of spread or variability even means for a categorical variable. They reviewed some options in textbooks that describe how observations are spread across categories, sometimes described as *diversity*.

Kiara and Leslie found several options for the *index of qualitative variation*, which quantified how much the observations are spread across categories of a categorical variable. While these indexes are computed in different ways, they all have a range from 0 to 1. The resulting values are *high* when observations are

FIGURE 2.15 Distribution of days of poor physical health showing median and IQR boundaries

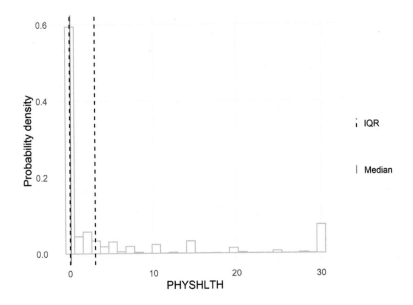

spread out among categories and *low* when they are not. For example, if a data set had a marital status variable and there were 3 people in each marital status category, the data would be considered perfectly spread across groups and the index value would be 1. Likewise, if everyone in the data set was in one category (e.g., unmarried), the index value would be 0 for no spread at all.

After reading through the R help documentation for the **qualvar** package, which includes several options, Kiara and Leslie found the *B index* to be their favorite.

They shared their finding with Nancy, who was playing on her phone because she had run out of things to code for the moment. Nancy had not used the B index, but she found B() in the **qualvar** package. She looked up the help documentation for the B() function and saw that the first argument is x, which is described as "a vector of frequencies." The PHYSHLTH variable is numeric, so it would not use the B index. Instead, Leslie went back to the TRNSGNDR variable. To get a vector of frequencies for TRNSGNDR, Nancy thought the table() function might work. Instead of making a table as a new object, Nancy added the table() code directly into the B() function. It worked perfectly.

```
# B index of TRNSGNDR variable
qualvar::B(x = table(brfss.2014.cleaned$TRNSGNDR))
## [1] 0.0009940017
```

The resulting value of 0.00099 is close to zero and therefore indicates that observations in this data set are not well spread out among the six categories of TRNSGNDR. While it is true that there are people in all categories, the "Not transgender" category contains a much larger number of observations than any of the other categories, so the small value of B reflects this lack of even spread of observations across categories of TRNSGNDR.

Leslie wanted to make sure she had the chance to practice reporting and interpreting the descriptive statistics for numeric variables, so she wrote a few sentences to make sure she understood.

The mean number of days of poor health per month for participants in the 2014 BRFSS was 4.22 ($s = 8.78$).

Leslie recognized that she would not report the mean and the median for the variable; instead, she would choose the most appropriate one. However, for the sake of practicing, she wrote an interpretation of the median.

The median number of days of poor health per month for participants in the 2014 BRFSS was 0 (IQR = 3).

The mode would not commonly be reported for the PHYSHLTH variable, so she reported the mode and B index for TRNSGNDR instead.

The most common response (mode) to the transgender question was "Not transgender." The responses were not spread out very evenly among the categories, with over 150,000 in the "Not transgender" category and just 116 in the "Gender non-conforming" category (B = .00099).

Kiara and Nancy approved of these interpretations and told Leslie her writing was similar to interpretations in published manuscripts.

2.6.5 ACHIEVEMENT 3: CHECK YOUR UNDERSTANDING

Find central tendency and spread for the age variable (**X_AGE80**). Examine the variable and the codebook first to see if it needs to be cleaned.

2.7 Achievement 4: Developing clear tables for reporting descriptive statistics

Although Leslie felt like she now had a great grasp of descriptive statistics, Kiara explained that they were only halfway done! After all, Kiara stated, statistics are only useful when people can understand them. In the case of descriptive statistics, she said, making a clear table is the key to good communication. Clear tables tend to have the following features:

- A title that explains what is in the table
  - The number of observations if possible
  - Key pieces of information that describe the sample such as the year of data collection and the data source
  - The units of measurement (people, organizations, etc.)
- Consistent use of the same number of decimal places throughout the table
- Numbers aligned to the right so that the decimal points line up
- Words aligned to the left
- Indentation and shading to differentiate rows or sections
- Limited internal lines
- Clearly labeled rows and columns

If the table contains only factor-type variables, Kiara explained, it may look like Table 2.1 including only percentages. They decided that reproducing that table would be good practice for making publication-quality tables. To reproduce Table 2.1, Kiara had Leslie note the variables included in the table and find them in the BRFSS codebook (https://www.cdc.gov/brfss/annual_data/2014/pdf/CODEBOOK14_LLCP.pdf). After she reviewed the variables in the codebook, the team got to work to reproduce Table 2.1. Kiara recommended they refer to this table as Table 2.1 as they work, with the understanding that it was a reproduction of the Table 1 printed in the Narayan et al. (2017) paper.

2.7.1 DATA CLEANING BEFORE ANALYSIS
2.7.1.1 CREATING A SMALLER DATA FRAME TO WORK WITH

Looking back at Table 2.1 and reviewing the Narayan et al. paper (2017), Leslie and Kiara determined that it contained only those who answered the transgender status question, were in the 40- to 74-year-old age groups, and were asked the mammogram question. They found these three variables in the codebook:

- `TRNSGNDR`: codebook page 83
- `_AGEG5YR`: codebook page 108
- `HADMAM`: codebook page 37

Kiara shared one of her favorite data management tips with Leslie, which was to create a smaller data set by limiting the data to the observations that will be analyzed. There are several ways to create a subset that contains only particular observations. One method is to simply grab the observations wanted using the square brackets `[ ]`. Kiara reminded Leslie that she had already used `[ ]` to get the 4th element of the `salaries` vector using `salaries[4]`. Vectors are one-dimensional, and therefore Leslie would just put one number inside the brackets. Data frames are two-dimensional, Kiara explained, since there are both rows and columns. So to index a data frame, the square brackets require two numbers, separated by a comma, and the order will always be `[rows, columns]`. Kiara wrote a few examples.

- Get the value of the 3rd row and 2nd column: `data.frame[3, 2]`.
- Get all of the values in the 5th column: `data.frame[ ,5]`. A blank in the rows part means "all," but it still needs to be separated by a comma.
- Get the values for rows 2 through 6 and columns 4 through 10: `data.frame[2:6, 4:10]`. The colon `:` can be read as "through."
- Get the values for rows 1, 7, 18 and columns 4 through 10: `data.frame[c(1, 7, 18), 4:10]`.

Since the R-Team has been using **tidyverse**, Nancy thought they should create a subset with the `filter()` function instead of the square brackets. She suggested that Leslie look up the help documentation for the `filter()` function on her own. Leslie found that `filter()` "choose[s] rows/cases where conditions are true." Nancy explained that this meant she should write a statement that is either `TRUE` or `FALSE` and R will use this to keep the observations where the statement is true and filter out the observations where the statement is false. Nancy knew the importance of understanding logical statements, so she gave Leslie a few examples to try before she wrote `filter()` code.

- Is the object on the left equal to the object on the right? Use `==`.
  - `3 == 9` is `FALSE` because 3 does not equal 9.
  - If `a = 10` and `b = 10`, then `a == b` is `TRUE`.

- Is the object on the left *not* equal to the object on the right? Use !=.
  - ○ 3 != 9 is TRUE because 3 does not equal 9.
  - ○ If a = 10 and b = 10, then a != b is FALSE.
- Is the object on the left greater than or less than the object on the right? Use > or <.
  - ○ 3 > 9 is FALSE.
  - ○ 3 < 9 is TRUE.
  - ○ 3 < 3 is FALSE.
  - ○ 3 <= 3 is TRUE.

Nancy then told Leslie that she could combine these logical statements. To require two conditions to both be true, use the &, so 3 < 9 & 4 == 4 would be TRUE. This is because *both* statements are true. However, 3 > 9 & 4 == 4 is FALSE. This is because the first statement 3 > 9 is FALSE, therefore it doesn't matter that the second part of the statement (4 == 4) is OK—the whole combined statement is FALSE.

Nancy explained that if you want to know if one *or* the other is true, use the | symbol. 3 > 9 | 4 == 4 is TRUE because 4 == 4 is TRUE.

Leslie had a better grasp of logical conditions after that and was ready to use filter(). When she reviewed the data frame before coding, Leslie noticed that the _AGEG5YR variable was imported with an X at the beginning of the variable name, so she incorporated this into the code.

```
# create a subset of the data set to keep
# transgender status of MtF OR FtM OR Gender non-conforming
# age group higher than group 4 and lower than group 12
# was asked mammogram question
brfss.2014.small <- brfss.2014.cleaned %>%
  filter(TRNSGNDR == 'Male to female'|
         TRNSGNDR == 'Female to male'|
         TRNSGNDR == 'Gender non-conforming') %>%
  filter(X_AGEG5YR > 4 & X_AGEG5YR < 12) %>%
  filter(!is.na(HADMAM))

# check the new data frame
summary(object = brfss.2014.small)
##                     TRNSGNDR      X_AGEG5YR         X_RACE
## Male to female        : 77    Min.   : 5.000   Min.    :1.000
## Female to male        :113    1st Qu.: 7.000   1st Qu.:1.000
## Gender non-conforming : 32    Median : 8.000   Median :1.000
## Not transgender       :  0    Mean   : 7.986   Mean    :2.054
## Not sure              :  0    3rd Qu.: 9.000   3rd Qu.:2.000
## Refused               :  0    Max.   :11.000   Max.    :9.000
##
##      X_INCOMG           X_EDUCAG           HLTHPLN1          HADMAM
## Min.    :1.000    Min.    :1.000    Min.    :1.000    Min.    :1.000
```

```
##    1st Qu.:2.000   1st Qu.:2.000   1st Qu.:1.000   1st Qu.:1.000
##    Median :4.000   Median :3.000   Median :1.000   Median :1.000
##    Mean   :3.685   Mean   :2.595   Mean   :1.108   Mean   :1.171
##    3rd Qu.:5.000   3rd Qu.:3.000   3rd Qu.:1.000   3rd Qu.:1.000
##    Max.   :9.000   Max.   :4.000   Max.   :2.000   Max.   :9.000
##
##       X_AGE80         PHYSHLTH
##    Min.   :40.00   Min.   : 0.000
##    1st Qu.:50.00   1st Qu.: 0.000
##    Median :57.00   Median : 1.000
##    Mean   :56.83   Mean   : 7.528
##    3rd Qu.:63.75   3rd Qu.:11.000
##    Max.   :74.00   Max.   :30.000
##                    NA's   :10
```

Leslie summarized what she wrote. The first `filter()` chose observations that were any one of the three categories of transgender included in the data. She used the | "or" operator for this `filter()`. The second `filter()` chose people in an age category above category 4 but below category 12, in the age categories 5 through 11. Leslie asked why they did not use the `X_AGE80` to choose people 40 to 74. Nancy replied that she had tried that first while Leslie was reading the codebook, but she found a few observations in `X_AGE80` to be coded strangely, and since the age categories variable `X_AGEG5YR` was the one used in the table they were trying to reproduce, she thought that was a better idea.

The last `filter()` used the `!is.na` to choose observations where the HADMAM variable was not NA. Applying all of these filters resulted in a smaller data frame with 222 observations. Leslie noticed that the breast cancer screening article included 220 people who fit the criteria and wondered why she and Nancy had 2 additional people in their data frame. She decided she would review the percentages closely in creating the table to see where these 2 people fit in and to determine if they should be excluded.

Kiara told Leslie that small mistakes seem to be common in published research, often due to errors in transferring numbers from statistical software into a word-processing program. She suggested that creating fully formatted tables directly in R or another software program could reduce errors and increase the reproducibility of published research.

Now that the data set contained the observations used to create the table, Kiara suggested that it may be useful to reduce the data set to contain only the variables used to create the table. In addition to transgender status, age categories, and mammogram information, the table contained percentages for race/ethnicity, income category, education category, and health insurance status. The complete list of variables for the table is as follows:

- TRNSGNDR
- X_AGEG5YR
- X_RACE
- X_INCOMG
- X_EDUCAG

- HLTHPLN1

- HADMAM

Nancy helped Leslie write some variable selection code to add to the filtering code they just wrote.

```
# create a subset of observations and variables
brfss.2014.small <- brfss.2014.cleaned %>%
    filter(TRNSGNDR == 'Male to female'|
            TRNSGNDR == 'Female to male'|
            TRNSGNDR == 'Gender non-conforming') %>%
    filter(X_AGEG5YR > 4 & X_AGEG5YR < 12) %>%
    filter(!is.na(HADMAM)) %>%
    select(TRNSGNDR, X_AGEG5YR, X_RACE, X_INCOMG, X_EDUCAG, HLTHPLN1, HADMAM)
```

Leslie used the `summary()` function to examine the new data set to see what it contained.

```
# summary statistics for the new data frame
summary(object = brfss.2014.small)
##                         TRNSGNDR        X_AGEG5YR          X_RACE
## Male to female        : 77   Min.   : 5.000   Min.   :1.000
## Female to male        :113   1st Qu.: 7.000   1st Qu.:1.000
## Gender non-conforming : 32   Median : 8.000   Median :1.000
## Not transgender       :  0   Mean   : 7.986   Mean   :2.054
## Not sure              :  0   3rd Qu.: 9.000   3rd Qu.:2.000
## Refused               :  0   Max.   :11.000   Max.   :9.000
##     X_INCOMG        X_EDUCAG        HLTHPLN1          HADMAM
## Min.   :1.000   Min.   :1.000   Min.   :1.000   Min.   :1.000
## 1st Qu.:2.000   1st Qu.:2.000   1st Qu.:1.000   1st Qu.:1.000
## Median :4.000   Median :3.000   Median :1.000   Median :1.000
## Mean   :3.685   Mean   :2.595   Mean   :1.108   Mean   :1.171
## 3rd Qu.:5.000   3rd Qu.:3.000   3rd Qu.:1.000   3rd Qu.:1.000
## Max.   :9.000   Max.   :4.000   Max.   :2.000   Max.   :9.000
```

Leslie noticed that some of the variables were the wrong data type, since R had computed the mean and median for each one when they were all categorical and should have been the factor data type. Luckily, Nancy knew of a variation on `mutate()` that could be used to change all the variables in this small data set to factor types. The `mutate_all()` function can be used to do something to every variable in a data frame. Nancy added `mutate_all(as.factor)` to the code and they tested to see if it worked.

```
# change variables to factor data types
brfss.2014.small <- brfss.2014.cleaned %>%
    filter(TRNSGNDR == 'Male to female'|
```

```
                TRNSGNDR == 'Female to male'|
                TRNSGNDR == 'Gender non-conforming') %>%
    filter(X_AGEG5YR > 4 & X_AGEG5YR < 12) %>%
    filter(!is.na(HADMAM)) %>%
    select(TRNSGNDR, X_AGEG5YR, X_RACE, X_INCOMG,
           X_EDUCAG, HLTHPLN1, HADMAM) %>%
    mutate_all(as.factor)

# summary statistics for the new data frame
summary(object = brfss.2014.small)
##                          TRNSGNDR    X_AGEG5YR     X_RACE     X_INCOMG X_EDUCAG
## Male to female          : 77   5 :27     1    :152    1:46     1:24
## Female to male          :113   6 :27     2    : 31    2:44     2:86
## Gender non-conforming:  32   7 :32     8    : 11    3:19     3:68
## Not transgender         :  0   8 :44     7    :  8    4:26     4:44
## Not sure                :  0   9 :44     5    :  7    5:65
## Refused                 :  0   10:24     4    :  6    9:22
##                                 11:24     (Other):  7
##
## HLTHPLN1 HADMAM
## 1:198    1:198
## 2: 24    2: 22
##          9:  2
##
##
##
##
```

2.7.1.2 ADDING LABELS TO VARIABLES

Leslie noticed that, while the variables were all factors, many did not have labels for each category. Nancy reminded Leslie that they could use `mutate()` and `recode_factor()` to add the category labels like they did for the TRNSGNDR variable. Leslie and Nancy reviewed the codebook and worked together to write the code to add the labels. Leslie was having some trouble with the apostrophe in "Don't know," and Nancy told her that adding the \ character before punctuation allows R to read the punctuation correctly. Leslie added the \ and it appeared to work.

```
# add labels to factor variables
brfss.2014.small <- brfss.2014.cleaned %>%
    filter(TRNSGNDR == 'Male to female'|
           TRNSGNDR == 'Female to male'|
           TRNSGNDR == 'Gender non-conforming') %>%
    filter(X_AGEG5YR > 4 & X_AGEG5YR < 12) %>%
```

```
    filter(!is.na(HADMAM)) %>%

    select (TRNSGNDR, X_AGEG5YR, X_RACE, X_INCOMG,
            X_EDUCAG, HLTHPLN1, HADMAM) %>%

    mutate_all(as.factor) %>%

    mutate(X_AGEG5YR = recode_factor(.x = X_AGEG5YR,
                                `5` = '40-44',
                                `6` = '45-49',
                                `7` = '50-54',
                                `8` = '55-59',
                                `9` = '60-64',
                                `10` = '65-69',
                                `11` = '70-74')) %>%

    mutate(X_INCOMG = recode_factor(.x = X_INCOMG,
                            `1` = 'Less than $15,000',
                            `2` = '$15,000 to less than $25,000',
                            `3` = '$25,000 to less than $35,000',
                            `4` = '$35,000 to less than $50,000',
                            `5` = '$50,000 or more',
                            `9` = 'Don\'t know/not sure/missing')) %>%

    mutate(X_EDUCAG = recode_factor(.x = X_EDUCAG,
                            `1` = 'Did not graduate high school',
                            `2` = 'Graduated high school',
                            `3` = 'Attended college/technical school',
                            `4` = 'Graduated from college/technical school',
                            `9` = NA_character_)) %>%

    mutate(HLTHPLN1 = recode_factor(.x = HLTHPLN1,
                            `1` = 'Yes',
                            `2` = 'No',
                            `7` = 'Don\'t know/not sure/missing',
                            `9` = 'Refused'))

# check the work so far
summary(object = brfss.2014.small)
##                      TRNSGNDR     X_AGEG5YR      X_RACE
## Male to female          : 77     40-44:27    1    :152
## Female to male          :113     45-49:27    2    : 31
## Gender non-conforming: 32        50-54:32    8    : 11
## Not transgender         :  0     55-59:44    7    :  8
## Not sure                :  0     60-64:44    5    :  7
## Refused                 :  0     65-69:24    4    :  6
##                                  70-74:24    (Other): 7
```

```
##                             X_INCOMG
## Less than $15,000           :46
## $15,000 to less than $25,000:44
## $25,000 to less than $35,000:19
## $35,000 to less than $50,000:26
## $50,000 or more             :65
## Don't know/not sure/missing :22
##
##                                   X_EDUCAG  HLTHPLN1  HADMAM
## Did not graduate high school          :24   Yes:198   1:198
## Graduated high school                 :86   No : 24   2: 22
## Attended college/technical school     :68             9:  2
## Graduated from college/technical school:44
##
##
##
```

Everything looked good so far, but X_RACE and HADMAM still needed to be recoded. Leslie noticed that, based on the percentages reported in Table 2.1, Pacific Islanders were included in the "Other race" category and not in the "Asian/Pacific Islander" category. To reproduce the exact percentages in the table, she needed to include Pacific Islanders as "Other." Reviewing the BRFSS codebook, page 106, she found the following:

1) White only, non-Hispanic

2) Black only, non-Hispanic

3) American Indian or Alaskan Native only, Non-Hispanic

4) Asian only, non-Hispanic

5) Native Hawaiian or other Pacific Islander only, Non-Hispanic

6) Other race only, non-Hispanic

7) Multiracial, non-Hispanic

8) Hispanic

9) Don't know/Not sure/Refused

Table 2.1 used the following categories:

1) White

2) Black

3) Native American

4) Asian/Pacific Islander

5) Other

Leslie mapped the categories in the codebook into the categories in the table.

- Category 1 (White only, non-Hispanic) from the BRFSS data was labeled as White in the table

- Category 2 (Black only, non-Hispanic) from the BRFSS data was labeled as Black in the table

- Category 3 (American Indian or Alaskan Native only, Non-Hispanic) from BRFSS was Native American in the table

- Category 4 (Asian only, non-Hispanic) from BRFSS was Asian/Pacific Islander in the table

- Due to the mistake in labeling in the paper, categories 5, 6, 7, and 8 from BRFSS were Other in the table

Nancy watched closely while Leslie wrote the recoding for the levels of X_RACE exactly as it was written in the 2017 paper for the purposes of reproducing the table.

```r
# add labels to factor variables
brfss.2014.small <- brfss.2014.cleaned %>%
  filter(TRNSGNDR == 'Male to female'|
           TRNSGNDR == 'Female to male'|
           TRNSGNDR == 'Gender non-conforming') %>%
  filter(X_AGEG5YR > 4 & X_AGEG5YR < 12) %>%
  filter(!is.na(HADMAM)) %>%
  select(TRNSGNDR, X_AGEG5YR, X_RACE, X_INCOMG,
         X_EDUCAG, HLTHPLN1, HADMAM) %>%
  mutate_all(as.factor) %>%
  mutate(X_AGEG5YR = recode_factor(.x = X_AGEG5YR,
                                   `5` = '40-44',
                                   `6` = '45-49',
                                   `7` = '50-54',
                                   `8` = '55-59',
                                   `9` = '60-64',
                                   `10` = '65-69',
                                   `11` = '70-74')) %>%
  mutate(X_INCOMG = recode_factor(.x = X_INCOMG,
                                  `1` = 'Less than $15,000',
                                  `2` = '$15,000 to less than $25,000',
                                  `3` = '$25,000 to less than $35,000',
                                  `4` = '$35,000 to less than $50,000',
                                  `5` = '$50,000 or more',
                                  `9` = 'Don\'t know/not sure/missing')) %>%
  mutate(X_EDUCAG = recode_factor(.x = X_EDUCAG,
                                  `1` = 'Did not graduate high school',
                                  `2` = 'Graduated high school',
```

```
                              `3` = 'Attended college/technical school',
                              `4` = 'Graduated from college/technical school',
                              `9` = NA_character_)) %>%
    mutate(HLTHPLN1 = recode_factor(.x = HLTHPLN1,
                              `1` = 'Yes',
                              `2` = 'No',
                              `7` = 'Don\'t know/not sure/missing',
                              `9` = 'Refused')) %>%
  mutate(X_RACE = recode_factor(.x = X_RACE,
                              `1` = 'White',
                              `2` = 'Black',
                              `3` = 'Native American',
                              `4` = 'Asian/Pacific Islander',
                              `5` = 'Other',
                              `6` = 'Other',
                              `7` = 'Other',
                              `8` = 'Other',
                              `9` = 'Other')) %>%
    mutate(HADMAM = recode_factor(.x = HADMAM,
                              `1` = 'Yes',
                              `2` = 'No',
                              `7` = 'Don\'t know/not sure/missing',
                              `9` = 'Refused'))

#check the work so far
summary(object = brfss.2014.small)
##                   TRNSGNDR    X_AGEG5YR                    X_RACE
##  Male to female        : 77   40-44:27   White                :152
##  Female to male        :113   45-49:27   Black                : 31
##  Gender non-conforming : 32   50-54:32   Native American      :  4
##  Not transgender       :  0   55-59:44   Asian/Pacific Islander:  6
##  Not sure              :  0   60-64:44   Other                : 29
##  Refused               :  0   65-69:24
##                               70-74:24
##                        X_INCOMG
##  Less than $15,000           :46
##  $15,000 to less than $25,000:44
##  $25,000 to less than $35,000:19
##  $35,000 to less than $50,000:26
##  $50,000 or more             :65
##  Don't know/not sure/missing :22
```

```
##
##                                        X_EDUCAG   HLTHPLN1       HADMAM
## Did not graduate high school              :24    Yes:198    Yes    :198
## Graduated high school                     :86    No : 24    No     : 22
## Attended college/technical school         :68               Refused:  2
## Graduated from college/technical school:44
##
##
##
```

2.7.1.3 CHECKING WORK AND RECODING PROBLEMATIC VALUES

Leslie wanted to figure out why there were 222 observations in her data frame and 220 in Table 2.1, which was showing the exact numbers from the Narayan et al. paper. Since the table only contained percentages, she thought she would review the percentages to find where the problem was. She remembered that percentages were produced with the `prop.table()` function, which needs a `table()` as input. To get a table of transgender status percentages, she used the following:

```
# get percents for TRNSGNDR
prop.table(x = table(brfss.2014.small$TRNSGNDR))
##
##       Male to female      Female to male Gender non-conforming
##            0.3468468           0.5090090             0.1441441
##      Not transgender            Not sure               Refused
##            0.0000000           0.0000000             0.0000000
```

These values were slightly different from those in the original table. Kiara thought this was likely due to the two-observation difference. Using her well-developed data-sleuthing skills, Kiara found that the difference was because the two observations where the HADMAM variable was coded as 9, or "Refused," were dropped before computing percentages of the TRNSGNDR variable but were kept for computing the percentages of all the other variables.

This was a really tricky data management problem! Leslie asked if they could change TRNSGNDR to NA when the HADMAM variable was category 9, which is the code for "Refused." Kiara said this would work, but it required learning a new function, if_else().

Kiara explained that the if_else() function takes three arguments. The first argument is a logical statement (or condition) that must be either TRUE or FALSE. The second argument is true =. This is where you tell R what to do if the statement from the first argument is TRUE. The third argument, false =, is what you want to happen if the statement from the first argument is FALSE. The second and third arguments have to be the same data type. Before they wrote the code, Kiara first had Leslie say out loud what she wanted the if_else() function to do. She responded with the following:

"For each person in the data set, if that person's value in HADMAM was *not* equal to 9, then leave their TRNSGNDR value as it is (do nothing). For everyone else that *does* have a value of 9 in HADMAM, change their TRNSGNDR value to be NA."

Kiara and Nancy looked at each other and were quite impressed with Leslie! Nancy added a line to the data management before `select()` and tested it.

```r
# complete data management code
brfss.2014.small <- brfss.2014.cleaned %>%
  filter(TRNSGNDR == 'Male to female'|
           TRNSGNDR == 'Female to male'|
           TRNSGNDR == 'Gender non-conforming') %>%
  filter(X_AGEG5YR > 4 & X_AGEG5YR < 12) %>%
  filter(!is.na(HADMAM)) %>%
  mutate(TRNSGNDR = if_else(condition = HADMAM != 9,
                            true = TRNSGNDR,
                            false = factor(NA))) %>%
  select(TRNSGNDR, X_AGEG5YR, X_RACE, X_INCOMG, X_EDUCAG, HLTHPLN1) %>%
  mutate_all(as.factor) %>%
  mutate(X_AGEG5YR = recode_factor(.x = X_AGEG5YR,
                                   `5` = '40-44',
                                   `6` = '45-49',
                                   `7` = '50-54',
                                   `8` = '55-59',
                                   `9` = '60-64',
                                   `10` = '65-69',
                                   `11` = '70-74')) %>%
  mutate(X_INCOMG = recode_factor(.x = X_INCOMG,
                                  `1` = 'Less than $15,000',
                                  `2` = '$15,000 to less than $25,000',
                                  `3` = '$25,000 to less than $35,000',
                                  `4` = '$35,000 to less than $50,000',
                                  `5` = '$50,000 or more',
                                  `9` = 'Don\'t know/not sure/missing')) %>%
  mutate(X_EDUCAG = recode_factor(.x = X_EDUCAG,
                                  `1` = 'Did not graduate high school',
                                  `2` = 'Graduated high school',
                                  `3` = 'Attended college/technical school',
                                  `4` = 'Graduated from college/technical school',
                                  `9` = NA_character_)) %>%
  mutate(HLTHPLN1 = recode_factor(.x = HLTHPLN1,
                                  `1` = 'Yes',
                                  `2` = 'No',
                                  `7` = 'Don\'t know/not sure/missing',
                                  `9` = 'Refused')) %>%
```

```
    mutate(X_RACE = recode_factor(.x = X_RACE,
                                   `1` = 'White',
                                   `2` = 'Black',
                                   `3` = 'Native American',
                                   `4` = 'Asian/Pacific Islander',
                                   `5` = 'Other',
                                   `6` = 'Other',
                                   `7` = 'Other',
                                   `8` = 'Other',
                                   `9` = 'Other')) %>%
  droplevels()

#check the work
prop.table(x = table(brfss.2014.small$TRNSGNDR))
##
##        Male to female        Female to male Gender non-conforming
##             0.3500000             0.5090909             0.1409091
```

It worked. The R-Team took a second to admire the results before continuing their conversation. Leslie noticed that there was now a `droplevels()` line at the end of the code. Nancy forgot to say she had snuck that into the code to remove the empty levels after recoding. After all that, Leslie vowed again that she would use good practices for organizing and annotating her code to avoid data management issues. She raised her right hand as if in court and swore to the team that she would annotate and organize her code. Kiara took that moment to explain another useful strategy for ensuring reproducibility, and that was to work with a *co-pilot* whenever coding. A co-pilot is another person who can write the code with you or run the code you have written and let you know if it worked.

2.7.2 CREATING A TABLE FROM THE CLEAN DATA

Creating well-formatted tables easily is one of the few things that R *does not do very well*. Nancy thought the **tableone** package (Yoshida, n.d.) was the best place to start, even though the tables it creates are not in the easiest format to use for formal reporting. The **tableone** package can create a table that includes all the variables in a data frame, and it automatically selects descriptive statistics to report based on the variable type. Nancy wrote a little code and showed Leslie how easy it is to create a table using `CreateTableOne()`.

```
# open tableone
library(package = "tableone")

# create a basic table
CreateTableOne(data = brfss.2014.small)
##
##                                                              Overall
```

```
##    n                                                222
##    TRNSGNDR (%)
##       Male to female                                 77 (35.0)
##       Female to male                                112 (50.9)
##       Gender non-conforming                          31 (14.1)
##    X_AGEG5YR (%)
##       40-44                                          27 (12.2)
##       45-49                                          27 (12.2)
##       50-54                                          32 (14.4)
##       55-59                                          44 (19.8)
##       60-64                                          44 (19.8)
##       65-69                                          24 (10.8)
##       70-74                                          24 (10.8)
##    X_RACE (%)
##       White                                         152 (68.5)
##       Black                                          31 (14.0)
##       Native American                                4 ( 1.8)
##       Asian/Pacific Islander                         6 ( 2.7)
##       Other                                          29 (13.1)
##    X_INCOMG (%)
##       Less than $15,000                              46 (20.7)
##       $15,000 to less than $25,000                   44 (19.8)
##       $25,000 to less than $35,000                   19 ( 8.6)
##       $35,000 to less than $50,000                   26 (11.7)
##       $50,000 or more                                65 (29.3)
##       Don't know/not sure/missing                    22 ( 9.9)
##    X_EDUCAG (%)
##       Did not graduate high school                   24 (10.8)
##       Graduated high school                          86 (38.7)
##       Attended college/technical school             68 (30.6)
##       Graduated from college/technical school       44 (19.8)
##    HLTHPLN1 = No (%)                                  24 (10.8)
```

After all the complicated data management, that was surprisingly easy! Leslie compared the table to Table 2.1 and noticed a few things to work on to reproduce it more closely:

- Table 2.1 only has percentages and not frequencies
- The HLTHPLN1 variable shows the "Yes" group in Table 2.1
- The headings for different sections are not variable names in Table 2.1
- The percent signs can be removed from the section headers

Nancy had used **tableone** only a few times, so she didn't know if these things could be changed. She checked the help documentation by typing `CreateTableOne` into the search box in the help tab. She noticed a `print()` function in the help documentation that had some options for changing how the table prints, including an option to add variable labels, which will address the third bullet. To use this feature, the variables must have labels in the data frame, though.

To check and see if the variables had labels, Nancy used `str(brfss.2014.small)`, which shows the *structure* of the data frame.

```
# check the labels for the data frame
str(object = brfss.2014.small)
## 'data.frame':    222 obs. of  6 variables:
## $ TRNSGNDR : Factor w/ 3 levels "Male to female",..: 1 1 2 3 1 3 2 1 1 2 ...
## $ X_AGEG5YR: Factor w/ 7 levels "40-44","45-49",..: 4 7 2 6 3 4 1 2 4 1 ...
## $ X_RACE   : Factor w/ 5 levels "White","Black",..: 1 1 5 5 1 1 1 1 1 5 ...
## $ X_INCOMG : Factor w/ 6 levels "Less than $15,000",..: 6 5 6 1 3 2 5 1
## 5 6 ...
## $ X_EDUCAG : Factor w/ 4 levels "Did not graduate high school",..: 2 4 4
## 1 2 2 4 2 4 1 ...
## $ HLTHPLN1 : Factor w/ 2 levels "Yes","No": 2 1 1 2 2 1 2 1 1 2 ...
```

The output from `str()` did not include anything that looked like labels. Nancy noticed that the **tableone** package uses labels created in the **labelled** package. She read the documentation for the **labelled** package and wrote some code to add labels to the `brfss.2014.small` data frame using `var_label()`, with the labels for the table listed in a vector. To indicate that the `TRNSGNDR` variable was missing two of the observations, Nancy included "($n = 220$)" in the label for the transgender status variable.

```
# add variable labels to print in table
labelled::var_label(x = brfss.2014.small) <- c("Transition status (n = 220)",
                                                 "Age category",
                                                 "Race/ethnicity",
                                                 "Income category",
                                                 "Education category",
                                                 "Health insurance?")

# check data frame for labels
str(object = brfss.2014.small)
## 'data.frame':    222 obs. of  6 variables:
## $ TRNSGNDR : Factor w/ 3 levels "Male to female",..: 1 1 2 3 1 3 2 1 1 2 ...
## ..- attr(*, "label")= chr "Transition status (n = 220)"
## $ X_AGEG5YR: Factor w/ 7 levels "40-44","45-49",..: 4 7 2 6 3 4 1 2 4 1 ...
## ..- attr(*, "label")= chr "Age category"
## $ X_RACE   : Factor w/ 5 levels "White","Black",..: 1 1 5 5 1 1 1 1 1 5 ...
```

```
## ..- attr(*, "label")= chr "Race/ethnicity"
## $ X_INCOMG : Factor w/ 6 levels "Less than $15,000",..: 6 5 6 1 3 2 5 1
5 6 ...
## ..- attr(*, "label")= chr "Income category"
## $ X_EDUCAG : Factor w/ 4 levels "Did not graduate high school",..: 2 4 4
1 2 2 4 2 4 1 ...
## ..- attr(*, "label")= chr "Education category"
## $ HLTHPLN1 : Factor w/ 2 levels "Yes","No": 2 1 1 2 2 1 2 1 1 2 ...
## ..- attr(*, "label")= chr "Health insurance?"
```

The data frame now showed labels with each variable. Now that the labels were in place, Nancy showed Leslie the `print()` function used with `CreateTableOne()`. To use `print()`, the table is first saved as an object with a name.

```
# create a basic table as an object
trans.hc.table <- CreateTableOne(data = brfss.2014.small)

# use print to show table with labels
print(x = trans.hc.table, varLabels = TRUE)
##
##                                        Overall
##   n                                    222
##   Transition status (n = 220) (%)
##      Male to female                     77 (35.0)
##      Female to male                    112 (50.9)
##      Gender non-conforming              31 (14.1)
##   Age category (%)
##      40-44                              27 (12.2)
##      45-49                              27 (12.2)
##      50-54                              32 (14.4)
##      55-59                              44 (19.8)
##      60-64                              44 (19.8)
##      65-69                              24 (10.8)
##      70-74                              24 (10.8)
##   Race/ethnicity (%)
##      White                             152 (68.5)
##      Black                              31 (14.0)
##      Native American                     4 ( 1.8)
##      Asian/Pacific Islander              6 ( 2.7)
##      Other                              29 (13.1)
##   Income category (%)
```

```
##      Less than $15,000                                  46 (20.7)
##      $15,000 to less than $25,000                       44 (19.8)
##      $25,000 to less than $35,000                       19 ( 8.6)
##      $35,000 to less than $50,000                       26 (11.7)
##      $50,000 or more                                    65 (29.3)
##      Don't know/not sure/missing                        22 ( 9.9)
##   Education category (%)
##      Did not graduate high school                       24 (10.8)
##      Graduated high school                              86 (38.7)
##      Attended college/technical school                  68 (30.6)
##      Graduated from college/technical school  44 (19.8)
##   Health insurance? = No (%)                            24 (10.8)
```

Now that the labels were working, the R-Team wanted to limit the numbers reported to just percentages. Nancy and Leslie read through all the help documentation under the help tab, and Nancy noticed a way to just print the percentages. She added the `format = "p"` argument to the `print()` function. She then saw that the percent (%) symbols could be removed with `explain = FALSE`, so she added this as well.

```
# use print to show table with labels and percent
print(x = trans.hc.table,
      varLabels = TRUE,
      format = "p",
      explain = FALSE)
##
##
##                                    Overall
##   n                                  222
##   Transition status (n = 220)
##      Male to female                  35.0
##      Female to male                  50.9
##      Gender non-conforming           14.1
##   Age category
##      40-44                           12.2
##      45-49                           12.2
##      50-54                           14.4
##      55-59                           19.8
##      60-64                           19.8
##      65-69                           10.8
##      70-74                           10.8
##   Race/ethnicity
```

```
##      White                                68.5
##      Black                                14.0
##      Native American                       1.8
##      Asian/Pacific Islander                2.7
##      Other                                13.1
##   Income category
##      Less than $15,000                    20.7
##      $15,000 to less than $25,000         19.8
##      $25,000 to less than $35,000          8.6
##      $35,000 to less than $50,000         11.7
##      $50,000 or more                      29.3
##      Don't know/not sure/missing           9.9
##   Education category
##      Did not graduate high school         10.8
##      Graduated high school                38.7
##      Attended college/technical school    30.6
##      Graduated from college/technical school 19.8
##   Health insurance? = No                  10.8
```

The last thing they wanted to fix was to show the "Yes" category for the health insurance variable; however, they did not see an option to do this in the help documentation. They decided to leave this for another day, and Leslie looked forward to figuring it out on her own before the next meeting, unless Nancy figured it out first!

Nancy and Leslie reviewed the table and found that it looked ready to use in a report or manuscript and had almost identical content to Table 2.1. Leslie complained that it felt like a lot more work than just retyping the numbers from R into a word-processing program. Kiara reminded her that this may be why they had to spend so much time to find the two observations and suggested three reasons to spend the time developing tables directly in R or another software program:

1. Transcribing the numbers can (and does) result in errors.

2. Small changes to table contents can be made more easily.

3. Code can be reused, so developing new tables will take less time after the first one is complete.

Leslie begrudgingly agreed and asked Nancy if they could try creating a table that included numeric variables as well. She explained that many of the articles she has read have long tables with both categorical and continuous variables displayed together.

Nancy thought this was a great idea, especially since it would allow her to write some more code. In order to create this table, the data frame needed to include continuous variables. Leslie went back to the data management code they created and added the PHYSHLTH variable to the select() list. PHYSHLTH shows the number of days of poor physical health in the last 30 days, so it is not categorical. Nancy removed the mutate_all(as.factor) %>% function since the recode_factor() worked to change these variables anyhow. Leslie wondered how long ago Nancy had realized that they did not need the mutate_all(as.factor) %>% once they had all the factors recoding with recode_factor().

```
# complete data management code
brfss.2014.small <- brfss.2014.cleaned %>%
  filter(TRNSGNDR == 'Male to female'|
         TRNSGNDR == 'Female to male'|
         TRNSGNDR == 'Gender non-conforming') %>%
  filter(X_AGEG5YR > 4 & X_AGEG5YR < 12) %>%
  filter(!is.na(HADMAM)) %>%
  mutate(TRNSGNDR = if_else(HADMAM != 9, TRNSGNDR, factor(NA))) %>%
  select(TRNSGNDR, X_AGEG5YR, X_RACE, X_INCOMG,
         X_EDUCAG, HLTHPLN1, PHYSHLTH) %>%
  mutate(X_AGEG5YR = recode_factor(.x = X_AGEG5YR,
                                   `5` = '40-44',
                                   `6` = '45-49',
                                   `7` = '50-54',
                                   `8` = '55-59',
                                   `9` = '60-64',
                                   `10` = '65-69',
                                   `11` = '70-74')) %>%
  mutate(X_INCOMG = recode_factor(.x = X_INCOMG,
                                  `1` = 'Less than $15,000',
                                  `2` = '$15,000 to less than $25,000',
                                  `3` = '$25,000 to less than $35,000',
                                  `4` = '$35,000 to less than $50,000',
                                  `5` = '$50,000 or more',
                                  `9` = 'Don\'t know/not sure/missing')) %>%
  mutate(X_EDUCAG = recode_factor(.x = X_EDUCAG,
                                  `1` = 'Did not graduate high school',
                                  `2` = 'Graduated high school',
                                  `3` = 'Attended college/technical school',
                                  `4` = 'Graduated from college/technical school',
                                  `9` = NA_character_)) %>%
  mutate(HLTHPLN1 = recode_factor(.x = HLTHPLN1,
                                  `1` = 'Yes',
                                  `2` = 'No',
                                  `7` = 'Don\'t know/not sure/missing',
                                  `9` = 'Refused')) %>%
  mutate(X_RACE = recode_factor(.x = X_RACE,
                                `1` = 'White',
                                `2` = 'Black',
                                `3` = 'Native American',
```

```
                              `4` = 'Asian/Pacific Islande',
                              `5` = 'Other',
                              `6` = 'Other',
                              `7` = 'Other',
                              `8` = 'Other',
                              `9` = 'Other')) %>%
  droplevels()

#check the work
prop.table(x = table(brfss.2014.small$TRNSGNDR))
##
##      Male to female      Female to male Gender non-conforming
##           0.3500000           0.5090909             0.1409091
```

To include PHYSHLTH in the table, they needed a variable label for it as well. Leslie added the variable label to the labeling code.

```
# add variable labels to print in table
labelled::var_label(x = brfss.2014.small) <- c("Transition status (n = 220)",
                                                "Age category",
                                                "Race/ethnicity",
                                                "Income category",
                                                "Education category",
                                                "Health insurance?",
                                                "Days/month poor physical health")

# check data frame for labels
str(object = brfss.2014.small)
## 'data.frame':    222 obs. of  7 variables:
##  $ TRNSGNDR : Factor w/ 3 levels "Male to female",..: 1 1 2 3 1 3 2 1 1 2 ...
##  ..- attr(*, "label")= chr "Transition status (n = 220)"
##  $ X_AGEG5YR: Factor w/ 7 levels "40-44","45-49",..: 4 7 2 6 3 4 1 2 4 1 ...
##  ..- attr(*, "label")= chr "Age category"
##  $ X_RACE   : Factor w/ 5 levels "White","Black",..: 1 1 5 5 1 1 1 1 1 5 ...
##  ..- attr(*, "label")= chr "Race/ethnicity"
##  $ X_INCOMG : Factor w/ 6 levels "Less than $15,000",..: 6 5 6 1 3 2 5 1
5 6 ...
##  ..- attr(*, "label")= chr "Income category"
##  $ X_EDUCAG : Factor w/ 4 levels "Did not graduate high school",..: 2 4 4
1 2 2 4 2 4 1 ...
```

```
## ..- attr(*, "label")= chr "Education category"
## $ HLTHPLN1 : Factor w/ 2 levels "Yes","No": 2 1 1 2 2 1 2 1 1 2 ...
## ..- attr(*, "label")= chr "Health insurance?"
## $ PHYSHLTH : num  30 5 4 30 0 NA 0 25 0 0 ...
## ..- attr(*, "label")= chr "Days/month poor physical health"
```

Then, Leslie copied the table code and ran it to see what would happen.

```
# create a basic table as an object
trans.hc.table <- CreateTableOne(data = brfss.2014.small)

# use print to show table with labels
print(x = trans.hc.table, varLabels = TRUE)
##
##                                              Overall
##    n                                         222
##    Transition status (n = 220) (%)
##        Male to female                         77 (35.0)
##        Female to male                        112 (50.9)
##        Gender non-conforming                  31 (14.1)
##    Age category (%)
##        40-44                                  27 (12.2)
##        45-49                                  27 (12.2)
##        50-54                                  32 (14.4)
##        55-59                                  44 (19.8)
##        60-64                                  44 (19.8)
##        65-69                                  24 (10.8)
##        70-74                                  24 (10.8)
##    Race/ethnicity (%)
##        White                                 152 (68.5)
##        Black                                  31 (14.0)
##        Native American                         4 ( 1.8)
##        Asian/Pacific Islander                  6 ( 2.7)
##        Other                                  29 (13.1)
##    Income category (%)
##        Less than $15,000                      46 (20.7)
##        $15,000 to less than $25,000           44 (19.8)
##        $25,000 to less than $35,000           19 ( 8.6)
##        $35,000 to less than $50,000           26 (11.7)
##        $50,000 or more                        65 (29.3)
```

```
##       Don't know/not sure/missing                 22 ( 9.9)
##     Education category (%)
##       Did not graduate high school                24 (10.8)
##       Graduated high school                       86 (38.7)
##       Attended college/technical school           68 (30.6)
##       Graduated from college/technical school     44 (19.8)
##     Health insurance? = No (%)                     24 (10.8)
##     Days/month poor physical health (mean (SD)) 7.53 (11.37)
```

The mean and standard deviation were added to the table! Kiara reminded Leslie that the mean and standard deviation were only good measures for the continuous variables when the variables were normally distributed. Leslie remembered that they had looked at the distribution of PHYSHLTH with a histogram. She took another look at Figure 2.16.

```
# make a histogram of PHYSHLTH (Figure 2.16)
brfss.2014.small %>%
  ggplot(aes(x = PHYSHLTH)) +
  geom_histogram()
```

The histogram confirmed that the variable is not normally distributed. Leslie remembered that median and IQR are good options for descriptive statistics when a variable is the numeric data type but not normally distributed. She looked in the documentation for the print() options for her table to see if there was any way to include the median and IQR instead of the mean and standard deviation. She found an argument for nonnormal = for adding the names of any numeric variables that are not normally distributed. Adding this to the print options, she got the following:

FIGURE 2.16 Distribution of the days of poor physical health variable

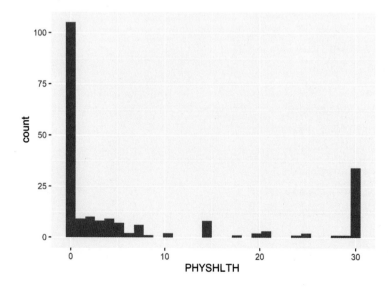

```
# use print to show table
print(x = trans.hc.table,
      varLabels = TRUE,
      nonnormal = 'PHYSHLTH')
##
##                                                       Overall
##   n                                                     222
##   Transition status (n = 220) (%)
##      Male to female                                   77 (35.0)
##      Female to male                                  112 (50.9)
##      Gender non-conforming                            31 (14.1)
##   Age category (%)
##      40-44                                            27 (12.2)
##      45-49                                            27 (12.2)
##      50-54                                            32 (14.4)
##      55-59                                            44 (19.8)
##      60-64                                            44 (19.8)
##      65-69                                            24 (10.8)
##      70-74                                            24 (10.8)
##   Race/ethnicity (%)
##      White                                           152 (68.5)
##      Black                                            31 (14.0)
##      Native American                                   4 ( 1.8)
##      Asian/Pacific Islander                            6 ( 2.7)
##      Other                                            29 (13.1)
##   Income category (%)
##      Less than $15,000                                46 (20.7)
##      $15,000 to less than $25,000                     44 (19.8)
##      $25,000 to less than $35,000                     19 ( 8.6)
##      $35,000 to less than $50,000                     26 (11.7)
##      $50,000 or more                                  65 (29.3)
##      Don't know/not sure/missing                      22 ( 9.9)
##   Education category (%)
##      Did not graduate high school                     24 (10.8)
##      Graduated high school                            86 (38.7)
##      Attended college/technical school               68 (30.6)
##      Graduated from college/technical school          44 (19.8)
##   Health insurance? = No (%)                       24 (10.8)
##   Days/month poor physical health (median [IQR]) 1.00 [0.00, 11.00]
```

The R-Team was happy with the final product. Nancy explained that there is an R package called **kableExtra** that is more difficult to use, but offers more flexibility in formatting. She wanted to show Leslie the alternate way using **kableExtra**, but she knew that it might be a little overwhelming. Leslie suggested a quick coffee break first ☕. Kiara said that sounded perfect. They would caffeinate and then regroup to figure out a **kableExtra** table.

2.7.3 CREATING A TABLE FROM CLEAN DATA (ANOTHER WAY)

2.7.3.1 CREATING A NEW DATA FRAME WITH SUMMARY STATISTICS

Leslie joked that they had promised if she organized and annotated her code that she would not have to redo her work, and yet here she was, making the same table again. Nancy and Kiara smiled. Instead of continuing to work with the **tidyverse** formatting, Nancy suggested working in base R to get the summary statistics for this second way of building the table. She found this to be more straightforward for categorical variables and valuable to practice in general. Nancy explained that what they needed was a data frame with all the descriptive statistics they wanted listed in the table. Leslie started by creating a table of the percentages for the TRNSGNDR variable.

```
# get percents for TRNSGNDR
( trans.p <- prop.table(x = table(brfss.2014.small$TRNSGNDR)) )
##
##       Male to female      Female to male Gender non-conforming
##            0.3500000           0.5090909             0.1409091
```

These percentages needed some work. Leslie tried multiplying them by 100 and then rounding them to one decimal place, like the percentages in the table in the manuscript.

```
# get percents for TRNSGNDR
( trans.perc <- round(x = 100 * prop.table(x = table(brfss.2014.small$TRNSG
NDR)), 1) )
##
##       Male to female      Female to male Gender non-conforming
##                 35.0                50.9                  14.1
```

Perfect! However, there were six more variables in the table. Nancy explained they could easily merge the percentages from all the variables in the brfss.2014.small data frame by converting each table of percentages into a data frame, giving the data frame a name, and using rbind() to merge the data frames, like this:

```
# get percents and assign a name for trans and race
# turn into data frames for easier merging
( trans.perc <- data.frame(round(x = prop.table(x = table(brfss.2014.small$
TRNSGNDR)) * 100, 1)) )
##                  Var1 Freq
## 1      Male to female 35.0
## 2      Female to male 50.9
## 3 Gender non-conforming 14.1
```

```
( race.perc <- data.frame(round(x = prop.table(x = table(brfss.2014.small
$X_RACE)) * 100, 1)) )
##                              Var1 Freq
## 1                          White 68.5
## 2                          Black 14.0
## 3                Native American  1.8
## 4 Asian/Pacific Islander          2.7
## 5                          Other 13.1
# merge together into one data frame
( table.perc <- rbind(trans.perc, race.perc) )
##                              Var1 Freq
## 1              Male to female 35.0
## 2              Female to male 50.9
## 3     Gender non-conforming 14.1
## 4                          White 68.5
## 5                          Black 14.0
## 6                Native American  1.8
## 7     Asian/Pacific Islander  2.7
## 8                          Other 13.1
```

Leslie thought Nancy must have had several cups of coffee on their break given how fast she typed the code.

2.7.3.2 USING A CUSTOM FUNCTION FOR REPEATED CODE

Leslie noted that `rbind()` worked great to create a data frame with each category and the percentage in that category. However, with seven variables to work with, Nancy suggested that they could be more efficient by writing their own *function*, known as a *custom function*. Kiara wondered if they could also use a *for loop*. Nancy thought this would work, too, but they would try writing a function first. Leslie thought they should just use `rbind()` to do the whole thing, which Nancy said would also work, but she wanted to at least try one custom function. Nancy showed Leslie that she could put the code used to get the percentages into a function with the name of the object being replaced by x. She reminded Leslie that function names are in upper camel case (Section 1.6.3.3) and began writing the `TableFun()` function.

```
# finding percents and rounding to one decimal place
# putting all percents in one column with cbind
TableFun <- function(x){
    data.frame(round(x = prop.table(x = table(x)) * 100, 1))
}
```

This code creates a function called `TableFun()` that would apply the code inside the curly brackets `{}` to any variable. To use `TableFun()` on a single variable, Nancy showed Leslie she could just type `TableFun()` with the name of the variable in parentheses, like this:

```
# using the TableFun function for the TRNSGNDR variable
TableFun(x = brfss.2014.small$TRNSGNDR)
##                            x Freq
## 1           Male to female 35.0
## 2           Female to male 50.9
## 3 Gender non-conforming 14.1
```

2.7.3.3 USING THE APPLY FAMILY

However, said Nancy, it is complicated to use the function on all the variables in the `brfss.2014.small` data set at one time. One way to do it is to use the `lapply()` function, which is part of the `apply` family of functions (Box 2.2). The `lapply()` function is used to apply some code to each item in a list. In this case, use `lapply()` to apply `TableFun()` to each variable in the `brfss.2014.small` data frame. Nancy told Leslie that data frames are a special type of list where each variable is an element of the list.

2.2 Nancy's fancy code: *apply* and *lapply*

The *apply* family of functions can be used to do something to every row or column or both of a data frame or matrix or list. For example, if there were a small data frame that included the number of hot dogs several cousins ate each year for the last 2 years, the `apply()` function could be used to find the mean for each cousin (the rows) or each year (the columns).

```
#vectors for each variable
hotdogs.2016 <- c(6, 2, 0, 3, 9, 1)
hotdogs.2017 <- c(8, 3, 0, 2, 6, 2)
cousins <- c("Therese", "Geoff", "Nick", "John", "Jim", "Karen")

#make a data frame from vectors
#use cousins vector as row name rather than variable
cuz.hot.dogs <- data.frame(hotdogs.2016, hotdogs.2017)
row.names(x = cuz.hot.dogs) <- cousins
cuz.hot.dogs
##           hotdogs.2016 hotdogs.2017
## Therese            6            8
## Geoff              2            3
## Nick               0            0
## John               3            2
## Jim                9            6
## Karen              1            2
```

To find the mean for each cousin, use `apply()` for rows. The `apply()` function takes three arguments: data frame or matrix name (`X =`), rows or columns (`MARGIN =`), and function name (`FUN =`). For rows, the `MARGIN =` argument would be 1. For columns, the `MARGIN =` argument would be 2.

```
# mean by observation
apply(X = cuz.hot.dogs, MARGIN = 1, FUN = mean)
## Therese   Geoff    Nick    John     Jim   Karen
##     7.0     2.5     0.0     2.5     7.5     1.5
```

To find the mean for each year, use `apply()` for columns.

```
# mean by variable
apply(X = cuz.hot.dogs, MARGIN = 2, FUN = mean)
## hotdogs.2016 hotdogs.2017
##          3.5          3.5
```

Use `lapply()` instead if there is a list rather than a data frame. Perhaps it is a list of the pets the cousins have and also their favorite ice cream flavor.

```
# make a list
cuz.list <- list(pet = c('cat', 'dog', 'dog', 'cat', 'bird', 'cat'),
                 ice.cream = c('vanilla', 'chocolate',
                              'chocolate', 'chocolate',
                              'strawberry', 'strawberry'))
# print the list
cuz.list
## $pet
## [1] "cat"  "dog"  "dog"  "cat"  "bird" "cat"
##
## $ice.cream
## [1] "vanilla"  "chocolate" "chocolate" "chocolate" "strawberry"
## [6] "strawberry"
```

To create a frequency table for each variable, use `lapply()` with two arguments. The first argument is the name of the list; the second is the function to use on each element of the list.

(Continued)

(Continued)

```
# make a table for each
# variable in cuzList list
lapply(X = cuz.list, FUN = table)
## $pet
##
## bird  cat  dog
##    1    3    2
##
## $ice.cream
##
##  chocolate strawberry    vanilla
##          3          2          1
```

Nancy went on to explain that using `lapply()` to apply `TableFun()` to the `brfss.2014.small` data frame would result in a list of tables of percentages, one table for each variable in the data frame. Once this list of tables is ready, she said, combine the tables using `rbind()` to merge objects by rows. Because there are seven tables to merge together, use the `do.call()` function to apply the `rbind()` function to each item in the list.

The `do.call()` function acts like a loop, conducting the same analyses for each element in the object, then starting over on the next element. So, Nancy summarized, `TableFun()` is applied to get tables of percentages from each variable in the `brfss.2014.small` data frame and then the `do.call()` function puts the table of percentages together using `rbind()` by going through and adding each table to the others one at a time. Leslie thought they should just have used `rbind()` and they would have been done by now.

Nancy explained that this process results in a new data frame containing each of the categories for each variable and the percentage of survey participants in the category. Leslie remembered that the `brfss.2014.small` data frame included the PHYSHLTH variable, which was not in the table. To exclude the PHYSHLTH variable from the calculations, they could take a subset of the variables by using the square brackets and subtracting the column where the variable was stored from the data frame. Leslie opened the data frame by clicking on it once under the Environment tab and counted to see that the PHYSHLTH variable was in column 7. They added −7 to the code to remove this column.

```
# use lapply to apply the TableFun function to
# all the variables in the data frame
# use the do.call function to call the rbind function
# to combine the list items into rows
( table.data <- do.call(rbind, (lapply(X = brfss.2014.small[ , -7],
                                       FUN = TableFun))) )
```

```
##                                                        x Freq
## TRNSGNDR.1                                Male to female 35.0
## TRNSGNDR.2                                Female to male 50.9
## TRNSGNDR.3                         Gender non-conforming 14.1
## X_AGEG5YR.1                                        40-44 12.2
## X_AGEG5YR.2                                        45-49 12.2
## X_AGEG5YR.3                                        50-54 14.4
## X_AGEG5YR.4                                        55-59 19.8
## X_AGEG5YR.5                                        60-64 19.8
## X_AGEG5YR.6                                        65-69 10.8
## X_AGEG5YR.7                                        70-74 10.8
## X_RACE.1                                          White 68.5
## X_RACE.2                                          Black 14.0
## X_RACE.3                                Native American  1.8
## X_RACE.4                        Asian/Pacific Islander  2.7
## X_RACE.5                                          Other 13.1
## X_INCOMG.1                         Less than $15,000 20.7
## X_INCOMG.2              $15,000 to less than $25,000 19.8
## X_INCOMG.3              $25,000 to less than $35,000  8.6
## X_INCOMG.4              $35,000 to less than $50,000 11.7
## X_INCOMG.5                             $50,000 or more 29.3
## X_INCOMG.6                 Don't know/not sure/missing 9.9
## X_EDUCAG.1              Did not graduate high school 10.8
## X_EDUCAG.2                     Graduated high school 38.7
## X_EDUCAG.3           Attended college/technical school 30.6
## X_EDUCAG.4  Graduated from college/technical school 19.8
## HLTHPLN1.1                                          Yes 89.2
## HLTHPLN1.2                                           No 10.8
```

After she had looked at the `table.data` object, Leslie noticed that there were 27 observations (or rows) with row labels and two variables per row, x for the category name, and `Freq` for the percentage in the category. The last row was the No category for health care, which was not in the original table. She removed the last row by taking a subset of the `table.data` data frame so it included just rows 1 through 26.

```
# remove health care No category
table.data <- data.frame(table.data[c(1:26), ])
```

Finally, Leslie labeled the columns of the data frame to be consistent with the table columns.

```
# label the columns
colnames(x = table.data) <- c("Survey participant demographics (n = 220)", "Percent")
```

Nancy reassured Leslie that all of the functions used here would be used and explained multiple times throughout their meetings, so not to worry if `rbind()` or `do.call()` or anything else was not yet 100% clear. There would be additional opportunities to use these and all the other functions. Nancy suggested copying and pasting any new functions Leslie was trying to use and changing little things to see what would happen. In this way, the purpose of each part of the code might become clearer. Nancy also suggested that the help documentation in the lower left pane of RStudio and searching online can be useful for finding examples of code to play with and use.

Nancy also reminded Leslie that, if a function seems like too much at this point, she could always use the `rbind()` method they used earlier and wait until she was more comfortable with R to write her own functions. Kiara still thought for loops might be better, so she wrote some instructions about for loops for Leslie to review if she wanted yet another option (Box 2.3).

2.3 Kiara's reproducibility resource: Using for loops instead of functions

The function worked well to get the data ready for a **kableExtra** table. However, Kiara suggested that some people prefer to write functions only when they will be useful for more than one project. For loops are another option and are a fundamental aspect of computer programming. There are for loops in all programming languages, not just R. They are a way of doing the same thing multiple times, or doing something *iteratively*. A for loop can be read as "for each item in (things you want to iterate over), do something." Kiara wrote the basic structure of a for loop.

```
# basic format of a for loop
for (i in 1:some number) {
    do something
}
```

The parts of the loop are as follows:

- The `1:some number` contains the elements you want to iterate over. For the **kableExtra** table, the same function would be used for the 7 variables from the `brfss.2014.small` data frame. This would be `1:7`. However, sometimes it is not clear how many iterations to do. For example, if you knew you wanted to do the same thing for each row in a data frame, but you didn't know off the top of your head how many rows there were, you could do `1:nrow(data.frame)`. The `nrow()` function counts the number of rows.

- The `i` stands for "each" and is the same type of `i` seen in equations. The top line then reads: "For each element in 1 through some number."

- The curly brackets `{ }` are around the body of the for loop. Whatever it is that should be done a lot of times, put that in the `{ }`.

- Most of the time the output would be stored, which requires one extra step of making an *empty* object that will store the output. This is called *initializing*.

For example, to use a for loop to square some numbers, here is how it might look:

```
# basic example of a for loop
squared.numbers <- NULL # initialize an empty vector that will
                        # contain the output
for (i in 1:10) {
  squared.numbers[i] <- i^2 # body of the for loop
}
# print out the result
print(squared.numbers)
##  [1]   1   4   9  16  25  36  49  64  81 100
```

Kiara wrote out the meaning in text.

First, make an empty vector called `squared.numbers`. For each item in numbers 1 through 10, take that number or `i` and square it (`i^2`). Whatever the result of squaring `i` is, store that result in the `squared.numbers` vector.

She thought it might be necessary to explain why there is an `[i]` next to `squared.numbers`. The `i` is the element. So on the first iteration, `i = 1`. The `squared.numbers[i]` bit is saying to store the result of the 1st iteration in the 1st location of `squared.numbers`. On the 7th iteration, `i = 7`, make sure to store that result in the 7th location of the output `squared.numbers`.

Kiara wrote the initial for loop to use this structure to make the data frame for the **kableExtra** table that contains percentage per category of all 7 factors in the `brfss.2014.small` data set. As she wrote, she thought, "For each variable (or column) in `brfss.2014.small`, get the percentages via the `prop.table` function, and then combine the results into a single data frame."

```
# initialize an empty data frame
table.data <- data.frame()

# make the for loop
for (i in 1:ncol(brfss.2014.small)) {

  # get the percents for a variable and put them in table.each
  table.each <-
    data.frame(round(x = prop.table(x = table(brfss.2014.small[,
i])) * 100, 1))
```

(Continued)

(Continued)

```
  # combine table.each with whatever is in table.data already
  table.data <- rbind(table.data, table.each)
}

# print table.data
table.data
## Var1 Freq
## 1 Male to female 35.0
## 2 Female to male 50.9
## 3 Gender non-conforming 14.1
## 4 40-44 12.2
## 5 45-49 12.2
## 6 50-54 14.4
## 7 55-59 19.8
## 8 60-64 19.8
## 9 65-69 10.8
## 10 70-74 10.8
## 11 White 68.5
## 12 Black 14.0
## 13 Native American 1.8
## 14 Asian/Pacific Islander 2.7
## 15 Other 13.1
## 16 Less than $15,000 20.7
## 17 $15,000 to less than $25,000 19.8
## 18 $25,000 to less than $35,000 8.6
## 19 $35,000 to less than $50,000 11.7
## 20 $50,000 or more 29.3
## 21 Don't know/not sure/missing 9.9
## 22 Did not graduate high school 10.8
## 23 Graduated high school 38.7
## 24 Attended college/technical school 30.6
## 25 Graduated from college/technical school 19.8
## 26 Yes 89.2
## 27 No 10.8
## 28 0 49.5
## 29 1 4.2
## 30 2 4.7
```

```
## 31                                              3   3.8
## 32                                              4   4.2
## 33                                              5   3.3
## 34                                              6   0.9
## 35                                              7   2.8
## 36                                              8   0.5
## 37                                             10   0.9
## 38                                             14   0.9
## 39                                             15   2.8
## 40                                             18   0.5
## 41                                             20   0.9
## 42                                             21   1.4
## 43                                             24   0.5
## 44                                             25   0.9
## 45                                             28   0.5
## 46                                             29   0.5
## 47                                             30  16.0
```

After this, there were still a couple details to work out. First, it was hard to tell which variable each of the categories was from in the first column, and the PHYSHLTH variable should have been excluded. Kiara edited the code to account for this by labeling the new data frame and removing the PHYSHLTH column from the loop.

```
# initialize an empty data frame
table.data <- data.frame()

# write the for loop
for (i in 1:(ncol(brfss.2014.small) - 1)) {
  # first, get the table
  table.each <-
    data.frame(round(x = prop.table(x = table(brfss.2014.small[,
i])) * 100, 1))

  # store the column name of that iteration for labels
  c.name <- colnames(brfss.2014.small[i])

  # make a new data frame that just contains the labels
  label.names <- data.frame(Variable = rep(c.name, times =
nrow(table.each)))
```

(Continued)

(Continued)

```
  # combine the label.names data frame and table.each data frame
via columns

  table.each.labelled <- cbind(label.names, table.each)

  # combine this with the table.data via rbind

  table.data <- rbind(table.data, table.each.labelled)
}

# print the new data frame

table.data
##       Variable                                    Var1 Freq
## 1     TRNSGNDR                         Male to female 35.0
## 2     TRNSGNDR                         Female to male 50.9
## 3     TRNSGNDR                  Gender non-conforming 14.1
## 4     X_AGEG5YR                                  40-44 12.2
## 5     X_AGEG5YR                                  45-49 12.2
## 6     X_AGEG5YR                                  50-54 14.4
## 7     X_AGEG5YR                                  55-59 19.8
## 8     X_AGEG5YR                                  60-64 19.8
## 9     X_AGEG5YR                                  65-69 10.8
## 10    X_AGEG5YR                                  70-74 10.8
## 11      X_RACE                                  White 68.5
## 12      X_RACE                                  Black 14.0
## 13      X_RACE                        Native American  1.8
## 14      X_RACE                 Asian/Pacific Islander  2.7
## 15      X_RACE                                  Other 13.1
## 16    X_INCOMG                     Less than $15,000 20.7
## 17    X_INCOMG          $15,000 to less than $25,000 19.8
## 18    X_INCOMG          $25,000 to less than $35,000  8.6
## 19    X_INCOMG          $35,000 to less than $50,000 11.7
## 20    X_INCOMG                        $50,000 or more 29.3
## 21    X_INCOMG          Don't know/not sure/missing 9.9
## 22    X_EDUCAG          Did not graduate high school 10.8
## 23    X_EDUCAG                 Graduated high school 38.7
## 24    X_EDUCAG      Attended college/technical school 30.6
## 25    X_EDUCAG Graduated from college/technical school 19.8
## 26    HLTHPLN1                                    Yes 89.2
## 27    HLTHPLN1                                     No 10.8
```

Two more adjustments were needed, making a subset of the `table.data` to exclude the last row and labeling the columns of the data frame to be consistent with the table columns.

```
# subset and add labels
table.data <- table.data[c(1:26), c(2:3)]
colnames(table.data) <- c("Survey participant demographics (n = 220)",
                          "Percent")

# print the new data frame
table.data
##             Survey participant demographics (n = 220) Percent
## 1                                      Male to female    35.0
## 2                                      Female to male    50.9
## 3                                Gender non-conforming    14.1
## 4                                               40-44    12.2
## 5                                               45-49    12.2
## 6                                               50-54    14.4
## 7                                               55-59    19.8
## 8                                               60-64    19.8
## 9                                               65-69    10.8
## 10                                              70-74    10.8
## 11                                              White    68.5
## 12                                              Black    14.0
## 13                                    Native American     1.8
## 14                              Asian/Pacific Islander     2.7
## 15                                              Other    13.1
## 16                                  Less than $15,000    20.7
## 17                          $15,000 to less than $25,000    19.8
## 18                          $25,000 to less than $35,000     8.6
## 19                          $35,000 to less than $50,000    11.7
## 20                                     $50,000 or more    29.3
## 21                         Don't know/not sure/missing     9.9
## 22                         Did not graduate high school    10.8
## 23                               Graduated high school    38.7
## 24                        Attended college/technical school    30.6
## 25                  Graduated from college/technical school    19.8
## 26                                                Yes    89.2
```

The `table.data` data frame was now ready to go into a **kableExtra** table in Section 2.7.3.4.

2.7.3.4 FORMATTING TABLES WITH *KABLE()*

Finally, with a clean data frame containing all the information for the table, Nancy showed Leslie that the pipe structure can be used to send the data frame to `kable()` for formatting. Two packages are used in creating well-formatted `kable` tables, **knitr** and **kableExtra**. The **knitr** package is used to get the basic table, while the **kableExtra** package is used for some of the formatting options like adding sections.

TABLE 2.2 Transgender Survey Participant Demographics

Variable	Survey participant demographics ($n = 220$)	Percent
TRNSGNDR.1	Male to female	35.0
TRNSGNDR.2	Female to male	50.9
TRNSGNDR.3	Gender non-conforming	14.1
X_AGEG5YR.1	40–44	12.2
X_AGEG5YR.2	45–49	12.2
X_AGEG5YR.3	50–54	14.4
X_AGEG5YR.4	55–59	19.8
X_AGEG5YR.5	60–64	19.8
X_AGEG5YR.6	65–69	10.8
X_AGEG5YR.7	70–74	10.8
X_RACE.1	White	68.5
X_RACE.2	Black	14.0
X_RACE.3	Native American	1.8
X_RACE.4	Asian/Pacific Islander	2.7
X_RACE.5	Other	13.1
X_INCOMG.1	Less than $15,000	20.7
X_INCOMG.2	$15,000 to less than $25,000	19.8
X_INCOMG.3	$25,000 to less than $35,000	8.6
X_INCOMG.4	$35,000 to less than $50,000	11.7
X_INCOMG.5	$50,000 or more	29.3
X_INCOMG.6	Don't know/not sure/missing	9.9
X_EDUCAG.1	Did not graduate high school	10.8
X_EDUCAG.2	Graduated high school	38.7
X_EDUCAG.3	Attended college/technical school	30.6
X_EDUCAG.4	Graduated from college/technical school	19.8
HLTHPLN1.1	Yes	89.2

```
# open libraries
library(package = "knitr")
library(package = "kableExtra")

# send the table.data to kable and add a title (Table 2.2)
table.data %>%
kable(format = "html",
      caption = "Transgender Survey Participant Demographics") %>%
kable_styling()
```

"Well, Table 2.2 is a start," thought Leslie after she finally found the table in the viewer pane. For the final formatting, Nancy showed Leslie how to add labels by using the pipe structure. For each variable, use the group_rows() argument with the name of the variable and the rows the variable categories are in. For example, rows 1 to 3 are the transition status, so the first group_rows() argument shows: group_rows("Transition status", 1, 3).

Unfortunately, group_rows() is one of those functions that is in more than one R package. It is in the **dplyr** package, which is part of the **tidyverse**, and it is in the **kableExtra** package. There are a couple of options to avoid the conflict: remove the **dplyr** package while creating the table, or use the :: format to specify that the group_rows() function should be from the **kableExtra** package. Since **dplyr** is used for most of the data management tasks, Leslie decided to go with the :: option and created Table 2.3.

```
# add the section names (Table 2.3)
table.data %>%
  kable(format = "html",
  caption = "Transgender Survey Participant Demographics",
      row.names = FALSE) %>%
kableExtra::group_rows(group_label = "Transition status",
            start_row = 1, end_row = 3) %>%
kableExtra::group_rows(group_label = "Age category",
            start_row = 4, end_row = 10) %>%
kableExtra::group_rows(group_label = "Race/ethnicity",
            start_row = 11, end_row = 15) %>%
kableExtra::group_rows(group_label = "Income category",
            start_row = 16, end_row = 21) %>%
kableExtra::group_rows(group_label = "Education category",
            start_row = 22, end_row = 25) %>%
kableExtra::group_rows(group_label = "Health insurance?",
            start_row = 26, end_row = 26)
```

Now that she had the manuscript table reproduced, Leslie was interested in making the bigger table with frequencies, and the median and IQR of PHYSHLTH. The first step, said Nancy, is to create a function (or

TABLE 2.3 Transgender Survey Participant Demographics

Variable Survey participant demographics (*n* = 220)	Percent
Transition status	
Male to female	35.0
Female to male	50.9
Gender non-conforming	14.1
Age category	
40–44	12.2
45–49	12.2
50–54	14.4
55–59	19.8
60–64	19.8
65–69	10.8
70–74	10.8
Race/ethnicity	
White	68.5
Black	14.0
Native American	1.8
Asian/Pacific Islander	2.7
Other	13.1
Income category	
Less than $15,000	20.7
$15,000 to less than $25,000	19.8
$25,000 to less than $35,000	8.6
$35,000 to less than $50,000	11.7
$50,000 or more	29.3
Don't know/not sure/missing	9.9
Education category	
Did not graduate high school	10.8
Graduated high school	38.7
Attended college/technical school	30.6
Graduated from college/technical school	19.8
Health insurance?	
Yes	89.2

expand `TableFun()`) to compute both frequencies and percentages. The `table()` function computes frequencies, so add it to `TableFun` and rename `TableFun` something logical like `TableFreqPerc`. Nancy wrote the code, but Leslie did not see the difference between `TableFun()` and `TableFreqPerc()`. Nancy showed her there was now a `table()` function before the `prop.table()` part.

```
# revise the TableFun function to compute both
# frequencies and percentages for Table 2.4
TableFreqPerc<- function(x){
    data.frame(table(x), round(x = prop.table(x = table(x)) * 100, 1))
}
# apply new function to brfss.2014.small data frame
bigger.table <- do.call(rbind, (lapply(X = brfss.2014.small, FUN =
TableFreqPerc)))
# click on the bigger.table object in the Environment
# pane to see the resulting table
# note that the categories show up twice in the data frame
# delete the second occurrence by making a subset of the data
bigger.table <- bigger.table[-3]
# remove Health insurance No category and PHYSHLTH numbers
bigger.table <- data.frame(bigger.table[c(1:26), ])
#add variable names
names(x = bigger.table) <- c("Survey participant demographics (n = 220)",
"Frequency", "Percent")
```

Now with a clean data frame, Leslie used the code from the smaller table—replacing `"table.data"` with `"bigger.table"`—to create a table with both frequencies and percentages (Table 2.4).

TABLE 2.4 Transgender Survey Participant Demographics

Survey participant demographics (*n* = 220)	Frequency	Percent
Transition status		
Male to female	77	35.0
Female to male	112	50.9
Gender non-conforming	31	14.1
Age category		
40–44	27	12.2
45–49	27	12.2
50–54	32	14.4
55–59	44	19.8

(Continued)

TABLE 2.4 (Continued)

Survey participant demographics (*n* = 220)	Frequency	Percent
60–64	44	19.8
65–69	24	10.8
70–74	24	10.8
Race/ethnicity		
White	152	68.5
Black	31	14.0
Native American	4	1.8
Asian/Pacific Islander	6	2.7
Other	29	13.1
Income category		
Less than $15,000	46	20.7
$15,000 to less than $25,000	44	19.8
$25,000 to less than $35,000	19	8.6
$35,000 to less than $50,000	26	11.7
$50,000 or more	65	29.3
Don't know/not sure/missing	22	9.9
Education category		
Did not graduate high school	24	10.8
Graduated high school	86	38.7
Attended college/technical school	68	30.6
Graduated from college/technical school	44	19.8
Health insurance?		
Yes	198	89.2

Although the original table creation was tedious, Leslie found that adding frequencies and rerunning the table code was not nearly as time-consuming.

The last thing, said Nancy, is to add the continuous PHYSHLTH variable to the table. Leslie reminded herself of the median and IQR for PHYSHLTH first.

```
# descriptive statistics for PHYSHLTH
median(x = brfss.2014.small$PHYSHLTH, na.rm = TRUE)
## [1] 1
IQR(x = brfss.2014.small$PHYSHLTH, na.rm = TRUE)
## [1] 11
```

The median days of poor physical health per month in this group was 1, and the IQR shows that there is an 11-day spread for the middle half of the people in this group. She hadn't been paying attention to the values in the `CreateTableOne` process and noticed that this was quite different from the median of 0 and the IQR of 3 for the full data set. This group of transgender survey participants had a higher median number of days of poor health and more variation than the full sample. The other thing she noticed was the spread of people across income categories. Large percentages were in the lowest income category and the highest income category, with fewer people in between. Leslie wondered how this compared to all people in this age group, not just people who are transgender.

Now that Leslie was aware of what she was looking for in the table, Nancy told her that adding the code to the table required a few steps. She wrote the code with lots of comments and then walked Leslie through it. She decided to remove the "($n = 220$)" from the column header now that they were expanding the table beyond reproducing Table 2.1.

```
# revise the TableFreqPerc function to compute
# frequencies and percents for factors
# median and IQR for numeric data types for Table 2.5
TableFreqPerc<- function(x){
  if(is.factor(x))
    data.frame(table(x), round(x = prop.table(x = table(x)) * 100, 1))
}

# apply new function to brfss.2014.small data frame
bigger.table <- do.call(rbind, (lapply(X = brfss.2014.small, FUN =
TableFreqPerc)))

# note that the categories show up twice in the data frame
# delete the second occurrence by making a subset of the data
bigger.table <- bigger.table[-3]

# remove Health insurance No category
bigger.table <- data.frame(bigger.table[c(1:26), ])

# add the age summary data
# make a small data frame for the age information
bigger.table <- rbind(bigger.table, data.frame(x="Poor health (days/mo)",
                          Freq = median(x = brfss.2014.small$PHYSHLTH,
                               na.rm = TRUE),
                          Freq.1 = IQR(x = brfss.2014.small$PHYSHLTH,
                               na.rm = TRUE)))

# add variable names
names(bigger.table) <- c("Survey participant demographics", "Frequency",
"Percent")
```

Once the values were all together in the new data frame, Nancy told Leslie that she could reuse code from earlier to create a formatted Table 2.5. Leslie left the "($n = 220$)" out of the "Survey participant demographics" column title and added the overall sample size and the sample size for the transition status variable since the table was no longer truly a reproduced version of Table 2.1. Finally, she added one more `kableExtra::` section for row 27 to add the `group_label = "Days poor physical health per month (median, IQR)"` to the last section.

TABLE 2.5 Transgender Survey Participant Demographics (*n* = 222)

Survey participant demographics	Frequency	Percent
Transition status (*n* = 220)		
Male to female	77	35.0
Female to male	112	50.9
Gender non-conforming	31	14.1
Age category		
40–44	27	12.2
45–49	27	12.2
50–54	32	14.4
55–59	44	19.8
60–64	44	19.8
65–69	24	10.8
70–74	24	10.8
Race/ethnicity		
White	152	68.5
Black	31	14.0
Native American	4	1.8
Asian/Pacific Islander	6	2.7
Other	29	13.1
Income category		
Less than $15,000	46	20.7
$15,000 to less than $25,000	44	19.8
$25,000 to less than $35,000	19	8.6
$35,000 to less than $50,000	26	11.7
$50,000 or more	65	29.3
Don't know/not sure/missing	22	9.9
Education category		
Did not graduate high school	24	10.8
Graduated high school	86	38.7
Attended college/technical school	68	30.6
Graduated from college/technical school	44	19.8
Health insurance?		
Yes	198	89.2
Days poor physical health per month (median, IQR)		
Poor health (days/mo)	1	11.0

Leslie took a few minutes to write an interpretation of the results and the information reported in Table 2.5.

> Of the participants in the 2014 BRFSS, 222 people identified as transgender, were 40–74 years old (the age range when mammograms are recommended), and were asked about having a mammogram. Of these, 77 were male-to-female (35.0%), 112 were female-to-male (50.9%), and 31 were gender non-conforming (14.1%). Most were White ($n = 152$; 68.5%) or Black ($n = 31$; 14.0%). The most common age groups were 50–54 ($n = 44$; 19.8%) and 55–59 ($n = 44$; 19.8%).

Kiara stopped Leslie before she finished to let her know that, when there is a table in a report or manuscript, it is usually not necessary to interpret every number in the table. In fact, she said, this can be seen as repetition and a poor use of space. Kiara recommended that Leslie report information from the table that is important to the study at hand or that is unusual in some way. Leslie thought that made sense, since the entire purpose of a table is to report results in a clear way. Kiara commented that the interpretation she started to write was correct and clear, just that it had more detail than needed.

Everyone was exhausted, but before quitting, they went back over what they had learned about R and about transgender health care. Leslie felt like she learned a lot about descriptive statistics but that they did not get too much into the issue of transgender health care and cancer screening other than learning that this group has a high median number of days of poor health per month and a strange distribution of income, which were both things that might be important to explore further. Nancy and Kiara agreed and thought they might have some meetings where this happens just due to what they had learned that day. The team made a plan to meet soon to learn about graphing, which, as Nancy reminded everyone, is one of the biggest strengths of R.

It had been so long since they walked into the café that Leslie was hungry for another snack. Nancy and Kiara were chatting while they walked toward the door when they noticed that Leslie was not with them. They turned around to see her back in the line for food. Leslie waved. "See you next time."

Kiara and Nancy paused for a second but decided not to wait. Nancy waved back. "Not if I see you first!" she joked.

Kiara just rolled her eyes, ready to head home and relax after such an intense meeting.

/// 2.8 CHAPTER SUMMARY

Congratulations! Like Leslie, you've learned and practiced the following in this chapter.

2.8.1 Achievements unlocked in this chapter: Recap

2.8.1.1 Achievement 1 recap: Understanding variable types and data types

The main variable types in social science are continuous and categorical, which are *numeric* and *factor* data types in R. True continuous variables can take any value along a continuum (e.g., height), while categorical variables are measured in categories (e.g., marital status).

2.8.1.2 Achievement 2 recap: Choosing and conducting descriptive analyses for categorical (factor) variables

Descriptive statistics most appropriate for factor-type variables are frequencies, which show the number of observations for each category, and percentages, which show the percentage of observations for each category.

2.8.1.3 Achievement 3 recap: Choosing and conducting descriptive analyses for continuous (numeric) variables

If a numeric variable is normally distributed, the appropriate descriptive statistics to report are the mean and standard deviation. The mean is a measure of central tendency that provides some idea of where the middle of the data is. The standard deviation is a measure of spread that indicates how spread out the values are. If a numeric variable is not normally distributed, the median and range or median and IQR are reported. The median is the middle value, while the IQR is the boundaries around the middle 50% of values.

2.8.1.4 Achievement 4 recap: Developing clear tables for reporting descriptive statistics

Computing the correct statistics is a great start, but organizing statistics in formats that are easy to understand is a key part of being an effective analyst. Creating tables that follow good formatting practices is one way to do this. Good formatting practices include number alignment, use of descriptive titles, choosing and reporting a consistent number of decimal places, and other formatting options.

2.8.2 Chapter exercises

The coder and hacker exercises are an opportunity to apply the skills from this chapter to a new scenario or a new data set. The coder edition evaluates the application of the concepts and functions learned in this R-Team meeting to new scenarios similar to those in the meeting. The hacker edition evaluates the use of the concepts and functions from this R-Team meeting in new scenarios, often going a step beyond what was explicitly explained.

The coder edition might be best for those who found some or all of the Check Your Understanding activities to be challenging or if they needed review before picking the correct responses to the multiple-choice questions. The hacker edition might be best if the Check Your Understanding activities were not too challenging and the multiple-choice questions were a breeze.

The multiple-choice questions and materials for the exercises are online at **edge.sagepub.com/harris1e**.

Q1: What is a measure of spread that is appropriate for each central tendency?

    a. Mean

    b. Median

    c. Mode

Q2: Which of the following measures would be most appropriate for describing the central tendency of a variable that is continuous and normally distributed?

    a. Mean

    b. Variance

    c. Median

    d. Mode

Q3: Which of the following measures would be most appropriate for describing the spread of a variable that is extremely right-skewed?

    a. Standard deviation

    b. Range

    c. IQR

    d. Mode

Q4: In R, categorical variables are best represented by the _____ data type and continuous variables are best represented by the _____ data type.

Q5: Custom functions are useful when doing which of the following?

    a. Loading a library

    b. Visualizing the distribution of one variable

    c. Working with continuous variables

    d. Doing the same thing multiple times

2.8.2.1 Chapter exercises: Coder edition

Use the BRFSS data in the **transgender_hc_ch2.csv** file at **edge.sagepub.com/harris1e** to create a table of appropriate descriptive statistics for *all* transgender participants in the 2014 BRFSS. Spend a few minutes looking through the BRFSS website before beginning. Include variables representing transition status, days of poor physical health (PHYSHLTH), race/ethnicity, income, education, age, and age category. Write a paragraph using the numbers in the table to describe the characteristics of the transgender participants of the 2014 BRFSS.

1) Open the **transgender_hc_ch2.csv** 2014 BRFSS data file.

2) Select the data including only transgender participants.

3) Select the data including only the variables of interest.

4) Check the data types of all the variables and fix any that seem incorrect (Achievement 1).

5) Based on the BRFSS codebook, code missing values and add category labels appropriately.

6) Choose and conduct appropriate descriptive statistics for all variables in the small data set (Achievements 2 and 3).

7) Develop a well-formatted table of results including all variables in the small data set (Achievement 4).

8) Add a prolog and comments to your code.

9) Summarize the characteristics of transgender survey participants in the 2014 BRFSS.

2.8.2.2 Chapter exercises: Hacker edition

Complete #1–#5 from the coder edition; then do the following:

6) Find the mean or median value of `PHYSHLTH` (whichever is most appropriate) and recode to create a new factor variable with values above the mean or median labeled as "poor physical health" and values below the mean labeled as "good physical health"; check your coding (Achievement 3).

7) Choose and conduct appropriate descriptive statistics for all variables in the small data set (Achievements 2 and 3).

8) Develop a well-formatted table of results including all variables in the small data set (Achievement 4).

9) Add a prolog and comments to your code.

10) Summarize the characteristics of transgender survey participants in the 2014 BRFSS.

2.8.2.3 Instructor note

Solutions to exercises can be found on the website for this book, along with ideas for gamification for those who want to take it further.

Visit **edge.sagepub.com/harris1e** to download the datasets, complete the chapter exercises, and watch R tutorial videos.

DATA VISUALIZATION

The R-Team and the Tricky Trigger Problem

It was just their third R-Team meeting, but Nancy and Kiara were impressed at how quickly Leslie had been learning R coding. They were meeting today at the business school of Leslie's university. Leslie had described a big open area with a lot of tables and a little coffee shop in the corner, which sounded perfect to Kiara and Nancy. Leslie was already on campus that morning, so she arrived first, but it was only a minute or two before Nancy and Kiara walked up. After a quick delay for coffee, they were all seated and ready to go.

"You're killing it on the coding front," said Kiara.

"Genius!" Nancy exclaimed. "Which means it's time to teach you all about one of the biggest strengths of R: making graphs! Graphs are so important for adding context to the numbers."

"For sure," Kiara said. "Remember last meeting when the `PHYSHLTH` histograms showed so clearly that it was not normally distributed?" A quick histogram review was enough evidence to suggest the appropriate descriptive statistics to use for the situation.

"I remember," said Leslie.

Nancy continued, "In addition to helping choose the right statistics to use, graphs are one of the best ways to communicate about data with various audiences."

"What are we waiting for?" Leslie asked.

"I like your enthusiasm," said Kiara.

Nancy explained that they would primarily use the `ggplot2` package from the `tidyverse` to create and format common graphs used to display data. She promised to cover which graphs are appropriate for different data types, the important features of a well-formatted graph, ways to avoid creating a misleading graph, and how to interpret graphs.

Nancy and Kiara created a list of achievements for Leslie's third R-Team meeting.

3.1 Achievements to unlock

- Achievement 1: Choosing and creating graphs for a single categorical variable
- Achievement 2: Choosing and creating graphs for a single continuous variable
- Achievement 3: Choosing and creating graphs for two variables at once
- Achievement 4: Ensuring graphs are well-formatted with appropriate and clear titles, labels, colors, and other features

3.2 The tricky trigger problem

Leslie's friend Leanne was very involved in an activist group called Moms Demand Action (https://momsdemandaction.org/) and had been sending Leslie information about guns and gun violence in the United States. Leslie had emailed Kiara and Nancy some of what she understood about this problem and the lack of research related to gun violence.

Note: In shaded sections throughout this text, the rows starting "##" show the output that will appear after running the R code just above it.

3.2.1 COMPARING GUN DEATHS TO OTHER CAUSES OF DEATH IN THE UNITED STATES

The United States has a high rate of gun ownership and a similarly high rate of gun injury and death (Giffords Law Center, n.d.). However, there has been relatively little research into gun injury and gun violence in recent decades after government funding was limited by the Dickey Amendment, a 1996 appropriations bill that cut $2.6 million from the Centers for Disease Control and Prevention (CDC) budget (Kellermann & Rivara, 2013). The Dickey Amendment, named after the Arkansas representative who introduced it, removed the funds in an effort by some members of the U.S. Congress to eliminate the National Center for Injury Prevention and Control (Kellermann & Rivara, 2013): "None of the funds made available for injury prevention and control at the Centers for Disease Control and Prevention may be used to advocate or promote gun control" (Omnibus Consolidated Appropriations Act of 1997, p. 244; Rubin, 2016). While the bill failed to eliminate the center, it was successful in eliminating funding for research on gun injury and violence.

An article published in the *Journal of the American Medical Association (JAMA)* used publicly available data to compare the amount of research money spent on each of the top 30 causes of death in the United States, including gun violence, between 2004 and 2015 (Stark & Shah, 2017). The authors also examined the number of publications describing research findings for the top 30 causes of death in the United States over the same time period. With the exception of falls, research on gun violence as a cause of death had the lowest research funding level of any of the top 30 causes of death. With the exception of drowning and asphyxia, gun violence was the topic of the fewest publications of any of the top 30 causes of death in the United States. Before their meeting, Nancy and Kiara requested the data for the gun violence article from the authors and reproduced some of the figures.

The figures in the article are *scatterplots*, which show one dot for each observation in the data set. In this case, each dot represents one of the top 30 causes of death in the United States. There is a label on each dot showing which cause of death it represents. The *x*-axis (horizontal) is the mortality rate, or the number of deaths per 100,000 people per year in the United States. The *y*-axis (vertical) shows the amount of funding spent on research. The relative position of each dot on the graph shows how many people the cause of death kills and how many dollars of funding are available for research. Causes with dots in the lower left have lower levels of mortality and lower levels of funding. Causes with dots in the upper right have higher mortality and higher research funding. Overall, as the mortality rate rises, the amount of research funding also rises. There are two exceptions, falls and gun violence, which are toward the middle of the group for rate of mortality but at the bottom for research funding levels. Overall, gun violence has the second lowest funding for research of the top 30 mortality causes (see Figure 3.1).

The second figure reproduced (Figure 3.2) from the paper (Stark & Shah, 2017) shows a similar pattern of number of publications on each topic on the *y*-axis and mortality rate on the *x*-axis. This time, there are four mortality causes that do not fit the pattern of more publications for higher mortality rates: drowning, asphyxia, aspiration, and gun violence. Of these, gun violence has the highest mortality rate. Overall, gun violence has the third lowest publication rate of the top 30 mortality causes.

3.2.2 WEAPONS USED IN HOMICIDE

To get a sense of the extent of gun violence in the United States, Nancy and Kiara looked up the annual Federal Bureau of Investigation (FBI) crime data reported in the Uniform Crime Reporting program (https://www.fbi.gov/services/cjis/ucr). They found that one of the data sources included the types of weapons used in homicides, such as firearms, knives or cutting instruments, blunt objects, and several other categories. Kiara and Nancy decided to make a bar chart of gun and non-gun homicides from the FBI data for the most recent 5 years reported. They flipped the axes so that the bars are horizontal. The *x*-axis shows the number of homicides, while the *y*-axis shows the year. In each year, the number of homicides by gun (green bars) was more than 2.5 times higher than all non-gun weapons combined (purple bars). For more than one of the years, there were three times as many homicides by gun as by all non-gun weapons combined (Figure 3.3).

FIGURE 3.1 Mortality rate versus funding from 2004 to 2015 for 30 leading causes of death in the United States

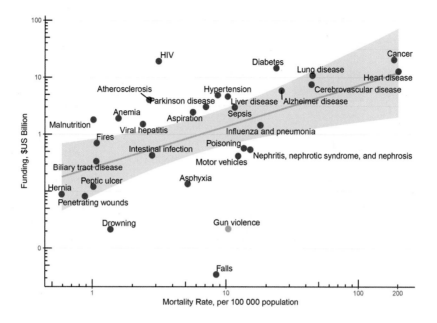

FIGURE 3.2 Mortality rate versus publication volume from 2004 to 2015 for 30 leading causes of death in the United States

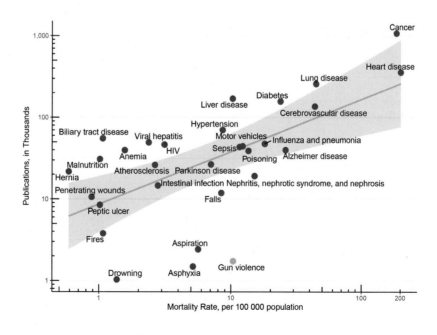

FIGURE 3.3 Homicides by guns and known non-gun weapons per year in the United States, 2012–2016

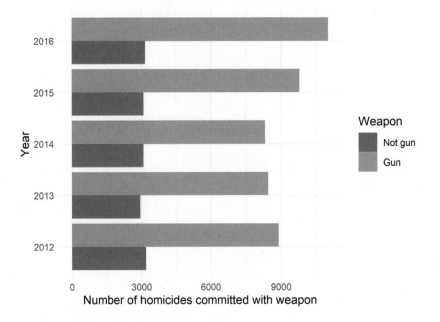

Source: FBI Uniform Crime Reports data.

Nancy and Kiara were interested in finding other patterns that might be useful in understanding gun violence.

3.2.3 TYPES OF GUNS USED IN HOMICIDE

Looking a little deeper into the FBI data, Nancy and Kiara found that within the firearms category are handguns, rifles, shotguns, other guns, and unknown gun type. They made another bar chart that suggested handguns were the most widely used type of gun for homicide in 2016. The graph includes all the homicides by gun for 2016 and shows the number of homicides by each type of gun. The *x*-axis has the number of homicides, while the *y*-axis has the type of gun (Figure 3.4).

3.2.4 THE ROLE OF GUN MANUFACTURERS IN REDUCING GUN DEATHS

Leslie remembered another article she had read recently from her friend Leanne. It was about the role that gun manufacturers could potentially play in reducing gun violence (Smith et al., 2017). The authors of this article argued that there is little information about how gun manufacturing is related to gun ownership or gun violence. They suggested that a better understanding of manufacturing could identify changes in manufacturing practices to increase safety and reduce injury and death. The authors used publicly available data from the Bureau of Alcohol, Tobacco, Firearms, and Explosives to examine how many guns were manufactured in the United States over a 25-year period from 1990 to 2015. The authors also examined the types of guns manufactured during this period and the types of guns confiscated after use in crime. Kiara and Nancy worked together to reproduce the graph from the article (Figure 3.5). This time it was a line graph, which is the type of graph often used to show change over time. In this case, time is on the *x*-axis and the number of firearms manufactured is on the *y*-axis.

FIGURE 3.4 Types of firearms used in homicides in the United States, 2016

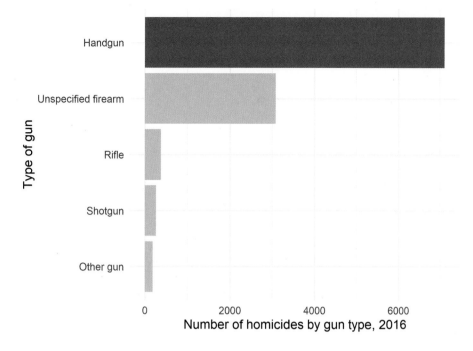

Source: FBI Uniform Crime Reports data.

FIGURE 3.5 Firearm types manufactured in the United States from 1990 to 2015

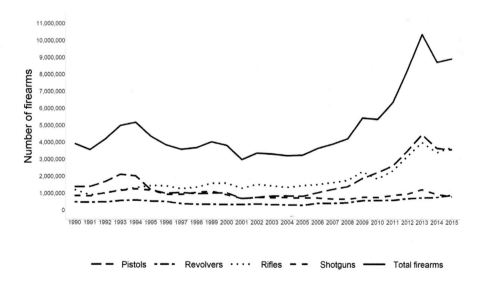

Source: U.S. Bureau of Alcohol, Tobacco, Firearms, and Explosives data.

FIGURE 3.6 Firearm types manufactured in the United States from 1990 to 2015

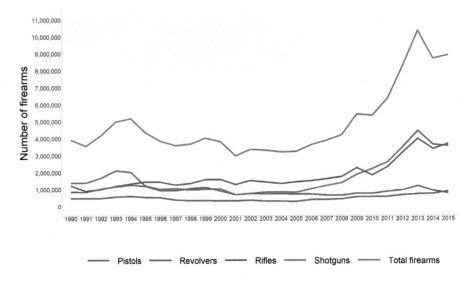

Pistols ——— Revolvers ——— Rifles ——— Shotguns ——— Total firearms

Source: U.S. Bureau of Alcohol, Tobacco, Firearms, and Explosives data.

Different types of lines show different types of guns being produced over time. Although the article used the line types to differentiate, Nancy and Kiara found it difficult to tell some of the line types apart, so they used solid lines and added color to the graph for easier reading. The resulting graph, Figure 3.6, showed a sharp increase in gun manufacturing after 2010, with the increase mostly being in the production of pistols and rifles.

Leslie, Nancy, and Kiara discussed how these four graphs tell a story about guns in the United States and may suggest policy solutions, such as funding research that examines the relationship, if any, between the types and quantities of guns manufactured and the number of gun homicides by weapon type. Nancy and Kiara explained to Leslie that the graphs shown here about gun research and manufacturing demonstrate just a few of the many ways to visualize data. *Data visualization*, or graphing, is one of the most powerful tools an analyst has for communicating information. Three graph types were demonstrated by Nancy and Kiara: the scatterplot, the bar chart, and the line graph. Kiara explained to Leslie that these are not the only types of graphs, but they are common types. She explained that, like descriptive statistics, there are different ways to visualize data that are appropriate for each data type.

3.3 Data, codebook, and R packages for graphs

Before they examined the data, Kiara made a list of all the data, documentation, and packages needed for learning about graphs.

- Two options for accessing the data
  - Download the three data files from **edge.sagepub.com/harris1e**
    - **nhanes_2011_2012_ch3.csv**

- **fbi_deaths_2016_ch3.csv**
- **gun_publications_funds_2004_2015_ch3.csv**
  - Download the raw data directly from the Internet for the FBI deaths data and the NHANES data by following the instructions in Box 3.1 and download **gun_publications_funds_2004_2015_ch3.csv** from **edge.sagepub.com/harris1e**
- Two options for accessing the codebooks
  - Download from **edge.sagepub.com/harris1e**
    - **nhanes_demographics_2012_codebook.html**
    - **nhanes_auditory_2012_codebook.html**
  - Access the codebooks online on the National Health and Nutrition Examination Survey (NHANES) website (https://wwwn.cdc.gov/nchs/nhanes/Search/DataPage.aspx?Component=Questionnaire&CycleBeginYear=2011)
- Install the following R packages if not already installed:
  - **tidyverse**, by Hadley Wickham (https://www.rdocumentation.org/packages/tidyverse/)
  - *ggmosaic*, by Haley Jeppson (https://github.com/haleyjeppson/ggmosaic)
  - *waffle*, by Bob Rudis (https://github.com/hrbrmstr/waffle)
  - *gridExtra*, by Baptiste Auguie (https://www.rdocumentation.org/packages/gridExtra/)
  - *readxl*, by Jennifer Bryan (https://www.rdocumentation.org/packages/readxl/)
  - *ggrepel*, by Kamil Slowikowski (https://www.rdocumentation.org/packages/ggrepel/)
  - *scales*, by Hadley Wickham (https://www.rdocumentation.org/packages/scales/)
  - *httr*, by Hadley Wickham (https://www.rdocumentation.org/packages/httr/)
  - **data.table** (Dowle & Srinivasan, 2019)
  - *RNHANES* (Susmann, 2016)

3.4 Achievement 1: Choosing and creating graphs for a single categorical variable

The first thing the team wanted to work on were graphs appropriate for displaying single variables. Before selecting a graph type, it is useful to think about the goal of the graph. Kiara suggested that making graphs to check whether something is normally distributed before calculating a mean is very different from making graphs to communicate information to an audience. The team decided to start by creating graphs that convey information from a single categorical variable. Kiara reminded Leslie that a categorical variable has categories that are either ordinal, with a logical order, or nominal, with no logical order. Categorical variables are the factor data type in R. Nancy explained that single categorical variables have several options for graphing. Some of the more commonly used graphs for a single categorical variable are the following:

- Pie chart
- Waffle chart
- Bar chart
- Point chart

Pie charts and waffle charts are similar; they are both used for showing parts of a whole. Bar charts and point charts tend to be used to compare groups. Leslie chose to start with the pie chart since it sounded delicious and she had always preferred dessert to breakfast!

3.4.1 PIE CHARTS

To create a pie chart for a single categorical variable, the team needed a variable to start with. Leslie suggested gun type from Figure 3.4. There were five categories of gun type represented in the graph: Other gun, Shotgun, Rifle, Unspecified firearm, and Handgun. Kiara thought focusing on one gun type might be one way to start understanding gun manufacturing. Maybe examining the type of gun with the highest (or lowest) quantity manufactured would be a good strategy? One way to do this would be to create a pie chart, like Figure 3.7.

Pie charts are meant to show parts of a whole. The pie, or circle, represents the whole. The slices of pie shown in different colors represent the parts. While pie charts are often seen in newspapers and other popular media, they are considered by most analysts as an unclear way to display data. A few of the reasons for this were summarized in an R-bloggers post (C, 2010):

- Pie charts are difficult to read since the relative size of pie pieces is often hard to determine.

- Pie charts take up a lot of space to convey little information.

- People often use fancy formatting like 3-D, which takes up more space and makes understanding the relative size of pie pieces even more difficult.

In fact, if you asked 100 data scientists, "Should I make a pie chart?" the answers might resemble Figure 3.8.

FIGURE 3.7 Firearm types manufactured in 2016 in the United States

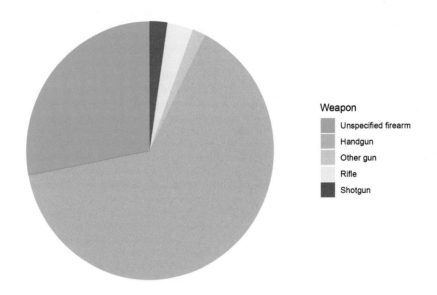

Weapon
- Unspecified firearm
- Handgun
- Other gun
- Rifle
- Shotgun

Source: U.S. Bureau of Alcohol, Tobacco, Firearms, and Explosives data.

FIGURE 3.8 Should I make a pie chart?

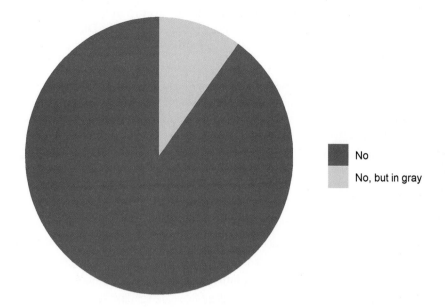

A *bar chart* and a *point chart* are more effective ways to present and compare the sizes of groups for a single variable. Instead of a pie chart, try a bar chart for showing responses to "Should I make a pie chart?" (Figure 3.9).

Nancy suggested that if a pie chart is truly the most appropriate way to communicate data (it isn't), or if you have been directed to make a pie chart, there is guidance on creating pie charts on many websites. As an alternative, Nancy told Leslie they would review how to make a waffle chart as a better way to show parts of a whole. Kiara suggested that they stick with the bar charts now that they have one example. Leslie hoped they were lemon bars because all this talk of pies and waffles has really made her hungry for something sweet.

FIGURE 3.9 Should I make a pie chart?

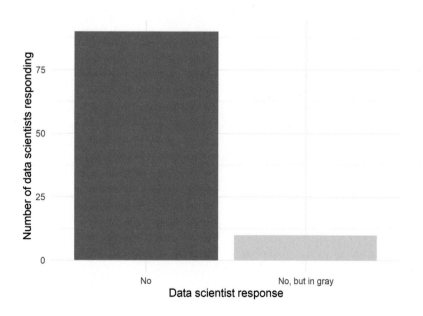

3.4.2 BAR CHARTS

One thing that might be useful to know in better understanding guns in the United States is the rate of gun use. Although publicly available data on gun use are rare because of the Dickey Amendment, Nancy knew of a few persistent researchers who had found ways to collect gun-related data.

3.1 Kiara's reproducibility resource: Bringing data in directly from the Internet

3.1.1 Excel data

Kiara explained that including the code to download data directly from the Internet improves reproducibility because it ensures that anyone reproducing the work is working with the same exact data set. The FBI data used in this meeting (saved as **fbi_deaths_2016_ch3.csv** at **edge.sagepub.com/harris1e**) were downloaded directly from the FBI's Uniform Crime Reporting database. To download this data set directly to create the **fbi_deaths_2016_ch3.csv** data set, follow these instructions.

The first thing to notice before importing a data set directly from the Internet is the format of the file. This file is saved with the file extension ".xls," which indicates that it is an Excel file. Excel files with the .xls extension cannot be imported using `read.csv()` because they are not csv files. Instead, these files can be imported using the **readxl** package. The **readxl** package does not read things directly from the Internet, so another package will have to be used to import the data first before they can be read by **readxl**. The **httr** package has the `GET()` function, which is useful for getting data directly from an online location (URL) and temporarily storing it. Once the data are temporarily stored in a local location, often the `tempfile, read_excel()` from the **readxl** package can be used to read in the data from the Excel file.

Kiara wrote out the exact instructions for downloading the data directly from their online source. She included lots of comments for each step.

```
# install and then load the readxl
# and httr packages
library(package = "readxl")
library(package = "httr")

# create a variable that contains the web
# URL for the data set
url1 <- "https://ucr.fbi.gov/crime-in-the-u.s/2016/crime-in-the-
u.s.-2016/tables/expanded-homicide-data-table-4.xls/output.xls"

# use the GET function in httr to put the URL
# in a temporary file and specify the .xls file extension
```

```
# temporary file is named tf in this example
GET(url = url1, write_disk(tf <- tempfile(fileext = ".xls")))

# use the read_excel function in readxl
# to get the temporary file tf
# skip the first 3 rows of the file because they
# are header rows and do not contain data
# specify the number of observations using n_max
fbi.deaths <- data.frame(read_excel(path = tf, sheet = 1, skip = 3,
n_max = 18))

# option to save the file to a folder called "data"
write.csv(x = fbi.deaths, file = "[data folder location]/data/fbi_
deaths_2016_ch3.csv", row.names = FALSE)
```

3.1.2 NHANES data

The data files for NHANES are available on the CDC website. Kiara noticed that each part of the survey is saved in a separate file in the SAS Transport or xpt format. Luckily, she recently learned about an R package called **RNHANES** that can be used to download demographic data and other NHANES data into a data frame for use in R. This package includes all the steps needed to download the data directly given the `file_name` and the `year` of the data of interest. These two pieces of information can be found on the NHANES website.

To download the NHANES data for the examples in this chapter, install the **RNHANES** package and run the following code:

```
# open package
library(package = "RNHANES")

# download audiology data (AUQ_G)
# with demographics
nhanes.2012 <- nhanes_load_data(file_name = "AUQ_G", year = "2011-2012",
                                demographics = TRUE)

# option to save the data to a "data" folder
write.csv(x = nhanes.2012, file = "[data folder location]/data/
nhanes_2011_2012_ch3.csv ",
row.names = FALSE)

# examine gun use variable (AUQ300)
summary(object = nhanes.2012$AUQ300)
```

(Continued)

To use the **RNHANES** package to open a different NHANES data set, find the data files available for download on the NHANES website and note the name and year of the data file of interest. Use the code provided, but change the `file_name = "AUQ_G"` to include the name of the file of interest and change the `year = "2011-2012"` to the year(s) for the data of interest. Kiara noted that the `nhanes_load_data()` process takes a few minutes on her laptop.

One example Nancy was aware of is a set of questions in the nationally representative *National Health and Nutrition Examination Survey*, or NHANES. Several administrations of the NHANES survey asked about gun use in the Audiology section concerned with how loud noise may influence hearing loss. The most recent year of NHANES data available with a gun use question was 2011–2012 (https://wwwn.cdc.gov/nchs/nhanes/Search/DataPage.aspx?Component=Questionnaire&CycleBeginYear=2011). One of the cool things about NHANES data is that an R package called **RNHANES** allows direct access to NHANES data from R, which is great for reproducibility. Kiara used **RNHANES** to download the 2011–2012 data (Box 3.1) and saved it for the R-Team as a csv file. Leslie used `read.csv()` to import the data and noticed that it had 82 variables, which is a lot for the `summary()` function. She checked that the import worked by using `head()` instead.

```
# import the data
nhanes.2012 <- read.csv(file = "[data folder location]/data/nhanes_
2011_2012_ch3.csv")

# check the import
head(x = nhanes.2012)
##     SEQN        cycle SDDSRVYR RIDSTATR RIAGENDR RIDAGEYR RIDAGEMN RIDRETH1
## 1 62161 2011-2012        7        2        1       22       NA        3
## 2 62162 2011-2012        7        2        2        3       NA        1
## 3 62163 2011-2012        7        2        1       14       NA        5
## 4 62164 2011-2012        7        2        2       44       NA        3
## 5 62165 2011-2012        7        2        2       14       NA        4
## 6 62166 2011-2012        7        2        1        9       NA        3
##   RIDRETH3 RIDEXMON RIDEXAGY RIDEXAGM DMQMILIZ DMQADFC DMDBORN4 DMDCITZN
## 1        3        2       NA       NA        2      NA        1        1
## 2        1        1        3       41       NA      NA        1        1
## 3        6        2       14      177       NA      NA        1        1
## 4        3        1       NA       NA        1       2        1        1
## 5        4        2       14      179       NA      NA        1        1
## 6        3        2       10      120       NA      NA        1        1
##   DMDYRSUS DMDEDUC3 DMDEDUC2 DMDMARTL RIDEXPRG SIALANG SIAPROXY SIAINTRP
## 1       NA       NA        3        5       NA       1        1        2
## 2       NA       NA       NA       NA       NA       1        1        2
## 3       NA        8       NA       NA       NA       1        1        2
```

```
## 4        NA      NA         4      1         2        1         2         2
## 5        NA       7        NA     NA        NA        1         1         2
## 6        NA       3        NA     NA        NA        1         1         2
##   FIALANG FIAPROXY FIAINTRP MIALANG MIAPROXY MIAINTRP AIALANGA  WTINT2YR
## 1       1        2        2       1        2        2        1 102641.406
## 2       1        2        2      NA       NA       NA       NA  15457.737
## 3       1        2        2       1        2        2        1   7397.685
## 4       1        2        2      NA       NA       NA       NA 127351.373
## 5       1        2        2       1        2        2        1  12209.745
## 6       1        2        2       1        2        2       NA  60593.637
##    WTMEC2YR SDMVPSU SDMVSTRA INDHHIN2 INDFMIN2 INDFMPIR DMDHHSIZ DMDFMSIZ
## 1 104236.583       1       91       14       14     3.15        5        5
## 2  16116.354       3       92        4        4     0.60        6        6
## 3   7869.485       3       90       15       15     4.07        5        5
## 4 127965.226       1       94        8        8     1.67        5        5
## 5  13384.042       2       90        4        4     0.57        5        5
## 6  64068.123       1       91       77       77       NA        6        6
##   DMDHHSZA DMDHHSZB DMDHHSZE DMDHRGND DMDHRAGE DMDHRBR4 DMDHREDU DMDHRMAR
## 1        0        1        0        2       50        1        5        1
## 2        2        2        0        2       24        1        3        6
## 3        0        2        1        1       42        1        5        1
## 4        1        2        0        1       52        1        4        1
## 5        1        2        0        2       33        2        2       77
## 6        0        4        0        1       44        1        5        1
##   DMDHSEDU AUQ054 AUQ060 AUQ070 AUQ080 AUQ090 AUQ100 AUQ110 AUQ136 AUQ138
## 1        5      2      1     NA     NA     NA      5      5      1      1
## 2       NA      1     NA     NA     NA     NA     NA     NA     NA     NA
## 3        4      2     NA     NA     NA     NA     NA     NA     NA     NA
## 4        4      1     NA     NA     NA     NA      4      5      2      2
## 5       NA      2     NA     NA     NA     NA     NA     NA     NA     NA
## 6        5      1     NA     NA     NA     NA     NA     NA     NA     NA
##   AUQ144 AUQ146 AUD148 AUQ152 AUQ154 AUQ191 AUQ250 AUQ255 AUQ260 AUQ270
## 1      4      2     NA     NA      2      2     NA     NA     NA     NA
## 2     NA     NA     NA     NA     NA     NA     NA     NA     NA     NA
## 3     NA     NA     NA     NA     NA     NA     NA     NA     NA     NA
## 4      4      2     NA     NA      2      1      5      1      2      1
## 5     NA     NA     NA     NA     NA     NA     NA     NA     NA     NA
## 6     NA     NA     NA     NA     NA     NA     NA     NA     NA     NA
##   AUQ280 AUQ300 AUQ310 AUQ320 AUQ330 AUQ340 AUQ350 AUQ360 AUQ370 AUQ380
## 1     NA      2     NA     NA      2     NA     NA     NA      2      1
```

## 2	NA	NA	NA	NA	NA	NA	NA	NA	NA	NA
## 3	NA	NA	NA	NA	NA	NA	NA	NA	NA	NA
## 4	1	1	2	1	2	NA	NA	NA	2	6
## 5	NA	NA	NA	NA	NA	NA	NA	NA	NA	NA
## 6	NA	NA	NA	NA	NA	NA	NA	NA	NA	NA

##	file_name	begin_year	end_year
## 1	AUQ_G	2011	2012
## 2	AUQ_G	2011	2012
## 3	AUQ_G	2011	2012
## 4	AUQ_G	2011	2012
## 5	AUQ_G	2011	2012
## 6	AUQ_G	2011	2012

Leslie looked through the audiology codebook and found the gun use question `AUQ300`, which asked participants, "Have you ever used firearms for any reason?" Before they started analyses, Leslie used `summary()` to check the `AUQ300` variable.

```
# check the data
summary(object = nhanes.2012$AUQ300)
##    Min. 1st Qu.  Median    Mean 3rd Qu.    Max.   NA's
##   1.000   1.000   2.000   1.656   2.000   7.000   4689
```

The gun use data imported as a numeric variable type. The audiology data codebook shows five possible values for `AUQ300`:

- 1 = Yes
- 2 = No
- 7 = Refused
- 9 = Don't know
- . = Missing

Using her skills from the earlier chapters, Leslie recoded the variable to a factor with these five levels and a more logical variable name.

```
# open tidyverse
library(package = "tidyverse")

# recode gun use variable
nhanes.2012.clean <- nhanes.2012 %>%
  mutate(AUQ300 = recode_factor(.x = AUQ300,
                                `1` = 'Yes',
                                `2` = 'No',
```

```
                                    `7` = 'Refused',
                                    `9` = 'Don\'t know'))

# check the recoding
summary(object = nhanes.2012.clean$AUQ300)

##      Yes       No Refused NA's
##     1613     3061       1 4689
```

Kiara noted there was a single `Refused` response to the gun use question and no `Don't know` responses. These categories are not likely to be useful for visualizing or analyzing this variable. Leslie recoded them as `NA` for missing. She also thought it would be easier to work with the gun use variable if the variable name were something more intuitive so she could remember it while coding. She almost asked Nancy if there was a function for renaming something, but she wanted to keep coding, so she looked up how to change variable names in R and found `rename()`. The `rename()` function works with the pipe structure. Filling the new name as the first argument of `rename()` and the old name as the second argument, Leslie renamed `AUQ300` to `gun.use`.

```
# recode gun use variable
nhanes.2012.clean <- nhanes.2012 %>%
  mutate(AUQ300 = na_if(x = AUQ300, y = 7)) %>%
  mutate(AUQ300 = recode_factor(.x = AUQ300,
                                `1` = 'Yes',
                                `2` = 'No')) %>%
rename(gun.use = AUQ300)

# check recoding
summary(object = nhanes.2012.clean$gun.use)
## Yes   No   NA's
## 1613 3061 4690
```

Kiara started by reminding Leslie about the `ggplot()` function from the **ggplot2** package to create a bar chart of gun use. The **ggplot2** package uses the *grammar of graphics*, which is what the *gg* stands for. Kiara reminded Leslie that graphs built with `ggplot()` are built in layers. The first layer starts with `ggplot()` and `aes()` or *aesthetics*, which contains the basic information about which variables are included in the graph and whether each variable should be represented on the *x*-axis, the *y*-axis, as a color, as a line type, or something else. The next layer typically gives the graph type—or graph geometry, in the grammar of graphics language—and starts with `geom_` followed by one of the available types. In this case, Leslie was looking for a bar chart, so `geom_bar()` was the geometry for this graph. Leslie remembered that `geom_bar()` is a layer of the plot, so it is added with a + instead of a `%>%`. She wrote the code for Figure 3.10, highlighted it, and held her breath while she clicked Run.

```
# plot gun use in US 2011-2012 (Figure 3.10)
nhanes.2012.clean %>%
  ggplot(aes(x = gun.use)) +
  geom_bar()
```

FIGURE 3.10 Gun use by NHANES 2011–2012 participants

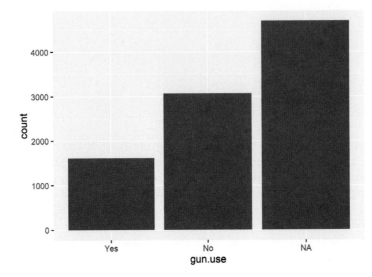

Leslie was again surprised at how quickly she could make a graph in R. While it needed a lot of work on the format, this was a good start. Leslie made a list of the things she wanted to change about this initial graph:

- Remove the NA bar from the graph.
- Change the labels on the axes to provide more information.
- Use a theme that does not use so much ink.

Leslie also thought she could

- Make each bar a different color.
- Show percentages instead of counts on the *y*-axis.

Kiara knew all of those things were possible, although adding the percentage on the *y*-axis could be tricky. She started with removing the NA bar using drop_na() for the gun.use variable before building the plot with ggplot(). Then she added a custom labels layer with labs(x = , y =) to add better labels on the two axes (Figure 3.11).

```
# omit NA category from gun.use plot and add axis labels (Figure 3.11)
nhanes.2012.clean %>%
  drop_na(gun.use) %>%
  ggplot(aes(x = gun.use)) +
  geom_bar() +
  labs(x = "Gun use", y = "Number of participants")
```

Before Kiara helped her add percentages to the *y*-axis, Leslie worked on the color. She remembered to add fill = gun.use to the aesthetics in aes(), and Kiara explained more about the aes() parentheses. She said that changing the way the graph looks based on the data should happen within aes(). For example, Leslie wanted the colors of the bars to be different depending on the gun use category, which comes from the

FIGURE 3.11 Gun use among 2011–2012 NHANES participants

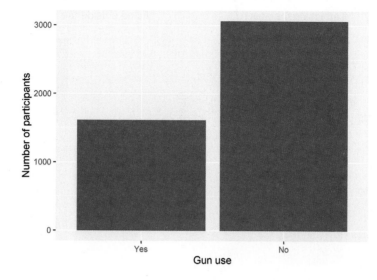

gun.use variable in the data set. Therefore, fill = should be within aes() like this: geom_bar(aes(fill = gun.use)). If Leslie wanted to make the bars a color without linking it to the categories of gun.use, Kiara explained, since this is *not* based on the data, Leslie would put the fill = *outside of* the aes() parentheses like this: geom_bar(fill = "purple"). Kiara wrote the code both ways to show Leslie and used the grid.arrange() function from the **gridExtra** package to show the plots side by side in Figure 3.12.

```
# fill bars inside aes
fill.aes <- nhanes.2012.clean %>%
  drop_na(gun.use) %>%
  ggplot(aes(x = gun.use)) +
  geom_bar(aes(fill = gun.use)) +
  labs(x = "Gun use", y = "Number of participants",
       subtitle = "Filled inside the aes()") +
  scale_fill_manual(values = c("#7463AC", "gray"), guide = FALSE) +
  theme_minimal()

# fill bars outside aes
fill.outside <- nhanes.2012.clean %>%
  drop_na(gun.use) %>%
  ggplot(aes(x = gun.use)) +
  geom_bar(fill = "#7463AC") +
  labs(x = "Gun use", y = "Number of participants",
       subtitle = "Filled outside the aes()") +
  theme_minimal()

# arrange the two plots side by side (Figure 3.12)
gridExtra::grid.arrange(fill.aes, fill.outside, ncol = 2)
```

FIGURE 3.12 Gun use among 2011–2012 NHANES participants

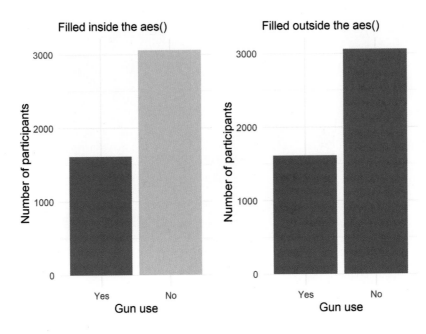

Leslie noticed that there were `aes()` options for both the `ggplot()` layer and the `geom_bar()` layer and asked what the difference was. Kiara thought that was a great question and explained that some aesthetics can be set in either place, like the color of the bars, for example. She made a quick change to the code and showed Leslie Figure 3.13 with the color set in the `ggplot()` layer `aes()` and in the `geom_bar()` layer `aes()`.

```
# fill inside aes for ggplot layer
fill.aes <- nhanes.2012.clean %>%
  drop_na(gun.use) %>%
  ggplot(aes(x = gun.use, fill = gun.use)) +
  geom_bar() +
  labs(x = "Gun use", y = "Number of participants", subtitle = "Filled in
ggplot layer") +
  scale_fill_manual(values = c("#7463AC", "gray"), guide = FALSE) +
  theme_minimal()

# fill inside aes for geom_bar layer
fill.outside <- nhanes.2012.clean %>%
  drop_na(gun.use) %>%
  ggplot(aes(x = gun.use)) +
  geom_bar(aes(fill = gun.use)) +
  labs(x = "Gun use", y = "Number of participants",
       subtitle = "Filled in geom_bar layer") +
```

```
    scale_fill_manual(values = c("#7463AC", "gray"), guide = FALSE) +
    theme_minimal()

# arrange the two plots side by side (Figure 3.13)
gridExtra::grid.arrange(fill.aes, fill.outside, ncol = 2)
```

Some aesthetics are specific to the type of graph geometry. For example, there is an aesthetic called `linetype =` that can make lines appear in different patterns, such as dotted. This is not an available aesthetic for graphs that have no lines in them. Kiara told Leslie that the aesthetics being relevant by geom is one reason why she prefers to put aesthetics in the `geom_` instead of in the `ggplot()` layer.

Kiara advised Leslie to save the URL for the Data Visualization Cheat Sheet from RStudio (https://www .rstudio.com/wp-content/uploads/2015/03/ggplot2-cheatsheet.pdf), which had the aesthetics available for the different geometries. Leslie opened the cheat sheet and saw many different types of graphs. Kiara pointed out that below the name of each type of `geom_` was a list, and these were the aesthetics available for that `geom_`. She pointed out the `geom_bar()` entry, which listed the following available aesthetics: x, alpha, color, fill, linetype, size, and weight (Figure 3.14).

FIGURE 3.13 Gun use among 2011–2012 NHANES participants

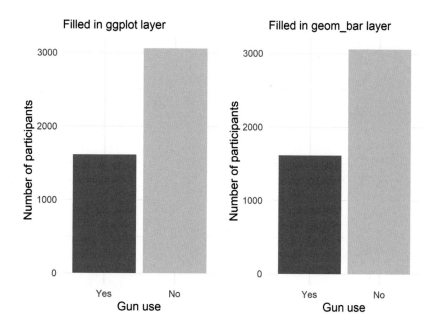

FIGURE 3.14 Entry in RStudio Data Visualization Cheet Sheet for the aesthetics available for geom_bar()

Leslie saved the URL. She knew this would be useful to have in the future.

They looked back at the graph and remembered that they had one more change to make. The change from the number of people to the percentage of people along the *y*-axis is tricky, although Leslie had seen it done before when Kiara wrote the code for her to create Figure 1.17. To get the *y*-axis to show percentage rather than count, the *y*-axis uses *special variables* with double periods around them. Special variables are statistics computed from a data set; the special variable *count* counts the number of observations. After reviewing Section 1.10.3, Kiara added the special variables to the aesthetics using `..count..` to represent the frequency of a category and `sum(..count..)` to represent the sum of all the frequencies. She multiplied by 100 to get a percent in Figure 3.15.

```
# formatted bar chart of gun use (Figure 3.15)
nhanes.2012.clean %>%
  drop_na(gun.use) %>%
  ggplot(aes(x = gun.use,
             y = 100*(..count..)/sum(..count..))) +
  geom_bar(aes(fill = gun.use)) +
  labs(x = "Gun use", y = "Percent of participants") +
  scale_fill_manual(values = c("#7463AC", "gray"), guide = FALSE) +
  theme_minimal()
```

Leslie wondered about why the *y*-axis of the graph only went to 60%. She had heard that people sometimes limit the range of the *y*-axis in order to make a difference between groups or a change over time look bigger (or smaller) than it actually is. Kiara showed her how to make the *y*-axis go to 100% by creating a `ylim()` layer in the `ggplot()`. The `ylim()` layer takes the lowest value for the *y*-axis and the highest value for the *y*-axis, separated by a comma. For a *y*-axis that goes from 0 to 100, it looks like this: `ylim(0, 100)` (Figure 3.16).

FIGURE 3.15 Gun use among 2011–2012 NHANES participants

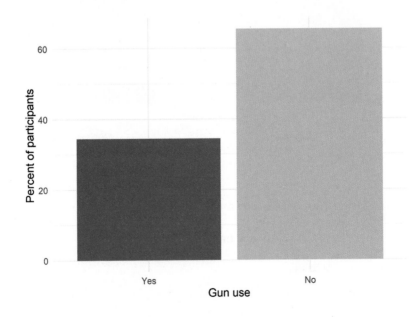

FIGURE 3.16 Gun use among 2011–2012 NHANES participants

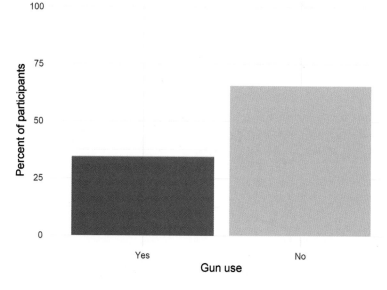

```
# formatted bar chart of gun use (Figure 3.16)
nhanes.2012.clean %>%
  drop_na(gun.use) %>%
  ggplot(aes(x = gun.use,
             y = 100*(..count..)/sum(..count..))) +
  geom_bar(aes(fill = gun.use)) +
  labs(x = "Gun use", y = "Percent of participants") +
  scale_fill_manual(values = c("#7463AC", "gray"), guide = FALSE) +
  theme_minimal() +
  ylim(0, 100)
```

The expanded *y*-axis did change the look of the graph, but the difference still seems large between the groups. The bar for the No group is about twice as large as the bar for the Yes group.

3.4.3 WAFFLE CHARTS

Waffle charts are similar to pie charts in showing the parts of a whole. However, the structure of a waffle chart visually shows the relative contributions of categories to the whole waffle more clearly. Nancy explained that, while pie may arguably be more delicious than waffles in real life, for reporting parts of a whole, waffles > pie.

Kiara suggested making a graph of the AUQ310 variable from the NHANES data set since it has more than two categories and so may be more interesting to view. The AUQ310 variable is the response to the question "How many total rounds have you ever fired?" for survey participants who reported that they had used a gun. The audiology data codebook shows eight categories for AUQ310:

- 1 = 1 to less than 100 rounds

- 2 = 100 to less than 1,000 rounds

- 3 = 1,000 to less than 10,000 rounds

- 4 = 10,000 to less than 50,000 rounds

- 5 = 50,000 rounds or more

- 7 = Refused

- 9 = Don't know

- . = Missing

Leslie added on to the existing data management code to add labels, change AUQ310 to a factor, and rename AUQ310 to fired, which was easier to remember and type.

```
# recode gun use variable
nhanes.2012.clean <- nhanes.2012 %>%
  mutate(AUQ300 = na_if(x = AUQ300, y = 7)) %>%
  mutate(AUQ300 = recode_factor(.x = AUQ300,
                                `1` = 'Yes',
                                `2` = 'No')) %>%
  rename(gun.use = AUQ300) %>%
  mutate(AUQ310 = recode_factor(.x = AUQ310,
                                `1` = "1 to less than 100",
                                `2` = "100 to less than 1000",
                                `3` = "1000 to less than 10k",
                                `4` = "10k to less than 50k",
                                `5` = "50k or more",
                                `7` = "Refused",
                                `9` = "Don't know")) %>%
  rename(fired = AUQ310)

#check recoding
summary(object = nhanes.2012.clean$fired)
##    1 to less than 100 100 to less than 1000 1000 to less than 10k
##                   701                   423                   291
##  10k to less than 50k           50k or more           Don't know
##                   106                    66                   26
##                  NA's
##                  7751
```

Now it was time to make the graph. Unfortunately, Nancy explained, there is no built-in geom_waffle() option for ggplot(), so they would use the **waffle** package instead. Before they started graphing, Leslie reviewed the package documentation (https://github.com/hrbrmstr/waffle).

FIGURE 3.17 Rounds shot by 1,613 gun users, NHANES 2011–2012

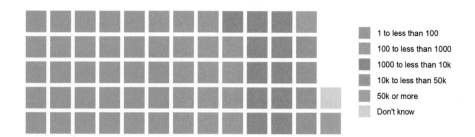

Note: One square represents 25 people.

The first argument for the `waffle()` is a table or vector of *summary statistics* used to make the waffle squares, sort of like the table used for the B index from their last meeting. That is, the data used by `waffle()` are not the *individual-level* data with one observation per row. Instead, the first argument is a frequency table or a vector of frequencies that shows how many observations are in each category. The `table()` code works well for use with `waffle()`.

By default, `waffle()` makes one square per observation. There are more than 1,000 observations in the `nhanes.2012` data frame, which seems like a lot of squares! Nancy suggested making each square represent 25 observations. Finally, the last argument for `waffle()` is the number of rows of squares. Leslie suggested they start with five rows and see what happens. Leslie made a table of the `fired` variable and named the table `rounds`. She then entered the `rounds` table into the `waffle()` function, divided by 25, and added `rows = 5` (Figure 3.17).

```
# open the waffle library
library(package = "waffle")

# make a table of rounds fired data
rounds <- table(nhanes.2012.clean$fired)

# each square is 25 people (Figure 3.17)
# 5 rows of squares
waffle(parts = rounds / 25, rows = 5)
```

It was clear from this waffle that the `1 to less than 100` category is the biggest.

Nancy suggested that color could be used to make a point about the size of a certain category. For example, if the goal was to examine people who own firearms but are less experienced in using firearms, they could use a bright color to highlight the group that had fired fewer rounds. Color is added by using a `colors =` option and listing the colors in a vector. Leslie added the RGB code for the purple color she had been using and then found some different shades of gray to include. Nancy showed her how to make sure the colors were assigned to the right parts of the waffle by entering the category labels for each color. If she did not enter the category labels, the list of colors would be assigned to the categories in alphabetical order, which could be tricky. After entering the colors, they reviewed Figure 3.18.

```
# change the colors (Figure 3.18)
waffle(parts = rounds / 25, rows = 5,
    colors = c("1 to less than 100" = "#7463AC",
               "100 to less than 1000" = "gray60",
               "1000 to less than 10k" = "gray90",
               "10k to less than 50k" = "black",
               "50k or more" = "gray40",
               "Don't know" = "gray80"))
```

FIGURE 3.18 Rounds shot by 1,613 gun users, NHANES 2011–2012

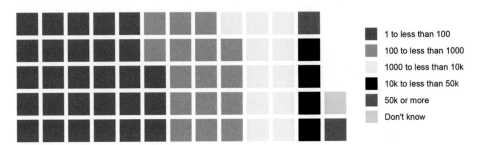

Note: One square represents 25 people.

The bright color for the `1 to less than 100` category made this category stand out. The two recommended graphs for displaying a single categorical or factor-type variable are bar charts and waffle charts. The bar chart is useful for showing relative group sizes. The waffle chart is an alternative to a pie chart and is best when demonstrating parts of a whole. Pie charts are available in R but are not recommended because they tend to be less clear for comparing group sizes.

3.4.4 ACHIEVEMENT 1: CHECK YOUR UNDERSTANDING

Create a bar chart for the gender variable (`RIAGENDR`) from the NHANES 2012 data set. Examine the codebook for coding hints and clean up the data first.

3.5 Achievement 2: Choosing and creating graphs for a single continuous variable

After making it through the options for graphing a single categorical variable, Leslie wanted to learn which graphs were appropriate for graphing a single continuous variable. Three commonly used options are histograms, *density plots*, and *boxplots*. Histograms and density plots are very similar to each other and show the overall shape of the data. These two types of graphs are especially useful in determining whether or not a variable has a *normal distribution* (see Figure 2.10). Boxplots show the central tendency and spread of the data, which is another way to determine whether a variable is normally distributed or skewed. Kiara added that *violin plots* are also useful when looking at a continuous variable and are like a combination of boxplots and density plots. Violin plots are commonly used to examine the distribution of a continuous variable for different levels (or groups) of a factor (or categorical) variable.

Kiara suggested focusing on histograms, density plots, and boxplots for now, and returning to violin plots when they are looking at graphs with two variables.

Kiara noted that the gun research data included a measure of the amount of research funding devoted to examining the different causes of death. Funding falls along a continuum and would be best examined as a continuous variable using a histogram, density plot, or boxplot. She helped Leslie with the coding needed to create each type of graph.

3.5.1 HISTOGRAMS

Kiara explained that histograms can be developed with **ggplot2**. She showed Leslie the data set they had received from the authors of the *JAMA* article (Stark & Shah, 2017) and Leslie imported it.

```
# bring in the data
research.funding <- read.csv(file = "[data folder location]/data/gun_
publications_funds_2004_2015_ch3.csv")

# check out the data
summary(object = research.funding)
##               Cause.of.Death Mortality.Rate.per.100.000.Population
##   Alzheimer disease    : 1    Min.   :  0.590
##   Anemia               : 1    1st Qu.:  1.775
##   Asphyxia             : 1    Median :  7.765
##   Aspiration           : 1    Mean   : 22.419
##   Atherosclerosis      : 1    3rd Qu.: 14.812
##   Biliary tract disease: 1    Max.   :201.540
##   (Other)              :24
##   Publications        Funding           Predicted.Publications
##   Min.   :   1034   Min.   :3.475e+06   8,759  : 2
##   1st Qu.:  12550   1st Qu.:3.580e+08   10,586 : 1
##   Median :  39498   Median :1.660e+09   11,554 : 1
##   Mean   :  93914   Mean   :4.137e+09   15,132 : 1
##   3rd Qu.:  54064   3rd Qu.:4.830e+09   16,247 : 1
##   Max.   :1078144   Max.   :2.060e+10   16,751 : 1
##                                         (Other):23
##   Publications..Studentized.Residuals.       Predicted.Funding
##   Min.   :-2.630                          $264,685,579   : 2
##   1st Qu.:-0.355                          $1,073,615,675 : 1
##   Median : 0.125                          $1,220,029,999 : 1
##   Mean   :-0.010                          $1,242,904,513 : 1
##   3rd Qu.: 0.745                          $1,407,700,121 : 1
##   Max.   : 1.460                          $1,417,564,256 : 1
##                                          (Other)        :23
##   Funding..Studentized.Residuals.
##   Min.   :-3.71000
```

```
##   1st Qu.:-0.53250
##   Median : 0.33500
##   Mean   :-0.02467
##   3rd Qu.: 0.57750
##   Max.   : 1.92000
##
```

Kiara showed Leslie the geometry for a histogram, `geom_histogram()`, and Leslie used it to start with a very basic histogram (Figure 3.19).

```
# make a histogram of funding (Figure 3.19)
histo.funding <- research.funding %>%
  ggplot(aes(x = Funding)) +
  geom_histogram()
histo.funding
```

Figure 3.19 shows frequency on the *y*-axis and mortality rate on the *x*-axis. Leslie noticed that the *x*-axis is shown using scientific notation. While she was familiar with scientific notation, which is useful for printing large numbers in small spaces, she knew it is not well understood by most audiences (Box 3.2). Kiara suggested changing the axis to show numbers that can be more easily interpreted; this can be done in several ways. One strategy is to convert the numbers from dollars to billions of dollars by dividing the `Funding` variable by 1,000,000,000 within the `aes()` for the `ggplot()` (Figure 3.20).

FIGURE 3.19 Research funding in billions for the top 30 mortality causes in the United States

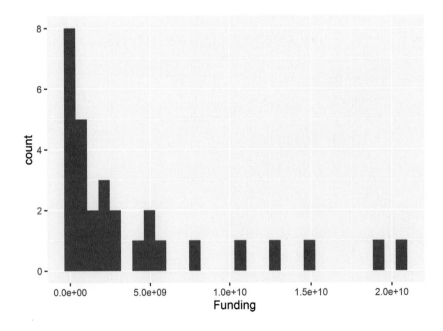

FIGURE 3.20 Research funding in billions for the top 30 mortality causes in the United States

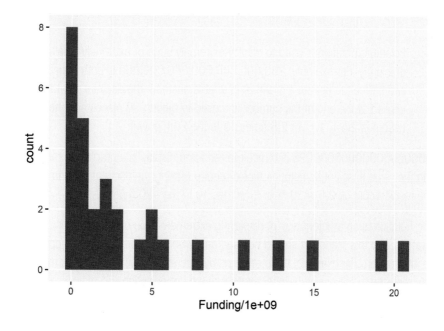

```
# make a histogram of funding (Figure 3.20)
histo.funding <- research.funding %>%
  ggplot(aes(x = Funding/1000000000)) +
  geom_histogram()
histo.funding
```

Now the values on the *x*-axis are easier to understand. From the histogram, it appears that most mortality causes are funded at 0 to $5 billion annually. However, several causes receive more than $5 billion, up to more than $25 billion. The very large values on the right of the graph suggested to Leslie that the *distribution* of the funding data is right-skewed.

Kiara reminded Leslie that each of the bars shown in the histogram is called a bin and contains a certain proportion of the observations. To show more bins, which may help to clarify the shape of the distribution, specify how many bins to see by adding `bins` = to the `geom_histogram()` layer. Leslie tried 10 bins in Figure 3.21.

```
# make a histogram of funding (Figure 3.21)
# adjust the number of bins to 10
histo.funding <- research.funding %>%
  ggplot(aes(x = Funding/1000000000)) +
  geom_histogram(bins = 10)
histo.funding
```

Scientific notation is used to display extremely large or extremely small numbers efficiently. For example, 250,000,000,000,000,000,000 is both difficult to read and difficult to use on a graph or in a table. Instead, the decimal point that is implied at the end of the number is moved to the left 20 places and the number becomes 2.5×10^{20} or 2.5 times 10 to the 20th power.

Likewise, .000000000000000000025 is difficult to read and display in a graph or a table. In this case, reporting the value in scientific notation would require moving the decimal point to the right 20 places. The result would be 2.5×10^{-20} or 2.5 times 10 to the −20th power.

While scientific notation is an efficient way of displaying extremely large or small values, it is not well understood. For this reason, it should be used only when there is not another option for displaying the information. For example, if the reported numbers could be divided by a million or a billion and then reported in millions or billions, this is a much better option.

When numbers are very large or very small, R will convert them to scientific notation. To turn off this option in R, type and run `options(scipen = 999)`. To turn it back on, type and run `options(scipen = 000)`.

FIGURE 3.21 Research funding for the top 30 mortality causes in the United States in 10-bin histogram

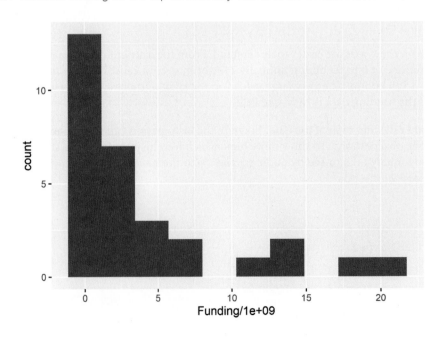

Leslie noticed that the range of the y-axis had changed when she changed the bins. Instead of the top value being 8, it was now 10. Nancy assured her that this was logical because the number of observations in each bar often changes when the bar is representing a different range of values. Nancy pointed to the first tall bar in Figure 3.20 and showed Leslie that the bar contains mortality causes with between 0 and maybe $0.5 billion in funding. Once `bins = 10` was added in Figure 3.21, the first tall bar represented mortality cases with between 0 and $1.25 billion in funding. With a wider range of funding values, there are more causes of mortality that fit into this first bar and therefore the bar is taller. Leslie thought she understood and noticed that there appear to be 8 causes of mortality with funding between 0 and $0.5 billion (Figure 3.20) but 13 causes of mortality with funding between 0 and $1.25 billion (Figure 3.21). Nancy confirmed that this is the case. Leslie was satisfied with this explanation and tried 50 bins next to see if it changed the shape (Figure 3.22).

```
# make a histogram of funding (Figure 3.22)
# adjust the number of bins to 50
histo.funding <- research.funding %>%
  ggplot(aes(x = Funding/1000000000)) +
  geom_histogram(bins = 50)
histo.funding
```

The 10-bin version looked best to Leslie, so she turned her attention to formatting, adding better titles for the axes in a `labs()` layer and making the graph printer-friendly to use less ink by adding a `theme_minimal()` layer (Figure 3.23).

FIGURE 3.22 Research funding for the top 30 mortality causes in the United States in 50-bin histogram

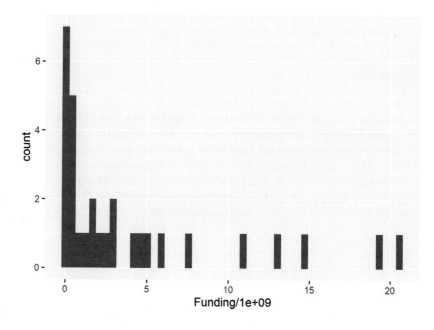

FIGURE 3.23 Research funding for the top 30 mortality causes in the United States

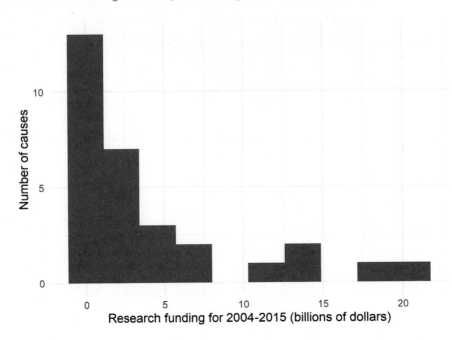

```
# make a histogram of funding (Figure 3.23)
# adjust the number of bins to 10
histo.funding <- research.funding %>%
  ggplot(aes(x = Funding/1000000000)) +
  geom_histogram(bins = 10) +
  labs(x = "Research funding for 2004-2015 (billions of dollars)",
       y = "Number of causes") +
  theme_minimal()
histo.funding
```

This looked even better to Leslie, so she asked Kiara and Nancy if they had any suggestions for other formatting that might make the graph easier to interpret. Kiara said she liked to add thin borders around the bins and fill the bins with white, similar to the plots in the previous chapter (e.g., Figure 2.15). Leslie asked her how to do this, and Kiara said that `geom_histogram()` can take arguments for `fill =`, which takes a color to fill each bin, and `color =`, which takes a color for the border of each bin. Leslie decided that since she is adding a `color` and `fill` based on what she wants, and not based on the data set, she should add these arguments to `geom_histogram()` *without* putting them in `aes()` (Figure 3.24).

```
# make a histogram of funding (Figure 3.24)
# formatting options
histo.funding <- research.funding %>%
  ggplot(aes(x = Funding/1000000000)) +
  geom_histogram(bins = 10, fill = "white", color = "gray") +
```

```
      labs(x = "Research funding for 2004-2015 (billions of dollars)",
           y = "Number of causes") +
    theme_minimal()
 histo.funding
```

The R-Team was happy with this final plot. Before moving on to density plots, they paused for a minute to discuss the shape of the distribution. Leslie noted that it is right-skewed and would therefore be best described using the median rather than the mean as they had discussed at the previous meeting (Section 2.6.2). She also thought that the IQR would probably be better than the range for reporting spread given how wide the range is (Section 2.6.4). Nancy and Kiara agreed with this assessment.

3.5.2 DENSITY PLOTS

A density plot is similar to a histogram but more fluid in appearance because it does not have the separate bins. Density plots can be created using `ggplot()` with a `geom_density()` layer. Leslie took the code from the histogram and replaced the `geom_histogram()` layer to see if that would work. Before she ran the code, Nancy stopped her to let her know that the y-axis is a different measure for this type of plot. Instead of frequency, it is the probability density, which is the probability of each value on the x-axis. The probability density is not very useful for interpreting what is happening at any given value of the variable on the x-axis, but it is useful in computing the percentage of values that are within a range along the x-axis. Leslie remembered seeing this on the y-axis of many of the histograms in their previous meeting and asked if it is used in histograms too. Nancy confirmed that probability density is the value of the y-axis for many different types of plots.

When she saw some confusion on Leslie's face, Nancy clarified that the area under the curve adds up to 100% of the data and the height of the curve is determined by the distribution of the data, which is scaled so that the area will be 100% (or 1). Leslie changed the `y =` option in the `labs()` layer to label the y-axis "Probability density" (Figure 3.25).

FIGURE 3.24 Research funding for the top 30 mortality causes in the United States

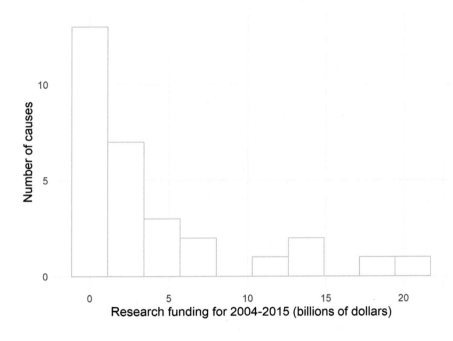

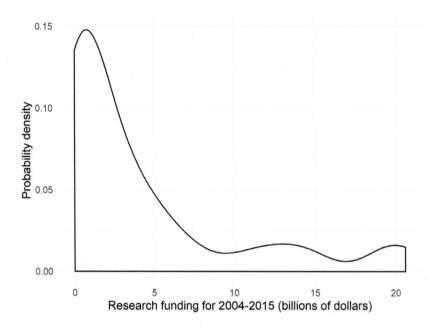

```
# density plot of research funding (Figure 3.25)
dens.funding <- research.funding %>%
    ggplot(aes(x = Funding/1000000000)) +
    geom_density() +
    labs(x = "Research funding for 2004-2015 (billions of dollars)",
        y = "Probability density") +
    theme_minimal()
dens.funding
```

Kiara tried to clarify some more. She told Leslie that the *area under the curve* in a density plot could be interpreted as the probability of a single observation or a range of observations. Probabilities are also useful for learning more about a population from a *sample*, or a subgroup selected from the *population*. She explained that they would discuss the use of density plots to demonstrate more about probability in their next meeting when they worked on probability concepts.

Leslie was not happy with the way the density plot looked. She added some color in order to be able to see the shape a little more. Nancy suggested trying a few values of bw = within the geom_density(), noting that bw usually takes much smaller values than bins. The bw stands for *bandwidth* in a density plot, which is similar to the bin width in a histogram. Leslie played with the bandwidth and some color in Figures 3.26 and 3.27.

```
# density plot of research funding (Figure 3.26)
# bw = .5
dens.funding <- research.funding %>%
```

```
  ggplot(aes(x = Funding/1000000000)) +
  geom_density(bw = .5, fill = "#7463AC") +
  labs(x = "Research funding for 2004-2015 (billions of dollars)",
       y = "Probability density") +
  theme_minimal()
dens.funding
```

```
# density plot of research funding (Figure 3.27)
# bw = 1.5
dens.funding <- research.funding %>%
  ggplot(aes(x = Funding/1000000000)) +
  geom_density(bw = 1.5, fill = "#7463AC") +
  labs(x = "Research funding for 2004-2015 (billions of dollars)",
       y = "Probability density") +
  theme_minimal()
dens.funding
```

It appeared that the higher the value used as a bandwidth in bw =, the smoother the graph looks. Leslie thought the final version with the bandwidth of 1.5 looked good. Nancy agreed but wanted to add one word of caution on density plots before they moved on. While density plots are generally similar to histograms, they do have one feature that some data scientists suggest is misleading. Compare Figure 3.24 with Figure 3.27. These are both from the same data; Figure 3.24 shows gaps where there are no observations, while Figure 3.27 has the appearance of data continuing without gaps across the full range of values. For this reason, data scientists sometimes recommend histograms over density plots, especially for small data sets where gaps in the data are more likely (Wilke, 2019).

FIGURE 3.26 Research funding for the top 30 mortality causes in the United States

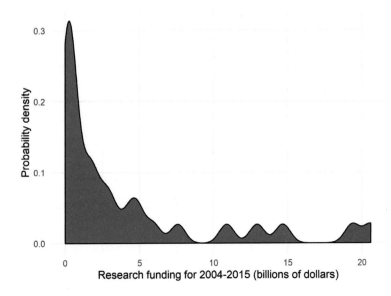

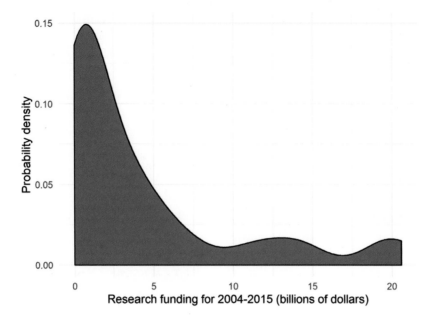

3.5.3 BOXPLOTS

Nancy explained that histograms and density plots were great for examining the overall shape of the data for a continuous variable, but that the boxplot was useful for identifying the middle value and the boundaries around the middle half of the data. Typically, boxplots consist of several parts:

1) A line representing the median value

2) A box containing the middle 50% of values

3) Whiskers extending to the value of the largest observation past the edge of the box, but not further than 1.5 times the IQR past the edge of the box

4) *Outliers* more than 1.5 times the IQR past the edge of the box

In `ggplot()`, the boxplot uses the `geom_boxplot()` function. Leslie copied her density plot code and changed the `geom_` type. Nancy explained that the boxplot would show the values of the variable along the *y*-axis by default, so instead of `x = Funding/1000000000`, Leslie needed to use `y = Funding/1000000000` in the plot aesthetics, `aes()`.

```
# boxplot of research funding (Figure 3.28)
box.funding <- research.funding %>%
  ggplot(aes(y = Funding/1000000000)) +
  geom_boxplot() +
  theme_minimal() +
  labs(y = "Research funding for 2004-2015 (billions of dollars)")
box.funding
```

FIGURE 3.28 Research funding for the top 30 mortality causes in the United States

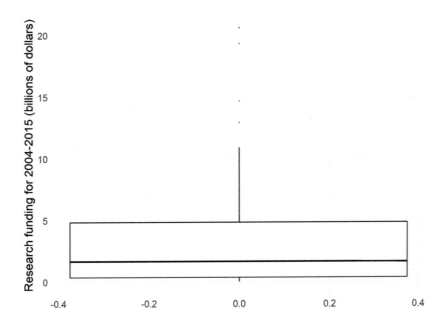

FIGURE 3.29 Research funding for the top 30 mortality causes in the United States

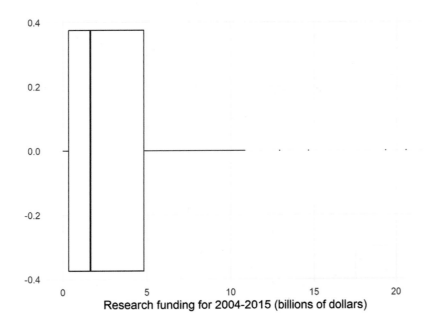

Figure 3.28 was a little difficult to interpret, so Kiara suggested that Leslie add a new layer of `coord_flip()` to flip the coordinates so that what used to be on the *y*-axis is now on the *x*-axis and vice versa in Figure 3.29.

```
# boxplot of research funding (Figure 3.29)
box.funding <- research.funding %>%
```

```
  ggplot(aes(y = Funding/1000000000)) +
  geom_boxplot() +
  theme_minimal() +
  labs(y = "Research funding for 2004-2015 (billions of dollars)") +
  coord_flip()
box.funding
```

She could then see the median funding level was about $2 billion based on the location of the thick black line in the middle of the box. Based on the boundaries of the box, she also determined that the middle half of the data appeared to be between about $1 billion and $5 billion.

Nancy pointed out that the right skew shown in the histogram and density plot can also be seen in this graph, with the long whisker to the right of the box and the outliers on the far right. The left whisker coming from the box and the right whisker coming from the box both extend to 1.5 times the value of the IQR away from the edge of the box (the box extends from the 25th percentile to the 75th percentile and contains the middle 50% of the data). Leslie noticed that the left whisker stopped at zero, because zero was the furthest value from the box even though it was not 1.5 × IQR below the value at the end of the box. The team agreed that each of the three graphs had strengths and weaknesses in revealing how the values of a numeric variable are distributed.

Nancy suggested they arrange the histogram, density plot, and boxplot together in order to see the similarities and differences between the three. Kiara had just the thing for that; the grid.arrange() function in the **gridExtra** package that she had used earlier to show the bar charts side by side (Figure 3.13) allows multiple graphs to be printed together. Leslie gave it a try, using the option nrow = 3 to display one graph per row rather than side by side in columns.

FIGURE 3.30 Three graphs for examining one continuous variable at a time

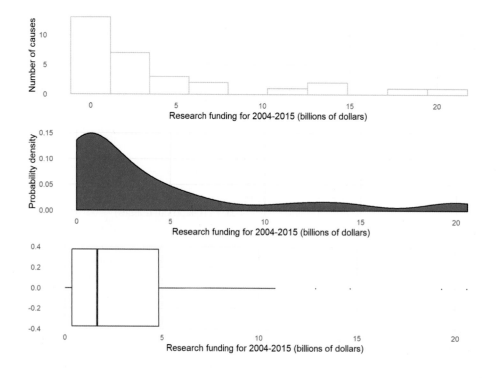

```
# plot all three options together (Figure 3.30)
gridExtra::grid.arrange(histo.funding,
                        dens.funding,
                        box.funding,
                        nrow = 3)
```

Looking at the three graphs together, it was clear that they tell a consistent story, but there are some different pieces of information to be learned from the different types of graphs. All three graphs show the right skew clearly, while the histogram and boxplot show gaps in the data toward the end of the tail. The boxplot is the only one of the three that clearly identifies the central tendency and spread of the variable. The R-Team was satisfied that they had good options for displaying a single continuous variable.

3.5.4 ACHIEVEMENT 2: CHECK YOUR UNDERSTANDING

Create a histogram, a boxplot, and a density plot to show the distribution of the age variable (RIDAGEYR) from the NHANES 2012 data set. Explain the distribution, including an approximate value of the median, what the boundaries are around the middle 50% of the data, and a description of the skew (or lack of skew).

3.6 Achievement 3: Choosing and creating graphs for two variables at once

Kiara and Nancy explained that graphs are also used to examine relationships among variables. As with single-variable graphs and descriptive statistics, choosing an appropriate plot type depends on the types of variables to be displayed. In the case of two variables, there are several different combinations of variable types:

- Two categorical/factor
- One categorical/factor and one continuous/numeric
- Two continuous/numeric

3.6.1 MOSAIC PLOTS FOR TWO CATEGORICAL VARIABLES

There are few options for visually examining the relationship between two categorical variables. One option is a *mosaic plot*, which shows the relative sizes of groups across two categorical variables. The NHANES data set used to demonstrate the waffle chart has many categorical variables that might be useful in better understanding gun ownership.

One of the first questions Leslie had was whether males were more likely than others to have used a gun. She had noticed that most, but not all, of the mass shootings in the United States had a male shooter and wondered if more males use guns overall. Nancy and Kiara thought that examining whether males were more likely than others to have used a gun was a good question to answer using mosaic and bar charts.

Leslie already had the gun.use variable ready but needed to know more about the sex or gender variables available in NHANES. She looked in the codebook to find how sex and gender were measured. She found a single sex- or gender-related variable called RIAGENDR that had the text "Gender of the participant." Leslie assumed that this was the biological sex variable and looked at the way it was categorized:

- 1 = Male
- 2 = Female
- . = Missing

Leslie checked the variable before recoding.

```
# check coding of RIAGENDR
table(nhanes.2012$RIAGENDR)
##
##    1    2
## 4663 4701
```

There were no missing values, so she added the labels to the two categories in her growing data management list and renamed the variable `sex`.

```
# recode sex variable
nhanes.2012.clean <- nhanes.2012 %>%
  mutate(AUQ300 = na_if(x = AUQ300, y = 7)) %>%
  mutate(AUQ300 = recode_factor(.x = AUQ300,
                                `1` = 'Yes',
                                `2` = 'No')) %>%
  rename(gun.use = AUQ300) %>%
  mutate(AUQ310 = recode_factor(.x = AUQ310,
                                `1` = "1 to less than 100",
                                `2` = "100 to less than 1000",
                                `3` = "1000 to less than 10k",
                                `4` = "10k to less than 50k",
                                `5` = "50k or more",
                                `7` = "Refused",
                                `9` = "Don't know")) %>%
  rename(fired = AUQ310) %>%
  mutate(RIAGENDR = recode_factor(.x = RIAGENDR,
                                  `1` = 'Male',
                                  `2` = 'Female')) %>%
  rename(sex = RIAGENDR)
```

Leslie checked her recoding before working on the graph.

```
#check recoding
summary(object = nhanes.2012.clean$sex)
##    Male Female
##    4663   4701
```

Leslie showed Kiara and Nancy that the variables were now ready for graphing. The `geom_mosaic()` function is not one of those included in `ggplot()`, so it requires use of the **ggmosaic** package. Leslie checked the documentation to see how it was used (https://github.com/haleyjeppson/ggmosaic). It looked like the `geom_mosaic()` layer was similar to the other `geom_` options, but the variables were added to the aesthetics in the `geom_mosaic()` layer rather than the `ggplot()` layer. She wrote the basic code to see how it would look in Figure 3.31.

```
# open library
library(package = "ggmosaic")

# mosaic plot of gun use by sex (Figure 3.31)
mosaic.gun.use.sex <- nhanes.2012.clean %>%
  mutate(gun.use, gun.use = na_if(x = gun.use, y = 7)) %>%
  ggplot() +
  geom_mosaic(aes(x = product(gun.use, sex), fill = gun.use))
mosaic.gun.use.sex
```

FIGURE 3.31 Firearm use by sex in the United States among 2011–2012 NHANES participants

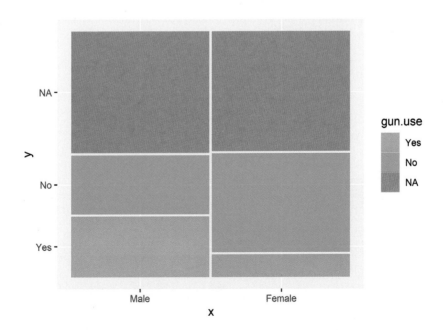

The resulting graph shows boxes representing the proportion of males and females who have used a gun and those who have not. There were a few things Leslie wanted to fix to make the graph more clearly convey the difference in gun use between males and females in this sample:

- Remove the NA category
- Add useful labels to the axes
- Remove the legend
- Change the colors to highlight the difference more clearly
- Change the theme so the graph is less cluttered

Nancy helped Leslie add a few of these options (Figure 3.32).

```
# formatted mosaic plot of sex and gun use (Figure 3.32)
# mosaic gun use by sex
mosaic.gun.use.sex <- nhanes.2012.clean %>%
  drop_na(gun.use) %>%
  ggplot() +
  geom_mosaic(aes(x = product(gun.use, sex), fill = gun.use)) +
  labs(x = "Participant sex", y = "Ever used firearm") +
  scale_fill_manual(values = c("#7463AC", "gray80"),
                    guide = FALSE) +
  theme_minimal()
mosaic.gun.use.sex
```

FIGURE 3.32 Firearm use by sex in the United States among 2011–2012 NHANES participants

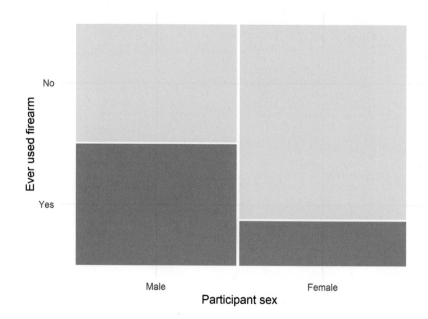

Figure 3.32 shows that the proportion of males who have used a firearm (purple bottom left) is higher than the proportion of females who have used a firearm (purple bottom right).

3.6.2 BAR CHARTS FOR TWO CATEGORICAL VARIABLES

Kiara was not a big fan of the mosaic plot. She complained that it might be OK for variables with a small number of categories like `gun.use`, but using a mosaic plot for variables with many categories is not useful. She said mosaic plots have some similarity to pie charts because it is hard to tell the relative sizes of some boxes apart, especially when there are more than a few.

Kiara preferred bar charts for demonstrating the relationship between two categorical variables. Bar charts showing frequencies across groups can take two formats: stacked or grouped. Like pie charts, *stacked bar charts* show parts of a whole. Also like pie charts, if there are many groups or parts that are similar in size, the stacked bar chart is difficult to interpret and *not* recommended.

Grouped bar charts are usually the best option. Kiara noted that stacked and grouped bar charts could be created with `ggplot()`, but that there are two types of `geom_` that work: `geom_bar()` and `geom_col()`. After reviewing the help page, Leslie learned that `geom_bar()` is used to display the number of cases in each group (parts of a whole), whereas `geom_col()` is used to display actual values like means and percentages rather than parts of a whole. This was a little confusing to Leslie, but she expected it would become more clear if she tried a few graphs. Since the R-Team was examining the proportion of gun use by sex, Leslie decided to start with `geom_bar()` and wrote some code to get Figure 3.33.

```
# stacked bar chart (Figure 3.33)
stack.gun.use.sex <- nhanes.2012.clean %>%
  ggplot(aes(x = sex, fill = gun.use)) +
  geom_bar()
stack.gun.use.sex
```

FIGURE 3.33 Firearm use by sex in the United States among 2011–2012 NHANES participants

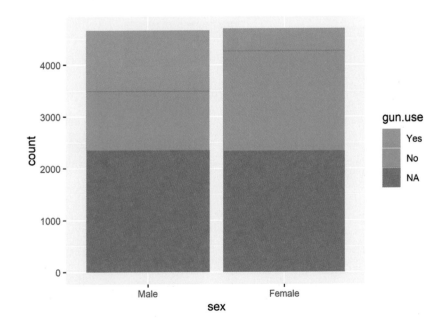

The resulting graph showed boxes representing the proportion of males and females who have ever used a gun or not used a gun. Like with the mosaic plot, there were a few things Leslie wanted to fix to make the graph more clearly convey the difference in gun use between males and females. Specifically, she wanted to remove the NA values, fix the titles, use the minimal theme, and add some better color. Leslie added some new layers to improve the graph (Figure 3.34).

```r
# formatted stacked bar chart (Figure 3.34)
stack.gun.use.sex <- nhanes.2012.clean %>%
  drop_na(gun.use) %>%
  ggplot(aes(x = sex, fill = gun.use)) +
  geom_bar() +
  theme_minimal() +
  labs(x = "Participant sex", y = "Number of participants") +
  scale_fill_manual(values = c("#7463AC", "gray80"),
                    name = "Firearm use")
stack.gun.use.sex
```

Leslie was curious about how to change this graph to a grouped bar chart since that was the recommended option. Nancy explained that the position = option for the geom_bar() layer is the place to specify whether the bars should be stacked or grouped. The default is stacked, so to get grouped, she suggested that Leslie add position = "dodge" to the geom_bar() layer. Leslie asked why "dodge" rather than "grouped" or something else. Nancy was not sure but thought it might have something to do with the use of group = for other purposes within the grammar of graphics. Leslie made this change to the code and tested it out in Figure 3.35.

FIGURE 3.34 Firearm use by sex in the United States among 2011–2012 NHANES participants

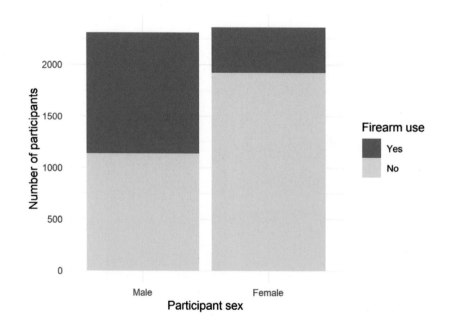

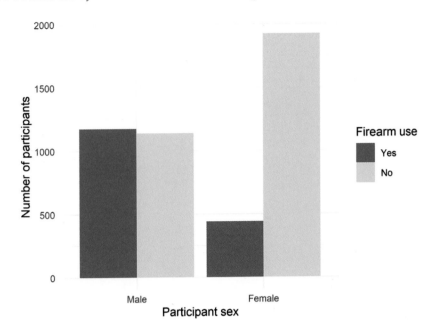

```
# formatted grouped bar chart (Figure 3.35)
group.gun.use.sex <- nhanes.2012.clean %>%
  drop_na(gun.use) %>%
  ggplot(aes(x = sex, fill = gun.use)) +
  geom_bar(position = "dodge") +
  theme_minimal() +
  labs(x = "Participant sex", y = "Number of participants") +
  scale_fill_manual(values = c("#7463AC", "gray80"),
                    name = "Firearm use")
group.gun.use.sex
```

Nancy noted that sometimes percentages are more useful than frequencies for a bar chart. Leslie reviewed the "Using special variables in graphs" section (Section 1.10.3) from their first meeting (Figure 1.17) to remind herself how this was done. To change to percentages, Leslie added a percent calculation to the *y*-axis in the `ggplot()` to create Figure 3.36.

```
# formatted grouped bar chart with percents (Figure 3.36)
group.gun.use.sex <- nhanes.2012.clean %>%
  drop_na(gun.use) %>%
  ggplot(aes(x = sex, fill = gun.use,
             y = 100*(..count..)/sum(..count..))) +
  geom_bar(position = "dodge") +
```

```
    theme_minimal() +
    labs(x = "Participant sex", y = "Percent of total participants") +
    scale_fill_manual(values = c("#7463AC", "gray80"),
                      name = "Firearm use")
group.gun.use.sex
```

FIGURE 3.36 Firearm use by sex in the United States among 2011–2012 NHANES participants

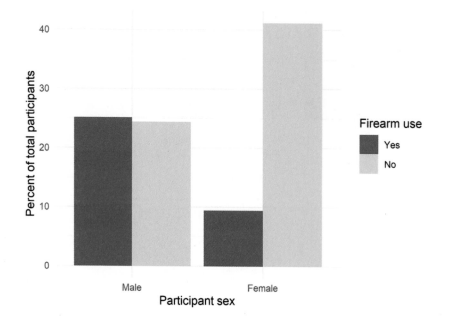

Leslie thought there was something odd about the percentages in this graph. She started estimating what they were and adding them together in her head. She figured out that all the bars together added up to 100%. This didn't seem quite right for comparing males to females since there could be more males than females overall or vice versa. She wondered if Nancy knew any code to change the percentages so that they added up to 100% *within each group*. Nancy said yes, as long as Leslie didn't mind learning some additional **tidyverse**. Leslie said she had time for one more graph, so Nancy jumped right in. Kiara worried that this code was too complicated to rely on a single comment at the top for reproducibility, and she asked Nancy if she could add in some extra comments as they went. Nancy was fine with this, and she edited the code with extra comments to get Figure 3.37.

```
# formatted grouped bar chart with percents (Figure 3.37)
group.gun.use.sex <- nhanes.2012.clean %>%
  drop_na(gun.use) %>%
  group_by(gun.use, sex) %>%      # make groups of gun.use by sex
  count() %>%                     # count how many are in each group
  group_by(sex) %>%              # pick the variable that will add
                                  # to 100%
```

```
    mutate(percent = 100*(n/sum(n))) %>%      # compute percents within
                                              # chosen variable

    ggplot(aes(x = sex, fill = gun.use,
              y = percent)) +                 # use new values from mutate
    geom_col(position = "dodge") +
    theme_minimal() +
    labs(x = "Participant sex",
         y = "Percent in sex group") +
    scale_fill_manual(values = c("#7463AC",
                                 "gray80"),
                      name = "Firearm use")
group.gun.use.sex
```

FIGURE 3.37 Firearm use by sex among 2011–2012 NHANES participants

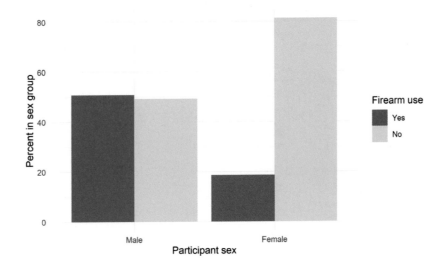

Nancy was pretty pleased with herself when this ran. Kiara was not happy with the documentation, but it was a start. While the code was long and Leslie was a little overwhelmed, Nancy reassured her that learning `ggplot()` code can be really complicated. Nancy shared a tweet from Hadley Wickham, the developer of **ggplot2** (Figure 3.38).

Leslie found that putting all of the options together in a grid to compare how well they do at conveying information was really useful for the single continuous variables, so she wrote one last section of code to compare the graph types for the two categorical variables (Figure 3.39).

```
# plot all three options together (Figure 3.39)
gridExtra::grid.arrange(mosaic.gun.use.sex,
                        stack.gun.use.sex,
                        group.gun.use.sex,
                        nrow = 2)
```

FIGURE 3.39 Three options for graphing two categorical variables together

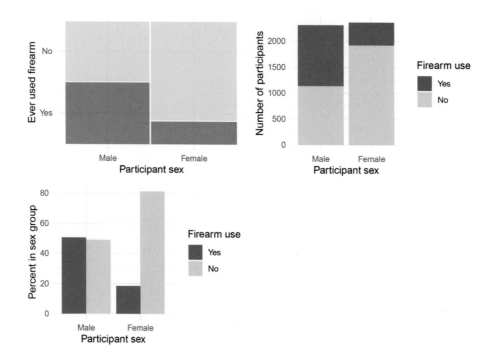

For Leslie, these graphs were pretty similar in the information they conveyed. The mosaic plot and stacked bar chart were almost the same, with the exception of the *y*-axis, which showed the number of participants for the stacked bar chart. The grouped bar chart did seem to convey the difference between the groups most clearly, making it easy to compare firearm use both within the male and female group and between the two groups. In terms of communicating statistical results, Leslie thought the grouped bar chart might become one of her favorites along with the boxplot.

3.6.3 BAR CHARTS, POINT CHARTS, BOXPLOTS, AND VIOLIN PLOTS FOR ONE CATEGORICAL AND ONE CONTINUOUS VARIABLE

Kiara suggested that bar charts can also be useful for examining how continuous measures differ across groups. For example, the NHANES data include a measure of age in years. The R-Team already knew that a higher percentage of males than females use firearms. They decided to also examine whether firearm users tend to be younger or older than those who do not use firearms. Age is measured in years, which is not *truly* continuous since partial years are not included, but the underlying concept is a continuous one, with age spanning across a continuum of years rather than being broken up into categories.

3.6.3.1 DATA MANAGEMENT

Age in years is measured along a continuum while firearm use is categorical, with two categories. A bar chart could show two bars for gun use (Yes and No) with the height of each bar based on the mean or median age of gun users or gun nonusers. Nancy eagerly started to type the code, but Leslie slid the laptop away from her and tried it herself by copying and editing the code from making Figure 3.15. After a couple of minutes, Nancy pulled the laptop back when she saw Leslie had gotten stuck on how to get the mean age on the *y*-axis. She showed Leslie how to add summary statistics in a bar chart by adding `stat = "summary"` to the `geom_bar()` layer. Once summary is specified, the layer also needs to know which summary statistic to use. Adding `fun.y = mean` will result in the mean of the `y =` variable from the aesthetics, which, in this case, is `y = RIDAGEYR` for age. Leslie nodded and pulled the laptop back to herself to edit some of the axis labels and run the code (Figure 3.40).

```
# bar chart with means for bar height (Figure 3.40)
bar.gun.use.age <- nhanes.2012.clean %>%
  drop_na(gun.use) %>%
  ggplot(aes(x = gun.use, y = RIDAGEYR)) +
  geom_bar(aes(fill = gun.use), stat = "summary", fun.y = mean) +
  theme_minimal() +
  labs(x = "Firearm use", y = "Mean age of participants") +
  scale_fill_manual(values = c("#7463AC", "gray80"),
                    guide = FALSE)
bar.gun.use.age
```

There was not much of a difference in the mean age of those who have used a firearm and those who have not used a firearm. Both groups were just under 45 years old as a mean. This graph was not a very

---

FIGURE 3.40 Mean age by firearm use for 2011–2012 NHANES participants

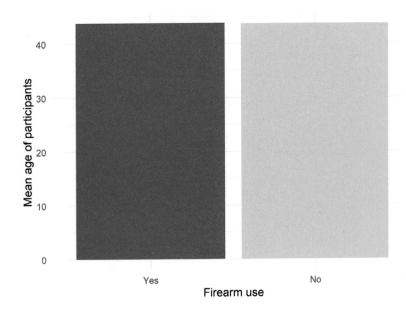

good use of space when just reporting that both means were 45 would suffice. Kiara was too busy looking over the code format to notice. Leslie thought back to the descriptive statistics meeting and remembered that the mean is only useful when the data are normally distributed. She suggested to Nancy that they check the distribution of age for people who do and do not use firearms. Nancy started typing immediately. Leslie looked over her shoulder as she made a density plot (Figure 3.41).

```
# density plots of age by firearm use category (Figure 3.41)
dens.gun.use.age <- nhanes.2012.clean %>%
  drop_na(gun.use) %>%
  ggplot(aes(x = RIDAGEYR)) +
  geom_density(aes(fill = gun.use), alpha = .8) +
  theme_minimal() +
  labs(x = "Age of participants", y = "Probability density") +
  scale_fill_manual(values = c("#7463AC", "gray80"),
                    name = "Used firearm")
dens.gun.use.age
```

Leslie was impressed! It looked like two density plots on top of each other. Nancy showed her the code and pointed out the `fill = gun.use` option in the `geom_density()` layer, which resulted in two density plots with two colors. Nancy also pointed out the `alpha = .8` in the `geom_density()` layer. The alpha sets the level of transparency for color, where 1 is not transparent and 0 is completely transparent. The .8 level allows for some transparency while the colors are mostly visible. She reminded Leslie that since the transparency level is not based on anything in the data set, the `alpha = .8` option should *not* be wrapped within the `aes()`. The rest of the graph was familiar to Leslie since it had the same options they had been using all day.

FIGURE 3.41 Distribution of age by firearm use for 2011–2012 NHANES participants

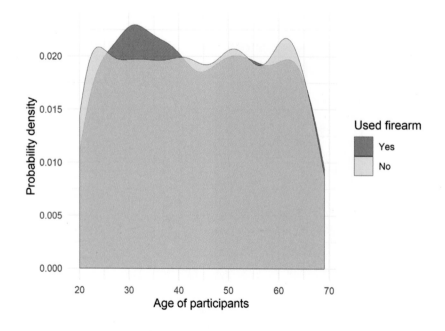

FIGURE 3.42 Example of a uniform distribution

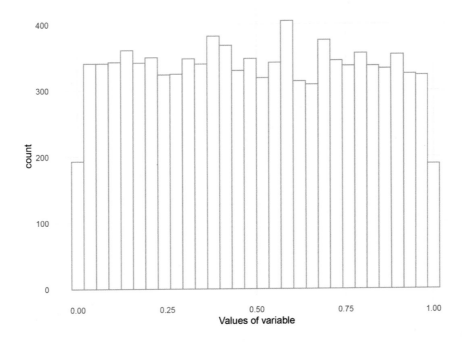

After talking through the code, Leslie looked at the graph. The distributions definitely did not look normal, she thought. But they did not look skewed either. Leslie remembered her stats class and looked through her old notes for distribution shapes. She found that this graph looked more like a *uniform distribution* than any of the other options. She read that a perfect uniform distribution had the same frequency for each value of the variable. Essentially, it looked like a rectangle. Nancy went ahead and plotted an example of a uniform distribution in Figure 3.42.

Leslie was not sure they needed an example, but this confirmed that the distribution of age for firearm users and nonusers had a uniform distribution. Since the distribution was not normally distributed, Leslie suggested they use the median instead of the mean. She started copying the code from the previous bar chart, replacing the `mean` with `median` in the `fun.y` = option of the `geom_bar()` layer (Figure 3.43).

```
# bar chart with median for bar height (Figure 3.43)
bar.gun.use.age.md <- nhanes.2012.clean %>%
  drop_na(gun.use) %>%
  ggplot(aes(x = gun.use, y = RIDAGEYR)) +
  geom_bar(aes(fill = gun.use), stat = "summary", fun.y = median) +
  theme_minimal() +
  labs(x = "Firearm use", y = "Median age of participants") +
  scale_fill_manual(values = c("#7463AC", "gray80"),
                    guide = FALSE)
bar.gun.use.age.md
```

FIGURE 3.43 Median age by firearm use for 2011–2012 NHANES participants

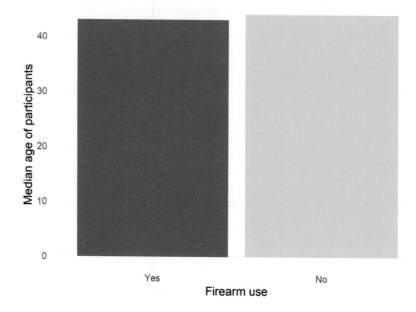

Leslie sighed. It still didn't look like a necessary plot. The median age of those who have used a firearm is maybe 1 or 2 years younger than the median age of those who have not used a firearm. Leslie thought this graph might be more useful if it included data spread, too. She remembered that measures of central tendency tend to be reported with measures of spread, and she asked Nancy if there was a way to add some indication of spread to the graph. Since they had decided on the median, was there a way to show its corresponding measure of spread, the IQR?

Nancy thought for a minute and remembered using a `geom_errorbar()` layer to add standard deviations to bar charts in the past, and thought this might also work to add IQR. She asked Leslie if she was up for more **tidyverse**. Leslie gave her two thumbs up, so Nancy started coding. Kiara noticed they were on to something new and wanted to make sure it was documented well for reproducibility. She squeezed in between Nancy and Leslie so she could suggest comments to write as they worked (Figure 3.44).

```
# bar chart with median for bar height and error bars (Figure 3.44)
gun.use.age.md.err <- nhanes.2012.clean %>%
  drop_na(gun.use) %>%
  group_by(gun.use) %>% # specify grouping variable
  summarize(central = median(RIDAGEYR),        # median, iqr by group
            iqr.low = quantile(x = RIDAGEYR, probs = .25),
            iqr.high = quantile(x = RIDAGEYR, probs = .75) ) %>%
  ggplot(aes(x = gun.use, y = central)) +      # use central tend for y-axis
  geom_col(aes(fill = gun.use)) +
  geom_errorbar(aes(ymin = iqr.low,            # lower bound of error bar
                    ymax = iqr.high,           # upper bound of error bar
```

```
                linetype = "IQR"),
           width = .2) +                        # width of error bar
    theme_minimal() +
    labs(x = "Firearm use", y = "Median age of participants") +
    scale_fill_manual(values = c("#7463AC", "gray80"),
                guide = FALSE) +
    scale_linetype_manual(values = 1, name = "Error bars")
  gun.use.age.md.err
```

While Leslie was happy that they had gotten error bars to show up, Figure 3.44 still wasn't all that interest-ing. Both groups had median ages in the early 40s, and about 50% of the observations in each group were between ages 30 and 60 based on the IQR error bars. The information in the graph could be easily reported in a single sentence rather than use so much space for so little information. She did notice that Nancy included `linetype =` in the `aes()` for the error bars. Nancy explained that she wanted it to be clear that the error bars were the IQR and not some other measure of spread. To specify IQR, she added a legend. Options included in the `aes()` (other than x and y) are added to a legend. By using `linetype = "IQR"`, she added a legend that would label the linetype as "IQR." Leslie noticed there was a line at the bottom of the code that included `scale_linetype_manual(values = 1, name = "")`. Nancy explained that, like the `scale_color_manual()` they had been using to specify colors, this allowed her to specify what type of line she wanted (she picked type 1) and several other options, such as whether or not to include the legend at all (`guide =`) and what the title of the legend should be (`name = "Error bars"`).

Kiara thought the same graph types with the FBI deaths data might show more variation and could be use-ful to add to their understanding of the role of gun types in homicides. Specifically, they could determine if there was a difference in the mean number of gun homicides per year by gun type. Leslie thought this was a good idea and would give her the chance to work with some of the great code that Nancy had created.

FIGURE 3.44 Median age with IQR for groups of firearm use for 2011–2012 NHANES participants

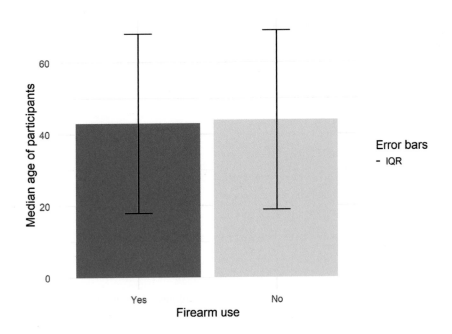

Nancy was interested to learn how she had downloaded the file, so Kiara copied the code and put it in Box 3.1 for Nancy to review. Leslie imported the **fbi_deaths_2016_ch3.csv** data set into R. Since it was a small data frame with just six variables, she used `summary()` to examine the data.

```
# import FBI data
fbi.deaths <- read.csv(file = "[data folder location]/data/fbi_deaths_2016_
ch3.csv")

# review the data
summary(object = fbi.deaths)
##                            Weapons X2012
##  Asphyxiation                  : 1 Min.   :     8.00
##  Blunt objects (clubs, hammers, etc.): 1 1st Qu.:    87.75
##  Drowning                      : 1 Median :   304.00
##  Explosives                    : 1 Mean   :  1926.28
##  Fire                          : 1 3rd Qu.:  1403.50
##  Firearms, type not stated     : 1 Max.   : 12888.00
##  (Other)                       :12
##      X2013                 X2014               X2015               X2016
##  Min.   :     2.00   Min.   :     7.0   Min.   :     1.00   Min.   :     1.0
##  1st Qu.:    87.25   1st Qu.:    75.5   1st Qu.:    87.75   1st Qu.:   100.2
##  Median :   296.50   Median :   261.0   Median :   265.00   Median :   318.0
##  Mean   :  1831.11   Mean   :  1825.1   Mean   :  2071.00   Mean   :  2285.8
##  3rd Qu.:  1330.00   3rd Qu.:  1414.2   3rd Qu.:  1410.00   3rd Qu.:  1428.8
##  Max.   : 12253.00   Max.   : 12270.0   Max.   : 13750.00   Max.   : 15070.0
##
```

It looks like each year was a variable in this data frame, and each observation was a type of weapon. Kiara thought a few things needed to happen before the data could be graphed. The most important thing to do would be to change the data set from wide, with one variable per year, to long. A long data set would have a variable called `year` specifying the year. Nancy knew what she wanted to do to make this happen and pulled the laptop over to write some code.

```
# make a long data frame
fbi.deaths.cleaned <- fbi.deaths %>%
  slice(3:7) %>%
  gather(key = "year", value = "number", X2012,
         X2013, X2014, X2015, X2016) %>%
  mutate(year, year = substr(x = year, start = 2, stop = 5)) %>%
  rename(weapons = Weapons)
```

Leslie asked Nancy to walk her through this code. Kiara suggested Leslie add comments as they went so that the code would be easier to understand later. Leslie agreed and Nancy started explaining. The first step was to isolate the different types of firearms in the data. One way to do this was to select the rows that had firearms in them. She suggested Leslie open the original data and identify the rows with firearm information. Leslie opened the original data set and saw that rows 3 to 7 had the five firearm types in them. Nancy then introduced `slice()`, which allows the selection of observations (or rows) by their position; in this case she used `slice(3:7)` to select rows 3 through 7. Kiara nudged Leslie to write a comment next to the `slice(3:7)` line. Leslie asked if `slice(3:7)` in this code would be like taking a subset. Would it be the same as `fbi.deaths[3:7,]`? Nancy confirmed that this was true.

Next, Nancy explained that `gather()` is a little tricky, but essentially it takes variables (i.e., columns) and turns them into observations (i.e., rows). The first two arguments were the new variable names (in quotes), and the last five arguments were the old variable names. Leslie was confused, but she wrote a comment and Nancy kept going.

The third task was `mutate()`, which was just used to remove the X from the beginning of the year values. The years were showing up as `X2012` instead of just `2012`. Using `substr()`, or substring, allows part of the word to be removed by specifying which letters to keep. By entering 2 and 5, `substr()` kept the values of the year variable starting at the second letter through the fifth letter.

Finally, `rename()` changed the variable named `Weapons` to a variable named `weapons`. Nancy preferred lowercase variable names for easier typing. Leslie understood, and Kiara was OK with the new comments in the code.

```
# make a long data frame
fbi.deaths.cleaned <- fbi.deaths %>%
    slice(3:7)                  %>% # selects rows 3 to 7
    gather(key = year, value = number, X2012,
            X2013, X2014, X2015, X2016) %>% # turn columns into rows
    mutate(year,
            year = substr(x = year,
                        start = 2,
                        stop = 5)) %>% # remove X from front of year entries
    rename(weapons = Weapons)
```

They decided it was time to make a bar chart.

3.6.3.2 BAR CHART

Kiara ran the same code she used for graphing mean age and gun use, but with the new data frame and variable names. She also changed the axis labels so they fit the data being graphed (Figure 3.45).

```
# plot number of homicides by gun type (Figure 3.45)
bar.homicide.gun <- fbi.deaths.cleaned %>%
    ggplot(aes(x = weapons, y = number)) +
    geom_bar(stat = "summary", fun.y = mean) +
    theme_minimal() +
    labs(x = "Firearm type", y = "Number of homicides committed")
bar.homicide.gun
```

FIGURE 3.45 Mean annual homicides committed by gun type in the United States, 2012–2016

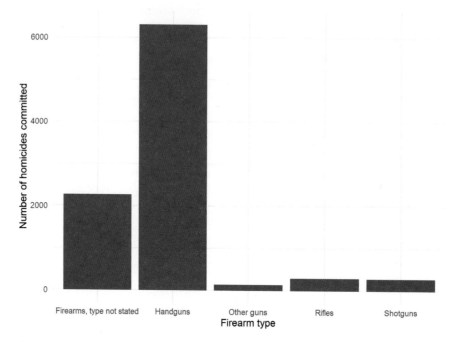

Leslie thought it might be easier to read this bar chart if it were flipped since some of the bar labels were complicated. Nancy flipped the coordinates by adding a `coord_flip()` layer. While she was working on it, she added some color to the bars using `scale_fill_brewer()` (Wickham et al., n.d.), which has a number of built-in color schemes (including many that are color-blind friendly) that are directly from the Color Brewer 2.0 website (http://colorbrewer2.org/). She tried a few of the palette options before choosing to use the Set2 palette by adding `palette = "Set2"` (Figure 3.46).

```
# flip the coordinates for better reading (Figure 3.46)
# add color and remove unnecessary legend
bar.homicide.gun <- fbi.deaths.cleaned %>%
  ggplot(aes(x = weapons, y = number)) +
  geom_bar(aes(fill = weapons), stat = "summary", fun.y = mean) +
  theme_minimal() +
  labs(x = "Firearm type", y = "Number of homicides committed") +
  coord_flip() +
  scale_fill_brewer(palette = "Set2", guide = FALSE)
bar.homicide.gun
```

The team discussed their strategies for using different options in the code to produce graphs that demonstrate a certain point or idea. For example, if the primary reason for creating the graph had been to highlight the role of handguns in homicide, using color to call attention to the length of the handgun bar would have been one way to highlight this fact. Nancy also suggested changing the order of the bars so that the bars would be in order by length. Leslie asked her to explain the code so she could practice it. Nancy said that `reorder()` can be used to order the bars from largest to smallest by the value of the number variable. She instructed Leslie to type `reorder()` in the `aes()` as part of the x = argument

FIGURE 3.46 Mean annual homicides by firearm type in the United States, 2012–2016

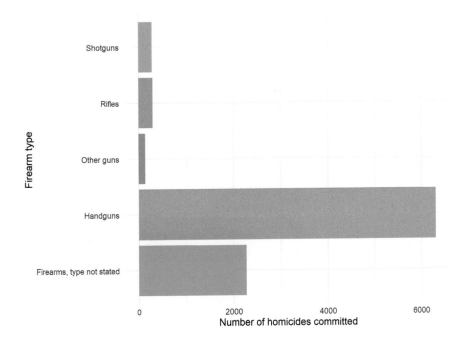

and then, within the parentheses, add the variable to be put in order and the variable that should be used to decide the order, like this: `reorder(weapons, -number)`. This means the factor `weapons` will be placed in order based on the numeric `number` variable. Leslie asked why the minus sign was in there. Nancy said this was to specify that the order should go from the smallest value to the largest value.

Kiara said they could use a strategy for assigning color to the bars similar to the one they used to assign color to categories in the waffle chart (Figure 3.18). Specifically, they could set each category equal to the name of the color to represent it. Leslie and Nancy both looked confused. Nancy quoted statistician Linus Torvalds when she said to Kiara, "Talk is cheap. Show me the code." Kiara added `reorder()` and the colors and showed her the code for Figure 3.47.

```
# highlight handguns using color (Figure 3.47)
bar.homicide.gun <- fbi.deaths.cleaned %>%
  ggplot(aes(x = reorder(x = weapons, X = -number), y = number)) +
  geom_bar(aes(fill = weapons), stat = "summary", fun.y = mean) +
  theme_minimal() +
  labs(x = "Firearm type", y = "Number of homicides") +
  coord_flip() +
  scale_fill_manual(values = c("Handguns" = "#7463AC",
                               "Firearms, type not stated" = "gray",
                               "Rifles" = "gray",
                               "Shotguns" = "gray",
                               "Other guns" = "gray"), guide=FALSE)

bar.homicide.gun
```

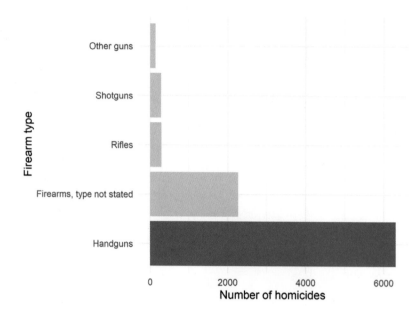

The R-Team agreed this use of color added emphasis to understanding the pattern of weapons used in homicides. Leslie asked if it was dishonest to emphasize a bar like this. Kiara thought the added emphasis was fine; dishonesty occurred when people changed the *x*-axis or *y*-axis or used other strategies to make differences look artificially bigger or smaller. In this case, handguns were the most used weapon, with a mean of more than 6,000 homicides per year by handgun.

3.6.3.3 POINT CHART

Nancy showed Leslie that the same data could be displayed with a single point rather than a bar. She used the code for the bar chart above and changed the `geom_bar()` layer to a `geom_point()` layer (Figure 3.48).

```
# gun deaths by gun type (Figure 3.48)
# highlight handguns using color
point.homicide.gun <- fbi.deaths.cleaned %>%
  ggplot(aes(x = reorder(x = weapons, X = -number), y = number)) +
  geom_point(aes(fill = weapons), stat = "summary", fun.y = mean) +
  theme_minimal() +
  labs(x = "Firearm type", y = "Number of homicides") +
  coord_flip() +
  scale_fill_manual(values = c("Handguns" = "#7463AC",
                               "Firearms, type not stated" = "gray",
                               "Rifles" = "gray",
                               "Shotguns" = "gray",
                               "Other guns" = "gray"), guide=FALSE)
point.homicide.gun
```

FIGURE 3.48 Mean annual homicides by firearm type in the United States, 2012–2016

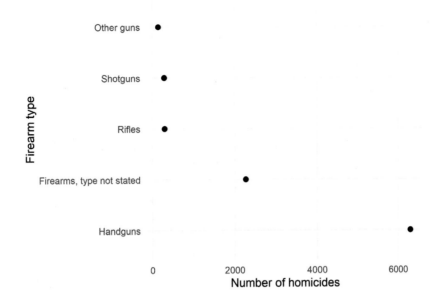

Leslie noticed that the colors did not show up in this new graph. Nancy fixed this by changing the term `fill =` to `color =`. She explained that `fill` is used to fill bars, while `color` works to color dots. Nancy thought this was also a good time to show off one more code trick, and she made the points larger using the `size =` option in the `geom_point()` layer (Figure 3.49).

```
# change fill to color add size to geom_point (Figure 3.49)
point.homicide.gun <- fbi.deaths.cleaned %>%
  ggplot(aes(x = reorder(x = weapons, X = -number), y = number)) +
  geom_point(aes(color = weapons, size = "Mean"),
             stat = "summary", fun.y = mean) +
  theme_minimal() +
  labs(x = "Firearm type", y = "Number of homicides") +
  coord_flip() +
  scale_color_manual(values = c("Handguns" = "#7463AC",
                                "Firearms, type not stated" = "gray",
                                "Rifles" = "gray",
                                "Shotguns" = "gray",
                                "Other guns" = "gray"), guide = FALSE) +
  scale_size_manual(values = 4, name = "")
point.homicide.gun
```

Leslie thought the bar chart was a little better at emphasizing, although this graph was not bad and would require less ink to print. Leslie asked Nancy if she could add the error bars to this graph, like she did with Figure 3.44. Nancy was up to the challenge and coded Figure 3.50. She took this opportunity to

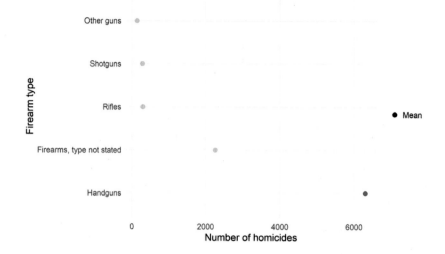

show Leslie one additional feature, which was to move the legend to another part of the graph, like the top or bottom. Leslie remembered seeing legends on the bottom of histograms in their previous meeting (Figure 2.7). Nancy confirmed that this was how they formatted those figures.

```
# add error bars (Figure 3.50)
point.homicide.gun <- fbi.deaths.cleaned %>%
  group_by(weapons) %>%
  summarize(central = mean(x = number),
            spread = sd(x = number)) %>%
  ggplot(aes(x = reorder(x = weapons, X = -central),
             y = central)) +
  geom_errorbar(aes(ymin = central - spread,
                    ymax = central + spread,
                    linetype = "Mean\n+/- sd"),
                width = .2) +
  geom_point(aes(color = weapons, size = "Mean"), stat = "identity") +
  theme_minimal() +
  labs(x = "Firearm type",
       y = "Number of homicides") +
  coord_flip() +
  scale_color_manual(values = c("Handguns" = "#7463AC",
                                "Firearms, type not stated" = "gray",
                                "Rifles" = "gray",
                                "Shotguns" = "gray",
```

```
                                    "Other guns" = "gray"), guide=FALSE) +
    scale_linetype_manual(values = 1, name = "") +
    scale_size_manual(values = 4, name = "") +
    theme(legend.position = "top")
point.homicide.gun
```

Leslie's first thought was that the means with their standard deviation error bars looked like TIE Fighters from *Star Wars*! She noticed that the standard deviations were very small for the `Other guns`, `Shotguns`, and `Rifles` groups. For these groups, the error bars did not even extend outside the dots. There was not much spread or variation in the number of homicide deaths by these three types of firearms. For `Handguns`, the error bar showed that the observations are spread to a few hundred homicides above and below the mean of 6,000. Leslie remembered that the data set was pretty small, based on just 5 years of data, which might be one of the reasons there was not a lot of spread or variation in the number of homicides per type of firearm. If the data were for more years, there might (or might not) be more variation due to mass homicide events, policy changes, or other factors.

Leslie was getting nervous that they might be using inappropriate measures of central tendency and spread since they did not know if the data were normally distributed. She thought the boxplots might be better at showing the distribution in each group so they could be sure they were choosing the most appropriate plots to interpret and report.

3.6.3.4 BOXPLOTS

Nancy slid the laptop over in front of her to make the boxplots. She used the code from the point chart and changed the `geom_` layer to make a boxplot (Figure 3.51).

FIGURE 3.50 Mean annual homicides by firearm type in the United States, 2012–2016

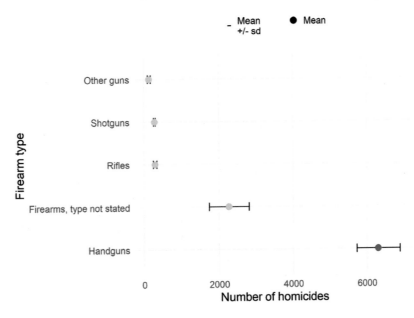

```
# change to boxplot (Figure 3.51)
box.homicide.gun <- fbi.deaths.cleaned %>%
  ggplot(aes(x = reorder(x = weapons, X = -number),
             y = number)) +
  geom_boxplot(aes(color = weapons)) +
  theme_minimal() +
  labs(x = "Firearm type", y = "Number of homicides") +
  coord_flip() +
  scale_color_manual(values = c("Handguns" = "#7463AC",
                                "Firearms, type not stated" = "gray",
                                "Rifles" = "gray",
                                "Shotguns" = "gray",
                                "Other guns" = "gray"), guide=FALSE)
box.homicide.gun
```

Nancy noted that boxplot color is specified with `fill =` in order to fill the boxplots instead of outlining them (Figure 3.52).

```
# fix color for boxplots (Figure 3.52)
box.homicide.gun <- fbi.deaths.cleaned %>%
  ggplot(aes(x = reorder(x = weapons, X = -number),
             y = number)) +
  geom_boxplot(aes(fill = weapons)) +
  theme_minimal() +
  labs(x = "Firearm type", y = "Number of homicides") +
  coord_flip() +
  scale_fill_manual(values = c("Handguns" = "#7463AC",
                               "Firearms, type not stated" = "gray",
                               "Rifles" = "gray",
                               "Shotguns" = "gray",
                               "Other guns" = "gray"), guide=FALSE)
box.homicide.gun
```

Nancy pushed the laptop back to Leslie so that she could practice. She was starting to feel bad that Leslie wasn't coding all that much. Leslie found that while the bar chart and point chart were great for comparing the means of the groups, the boxplot provided more information about the distribution in each group. For example, over the 2012–2016 time period, the number of handguns and unspecified firearms used in homicides varied a lot more than the use of the other three firearm types. She could tell this was the case because the boxes encompassing the middle 50% of the data were wider, so the IQR was larger. This might suggest that a closer examination of the trends in the production and use of handguns could be useful for understanding what was going on.

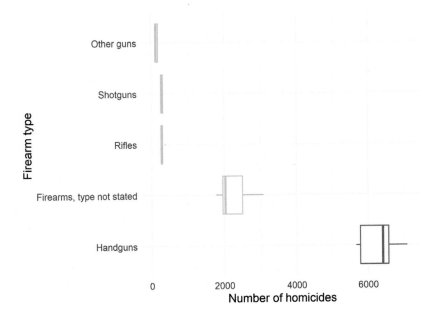

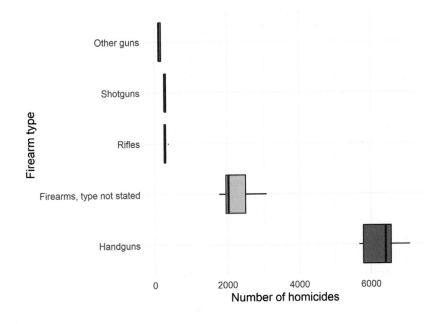

Leslie noticed that the boxplot also suggested that the distributions for the `Firearms, type not stated` and `Handguns` categories were skewed. She could tell because for the `Firearms, type not stated` category, the median is on the far left of the box, indicating that there are some larger values on the right of this distribution. She remembered what she had learned about calculating means and medians and thought that the mean values they had been reviewing might have been misleading for this group since the large values would make the mean seem larger (just like Bill Gates's salary would make the mean salary of your friends seem larger). Likewise, Leslie noticed that the median was toward the right-hand side of the `Handguns` box. This indicated there might be small values in this group that would have resulted in a smaller mean value. Given the skew, Leslie thought they would be better off using the boxplot or changing the bar chart or point chart to medians rather than means.

Nancy was not all that interested in the statistical concepts but wanted to show Leslie one more code trick. She knew a way to show the data points and the boxplots at the same time. Leslie liked this idea since it would help her to understand why the boxplots seem to show some skew. Nancy took over the keyboard and added a new `geom_jitter()` layer to the `ggplot()`. She also used the `alpha = .8` option with the boxplots to make the color a little less bright so that it was easier to see the data in Figure 3.53.

```
# Add points to boxplots (Figure 3.53)
box.homicide.gun <- fbi.deaths.cleaned %>%
  ggplot(aes(x = reorder(x = weapons, X = -number),
             y = number)) +
  geom_boxplot(aes(fill = weapons), alpha = .8) +
  geom_jitter() +
  theme_minimal() +
  labs(x = "Firearm type", y = "Number of homicides") +
  coord_flip() +
  scale_fill_manual(values = c("Handguns" = "#7463AC",
                               "Firearms, type not stated" = "gray",
                               "Rifles" = "gray",
                               "Shotguns" = "gray",
                               "Other guns" = "gray"), guide=FALSE)
box.homicide.gun
```

Leslie loved the addition of the data to the plot! Although this data set was very small, she could imagine how putting the points with the boxes for a larger data set would be very useful for seeing how well the boxes were capturing the distribution of the underlying data.

Kiara looked over the code and asked about the `geom_jitter()` layer. She asked why Nancy hadn't just used `geom_point()` like they had before when they wanted to see points on a graph. Nancy explained that `geom_jitter()` is a shortcut code for `geom_point(position = "jitter")`. She added that both of these would do the same thing, which is place the points on the graph, but add some "jitter" so that they are not all along a straight line. Having points all along a line makes it difficult to see patterns, especially in large data sets where many of the data points may be overlapping. Kiara was satisfied and did not think they needed to add more documentation.

3.6.3.5 VIOLIN PLOTS

Nancy described violin plots as somewhere between boxplots and density plots, typically used to look at the distribution of continuous data within categories. Leslie copied the code from above, removing the `geom_jitter` and changing `geom_boxplot` to `geom_violin` (Figure 3.54).

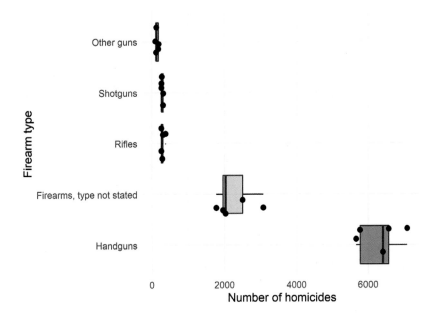

```
# violin plot (Figure 3.54)
violin.homicide.gun <- fbi.deaths.cleaned %>%
  ggplot(aes(x = reorder(x = weapons, X = -number),
             y = number)) +
  geom_violin(aes(fill = weapons)) +
  theme_minimal() +
  labs(x = "Firearm type", y = "Number of homicides") +
  coord_flip() +
  scale_fill_manual(values = c('gray', "#7463AC", 'gray',
                               'gray', 'gray'), guide=FALSE)
violin.homicide.gun
```

Leslie, Nancy, and Kiara agreed that this graph type did not work for these data. Kiara suggested that this was because, as they learned from the other plots above, there were too few cases per group for some graphs to be appropriate. Nancy still wanted to illustrate to Leslie the utility of violin plots because in many scenarios, they are useful. She wrote some quick code using the nhanes.2012.clean data from above to look at whether the distributions of age were the same for males and females (Figure 3.55).

```
# violin plot of age by sex for NHANES (Figure 3.55)
nhanes.2012.clean %>%
  ggplot(aes(x = sex, y = RIDAGEYR)) +
  geom_violin(aes(fill = sex)) +
```

```
scale_fill_manual(values = c("gray", "#7463AC"), guide = FALSE) +
labs(y = "Age in years", x = "Sex") +
theme_minimal()
```

FIGURE 3.54 Annual homicides by firearm type in the United States, 2012–2016

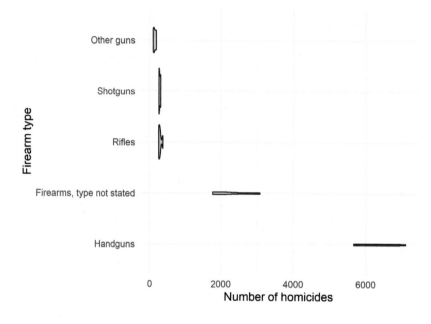

FIGURE 3.55 Distribution of age by sex for participants in the 2011–2012 NHANES survey

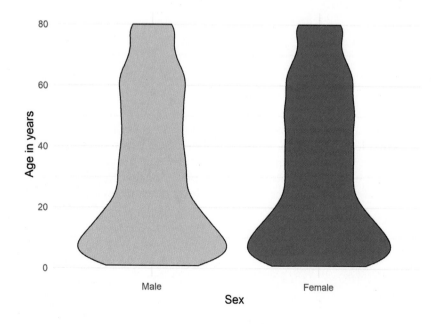

Although there didn't seem to be much of a difference in the distribution of ages between males and females, Leslie saw how she could tell the distribution by group from this plot, which might be useful for future projects. She was also amused that the shapes looked like beakers from a chemistry lab.

Before they moved to the last section, Leslie wanted to look at the different graph types of the weapons used in homicide one last time. The violin plots didn't work well, but the other three were good, so she copied her code from the previous section and added the new graph names (Figure 3.56).

```
# plot all three options together (Figure 3.56)
gridExtra::grid.arrange(bar.homicide.gun,
                        point.homicide.gun,
                        box.homicide.gun,
                        ncol = 2)
```

Leslie thought the purple bar in the bar chart stood out the most, probably because it was a lot of color in one place. This might be a good choice if the goal was to clearly and quickly communicate how big the mean is for the Handgun group compared to all the other means. Both the point chart and the boxplot were better at showing spread in addition to the central tendency. The boxplot gave the most information about the actual data underlying the plot. Leslie reminded them that whichever graph they chose, the median and IQR were better to show than the mean and standard deviation, given the skew they could see in the boxplot. Of all these graphs, she would choose the boxplot. Nancy and Kiara agreed.

FIGURE 3.56 Graph types for one factor and one numeric variable

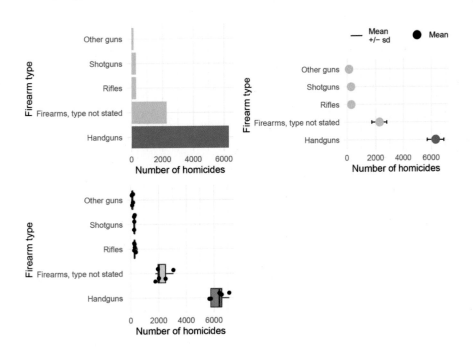

3.6.4 LINE GRAPHS AND SCATTERPLOTS FOR TWO CONTINUOUS VARIABLES

Now it was time to see what was useful for examining the relationship between two numeric variables. Nancy looked through the data they had discussed so far and found the Number of handguns produced and the Year variables. She explained that the production of handguns over time could be examined using a scatterplot or a line graph. These two types of graphs are useful for examining the relationship between two numeric variables that have values that are along a continuum, whether they are truly continuous or just close to continuous. The number of handguns produced is most like a continuous variable because it spans a continuum from zero to some upper limit. The year of production might be considered continuous if the underlying idea is to examine how things changed over a continuous measure of time. In other cases, the year might be considered a categorical idea rather than continuous, with each year treated as a category.

```
# bring in the data
guns.manu <- read.csv(file = "[data folder location]/data/total_firearms_
manufactured_US_1990to2015.csv")
summary(object = guns.manu)
##      Year          Pistols           Revolvers           Rifles
## Min.   :1990   Min.   : 677434   Min.   :274399   Min.   : 883482
## 1st Qu.:1996   1st Qu.: 989508   1st Qu.:338616   1st Qu.:1321474
## Median :2002   Median :1297072   Median :464440   Median :1470890
## Mean   :2002   Mean   :1693216   Mean   :476020   Mean   :1796195
## 3rd Qu.:2009   3rd Qu.:2071096   3rd Qu.:561637   3rd Qu.:1810749
## Max.   :2015   Max.   :4441726   Max.   :885259   Max.   :3979568
##     Shotguns        Total.firearms
## Min.   : 630663   Min.   : 2962002
## 1st Qu.: 735563   1st Qu.: 3585090
## Median : 859186   Median : 3958740
## Mean   : 883511   Mean   : 4848942
## 3rd Qu.:1000906   3rd Qu.: 5300686
## Max.   :1254924   Max.   :10349648
```

Nancy looked at the data and noticed that each firearm type was included as a different variable. Instead of this, she thought that gun type should be one factor variable with each type of gun as a category of the factor. This is another case of wide data that should be long. Nancy looked back at her code for making wide data long and applied the same code here along with a line of code to ensure that the new gun.type variable was the factor data type.

```
# make wide data long
guns.manu.cleaned <- guns.manu %>%
  gather(key = gun.type, value = num.guns, Pistols,
         Revolvers, Rifles, Shotguns, Total.firearms) %>%
  mutate(gun.type = as.factor(gun.type))
```

```
# check the data
summary(object = guns.manu.cleaned)
##       Year                  gun.type         num.guns
##  Min.    :1990    Pistols        :26    Min.    :   274399
##  1st Qu. :1996    Revolvers      :26    1st Qu. :   741792
##  Median  :2002    Rifles         :26    Median  :  1199178
##  Mean    :2002    Shotguns       :26    Mean    :  1939577
##  3rd Qu. :2009    Total.firearms :26    3rd Qu. :  3119839
##  Max.    :2015                          Max.    : 10349648
```

3.6.4.1 LINE GRAPHS

Once the data were formatted, Nancy hurried on to the graphing. She started by piping the new data frame into the `ggplot()` function with `geom_line()` to create a *line graph*. To reproduce the line graph in Figure 3.5, Nancy used a different line for each gun type by adding `linetype = gun.type` to the `aes()` (Figure 3.57).

```
# plot it (Figure 3.57)
line.gun.manu <- guns.manu.cleaned %>%
  ggplot(aes(x = Year, y = num.guns)) +
  geom_line(aes(linetype = gun.type))
line.gun.manu
```

FIGURE 3.57 Firearms manufactured in the United States over time (1990–2015)

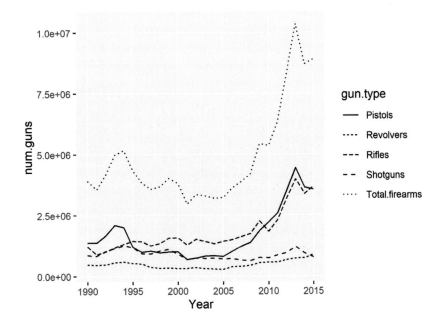

The graph was a good start, but Nancy was not satisfied with it. She made herself a list of the things to change:

- Convert the scientific notation on the *y*-axis to regular numbers
- Add a theme to get rid of the gray background
- Make better labels for the axes and legend
- Add color to the lines to help differentiate between gun types

```
# update the y-axis, theme, line color, labels (Figure 3.58)
line.gun.manu <- guns.manu.cleaned %>%
  ggplot(aes(x = Year, y = num.guns/100000)) +
  geom_line(aes(color = gun.type)) +
  theme_minimal() +
  labs(y = "Number of firearms (in 100,000s)") +
  scale_color_brewer(palette = "Set2", name = "Firearm type")
line.gun.manu
```

Kiara suggested that more formatting options could be changed to reproduce Figure 3.5 exactly, but Figure 3.58 was actually easier to read. She wondered if Nancy knew a way to make the lines thicker so they were easier to tell apart.

Leslie was still interested in handguns after learning how many more were used in homicides. Pistols and revolvers are both types of handguns, so to see more clearly whether the number of handguns has increased, she asked if Nancy knew an easy way to sum these two values for each year. Nancy said this could be done in the original data set before creating the long data set used to graph. Nancy was delighted to show off yet another of her code skills and wrote some code for Figure 3.59.

FIGURE 3.58 Firearms manufactured in the United States over time (1990–2015)

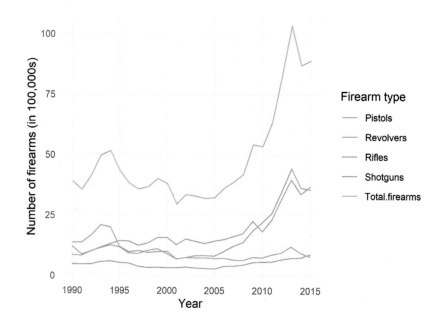

```
# make a handguns category that is pistols + revolvers
# remove pistols and revolvers from graph
guns.manu.cleaned <- guns.manu %>%
  mutate(Handguns = Pistols + Revolvers) %>%
  gather(key = gun.type, value = num.guns, Pistols, Revolvers,
         Rifles, Shotguns, Total.firearms, Handguns) %>%
  mutate(gun.type, gun.type = as.factor(gun.type)) %>%
  filter(gun.type != "Pistols" & gun.type != "Revolvers")

# update the line graph with new data and thicker lines (Figure 3.59)
line.gun.manu <- guns.manu.cleaned %>%
  ggplot(aes(x = Year, y = num.guns/100000)) +
  geom_line(aes(color = gun.type), size = 1) +
  theme_minimal() +
  labs(y = "Number of firearms (in 100,000s)") +
  scale_color_brewer(palette = "Set2", name = "Firearm type")
line.gun.manu
```

The graph suggested the number of handguns manufactured increased steadily from 2005 to 2013, and handguns were the most manufactured type of gun from 2009 to 2015. The team was happy with this graph and found it easier to read than Figure 3.5, so they moved on to the next graph type for two numeric variables.

FIGURE 3.59 Firearms manufactured in the United States over time (1990–2015)

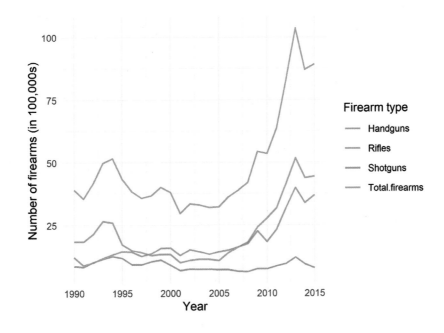

3.6.4.2 SCATTERPLOTS

Nancy explained that a scatterplot is also useful to show the relationship between two continuous variables. In a scatterplot, instead of connecting data points to form a line, one dot is used to represent each data point. Leslie had recently learned about the situations where a line graph was more useful than a scatterplot: (a) when the graph is showing change over time, and (b) when there is not a lot of variation in the data. Relationships where there is no measure of time and data that include a lot of variation are better shown with a scatterplot. Leslie slid the laptop away from Nancy while she still could and started to work on the code. Nancy suggested that they try their usual strategy of changing the `geom_line()` layer to `geom_point()` to see how a scatterplot would work for the graph they just built (Figure 3.60).

```
# use scatterplot instead of line (Figure 3.60)
scatter.gun.manu <- guns.manu.cleaned %>%
  ggplot(aes(x = Year, y = num.guns/100000)) +
  geom_point(aes(color = gun.type)) +
  theme_minimal() +
  labs(y = "Number of firearms (in 100,000s)") +
  scale_color_brewer(palette = "Set2", name = "Firearm type")
scatter.gun.manu
```

The three of them looked at the graph and rolled their eyes. It appeared that the guidance Leslie had received was correct; data over time are better shown with a line graph than a scatterplot. Leslie thought about the graphs they had been examining and remembered Figure 3.1 and Figure 3.2.

FIGURE 3.60 Firearms manufactured in the United States over time (1990–2015)

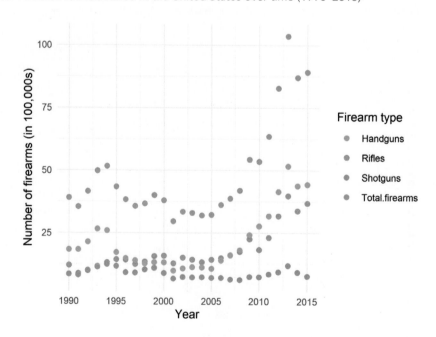

These graphs showed the amount of funding for research for the top 30 causes of death. Both included a lot of variation, and the information they conveyed was clear with the scatterplot. Kiara checked the `research.funding` data frame and wrote some code using `ggplot()` with a `geom_point()` layer to show the variation in funding by cause of death (Figure 3.61).

```
# scatterplot of gun research by funding (Figure 3.61)
scatter.gun.funding <- research.funding %>%
  ggplot(aes(x = Mortality.Rate.per.100.000.Population, y = Funding))+
    geom_point()
scatter.gun.funding
```

Leslie was surprised that Figure 3.61 did not look at all like Figure 3.1. She was curious about changing this graph to a line graph where the dots would be connected instead of separate dots.

```
# Line graph of gun research by funding (Figure 3.62)
line.gun.funding <- research.funding %>%
  ggplot(aes(x = Mortality.Rate.per.100.000.Population, y = Funding))+
    geom_line()
line.gun.funding
```

Figure 3.62 looked even worse. Clearly a scatterplot was a better idea, but Leslie wondered why the first graph looked so different from the original Figure 3.1. In the interest of reproducibility, Kiara took a

FIGURE 3.61 Research funding for the top 30 causes of mortality in the United States

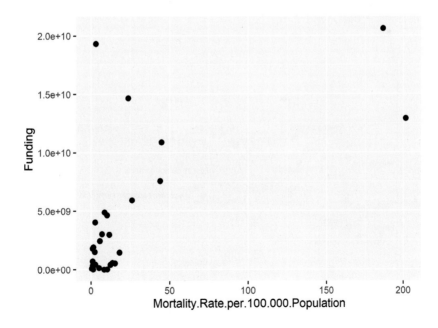

closer look at the Figure 3.1 graph (copied to Figure 3.63). She noticed that the *x*- and *y*-axes in the original figure did not have even spacing between numbers.

There was a large distance between 1 and 10, but the distance between 10 and 100 was about the same even though this should be nine times as far. Leslie thought it looked like a variable transformation. That is, the values of the variable had been transformed by adding, multiplying, or performing some

FIGURE 3.62 Research funding for the top 30 causes of mortality in the United States

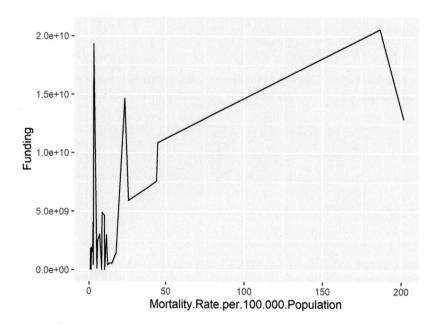

FIGURE 3.63 Reproduced figure showing mortality rate versus funding from 2004 to 2015 for the 30 leading causes of death in the United States

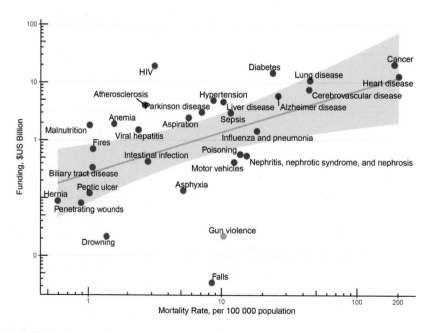

other mathematical operation. Kiara looked in the methods section of the paper that reported the graph and found this sentence: "The predictor and outcomes were log-transformed" (Stark & Shah, 2017, p. 84). As soon as they found this information, Nancy was ready to code it! Leslie wanted to decide what would be best, though. Nancy had an idea: Since they were not doing any analyses with the transformed variable, she could just use a log scale for the axes of the figure. Kiara and Leslie agreed and slid the laptop to Nancy to code it.

Leslie reminded Nancy that they might also want to add a *trend line* to provide an additional visual cue about the relationship between the variables. For example, while connecting all the dots with a line was not useful, a line showing the general relationship between cause of mortality and research funding could help clarify the relationship between the two variables. Nancy had just the trick. She would add layers for scaling with `scale_x_log10()` and `scale_y_log10()` for the axes and a layer with `stat_smooth()` for a smooth line through the dots. Nancy decided to reproduce the labels for the *x*- and *y*-axes from the original as well while she was working on the code. The *y*-axis layer appears to be in billions, so the funding variable should be divided by billions to make this true (Figure 3.64).

```
# scatterplot of gun research by funding (Figure 3.64)
# with axes showing a natural log scale
scatter.gun.funding <- research.funding %>%
  ggplot(aes(x = Mortality.Rate.per.100.000.Population,
             y = Funding/1000000000))+
  geom_point() +
  stat_smooth() +
  scale_x_log10() +
  scale_y_log10() +
  labs(y = "Funding, $US billion",
       x = "Mortality rate, per 100 000 population")
scatter.gun.funding
```

FIGURE 3.64 Research funding for the top 30 causes of mortality in the United States

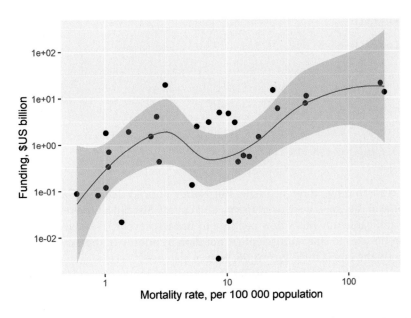

That line does not look right, thought Nancy. She had forgotten to use the `method` = `lm` or linear model option to add a straight line with the `stat_smooth()` function. She added this and used `theme_minimal()` to get rid of the gray background (Figure 3.65).

```
#scatterplot of gun research by funding (Figure 3.65)
#with axes showing a natural log scale
scatter.gun.funding <- research.funding %>%
  ggplot(aes(x = Mortality.Rate.per.100.000.Population,
             y = Funding/1000000000))+
  geom_point() +
  stat_smooth(method = "lm") +
  scale_x_log10() +
  scale_y_log10() +
  labs(y = "Funding, $US billion",
       x = "Mortality rate, per 100 000 population") +
  theme_minimal()
scatter.gun.funding
```

Nancy showed off one last `ggplot()` skill with some additional options to label the points, highlight the point representing gun violence, and make the formatting better match the original (Figure 3.66).

```
# fancy graph (Figure 3.66)
scatter.gun.funding.lab <- research.funding %>%
  ggplot(aes(x = Mortality.Rate.per.100.000.Population,
             y = Funding/1000000000))+
  geom_point() +
  stat_smooth(method = "lm") +
  scale_x_log10() +
  scale_y_log10() +
  labs(y = "Funding, $US billion",
       x = "Mortality rate, per 100 000 population") +
  theme_minimal() +
  geom_text(aes(label = Cause.of.Death))
scatter.gun.funding.lab
```

This was pretty close to done, thought Leslie. But Nancy noticed that the *y*-axis was still in scientific notation, and some of the labels were overlapping and cut off. She did a little research to see if she could fix these things and came up with a new package to use to prevent label overlapping, **ggrepel**, and an idea for fixing the axes to show nonscientific notation by adding in the exact numbers for each axis (Figure 3.67). To fix the labels for Figure 3.66, Nancy also used `library(package = "scales")` to open the `scales` package before running the Figure code.

FIGURE 3.65 Research funding for the top 30 causes of mortality in the United States

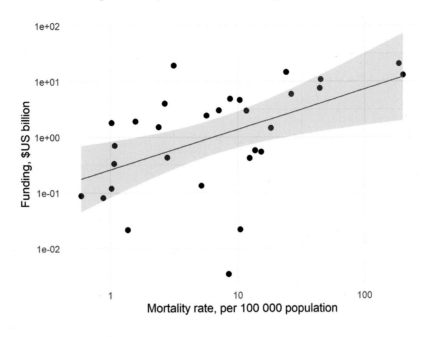

FIGURE 3.66 Research funding for the top 30 causes of mortality in the United States

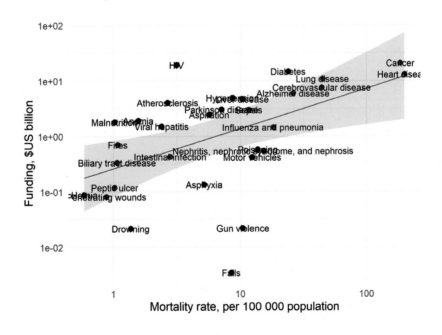

```
# fancy graph with better labels (Figure 3.67)
scatter.gun.funding.lab <- research.funding %>%
  ggplot(aes(x = Mortality.Rate.per.100.000.Population,
         y = Funding/1000000000)) +
```

```
    geom_point() +
    stat_smooth(method = "lm") +
    scale_x_log10(breaks = c(1,10,100), labels = comma) +
    scale_y_log10(breaks = c(1,10,100), labels = comma) +
    labs(y = "Funding, $US billion",
         x = "Mortality rate, per 100 000 population") +
    theme_minimal() +
    ggrepel::geom_text_repel(aes(label = Cause.of.Death), size = 3.5)
scatter.gun.funding.lab
```

It might not be perfect, but the team thought Figure 3.67 was good enough. The final scatterplot pretty clearly showed the relationship between funding and mortality rate, with some outliers like falls, gun violence, and HIV. Kiara put together the graph options for two numeric variables in Figure 3.68.

```
# show graph types (Figure 3.68)
gridExtra::grid.arrange(line.gun.manu,

                        scatter.gun.funding,

                        nrow = 2)
```

The type of graph clearly had to match the data when working with two numeric variables. Line graphs were useful to show change over time or to graph data with little variation. Scatterplots were better

---

FIGURE 3.67 Research funding for the top 30 causes of mortality in the United States

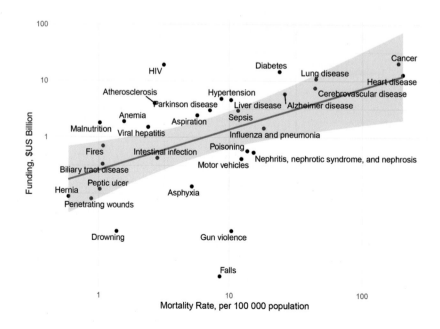

FIGURE 3.68 Graph types for two continuous or numeric variables

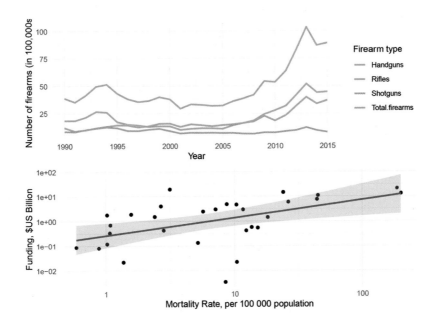

for when there was some variation in the relationship between the two variables. Nancy thought they were done with graphs, but Kiara had one more thing she wanted to discuss. Because graphs are such an important part of communicating data, it is extremely important that they are well-formatted. Formatting graphs well is also key for making sure your work is reproducible.

3.6.5 ACHIEVEMENT 3: CHECK YOUR UNDERSTANDING

Plot an appropriate graph to show the relationship between marital status (DMDMARTL) and sex (RIAGENDR) in the NHANES data. Explain why you chose this graph and not the others available.

3.7 Achievement 4: Ensuring graphs are well-formatted with appropriate and clear titles, labels, colors, and other features

In addition to choosing an appropriate graph, Kiara reminded Leslie that the primary goal was to be clear and for the graph to stand alone without relying on additional text to explain it. For a graph to stand alone, it should have as many of these features as possible:

- Clear labels and titles on both axes
- An overall title describing what is in the graph along with
  - Date of data collection
  - Units of analysis (e.g., people, organizations)
  - Sample size

In addition, researchers often use the following to improve a graph:

- Scale variables with very large or very small values (e.g., using millions or billions)
- Color to draw attention to important or relevant features of a graph

Leslie reviewed the graphs they had created so far and saw that Nancy and Kiara had been demonstrating these concepts and that most of the graphs they worked on had most of these features. The R-Team was once again exhausted from so much R and was ready to call it a day.

Leslie thought about everything they had learned through graphing. They had discovered that a higher percentage of males use guns than females, and that median age was nearly the same for gun users compared to nonusers. They had also learned that handguns were responsible for homicides at a far greater rate than were other types of guns, and that more handguns were manufactured than other types of guns. They confirmed through reproducing a published graph that funding for gun violence research was the third lowest of the top 30 mortality causes.

Leslie was so eager to text Leanne and share the graphs that she almost forgot to say goodbye to Nancy and Kiara. She thought the information they gained by exploring the data with graphs might be useful for Leanne's work with Moms Demand Action.

When she turned around to wave, she saw that Nancy was lost in her phone checking emails and had nearly collided with a large group of students who were just walking into the business school.

She waved to Nancy and looked around for Kiara. She saw Kiara across far ahead, no phone in sight and almost to the parking garage. "See you later!" Leslie yelled.

Kiara turned around and waved. "Looking forward to it!" she yelled back.

/// 3.8 CHAPTER SUMMARY

3.8.1 Achievements unlocked in this chapter: Recap

Congratulations! Like Leslie, you've learned and practiced the following in this chapter.

3.8.1.1 Achievement 1 recap: Choosing and creating graphs for a single categorical variable

Bar charts and waffle charts are the best options to plot a single categorical variable. Even if it makes the R-Team hungry just thinking about it, waffle charts are a better option than pie charts for showing parts of a whole.

3.8.1.2 Achievement 2 recap: Choosing and creating graphs for a single continuous variable

Histograms, density plots, and boxplots demonstrate the distribution of a single continuous variable. It is easier to see skew in histograms and density plots, but central tendency is easier to identify in boxplots.

3.8.1.3 Achievement 3 recap: Choosing and creating graphs for two variables at once

For two categorical variables, a mosaic plot or a bar chart with grouped or stacked bars are recommended. For one categorical and one continuous variable, boxplots are a good choice and the two types of bar charts work well. To examine distribution across groups, grouped histograms and density plots (and violin plots) can also be used. Line graphs and scatterplots are useful for two continuous variables. Line graphs are good for graphing change over time and for when there is little variability in the data; scatterplots are better for data with a lot of variability.

3.8.1.4 Achievement 4 recap: Ensuring graphs are well-formatted with appropriate and clear titles, labels, colors, and other features

Graphs should be able to stand alone. They should include clear labels and titles on both axes and an overall title that includes date of data collection, units of analysis, and sample size. In addition, researchers could scale variables with very large or very small values (e.g., using millions or billions) and use color to draw attention to important or relevant features of a graph.

3.8.2 Chapter exercises

The coder and hacker exercises are an opportunity to apply the skills from this chapter to a new scenario or a new data set. The coder edition evaluates the application of the concepts and functions learned in this R-Team meeting to scenarios similar to those in the meeting. The hacker edition evaluates the use of the concepts and functions from this R-Team meeting in new scenarios, often going a step beyond what was explicitly explained.

The coder edition might be best for those who found some or all of the Check Your Understanding activities to be challenging or if they needed review before picking the correct responses to the multiple-choice questions. The hacker edition might be best if the Check Your Understanding activities were not too challenging and the multiple-choice questions were a breeze.

The multiple-choice questions and materials for the exercises are online at **edge.sagepub.com/harris1e**.

Q1: Which of the following is appropriate to graph a single categorical variable?
   a. Histogram
   b. Bar chart
   c. Boxplot
   d. Scatterplot

Q2: Which of the following is appropriate to graph a single continuous variable?
   a. Waffle chart
   b. Histogram
   c. Bar chart
   d. Pie chart

Q3: A mosaic plot is used when graphing
   a. the relationship between two continuous variables.
   b. the relationship between one continuous and one categorical variable.
   c. the relationship between two categorical variables.
   d. data that are not normally distributed by group.

Q4: Which of the following is not a recommended type of graph:
   a. Pie chart
   b. Bar chart
   c. Waffle chart
   d. Density plot

Q5: Density plots, histograms, and boxplots can all be used to
   a. examine frequencies in categories of a factor.
   b. examine the relationship between two categorical variables.
   c. determine whether two continuous variables are related.
   d. examine the distribution of a continuous variable.

3.8.2.1 Chapter exercises: Coder edition

Use the NHANES data to examine gun use in the United States. Spend a few minutes looking through the NHANES website before you begin. Create well-formatted, appropriate graphs using the NHANES 2011–2012 data (available at **edge.sagepub.com/harris1e** or by following the instructions in Box 3.1) examining each of the variables listed below. Be sure to code missing values appropriately.

1) Income (Achievements 2 and 4)
2) Marital status (Achievements 1 and 4)
3) Race (Achievements 1 and 4)
4) Income and gun use (Achievements 3 and 4)
5) Race and gun use (Achievements 3 and 4)
6) Marital status and gun use (Achievements 3 and 4)

Use good code-formatting practices, and include a sentence after each graph in the comments that explains what the graph shows.

3.8.2.2 Chapter exercises: Hacker edition

Complete the coder edition with the following additional features:

- Format Graphs 3 and 5 to use color to highlight the group with the highest gun usage.

- In the percentage graph for Graph 1, highlight the highest percentage group with a different color.

3.8.2.3 Chapter exercises: Ultra hacker edition

Use the FBI data to re-create Figure 3.3.

3.8.2.4 Instructor note

Solutions to exercises can be found on the website for this book, along with ideas for gamification for those who want to take it further.

Visit **edge.sagepub.com/harris1e** to download the datasets, complete the chapter exercises, and watch R tutorial videos.

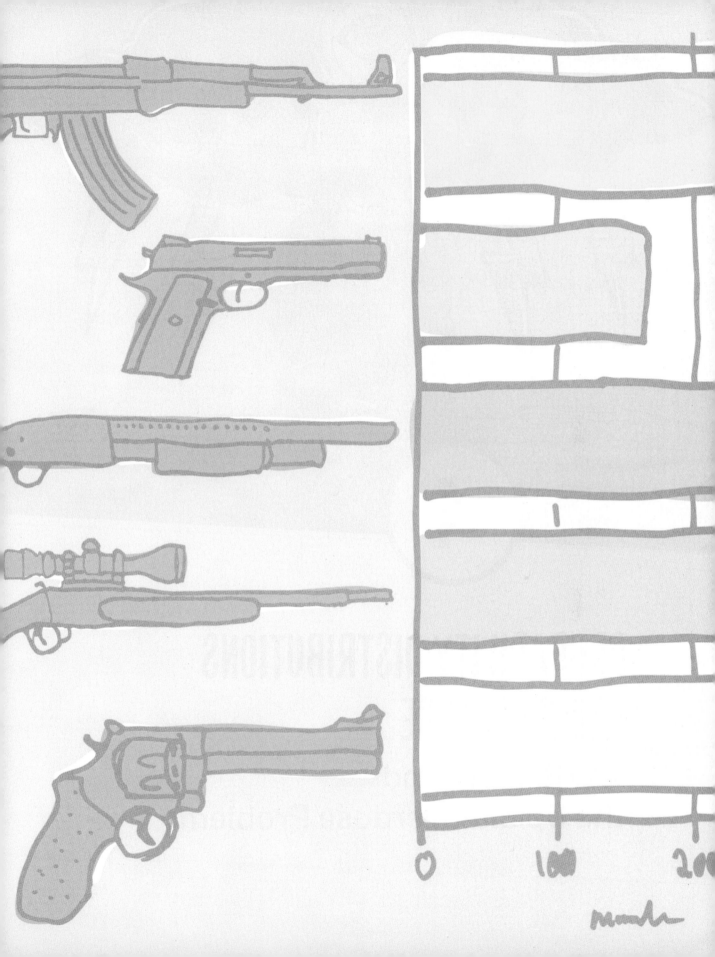

4

PROBABILITY DISTRIBUTIONS AND INFERENCE

The R-Team and the Opioid Overdose Problem

Nancy reserved her favorite conference room at work for their meeting, and Leslie showed up with a pan of brownies to share.

"Nice baking work," said Nancy, between mouthfuls.

"And nice work on descriptive statistics and graphs so far. You've laid a good foundation," said Kiara.

"Definitely," agreed Nancy. "Next, let's introduce Leslie to *statistical inference*."

"Pass the brownies over here first, Nancy," Kiara said. After helping herself, she explained, "Statistical inference is one of the foundational ideas in statistics. Since it is often impossible to collect information on every single person or organization, scientists take samples of people or organizations and examine the observations in the sample. Inferential statistics are then used to take the information from the sample and use it to understand (or infer to) the population."

Nancy chimed in, "Much of statistical inference is based on the characteristics of different distributions. The normal distribution that we talked about a little [Section 2.6.2.1] is just one of many distributions used to determine how probable it is that something happening in a sample is also happening in the population that the sample came from."

"I'm ready to learn," said Leslie.

Then, together, they set out to learn two of the most commonly used distributions and how they are used to infer information about populations from samples. Kiara created the outline of achievements for the day.

4.1 Achievements to unlock

- Achievement 1: Defining and using probability distributions to infer from a sample
- Achievement 2: Understanding the characteristics and uses of a binomial distribution of a binary variable
- Achievement 3: Understanding the characteristics and uses of the normal distribution of a continuous variable
- Achievement 4: Computing and interpreting z-scores to compare observations to groups
- Achievement 5: Estimating population means from sample means using the normal distribution
- Achievement 6: Computing and interpreting confidence intervals around means and proportions

4.2 The awful opioid overdose problem

Leslie's friend Corina had been doing a lot of research on the opioid epidemic in the United States. When they met for coffee, Corina told Leslie about the alarming increases in drug overdoses in the United States in recent years and showed her the County Health Rankings & Roadmaps website (http://www.countyhealthrankings .org/explore-health-rankings/rankings-data-documentation), which includes data on overdose deaths per 100,000 U.S. residents for each year. Since Corina was a data

⑤SAGE edge™
Visit **edge.sagepub .com/harris1e** to watch an R tutorial

person too, she had graphed the County Health Rankings data to demonstrate the steady rise of drug overdose deaths from 2014–2017 (Figure 4.1).

Leslie could not stop thinking about these data and spent some time looking through the County Health Roadmap website later that day. She did some more searching and found the CDC WONDER website (https://wonder.cdc.gov/ucd-icd10.html), which has data on the underlying cause of each death in the United States. For drug deaths, the CDC WONDER data include the drug implicated in each death, if available. One graph shown on the CDC website (Figure 4.2) demonstrated a sharp increase in opioid-related deaths, accounting for some of the increase in overall drug overdose deaths that Corina was working on.

Leslie was curious about policies and programs that might address this growing problem. After a little more research, she found that states had begun to adopt policies to try to combat the opioid epidemic. Some of the state-level policy solutions to addressing the increasing number of opioid overdoses were as follows (Haegerich, Paulozzi, Manns, & Jones, 2014):

- Imposition of quantity limits
- Required prior authorization for opioids
- Use of clinical criteria for prescribing opioids
- Step therapy requirements
- Required use of prescription drug monitoring programs

Leslie looked into these different strategies and found that *quantity limit policies* set limits on the supply of opioids prescribed in an initial prescription. States limit first-time prescriptions to 3, 5, 7, or 14 days. *Prior authorization* is the requirement of a medical justification for an opioid prescription before an insurer will cover the prescription (Hartung et al., 2018). *Clinical criteria for prescribing opioids* are

FIGURE 4.1 Drug overdose deaths per 100,000 U.S. residents 2014–2017

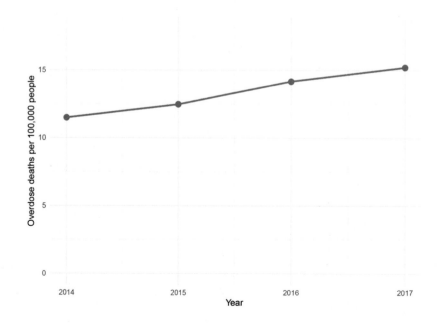

Source: County Health Rankings data.

FIGURE 4.2 Drugs involved in U.S. overdose deaths, 2000–2016

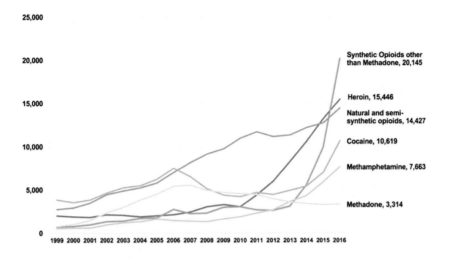

Source: CDC (https://d14rmgtrwzf5a.cloudfront.net/sites/default/files/overdosedeaths1.jpg).

guidelines for physicians making decisions about opioids, including selection of the type, dose, duration, discontinuation, and associated potential risks. *Step therapy* requires patients to try certain drugs before other drugs, so certain opioids may not be available until patients have tried nonopioid or alternative opioid options. *Prescription drug monitoring programs* are active programs that collect, monitor, and analyze data on prescriptions from prescribers and pharmacies in order to identify problematic prescribing patterns and aid in understanding the epidemic.

The Kaiser Family Foundation (KFF) keeps track of the adoption of these policies across all 50 states and the District of Columbia (Smith et al., 2016). After reading through the report on the KFF website, Leslie noticed that the number of state policies being adopted is increasing. This observation is what made Leslie decide to bring the idea of opioid overdoses to the R-Team as a possible problem.

She summarized everything she had found above and showed the team the data sources at County Roadmaps, the CDC, and KFF. She showed them a copy of Figure 4.1 and explained that when she was reading the report on the KFF website (Smith et al., 2016), she thought it showed an increase in the number of states adopting policies that might address the increases in drug overdoses, especially in opioid overdoses. Nancy was eager, as usual, to start coding. She went to the KFF website so she could start importing the data into R and found one of her very favorite things: messy data saved in inconsistent formats. It took her a little time, but she eventually got the data to cooperate and created a line graph showing state opioid policies from 2015 to 2017 (Figure 4.3). Leslie was interested in how Corina got the County Health Roadmap data together to make Figure 4.1, so Nancy figured it out and sent her the code so she could review it later (Box 4.1).

Nancy was interested in treatment programs as well as policies. Nancy's friend Robert had a son who had become addicted to opioids after they were prescribed following a minor surgery. Robert did some research and found that medication-assisted therapies were twice as effective as other forms of treatment (Connery, 2015), but unfortunately, there were no treatment facilities with medication-assisted therapies (Volkow, Frieden, Hyde, & Cha, 2014) in the rural area where he and his son lived. The nearest facility with these therapies was in a larger town about 40 miles away, which put an additional barrier in Robert's way to getting effective help for his son.

FIGURE 4.3 Number of states adopting prescription drug policies, 2015–2017

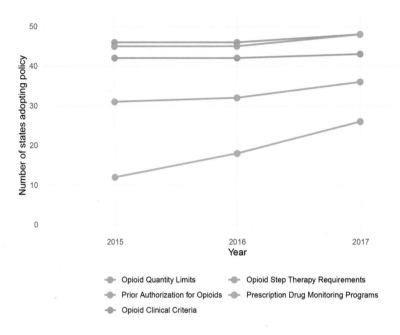

Source: Smith et al. (2016).

4.1 Nancy's fancy code: Importing data directly from csv files on the Internet

The County Health Rankings data sets are saved on the Rankings Data & Documentation section of the County Health Rankings & Roadmaps website (http://www.countyhealthrankings.org/explore-health-rankings/rankings-data-documentation). While the links on the website look consistent over time, the data files have been saved inconsistently. This is very common for online data sources and often requires some extra time to understand the data and write code to import it in a useful way.

For example, the 2017 data file from the website has labels for the variables in the first row and the variable names in the second row (Figure 4.4).

FIGURE 4.4 Example from the first two rows in the County Health Rankings 2017 data set

HW	HX
Drug Overdose Deaths Numerator	Drug Overdose Deaths Denominator
measure_138_numerator	measure_138_denominator
2,057	14,542,078
16	165,988
103	599,360

FIGURE 4.5 Example from the first two rows in the County Health Rankings 2014 data set

JT	JU
measure_138_numerator	measure_138_denominator
Drug poisoning deaths Numerator	Drug poisoning deaths Denominator
3,259	32,658,235
27	363,758
176	1,196,472

The 2014 file with the same name from the same website has the variable names in the first row and the variable labels in the second row (Figure 4.5).

Although the data are essentially the same, the data files require different code to import in order to be consistent. The `skip =` argument for the `read_csv()` function from the **tidyverse** package allows skipping any number of rows at the beginning of a file, which works well to import the 2017 data directly from the website. Using `read_csv()` and skipping 1 row for the 2017 data will import the data with variable names but without labels.

```
# load data skip first row
library(package = "tidyverse")

counties.2017.demo <- read_csv(file = "http://www.countyhealthrankings
.org/sites/default/files/2017CHR_CSV_Analytic_Data.csv", skip = 1)

# check the first few observations
head(x = counties.2017.demo)
```

For the 2014 data, the first row is important to keep because it has the variable names. However, the second row can be skipped because it contains variable labels and not actual data. The `read_csv` code can be used, but the `skip =` feature is not useful here since it skips rows only at the beginning of the file. Instead, try using the square brackets to make a subset of the data, removing the first row by adding `-1` as the first entry in the subsetting brackets, `[-1, ]`.

```
# load data skip first row after header
counties.2014.demo <- read_csv(file = "http://www.
countyhealthrankings.org/sites/default/files/analytic_data2014.csv")
[-1, ]

# check the first few observations
head(x = counties.2014.demo)
```

(Continued)

(Continued)

To put all the data sets together into one for graphing requires bringing in each one in a unique way based on how the file was saved so that they are all consistent and then merging them together.

```
# import 2014
# examine the data at http://www.countyhealthrankings.org/sites/
# default/files/2014%20CHR%20analytic%20data.csv
# the variable names are on the first row
# get the variable names first to add them to the data
colNames2014 <- names(x = read_csv(file = "http://www.
countyhealthrankings.org/sites/default/files/2014%20CHR%20
analytic%20data.csv", n_max = 0))

# then get the data
# add the variable names using col_names
counties2014 <- read_csv(file = "http://www.countyhealthrankings.
org/sites/default/files/2014%20CHR%20analytic%20data.csv",
                         col_names = colNames2014, skip=2)


# 2017 has variable names in the second row
# data location http://www.countyhealthrankings.org/sites/default/
# files/2017CHR_CSV_Analytic_Data.csv
# get the names and save them, skip one row to get the names from
# second row
colNames2017 <- names(x = read_csv(file = "http://www.
countyhealthrankings.org/sites/default/files/2017CHR_CSV_Analytic_
Data.csv", skip=1, n_max = 0))


# then get the data
# add the variable names using col_names
counties2017 <- read_csv(file = "http://www.countyhealthrankings
.org/sites/default/files/2017CHR_CSV_Analytic_Data.csv",
                         col_names = colNames2017, skip=2)


# 2015 & 2016 have no var names
# URL: http://www.countyhealthrankings.org/sites/default/
# files/2015%20CHR%20Analytic%20Data.csv
counties2015 <- read_csv(file = "http://www.countyhealthrankings
.org/sites/default/files/2015%20CHR%20Analytic%20Data.csv")


# URL: http://www.countyhealthrankings.org/sites/default/
# files/2016CHR_CSV_Analytic_Data_v2.csv
```

```
counties2016 <- read_csv(file = "http://www.countyhealthrankings.org/
sites/default/files/2016CHR_CSV_Analytic_Data_v2.csv")
# the columns for 2015 and 2016 are named with the labels rather
# than the variable names
# rename these columns to be consistent with 2014 and 2017
# overdose numerator column should be renamed measure_138_numerator
# overdose denominator column should be renamed measure_138_
# denominator
counties2015 <- rename(.data = counties2015,
                       measure_138_numerator =
                           "Drug poisoning deaths Numerator")
counties2015 <- rename(.data = counties2015,
                       measure_138_denominator =
                           "Drug poisoning deaths Denominator")

# rename the 2016 columns
counties2016 <- rename(.data = counties2016,
                       measure_138_numerator =
                           "Drug Overdose Deaths Numerator")
counties2016 <- rename(.data = counties2016,
                       measure_138_denominator =
                           "Drug Overdose Deaths Denominator")
```

Now there are four data sets, with each data set having `measure_138_numerator`, which is the numerator for calculating the drug poisoning deaths in the county, and `measure_138_denominator`, which is the *denominator*, or the part of the fraction below the line, for calculating the drug poisoning deaths in the county. Since there are four data sets, a function would be helpful so that the overdose death rate doesn't have to be computed four separate times.

The function should sum the numerator variable values to get the total number of overdose deaths across all counties, and divide this by the sum of the denominator variable, which is the sum of the populations of the counties. The denominator number can then be multiplied by 100,000 to get the rate of overdose deaths per 100,000 people in a county. The formula in the function should be as shown in Equation (4.1).

$$od.death.rate = \frac{measure.138.numerator}{100,000 \times measure.138.denominator} \qquad (4.1)$$

The `OverdoseFunc()` function employs Equation (4.1).

```
# overdose rates function
OverdoseFunc <- function(x) {
```

(Continued)

(Continued)

```
  (sum(x$measure_138_numerator, na.rm = TRUE)/sum(x$measure_138_
  denominator, na.rm = TRUE)) * 100000

  }
```

To use the function to get the overdose rate for each year and put all the rates in a data frame to graph, apply it to each data frame, `counties2014`, `counties2015`, `counties2016`, and `counties2017`.

```
# overdose rates vector
overdose.per.100k <- c(OverdoseFunc(x = counties2014),
                       OverdoseFunc(x = counties2015),
                       OverdoseFunc(x = counties2016),
                       OverdoseFunc(x = counties2017))

# year vector
year <- c(2014, 2015, 2016, 2017)

# combine vectors into small data frame
od.rates.year <- data.frame(overdose.per.100k, year)
```

Finally, the small data frame can be used to make a completely reproducible version of Figure 4.1, as long as the data sets are available in the same format.

```
# make the graph (Figure 4.1)
od.rates.year %>%
  ggplot(aes(x = year, y = overdose.per.100k)) +
  geom_line(color = '#7463AC', size = 1) +
  geom_point(color = '#7463AC', size = 3) +
  theme_minimal() +
  ylim(0, 18) +
  labs(y = "Overdose deaths per 100,000 people", x = "Year")
```

Having lived in a larger city most of her life, Leslie had never considered distance as a factor in why and how people get health care and treatment. She searched for information about this and found *amfAR*, the Foundation for AIDS Research, which has an Opioid & Health Indicators Database (https://opioid .amfar.org). The data in amfAR's database included distance to the nearest substance abuse treatment facility that has medication-assisted therapies. Kiara thought this sounded like good data to use to learn about the normal distribution. She looked through the database and noticed that it included a lot of different data at both the state and county levels. The state-level data gave rates of different health outcomes and characteristics of health services for entire states. The county-level data gave the same information, but for each county. Some variables were not available at the county level because the number of people living in the county was too small and the data could compromise privacy. The team was satisfied that they had some meaningful data to learn more about policies and programs that address the ongoing opioid problem in the United States. They were ready to start learning about distributions and inference.

4.3 Data, codebook, and R packages for learning about distributions

Before they examined the data, Kiara made a list of all the data, documentation, and packages needed for learning about distributions.

- Options for accessing the data
  - Download clean data sets **pdmp_2017_kff_ch4.csv** and **opioid_dist_to_facility_2017_ch4.csv** from **edge.sagepub.com/harris1e**
  - Download the county-level distance data files directly from the amfAR website (https://opioid .amfar.org/indicator/dist_MAT) and use `read_csv()` to import the files; note that the data on the amfAR website are periodically updated to improve accuracy, so results may be slightly different from what is shown in the text when importing data directly from amfAR
  - Import and clean the data for 2017 from Table 19 in the online report on the KFF website (Smith et al., 2016)
- Two options for accessing the codebook
  - Download the codebook file **opioid_county_codebook.xlsx** from **edge.sagepub.com/harris1e**
  - Use the online version of the codebook from the amfAR Opioid & Health Indicators Database website (https://opioid.amfar.org)
- Install the following R package if not already installed
  - **`tidyverse`**, by Hadley Wickham (https://www.rdocumentation.org/packages/tidyverse/)

4.4 Achievement 1: Defining and using the probability distributions to infer from a sample

Based on Figure 4.3, Leslie was right that the number of state-level drug monitoring programs increased over the 2015 to 2017 time period. She had heard that there was emerging evidence that prescription drug monitoring programs (PDMPs) were an effective tool in understanding the opioid crisis and in reducing opioid overdoses and deaths (Haegerich et al., 2014). As of 2017, just over half of all U.S. states had adopted a PDMP, which can be represented in a *probability distribution*. A probability distribution is the set of probabilities that each possible value (or range of values) of a variable occurs.

Kiara started to explain to Nancy what a probability distribution was, but Nancy was busy texting Robert to check in on his son, so she turned to Leslie and explained that if she were to put the names of states on slips of paper and select one without looking, the probability that the state she selected would have a monitoring program in 2017 would be 26 out of 51 (50 states plus Washington, DC), which is 51%. The probability that she selected a state with no monitoring program would be 25/51 or 49%. The set of these probabilities together is the probability distribution for the PDMP policy. Leslie remembered some of this from her statistics class, although she admitted it had been a while since she had thought about probability distributions.

4.4.1 CHARACTERISTICS OF PROBABILITY DISTRIBUTIONS

Kiara continued to explain that probability distributions have two important characteristics:

1. The probability of each real value of some variable is non-negative; it is either zero or positive.

2. The sum of the probabilities of all possible values of a variable is 1.

It had started to come back to Leslie. She remembered that there are many different probability distributions, with each one falling into one of two categories: *discrete* or continuous. Discrete probability distributions show probabilities for variables that can have only certain values, which includes categorical variables and variables that must be measured in whole numbers, such as "number of people texting during class." Continuous probability distributions show probabilities for values, or ranges of values, of a continuous variable that can take any value in some range.

4.4.2 TYPES OF PROBABILITY DISTRIBUTIONS

These two categories of probability distributions are the foundation for most statistical tests in social science. Kiara suggested that there are two probability distributions in particular that are commonly used and good examples for learning how a probability distribution works: the binomial distribution and the normal distribution. The binomial distribution is a discrete probability distribution and applies to probability for binary categorical variables with specific characteristics. The normal distribution is a continuous probability distribution and applies to probability for continuous variables.

4.4.3 ACHIEVEMENT 1: CHECK YOUR UNDERSTANDING

The binomial distribution is a probability distribution for _____ variables, while the normal distribution is a probability distribution for _____ variables.

Thirty-six of 51 states have opioid step therapy requirements. What are the probabilities that would make up the probability distribution for states having opioid step therapy requirements?

4.5 Achievement 2: Understanding the characteristics and uses of a binomial distribution of a binary variable

The binomial distribution is a discrete probability distribution used to understand what may happen when a variable has two possible outcomes, such as "eats brownies" and "does not eat brownies." The most common example is flipping a coin, but there are many variables that have two outcomes: alive or dead, smoker or nonsmoker, voted or did not vote, depressed or not depressed. Kiara suggested to Leslie that whether a state did or did not adopt an opioid policy is another example of a variable with two possible outcomes: policy, no policy. More specifically, the binomial distribution is used to represent the distribution of a *binomial random variable*, which has the following properties:

- A variable is measured in the same way n times.

- There are only two possible values of the variable, often called "success" and "failure."

- Each observation is *independent* of the others.

- The probability of "success" is the same for each observation.

- The random variable is the number of successes in n measurements.

The binomial distribution is defined by two things:

- *n*, which is the number of observations (e.g., coin flips, people surveyed, states selected)
- *p*, which is the probability of success (e.g., 50% chance of heads for a coin flip, 51% chance of a state having a PDMP)

Leslie thought that this seemed overly complicated so far. If she knows that 51% of states have monitoring programs and 49% do not, why not just report those percentages and be done with it?

4.5.1 USING DISTRIBUTIONS TO LEARN ABOUT POPULATIONS FROM SAMPLES

Nancy was done texting and joined the conversation to explain that researchers often work with samples instead of populations. In the case of the state data on opioid policies, all states are included, so this is the entire population of states. When it is feasible to measure the entire population, reporting the percentages like Leslie suggested is usually sufficient. However, populations are often expensive and logistically difficult or impossible to measure, so a subset of a population is measured instead. This subset is a sample. If, for example, Leslie were working on her dissertation and wanted to study how the number of opioid deaths in a state relates to one or two characteristics of states, she might choose a sample of 20 or 30 states to examine.

4.5.2 STATISTICAL PROPERTIES OF A BINOMIAL RANDOM VARIABLE

If Leslie did not know which states had PDMPs (she just knew it was 51% of states) and decided her sample of states needed to include exactly 10 states with PDMPs, she could use the binomial distribution to decide how many states to include in a sample in order to have a good chance of picking 10 with PDMPs. Before she could use the binomial distribution, she would need to ensure that the PDMP variable had the properties of a binomial random variable:

- The existence of a monitoring program would be determined for each state.
- The only two possible values are "success" for having a PDMP and "failure" for not having a PDMP.
- Each state is independent of the other states.
- The probability of having a program is the same for each state.

Leslie was concerned about the third and fourth assumptions of states being independent of other states and having the same probability of having a program. She thought that state lawmakers are independent of each other, but she had read that neighboring states will often be more similar to each other than they are to states in other parts of the country. They discussed it for a few minutes and decided that the influence of geography is complex and should be seriously considered before publishing any research with these data, but that they felt OK using these data to explore the statistical concepts. For today, they would consider the states and counties in the data as independent of each other. This made Kiara a little nervous, and she vowed to put a big emphasis on meeting the underlying assumptions about statistical properties for all the data they would select and use in the remaining meetings.

After that detour, they returned to their discussion of the binomial distribution. The *expected value* of a binomial random variable is *np*, where *n* is the sample size and *p* is the probability of a success. In this example, if the sample size is 20 and the probability of success (having a PDMP) is 51%, which is formatted as a proportion rather than a percentage for the purposes of this calculation, the expected value of the binomial random variable after taking a sample of 20 states would be $20 \times .51$ or 10.2. This means that a sample of 20 states is likely to have 10.2 states with PDMPs.

The expected value is useful, but since the value of p is a probability (not a certainty), the expected value will not occur every time a sample is taken. Kiara explained that they could use the *probability mass function* for the binomial distribution to compute the probability that any given sample of 20 states would have *exactly* 10 states with PDMPs. A probability mass function computes the probability that an *exact* number of successes happens for a discrete random variable, given n and p. Nancy was getting bored with all this terminology, so Leslie summarized it in practical terms. She explained that the probability mass function will give them the probability of getting 10 states with a PDMP if they selected 20 states at random from the population of states where the likelihood of any one state having a PDMP was 51%. In the probability mass function in Equation (4.2), x represents the specific number of successes of interest, n is the sample size, and p is the probability of success.

$$f(x, n, p) = \binom{n}{x} p^x (1-p)^{(n-x)}$$

(4.2)

Leslie substituted the values of x, n, and p from the scenario into Equation (4.2) to get Equation (4.3).

$$f(10, 20, .51) = \binom{20}{10} .51^{10} (1-.51)^{(20-10)} = .175$$

(4.3)

Leslie confirmed that there is a 17.5% probability of choosing *exactly* 10 states with PDMPs if she chooses 20 states at random from the population of states where 51% of states have a PDMP. Nancy saw her chance to get some code into the discussion and showed Leslie that R has a function built in for using the binomial distribution. She showed them how to use the `dbinom()` function in base R, which uses Equation (4.2) to compute the probability given the number of successes (x), the sample size (size =), and the probability of success (prob =).

```
# where successes = 10, n = 20, prob = .51
dbinom(x = 10, size = 20, prob = .51)
## [1] 0.1754935
```

4.5.3 VISUALIZING AND USING THE BINOMIAL DISTRIBUTION

Kiara let Leslie know that the binomial distribution can also be displayed graphically and used to understand the probability of getting a specific number of successes or a range of successes (e.g., 10 or more successes). She created a plot of the probability mass function showing the distribution of probabilities of different numbers of successes. Nancy created an example graph showing the probability of getting a certain number of states with monitoring programs in a sample when 20 are selected (Figure 4.6).

Along the x-axis in the plot are the number of states selected that have a PDMP program (in a sample where $n = 20$ and $p = .51$). Along the y-axis is the probability of selecting *exactly* that many states. For example, it looks like there is about a 1% chance of exactly five successes. In choosing 20 states at random from all the states, there is approximately a 1% chance that *exactly* 5 of them will have a PDMP. Kiara used the R code Nancy showed them to confirm this observation:

```
# 5 successes from a sample of 20 with 51% probability of success
dbinom(x = 5, size = 20, prob = .51)
## [1] 0.01205691
```

FIGURE 4.6 Probability mass function plot showing probability of number of selected states with PDMPs out of 20 total selected when 51% have PDMPs overall

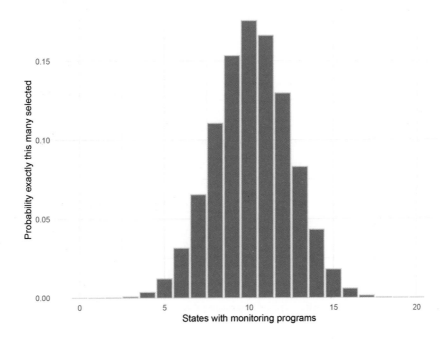

By multiplying the result by 100, Leslie determined there was a 1.21% chance of choosing 20 states at random from a population where 51% have PDMPs and the sample has exactly 5 with a PDMP. She wondered what would happen if the percentage of states with programs increased. Or if 75% of states had programs, what would the probability be that exactly 5 out of 20 selected at random would have a PDMP?

Nancy saw her chance to write some more code and plotted a binomial distribution for a sample size of 20 with a 75% probability of success. An examination of the graph reveals that the probability of *exactly* five successes is very low, near zero (Figure 4.7). Leslie could not even see the purple in the left tail of the graph.

Leslie pointed out that the distribution had shifted to the right on the *x*-axis and that getting exactly five states with PDMPs was even less probable than before when the probability of PDMPs per state was 51%. Kiara thought this made sense; it would be weird to get so few states with PDMPs in a sample if 75% of all states had this program. Nancy just wanted to code and wrote the `dbinom()` to check how low the probability of five successes (states with PDMPs) actually was.

```
# 5 successes from 20 selections with 75% probability of success
dbinom(x = 5, size = 20, prob = .75)
## [1] 3.426496e-06
```

Leslie remembered that the −06 in the output was scientific notation (see Box 3.2). When 75% of states have PDMPs, she determined there is a 0.00034% chance (0.0000034 × 100) of choosing exactly 5 states with PDMPs out of 20 selected.

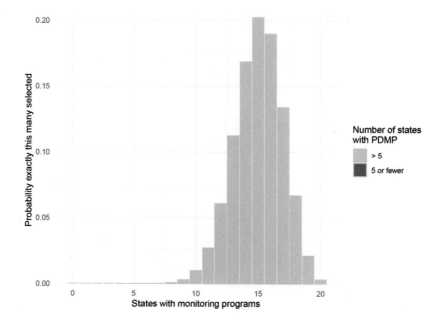

So far, the probabilities were very small for scenarios of getting exactly five or exactly 10 states with PDMPs in a sample. Kiara explained that the ***cumulative distribution function*** for the binomial distribution can determine the probability of getting some *range of values*, which is often more useful than finding the probability of one specific number of successes. For example, what is the probability of selecting 20 states and getting five *or fewer* states with PDMPs? Likewise, what is the probability of getting 10 *or more* states with PDMPs in a sample of 20? Leslie wrote out the equation for the cumulative distribution function in Equation (4.4).

$$f(x,n,p) = \sum_{x=0}^{x_{floor}} \binom{n}{x} p^x (1-p)^{(n-x)} \qquad (4.4)$$

where x is the number of successes, x_{floor} is the largest integer less than or equal to x, n is the sample size, and p is the probability of success. Kiara mentioned that the cumulative distribution function computes the probability of getting x *or fewer* successes.

Leslie asked Nancy if she could edit the graph to show the probability of 5 or fewer states with PDMPs in a sample of 20 where 51% of states overall have PDMPs. She edited the graph so that the purple showed the range where there were five or fewer successes (Figure 4.8).

Leslie and Kiara thought it looked like less than a 2% chance of five or fewer given the size of the purple section of Figure 4.8. Nancy introduced `pbinom()`, which uses Equation (4.4) to compute the probability of five or fewer successes (q = 5) in a sample of 20 (`size = 20`) from a population with a 51% probability of success (`prob = .51`):

```
# 5 or fewer successes from 20 selections
# with 51% probability of success
pbinom(q = 5, size = 20, prob = .51)
## [1] 0.01664024
```

FIGURE 4.8 Probability of 5 or fewer selected states with PDMPs out of 20 total selected when 51% have PDMPs overall

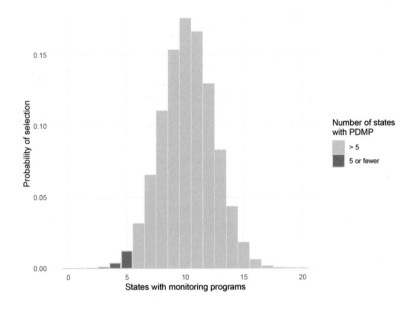

FIGURE 4.9 Probability of 10 or more selected states with PDMPs out of 20 total selected when 51% have PDMPs overall

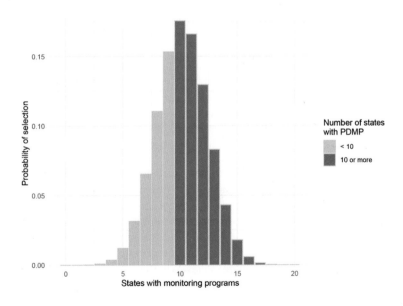

The probability of 0.0166 or 1.66% makes sense. The purple section of Figure 4.8 appears to be quite small. Leslie wanted to try computing the probability for 10 successes *or more*. Nancy created Figure 4.9 to start.

Leslie thought this looked like more than half the time. She asked Nancy to use `pbinom()` to compute the value. This time, the range of values she wanted to get the probability for was on the right side of the graph instead of the left side, so she looked at the help documentation and found that there was a setting for pbinom() to get the right side of the graph but specifying lower.tail = FALSE. The lower.tail = option has the default value of TRUE, so it did not need to be included when estimating the lower tail, but it needs to be added when it is the upper tail on the right being estimated.

```
# 10 or more successes from 20 selections
# with 51% probability of success
# get right side of graph
pbinom(q = 10, size = 20, prob = .51, lower.tail = FALSE)
## [1] 0.4474504
```

This did not seem right to Kiara and Leslie. It did not match the graph, which clearly showed more than half of the histogram was shaded purple. Leslie had an idea. The pbinom() calculation with the default of lower.tail = TRUE is for 10 or fewer successes; maybe the lower.tail = FALSE is computing *higher than 10* rather than *10 or higher,* so it is missing some of the graph in the middle. Leslie thought a change to the arguments for pbinom() might work to get the probability of *10 or more* successes:

```
# 10 or more successes from 20 selections
# with 51% probability of success
pbinom(q = 9, size = 20, prob = .51, lower.tail = FALSE)
## [1] 0.6229439
```

This seemed like a more accurate value for the purple part of Figure 4.9. Leslie interpreted the results as a 62.29% probability of selecting 10 or more states with PDMPs in a sample of 20 from a population of states where 51% have PDMPs.

Leslie was not that excited about this day of R so far. It had not seemed all that useful, and there had not been much coding fun yet. Kiara suggested that bringing in some actual data and testing the methods on the real data might help. Unfortunately, the first opioid policy data from the KFF from 2015 to 2017 were summary data that did not list the specific states that had passed the opioid policies. Leslie searched the KFF website and found a table with available downloadable data showing the actual states and their opioid policy adoption as of 2017 (Smith et al., 2016).

Nancy sprang into action and began to code. She tried to bring the data directly into R from the KFF website, but the way the website was formatted, it was better to download and save the data and use the saved data file. She downloaded the file from the website, opened it in Excel, and removed a few rows at the top and bottom of the file that contained notes (not data), then sent it to Leslie. Kiara was a little annoyed by this because removing things by hand is not a reproducible research practice, but she let it go for now.

Leslie imported the file and used summary() to review what was there.

```
# bring in the opioid policy data and check it out
opioid.policy.kff <- read.csv(file = "[data folder location]/data/pdmp_2017_
kff_ch4.csv")

# check the data frame
summary(object = opioid.policy.kff)
```

```
##              X       Opioid.Quantity.Limits Clinical.Edits.in.Claim.System
## Alabama    : 1    No : 1                 No : 3
## Alaska     : 1    Yes:50                 Yes:48
## Arizona    : 1
## Arkansas   : 1
## California : 1
## Colorado   : 1
## (Other)    :45
## Opioid.Step.Therapy.Requirements
## No :12
## Yes:39
##
##
##
##
##
## Other.Prior.Authorization.Requirements.for.Opioids
## No : 7
## Yes:44
##
##
##
##
##
## Required.Use.of.Prescription.Drug.Monitoring.Programs
## No :19
## Yes:32
##
##
##
##
##
## Any.Opioid.Management.Strategies.In.Place
## Yes:51
##
##
##
##
##
##
```

Leslie was unsure about how to proceed. Kiara explained that they could pretend that they only had a budget to collect data from a sample of states and then use the binomial distribution with that sample to see if they could get close to what the true value is. Kiara suggested they take a sample of 25 states and see if the sample of 25 states has 15 or more states with PDMPs. First, they should see what the binomial distribution tells them about the probability of getting a sample with 15 or more PDMPs out of 25 states. For this, they would need the percentage of states that currently have PDMPs (the success rate). Leslie examined the KFF data and saw that 32/51, or 63% of states, had PDMPs as of 2017. Leslie copied the `pbinom()` code and revised it for the new scenario:

```
# 15 or more successes from 25 selections
# with 63% probability of success
# pbinom computes left tail, so use lower.tail = FALSE
pbinom(q = 14, size = 25, prob = .63, lower.tail = FALSE)
## [1] 0.7018992
```

The probability of selecting a sample of 25 states where 15 or more states have PDMPs is 70.19%. Leslie did not know what to do next. Luckily, Nancy had some R code to help. Before they started sampling, Kiara chimed in to tell Leslie and Nancy that the `set.seed()` function is useful when conducting random sampling since it will result in the same sample to be taken each time the code is run, which makes sampling more reproducible (see Box 4.2).

4.2 Kiara's reproducibility resource: Using `set.seed()`

Kiara never missed an opportunity to teach Leslie about reproducibility. While she thought it was a little early in Leslie's R education to introduce the `set.seed()` function, she decided to do it anyway.

Kiara explained that some procedures in statistics are conducted by first selecting a subset of values at random from a larger group of values. When values are randomly selected, there is usually no way to find the same set of values again. However, the `set.seed()` function in R allows the analyst to set a starting point for the random selection process. The selection process can then be reproduced by setting the same seed. When a random selection process starts in the same place, the same random sample of values is selected.

Try an example to see what happens when no `set.seed()` function is used with the `opioid.policy.kff` data frame.

```
# sample 25 states at random and get some frequencies
opioid.policy.kff %>%
  select(Required.Use.of.Prescription.Drug.Monitoring.Programs) %>%
  sample_n(size = 25) %>%
  summary()
```

```
## Required.Use.of.Prescription.Drug.Monitoring.Programs
## No :11
## Yes:14

# sample another 25 states at random using the same code
opioid.policy.kff %>%
  select(Required.Use.of.Prescription.Drug.Monitoring.Programs) %>%
  sample_n(size = 25) %>%
  summary()

## Required.Use.of.Prescription.Drug.Monitoring.Programs
## No :13
## Yes:12
```

The frequencies for the two samples are different because they include different states. Leslie noticed she got different values than Kiara when she took the samples on her laptop. Now choose a seed value and set the same seed value before each sample:

```
# set seed value
set.seed(seed = 35)
# sample 25 states at random
opioid.policy.kff %>%
  select(Required.Use.of.Prescription.Drug.Monitoring.Programs) %>%
  sample_n(size = 25) %>%
  summary()
## Required.Use.of.Prescription.Drug.Monitoring.Programs
## No :13
## Yes:12

# set seed value
set.seed(seed = 35)
# sample 25 states at random
opioid.policy.kff %>%
  select(Required.Use.of.Prescription.Drug.Monitoring.Programs) %>%
  sample_n(size = 25) %>%
  summary()
```

(Continued)

(Continued)

```
##   Required.Use.of.Prescription.Drug.Monitoring.Programs
##   No :13
##   Yes:12
```

The frequencies are the same because the same states are in each sample.

Kiara had one more piece of information about `set.seed()` to share with Leslie. The random number generator (RNG) that R used for sampling was changed in R version 3.6.0, which was released in early 2019 and is often referred to as *R-3.6.0*. Any analyses that were done using `set.seed()` before this version would not be reproducible with `set.seed()` and the same seed number. Instead, to reproduce older results that had used `set.seed()`, another function was required to specify the random number generator default from earlier versions of R. Kiara wrote the code they would use in this situation, using the example of `seed = 35` that they had just examined.

```
# reproduce R results from analyses prior
# to R version 3.6.0
RNGkind(sample.kind = "Rounding")
set.seed(seed = 35)

# sample 25 states at random
opioid.policy.kff %>%
  select(Required.Use.of.Prescription.Drug.Monitoring.Programs) %>%
  sample_n(size = 25) %>%
    summary()
##   Required.Use.of.Prescription.Drug.Monitoring.Programs
##   No : 6
##   Yes:19
```

Leslie saw that the sample was different from the previous samples using the seed value of 35. Kiara explained that these results would be consistent with samples taken prior to R version 3.6.0. She explained that the current default RNG algorithm for sampling is "Rejection," whereas R versions before 3.6.0 had used the "Rounding" algorithm as the default. She changed the `sample.kind` argument to "Rejection" to demonstrate.

```
# reproduce R results from analyses from
# R version 3.6.0 and later
```

```
RNGkind(sample.kind = "Rejection")
set.seed(seed = 35)

# sample 25 states at random
opioid.policy.kff %>%
  select(Required.Use.of.Prescription.Drug.Monitoring.Programs) %>%
  sample_n(size = 25) %>%
  summary()

##   Required.Use.of.Prescription.Drug.Monitoring.Programs
##   No :13
##   Yes:12
```

The results were now the same as what they had obtained the first time they used `set.seed()` with the seed of 35. Kiara noted that "Rejection" was now the default. As long as analysis was conducted using a version of R that was 3.6.0 or later, reproducing the analysis in a version of R that was 3.6.0 or later did not require setting the `RNGkind()` to "Rejection" since this was the default. That is, they could just use the `set.seed()` and it would default to the "Rejection" style of RNG. Leslie asked why the `set.seed()` function had changed and Kiara explained that the previous RNG had not worked well for taking very large samples (https://bugs.r-project.org/bugzilla/show_bug.cgi?id=17494), so this change was made to address that limitation.

Leslie was a little nervous about using the `set.seed()` function for the rest of the work today after they had been changing the default settings. Kiara suggested they reset the random number generator to its default settings before they went on to the rest of the work. The `RNGversion()` function can be used for this. Adding `getRversion()` as the argument will result in R using the defaults for the current version of R being used. Leslie was confused. Kiara showed her the code.

```
# reinstate default RNG settings of
# version of R being used
RNGversion(vstr = getRversion())
```

Kiara reassured Leslie that, as long as she was using a recent version of R (at least 3.6.0), she would not have to worry about the RNG settings and could just use `set.seed()` to make sure her work was reproducible. Leslie was relieved since she had R-3.6.0 and did not plan on going back to an older version of the software.

Being able to select the same value as a starting point for sampling or analyses is useful for ensuring that other people can reproduce statistical results. Without a starting seed for the samples, reproduced results would often be close but not the same as the results shown. In addition to sampling, there are other uses for `set.seed()` in some sophisticated statistical models that use simulation to estimate values.

It is often difficult or even impossible to measure a single characteristic of a population, even for a characteristic that does not seem complex. For example, consider measuring the age of every person in the United States. With more than 325 million people and people being born and dying constantly, there is just no feasible way. Instead, researchers take samples or subsets of the population. There are many methods of sampling that serve different purposes, but one common choice researchers have to make is whether they will sample with or without replacement.

In **sampling with replacement**, a person selected to be in a sample would then be *replaced* into the population before the next selection. This means the probability of any given person being selected remains exactly the same because the sample size remains exactly the same. However, it also means that same person could be selected multiple times, although this is rare when the population is very large. **Sampling without replacement** changes the sample size with each selection, but each person in the population can be represented in the sample only one time.

As she wrote the code, Nancy explained that `sample_n()` can be used to take a sample. The arguments for `sample_n()` are `size =`, which is where to put the size of the sample to take, and `replace =`, which is where you choose whether you want R to sample *with replacement* (replacing each value into the population after selection so that it could be selected again) or *without replacement* (leaving a value out of the sampling after selection). Leslie had learned about sampling with and without replacement in her previous statistics class and shared some of her notes with Kiara and Nancy for later (Box 4.3).

Nancy wrote the code to take the sample and to get the percentage of states in the sample with a PDMP. She made a note to herself that it might be worth renaming the variables since they have very long names in the imported data frame.

```
# set a starting value for sampling
set.seed(seed = 3)

# sample 25 states and check file
opioid.policy.kff %>%
  select(Required.Use.of.Prescription.Drug.Monitoring.Programs) %>%
  sample_n(size = 25) %>%
  summary()
##  Required.Use.of.Prescription.Drug.Monitoring.Programs
##  No :8
##  Yes:17
```

The output shows `No  :8` and `Yes:17`, so the sample has 17 states with PDMPs. Leslie was satisfied. The binomial distribution indicated there was a 70.19% chance they would see 15 or more states with PDMPs in a sample this big, and they did. Nancy thought they should take a few more samples with different seeds just to see what would happen.

```
# set a starting value for sampling
set.seed(seed = 10)

# sample 25 states and check file
opioid.policy.kff %>%
  select(Required.Use.of.Prescription.Drug.Monitoring.Programs) %>%
  sample_n(size = 25) %>%
  summary()
##  Required.Use.of.Prescription.Drug.Monitoring.Programs
##  No :10
##  Yes:15
```

This sample has 15 states with PDMPs. Nancy thought they should try at least one more.

```
# set a starting value for sampling
set.seed(seed = 999)

# sample 25 states and check file
opioid.policy.kff %>%
  select(Required.Use.of.Prescription.Drug.Monitoring.Programs) %>%
  sample_n(size = 25) %>%
  summary()
##  Required.Use.of.Prescription.Drug.Monitoring.Programs
##  No :11
##  Yes:14
```

This one has 14 states with PDMPs. Out of three samples of 25 states, two samples had 15 or more states with PDMPs and one sample had fewer than 15 states with PDMPs. This was consistent with the binomial distribution prediction that 70.19% of the time a sample of size 25 will have at least 15 states with PDMPs. Leslie agreed that it is a lot easier to use `pbinom()` than to take a bunch of samples to see what happens. She finally saw the value of this distribution for selecting a sample size. Kiara was glad this clarified things, and they prepared for the next achievement on the list.

4.5.4 ACHIEVEMENT 2: CHECK YOUR UNDERSTANDING

Forty-eight states (94%) had implemented an opioid quantity limits policy by 2017. Nancy created the graph shown in Figure 4.10 to show the probability for having an opioid quantity policy in a sample of 30 states when the probability in the population of states is 94%. Based on the graph, how likely do you think it is that exactly 30 states in a sample of 30 states would have this policy?

FIGURE 4.10 Probability of states having an opioid quantity limits policy out of 30 total selected when 94% have the policy overall

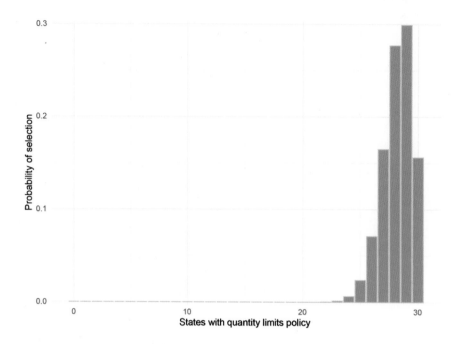

Use `dbinom()` to determine the probability of choosing 30 states and having exactly 30 of them with an implemented opioid quantity limits policy in 2017. Interpret the result for Leslie and note how well the result matches what could be estimated based on Figure 4.10.

4.6 Achievement 3: Understanding the characteristics and uses of the normal distribution of a continuous variable

Kiara reminded Leslie that many of the variables of interest in social science are not binary, so the binomial distribution and its related functions would not be all that useful. Instead, Kiara explained, the probability distribution for a continuous variable is the normal distribution. Just as the shape of the binomial distribution is determined by n and p, the shape of the normal distribution for a variable in a sample is determined by μ and σ, the population mean and standard deviation, which are estimated by the sample mean and standard deviation, m and s.

4.6.1 PROBABILITY DENSITY FUNCTION

Kiara explained that the normal distribution is used to find the likelihood of a certain value or range of values for a continuous variable. For example, she had calculated the mean distance to the nearest substance abuse facility providing medication-assisted treatment for all the counties in the amfAR data set and found that it was 24.04 miles with a standard deviation of 22.66 miles. Like the probabilities from the binomial distribution that are shown visually in a probability mass function graph, the normal distribution has a *probability density function* graph. Using the mean and standard deviation of 24.04 and 22.66, the probability density function graph would look like Figure 4.11.

FIGURE 4.11 Probability density for a variable with a mean of 24.04 and a standard deviation of 22.66

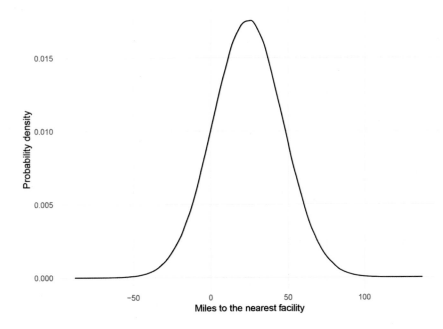

Leslie noticed that this graph extended into negative numbers, which did not make sense for a measure of distance. There is no way to walk or drive –2 miles. She thought back to Section 2.6.3 and guessed that this variable might be *skewed* to the right rather than normally distributed, given the large standard deviation relative to its mean. Her first thought had been *leptokurtic*, but since the left side of the distribution of this variable has to stop at zero, it seemed more likely that it was right skewed. Kiara thought this sounded likely and suggested that they **transform** the variable so that they could continue to discuss the normal distribution. For variables that are right skewed, a few transformations that could work to make the variable more normally distributed are square root, cube root, reciprocal, and log (Manikandan, 2010).

Leslie imported the distance data from amfAR and reviewed it before they worked on data transformation.

```
# distance to substance abuse facility with medication-assisted treatment
dist.mat <- read.csv(file = "[data folder location]/data/opioid_dist_to_
facility_2017_ch4.csv")

# review the data
summary(object = dist.mat)
##      STATEFP          COUNTYFP          YEAR           INDICATOR
## Min.   : 1.00    Min.   :   1.0    Min.   :2017    dist_MAT:3214
## 1st Qu.:19.00    1st Qu.:  35.0    1st Qu.:2017
## Median :30.00    Median :  79.0    Median :2017
## Mean   :31.25    Mean   : 101.9    Mean   :2017
## 3rd Qu.:46.00    3rd Qu.: 133.0    3rd Qu.:2017
## Max.   :72.00    Max.   : 840.0    Max.   :2017
##
```

```
##       VALUE                STATE          STATEABBREVIATION
##   Min.   :   0.00    Texas   : 254    TX     : 254
##   1st Qu.:   9.25    Georgia : 159    GA     : 159
##   Median :  18.17    Virginia: 127    VA     : 127
##   Mean   :  24.04    Kentucky: 120    KY     : 120
##   3rd Qu.:  31.00    Missouri: 115    MO     : 115
##   Max.   : 414.86    Kansas  : 105    KS     : 105
##                      (Other) :2334    (Other):2334
##                 COUNTY
##   Washington County:   30
##   Jefferson County :   25
##   Franklin County  :   24
##   Jackson County   :   23
##   Lincoln County   :   23
##   Madison County   :   19
##   (Other)          :3070
```

Nancy summarized the variables in the data frame as follows:

- STATEFP: Unique Federal Information Processing Standards (FIPS) code representing each state
- COUNTYFP: Unique FIPS code representing each county
- YEAR: Year data were collected
- INDICATOR: Label for value variable
- VALUE: Distance in miles to nearest substance abuse facility with medication-assisted treatment (MAT)
- STATE: Name of state
- STATEABBREVIATION: Abbreviation for state
- COUNTY: Name of county

Before they began to work on the data, Nancy wanted to clarify that the data were *county-level* data. The distances contained in the data frame were the distances from the middle of each county to the nearest treatment facility with medication-assisted therapy (MAT) for substance abuse. Leslie and Kiara were glad Nancy reminded them and understood that they were working with counties and not with states or people. Leslie repeated that, for these data, the observations were counties. Nancy nodded yes and Leslie went ahead and graphed the distance variable, VALUE, to confirm whether skew was a problem (Figure 4.12).

```
# open tidyverse
library(package = "tidyverse")

# graph the distance variable (Figure 4.13)
dist.mat %>%
```

```r
ggplot(aes(x = VALUE)) +
  geom_histogram(fill = "#7463AC", color = "white") +
  theme_minimal() +
  labs(x = "Miles to nearest substance abuse facility",
       y = "Number of counties")
```

The distance variable was skewed for sure! Leslie tried the four transformations to see which was more useful for making the distance variable more normally distributed (Figure 4.13).

```r
# transforming the variable
dist.mat.cleaned <- dist.mat %>%
  mutate(miles.cube.root = VALUE^(1/3)) %>%
  mutate(miles.log = log(x = VALUE)) %>%
  mutate(miles.inverse = 1/VALUE) %>%
  mutate(miles.sqrt = sqrt(x = VALUE))

# graph the transformations (Figure 4.13)
cuberoot <- dist.mat.cleaned %>%
  ggplot(aes(x = miles.cube.root)) +
  geom_histogram(fill = "#7463AC", color = "white") +
  theme_minimal() +
  labs(x = "Cube root of miles to nearest facility", y = "Number of counties")

logged <- dist.mat.cleaned %>%
  ggplot(aes(x = miles.log)) +
  geom_histogram(fill = "#7463AC", color = "white") +
  theme_minimal() +
  labs(x = "Log of miles to nearest facility", y = "")

inversed <- dist.mat.cleaned %>%
  ggplot(aes(x = miles.inverse)) +
  geom_histogram(fill = "#7463AC", color = "white") +
  theme_minimal() + xlim(0, 1) +
  labs(x = "Inverse of miles to nearest facility", y = "Number of counties")

squareroot <- dist.mat.cleaned %>%
  ggplot(aes(x = miles.sqrt)) +
  geom_histogram(fill = "#7463AC", color = "white") +
  theme_minimal() +
  labs(x = "Square root of miles to nearest facility", y = "")

gridExtra::grid.arrange(cuberoot, logged, inversed, squareroot)
```

FIGURE 4.12 Miles from county to the nearest substance abuse treatment facility with medication-assisted therapy (2017)

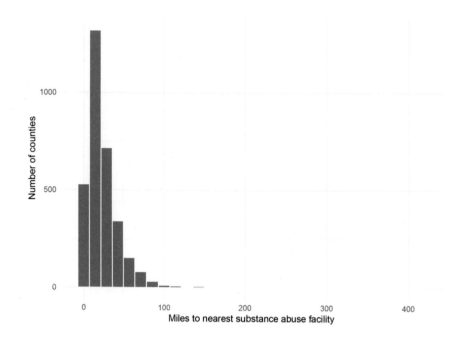

FIGURE 4.13 Selecting a transformation to make the distance variable more normally distributed for analysis

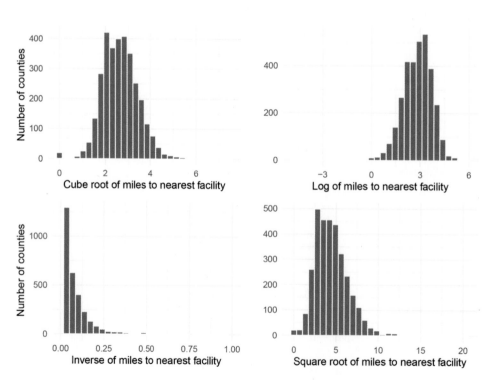

Leslie found that the cube root was the best of the four transformations for making the distribution appear normal, or *normalizing* the variable. The inverse did not work at all and made the variable appear even more skewed than it originally was. The log and square root both were fine, but Leslie decided the cube root was closest to normal and chose this transformation. Nancy proceeded to get the mean and standard deviation of the cube root of distance so they could get back to plotting the probability distribution.

```
# mean and standard deviation for cube root of miles
dist.mat.cleaned %>%
  summarize(mean.tran.dist = mean(x = miles.cube.root),
            sd.tran.dist = sd(x = miles.cube.root))
##   mean.tran.dist sd.tran.dist
## 1      2.662915    0.7923114
```

Nancy plotted the probability distribution with these new summary statistics (Figure 4.14).

That looked good for the purpose of discussing the probabilities. They returned to the original topic, and Kiara explained that the area under the Figure 4.14 curve represents 100% of observations. Using this probability density function graph to determine probabilities is a little different from using the probability mass function graph from the binomial distribution in the previous examples. With continuous variables, the probability of any one specific value is going to be extremely low, often near zero. Instead, probabilities are usually computed for a range of values.

Nancy created an example of this with the shading under the curve representing U.S. counties with the cube root of miles to a treatment facility being 4 or more, which is 4 cubed or 64 miles or more to the nearest substance abuse treatment facility with MAT (Figure 4.15).

FIGURE 4.14 Probability density function for a variable with a mean of 2.66 and a standard deviation of .79

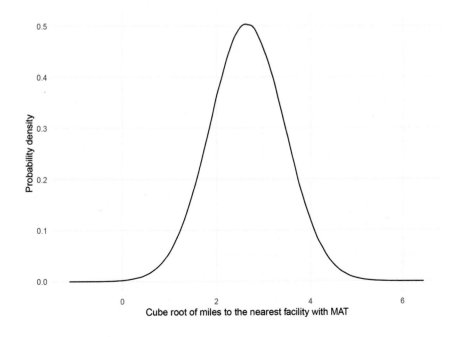

FIGURE 4.15 Probability density function for the cube root of the distance to treatment facility variable with a mean of 2.66 and a standard deviation of .79

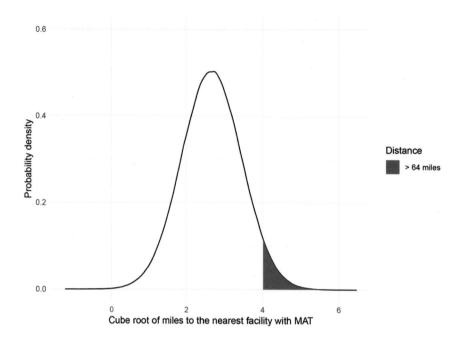

4.6.2 FINDING THE AREA UNDER THE CURVE

Nancy told Leslie that the `pnorm()` function is useful for finding the actual probability value for the shaded area under the curve. In this case, `pnorm()` could be used to determine the proportion of counties that are 4 cube root miles or more to the nearest facility with MAT. The `pnorm()` function takes three arguments: the value of interest (q), the mean (m), and the standard deviation (s).

```
# shaded area under normal curve > 4
# when curve has mean of 2.66 and sd of .79
pnorm(q = 4, mean = 2.66, sd = .79)
## [1] 0.9550762
```

Kiara asked Leslie if 95.5% seemed right. Did the shaded area in Figure 4.15 look like 95.5% of the area under the curve? Leslie shook her head no.

Nancy let them both know that the `pnorm()` function finds the area under the curve starting on the left up to, but not including, the q value entered, which in this case is 4. To get the area from 4 to ∞ under the right tail of the distribution, add the `lower.tail = FALSE` option.

```
# shaded area under normal curve
# when curve has mean of 2.66 and sd of .79
pnorm(q = 4, mean = 2.66, sd = .79, lower.tail = FALSE)
## [1] 0.04492377
```

Yes, this was much better! It looked like 4.49% of observations were in the shaded part of this distribution and therefore had a value for the distance variable of 4 or greater. Reversing the transformation, this indicated that residents of 4.49% of counties have to travel 4^3 or 64 miles or more to get to the nearest substance abuse facility providing medication-assisted treatment. This seemed really far to Leslie to travel to get treatment, especially for people struggling with an opioid addiction or trying to help their family members and friends. Kiara agreed, 64 miles of travel could be an insurmoutable challenge for people trying to get care.

4.6.3 ACHIEVEMENT 3: CHECK YOUR UNDERSTANDING

Figure 4.16 shows shading for the part of the distribution that is less than 2. Estimate (without computing the answer) the percentage of counties in the shaded area.

Use pnorm() to compute the percentage of counties in the shaded area. Compare the answer with your estimate to see if it seems accurate, and make adjustments to the code if needed. Interpret the final computed value.

FIGURE 4.16 Probability density function for a variable with a mean of 2.66 and a standard deviation of .79

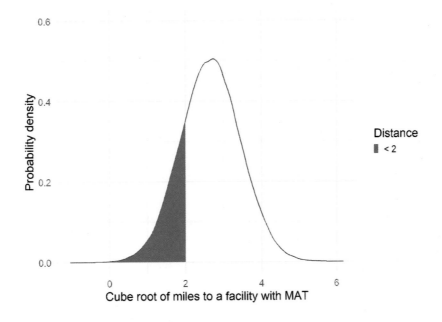

4.7 Achievement 4: Computing and interpreting z-scores to compare observations to groups

Kiara chimed in to show off her favorite useful feature of the normal distribution. She told Leslie that, regardless of what the mean and standard deviation are, a normally distributed variable has approximately

- 68% of values within one standard deviation of the mean
- 95% of values within two standard deviations of the mean
- 99.7% of values within three standard deviations of the mean

These characteristics of the normal distribution can be used to describe and compare how far individual observations are from a mean value. For example, in the example above, about 68% of counties are between 2.66 − .79 = 1.87 and 2.66 + .79 = 3.45 cube root miles from the nearest substance abuse facility with MAT. Transforming these values back into miles would be cubing them, so 6.54 to 41.06 miles. In addition, about 95% of counties would be between 2.66 − (.79 × 2) and 2.66 + (.79 × 2) miles, which would be cubed to equal 1.26 and 76.23 miles, from the nearest substance abuse facility with MAT.

Kiara explained that this information was used to create z-scores, which allow description and comparison of where an observation falls compared to the other observations for a normally distributed variable.

4.7.1 DEFINING THE z-SCORE

Kiara gave Leslie the z-score formula in Equation (4.5) and explained that the *z-score* is the number of standard deviations an observation is away from the mean.

$$z_i = \frac{x_i - m_x}{s_x} \tag{4.5}$$

The x_i in Equation (4.5) represents the value of variable x for a single observation, m_x is the mean of the x variable, and s_x is the standard deviation of the x variable. So, z_i is the difference between the observation value and the mean value for a variable and is converted by the denominator into standard deviations. The final z-score for an observation is the number of standard deviations it is from the mean.

4.7.2 CALCULATING AND INTERPRETING z-SCORES

Leslie tried using Equation (4.5) to calculate z for a county with residents who have to travel 50 miles to the nearest facility. In the transformed miles variable, this would be the cube root of 50, or a value of 3.68. Leslie substituted the values into Equation (4.5) and computed z.

$$z = \frac{3.68 - 2.66}{.79} = 1.29 \tag{4.6}$$

Equation (4.6) produced $z = 1.29$, which indicated that the transformed distance to a facility with MAT for this example county was 1.29 standard deviations above the mean transformed distance from a county to a facility with MAT. This county was farther away from MAT than the mean distance for a county.

In Equation (4.7), Leslie found that a county with a 10-mile distance to a facility with MAT, which is a value of 2.15 in the transformed distance variable, was .65 standard deviations *below* the mean transformed distance ($z = -.65$):

$$z = \frac{2.15 - 2.66}{.79} = -.65 \tag{4.7}$$

Leslie noticed that the z-score was a positive value for a county with a distance that was higher than the mean and a negative value for a county with a distance that was lower than the mean. The z-score not only indicated how many standard deviations away from the mean an observation was, but whether the observed value was above or below the mean.

4.7.3 ACHIEVEMENT 4: CHECK YOUR UNDERSTANDING

Use Equation (4.5) to calculate the z-score for a county where you have to drive 15 miles to the nearest substance abuse treatment facility with MAT. Remember to transform the 15-mile distance first before computing z. Interpret your result.

4.8 Achievement 5: Estimating population means from sample means using the normal distribution

4.8.1 SAMPLES AND POPULATIONS

Kiara explained that the characteristics of the normal curve are exceptionally useful in better understanding the characteristics of a population when it is impossible to measure the entire population. She stated that, for example, there was no real way to measure the height or weight or income of every single person in the United States. Instead, researchers often use a representative sample from the population they are interested in and use properties of the normal distribution to understand what is likely happening in the whole population.

A *representative sample* is a sample taken carefully so that it does a good job of representing the characteristics of the population. For example, if a sample of U.S. citizens were taken and the sample was 75% female, this would not be representative of the distribution of sex in the population. There are many strategies for sampling that help to ensure a representative sample. Kiara suggested that Leslie read about sampling if she is ever going to collect her own data.

4.8.2 USING THE NORMAL DISTRIBUTION AND SAMPLES TO UNDERSTAND POPULATIONS

To see how the normal distribution can use sample data to understand the population, Leslie suggested using the distance to a treatment facility variable. Kiara thought that would work and explained that they do not have to transform the variable for this demonstration because the theory they are using works for continuous variables whether they are normally distributed or not.

Before they started, Leslie used the `rename()` code from Section 3.4.2 to give the distance variable the name `distance` since that was easier to remember. She also used `summarize()` to remind them all of the mean and standard deviation of the `distance` variable.

```
# rename variable
dist.mat.cleaned <- dist.mat %>%
  rename('distance' = VALUE)

# get mean and sd from cleaned data
dist.mat.cleaned %>%
  summarize(mean.dist = mean(x = distance),
            sd.dist = sd(x = distance),
            n = n())
##   mean.dist  sd.dist    n
## 1  24.04277 22.66486 3214
```

Leslie found that the mean distance to the nearest substance abuse facility that provides at least one type of MAT is 24.04 miles away, with a standard deviation of 22.66 miles. She also noted that there were 3,214 counties in the data set representing all (or almost all) of the counties in the United States; thus, this is not a sample of counties, it is the population of counties.

Kiara then asked Leslie how close she thought they could get to the true mean distance to a facility ($m = 24.04$) if they had only enough time and money to collect data on distances from 500 counties rather than all 3,214 counties?

4.8.3 EXAMINING A SAMPLE FROM A POPULATION

Leslie was unsure about whether a sample would have a mean distance anywhere near the mean distance in the population. Luckily Nancy had some R code to help. Before they started sampling, Kiara reminded Leslie and Nancy that the `set.seed()` function is useful for reproducibility (Box 4.2). With Nancy's help, Leslie wrote the first code to take a sample of 500 counties, using `set.seed()` and finding the mean of the distances in the sample with `summarize()`. Leslie explained that they were sampling with replacement since each observation having the same exact chance of selection is part of the definition of the Central Limit Theorem, which is what they were going to explore.

```
# set a starting value for sampling
set.seed(seed = 1945)

# sample 500 counties at random
counties.500 <- dist.mat.cleaned %>%
  sample_n(size = 500, replace = TRUE)

# compute the mean distance in the sample
counties.500 %>%
  summarize(mean.s1 = mean(x = distance))
##    mean.s1
## 1 24.40444
```

The result is 24.40 miles, which is close to the population mean of 24.04 miles, but not exactly the same. Leslie tried it again with a different seed value to choose a different set of 500 counties.

```
# set a different starting value for sampling
set.seed(seed = 48)

# sample 500 counties at random
counties.500.2 <- dist.mat.cleaned %>%
  sample_n(size = 500, replace = TRUE)

# compute the mean distance in the sample
counties.500.2 %>%
  summarize(mean.s2 = mean(x = distance))
##    mean.s2
## 1 23.49652
```

This time the mean distance was 23.50 miles, which is lower than the first sample mean of 24.40 miles and a little under the population value of 24.04 miles.

4.8.4 EXAMINING A SAMPLE OF SAMPLES FROM A POPULATION

Leslie wondered what would happen if she took 20 samples of counties where each sample had 500 counties in it. Nancy had done this before and had some code to work with. She used the `replicate()` function with the argument `n = 20` to repeat the sampling 20 times. She then used `bind_rows()` to combine the 20 samples into a data frame.

After collecting and combining all the samples, she used `group_by()` and `summarize()` to get the mean distance for each sample.

```
# get 20 samples
# each sample has 500 counties
# put samples in a data frame with each sample having
# a unique id called sample_num
set.seed(seed = 111)
samples.20 <- bind_rows(replicate(n = 20, dist.mat.cleaned %>%
                            sample_n(size = 500, replace = TRUE),
                            simplify = FALSE), .id = "sample_num")

# find the mean for each sample
sample.20.means <- samples.20 %>%
  group_by(sample_num) %>%
  summarize(mean.distance = mean(x = distance, na.rm = TRUE))
sample.20.means
## # A tibble: 20 x 2
##     sample_num mean.distance
##     <chr>          <dbl>
## 1  1             24.2
## 2  10            22.0
## 3  11            23.9
## 4  12            23.8
## 5  13            23.1
## 6  14            23.0
## 7  15            22.6
## 8  16            24.4
## 9  17            24.4
## 10 18            24.0
## 11 19            23.7
## 12 2             24.2
## 13 20            23.1
## 14 3             23.9
## 15 4             24.4
## 16 5             24.7
```

```
## 17  6                   22.8
## 18  7                   24.2
## 19  8                   23.9
## 20  9                   24.2
```

Now that they had the mean distance to substance abuse facilities for each of 20 samples, with each sample including 500 counties, Kiara suggested they take the mean of the sample means. Before they did that, Leslie asked what a `tibble` is since she had seen it in output like the list of means. Kiara explained that a tibble is a type of data frame in R that has better options for printing, especially when data files are very large. Leslie was satisfied with that explanation and wanted to get her hands back on the code, so she asked Nancy for the laptop to get the mean of all the sample means.

```
# find the mean of the 20 sample means
sample.20.means %>%
  summarize(mean.20.means = mean(x = mean.distance))
## # A tibble: 1 x 1
##    mean.20.means
##            <dbl>
## 1          23.7
```

The mean of the 20 sample means is 23.7, which is closer to the population mean of 24.04 than either of the first two individual samples were. Leslie copied the code and changed the n = 20 to n = 100 for 100 samples and found the mean of the 100 sample means.

```
# get 100 samples
set.seed(seed = 143)
samples.100 <- bind_rows(replicate(n = 100, dist.mat.cleaned %>%
                          sample_n(size = 500, replace = TRUE),
                          simplify = FALSE), .id = "sample_num")

# find the mean for each sample
sample.100.means <- samples.100 %>%
  group_by(sample_num) %>%
  summarize(mean.distance = mean(x = distance))

# find the mean of the 100 sample means
sample.100.means %>%
  summarize(mean.100.means = mean(mean.distance))
## # A tibble: 1 x 1
##    mean.100.means
##             <dbl>
## 1           24.0
```

The mean of 100 sample means is 24.0, which is even closer to the true population mean of 24.04 than the individual samples or the mean of the 20 samples.

Nancy told Leslie that they could get closer to the population mean if they used more samples and larger sample sizes.

Leslie tried taking 1,000 samples and graphing the mean distances from the samples. She noticed that the code took a little while to run on her laptop this time. Kiara explained that taking 1,000 samples requires more processing than a single sample. Kiara said it might take a few minutes.

```
# get 1000 samples
set.seed(seed = 159)
samples.1000 <- bind_rows(replicate(n = 1000, dist.mat.cleaned %>%
                          sample_n(size = 500, replace = TRUE),
                          simplify = FALSE), .id = "sample_num")

# find the mean for each sample
sample.1000.means <- samples.1000 %>%
  group_by(sample_num) %>%
  summarize(mean.distance = mean(x = distance))

# find the mean of the sample means
sample.1000.means %>%
  summarize(mean.1000.means = mean(x = mean.distance))
## # A tibble: 1 x 1
##    mean.1000.means
##             <dbl>
## 1            24.0

# histogram of the 1000 means (Figure 4.17)
sample.1000.means %>%
  ggplot(aes(x = mean.distance)) +
  geom_histogram(fill = "#7463AC", color = "white") +
  labs(x = "Mean distance to facility with MAT",
       y = "Number of samples") +
  theme_minimal()
```

Leslie noticed that the mean of the sample means of 24.0 is very close to the population mean of 24.04, and the graph of the sample means looks a lot like a normal distribution (Figure 4.17). Kiara explained that taking a lot of large samples and graphing their means results in a sampling distribution that looks like a normal distribution, and, more importantly, *the mean of the sample means is nearly the same as the population mean.* A *sampling distribution* is the distribution of summary statistics from repeated samples taken from a population.

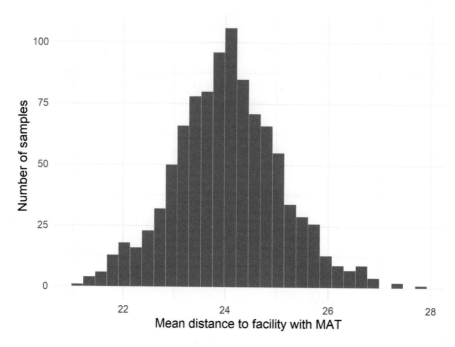

4.8.5 THE CENTRAL LIMIT THEOREM

Kiara explained that this phenomenon is called the *Central Limit Theorem* and that it holds true for continuous variables that both are and are not normally distributed. The Central Limit Theorem is one of the most important ideas for *inferential statistics*, or statistical approaches that infer population characteristics based on sample data.

Another characteristic of the Central Limit Theorem is that the standard deviation of the sample means can be estimated using the population standard deviation and the size of the samples that make up the distribution with Equation (4.8).

$$s_{samp.dist} = \frac{\sigma}{\sqrt{n}} \tag{4.8}$$

where σ is the *population* standard deviation and *n* is the size of the samples used to make the sampling distribution. Since they had all the counties (the population), Leslie computed σ for the population distance variable and used it to compute the standard deviation of the sampling distribution. Unfortunately, the sd() function will not work to compute σ because the underlying calculations for sd() include *n* – 1 in the denominator to account for data being a sample rather than a population. Leslie learned about this once in one of her statistics classes: The *n* – 1 is called the Bessel correction (Upton & Cook, 2014), and when calculating the *population* standard deviation, it is not needed. Leslie went back and copied Equation (2.4) to remind the team about the calculation of the sample standard deviation with Equation (4.9).

$$s_x = \sqrt{\frac{\sum_{i=1}^{n}(x_i - m_x)^2}{n-1}} \tag{4.9}$$

Then she wrote the formula for σ, the population standard deviation, as Equation (4.10):

$$\sigma_x = \sqrt{\frac{\sum_{i=1}^{n}(x_i - \mu_x)^2}{n}} \tag{4.10}$$

Kiara had an idea. She remembered that the standard deviation was the square root of the variance and that the sample variance was calculated using Equation (4.11).

$$s_x^2 = \frac{\sum_{i=1}^{n}(x_i - m_x)^2}{n-1} \tag{4.11}$$

She thought they could use a little algebra to reverse the Bessel correction by multiplying the variance, which is under the square root sign in the standard deviation formula, by $\frac{n-1}{n}$. The $n-1$ in the numerator would cancel out the $n-1$ in the denominator of the variance calculation, leaving n in the denominator. Kiara suggested they use this strategy to calculate the population standard deviation (σ) using Equation (4.10).

$$\sigma_x = \sqrt{\frac{\sum_{i=1}^{n}(x_i - \mu_x)^2}{n-1} \times \frac{n-1}{n}}$$

Nancy thought about how to do this in R and decided she could use `var()*((n-1)/n)` to get the population variance of σ^2 and then use `sqrt()` from there to get population standard deviation (σ). This could then be used to get the estimate of the sampling standard deviation like Equation (4.8). Leslie thought that sounded like a good plan and wrote some code.

```
# compute estimated standard dev of sampling dist
dist.mat.cleaned %>%
  drop_na(distance) %>%
  summarize(n = n(),
            pop.var = var(x = distance)*((n - 1)/n),
            pop.s = sqrt(x = pop.var),
            s.samp.dist.est = pop.s/sqrt(x = 500))

##        n pop.var    pop.s s.samp.dist.est
## 1 3214 513.536 22.66133        1.013446
```

Nancy reminded her that she could also compute the standard deviation of the sampling distribution directly since they had the 1,000 sample means saved in a data frame. That sounded easier and Leslie tried it.

```
# computing the samp dist standard devation
# directly from the 1000 sample means
sd(x = sample.1000.means$mean.distance, na.rm = T)
## [1] 1.04966
```

They noticed that the results were similar (1.01 and 1.05), but not identical.

4.8.6 THE STANDARD ERROR

Kiara explained that, since the mean of the sample means in the sampling distribution is very close to the population mean, the standard deviation of the sampling distribution shows how much we expect sample means to vary from the population mean. Specifically, given that the distribution of sample means is relatively normally distributed, 68% of sample means will be within one standard deviation of the mean of the sampling distribution, and 95% of sample means will be within two standard deviations of the sampling distribution mean. Since the sampling distribution mean is a good estimate of the population mean, it follows that most of the sample means are within one or two standard deviations of the population mean.

Since it is unusual to have the entire population for computing the population standard deviation, and it is also unusual to have a large number of samples from one population, a close approximation to this value is called the *standard error of the mean* (often referred to simply as the "standard error"). The standard error is computed by dividing the standard deviation of a variable by the square root of the sample size (Equation [4.12]).

$$se = \frac{s}{\sqrt{n}} \tag{4.12}$$

where *s* is the sample standard deviation of the variable of interest and *n* is the sample size.

Leslie tried computing the standard error for the mean of distance in the first sample of 500 counties:

```
# mean, sd, se for first sample of 500 counties
counties.500 %>%
  summarize(mean.dist = mean(x = distance),
            sd.dist = sd(x = distance),
            se.dist = sd(x = distance)/sqrt(x = length(x = distance)))
##    mean.dist  sd.dist  se.dist
## 1   24.40444 23.79142 1.063985
```

She could also compute the mean, standard deviation, and standard error of distance for the second sample she took:

```
# mean, sd, se for second sample
counties.500.2 %>%
  summarize(mean.dist = mean(x = distance),
            sd.dist = sd(x = distance),
            se.dist = sd(x = distance)/sqrt(x = length(x = distance)))
##    mean.dist sd.dist   se.dist
## 1   23.49652 20.08756 0.8983431
```

Both of the standard error (*se*) values are close to the sampling distribution standard deviation of 1.05, but they are not exactly the same. The first sample standard error of 1.06 was a little above and the second sample standard error of .90 was a little below.

Kiara wanted to summarize what they had just done because it felt important and confusing:

- The standard deviation of the sampling distribution is 1.05.
- The standard error from the first sample is 1.06.
- The standard error from the second sample is 0.90.

Most of the time, she explained, researchers have a single sample and so the only feasible way to determine the standard deviation of the sampling distribution is by computing the standard error of the single sample. This value tends to be a good estimate of the standard deviation of sample means. As Kiara explained, if

- about 68% of sample means are within one standard deviation of the sampling distribution mean (i.e., mean-of-sample-means),

- about 95% of sample means are within two standard deviations of the sampling distribution mean (i.e., mean-of-sample-means),

- the mean of a sampling distribution tends to be close to the population mean, and

- the sample standard error is a good estimate of the sampling distribution standard deviation,

then the mean of a variable from any given sample (given good data collection practices) is likely to be within two standard errors of the population mean for that variable. This is one of the foundational ideas of inferential statistics.

4.8.7 STANDARD DEVIATION VERSUS STANDARD ERROR

Leslie stopped Kiara to make sure she understood the difference between a sample standard deviation and a sample standard error. Kiara said the standard deviation is a measure of the variability in the sample, while the standard error is an estimate of how closely the sample represents the population.

If there were no way to measure every county to get the population mean for the distance to the nearest substance abuse facility in a county, Leslie could use the first sample of 500 counties to estimate that there is a good chance that the population mean distance is between 24.40 – 1.06 and 24.40 + 1.06 or 23.34 and 25.46. There is an even higher probability that the population mean distance is between 24.40 – (1.06 × 2) and 24.40 + (1.06 × 2) or 22.28 and 26.52. While it is unusual to have the population mean to compare sample results to, this time the team has it and can see that the population mean of 24.04 miles to the nearest substance abuse facility is represented well by the sample mean of 24.40 and its standard error of 1.06.

4.8.8 ACHIEVEMENT 5: CHECK YOUR UNDERSTANDING

Take a sample of 200 counties and compute the mean, standard deviation, and standard error for the distance to the nearest substance abuse treatment facility with medication-assisted therapy. Based on the sample mean and standard error, find the range of values where the population mean distance could be. Explain your results.

4.9 Achievement 6: Computing and interpreting confidence intervals around means and proportions

Leslie wanted to be sure she had the standard error concept correct because it is important. Kiara stated that the range around the sample mean where the population mean *might* be shows the uncertainty of computing a mean from a sample.

These ranges around the sample mean, Kiara explained, are reported as *confidence intervals* (or CIs). Leslie looked confused. Kiara clarified that *confidence* in this context is not about an emotion or feeling, but about how much uncertainty there is in the results. Most of the time, social scientists report 95% intervals or 95% confidence intervals, which show the range where the population value would likely be 95 times if the study were conducted 100 times. Sometimes, smaller or larger intervals are reported, like a 68% confidence interval (68% CI) or a 99% confidence interval (99% CI), but usually it's a 95% confidence interval.

Leslie repeated the 95% interval idea as she understood it:

- About 95% of values lie within two standard deviations of the mean for a variable that is normally distributed.

- The standard error of a sample is a good estimate of the standard deviation of the sampling distribution, which is normally distributed.

- The mean of the sampling distribution is a good estimate of the population mean.

- So, most sample means will be within two standard errors of the population mean.

Perfect, thought Kiara, with one minor correction. While it is common to hear two standard deviations, Kiara explained that the number of standard deviations away from the mean containing 95% of observations in a normal curve is actually 1.96. Kiara repeated what she said to draw Leslie's attention to how she explained 1.96 as the number of standard deviations away from the mean. She reminded Leslie that the number of standard deviations some observation is away from the mean is called a *z*-score. She also thought it might be a good time to mention that the 95% of observations being within 1.96 standard deviations of the mean leaves 5% of observations in the tails of the distribution, outside the confidence interval, as in Figure 4.18.

Leslie confirmed that when they took the first sample of 500 counties, they found the mean distance to a facility with MAT was 24.40 miles with a standard error of 1.06. She asked Kiara if they could use this information to report this as a mean and its 95% confidence interval. Kiara nodded yes. The 95% confidence interval for a mean is constructed from the mean, its standard error, and the *z*-score of 1.96.

FIGURE 4.18 Normal distribution with mean, 95% CI, and 2.5% shaded in each tail outside the 95% CI

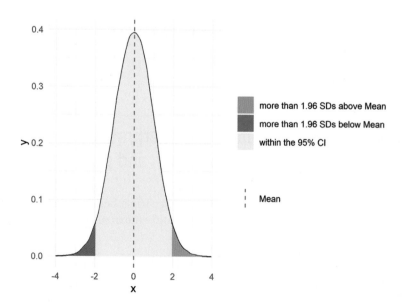

4.9.1 COMPUTING AND INTERPRETING A 95% CONFIDENCE INTERVAL FOR A MEAN

Once she thought she understood how the confidence interval works, Leslie started to compute the CI by hand, but Nancy had a better idea.

```
# add CI to summary statistics
summ.500.counties <- counties.500 %>%
  summarize(mean.s1 = mean(x = distance),
            sd.s1 = sd(x = distance),
            se.s1 = sd(x = distance)/sqrt(x = length(x = distance)),
            lower.ci.s1 = mean.s1 - 1.96 * se.s1,
            upper.ci.s1 = mean.s1 + 1.96 * se.s1)
summ.500.counties
##     mean.s1    sd.s1    se.s1 lower.ci.s1 upper.ci.s1
## 1 24.40444 23.79142 1.063985    22.31903    26.48985
```

The 95% confidence interval for the mean distance from the sample of 500 counties was 22.32–26.49. Kiara interpreted the results for the team:

> The mean distance in miles to the nearest substance abuse treatment facility with MAT in a sample of 500 counties is 24.40; the true or population mean distance in miles to a facility likely lies between 22.32 and 26.49 (m = 24.40; 95% CI = 22.32–26.49).

Nancy thought now was a good time to go back to the visuals and examine this confidence interval with a histogram. She created a histogram of the distance to a treatment facility showing the mean and the 95% confidence interval around the mean (Figure 4.19).

FIGURE 4.19 Miles to the nearest substance abuse treatment facility with MAT from a 2017 sample of 500 counties in the United States

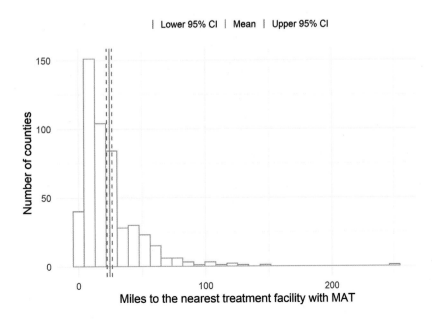

FIGURE 4.20 Miles to the nearest substance abuse treatment facility with MAT from a 2017 sample of 500 counties in the United States

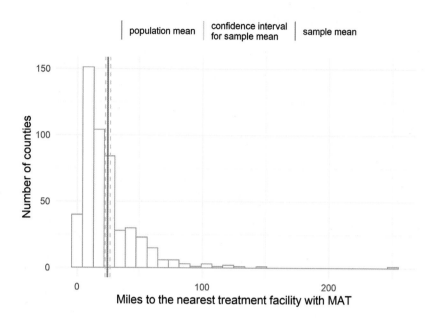

Wow, the confidence interval was really narrow, thought Leslie. Leslie noticed that the mean seemed to be a little to the right of where she would have guessed, but also noticed that the histogram was right-skewed, so it made sense that the mean was a little larger than it seemed like it should be. She remembered back to Section 2.6.2, which explained what skew does to the value of the mean and why the median might be a better measure of central tendency in this situation.

Since they had the unusual benefit of knowing the population mean of the distance variable, Nancy thought it might be a good idea to add the mean for the population to the graph to see how well this sample was doing at representing the population. She added another vertical line to show where the population mean was in relation to the sample mean and its confidence interval (Figure 4.20).

The population mean was inside the confidence interval and just below the sample mean, which was not easy to see since the two means were so close together. Leslie wondered what the mean and confidence interval looked like for the second sample, so she used Nancy's trick to calculate it.

```
# add CI to summary statistics other sample
counties.500.2 %>%
  summarize(mean = mean(x = distance),
            sd = sd(x = distance),
            se = sd(x = distance)/sqrt(x = length(x = distance)),
            lower.ci = mean - 1.96 * se,
            upper.ci = mean + 1.96 * se)
##       mean       sd        se lower.ci upper.ci
## 1 23.49652 20.08756 0.8983431 21.73577 25.25727
```

FIGURE 4.21 Miles to the nearest substance abuse treatment facility with MAT from a 2017 sample of 500 counties in the United States

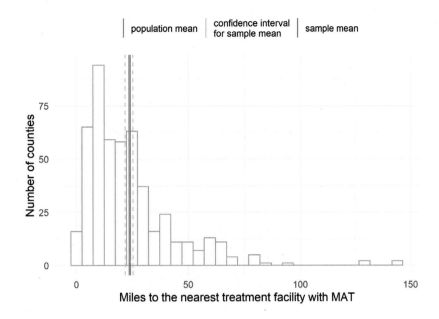

This sample mean is a smaller value than the first sample mean. Leslie asked Nancy if she could plot the mean with its CI and the population mean again so she could see the sample mean, confidence interval, and population mean all together (Figure 4.21).

Again the population mean is inside the confidence interval and near the sample mean. This made Leslie wonder about the confidence intervals when they took 20, 100, and 1,000 samples. Nancy thought they could find these values by using group_by() and summarize(). Nancy tried the 20-samples data.

```
# add CI to summary statistics other sample
samp.20.stats <- samples.20 %>%
  group_by(sample_num) %>%
  summarize(means = mean(x = distance),
            sd = sd(x = distance),
            se = sd(x = distance)/sqrt(x = length(x = distance)),
            lower.ci = means - 1.96 * se,
            upper.ci = means + 1.96 * se)
samp.20.stats
## # A tibble: 20 x 6
##    sample_num means   sd    se lower.ci upper.ci
##    <chr>      <dbl> <dbl> <dbl>   <dbl>    <dbl>
## 1 1           24.2  24.5  1.09    22.0     26.3
## 2 10          22.0  17.1  0.765   20.5     23.5
## 3 11          23.9  20.0  0.895   22.1     25.6
```

```
##  4 12         23.8  20.7 0.924    21.9        25.6
##  5 13         23.1  20.8 0.931    21.2        24.9
##  6 14         23.0  22.3 0.999    21.0        24.9
##  7 15         22.6  19.7 0.880    20.9        24.3
##  8 16         24.4  21.9 0.979    22.5        26.3
##  9 17         24.4  21.6 0.965    22.5        26.3
## 10 18         24.0  22.9 1.02     22.0        26.0
## 11 19         23.7  21.4 0.958    21.9        25.6
## 12 2          24.2  19.6 0.878    22.4        25.9
## 13 20         23.1  21.4 0.957    21.2        25.0
## 14 3          23.9  22.4 1.00     22.0        25.9
## 15 4          24.4  21.7 0.971    22.5        26.3
## 16 5          24.7  22.6 1.01     22.7        26.7
## 17 6          22.8  19.1 0.853    21.1        24.5
## 18 7          24.2  23.5 1.05     22.2        26.3
## 19 8          23.9  21.9 0.978    22.0        25.8
## 20 9          24.2  22.4 1.00     22.3        26.2
```

Looking at the `lower.ci` and `upper.ci`, which are the lower and upper bounds of the 95% confidence interval for each sample mean, Leslie could see that all except one of them contained the population mean of 24.04 miles. Nancy thought a graph would be easier to examine and went back to Section 3.6.3.3 to copy the code using `geom_errorbar()` with `geom_point()`. She created a graph showing the population mean of 24.04 miles and the means and 95% confidence intervals for the 20 samples (Figure 4.22).

```
# graph means and CI for 20 samples (Figure 4.22)
samp.20.stats %>%
  ggplot(aes(y = means, x = sample_num)) +
  geom_errorbar(aes(ymin = lower.ci,
                    ymax = upper.ci,
                linetype = "95% CI of\nsample mean"), color = "#7463AC") +
  geom_point(stat = "identity", aes(color = "Sample mean")) +
  geom_hline(aes(yintercept = 24.04, alpha = "Population mean"),
             color = "deeppink") +
  labs(y = "Mean distance to treatment facility (95% CI)",
       x = "Sample") +
  scale_color_manual(values = "#7463AC", name = "") +
  scale_linetype_manual(values = c(1, 1), name = "") +
  scale_alpha_manual(values = 1, name = "") +
  theme_minimal()
```

FIGURE 4.22 Means and 95% confidence intervals of miles to the nearest substance abuse treatment facility with MAT from 20 samples of counties in the United States

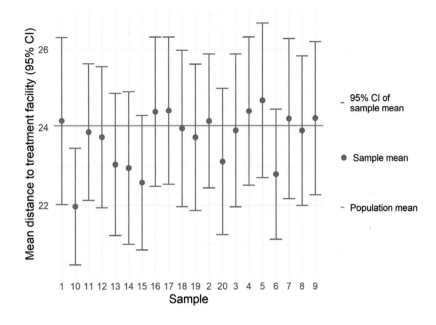

Leslie noticed that the 95% confidence intervals for 19 of the 20 samples contained the population mean and wondered about the 100 samples. She copied Nancy's graphing code and started editing it. Nancy suggested that 100 samples were a lot to put on one graph, especially to read the sample numbers on the *x*-axis. Leslie tried it and agreed. Nancy showed her a trick to remove the text from the *x*-axis with one more layer in her graph code (Figure 4.23).

FIGURE 4.23 Means and 95% confidence intervals of miles to the nearest substance abuse treatment facility with MAT from 20 samples of counties in the United States

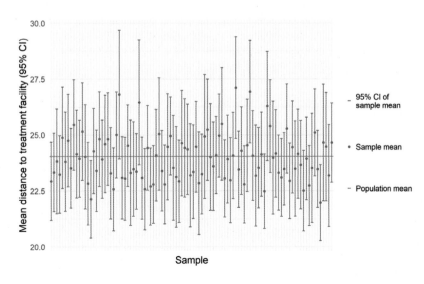

```
# get sample statistics
samp.100.stats <- samples.100 %>%
  group_by(sample_num) %>%
  summarize(means = mean(x = distance),
            sd = sd(x = distance),
            se = sd(x = distance)/sqrt(x = length(x = distance)),
            lower.ci = means - 1.96*se,
            upper.ci = means + 1.96*se)

# graph means and CI for 100 samples (Figure 4.23)
samp.100.stats %>%
  ggplot(aes(y = means, x = sample_num)) +
  geom_errorbar(aes(ymin = lower.ci,
                    ymax = upper.ci,
                    linetype = "95% CI of\nsample mean"), color = "#7463AC") +
  geom_point(stat = "identity", aes(color = "Sample mean")) +
  geom_hline(aes(yintercept = 24.04, alpha = "Population mean"),
             color = "deeppink") +
  labs(y = "Mean distance to treatment facility (95% CI)",
       x = "Sample") +
  scale_color_manual(values = "#7463AC", name = "") +
  scale_linetype_manual(values = c(1, 1), name = "") +
  scale_alpha_manual(values = 1, name = "") +
  theme_minimal() +
  theme(axis.text.x = element_blank())
```

Leslie reviewed the graph and saw four confidence intervals that did not cross over the population mean. She asked Nancy if there was any way to highlight these in the graph. Nancy looked at the graph and saw the confidence intervals Leslie had noticed. She thought they could add to the summary statistics in order to highlight any confidence intervals that ended above or below the population mean. She played with the code a little and came up with Figure 4.24.

```
# get sample statistics
samp.100.stats <- samples.100 %>%
  group_by(sample_num) %>%
  summarize(means = mean(x = distance),
            sd = sd(x = distance),
            se = sd(x = distance)/sqrt(x = length(x = distance)),
            lower.ci = means - 1.96*se,
            upper.ci = means + 1.96*se,
            differs = lower.ci > 24.04 | upper.ci < 24.04)
```

```
# graph means and CI for 100 samples (Figure 4.24)

samp.100.stats %>%

  ggplot(aes(y = means, x = sample_num)) +

  geom_errorbar(aes(ymin = lower.ci,

                    ymax = upper.ci,

                color = differs)) +

  geom_point(stat = "identity", aes(fill = "Sample mean"), color = "#7463AC") +

  geom_hline(aes(yintercept = 24.04, linetype = "Population mean"),

          color = "dodgerblue2") +

  labs(y = "Mean distance to treatment facility with MAT (95% CI)",

     x = "Sample") +

  scale_fill_manual(values = "#7463AC", name = "") +

  scale_color_manual(values = c("#7463AC", "deeppink"), name = "",

                       labels = c("95% CI of sample mean", "95% CI of sample mean")) +

  scale_linetype_manual(values = c(1, 1), name = "") +

  theme_minimal() +

  theme(axis.text.x = element_blank())
```

Leslie was delighted by this new graph. It clearly showed how the means of samples from a population can come close to the population mean much of the time. For 4 of the 100 samples, the population mean was outside the confidence interval, but for 96 of the 100 samples, the population mean was within 1.96 standard errors of the sample mean. Leslie thought that being able to say with some certainty *how close* the characteristics of a sample are to the population was powerful. Kiara agreed that the Central Limit Theorem is awesome.

FIGURE 4.24 Means and 95% confidence intervals of miles to the nearest substance abuse treatment facility with MAT from 20 samples of counties in the United States

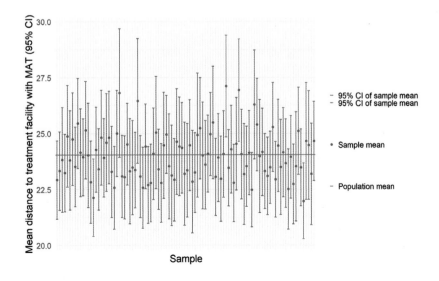

4.9.2 CONFIDENCE INTERVALS FOR PERCENTAGES

Leslie started thinking about the binomial distribution and the data from earlier in the day. She wondered if they could learn anything more about the percentage of states that are implementing opioid policies. She asked Kiara if there was such a thing as a confidence interval around the proportion of *successes* for a binary variable. Kiara said that this absolutely exists, and they did not even need a new strategy to be able to compute the 95% confidence interval around a proportion since the sampling distribution for a binary variable is normally distributed. Given the normally distributed sampling distribution, the same strategy for computing confidence intervals can be used. Leslie was a little confused since confidence intervals require means and standard errors, which do not seem like measures to compute for binary variables. Kiara explained that, for variables that have only two values (e.g., Yes and No, success and failure, 1 and 0), the mean of the variable is the same as the percentage of the group of interest. For example, consider a survey of 10 people that asked if they drink coffee or do not drink coffee, where drinking coffee is coded as 1 and not drinking coffee is coded as 0. The data set might look like this:

```
# do you drink coffee?
coffee <- c(1, 0, 1, 1, 0,
            0, 0, 1, 1, 1)
```

Finding the mean of this data set, like finding any other mean, would entail adding up the values and dividing by how many observations there were. Adding up the ones and zeros would be $1 + 0 + 1 + 1 + 0 + 0 + 0 + 1 + 1 + 1$ or 6. Six divided by 10 is .6. This is also the proportion or, after multiplying by 100, the percentage of people in this sample who drink coffee.

```
# mean of coffee variable
mean(x = coffee)
## [1] 0.6
```

This means that the percentage of people in a sample who have the variable category of interest is the mean of the sample for that variable. The mean of a binary variable like this one is typically abbreviated as p for proportion rather than m for mean. Nancy imported the opioid program data and did a little data management so that it was easier to work with.

```
# open state opioid program data
state.opioid.pgm.2017 <- read.csv(file = "[data folder location]/data/
pdmp_2017_kff_ch4.csv")

# recode Yes to 1 and No to 0
# change long name to pdmp
state.opioid.pgm.2017.cleaned <- state.opioid.pgm.2017 %>%
  rename(pdmp = Required.Use.of.Prescription.Drug.Monitoring.Programs) %>%
  mutate(pdmp = as.numeric(x = pdmp) - 1)

# find the mean of pdmp
state.opioid.pgm.2017.cleaned %>%
```

```
summarize(p = mean(x = pdmp))
##           p
## 1 0.627451
```

Leslie stopped her and asked her to explain why she subtracted 1 from the `pdmp` variable after making it numeric with `as.numeric()`. Nancy explained that R does not use zero for `as.numeric()`, so the two categories get recoded to be No is 1 and Yes is 2. These values will not work for computing the mean; the variable needs to be coded as 0 and 1 for this. By subtracting 1, the variable is coded 0 for No and 1 for Yes, which works for computing the mean. After explaining, Nancy computed the mean to demonstrate and found that it was .6275, so 62.75% of the states have a PDMP.

Now that the data were imported and they knew the mean, Nancy copied her earlier code to take some samples of the states and compute the sample means. Using `bind_rows()` to combine the samples taken with `replicate()`, which repeats some task *n* times (as specified), Nancy took 100 samples with each sample having 30 states in it. The `replicate()` code includes the *n* argument, the task to be completed, a `simplify` = argument that keeps all the results, and an `.id` = argument to give the replication number a variable name in the object that results from the code. She then found the means of all the samples.

```
# get 100 samples
# each sample has 30 states
# put samples in a data frame with each sample having
# a unique id called sample_num
set.seed(seed = 143)
samples.30.states <- bind_rows(replicate(n = 100,
                                state.opioid.pgm.2017.cleaned %>%
                    sample_n(size = 30, replace = TRUE),
                    simplify = FALSE), .id = "sample_num")

# find the mean for each sample
sample.30.means.states <- samples.30.states %>%
  group_by(sample_num) %>%
  summarize(p.pdmp = mean(x = pdmp))
sample.30.means.states
## # A tibble: 100 x 2
##    sample_num p.pdmp
##    <chr>       <dbl>
## 1 1           0.6
## 2 10          0.633
## 3 100         0.5
## 4 11          0.633
## 5 12          0.467
## 6 13          0.567
```

```
##  7 14          0.767
##  8 15          0.433
##  9 16          0.6
## 10 17          0.667
## # ... with 90 more rows
```

Nancy then graphed the sampling distribution of 100 sample means from 100 samples with each sample having 30 states (Figure 4.25).

Leslie noticed that the sampling distribution looked relatively normally distributed. Kiara explained that it would look even more normally distributed with more samples. Given that the sampling distribution is normally distributed, 95% of sample means would be within two standard deviations of the mean of the means. For any given sample, then, the 95% confidence interval for the mean (which is the percentage in the category of interest) can be computed using the same formula of $m + (1.96 \times se)$ and $m - (1.96 \times se)$. The only thing they needed, Kiara explained, was the standard error. For binary variables, the standard error is computed by following Equation (4.13).

$$se_p = \sqrt{\frac{p(1-p)}{n}} \tag{4.13}$$

where p is the mean (proportion of 1s) and n is the sample size. This seemed almost too easy to Leslie. She copied some of Nancy's code from earlier and made some revisions to get the means and confidence intervals for the samples and to plot the results like they did for the distance variable in Figure 4.24.

Leslie noticed that 98 of the 100 samples had a 95% confidence interval that included the population mean of 62.75% of states with PDMPs (Figure 4.26).

FIGURE 4.25 Histogram of 100 samples of states with PDMPs (2017)

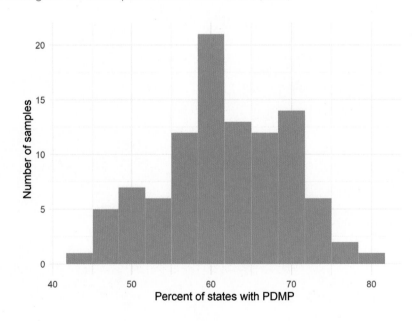

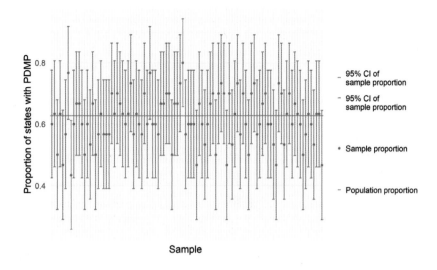

4.9.3 OTHER CONFIDENCE INTERVALS

Kiara wanted to mention two last things before they were done with distributions and inference for the day. While 95% confidence intervals are very common, sometimes confidence intervals that are wider or narrower are useful. To compute a wider or narrower confidence interval, replace the 1.96 with the *z*-score for the interval of interest. The three most common intervals have the following *z*-scores:

- 90% confidence interval *z*-score = 1.645
- 95% confidence interval *z*-score = 1.96
- 99% confidence interval *z*-score = 2.576

Kiara suggested that other *z*-scores for other confidence intervals can be found on many statistics websites. The last thing Kiara wanted to say was that confidence intervals for small samples, usually defined as samples with fewer than 30 observations (Field, 2013), use a *t*-statistic instead of a *z*-score in computing confidence intervals for means and in other types of analyses.

The *t*-statistic is from the *t*-distribution and, like the *z*-score, it measures the distance from the mean. However, the *t*-statistic does this using the standard deviation of the *sampling distribution*, also known as the standard error, rather than the standard deviation of the *sample*. Specifically, the *t*-statistic is computed using the formula in Equation (4.14),

$$t = \frac{m}{\frac{s}{\sqrt{n}}} \tag{4.14}$$

where *m* is the sample mean for a variable, *s* is the sample standard deviation for the same variable, and *n* is the sample size. Note that the denominator for *t* is $\frac{s}{\sqrt{n}}$, which is the standard error.

The main practical difference between the two is that the *t*-statistic works better when samples are small; once samples are very large ($n > 1,000$), the two values will be virtually identical. The R-Team will discuss the *t*-statistic and *t*-distribution in much more detail later (Chapter 6).

Leslie felt like she had learned a lot about statistics and about the seriousness of the opioid problem. She was surprised to learn that people travel a mean of 24.04 miles just to get to a treatment facility where they can get medication-assisted therapy. She had also learned that, while there are some effective policies for reducing opioid use, not all states have adopted these policies. However, she knew she should keep in mind that the assumptions they made about states being independent needed more attention before adopting today's conclusions as truth. As she started to learn more about how inferential statistics were used, Leslie knew she would be better able to contribute to the research on all of these complex problems.

Leslie thought about calling Corina to discuss what she had learned and to tell her about some of the data sources they had used, but first she had to get her other homework done.

"I wouldn't be disappointed if someone brought brownies every time we met," Kiara casually mentioned while looking right at Leslie.

Leslie smiled. "I'll see what I can do."

Leslie thanked Nancy and Kiara for their help and picked up her bag. Kiara was ready to leave, too. Nancy walked Kiara and Leslie to the elevator. She had a little more work to do before she could leave.

"I hope you don't have to stay too late!" said Leslie as they got on the elevator and she realized Nancy was not coming with them.

"Me too!" Nancy exclaimed and waved as the elevator door closed. "See you next time."

4.9.4 ACHIEVEMENT 6: CHECK YOUR UNDERSTANDING

Describe what a confidence interval is in your own words.

/// 4.10 CHAPTER SUMMARY

4.10.1 Achievements unlocked in this chapter: Recap

Congratulations! Like Leslie, you've learned and practiced the following in this chapter.

4.10.1.1 Achievement 1 recap: Defining and using the probability distributions to infer from a sample

A probability distribution is the numeric or visual representation of the probability of a value or range of values of a variable occurring.

4.10.1.2 Achievement 2 recap: Understanding the characteristics and uses of a binomial distribution of a binary variable

The binomial distribution is the probability distribution used to represent the distribution of a binomial random variable, which has the following properties:

- A variable is measured in the same way *n* times.

- There are only two possible values of the variable, often called "success" and "failure."

- Each observation is independent of the others.

- The probability of success is the same for each observation.

- The random variable is the number of successes in n measurements.

The binomial distribution is defined by two things:

- n, which is the number of observations (e.g., coin flips, people surveyed, states selected)

- p, which is the probability of success (e.g., 50% chance of heads for a coin flip, 51% chance of a state having a PDMP)

4.10.1.3 Achievement 3 recap: Understanding the characteristics and uses of the normal distribution of a continuous variable

The normal distribution is the probability distribution used to represent the distribution of a continuous variable. The normal distribution is defined by the mean and standard deviation of a variable.

A normally distributed variable has 68% of its values within one standard deviation of the mean and 95% of its values within two standard deviations of the mean.

4.10.1.4 Achievement 4 recap: Computing and interpreting z-scores to compare observations to groups

A z-score is the number of standard deviations away from the mean an observation is.

4.10.1.5 Achievement 5 recap: Estimating population means from sample means using the normal distribution

The Central Limit Theorem demonstrates that a sample mean will be within one standard error of the population mean 68% of the time and within two standard errors 95% of the time. A sample mean is often a good approximation of a population mean.

4.10.1.6 Achievement 6 recap: Computing and interpreting confidence intervals around means and proportions

Confidence intervals quantify where the population value likely lies with some level of probability based on how the interval is computed. Most of the time, social scientists report 95% intervals or 95% confidence intervals, which show the range where the population value will likely be 95 times if the study were conducted 100 times. Sometimes smaller or larger intervals are reported, like a 68% confidence interval or a 99% confidence interval. Small samples use t instead of z to compute the confidence interval upper and lower values.

4.10.2 Chapter exercises

The coder and hacker exercises are an opportunity to apply the skills from this chapter to a new scenario or a new data set. The coder edition evaluates the application of the concepts and functions learned in this R-Team meeting to scenarios similar to those in the meeting. The hacker edition evaluates the use of the concepts and functions from this R-Team meeting in new scenarios, often going a step beyond what was explicitly explained.

The coder edition might be best for those who found some or all of the Check Your Understanding activities to be challenging or if they needed review before picking the correct responses to the multiple-choice questions. The hacker edition might be best if the Check Your Understanding activities were not too challenging and the multiple-choice questions were a breeze.

The multiple-choice questions and materials for the exercises are online at **edge.sagepub.com/harris1e**.

Q1: The binomial distribution depends on which of the following?
   a. Mean and standard deviation
   b. Sample size and probability of success
   c. Standard deviation and number of successes
   d. Mean and probability of success

Q2: The normal distribution depends on which of the following?
   a. Mean and standard deviation
   b. Sample size and probability of success
   c. Standard deviation and number of successes
   d. Mean and probability of success

Q3: In a normal distribution, about 95% of observations are
   a. within one standard deviation of the mean.
   b. included in computing the mean.
   c. within two standard deviations of the mean.
   d. divided by the sample size to get the standard deviation.

Q4: A sampling distribution shows
   a. the distribution of means from multiple samples.
   b. the distribution of sample sizes over time.

c. the distribution of scores in the population.

d. the distribution of observations from a single sample.

Q5: The *z*-score is

a. the number of standard errors between the mean and some observation.

b. the difference between the sample mean and population mean.

c. the width of the 95% confidence interval.

d. the number of standard deviations an observation is from the mean.

4.10.2.1 Chapter exercises: Coder edition

Use the **pdmp_2017_kff_ch4.csv** file from **edge.sagepub.com/harris1e** to examine the opioid step therapy requirements variable. This variable is coded as Yes if the state had adopted step therapy guidelines as of 2017 and No if the state had not adopted step therapy guidelines. Recode the variable so that it is 1 for Yes and 0 for No. Give the variable a new name that is easier to use. Answer the following questions:

1. What percentage of states (including Washington, DC) adopted the step therapy guideline as of 2017? What percentage of states did not adopt the step therapy?

2. If 10 states were chosen at random, what is the probability that exactly 5 of them would have adopted the step therapy policy? (Achievement 2)

3. If 15 states were chosen at random, what is the probability that 5 of the 15 would have adopted step therapy policy? (Achievement 2)

4. Take a sample of 30 states, compute the proportion of states in the sample that have step therapy guidelines, and compute the 95% confidence interval for the proportion. Interpret your results. Compare the sample proportion to the population proportion computed in #1. Was the population proportion in the 95% confidence interval for the sample proportions? (Achievement 6)

amfAR, The Foundation for AIDS Research, also publishes data on the distance to needle exchange programs. Needle exchange programs are important for preventing the spread of disease among intravenous drug users, including opioid users. Bring in the **opioid_dist_to_needle_exchange_2018.csv** file and examine the codebook **opioid_county_codebook .xlsx** from **edge.sagepub.com/harris1e**.

5. Find the population mean and standard deviation of distance to needle exchange. The variable name is `VALUE`.

6. View the data, pick one county, and compute its *z*-score for distance to needle exchange. Interpret the *z*-score. (Achievements 3 and 4)

7. Take a random sample of 500 counties and find the mean, standard deviation, and standard error of distance for the sample. (Achievement 6)

8. Compare the population mean for `VALUE` with the sample mean and sample standard error. (Achievement 6)

9. Compute a 95% confidence interval around the sample mean for distance to needle exchange. Interpret the mean and confidence interval. (Achievement 6)

4.10.2.2 Chapter exercises: Hacker edition

Complete the questions from the coder edition plus the following:

10. For the distance data set in the coder edition, take 100 samples with an adequate number of observations per sample. Compute and graph the distribution of the sample means (the sampling distribution). Discuss the process, the shape of the distribution, and how the shape of the distribution is related to the Central Limit Theorem.

4.10.2.3 Instructor note

Solutions to exercises can be found on the website for this book, along with ideas for gamification for those who want to take it further.

Visit **edge.sagepub.com/harris1e** to download the datasets, complete the chapter exercises, and watch R tutorial videos.

5

COMPUTING AND INTERPRETING CHI-SQUARED

The R-Team and the
Vexing Voter Fraud Problem

It was Kiara's turn to host, and she had the perfect spot at work in a meeting space on the third floor with a view of the city. When Nancy and Leslie arrived, they found the entrance locked for the weekend and texted Kiara. She walked down the stairs to let them in. When she opened the door, Leslie was already talking about their previous meeting.

"I think it's so cool how sampling distributions can be used to compute confidence intervals that provide insight into a population based on the characteristics of a sample," Leslie said.

"I'm glad you think so," said Kiara. She reminded her that using information from a sample to make claims about a population is called inference and that statistical methods used for inference are inferential statistics. For example, the confidence intervals for the sample mean and sample percentage are ranges where the population mean or population percentage likely lies. Essentially, the idea of inferential statistics is that samples can be used to understand populations.

Kiara explained, "This is just the beginning when it comes to inference."

"Definitely," Nancy agreed. "Let's teach Leslie how to conduct commonly used inferential statistical tests in R."

They decided to start with the *chi-squared* test of independence, which is a statistical test to understand whether there is a relationship between two categorical variables. The chi-squared test of independence is one of a few bivariate, or two-variable, tests that are widely used in statistical analyses across many fields. Kiara also mentioned that when a chi-squared test of independence indicates that there may be a relationship between two things, there are several follow-up tests to find out more about the relationship.

"Let's get started!" Leslie exclaimed.

Nancy put together a list of achievements for the day.

5.1 Achievements to unlock

- Achievement 1: Understanding the relationship between two categorical variables using bar charts, frequencies, and percentages

- Achievement 2: Computing and comparing observed and expected values for the groups

- Achievement 3: Calculating the chi-squared statistic for the test of independence

- Achievement 4: Interpreting the chi-squared statistic and making a conclusion about whether or not there is a relationship

- Achievement 5: Using Null Hypothesis Significance Testing to organize statistical testing

- Achievement 6: Using standardized residuals to understand which groups contributed to significant relationships

- Achievement 7: Computing and interpreting effect sizes to understand the strength of a significant chi-squared relationship

- Achievement 8: Understanding the options for failed chi-squared assumptions

SAGE edge™

Visit **edge.sagepub .com/harris1e** to watch an R tutorial

5.2 The voter fraud problem

With another big election coming up, Leslie had been noticing a lot of news related to voting rights and voter registration. Her cousin Kristen lives in Oregon and mentioned that in 2015, voters had passed the Oregon Motor Voter Act (https://sos.oregon.gov/voting/Pages/motor-voter-faq.aspx), which made Oregon the first state to use automatic voter registration. Oregon residents who get a driver's license, permit, or state-issued identification card are automatically registered to vote. They are then sent a notification so that they can opt out of being registered to vote if they want to. This was very different from what Leslie had experienced registering to vote in her home state. She had filled out a form and sent it through the mail, and then waited for a very long time to get a reply. She was currently debating whether to change her voter registration from her home state to where she is going to school, but it felt like a big hassle.

Kiara remembered hearing several stories in the news after the 2018 midterm elections about how some state laws are making it more difficult, rather than easier, to register and vote. Leslie looked up voting laws and found a website from the Brennan Center for Justice that showed that 99 bills making it more difficult to vote, mostly through stricter voter identification requirements, had been introduced across 31 states in 2017 and that 25 states had put in new voting restrictions since 2010. Nancy pulled up the website and found that it wasn't all bad news: A total of 531 bills to expand voting access were introduced in 30 states in 2017, including several automatic voter registration bills ("New Voting Restrictions in America," n.d.).

Kiara and Leslie felt like they understood why the bills making it easier to register and vote were being introduced and passed, but they were also interested in why states were simultaneously introducing and supporting bills that made it more difficult to vote. Nancy thought she understood what was going on with the new voter identification laws. She had visited her uncles in a neighboring state last summer. She had learned that in that state, people were required to show proof of identification before they could vote. The state said this was to prevent voter fraud. Her uncles were concerned about voter fraud and thought this was a good solution. Leslie looked up some information on voter fraud and found that evidence suggests voter fraud does happen but is rare (Khan & Carson, 2012; Levitt, 2014; Minnite, 2017). She also found that Nancy's uncles were not the only ones who feel that fraud is a problem. She read one paper that showed that 23% of people think that people voting more than once in an election is very common or occasionally happens; 30% think that noncitizens voting is very common or occasionally happens; and 24% think voter impersonation is very common or occasionally happens. Similar percentages were found for vote theft (21%) and absentee ballot fraud (28%) (Stewart, Ansolabehere, & Persily, 2016).

Nancy found some additional research that was not related directly to voter registration, but to election fraud instead. Specifically, just over 70% of people in one survey thought election officials were fair very often or fairly often, and 80% thought votes were counted fairly very often or fairly often (Bowler, Brunell, Donovan, & Gronke, 2015), leaving a large percentage of U.S. citizens believing officials and vote counting are not fair. Republicans were more likely to believe voter fraud is widespread (Stewart et al., 2016) and consider elections to be unfair (Bowler et al., 2015; Wolak, 2014). However, they were not the only ones. About half the percentage of Democrats as Republicans think voter fraud is frequent (Stewart et al., 2016). Also, women, minorities, younger people, people with less education, and "sore losers" (people whose candidate lost an election) are more likely to think that elections are unfair (Bowler et al., 2015; Wolak, 2014). Some research shows that people who believe voter fraud is widespread are more likely to support voter identification laws (Stewart et al., 2016), although this relationship differs a lot by political party and by the amount and sources of information a person has (Kane, 2017; Stewart et al., 2016; Wilson & Brewer, 2013).

Given the ongoing policy battles over voter registration and all the information out there about voting fraud and voter identification, Nancy and Kiara thought it would be a great topic to focus on for learning

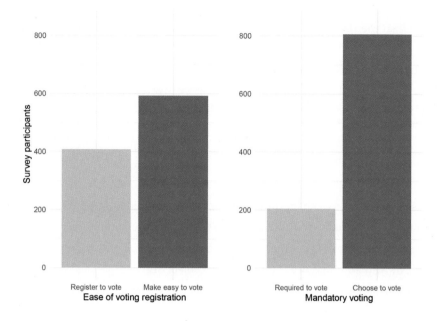

Source: "Public Supports Aim" (2017).

about chi-squared. Before they began, Kiara wanted to get everyone on the same page with the basics, so she showed Nancy and Leslie the χ^2 symbol and confirmed that it is pronounced "kai"-squared, not "chai"-squared! Nancy, ever eager to get to the actual coding, found some data from 2017 on the Pew Internet & American Life website ("Public Supports Aim," 2017). In the survey that resulted in this data set, participants were asked to choose which statement best represented their views on voting:

- Citizens should have to prove they really want to vote by registering ahead of time [OR] Everything possible should be done to make it easy for every citizen to vote.

- All citizens should be required to vote in national elections [OR] Every citizen should be able to decide for themselves whether or not to vote in national elections.

She downloaded the data set, which contained 1,028 observations, and quickly wrote some code to graph the responses to these two questions (Figure 5.1). It looked like about 40% of people thought that citizens should have to prove they want to vote by registering, and 60% thought voting should be made as easy as possible. The split was bigger with making voting a requirement, with about 80% of people who thought voting should be a choice.

With this background and data, the team felt ready to embark on a chi-squared adventure.

5.3 Data, documentation, and R packages for learning about chi-squared

Before they began, Kiara made a list of all the data and R packages for learning chi-squared so they could download and install everything first.

- Two options for accessing the data
  - Download the data set **pew_apr_19-23_2017_weekly_ch5.sav** from **edge.sagepub.com/harris1e**
  - Download the data set from the Pew Research Center website (https://www.people-press.org/2017/06/28/public-supports-aim-of-making-it-easy-for-all-citizens-to-vote/)
- Two options for accessing the documentation
  - Download the documentation files **pew_voting_april_2017_ch5.pdf**, **pew_voting_demographics_april_2017_ch5.docx**, and **pew_chap5_readme.txt** from **edge.sagepub.com/harris1e**
  - Download the data set from the Pew Research Center website and the documentation will be included with the zipped file
- Install the following R packages if not already installed:
  - **haven**, by Hadley Wickham (https://www.rdocumentation.org/packages/haven/)
  - **tidyverse**, by Hadley Wickham(https://www.rdocumentation.org/packages/tidyverse/)
  - **descr**, by Jakson Alves de Aquino (https://www.rdocumentation.org/packages/descr/)
  - *fmsb*, by Minato Nakazawa (https://cran.r-project.org/web/packages/fmsb/index.html)
  - *lsr*, by Daniel Navarro (https://cran.r-project.org/web/packages/lsr/index.html)

5.4 Achievement 1: Understanding the relationship between two categorical variables using bar charts, frequencies, and percentages

Before conducting any sort of inferential analyses that use sample data to understand a population, it is a best practice to get to know the sample data using descriptive statistics and graphics. This step in research is often called *exploratory data analysis* or EDA. The descriptive statistics for EDA examining categorical variables are frequencies and percentages (Section 2.5).

Kiara had downloaded the survey data from the Pew website, which resulted in a zipped folder with the survey questions, data, and a few other documents, so she did not attempt to import the data directly into R from the website given how complex the file was, although she guessed it was possible. The data set was saved with a .sav file extension, which meant it was SPSS-formatted data. There are several ways to import SPSS data into R. Kiara suggested to Leslie that she use the **haven** package because the format of the imported data from this package works well with **tidyverse**.

Leslie imported the data using `read_sav()` from the **haven** package. She noticed that there were 49 variables in the data frame, which is more than they needed to work with that day. To make the data frame more manageable, Leslie decided to keep just the variables of interest. She looked at the documentation and decided to keep the two voting questions, `pew1a` and `pew1b`, along with `race`, `sex`, `mstatus` (marital status), `ownhome` (home ownership), `employ`, and `polparty` (political party affiliation). All of the variables were categorical and nominal. Leslie reminded herself that nominal variables are categorical variables that have no inherent order to the categories, while ordinal variables are categorical variables that do have an inherent order to the categories (Section 1.7.5).

```
# open haven to import the April 17-23 Pew Research Center data
library(package = "haven")

# import the voting data
vote <- read_sav(file = "[data folder location]/data/pew_apr_19-23_2017_weekly_ch5.sav")

# open tidyverse
library(package = "tidyverse")

# select variables of interest
vote.cleaned <- vote %>%
  select(pew1a, pew1b, race, sex, mstatus, ownhome, employ, polparty)

# check data
summary(object = vote.cleaned)
##      pew1a           pew1b           race            sex
##  Min.   :1.000   Min.   :1.000   Min.   : 1.000   Min.   :1.000
##  1st Qu.:1.000   1st Qu.:2.000   1st Qu.: 1.000   1st Qu.:1.000
##  Median :2.000   Median :2.000   Median : 1.000   Median :2.000
##  Mean   :1.717   Mean   :1.897   Mean   : 4.482   Mean   :1.518
##  3rd Qu.:2.000   3rd Qu.:2.000   3rd Qu.: 2.000   3rd Qu.:2.000
##  Max.   :9.000   Max.   :9.000   Max.   :99.000   Max.   :2.000
##     mstatus         ownhome          employ          polparty
##  Min.   :1.000   Min.   :1.000   Min.   :1.000   Min.   :0.000
##  1st Qu.:2.000   1st Qu.:1.000   1st Qu.:1.000   1st Qu.:1.000
##  Median :3.000   Median :1.000   Median :2.000   Median :2.000
##  Mean   :3.219   Mean   :1.481   Mean   :2.527   Mean   :2.475
##  3rd Qu.:5.000   3rd Qu.:2.000   3rd Qu.:3.000   3rd Qu.:3.000
##  Max.   :9.000   Max.   :9.000   Max.   :9.000   Max.   :9.000
```

Leslie sighed and leaned back. Based on summary() showing means and medians, it appeared that all of the variables were imported into R as numeric data type variables when they should be factor data type. Kiara shrugged and suggested that they were probably going to have to recode most of them anyway to make sure the missing values were appropriately handled. Leslie got out the documentation to start the data management.

5.4.1 DATA CLEANING

Leslie decided to start with the voting variables. Figure 5.2 shows the survey questions for the voting variables.

Nancy took one look at the survey and wanted to fix something before Leslie continued her coding. Nancy slid the laptop over and started to type. She knew that read_sav() imported the file in a "**haven**-labeled"

FIGURE 5.2 Screenshot of Pew Research Center April 19–23, 2017, survey document page 1

PEW RESEARCH CENTER
April 19-23, 2017 OMNIBUS
FINAL QUESTIONNAIRE

ASK ALL:

PEW.1 I'm going to read you some pairs of statements that will help us understand how you feel about a number of things. As I read each pair, tell me whether the FIRST statement or the SECOND statement comes closer to your own views — even if neither is exactly right. The first pair is **[READ AND RANDOMIZE <u>AND</u> RANDOMIZE STATEMENTS WITHIN PAIRS]**. Next, **[NEXT PAIR] [IF NECESSARY:** "Which statement comes closer to your views, even if neither is exactly right?"]

a. Citizens should have to prove they really want to vote by registering ahead of time [OR]
Everything possible should be done to make it easy for every citizen to vote

b. All citizens should be required to vote in national elections [OR]
Every citizen should be able to decide for themselves whether or not to vote in national elections

c. I am willing to give up some of my personal privacy if it helps keep the country safe [OR]
I'm not willing to give up any of my personal privacy, even if it helps keep the country safe

d. The government has the right to set some restrictions on the use of private property [OR]
The way private property is used should be left entirely up to the property owner

e. If the gap between the rich and poor continues to grow, it will pose a threat to American democracy [OR]
American democracy can function well even if the gap between the rich and poor continues to grow

RESPONSE CATEGORIES:

1 Statement #1
2 Statement #2
5 Neither/Both equally **(VOL.)**
9 Don't know/Refused **(VOL.)**

FIGURE 5.3 Screenshot of data frame with long labels

pew1a PEW-1a. As I read each pair, tell me whether the FIRST statement ...	**pew1b** PEW-1b. As I read each pair, tell me whether the FIRST statement ...	**race** Race of Respondent	**sex** Enter Sex of Respondent
2	2	2	2
1	2	1	2
9	9	1	1
2	1	1	2
1	1	1	2
2	2	2	1

format, which was a little tricky to use, and that changing the variables to factors would result in using the current labels, which were extremely long! Leslie wanted to see these super-long labels, so Nancy clicked twice on the data frame name in the Environment tab and the data frame popped up (Figure 5.3). Leslie saw the variable names of `pew1a` and `pew1b` at the top with a long statement under each. Nancy explained that those are the **haven** labels; they are the full text of the question asked for each variable. Leslie now understood what Nancy meant and why she wanted to remove them.

Nancy added `zap_labels()` to the data management to remove the super-long labels. She slid the laptop back to Leslie so she could get some practice with `recode_factor()`. Leslie worked on the `pew1a` and `pew1b` voting variables first to recode them and give them more descriptive variable names, `ease.vote` and `require.vote`.

```
# select variables of interest and clean them
vote.cleaned <- vote %>%
```

```
  select(pew1a, pew1b, race, sex, mstatus, ownhome, employ, polparty) %>%
  zap_labels() %>%
  mutate(pew1a = recode_factor(.x = pew1a,
                                `1` = 'Register to vote',
                                `2` = 'Make easy to vote',
                                `5` = NA_character_,
                                `9` = NA_character_)) %>%
  rename(ease.vote = pew1a) %>%
  mutate(pew1b = recode_factor(.x = pew1b,
                                `1` = 'Require to vote',
                                `2` = 'Choose to vote',
                                `5` = NA_character_,
                                `9` = NA_character_)) %>%
  rename(require.vote = pew1b)

# check voting variables
summary(object = vote.cleaned)
##           ease.vote            require.vote        race
##   Register to vote :408   Require to vote:205   Min.   : 1.000
##   Make easy to vote:593   Choose to vote :806   1st Qu.: 1.000
##   NA's             : 27   NA's           : 17   Median : 1.000
##                                                 Mean   : 4.482
##                                                 3rd Qu.: 2.000
##                                                 Max.   :99.000
##      sex           mstatus         ownhome          employ
##   Min.   :1.000   Min.   :1.000   Min.   :1.000   Min.   :1.000
##   1st Qu.:1.000   1st Qu.:2.000   1st Qu.:1.000   1st Qu.:1.000
##   Median :2.000   Median :3.000   Median :1.000   Median :2.000
##   Mean   :1.518   Mean   :3.219   Mean   :1.481   Mean   :2.527
##   3rd Qu.:2.000   3rd Qu.:5.000   3rd Qu.:2.000   3rd Qu.:3.000
##   Max.   :2.000   Max.   :9.000   Max.   :9.000   Max.   :9.000
##      polparty
##   Min.   :0.000
##   1st Qu.:1.000
##   Median :2.000
##   Mean   :2.475
##   3rd Qu.:3.000
##   Max.   :9.000
```

Leslie looked happy with the recoding so far. She worked on the race, sex, and ownhome variables next. Luckily, these variable names were already easy to understand, so the recoding was more straightforward. Before recoding race, Leslie examined a table to see how many people were in each category.

```
# examine race variable before recoding
table(vote.cleaned$race)
##
##    1    2    3    4    5    6    7    8    9   10   99
##  646  129   63   26   61   22   19    2    1   34   25
```

Leslie reviewed the documentation to see what these category numbers represented. She was concerned about some of the categories with so few people in them. The survey responses (Figure 5.4) did not seem to match the data since the variable in the data set had 11 categories and the survey showed 8 categories. She also noticed that the variable was called race in the data and race1 in the survey.

Leslie examined the other documentation with the data source to see if she could figure out what was happening. She found a text file called readme.txt with the downloaded data that included recommendations from the Pew Research Center on how to recode race (Figure 5.5).

Although the recommended recoding (Figure 5.5) used a different coding language than R, Leslie thought she understood what to do. The code suggested that Pew recommended recoding into five categories of race-ethnicity:

- White non-Hispanic
- Black non-Hispanic
- Hispanic
- Other
- Don't know/refused

FIGURE 5.4 Screenshot of Pew Research Center voting data survey document page 5

ASK ALL:
race1   Do you consider yourself white, black or African American, Asian, Native American, Pacific Islander, mixed race or some other race? **[ENTER ONE ONLY][IF RESPONDENT SAYS HISPANIC ASK:** Do you consider yourself a white Hispanic or a black Hispanic?] **[INTERVIEWER NOTE: CODE AS WHITE (1) OR BLACK (2). IF RESPONDENTS REFUSED TO PICK WHITE OR BLACK HISPANIC, RECORD HISPANIC AS "OTHER"]**

        1   White
        2   Black or African American
        3   Asian/Chinese/Japanese
        4   Native American/American Indian/Alaska Native
        5   Native Hawaiian and Other Pacific Islander
        6   Mixed
        0   Other **(SPECIFY)** _____
        9   Refused **(VOL.)**

FIGURE 5.5 Screenshot of Pew Research Center voting data readme file

```
**The race-ethnicity variable (racethn) was computed using the following syntax**
recode race (3 thru 5=3)(6 thru 10=4)(99=9)(else=copy) into racethn.
val label racethn 1'White non-Hispanic' 2 'Black non-Hispanic' 3'Hispanic' 4'Other' 9'Don't know/Refused (VOL.)'.
var label racethn 'Race-Ethnicity'.
```

Leslie consulted with Nancy and Kiara, and they decided to code Don't know/refused as NA since there were just 25 people in this category. Leslie added the race variable recoding to the data management so far. She then went ahead with the sex and ownhome variables, which were clearer in the survey.

```
# select variables of interest and clean them
vote.cleaned <- vote %>%
  select(pew1a, pew1b, race, sex, mstatus, ownhome, employ, polparty) %>%
  zap_labels() %>%
  mutate(pew1a = recode_factor(.x = pew1a,
                              `1` = 'Register to vote',
                              `2` = 'Make easy to vote',
                              `5` = NA_character_,
                              `9` = NA_character_)) %>%
  rename(ease.vote = pew1a) %>%
  mutate(pew1b = recode_factor(.x = pew1b,
                              `1` = 'Require to vote',
                              `2` = 'Choose to vote',
                              `5` = NA_character_,
                              `9` = NA_character_)) %>%
  rename(require.vote = pew1b) %>%
  mutate(race = recode_factor(.x = race,
                              `1` = 'White non-Hispanic',
                              `2` = 'Black non-Hispanic',
                              `3` = 'Hispanic',
                              `4` = 'Hispanic',
                              `5` = 'Hispanic',
                              `6` = 'Other',
                              `7` = 'Other',
                              `8` = 'Other',
                              `9` = 'Other',
                              `10` = 'Other',
                              `99` = NA_character_)) %>%
  mutate(sex = recode_factor(.x = sex,
                              `1` = 'Male',
                              `2` = 'Female')) %>%
  mutate(ownhome = recode_factor(.x = ownhome,
                              `1` = 'Owned',
                              `2` = 'Rented',
                              `8` = NA_character_,
                              `9` = NA_character_))
```

```
# check recoding
summary(object = vote.cleaned)
##                ease.vote              require.vote                    race
##   Register to vote :408     Require to vote:205     White non-Hispanic:646
##   Make easy to vote:593     Choose to vote :806     Black non-Hispanic:129
##   NA's             : 27     NA's           : 17     Hispanic          :150
##                                                     Other             : 78
##                                                     NA's              : 25
##
##       sex           mstatus            ownhome          employ          polparty
##   Male  :495    Min.   :1.000     Owned :678     Min.   :1.000    Min.   :0.000
##   Female:533    1st Qu.:2.000     Rented:328     1st Qu.:1.000    1st Qu.:1.000
##                 Median :3.000     NA's  : 22     Median :2.000    Median :2.000
##                 Mean   :3.219                    Mean   :2.527    Mean   :2.475
##                 3rd Qu.:5.000                    3rd Qu.:3.000    3rd Qu.:3.000
##                 Max.   :9.000                    Max.   :9.000    Max.   :9.000
```

Leslie checked the recoding and it was correct; they were ready to continue.

5.4.2 USING DESCRIPTIVE STATISTICS TO EXAMINE THE RELATIONSHIP BETWEEN TWO CATEGORICAL VARIABLES

First, Leslie decided to examine the relationship between ease of voting and sex. The first step was examining frequencies and a graph in order to understand the relationship between the two. Leslie started to type `table()` and Nancy scooted the laptop away. She wanted to show Leslie another option from the **tidyverse**. Nancy introduced `spread()`, which can be used to spread data out into columns. Leslie did not understand what she was talking about, so Nancy showed her how it looked without `spread()`:

```
# voting ease by race-eth no spread
vote.cleaned %>%
  drop_na(ease.vote) %>%
  drop_na(race) %>%
  group_by(ease.vote, race) %>%
  summarize(freq.n = n())
## # A tibble: 8 x 3
## # Groups:   ease.vote [2]
##   ease.vote          race                  freq.n
##   <fct>              <fct>                  <int>
## 1 Register to vote   White non-Hispanic       292
## 2 Register to vote   Black non-Hispanic        28
```

```
## 3 Register to vote  Hispanic             51
## 4 Register to vote  Other                27
## 5 Make easy to vote White non-Hispanic   338
## 6 Make easy to vote Black non-Hispanic   98
## 7 Make easy to vote Hispanic             97
## 8 Make easy to vote Other                46
```

Then Nancy showed her how it looked with `spread()`:

```
# voting ease by race-eth with spread
vote.cleaned %>%
  drop_na(ease.vote) %>%
  drop_na(race) %>%
  group_by(ease.vote, race) %>%
  summarize(freq.n = n()) %>%
  spread(key = race, value = freq.n)
## # A tibble: 2 x 5
## # Groups:   ease.vote [2]
##   ease.vote        `White non-Hispanic` `Black non-Hispani~ Hispanic Other
##   <fct>                    <int>               <int>             <int>   <int>
## 1 Register to vote   292                   28                   51       27
## 2 Make easy to vote  338                   98                   97       46
```

Leslie rolled her eyes and reached over to type:

```
# voting ease by race-eth with table
table(vote.cleaned$ease.vote, vote.cleaned$race)
##
##                     White non-Hispanic Black non-Hispanic Hispanic Other
##   Register to vote          292                  28          51     27
##   Make easy to vote         338                  98          97     46
```

Nancy nodded. She agreed that, in this situation, using `table()` was faster. However, there might be times when `spread()` would be the easier solution, so it is good to know that it exists. Leslie agreed.

Leslie noticed that it was not easy to determine whether there was a higher percentage of people in either vote category across the four race-ethnicity groups. Leslie thought that some percentages might help make this comparison easier. While she was typing the `prop.table()` function, Nancy told her about an option to label her table. Row and column labels can be added to the `table()` function and will be printed in the output. She told Leslie to put `Voting.ease =` before the `ease.vote` variable and `Race.eth =` before the `race` variable. Leslie tried it.

```
# table of percents voting ease by race-eth
prop.table(x = table(Voting.ease = vote.cleaned$ease.vote,
                     Race.eth = vote.cleaned$race))
##                      Race.eth
## Voting.ease          White non-Hispanic Black non-Hispanic   Hispanic
##    Register to vote           0.29887410         0.02865916 0.05220061
##    Make easy to vote          0.34595701         0.10030706 0.09928352
##                      Race.eth
## Voting.ease              Other
##    Register to vote 0.02763562
##    Make easy to vote 0.04708291
```

The row and column labels were helpful, but it was still difficult to interpret since the percentages added up to 100% for the whole table and so were out of the total rather than being for each category of race-ethnicity. It was not all that useful to know that 29.88% of all participants were both White non-Hispanic and in favor of voter registration. What Leslie wanted to know was whether people who are White non-Hispanic are more in favor of voter registration *or* making it easier for people to vote. Kiara checked the help documentation for prop.table() and found an argument to use to compute either the row percentages with margin = 1 or the column percentages with margin = 2. Since Leslie was interested in column percentages, she added the option to make these appear.

```
# table of percents voting ease by race-eth
prop.table(x = table(Voting.ease = vote.cleaned$ease.vote,
                     Race.eth = vote.cleaned$race),
           margin = 2)
##                      Race.eth
## Voting.ease          White non-Hispanic Black non-Hispanic  Hispanic
##    Register to vote            0.4634921          0.2222222 0.3445946
##    Make easy to vote           0.5365079          0.7777778 0.6554054
##                      Race.eth
## Voting.ease             Other
##    Register to vote 0.3698630
##    Make easy to vote 0.6301370
```

To make sure she had the right percentages, Leslie added up the columns. Each column added up to 1 or 100%, so the margin = 2 argument worked as expected.

Leslie noticed that White non-Hispanic participants were fairly evenly divided between those who thought people should register if they want to vote and those who thought voting should be made as easy as possible. The other three race-ethnicity groups had larger percentages in favor of making it as easy as possible to vote, with Black non-Hispanic participants having the highest percentage (77.78%) in favor of making it easy to vote. In this initial table, the voting registration policy a person favors differed by race-ethnicity. Leslie used the same code to examine the voting requirement.

```
# table of percents voting required by race-eth
prop.table(x = table(Voting.requirement = vote.cleaned$require.vote,
                      Race.eth = vote.cleaned$race),
           margin = 2)
##                     Race.eth
## Voting.requirement White non-Hispanic Black non-Hispanic   Hispanic
##    Require to vote            0.1502347          0.3228346 0.3401361
##    Choose to vote             0.8497653          0.6771654 0.6598639
##                     Race.eth
## Voting.requirement     Other
##    Require to vote 0.1891892
##    Choose to vote  0.8108108
```

This time, most participants from the White non-Hispanic group were in favor of letting people choose whether to vote, while the percentage in favor of being required to vote was more than twice as high for Black non-Hispanic and Hispanic participants. The Other group was more similar to the non-Hispanic White group. Being required to vote or choosing to vote was different by race-ethnicity.

5.4.3 USING GRAPHS TO EXAMINE THE RELATIONSHIP BETWEEN TWO CATEGORICAL VARIABLES

Leslie decided to graph these relationships to see if a data visualization provided any additional information. Kiara said that grouped bar graphs like the ones in Section 3.6.2 would be the best option here. Nancy suggested using `grid.arrange()` to put the two plots together and pulled the laptop in front of her to work on the code (Figure 5.6).

```
# open gridExtra to put graphs together (Figure 5.6)
library(package = "gridExtra")

# graph the relationship between registration ease and race eth
ease.graph <- vote.cleaned %>%
  drop_na(ease.vote) %>%
  drop_na(race) %>%
  group_by(ease.vote, race) %>%
  count() %>%
  group_by(race) %>%
  mutate(perc = 100*n/sum(n)) %>%
  ggplot(aes(x = race, y = perc, fill = ease.vote)) +
  geom_bar(position = "dodge", stat = "identity") +
  theme_minimal() +
  scale_fill_manual(values = c("gray", "#7463AC"),
                    name = "Opinion on \nvoter registration") +
```

```
    labs(x = "", y = "Percent within group") +
    theme(axis.text.x = element_blank())

# graph the relationship between required voting and race eth
req.graph <- vote.cleaned %>%
    drop_na(require.vote) %>%
    drop_na(race) %>%
    group_by(require.vote, race) %>%
    count() %>%
    group_by(race) %>%
    mutate(perc = 100*n/sum(n)) %>%
    ggplot(aes(x = race, y = perc, fill = require.vote)) +
    geom_bar(position = "dodge", stat = "identity") +
    theme_minimal() +
    scale_fill_manual(values = c("gray", "#7463AC"),
                      name = "Opinion on voting") +
    labs(x = "Race-ethnicity group", y = "Percent within group")

grid.arrange(ease.graph, req.graph, nrow = 2)
```

FIGURE 5.6 Opinion on voter registration and voting requirements by race-ethnicity from Pew Research Center ($n = 1,028$)

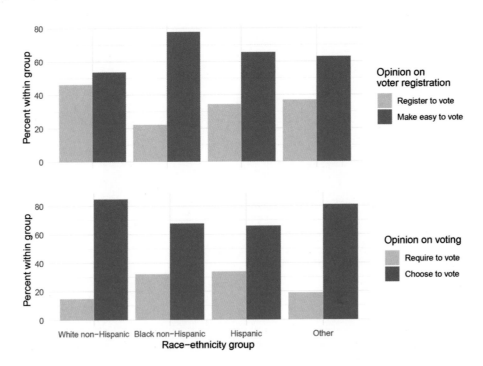

This was easier to examine than the tables, and the differences were quickly clear. Based on the descriptive and visual exploratory data analysis (EDA), race-ethnicity was related to opinions about voter registration and voting requirements. Specifically, there was a higher percentage of White non-Hispanic participants supporting choosing to vote, while the highest percentage supporting making it easy to vote were Black non-Hispanic participants.

5.4.4 ACHIEVEMENT 1: CHECK YOUR UNDERSTANDING

Make an appropriate table or a graph to examine the relationship between sex and voting requirements. Explain the results.

5.5 Achievement 2: Computing and comparing observed and expected values for the groups

5.5.1 OBSERVED VALUES

Kiara examined what Leslie had done so far and agreed that it looked like there were some differences among the race-ethnicity groups in support for ease of voter registration and for requirements to vote. Kiara explained that the chi-squared test is useful for testing to see if there may be a statistical relationship between two categorical variables. The chi-squared test is based on the observed values, like the ones in the tables in Section 5.4.2, and the values expected to occur if there were no relationship between the variables.

That is, given overall frequencies for the two variables from the data summary, how many people would Leslie *expect* to be in each of the cells of the table just shown?

5.5.2 EXPECTED VALUES

Given these frequencies from the data summary, what would the R-Team expect to see in the blank cells of this table created from the **stargazer** package by Marek Hlavac (https://www.rdocumentation.org/packages/stargazer/)?

```
## ==========================================================================
##                    White non-Hispanic Black non-Hispanic Hispanic Other Total
## ------------------------------------------------------------------------
## Register to vote                                                     398
## Make easy to vote                                                    579
## Total                  630                126              148    73   977
## ------------------------------------------------------------------------
```

Without knowing anything else, it would be tempting to just put half the White non-Hispanic people in the "Register to vote" category and half in the "Make easy to vote" category. However, overall, about 60% of the people want to make it easy to vote and about 40% want voter registration. This complicated things. Kiara let Leslie think about how she would fill in this table for a few minutes before explaining that there was an easy way to compute the expected values while taking the overall percentages into consideration by using the row and column totals.

For each cell in the table, multiply the row total for that row by the column total for that column and divide by the overall total, as in Equation (5.1).

$$\frac{row\,Total \times column\,Total}{Total} \tag{5.1}$$

```
##
## ==============================================================================
##          White non-Hispanic Black non-Hispanic  Hispanic     Other    Total
## ------------------------------------------------------------------------------
## Register to vote    398x630/977      398x126/977  398x148/977 398x73/977   398
## Make easy to vote 579x630/977      579x126/977  579x148/977 579x73/977   579
## Total                        630              126          148         73    977
## ------------------------------------------------------------------------------
```

In multiplying it all out, the expected values would be somewhat different from the observed values. The next table shows expected values *below* the observed values for each cell. Many of the cells have observed and expected values that are very close to each other. For example, the observed number of Other race-ethnicity people who want to make it easy to vote is 46, while the expected is 43.3. Some categories show bigger differences. For example, the observed number of Black non-Hispanics who think people should register to vote is 28, and the expected value is nearly twice as high at 51.3.

	White non-Hispanic	Black non-Hispanic	Hispanic	Other	Total
Register to vote (observed)	292	28	51	27	398
Register to vote (expected)	256.6	51.3	60.3	29.7	398
Make easy to vote (observed)	338	98	97	46	579
Make easy to vote (expected)	373.4	74.7	87.7	43.3	579
Total	630	126	148	73	977

5.5.3 COMPARING OBSERVED AND EXPECTED VALUES

Kiara explained that, if there were no relationship between opinions on voting ease and race-ethnicity, the observed and expected values would be the same. That is, the observed data would show that 373.4 White non-Hispanic people wanted to make it easy to vote.

Differences between observed values and expected indicates that there may be a relationship between the variables. In this case, it looks like there are more people than expected who want to make voting easier in all the categories, except non-Hispanic White. In the non-Hispanic White category, there are more people than expected who want people to prove they want to vote by registering. This suggests that there may be some relationship between opinions about the ease of voting and race-ethnicity.

5.5.4 THE ASSUMPTIONS OF THE CHI-SQUARED TEST OF INDEPENDENCE

While they were talking about observed and expected values, Kiara decided it was a good time to bring up the *assumptions* of the chi-squared test. Leslie had heard about assumptions before and knew they were typically lists of requirements that must be met before using a statistical test. Kiara confirmed that this was correct and reminded Leslie that they had already talked about one assumption, the assumption of a normal distribution for using the mean and standard deviation. She listed the assumptions for conducting a chi-squared test (McHugh, 2013):

- The variables must be nominal or ordinal (usually nominal).

- The expected values should be 5 or higher in at least 80% of groups.

- The observations must be independent.

These assumptions were confusing to Leslie, and she asked if they could walk through them for the voting ease and race example. Kiara agreed. She listed the assumptions, and they worked together to show how the data for the voting example met or did not meet each one.

5.5.4.1 ASSUMPTION 1: THE VARIABLES MUST BE NOMINAL OR ORDINAL

Race has categories that are in no particular order, so it is nominal. The ease of voting variable has categories that are in no particular order, so it is also nominal. This assumption is met.

5.5.4.2 ASSUMPTION 2: THE EXPECTED VALUES SHOULD BE 5 OR HIGHER IN AT LEAST 80% OF GROUPS

Kiara explained that the groups are the different cells of the table, so White non-Hispanic participants who think people should register to vote is one group. In this example, there are 8 groups, so 80% of this would be 6.4 groups. Since there is no way to have .4 of a group, 7 or more of the groups should have expected values of 5 or more. None of the groups have expected values even close to 5; all are much higher. This assumption is met.

5.5.4.3 ASSUMPTION 3: THE OBSERVATIONS MUST BE INDEPENDENT

There are a couple of ways observations can be nonindependent. One way to violate this assumption would be if the data included the same set of people before and after some intervention or treatment. Kiara explained that another way to violate this assumption would be for the data to include siblings or parents and children or spouses or other people who are somehow linked to one another. Since people who are linked to each other often have similar characteristics, statistical tests on related observations need to be able to account for this, and the chi-squared test does not. Leslie thought she understood and pointed out that the Pew data included independent observations (not siblings or other related people and not the same people measured more than once), so this assumption is met.

Leslie asked what happens when the assumptions are not met for a statistical test. Kiara explained that, often, another test could be used, depending on which of the assumptions has not been met. For chi-squared, the assumption that is often a problem is the assumption about expected values being at least 5 in most cells. Kiara said they would look at an option for addressing this assumption violation as they walked through some examples.

5.5.5 ACHIEVEMENT 2: CHECK YOUR UNDERSTANDING

Which of the following is true about the observed and expected values for voting ease and race-ethnicity? (Choose all that apply.)

- There are more people than expected who want to make it easy to vote and are Hispanic.
- There are more people than expected who want to make it easy to vote and are Black non-Hispanic.
- There are more people than expected who want people to register to vote and are Black non-Hispanic.

5.6 Achievement 3: Calculating the chi-squared statistic for the test of independence

5.6.1 SUMMING THE DIFFERENCES BETWEEN OBSERVED AND EXPECTED VALUES

The differences between observed values and expected values can be combined into an overall statistic showing how much observed and expected differ across all the categories (Kim, 2017). However, since some expected values are higher than observed values and some are lower, and the observed and expected will always have the same total when summed, combining the differences will always result in zero, like in Equation (5.2).

$$(292 - 256.6) + (28 - 51.3) + \ldots + (46 - 43.3) = 0 \tag{5.2}$$

5.6.2 SQUARING THE SUMMED DIFFERENCES

Squaring the differences before adding them up will result in a positive value that is larger when there are larger differences between observed and expected and smaller when there are smaller differences. This value captures the magnitude of the difference between observed and expected values. Kiara noted that there was one additional step to compute a chi-squared (χ^2) statistic. In order to account for situations when the observed and expected values are very large, which could result in extremely large differences between observed and expected, the squared differences are divided by the expected value in each cell, like in Equations (5.3) and (5.4).

$$\chi^2 = \Sigma \frac{(observed - expected)^2}{expected} \tag{5.3}$$

$$\chi^2 = \frac{(292-256.6)^2}{256.6} + \frac{(28-51.3)^2}{51.3} + \frac{(51-60.3)^2}{60.3} + \frac{(338-373.4)^2}{373.4} +$$

$$\frac{(98-74.7)^2}{74.7} + \frac{(97-87.7)^2}{87.7} + \frac{(46-43.3)^2}{43.3} = 28.952 \qquad (5.4)$$

5.6.3 USING R TO COMPUTE CHI-SQUARED

Equation (5.4) shows a chi-squared statistic computed by hand for the voting data. The same statistic can be computed by R through a number of different methods. In base R, the `chisq.test()` function is useful. Looking at the help documentation, Leslie noticed that the test takes arguments for x and y along with some other possible choices. Nancy suggested starting simply and specifying *x* and *y* as `ease.vote` and `race`.

```
# chi-squared statistic for ease of voting
# and race
chisq.test(x = vote.cleaned$ease.vote,
           y = vote.cleaned$race)
##
##   Pearson's Chi-squared test
##
## data: vote.cleaned$ease.vote and vote.cleaned$race
## X-squared = 28.952, df = 3, p-value = 2.293e-06
```

Leslie noted that the "X-squared" value was the same as the hand-calculated results. However, the output also provided two other values, `df = 3` and `p-value < 2.293e-16`. Kiara asked Leslie how much she remembered about probability distributions from their previous meeting (Section 4.4). She explained that the same concepts can be applied to interpreting a chi-squared statistic and the corresponding *p*-value.

5.6.4 ACHIEVEMENT 3: CHECK YOUR UNDERSTANDING

The way to compute a chi-squared statistic is to add up all the observed values and subtract the sum of all the expected values. Then, square the total.

- True
- False

When computing a chi-squared statistic, square any negative values but not the positive ones.

- True
- False

5.7 Achievement 4: Interpreting the chi-squared statistic and making a conclusion about whether or not there is a relationship

5.7.1 VISUALIZING THE CHI-SQUARED DISTRIBUTION

Kiara explained that the chi-squared distribution was made up of all the possible values of the chi-squared statistic and how often each value would occur when there is *no relationship between the variables*. The chi-squared distribution looks different from the binomial and normal distributions. The binomial distribution has two *parameters*, n and p, that define its shape (Section 4.5), and the normal distribution shape is defined by the mean (m or μ) and the standard deviation (s or σ). The chi-squared distribution has a single parameter, the *degrees of freedom* or df, which is the population mean for the distribution. The df can be used to find the population standard deviation for the distribution, $\sqrt{2\,df}$.

Since the chi-squared statistic is the sum of *squared* differences, it will never go below zero, and extreme values, where the observed values are much different from what was expected, are always large and positive. While Kiara explained chi-squared distributions to Leslie, Nancy practiced her fancy coding skills by graphing a few chi-squared distributions to demonstrate (Figure 5.7).

Leslie noticed that the chi-squared distributions Nancy created were all a similar shape but were not exactly the same, and that the difference appeared to be related to how many degrees of freedom the distribution had. This made sense given that distributions with different degrees of freedom have different means and standard deviations and so are likely to look different, just like the normal distribution has a different shape given the mean and standard deviation of the variable.

FIGURE 5.7 Chi-squared probability distributions

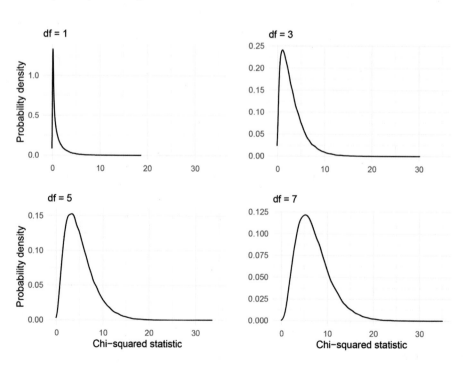

To get the value of the degrees of freedom for any chi-squared test, subtract 1 from the number of categories for each of the variables in the test, then multiply the resulting numbers together. For the ease of voting (2 categories) and race (4 categories), the chi-squared distribution would have $(2 - 1)(4 - 1)$ degrees of freedom, which is 3 degrees of freedom. A chi-squared distribution with 3 degrees of freedom has a population standard deviation of $\sqrt{2 \times 3}$ or 2.449.

5.7.2 AREA UNDER THE CURVE

Kiara explained that the chi-squared distribution shown, which is the chi-squared *probability density function,* shows the probability of a value of chi-squared occurring when there is no relationship between the two variables contributing to the chi-squared. For example, a chi-squared statistic of exactly 10 with 5 degrees of freedom would have a probability of occurring a little less than 3% of the time, as shown in the graph where the vertical line hits the distribution (Figure 5.8).

If there were no relationship between two variables, the probability that the differences between observed and expected values would result in a chi-squared of exactly 10 is pretty small. It might be more useful to know what the probability is of getting a chi-squared of 10 *or higher*. The probability of the chi-squared value being 10 or higher would be the area under the curve from 10 to the end of the distribution at the far right, shown as the shading under the curve in Figure 5.9.

While not as small as 3%, it is still a relatively small number. The probability of the squared differences between observed and expected adding up to 10 or more is low when there is no relationship between the variables. The observed values, therefore, are quite different from what we would expect if there were no relationship between the variables. Kiara reminded Leslie that the expected values are the values that would occur if there were no relationship between the two variables. When the chi-squared is large, it is because the observed values are different from expected, suggesting a relationship between the variables.

FIGURE 5.8 Chi-squared probability distribution ($df = 5$)

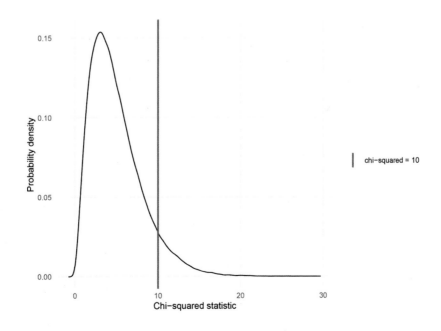

FIGURE 5.9 Chi-squared probability distribution (*df* = 5)

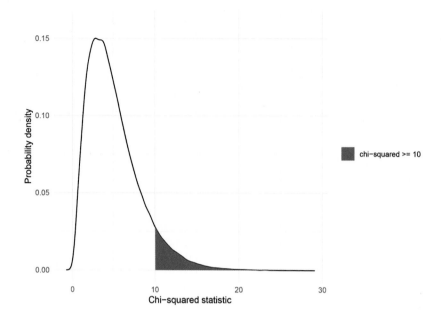

Kiara explained that, with samples being selected to represent populations, and with sample statistics often being a good representation of the population (Section 4.8), this statement could be even more specific. That is, she said, the probability density function in Figure 5.9 shows the probability of a chi-squared value of 10 or bigger when there is no relationship between the two variables *in the population* that was sampled.

5.7.3 USING THE CHI-SQUARED DISTRIBUTION TO DETERMINE PROBABILITY

Leslie was a little confused. Kiara continued but switched to the voting data as a more concrete example. The chi-squared from the voting data was 28.952 with *df* = 3.

```
##
##   Pearson's Chi-squared test
##
## data: vote.cleaned$ease.vote and vote.cleaned$race
## X-squared = 28.952, df = 3, p-value = 2.293e-06
```

Graphing the probability density function curve far enough to the right to capture the chi-squared value of 28.952 results in Figure 5.10.

By the time the distribution gets to chi-squared = 20, there is so little space under the curve that it is impossible to see. Obtaining a value of chi-squared as large as 28.952 or larger in this sample has an

FIGURE 5.10 Chi-squared probability distribution ($df = 3$)

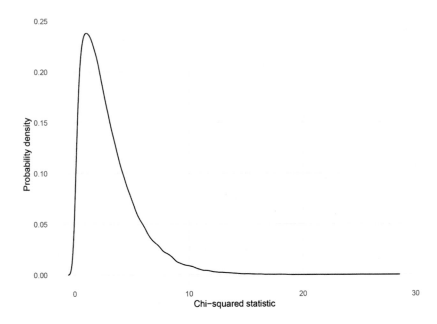

extremely low probability if there were no relationship between the two variables in the population that was sampled. Kiara reminded Leslie of the results of the chi-squared test from earlier:

```
##
##   Pearson's Chi-squared test
##
## data: vote.cleaned$ease.vote and vote.cleaned$race
## X-squared = 28.952, df = 3, p-value = 2.293e-06
```

The part of this output associated with the probability of a chi-squared value being 28.952 or higher in the sample when there is no relationship between the two variables in the population sampled is the **p-value**. In this case, the *p*-value is shown as < 2.293e-06. From earlier, Leslie knew that this is scientific notation and the *p*-value is .000002293. The probability of getting a chi-squared of 28.953 is very tiny, close to—but not exactly—zero. This is consistent with the graph showing very little space between the distribution curve and the *x*-axis. A chi-squared this big, and the corresponding *p*-value this small, means the observed values were much different from what Leslie would have expected to see if there were no relationship between opinion on voter registration and race-ethnicity in the population sampled.

Probabilities as small as .000002293 are reported as suggesting that the differences between observed and expected are *statistically significant*. This does not necessarily mean the differences are important or practically significant, just that they are bigger than what would most likely have happened if there were no relationship in the population between the variables involved.

While $p = .000002293$ would almost always be considered statistically significant, other probabilities could suggest that the differences between observed and expected are not big enough to be statistically significant. Thresholds for what is considered statistically significant are set by the analyst *before* conducting analyses. Usually in the social sciences, a p-value less than .05 is considered statistically significant. That is, the decision about which threshold to use is made ahead of time (before analyses are completed) and is referred to in statistics as the *alpha* or α. A p-value of less than .05 indicates less than a 5% probability of calculating a chi-squared statistic that big *or bigger* if the observed values were what was expected (i.e., that there was no relationship between the variables).

5.7.4 SELECTING THE THRESHOLD FOR STATISTICAL SIGNIFICANCE

Occasionally, analysts will set a higher statistical significance threshold for a p-value like $\alpha = .10$ or a lower threshold like $\alpha = .001$. The higher threshold is easier to meet because it does not require as much of a difference between observed and expected values to reach statistical significance. Smaller differences between observed and expected, therefore, would be reported as statistically significant with a p-value threshold of $\alpha = .10$. On the other hand, the difference between observed and expected would have to be larger to reach statistical significance if the threshold were set to $\alpha = .001$. A low threshold like this might be set in cases where reporting statistical significance could result in policy or program changes that are very expensive or have a direct impact on the health of living things.

Kiara summarized the result of the chi-squared test for Leslie as follows:

> There was a statistically significant association between views on voting ease and race-ethnicity [$\chi^2(3) = 28.95; p < .05$].

When possible, use the actual p-value rather than $p < .05$. In this case, the p-value of .000002293 has too many decimal places for easy reporting, so using $< .05$ or using the less than symbol $<$ with whatever the chosen threshold, α, was (e.g., $< .10$ or $< .001$) will work.

Kiara and Leslie decided that, for the sake of ease, they would adopt an $\alpha = .05$ for their remaining statistical tests today and for the rest of their meetings. Nancy agreed with this decision.

5.7.5 ACHIEVEMENT 4: CHECK YOUR UNDERSTANDING

Which of the following is a good representation of p-value $< 2.2e-4$?

- $p < .00022$
- $p < -1.8$
- $p < -8.8$
- $p < .000022$

Which of these is a common value for an alpha in many fields?

- 1
- 0
- .05
- .5

5.8 Achievement 5: Using Null Hypothesis Significance Testing to organize statistical testing

Kiara mentioned to Leslie that one process to organize statistical tests like chi-squared is *Null Hypothesis Significance Testing* or NHST. Leslie asked if this was the same as the chi-squared goodness-of-fit test that she remembered from her stats class. Kiara shook her head no, so Leslie decided she would look that up later (Box 5.1). Kiara wrote out the steps of NHST:

1. Write the null and alternate hypotheses.

2. Compute the test statistic.

3. Calculate the probability that your test statistic is at least as big as it is if there is no relationship (i.e., the null is true).

4. If the probability that the null is true is very small, usually less than 5%, reject the null hypothesis.

5. If the probability that the null is true is not small, usually 5% or greater, retain the null hypothesis.

5.8.1 NHST STEP 1: WRITE THE NULL AND ALTERNATE HYPOTHESES

Kiara explained that the *null hypothesis* is usually a statement that claims there is *no difference* or *no relationship* between things, whereas the *alternate hypothesis* is the claim that there *is* a difference or a relationship between things. The null (H0) and alternate (HA) hypotheses are written about the *population* and are tested using a *sample* from the population. Here are the null and alternate hypotheses for the voting data:

H0: People's opinions on voter registration are the same across race-ethnicity groups.

HA: People's opinions on voter registration are *not* the same across race-ethnicity groups.

Nancy noted that HA was sometimes written as H1.

5.8.2 NHST STEP 2: COMPUTE THE TEST STATISTIC

The test statistic to use when examining a relationship between two categorical variables is the chi-squared statistic, χ^2. This can be computed by hand or by using one of the R functions available.

```
# chi-squared statistic for ease of voting
# and race
chisq.test(x = vote.cleaned$ease.vote,
           y = vote.cleaned$race)
##
##  Pearson's Chi-squared test
```

```
##
## data:  vote.cleaned$ease.vote and vote.cleaned$race
## X-squared = 28.952, df = 3, p-value = 2.293e-06
```

The test statistic is $\chi^2 = 28.95$.

5.8.3 NHST STEP 3: CALCULATE THE PROBABILITY THAT YOUR TEST STATISTIC IS AT LEAST AS BIG AS IT IS IF THERE IS NO RELATIONSHIP (I.E., THE NULL IS TRUE)

The probability of seeing a chi-squared as big as 28.95 in our sample if there were no relationship in the population between opinion on voting ease and race-ethnicity group would be 0.000002293 or $p < .05$.

5.8.4 NHST STEP 4: IF THE PROBABILITY THAT THE NULL IS TRUE IS VERY SMALL, USUALLY LESS THAN 5%, REJECT THE NULL HYPOTHESIS

The probability that the null hypothesis, "People's opinions on voter registration are the same across race-ethnicity groups," is true in the population based on what we see in the sample is 0.000002293 or $p < .05$. This is a very small probability of being true and indicates that the null hypothesis is not likely to be true and should therefore be *rejected*.

5.8.5 NHST STEP 5: IF THE PROBABILITY THAT THE NULL IS TRUE IS NOT SMALL, USUALLY 5% OR GREATER, RETAIN THE NULL HYPOTHESIS

Step 5 does not apply in this situation.

Leslie liked this way of organizing the statistical test and wrote up a full interpretation of the work.

We used the chi-squared test to test the null hypothesis that there was no relationship between opinions on voter registration and race-ethnicity group. We rejected the null hypothesis and concluded that there was a statistically significant association between views on voter registration and race-ethnicity [$\chi^2(3) = 28.95$; $p < .05$].

5.8.6 ACHIEVEMENT 5: CHECK YOUR UNDERSTANDING

Which of the following statements are true about the chi-squared test (choose all that apply)?

- Chi-squared compares means of groups.
- Chi-squared can be negative or positive.
- Chi-squared is larger when there is a bigger difference between observed and expected.
- Chi-squared and χ^2 are two ways to represent the same thing.

The chi-squared test of independence tests whether there is a relationship between two categorical variables. The chi-squared goodness-of-fit test is used in a different situation. Specifically, the ***chi-squared goodness-of-fit*** test is used for comparing the values of a single categorical variable to values from a hypothesized or population variable. The goodness-of-fit test is often used when trying to determine if a sample is a good representation of the population.

For example, compare the observed values of the race-ethnicity variable to what would be expected in each category if the representation of race-ethnicity in the sample accurately captured the race-ethnicity of people in the U.S. population. The test statistic for this comparison is chi-squared. The test statistic itself is computed using the hypothesized or population values as the expected values. Leslie worked through an example using NHST to organize and using the race-ethnicity variable from the Pew Research Center data.

Step 1: Write the null and alternate hypotheses

HO: The proportions of people in each race-ethnicity category in the sample are the same as the proportions of people in each race-ethnicity category in the U.S. population.

HA: The proportions of people in each race-ethnicity category in the sample are *not* the same as the proportions of people in each race-ethnicity category in the U.S. population.

Step 2: Compute the test statistic

Leslie looked at the Wikipedia page for U.S. demographics. She found the distribution in the 2000 census and matched it to the categories in the Pew Research Center data. The U.S. population is

- 69.1% White non-Hispanic,
- 12.1% Black non-Hispanic,
- 12.5% Hispanic, and
- 6.3% Other.

To compare the distribution of race in the sample to this population distribution, she will need a vector of the frequencies in the sample to compare to these percentages. The `count()` function will count the number of observations in each category and add a variable called `n` to the new `race-eth` data frame.

(Continued)

(Continued)

```
# frequencies of race-ethnicity from pew data
race.eth <- vote.cleaned %>%
  drop_na(race) %>%
  count(race)
race.eth
## # A tibble: 4 x 2
##   race                  n
##   <fct>             <int>
## 1 White non-Hispanic  646
## 2 Black non-Hispanic  129
## 3 Hispanic            150
## 4 Other                78
```

The vector of frequencies for number of people in each race-ethnicity group is `race.eth$n`. The `chisq.test()` can be used by entering the frequency vector and then entering the population proportions for each race-ethnicity in the same order as the values in the vector. The two arguments are `x` = for the observed vector and `p` = for the population vector.

```
# chi-squared comparing observed race-eth to population race-eth
race.gof <- chisq.test(x = race.eth$n, p = c(.691, .121, .125, .063))
race.gof
##
##   Chi-squared test for given probabilities
##
## data: race.eth$n
## X-squared = 11.986, df = 3, p-value = 0.007432
```

Step 3: Calculate the probability that your test statistic is at least as big as it is if there is no relationship (i.e., the null is true)

The probability that the null hypothesis is true is 0.007.

Step 4: If the probability that the null is true is very small, usually less than 5%, reject the null hypothesis

A chi-squared goodness-of-fit test comparing the frequencies of race-ethnicity groups in the Pew Research Center data to the proportions of each race-ethnicity group in the U.S. population found a statistically significant difference between the observed and the population values [$\chi^2(3) = 11.99$; $p = 0.007$].

Step 5: If the probability that the null is true is not small, usually 5% or greater, retain the null hypothesis

Not applicable.

Leslie thought they should take a look at a graph to better understand these results (Figure 5.11).

```
# add percents of race-ethnicity from Pew data to make a data frame
# for graphing
race.eth.graph.data <- vote.cleaned %>%
  drop_na(race) %>%
  group_by(race) %>%
  summarize(n = n()) %>%
  mutate(sample = n/sum(n),
         population = c(.691, .121, .125, .063)) %>%
  gather(key = samp.or.pop, value = perc, sample, population)
race.eth.graph.data
## # A tibble: 8 x 4
##   race                  n samp.or.pop     perc
##   <fct>             <int> <chr>          <dbl>
## 1 White non-Hispanic   646 sample        0.644
## 2 Black non-Hispanic   129 sample        0.129
## 3 Hispanic             150 sample        0.150
## 4 Other                 78 sample        0.0778
## 5 White non-Hispanic   646 population    0.691
## 6 Black non-Hispanic   129 population    0.121
## 7 Hispanic             150 population    0.125
## 8 Other                 78 population    0.063
# Make the graph (Figure 5.11)
race.eth.graph.data %>%
  ggplot(aes(x = race, y = 100*perc, fill = samp.or.pop)) +
  geom_bar(position = "dodge", stat = "identity") +
  theme_minimal() +
  scale_fill_manual(values = c("gray", "#7463AC"),
                    name = "Population\nor sample") +
  labs(y = "Percent of people", x = "Race-ethnicity group")
```

(Continued)

(Continued)

FIGURE 5.11 Comparison of race-ethnicity distribution between population and sample

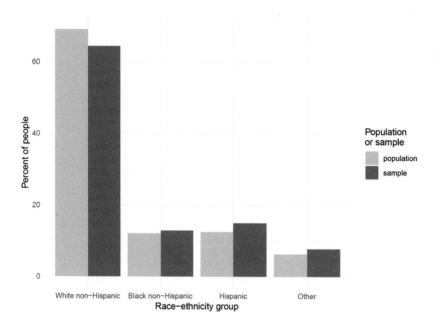

Leslie didn't think the groups looked all that different from each other. There were fewer White non-Hispanic and more Hispanic and Other in the sample, but none of the differences was huge. Leslie had learned from Nancy that she could examine the standardized residuals (see Section 5.9) from the `race.gof` object. She looked up the `chisq.test()` in the help documentation (https://www.rdocumentation.org/packages/stats/versions/3.6.0/topics/chisq.test) to determine what the standardized residuals were called in the `race.gof` object. In this case, the `race .gof` object resulting from the goodness-of-fit test included `stdres`, the standardized residuals.

```
# standardized residuals from race.gof object
race.gof$stdres
## [1] -3.2166451 0.7394098 2.3510764 1.9248365
```

The standardized residuals were in the same order as the categories of race-ethnicity, so it appeared that the proportion of White non-Hispanic in the sample was much lower than expected (standardized residual = −3.22), while the proportion of Hispanic participants in the sample was much higher than expected (standardized residual = 2.35). Leslie wrote her full interpretation:

A chi-squared goodness-of-fit test comparing the proportion of participants in race-ethnicity groups in the Pew Research Center data to the proportion in each race-ethnicity group in the U.S. population (from Wikipedia) found a statistically significant difference between the observed sample and the population values [$\chi^2(3) = 11.99$; $p = 0.007$]. Standardized residuals indicated there were fewer White non-Hispanic participants and more Hispanic participants in the sample than would be expected based on the population proportions.

5.9 Achievement 6: Using standardized residuals to understand which groups contributed to significant relationships

One limitation of the chi-squared independence test is that it determines whether or not there is a statistically significant relationship between two categorical variables but does not identify what makes the relationship significant. The name for this type of test is *omnibus*. An omnibus statistical test identifies that there is some relationship going on, but not what that relationship is. For example, is the relationship between opinions on voting ease and the race-ethnicity category significant because there are more non-Hispanic White people than expected who think people should register to vote? Or is it significant because fewer non-Hispanic Black people than expected think people should register to vote? Where are the largest differences between observed and expected?

5.9.1 USING STANDARDIZED RESIDUALS FOLLOWING CHI-SQUARED TESTS

Nancy explained that standardized residuals (like *z*-scores) can aid analysts in determining which of the observed frequencies are significantly larger or smaller than expected. The standardized residual is computed by subtracting the expected value in a cell from the observed value in a cell and dividing by the square root of the expected value, as in Equation (5.5).

$$standardized. residual = \frac{observed - expected}{\sqrt{expected}} \tag{5.5}$$

The resulting value is the standardized residual and is distributed like a *z*-score. Values of the standardized residuals that are higher than 1.96 or lower than –1.96 indicate that the observed value in that group is much higher or lower than the expected value. These are the groups that are contributing the most to a large chi-squared statistic and could be examined further and included in the interpretation.

Nancy explained that standardized residuals are available with the chi-squared statistic from the `CrossTable()` function in the **descr** package. She said that `CrossTable()` is one of the functions that has a lot of possible arguments to include, and choosing which arguments is important. She recommended including arguments in the code to show expected values and standardized residuals. Kiara made some notes about arguments and argument names in R code for Leslie to review later (Box 5.2).

Nancy wrote the code for the voting and race chi-squared test. Her code showed `CrossTable()` with arguments for showing the expected values, `expected = TRUE`, the standardized residuals, `sresid = TRUE`, and the chi-squared, `chisq = TRUE`. Nancy had a few other arguments in her code and Leslie asked about them. Specifically, why are `prop.c = FALSE`, `prop.t = FALSE`, and `prop.chisq = FALSE` in the code? Nancy explained that the default for `CrossTable()` is to include proportions in the columns (`prop.c`), proportions out of total (`prop.t`), and proportions of the chi-squared (`prop.chisq`) for each group in the table. Using options like `prop.c = FALSE` removes all this extra information so they can create a clearer table. Kiara created some additional guidance about this for Leslie to ponder later (Box 5.2).

```
# open descr
library(package = "descr")

# chi-squared examining ease of voting and race
CrossTable(x = vote.cleaned$ease.vote,
           y = vote.cleaned$race,
           expected = TRUE,
           prop.c = FALSE,
           prop.t = FALSE,
           prop.chisq = FALSE,
           chisq = TRUE,
           sresid = TRUE)
## Cell Contents
## |-------------------------|
## |                       N |
## |              Expected N |
## |           N / Row Total |
## |            Std Residual |
## |-------------------------|
##
## ========================================================================
##                  vote.cleaned$race
## vot.clnd$s.vt   Whit nn-Hspnc   Blck nn-Hspnc   Hispanic   Other   Total
## ------------------------------------------------------------------------
## Register t vt            292             28          51        27     398
##                        256.6           51.3        60.3      29.7
##                        0.734          0.070       0.128     0.068   0.407
##                        2.207         -3.256      -1.197    -0.502
## ------------------------------------------------------------------------
## Make esy t vt            338             98          97        46     579
##                        373.4           74.7        87.7      43.3
##                        0.584          0.169       0.168     0.079   0.593
##                       -1.830          2.700       0.992     0.416
## ------------------------------------------------------------------------
## Total                    630            126         148        73     977
## ========================================================================
##
## Statistics for All Table Factors
##
## Pearson's Chi-squared test
## ------------------------------------------------------------------
## Chi^2 = 28.95154      d.f. = 3      p = 2.29e-06
```

5.2 Kiara's reproducibility resource: Specifying arguments in code

Kiara sensed an opportunity to teach Leslie about coding practices that improve reproducibility. She noticed that Nancy had been great about using argument names in code but that they had not explained this quirk of R to Leslie yet. Because `CrossTable()` has so many arguments that can be used, Kiara thought this was a good example.

The `CrossTable()` function requires two arguments, an *x* and a *y*. Check the help documentation shown in Figure 5.12 to see these arguments.

In the help documentation, it shows that `CrossTable` interprets the first value entered after the opening parenthesis as the *x* and the second value as the *y*. The *x* is then used for the rows while the *y* is used for the columns in the table. If Leslie enters the two variables into the `CrossTable()` function with `ease.vote` first and `race` second, the `ease.vote` variable will be considered *x* and put in the rows, while the `race` variable will be considered *y* and put in columns, like this:

FIGURE 5.12 CrossTable help documentation

Cross tabulation with tests for factor independence

Description

An implementation of a cross-tabulation function with output similar to S-Plus crosstabs() and SAS Proc Freq (or SPSS format) with Chi-square, Fisher and McNemar tests of the independence of all table factors.

Usage

```
CrossTable(x, y,
        digits = list(expected = 1, prop = 3, percent = 1, others = 3),
        max.width = NA, expected = FALSE,
        prop.r = TRUE, prop.c = TRUE, prop.t = TRUE,
        prop.chisq = TRUE, chisq = FALSE, fisher = FALSE,
        mcnemar = FALSE, resid = FALSE, sresid = FALSE,
        asresid = FALSE, missing.include = FALSE,
        drop.levels = TRUE, format = c("SAS","SPSS"),
        dnn = NULL, cell.layout = TRUE,
        row.labels = !cell.layout,
        percent = (format == "SPSS" && !row.labels),
        total.r, total.c, xlab = NULL, ylab = NULL, ...)
```

Arguments

x	A vector or a matrix. If y is specified, x must be a vector.
y	A vector in a matrix or a dataframe.
digits	Named list with number of digits after the decimal point for four categories of statistics: expected values, cell proportions, percentage and others statistics. It can also be a numeric vector with a single number if you want the same number of digits in all statistics.
max.width	In the case of a 1 x n table, the default will be to print the output horizontally. If the number of columns exceeds max.width, the table will be wrapped for each successive increment of max.width columns. If you want a single column vertical table, set max.width to 1.
prop.r	If TRUE, row proportions will be included.
prop.c	If TRUE, column proportions will be included.
prop.t	If TRUE, table proportions will be included.
expected	If TRUE, expected cell counts from the *Chi-Square* will be included.
prop.chisq	If TRUE, chi-square contribution of each cell will be included.
chisq	If TRUE, the results of a chi-square test will be printed after the table.
fisher	If TRUE, the results of a Fisher Exact test will be printed after the table
mcnemar	If TRUE, the results of a McNemar test will be printed after the table.
resid	If TRUE, residual (Pearson) will be included.
sresid	If TRUE, standardized residual will be included.

(Continued)

(Continued)

```
# chi-squared examining ease of voting and race-eth category
# no specification of argument names
CrossTable(vote.cleaned$ease.vote,
           vote.cleaned$race)
##    Cell Contents
## |-------------------------|
## |-----------------------N |
## | Chi-square contribution |
## |           N / Row Total |
## |           N / Col Total |
## |         N / Table Total |
## |-------------------------|
##
## ================================================================
##                   vote.cleaned$race
## vot.clnd$s.vt  Whit nn-Hspnc  Blck nn-Hspnc  Hispanic  Other  Total
## ----------------------------------------------------------------
## Register t vt           292            28         51     27    398
##                       4.871        10.603      1.432  0.252
##                       0.734         0.070      0.128  0.068  0.407
##                       0.463         0.222      0.345  0.370
##                       0.299         0.029      0.052  0.028
## ----------------------------------------------------------------
## Make esy t vt           338            98         97     46    579
##                       3.348         7.288      0.984  0.173
##                       0.584         0.169      0.168  0.079  0.593
##                       0.537         0.778      0.655  0.630
##                       0.346         0.100      0.099  0.047
## ----------------------------------------------------------------
## Total                   630           126        148     73    977
##                       0.645         0.129      0.151  0.075
## ================================================================
```

Putting the `race` variable first and the `ease.vote` variable second without specifying the argument names will result in a different table.

```
# chi-squared examining ease of voting and race-eth category
# no specification of argument names
CrossTable(vote.cleaned$race,
           vote.cleaned$ease.vote)
## Cell Contents
## |-------------------------|
## |                       N |
## | Chi-square contribution |
## |           N / Row Total |
## |           N / Col Total |
## |         N / Table Total |
## |-------------------------|
##
## ===================================================================
##                         vote.cleaned$ease.vote
## vote.cleaned$race   Register to vote   Make easy to vote    Total
## -------------------------------------------------------------------
## White non-Hispanic            292                 338        630
##                             4.871               3.348
##                             0.463               0.537      0.645
##                             0.734               0.584
##                             0.299               0.346
## -------------------------------------------------------------------
## Black non-Hispanic             28                  98        126
##                            10.603               7.288
##                             0.222               0.778      0.129
##                             0.070               0.169
##                             0.029               0.100
## -------------------------------------------------------------------
## Hispanic                       51                  97        148
##                             1.432               0.984
##                             0.345               0.655      0.151
##                             0.128               0.168
##                             0.052               0.099
## -------------------------------------------------------------------
## Other                          27                  46         73
```

(Continued)

```
##                                        0.252              0.173
##                                        0.370              0.630      0.075
##                                        0.068              0.079
##                                        0.028              0.047
## ----------------------------------------------------------------------------
## Total                                   398                 579        977
##                                        0.407              0.593
## ============================================================================
```

If argument names are included, x = vote.cleaned$ease.vote and y = vote
.cleaned$race, then their order does not matter in the CrossTable() code. Using the
argument names of x = and y = clarifies which variable is in the rows and which is in the columns.
Argument names override the default order in which the arguments are placed inside the parentheses.

```
# chi-squared examining ease of voting and race-eth category
# specification of argument names
CrossTable(y = vote.cleaned$race,
           x = vote.cleaned$ease.vote)
## Cell Contents
## |-------------------------|
## |                       N |
## | Chi-square contribution |
## |           N / Row Total |
## |           N / Col Total |
## |         N / Table Total |
## |-------------------------|
##
## ============================================================================
##                      vote.cleaned$race
## vot.clnd$s.vt  Whit nn-Hspnc  Blck nn-Hspnc  Hispanic  Other  Total
## ----------------------------------------------------------------------------
## Register t vt           292             28         51      27    398
##                       4.871         10.603      1.432   0.252
##                       0.734          0.070      0.128   0.068  0.407
##                       0.463          0.222      0.345   0.370
```

```
## 	            0.299 	      0.029 	  0.052  0.028
## ---------------------------------------------------------------
## Make esy t vt 	      338 	         98 	     97 	  46 	 579
## 	            3.348 	      7.288 	  0.984  0.173
## 	            0.584 	      0.169 	  0.168  0.079 0.593
## 	            0.537 	      0.778 	  0.655  0.630
## 	            0.346 	      0.100 	  0.099  0.047
## ---------------------------------------------------------------
## Total 	          630 	        126 	    148 	  73 	 977
## 	            0.645 	      0.129 	  0.151  0.075
## ===============================================================
```

The output is the same when the variables are entered in another order but have specified the argument names.

```
# chi-squared examining ease of voting and race-eth category
# specification of argument names
CrossTable(x = vote.cleaned$ease.vote,
           y = vote.cleaned$race)
## Cell Contents
## |-------------------------|
## |                       N |
## | Chi-square contribution |
## |           N / Row Total |
## |           N / Col Total |
## |         N / Table Total |
## |-------------------------|
##
## ===============================================================
##                   vote.cleaned$race
## vot.clnd$s.vt  Whit nn-Hspnc  Blck nn-Hspnc  Hispanic  Other  Total
## ---------------------------------------------------------------
## Register t vt 	      292 	         28 	     51 	  27 	 398
## 	            4.871 	     10.603 	  1.432  0.252
## 	            0.734 	      0.070 	  0.128  0.068 0.407
```

(Continued)

(Continued)

```
##                              0.463        0.222    0.345  0.370
##                              0.299        0.029    0.052  0.028
## ------------------------------------------------------------------
## Make esy t vt         338              98       97      46    579
##                              3.348        7.288    0.984  0.173
##                              0.584        0.169    0.168  0.079  0.593
##                              0.537        0.778    0.655  0.630
##                              0.346        0.100    0.099  0.047
## ------------------------------------------------------------------
## Total                 630             126      148      73    977
##                              0.645        0.129    0.151  0.075
## ==================================================================
```

After the `x =` and `y =` arguments, the documentation shows a lot of other arguments that can be specified in order to include (or not include) certain things in the output or to conduct analyses in a specific way. The defaults are shown under the Usage heading in Figure 5.12. In this figure, it looks like the *expected* values will not show by default given `expected = FALSE`, but this can be changed to override the default by adding `expected = TRUE` to the code. It also appears that the proportions for the row (`prop.r`), the column (`prop.c`), and the total (`prop.t`) are all included by default along with something called `prop.chisq`. To clean up the output of `CrossTable()`, decide on which pieces of information are useful (usually row *or* column proportions, but not both, should be included) and change the rest to `FALSE`, like this:

```
# chi-squared examining ease of voting and race-eth category
# specification of arguments
CrossTable(x = vote.cleaned$ease.vote,
           y = vote.cleaned$race,
           expected = TRUE,
           prop.c = FALSE,
           prop.t = FALSE,
           prop.chisq = FALSE,
           chisq = TRUE,
           sresid = TRUE)
##    Cell Contents
## |-------------------------|
## |                       N |
```

```
## |              Expected N |
## |          N / Row Total |
## |            Std Residual |
## |------------------------|
##
## ========================================================================
##                        vote.cleaned$race
## vot.clnd$s.vt  Whit nn-Hspnc  Blck nn-Hspnc  Hispanic  Other  Total
## ------------------------------------------------------------------------
## Register t vt            292            28         51     27    398
##                        256.6          51.3       60.3   29.7
##                        0.734         0.070      0.128  0.068  0.407
##                        2.207        -3.256     -1.197 -0.502
## ------------------------------------------------------------------------
## Make esy t vt            338            98         97     46    579
##                        373.4          74.7       87.7   43.3
##                        0.584         0.169      0.168  0.079  0.593
##                       -1.830         2.700      0.992  0.416
## ------------------------------------------------------------------------
## Total                    630           126        148     73    977
## ========================================================================
##
## Statistics for All Table Factors
##
## Pearson's Chi-squared test
## ------------------------------------------------------------------------
## Chi^2 = 28.95154      d.f. = 3      p = 2.29e-06
```

This output has observed frequencies, expected frequencies, observed row proportions, and standardized residuals in the table. Below the table, the `chisq = TRUE` has resulted in printing the chi-squared statistic with *df* and *p*.

Taking a little time to specify arguments in code can improve the readability of output and ensure that whatever was intended actually happens regardless of the order in which arguments are entered.

5.9.2 INTERPRETING STANDARDIZED RESIDUALS AND CHI-SQUARED RESULTS

The standardized residuals are shown in the last row of each cell (see the key at the top of the table to figure this out) with an absolute value higher than 1.96 in the White non-Hispanic group for "Register to vote" (std. res. = 2.207) and Black non-Hispanic group for both categories; the standardized residual was –3.256 for "Register to vote" and 2.700 for "Make easy to vote." The 2.207 value for White non-Hispanic who selected "Register to vote" indicates that more White non-Hispanic people than expected selected that option. The –3.256 for Black non-Hispanic indicated that fewer Black non-Hispanic people than expected selected "Register to vote." Finally, the 2.700 for Black non-Hispanic indicated that more Black non-Hispanic people than expected selected "Make easy to vote." The Hispanic and Other race-ethnicity groups did not have more or fewer than expected observations in either category. The significant chi-squared result was driven by more White non-Hispanic and fewer Black non-Hispanic people feeling that people should prove they want to vote by registering and more Black non-Hispanic people feeling that the process for voting should be made easier.

Leslie adds this information to her interpretation:

> We used the chi-squared test to test the null hypothesis that there was no relationship between opinions on voter registration by race-ethnicity group. We rejected the null hypothesis and concluded that there was a statistically significant association between views on voter registration and race-ethnicity [$\chi^2(3) = 28.95$; $p < .05$]. Based on standardized residuals, the statistically significant chi-squared test result was driven by *more White non-Hispanic* participants and *fewer Black non-Hispanic* participants than expected believe that people should prove they want to vote by registering, and more Black non-Hispanic participants than expected believe that the voting process should be made easier.

5.9.3 ACHIEVEMENT 6: CHECK YOUR UNDERSTANDING

A standardized residual of –3.56 would indicate which of the following?

- The observed value is greater than the expected value in the cell.
- The observed value is less than the expected value in the cell.
- The chi-squared is not statistically significant.
- The chi-squared is a lower value than expected.

5.10 Achievement 7: Computing and interpreting effect sizes to understand the strength of a significant chi-squared relationship

5.10.1 COMPUTING THE CRAMÉR'S V STATISTIC

Now that Leslie could determine if two categorical variables are related and what might be driving that relationship, Kiara suggested they discuss one more detail about chi-squared that is useful. While the voting data showed a relationship between preference on voter registration and race-ethnicity, the strength of the relationship was not clear. Kiara explained that the strength of a relationship in statistics is referred to as *effect size*. For chi-squared, there are a few options, including the commonly used effect size statistic of *Cramér's V* (Kim, 2017), which is computed in Equation (5.6).

$$V = \sqrt{\frac{\chi^2}{n(k-1)}} \qquad (5.6)$$

In Equation (5.6), the chi-squared is the test statistic for the analysis, n is the sample size, and k is the number of categories in the variable with the *fewest* categories.

Computing the value by hand is one option. The voting easy variable has two categories, so $k = 2$ in this case, and substituting the values into Equation (5.6) results in Equation (5.7).

$$V = \sqrt{\frac{28.952}{977(2-1)}} = .17 \qquad (5.7)$$

There are several packages in R that compute the V statistic. The **lsr** package is a good option because it takes the same arguments as `CrossTabs()` and `chisq.test()`, so it is easy to use.

```
# compute Cramér's V for voting ease and race
# chi-squared analysis
library(package = "lsr")
cramersV(x = vote.cleaned$ease.vote,
         y = vote.cleaned$race)
## [1] 0.1721427
```

5.10.2 INTERPRETING CRAMÉR'S V

Leslie noticed the effect size is .17, but how is that interpreted? What does it mean? Kiara said the general rule was that values of Cramér's V are interpreted as follows:

- Small or weak effect size for $V = .1$
- Medium or moderate effect size for $V = .3$
- Large or strong effect size for $V = .5$

In this case, the effect size is between small and medium. There is a statistically significant relationship between opinions on voter registration and race-ethnicity, and the relationship is weak to moderate. This is consistent with the frequencies, which are different from expected, but not by an enormous amount in most of the groups.

```
## Cell Contents
## |-------------------------|
## |                     N |
## |            Expected N |
## |        N / Row Total |
## |          Std Residual |
## |-------------------------|
```

```
##
## =======================================================================
##                        vote.cleaned$race
## vot.clnd$s.vt    Whit nn-Hspnc   Blck nn-Hspnc   Hispanic   Other   Total
## ----------------------------------------------------------------------
## Register t vt            292            28         51        27     398
##                        256.6          51.3       60.3      29.7
##                        0.734         0.070      0.128     0.068   0.407
##                        2.207        -3.256     -1.197    -0.502
## ----------------------------------------------------------------------
## Make esy t vt            338            98         97        46     579
##                        373.4          74.7       87.7      43.3
##                        0.584         0.169      0.168     0.079   0.593
##                       -1.830         2.700      0.992     0.416
## ----------------------------------------------------------------------
## Total                    630           126        148        73     977
## =======================================================================
##
## Statistics for All Table Factors
##
## Pearson's Chi-squared test
## ----------------------------------------------------------------
## Chi^2 = 28.95154       d.f. = 3       p = 2.29e-06
```

There are additional options for effect size when both variables in the chi-squared analysis are binary with two categories.

5.10.3 AN EXAMPLE OF CHI-SQUARED FOR TWO BINARY VARIABLES

Kiara remembered there was a binary variable that classified people as owning or renting their home. She used NHST to conduct a chi-squared test with ease.vote.

5.10.3.1 NHST STEP 1: WRITE THE NULL AND ALTERNATE HYPOTHESES

H0: Opinions on voter registration are the same by home ownership status.

HA: Opinions on voter registration are *not* the same by home ownership status.

5.10.3.2 NHST STEP 2: COMPUTE THE TEST STATISTIC

```
# chi-squared examining ease of voting and race-ethnicity category
CrossTable(x = vote.cleaned$ease.vote,
           y = vote.cleaned$ownhome,
```

```
          expected = TRUE,
          prop.c = FALSE,
          prop.t = FALSE,
          prop.chisq = FALSE,
          chisq = TRUE,
          sresid = TRUE)
## Cell Contents
## |-------------------------|
## |                       N |
## |              Expected N |
## |           N / Row Total |
## |           Std Residual  |
## |-------------------------|
##
## ===================================================
##                        vote.cleaned$ownhome
## vote.cleaned$ease.vote   Owned    Rented    Total
## ---------------------------------------------------
## Register to vote          287       112      399
##                           269       130
##                         0.719     0.281    0.406
##                         1.099    -1.580
## ---------------------------------------------------
## Make easy to vote         375       208      583
##                           393       190
##                         0.643     0.357    0.594
##                        -0.909     1.307
## ---------------------------------------------------
## Total                     662       320      982
## ===================================================
##
## Statistics for All Table Factors
##
## Pearson's Chi-squared test
## ------------------------------------------------------------
## Chi^2 = 6.240398      d.f. = 1      p = 0.0125
##
## Pearson's Chi-squared test with Yates' continuity correction
## ------------------------------------------------------------
## Chi^2 = 5.898905      d.f. = 1      p = 0.0152
```

5.10.3.3 NHST STEP 3: CALCULATE THE PROBABILITY THAT YOUR TEST STATISTIC IS AT LEAST AS BIG AS IT IS IF THERE IS NO RELATIONSHIP (I.E., THE NULL IS TRUE)

The *p*-value is .0152.

5.10.3.4 NHST STEPS 4 AND 5: INTERPRET THE PROBABILITY AND WRITE A CONCLUSION

Leslie found that there was a statistically significant relationship between opinion on registering to vote and home ownership [$\chi^2(1) = 5.90$; $p = .02$].

5.10.4 INTERPRETING THE YATES CONTINUITY CORRECTION

Leslie noticed that two different chi-squared statistics were printed in the results of this analysis. Kiara explained that the *Yates continuity correction* for the second version of the chi-squared subtracts an additional .5 from the difference between observed and expected in each group, or cell of the table, making the chi-squared test statistic value smaller, making it harder to reach statistical significance. This correction is used when both variables have just two categories because the chi-squared distribution is not a perfect representation of the distribution of differences between observed and expected of a chi-squared in the situation where both variables are binary. The `CrossTable()` function used for this analysis gives both the uncorrected and the corrected chi-squared, while the `chisq.test()` function gives only the corrected result unless an argument is added.

```
# checking chisq.test function
chisq.test(x = vote.cleaned$ease.vote,
           y = vote.cleaned$ownhome)

##
##   Pearson's Chi-squared test with Yates' continuity correction
##
## data:  vote.cleaned$ease.vote and vote.cleaned$ownhome
## X-squared = 5.8989, df = 1, p-value = 0.01515

# removing the Yates correction
chisq.test(x = vote.cleaned$ease.vote,
           y = vote.cleaned$ownhome,
           correct = FALSE)

##
##   Pearson's Chi-squared test
##
## data:  vote.cleaned$ease.vote and vote.cleaned$ownhome
## X-squared = 6.2404, df = 1, p-value = 0.01249
```

Kiara suggested Leslie pay close attention to the chi-squared results for two binary variables that produce 2 × 2 tables. Leslie should make sure she picks the version of the chi-squared (with or without the Yates correction) she wants to report and accurately describes it. Kiara explained that this is yet another reproducibility-related suggestion.

5.10.4.1 COMPUTING AND INTERPRETING THE EFFECT SIZE

Once the analysis reveals a significant relationship, the standardized residuals and effect size are useful in better understanding the relationship. In the initial analyses above, it appears that all of the standardized residuals were of a smaller magnitude. The group with the largest standardized residual was the one made up of those renting their homes who feel that people should have to register to vote. This group had a –1.58 standardized residual, indicating fewer people than expected were in this group. None of the standardized residuals were outside the –1.96 to 1.96 range, though.

```
# compute Cramér's V for voting ease and home owning
cramersV(x = vote.cleaned$ease.vote,
         y = vote.cleaned$ownhome)
## [1] 0.07750504
```

The value of V for this analysis falls into the weak or small effect size range. This makes sense given that the observed and expected values were not very different from each other for any of the groups. Leslie wrote the full interpretation:

We used the chi-squared test to test the null hypothesis that there was no relationship between opinions on voter registration by home ownership group. We rejected the null hypothesis and concluded that there was a statistically significant association between views on voter registration and home ownership [$\chi^2(3) = 6.24$; $p = .01$]. Based on standardized residuals, the statistically significant chi-squared test results were driven by fewer people than expected who were renters and thought people should have to register to vote. Although statistically significant, the relationship was weak ($V = .08$).

5.10.5 THE PHI COEFFICIENT EFFECT SIZE STATISTIC

Leslie remembered that sometimes a different statistic is reported with a chi-squared. Kiara thought she might know what Leslie was referring to; she explained that, when computing for 2 × 2 tables, the $k - 1$ term in the denominator of the Cramér's V formula is always 1, so this term is not needed in the calculation. The formula without this term is called the *phi coefficient* and is computed using the formula in Equation (5.8).

$$\phi = \sqrt{\frac{\chi^2}{n}}$$

(5.8)

There is no reason to use a different R package to compute the phi coefficient since it is just a special case of Cramér's V. Kiara mentioned that the phi calculation uses the version of chi-squared that is *not* adjusted by the Yates correction. Leslie asked why this is only used for 2 × 2 tables, since any chi-squared where one of the variables has two categories would have $k - 1 = 1$. Kiara thought she was right but did not know why. Leslie did a little digging and found some information on why the phi coefficient tends to be used only for 2 × 2 tables. Nancy was getting bored and asked if they could discuss it some other time; she wanted to talk about the odds ratio. Leslie wrote up a few notes so she would remember what she found (Box 5.3).

5.10.6 THE ODDS RATIO FOR EFFECT SIZE WITH TWO BINARY VARIABLES

Another effect size useful when both variables are binary is the odds ratio (OR) (Kim, 2017). The *odds ratio* measures the odds of some event or outcome occurring given a particular exposure compared to the odds of it happening without that exposure. In this case, the *exposure* would be home ownership, and the *outcome* would be opinion on ease of voting. The odds ratio would measure the odds of thinking people should register to vote given owning a home, compared to the odds of thinking people should register to vote given not owning a home.

The calculation uses the frequencies in the 2 × 2 table where the rows are the exposure and the columns are the outcome.

```
##
##          Register to vote Make easy to vote
##  Owned               287               375
##  Rented              112               208
```

5.10.6.1 CALCULATING THE ODDS RATIO

The odds ratio is calculated using the formula in Equation (5.9) (Szumilas, 2010).

$$OR = \frac{exposed.with.outcome \,/\, unexposed.with.outcome}{exposed.no.outcome \,/\, unexposed.no.outcome} \tag{5.9}$$

Leslie substituted in the values and computed the odds ratio in Equation (5.10).

$$OR = \frac{287 \,/\, 112}{375 \,/\, 208} = \frac{2.5625}{1.802885} = 1.42 \tag{5.10}$$

5.10.6.2 INTERPRETING THE ODDS RATIO

The numerator shows that the odds of an outcome for those who reported being exposed compared to those who reported not being exposed are 2.56. The denominator shows that the odds of no outcome for those who reported being exposed compared to those who reported not being exposed are 1.80. Dividing the 2.56 by 1.80, the resulting odds ratio is 1.42 and could be interpreted in a couple of ways:

- Home owners have 1.42 times the odds of thinking people should register to vote compared to people who do not own homes.

- Home owners have 42% higher odds of thinking people should register to vote compared to people who do not own homes.

Consistent with the Cramér's V or the phi coefficient value showing a weak effect, this odds ratio also shows a small effect of home ownership on opinion about voting ease. Odds ratios interpretation depends mostly on whether the OR is above or below 1. An odds ratio of 1 would be interpreted as having equal odds. Odds ratios above or below 1 are interpreted as follows:

- OR > 1 indicates higher odds of the outcome for exposed compared to unexposed

- OR < 1 indicates lower odds of the outcome for exposed compared to unexposed

An odds ratio of .85 would be interpreted in a couple of ways:

- People with the exposure have .85 times the odds of having the outcome compared to people who were not exposed.

- People with the exposure have 15% lower odds of having the outcome compared to people who were not exposed.

In addition to computing the OR by hand, there is an `oddsratio()` function in the **fmsb** package. Leslie and Kiara looked at the help documentation, and it appeared that the use of the `oddsratio()` function has this format: `oddsratio(a, b, c, d)`, where

- a is exposed with outcome,

- b is not exposed with outcome,

- c is exposed no outcome, and

- d is not exposed no outcome.

Leslie tried entering the voting and home ownership frequencies into the function to test it.

```
# open fmsb
library(package = "fmsb")

# odds ratio from frequencies
oddsratio(a = 287,
          b = 112,
          c = 375,
          d = 208)
##          Disease Nondisease Total
## Exposed      287        375   662
```

```
## Nonexposed       112        208    320
## Total            399        583    982
##
##   Odds ratio estimate and its significance probability
##
## data:  287 112 375 208
## p-value = 0.01253
## 95 percent confidence interval:
##   1.078097 1.873847
## sample estimates:
## [1] 1.421333
```

The results include "sample estimates," which looks like a confirmation of the 1.42 odds ratio just as computed by hand. The results also show a table with the frequencies, a *p*-value, and a 95% confidence interval. Kiara suggested to Leslie that they already knew the relationship was statistically significant given the results of the chi-squared test, but Leslie was still interested in the meaning of the *p*-value and confidence interval for the odds ratio.

Kiara explained that the *p*-value for the odds ratio has the same broad meaning as the *p*-value for the chi-squared, but instead of being based on the area under the curve for the chi-squared distribution, it is based on the area under the curve for the log of the odds ratio, which is approximately normally distributed. The odds ratio can only be a positive number, and it results in a right-skewed distribution, which the log function can often transform to something close to normal, as they saw earlier in Section 4.6.1.

Likewise, Kiara explained, the 95% confidence interval has a similar meaning to the 95% confidence intervals for means computed in Section 4.9. In this case, the odds ratio is 1.42 in the sample, and the odds ratio likely falls between 1.078 and 1.875 in the population that was sampled. In the sample, home owners had 42% higher odds of thinking people should register to vote compared to people who are renters. In the population, home owners had 7.8% to 87.4% higher odds of thinking people should register to vote compared to people who rent (OR = 1.42; 95% CI: 1.078–1.874).

5.10.7 ACHIEVEMENT 7: CHECK YOUR UNDERSTANDING

Describe what Cramér's *V*, the phi coefficient, and odds ratios are and how they differ.

5.11 Achievement 8: Understanding the options for failed chi-squared assumptions

Before they were done for the day, Leslie also wanted to discuss the assumptions of chi-squared and what to do when each one is violated. Kiara was fine with this, although she thought the expected cell size being less than 5 in a lot of cells was going to be the most likely assumption to cause problems. Leslie listed the assumptions again and they discussed the options for when each assumption is violated.

5.11.1 VIOLATING THE ASSUMPTION THAT THE VARIABLES MUST BE NOMINAL OR ORDINAL

Kiara promised this one was easy! Use a different statistical test. Chi-squared is only appropriate for categorical variables.

5.11.2 VIOLATING THE ASSUMPTION OF EXPECTED VALUES OF 5 OR HIGHER IN AT LEAST 80% OF GROUPS

The sampling distribution for the chi-squared statistic approximates the actual chi-squared distribution but does not capture it completely accurately. When a sample is large, the approximation is better and using the chi-squared distribution to determine statistical significance works well. However, for very small samples, the approximation is not great, so a different method of computing the p-value is better. The method most commonly used is the *Fisher's exact test*. The Fisher's exact test computes a different p-value for the chi-squared statistic (Kim, 2017). In R, the Fisher's exact test can be conducted with the `fisher.test()` function. The process of NHST and the interpretation of the results are the same as for the chi-squared, just with a different method of computing the p-value to reject or retain the null hypothesis.

5.11.3 VIOLATING THE INDEPENDENT OBSERVATIONS ASSUMPTION

Leslie then asked what would happen if the observation of independent assumptions was violated. Kiara looked at her with a straight face and said, "It *depends*," and started laughing. "Seriously, though," she explained, "there are a few ways observations can be non-independent." She went on to say that if the data were collected in order to examine nonindependent observations, such as some characteristic of the same set of people before and after an intervention, or whether two siblings share some characteristic or opinion, *McNemar's test* is a good alternative to the chi-squared test, but only when both of the variables are binary, or have two categories (McCrum-Gardner, 2008). McNemar's test is available in R with the `mcnemar.test()` function.

If there are three or more groups for one variable and a binary second variable, *Cochran's Q-test* is an option (McCrum-Gardner, 2008) and is available in R in the **nonpar** package by D. Lukke Sweet (https://cran.r-project.org/web/packages/nonpar/index.html). If the data were collected in a sloppy way and this resulted in a few people being surveyed twice, for example, it is probably best to clean the data as much as possible and stick to using descriptive statistics and graphs because the data are not independent and there is not a good way to make them independent.

Leslie was overwhelmed by all of these different tests! How would she ever remember which test to use? Kiara reassured her that *most* of what she would need to do as a data scientist would be among the descriptive statistics and inferential tests they had already covered and planned to talk about in the upcoming weeks. She also explained that almost all of the inferential tests she was going to use can follow the same NHST process she used with the chi-squared test. The things that usually differ from test to test are the test statistic and the underlying distribution used to get the p-value. Leslie felt a little better but was still nervous. Nancy let her know that the next set of tests they would learn involved beer. That sounded fun, so Leslie relaxed a little.

Before they headed their separate ways for the evening, Leslie wanted to summarize what they had learned. Using chi-squared to examine relationships between two categorical variables, they had learned that opinions about voter registration differed significantly by race-ethnicity and by home ownership. Specifically, White non-Hispanic survey participants were in favor of having people registering to vote, while black non-Hispanic participants were in favor of the voting process being made easier.

In addition, fewer renters than expected thought people should have to register to vote. Leslie thought this was a good start and was interested in the other voting question about whether people should be required to vote or should choose to vote. Kiara said that worked well because she and Nancy had some exercises Leslie could do to work on her new chi-squared skills before their next meeting.

As they all started to pack up, Nancy suddenly remembered it was her uncle's birthday tomorrow! "Should I tell him about the voting statistics?" she asked, jokingly.

"Nah," said Kiara, "save it for a big awkward family dinner!"

"Sounds about right," Leslie added.

"Great idea!" Nancy said, laughing.

Kiara noticed Leslie and Nancy were both packed and ready to leave. "Don't let me forget to turn off the main lights as we leave," she said as she closed her laptop and put it in her bag.

"We won't," Nancy and Leslie said in unison as they all walked out of the conference room and toward the stairs.

/// 5.12 CHAPTER SUMMARY

5.12.1 Achievements unlocked in this chapter: Recap

Congratulations! Like Leslie, you've learned and practiced the following in this chapter.

5.12.1.1 Achievement 1 recap: Understanding the relationship between two categorical variables using bar charts, frequencies, and percentages

Prior to conducting inferential statistical tests like chi-squared, it is useful to get some idea of the characteristics and relationships in your data. Descriptive statistics and graphs, or exploratory data analysis (EDA), can serve two purposes: It can help you better understand the people, things, or phenomena you are studying; and it can help you make an educated prediction about the likely results of a statistical test, which can aid in identifying issues if (or when) the test is not properly conducted.

5.12.1.2 Achievement 2 recap: Computing and comparing observed and expected values for the groups

When there is a relationship between two categorical variables, the frequencies observed are typically different from what would be expected to happen if there were no relationship. The differences between observed and expected are used to calculate chi-squared and determine whether a relationship exists. Chi-squared has a number of assumptions that should be met in order for the test to be used appropriately.

5.12.1.3 Achievement 3 recap: Calculating the chi-squared statistic for the test of independence

Chi-squared is the sum of the squared differences between observed frequencies and expected frequencies when two categorical variables are examined together. There are several options for computing the chi-squared statistic in R, including `chisq.test()` and `CrossTable()`.

5.12.1.4 Achievement 4 recap: Interpreting the chi-squared statistic and making a conclusion about whether or not there is a relationship

The chi-squared statistic is interpreted based on where it falls in the probability distribution determined by the degrees of freedom for the test. A very large chi-squared is likely to be statistically significant, showing a large difference between observed and expected frequencies in the sample, which suggests a relationship between the two variables in the population.

5.12.1.5 Achievement 5 recap: Using Null Hypothesis Significance Testing to organize statistical testing

The process of null hypothesis significance testing (NHST) can help to organize the process of statistical tests and clarify what a test and its results mean.

5.12.1.6 Achievement 6 recap: Using standardized residuals to understand which groups contributed to significant relationships

Standardized residuals show the standardized difference between observed and expected values in each cell, allowing identification of the frequencies contributing the most to the chi-squared statistic. Standardized residuals above 1.96 or below −1.96 show frequencies contributing a significant amount to the chi-squared value.

5.12.1.7 Achievement 7 recap: Computing and interpreting effect sizes to understand the strength of a significant chi-squared relationship

Chi-squared is an omnibus test, which means that it shows whether or not there is a relationship between variables but gives no indication of how strong the relationship is. Cramér's V, ϕ, or an odds ratio can provide this information for significant chi-squared statistical tests.

5.12.1.8 Achievement 8 recap: Understanding the options for failed chi-squared assumptions

When chi-squared assumptions fail, there are other options, including recoding data to combine groups, choosing a different statistical test, or using descriptive statistics and graphs without a chi-squared analysis. Which options are most useful depends on which assumption(s) failed and how they failed.

5.12.2 Chapter exercises

The coder and hacker exercises are an opportunity to apply the skills from this chapter to a new scenario or a new data set. The coder edition evaluates the application of the concepts and functions learned in this R-Team meeting to scenarios similar to those in the meeting. The hacker edition evaluates the use of the concepts and functions from this R-Team meeting in new scenarios, often going a step beyond what was explicitly explained.

The coder edition might be best for those who found some or all of the Check Your Understanding activities to be challenging or if they needed review before picking the correct responses to the multiple-choice questions. The hacker edition might be best if the Check Your Understanding activities were not too challenging and the multiple-choice questions were a breeze.

The multiple-choice questions and materials for the exercises are online at **edge.sagepub.com/harris1e**.

Q1: The chi-squared test can be used to understand the relationship between

- a. any two variables.
- b. two categorical variables.
- c. two continuous variables.
- d. one categorical and one continuous variable.

Q2: The chi-squared statistic is computed by first squaring the differences between

- a. observed frequencies and expected frequencies.
- b. observed frequencies and the total sample size.
- c. observed frequencies and observed percentages.
- d. expected values and observed percentages.

Q3: The chi-squared distribution often has what type of skew?

- a. Left
- b. Right
- c. It depends
- d. It is not skewed

Q4: To learn which cells are contributing the most to the size of a chi-squared statistic, compute

- a. the standardized residuals.
- b. the p-value.
- c. the odds ratio.
- d. Cramér's V.

Q5: Which of the following is *not* an effect size for chi-squared?

- a. Cramér's V
- b. Odds ratio
- c. Phi
- d. p-value

5.12.2.1 Chapter exercises: Coder edition

Use the data from this chapter to better understand who holds the two different opinions about ease of voting. Examine the relationships between the ease of voting variable and sex, political party membership, and employment status.

1) Open the data using the strategy shown in this chapter, and follow the data-cleaning steps in Section 5.4.1.

2) Clean the remaining variables in the data set so they have clear variable names, category labels, and missing value coding. For the employ variable, the category labels are 1 = Employed full-time, 2 = Employed part-time, 3 through 8 = Not employed, 9 = Refused.

3) Compute the appropriate descriptive statistics to examine the relationships between the ease of voting variable and sex, marital status, employment status, and political party (Achievement 1).

4) Use the NHST process and test whether or not there is a relationship between opinion on ease of voting and sex, marital status, employment status, and political party (Achievements 2–5).

5) For any significant chi-squared results, use standardized residuals to identify which groups have lower or higher frequencies than expected and discuss the differences between observed and expected for these groups (Achievement 6).

6) For any significant chi-squared results, compute, report, and interpret Cramér's V (Achievement 7).

7) Check the assumptions and report whether they were met; for any unmet assumptions, explain a possible alternate strategy for analysis (Achievements 2 and 8).

8) Add a prolog and comments to your code.

5.12.2.2 Chapter exercises: Hacker edition

Complete #1–#7 from the coder edition, and then do the following:

8) Create a grouped bar graph for each of the analyses and describe how the graph and your results are consistent or not (Achievement 1).

9) Add a prolog and comments to your code.

5.12.2.3 Instructor's note

Solutions to exercises can be found on the website for this book, along with ideas for gamification for those who want to take it further.

Visit **edge.sagepub.com/harris1e** to download the datasets, complete the chapter exercises, and watch R tutorial videos.

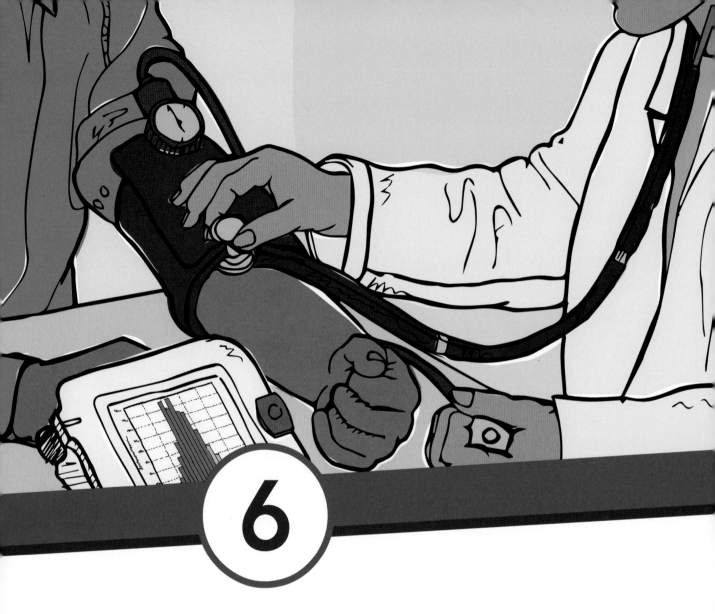

6

CONDUCTING AND INTERPRETING *t*-TESTS

The R-Team and the Blood Pressure Predicament

The R-Team held their next meeting at a pub. Leslie spotted Nancy and Kiara waving at her and walked over to their table and took a seat.

After giving the waiter her order, she said, "OK, guys, I'm ready to move on to my next inferential statistical test."

"All right," said Kiara. "Today we've decided to work on t-tests, which are used to compare two means to see if they are different from each other. The test is often used to compare the mean of some continuous variable across two groups. For example, it might be used to compare the mean income of college graduates and people who have not graduated from college."

Nancy added, "A t-test can also be used like the goodness-of-fit chi-squared to compare the mean from one group to a population mean. For example, the t-test could be used to see if the mean age in a sample is the same as the mean age in the population that was sampled."

Leslie knew that the t-statistic had come up before when they were looking at the confidence intervals. She said, "I remember when you said that the t-statistic was used in place of z when sample sizes were small."

"You've really been paying attention," said Kiara, smiling. "The t-statistic is also used as the test statistic for a t-test to compare the means of two groups to see whether they are different." Kiara continued to explain that there are several versions of the t-test to use, depending on the situation. She suggested they should discuss the *one-sample* **t-test**, the *independent-samples* **t-test**, and the *dependent-samples* **t-test** (also known as the *paired-samples* **t-test** or paired t-test). All three of these tests compare two means, but each test is used in a different situation, similar to how the goodness-of-fit chi-squared and the chi-squared test of independence were used in the two different situations.

Nancy said, "As with the chi-squared test, we will use the NHST process to organize the statistical testing. Also as with chi-squared, we will check the assumptions of each t-test and discuss alternate analysis methods when the assumptions are not met."

Right then, the waiter delivered their drinks.

Leslie and Kiara had both ordered pale ales, but Nancy's beverage was very dark and had a creamy foam on top.

"What are you drinking?" Leslie asked Nancy.

"Guinness, of course!" Nancy exclaimed. "Because it ties in with the theme of today's meeting."

Leslie looked intrigued.

"Stay tuned," said Nancy, winking.

"OK," Leslie said. "We should get this meeting started."

"Cheers to that!" said Kiara and Nancy, and they all clinked glasses.

Kiara put together a list of achievements for the day.

$SAGE edge

Visit **edge.sagepub.com/harris1e** to watch an R tutorial

6.1 Achievements to unlock

- Achievement 1: Understanding the relationship between one categorical variable and one continuous variable using histograms, means, and standard deviations
- Achievement 2: Comparing a sample mean to a population mean with a one-sample *t*-test
- Achievement 3: Comparing two unrelated sample means with an independent-samples *t*-test
- Achievement 4: Comparing two related sample means with a dependent-samples *t*-test
- Achievement 5: Computing and interpreting an effect size for significant *t*-tests
- Achievement 6: Examining and checking the underlying assumptions for using the *t*-test
- Achievement 7: Identifying and using alternate tests when *t*-test assumptions are not met

6.2 The blood pressure predicament

As they sipped their drinks, Leslie described a recent conversation with her parents. Her dad had had a physical exam and learned he had high blood pressure. Now her parents were concerned about the health implications of high blood pressure. Leslie, Nancy, and Kiara all admitted they didn't know much about blood pressure. Leslie said the conversation with her parents made her realize that she did not have a good understanding of the relationship of blood pressure (or other vital signs, if she was being honest) to the health behaviors she and some of her friends participated in, such as alcohol and marijuana use, smoking, or physical activity.

The R-Team decided this could be a good thing to know, and they started by reading about the two blood pressure measures, systolic and diastolic. They found that systolic blood pressure is measured in millimeters of mercury, or mmHG, and ranges from 74 to 238; diastolic blood pressure is also measured in mmHG and ranges from 0 to 120. Kiara did some searching and found that the National Health and Nutrition Examination Survey (NHANES) conducted regularly by the Centers for Disease Control and Prevention (CDC) collects blood pressure measurements from participants. Before they read more, they visited the CDC website and explored the NHANES data and codebook for 2015–2016 (CDC, 2017).

6.3 Data, codebook, and R packages for learning about *t*-tests

Before they examined the data, Kiara made a list of all the data, documentation, and packages needed for learning about *t*-tests.

- Two options for accessing the data
  - Download the data set **nhanes_2015–2016_ch6.csv** from **edge.sagepub.com/harris1e**
  - Follow the instructions in Box 6.1 to import the data directly from the Internet into R
- Two options for accessing the codebook
  - Download the codebook files **nhanes_demographics_20152016_codebook.html** and **nhanes_examination_20152016_codebook.html** from **edge.sagepub.com/harris1e**
  - Use the online version of the codebook on the NHANES website (https://www.cdc.gov/nchs/nhanes/index.htm)

- Install the following R packages if not already installed
  - **RNHANES**, by Herb Susmann (https://cran.r-project.org/web/packages/RNHANES/vignettes/introduction.html)
  - `lsr`, by Daniel Navarro (https://cran.r-project.org/web/packages/lsr/index.html)
  - **tidyverse**, by Hadley Wickham (https://www.rdocumentation.org/packages/tidyverse/)
  - *car*, by John Fox (https://www.rdocumentation.org/packages/car/)
  - *BSDA*, by Alan T. Arnholt (https://www.rdocumentation.org/packages/BSDA/)
  - *rcompanion*, by Salvatore Mangiafico (https://www.rdocumentation.org/packages/rcompanion/)

6.1 Kiara's reproducibility resource: Importing NHANES data directly into R with RNHANES

The **RNHANES** package was developed in order to access the NHANES data directly, and it can be imported into R for analyses with a single line of code (https://cran.r-project.org/web/packages/RNHANES/vignettes/introduction.html). The package uses the function `nhanes_load_data()` to load the NHANES data sets, and it takes three arguments for basic importing: `file_name =`, `year =`, and `demographics =`.

The file name is found in the list of data files on the NHANES website. For example, the file name for the file with blood pressure data in it is **BPX**. The year argument takes the range when the data were collected. In this case, the data were collected from 2015–2016, so this is the value to enter for year. Finally, the demographics argument is logical and takes TRUE in order to include demographic variables in the download or FALSE to exclude them. Demographic variables include age, education, sex, and many other characteristics of the participants that are often useful.

Unfortunately, the **RNHANES** package only accesses NHANES data prior to 2015, so a blood pressure file from 2014 or earlier could be downloaded by installing **RNHANES** and then using this code:

```
# import nhanes 2013-2014 BPX file with demographics
nhanes.2013 <- RNHANES::nhanes_load_data(file_name = "BPX",
                                         year = "2013-2014",
                                         demographics = TRUE)
```

For the 2015–2016 data, the **RNHANES** package developer has a new version of the package on GitHub to access the data. This package can be used the same as the CRAN version of

(Continued)

(Continued)

RNHANES, with the one difference being that it should be installed directly from GitHub using the *devtools* package and `install_github()` function. First, install the **devtools** package, then use this code for accessing the NHANES 2015–2016 data via this developer version of **RNHANES**:

```
# installing new RNHANES package from GitHub
devtools::install_github("silentspringinstitute/RNHANES")

# import nhanes 2015-2016 BPX file with demographics
nhanes.2016 <- RNHANES::nhanes_load_data(file_name = "BPX",
                                         year = "2015-2016",
                                         demographics = TRUE)
```

Importing the NHANES data directly from the Internet into a code file increases reproducibility since the data will be the same regardless of who uses the code, as long as the online version of the data remains the same. Once a data file is downloaded and accessed from a local location, any changes to the data file locally can result in inconsistent results.

6.4 Achievement 1: Understanding the relationship between one categorical variable and one continuous variable using histograms, means, and standard deviations

To get started, Kiara downloaded and saved the 2015–2016 NHANES data set in a csv file so they had a local copy that was easy to open. She wanted to make sure that Leslie knew about the **RNHANES** package she used for the download that allows access to most NHANES data in R directly from the CDC website with a single function (Box 6.1).

```
# import nhanes 2015-2016
nhanes.2016 <- read.csv(file = "[data folder location]/data/nhanes_2015-2016_
ch6.csv")
```

Nancy noticed a lull in activity and jumped in to write the code to learn about the distribution of the systolic blood pressure variable. Because systolic and diastolic blood pressure are measured along a continuum, she reviewed the graphs from Section 3.5 for graphing a single continuous variable and chose a histogram to easily see the shape of the distribution. She looked up the name of the blood pressure variables in the NHANES examination codebook and found that systolic blood pressure was variable BPXSY1. She used the colors and theme they had been using and added labels to the axes for a well-formatted graph (Figure 6.1).

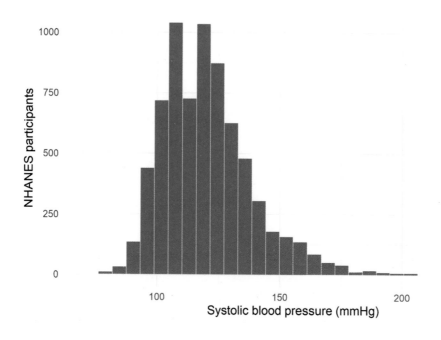

```
# open tidyverse for graphing with ggplot2
library(package = "tidyverse")

# graph systolic blood pressure variable BPXSY1 (Figure 6.1)
sbp.histo <- nhanes.2016 %>%
  ggplot(aes(x = BPXSY1)) +
  geom_histogram(fill = "#7463AC", color = "white") +
  theme_minimal() +
  labs(x = "Systolic blood pressure (mmHg)",
       y = "NHANES participants")
sbp.histo
```

Leslie suggested that it was close to normally distributed with a little right skew. The graph showed that most people have systolic blood pressure between 100 and 150. She found that the CDC defined normal systolic blood pressure as below 120 mmHg, at-risk between 120–139, and high systolic blood pressure as 140 mmHg and above (https://www.cdc.gov/bloodpressure/measure.htm). She thought that viewing these ranges in the histogram might be useful, so she searched for how to fill ranges with different colors. She found that she could add a logical statement to fill = that allowed her to fill the histogram based on the statement. In this case, she added BPXSY1 > 120 so that she could fill the histogram with one color when R evaluated the statement and found that it was FALSE and another color when R evaluated the statement and found that it was TRUE. She then added the two colors for BPXSY1 > 120 is TRUE and BPXSY1 > 120 is FALSE to the scale_fill_manual() layer along with labels corresponding to the two groups. This resulted in a histogram with purple

FIGURE 6.2 Distribution of systolic blood pressure in mmHg for 2015–2016 NHANES participants

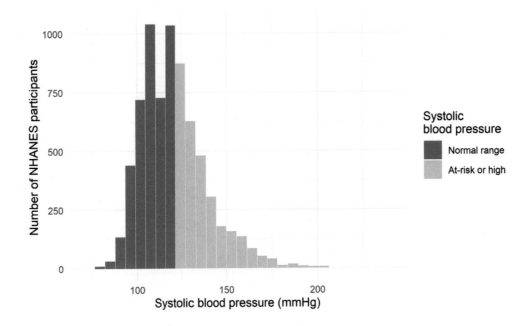

representing normal systolic blood pressure and gray representing at-risk or high systolic blood pressure (Figure 6.2).

```
# graph systolic bp BPXSY1 (Figure 6.2)
sbp.histo <- nhanes.2016 %>%
  ggplot(aes(x = BPXSY1, fill = BPXSY1 > 120)) +
  geom_histogram(color = "white") +
  theme_minimal() +
  scale_fill_manual(values = c("#7463AC","gray"),
                    labels = c("Normal range", "At-risk or high"),
                    name = "Systolic\nblood pressure") +
  labs(x = "Systolic blood pressure (mmHg)",
       y = "Number of NHANES participants")
sbp.histo
```

For diastolic blood pressure, Leslie found that the CDC defined normal as < 80 mmHG, at-risk as 80–89 mmHG, and high as 90+ mmHg. She used the same code and changed the variable name to BPXDI1 and the threshold to 80mmHG (Figure 6.3).

```
# graph diastolic bp BPXDI1 (Figure 6.3)
nhanes.2016 %>%
```

```
ggplot(aes(x = BPXDI1, fill = BPXDI1 > 80)) +

geom_histogram(color = "white") +

theme_minimal() +

scale_fill_manual(values = c("#7463AC", "gray"),

                  labels = c("Normal range", "At-risk or high"),

                  name = "Blood pressure") +

labs(x = "Diastolic blood pressure (mmHg)",

     y = "Number of NHANES participants")
```

The diastolic histogram had a tiny bar all the way at 0, which seemed like a terrible blood pressure, and Leslie thought she would check those observations later. They were probably a data entry problem or some missing value coding they had missed in the codebook.

It appeared that more people were within the normal range for diastolic blood pressure than were in the normal range for systolic blood pressure. Looking at these two distributions, Leslie thought that the mean systolic blood pressure in the sample was likely higher than the 120 threshold for healthy. Kiara agreed and said that one of the *t*-tests they were going to talk about today could help to test this hypothesis.

Based on observing the histograms, Leslie had predicted that the mean systolic blood pressure in the sample was higher than 120. In addition to the histogram, she could check this with the mean and standard deviation.

FIGURE 6.3 Distribution of diastolic blood pressure in mmHg for 2015–2016 NHANES participants

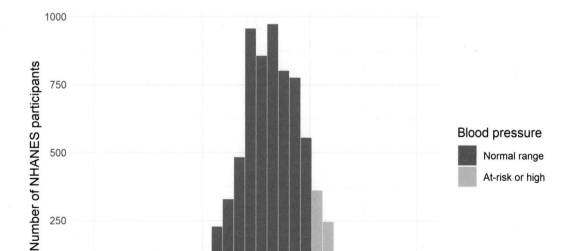

```
# mean and sd of systolic blood pressure
nhanes.2016 %>%
  drop_na(BPXSY1) %>%
  summarize(m.sbp = mean(x = BPXSY1),
            sd.sbp = sd(x = BPXSY1))
##       m.sbp    sd.sbp
## 1 120.5394 18.61692
```

Leslie was surprised when she found that the observed mean was 120.54, which was just slightly higher than the threshold of 120. While it did not seem like a big difference, she looked at Figure 6.2 again and wondered if the 120.54 was different enough from 120 for the difference to be statistically significant.

6.4.1 ACHIEVEMENT 1: CHECK YOUR UNDERSTANDING

In addition to a histogram, which graphs could be used to determine if the distributions of the blood pressure variables are normal (check all that apply)?

- Density plot
- Scatterplot
- Boxplot
- Line graph

Try using one of the graphs appropriate for examining the distribution to graph the diastolic blood pressure variable. What new information, if any, did the graph provide?

6.5 Achievement 2: Comparing a sample mean to a population mean with a one-sample *t*-test

Kiara explained that comparing the mean in the NHANES data to a hypothesized value like 120 can be done with a one-sample *t*-test. The one-sample *t*-test compares a *sample* mean to a *hypothesized* or *population* mean. It is one of three types of *t*-tests. Kiara wrote a short overview of the three *t*-tests:

- *One-sample* t-*test*: compares a mean to a population or hypothesized value
- *Independent-samples* t-*test*: compares the means of two unrelated groups
- *Dependent-samples* t-*test*: compares the means of two related groups

Leslie was ready to go. She looked at her notes from their chi-squared meeting (Section 5.8) to remind herself of the NHST process.

1. Write the null and alternate hypotheses.
2. Compute the test statistic.
3. Calculate the probability that your test statistic is at least as big as it is if there is no relationship (i.e., the null hypothesis is true).

4. If the probability that the null hypothesis is true is very small, usually less than 5%, reject the null hypothesis.

5. If the probability that the null hypothesis is true is not small, usually 5% or greater, retain the null hypothesis.

6.5.1 NHST STEP 1: WRITE THE NULL AND ALTERNATE HYPOTHESES

The first step was to write the null hypothesis for statistical testing. Kiara reminded Leslie that the null hypothesis was usually a statement that claimed there was no difference or no relationship between things. In this case, the null hypothesis should state that the mean systolic blood pressure of adults in the United States is no different from the hypothesized value of 120. Leslie wrote the following:

H0: There is no difference between mean systolic blood pressure in the United States and the cutoff for normal blood pressure, 120 mmHG.

HA: There is a difference between mean systolic blood pressure in the United States and the cutoff for normal blood pressure, 120 mmHG.

6.5.2 NHST STEP 2: COMPUTE THE TEST STATISTIC

The one-sample t-test uses the t-statistic (sort of like a z-statistic) as the test statistic as shown in Equation (6.1).

$$t = \frac{m_x - \mu_x}{\frac{s_x}{\sqrt{n_x}}}$$

(6.1)

In the formula for t, the m_x represents the mean of the variable x, the variable to be tested, μ_x is the population mean or hypothesized value of the variable, s_x is the sample standard deviation of x, and n_x is the sample size. Leslie remembered the z-statistic calculation and noticed how similar this was. The difference was that the denominator was the *standard error* rather than the *standard deviation*. Kiara reminded her that the standard error approximates the standard deviation of the sampling distribution (Section 4.8.6). This difference means that z shows how many sample standard deviations some value is away from the mean, while t shows how many standard errors (i.e., population standard deviations) some value is away from the mean.

Nancy noticed that they did not currently have the value of n and she jumped on the laptop to add it. Leslie was confused. Why would they not just use the n of 9,544 shown in the Environment pane? Nancy told her to wait a second for the code, suggesting it might help her figure it out.

```
# mean and sd of systolic blood pressure
nhanes.2016 %>%
  drop_na(BPXSY1) %>%
  summarize(m.sbp = mean(x = BPXSY1),
            sd.sbp = sd(x = BPXSY1),
            n.spb = n())
##      m.sbp    sd.sbp n.spb
## 1 120.5394  18.61692  7145
```

Leslie noticed that the value of n.sbp in the output was much lower than the 9,544 observations shown in the Environment pane. Nancy explained that drop_na(BPXSY1) had removed all the people from the sample who were missing data on the BPXSY1 variable, which was over 2,000 people. Leslie added the values into Equation (6.1) and calculated t using Equation (6.2).

$$t = \frac{120.5394 - 120}{\frac{18.61692}{\sqrt{7145}}} = 2.45 \tag{6.2}$$

With a t of 2.45, the sample mean of 120.54 was 2.45 standard errors above the hypothesized value of 120.

After Leslie computed the t-statistic by hand, Kiara mentioned that there were ways to do these calculations in R. In base R, the t.test() function is useful for getting the t for a one-sample t-test. The function arguments include the name of the variable and the hypothesized or population value (μ) to compare it to. The name of the variable was BPXSY1 and the hypothesized value was 120, so the function was as follows:

```
# comparing mean of BPXSY1 to 120
t.test(x = nhanes.2016$BPXSY1, mu = 120)
##
##   One Sample t-test
##
## data:  nhanes.2016$BPXSY1
## t = 2.4491, df = 7144, p-value = 0.01435
## alternative hypothesis: true mean is not equal to 120
## 95 percent confidence interval:
##   120.1077 120.9711
## sample estimates:
## mean of x
##   120.5394
```

The output contained a lot of information. The first row confirmed the variable examined by the t.test() function was nhanes.2016$BPXSY1. The second row starts with $t = 2.4491$, which was the same as the hand-calculated value. The next part of the output was $df = 7,144$. Kiara explained that, in this context, the degrees of freedom (df) are not computed using rows and columns like the chi-squared degrees of freedom. For the one-sample t-test, the df value is computed by subtracting 1 from the sample size. A $df = 7,144$ would therefore indicate the sample size is 7,145. This was consistent with the n of 7,145 from summarize() when they examined the variable earlier. The next number in the t.test() output is the p-value of 0.01435, which took Leslie to Step 3 of the NHST.

6.5.3 NHST STEP 3: CALCULATE THE PROBABILITY THAT YOUR TEST STATISTIC IS AT LEAST AS BIG AS IT IS IF THERE IS NO RELATIONSHIP (I.E., THE NULL IS TRUE)

The t-statistic was 2.4491. Like the chi-squared statistic, the t-statistic has a distribution made up of all the possible values of t and how probable each value is to occur. In the case of t, the distribution looks similar to a normal distribution. Nancy looked up from texting and saw an opportunity to code. She plotted a t-distribution with 7,144 degrees of freedom (Figure 6.4).

FIGURE 6.4 *t*-distribution with *df* = 7,144

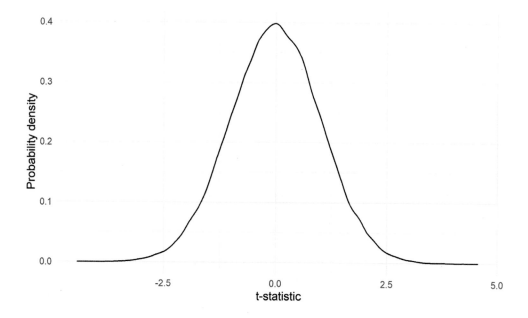

Kiara suggested shading under the curve for the *t*-statistic value of 2.4491 and higher like they had been doing with other statistical tests. Nancy added the shading to represent the probability of getting a *t*-statistic that is 2.4491 or greater if the null hypothesis were true (Figure 6.5).

The shaded section of Figure 6.5 is very small, indicating that a *t*-statistic of 2.4491 or greater has a low probability when the null hypothesis is true. The output from the *t*-test showed that this probability

FIGURE 6.5 *t*-distribution (*df* = 7,144) shaded for values of 2.4491 or higher

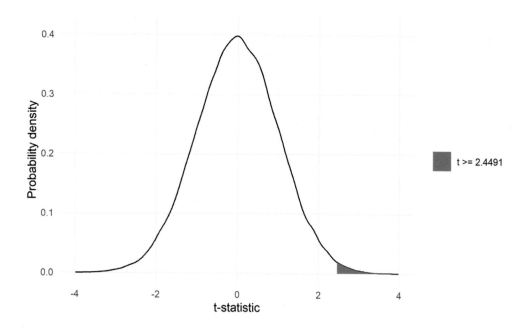

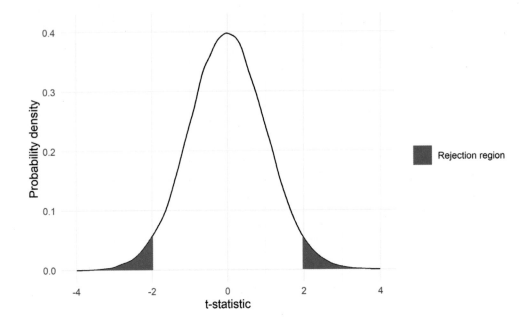

was 0.014, the *p*-value. The interpretation of this value is that there is a 1.4% probability that a *t*-statistic would be 2.4491 or greater if the null hypothesis were true. That is, there is a 1.4% probability of getting a *t*-statistic of 2.4491 or greater for a mean of 120.54 in this sample if it came from a population with a mean systolic blood pressure of 120.

Usually a *t*-statistic, or any test statistic, with a probability of occurring less than 5% of the time is considered to be statistically significant. For a *t*-distribution with 7,144 degrees of freedom, the cutoff for values of the *t*-statistic that would occur less than 5% of the time are shown by the shaded areas in Figure 6.6. The shaded areas together make up the *critical region* or *rejection region* for the null hypothesis since the values of *t* in these shaded areas happen so infrequently when the null hypothesis is true that it should be rejected. The *t*-statistics falling into this critical region therefore suggest a statisti-cally significant result (Figure 6.6).

Any value of the *t*-statistic that is in the shaded tails of the distribution happens with a probability of less than α, which is often 5%, when the null hypothesis is true.

6.5.4 NHST STEPS 4 AND 5: INTERPRET THE PROBABILITY AND WRITE A CONCLUSION

In this case, the *t*-statistic is in the shaded region, which is the rejection region. This is sufficient evi-dence to reject the null hypothesis in favor of the alternate hypothesis. Even though the difference between the mean systolic blood pressure of 120.54 and the hypothesized value of 120 is small, it is sta-tistically significant. The probability of this sample coming from a population where the mean systolic blood pressure is actually 120 is just 1.4%. This sample is likely to be from a population with a higher mean blood pressure.

Leslie summarized the results of this *t*-test:

The mean systolic blood pressure in a sample of 7,145 people was 120.54 (sd = 18.62). A one-sample t-test found this mean to be statistically significantly different from the hypothesized mean of 120 [$t(7144)$ = 2.449; p = 0.014]. The sample likely came from a population with a mean systolic blood pressure not equal to 120.

6.5.5 ACHIEVEMENT 2: CHECK YOUR UNDERSTANDING

Interpret the results of the same one-sample t-test conducted after limiting the NHANES sample to people 65 years old or older.

```
# create a subset of the data frame of people 65+ years old
nhanes.2016.65plus <- nhanes.2016 %>%
  filter(RIDAGEYR >= 65)

# comparing mean of BPXSY1 to 120
t.test(x = nhanes.2016.65plus$BPXSY1, mu = 120)

##
## One Sample t-test
##
## data: nhanes.2016.65plus$BPXSY1
## t = 29.238, df = 1232, p-value < 2.2e-16
## alternative hypothesis: true mean is not equal to 120
## 95 percent confidence interval:
##   135.4832 137.7106
## sample estimates:
## mean of x
##   136.5969
```

6.6 Achievement 3: Comparing two unrelated sample means with an independent-samples t-test

Leslie thought this was cool for checking to see how well a sample represents a population for a single variable like the goodness-of-fit chi-squared test (Box 5.1) and asked if the t-test could be used for anything else. Kiara reminded her that there are two additional types of t-test. Instead of comparing one mean to a hypothesized or population mean, the independent-samples t-test compares the means of two groups to each other. For example, the NHANES data set includes sex measured in two categories: males and females. Kiara suggested that they might be interested in whether the mean systolic blood pressure was the same for males and females in the population. That is, do males and females in the sample come from a population where males and females have the same mean systolic blood pressure?

Kiara explained that the independent-samples t-test could be used to find out the answer. Before conducting NHST, Leslie started with some descriptive and visual EDA. She noted that they have the blood pressure variable measured on a continuum and treated as continuous, and the sex variable that is

FIGURE 6.7 NHANES 2015–2016 demographics codebook: Gender variable

RIAGENDR - Gender

Variable Name:	RIAGENDR
SAS Label:	Gender
English Text:	Gender of the participant.
Target:	Both males and females 0 YEARS - 150 YEARS

Code or Value	Value Description	Count	Cumulative	Skip to Item
1	Male	4892	4892	
2	Female	5079	9971	
.	Missing	0	9971	

categorical with only two categories measured by the NHANES. Since they were comparing blood pressure across groups, she decided to start with some group means.

```
# compare means of BPXSY1 across groups
# sex variable is RIAGENDR
nhanes.2016 %>%
  drop_na(BPXSY1) %>%
  group_by(RIAGENDR) %>%
  summarize(m.sbp = mean(x = BPXSY1))
## # A tibble: 2 x 2
##    RIAGENDR m.sbp
##       <int> <dbl>
## 1         1  122.
## 2         2  119.
```

It certainly looked like there might be a difference, but it was unclear who has higher or lower blood pressure since the categories of sex are not labeled clearly. Nancy slid the laptop over and did some cleaning for both the variables. She looked in the codebook to find out how the RIAGENDR variable was coded. She found the entry for RIAGENDR in the demographics codebook (Figure 6.7).

The codebook showed that 1 is Male and 2 is Female. Nancy added the labels and renamed the RIAGENDR variable to sex. While she was working on this, she also renamed the BPXSY1 variable to systolic so that it was easier to remember and type.

```
# add labels to sex and rename variables
nhanes.2016.cleaned <- nhanes.2016 %>%
  mutate(RIAGENDR = recode_factor(.x = RIAGENDR,
                          `1` = 'Male',
                          `2` = 'Female')) %>%
```

```
  rename(sex = RIAGENDR) %>%
  rename(systolic = BPXSY1)
```

Once the recoding was done, Nancy updated the means calculations with the new data frame name and variable names.

```
# compare means of systolic by sex
nhanes.2016.cleaned %>%
  drop_na(systolic) %>%
  group_by(sex) %>%
  summarize(m.sbp = mean(x = systolic))
## # A tibble: 2 x 2
##    sex       m.sbp
##    <fct>     <dbl>
## 1 Male        122.
## 2 Female      119.
```

It appeared that males had a higher mean systolic blood pressure than females in the sample. Leslie thought a graph might provide a little more perspective, so she decided on a density plot (Section 3.6.3) and created Figure 6.8.

FIGURE 6.8 Distribution of systolic blood pressure by sex in mmHg for 2015–2016 NHANES participants

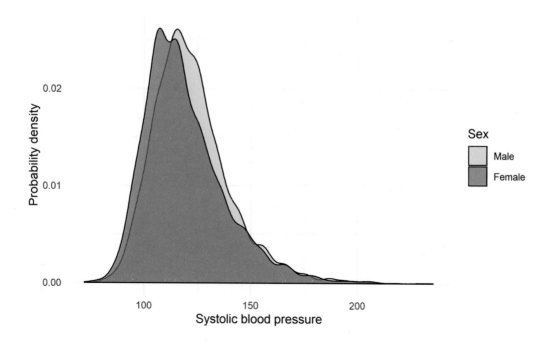

```
# density plot of systolic by sex (Figure 6.8)
dens.sex.bp <- nhanes.2016.cleaned %>%
  ggplot(aes(x = systolic,
             fill = sex)) +
  geom_density(alpha = .8) +
  theme_minimal() +
  labs(x = "Systolic blood pressure", y = "Probability density") +
  scale_fill_manual(values = c('gray', '#7463AC'),
                    name = "Sex")
dens.sex.bp
```

Figure 6.8 showed distributions that were right skewed, with the distribution for males shifted to the right of the distribution for females and showing higher values overall. Now that she knew what to look for, Leslie was ready for the independent-samples *t*-test. She used the NHST to organize her work.

6.6.1 NHST STEP 1: WRITE THE NULL AND ALTERNATE HYPOTHESES

H0: There is no difference in mean systolic blood pressure between males and females in the U.S. population.

HA: There is a difference in mean systolic blood pressure between males and females in the U.S. population.

6.6.2 NHST STEP 2: COMPUTE THE TEST STATISTIC

The test statistic for the independent-samples *t*-test is a little more complicated to calculate since it now includes the means from both the groups in the numerator and the standard errors from the groups in the denominator. In the independent-samples *t*-test formula shown in Equation (6.3), m_1 is the mean of one group and m_2 is the mean of the other group; the difference between the means makes up the numerator. The larger the difference between the group means, the larger the numerator will be and the larger the *t*-statistic will be!

The denominator of Equation (6.3) contains the variances for the first group, s_1^2, and the second group, s_2^2, along with the sample sizes for each group, n_1 and n_2.

$$t = \frac{m_1 - m_2}{\sqrt{\dfrac{s_1^2}{n_1} + \dfrac{s_2^2}{n_2}}} \tag{6.3}$$

Nancy added the variance and sample size *n* for each group to the `summarize` statistics so they could get an idea of what the differences look like.

```
# compare means of systolic by sex
nhanes.2016.cleaned %>%
  drop_na(systolic) %>%
  group_by(sex) %>%
```

```
  summarize(m.sbp = mean(x = systolic),
            var.sbp = var(x = systolic),
            samp.size = n()) %>%
  mutate_if(is.numeric, format, 4)
# A tibble: 2 x 4
## sex           m.sbp         var.sbp        samp.size
## <fctr>        <dbl>         <dbl>          <int>
## Male          122.1767      329.2968       3498
## Female        118.9690      358.2324       3647
```

In Equation (6.4), Leslie substituted the values from `summarize()` into the *t*-statistic formula from Equation (6.3).

$$t = \frac{122.1767 - 118.9690}{\sqrt{\dfrac{329.2968}{3498} + \dfrac{358.2324}{3647}}} = 7.31 \qquad (6.4)$$

After watching Leslie substitute the values into the equation and do the math, Nancy typed a line of code.

```
# compare systolic blood pressure for males and females
twosampt <- t.test(formula = nhanes.2016.cleaned$systolic ~
                   nhanes.2016.cleaned$sex)
twosampt
##
##   Welch Two Sample t-test
##
## data:  nhanes.2016.cleaned$systolic by nhanes.2016.cleaned$sex
## t = 7.3135, df = 7143, p-value = 2.886e-13
## alternative hypothesis: true difference in means is not equal to 0
## 95 percent confidence interval:
##   2.347882 4.067432
## sample estimates:
##    mean in group Male mean in group Female
##             122.1767             118.9690
```

This time, instead of the first argument being `x =`, Nancy typed `formula =`. In R, a formula typically (but not always) has a single variable on the left, followed by a ~ (tilde), followed by one or more objects that somehow predict or explain whatever was on the left-hand side. In a lot of statistical tests, the object on the left-hand side of the formula is the outcome or *dependent variable* while the object(s) on the right-hand side of the formula are the *predictors* or *independent variables*. In this case, systolic blood pressure is the *outcome* being explained by the *predictor* of sex.

Before they reviewed the output, Nancy explained to Leslie that Equation 6.3 and the output from R both use a variation of the *t*-test called the *Welch's t-test*. She explained that the formula for the

Welch's *t*-test is slightly different from the original formula for *t*, which used *pooled variance* in the denominator. Pooled variance assumes that the variances in the two groups are equal and combines them. When the variances are unequal, which happens frequently, the equal variances *t*-test can produce biased results, so the Welch's *t*-test formula is typically recommended and is the default test for `t.test()` in R (Delacre, Lakens, & Leys, 2017).

The `t.test()` output shows a *t*-statistic of 7.31, which was consistent with what Leslie calculated. The degrees of freedom are 7,143, which is the sample size of 7,145 minus 2 because there are two groups. In the case of the independent-samples *t*-test, the degrees of freedom are computed as $n - k$, where *n* is the sample size and *k* is the number of groups. Leslie noticed that there was a 95% confidence interval in the `t.test()` output. Kiara explained that this was the 95% confidence interval around the difference between the two groups. In the sample, the difference between male systolic blood pressure ($m = 122.18$) and female systolic blood pressure ($m = 118.97$) is 3.21. In the population this sample came from, the difference between the mean male and female systolic blood pressure is likely to be between 2.35 and 4.07 (the 95% confidence interval). Kiara noted that the range does not contain zero, so in the population this sample came from, the difference between male and female blood pressure is not likely to be zero. Based on the difference in the sample and the other characteristics of the sample, there is likely some difference between male and female blood pressure in the sampled population.

Leslie took a look at the help documentation for `t.test()` to see what else it had to offer. She noticed that the help documentation calls the *t*-test "*Student's t-test*" even though Nancy had told her R code defaulted to the Welch's *t*-test. (Figure 6.9).

Leslie asked, "Is it called Student's *t*-test because it is one of the first statistical tests taught to students?"

"Nope," Kiara answered. "'Student' was a pseudonym used by the statistician who first developed the *t*-test."

"Which is the original version of the *t*-test with pooled variances that I mentioned earlier. He developed it while working for Guinness!" Nancy exclaimed. "And why I'm drinking one in his honor tonight." Nancy showed Leslie one of her books from grad school. She had brought it so Leslie could read the story of William Sealy Gossett, the Guinness brewery, and the *t*-test (Box 6.2).

FIGURE 6.9 *t*-test help documentation

t.test {stats}   R Documentation

Student's t-Test

Description

Performs one and two sample t-tests on vectors of data.

Usage

```
t.test(x, ...)

## Default S3 method:
t.test(x, y = NULL,
       alternative = c("two.sided", "less", "greater"),
       mu = 0, paired = FALSE, var.equal = FALSE,
       conf.level = 0.95, ...)

## S3 method for class 'formula'
t.test(formula, data, subset, na.action, ...)
```

6.2 Leslie's stats stuff: What does the *t*-test have to do with beer?

Leslie read the material Nancy shared and learned that the *t*-test was developed by William Sealy Gosset, who was hired in 1900 by Guinness, the Irish beer brewer, along with a group of young scientists. Their charge was to apply scientific expertise to improve the brewing process (Box, 1987; Cals & Winkens, 2018; Connelly, 2011). Among the scientists, Gosset stood out for having experience with math and was recruited to analyze the data during and after 7 years of experiments to better understand the influence of weather and soil on growing barley (Box, 1987). It was during these 7 years that Gosset, with help from Karl Pearson (another influential statistician), developed the *t*-test in order to handle the small samples and the limitations of using sample values of *s* and *m* rather than population values of σ and μ. Gosset's analyses identified the barley that produced the highest yield and quality, allowing Guinness to identify and purchase the best barley for their growing area. Guinness opposed the publication of Gosset's work, specifically its ties to the Guinness brewery. However, the board agreed that he could publish his work if he used a pseudonym, and he chose Student (Box, 1987). So, the widely used *t*-test was developed in order to make beer better.

6.6.3 NHST STEP 3: CALCULATE THE PROBABILITY THAT YOUR TEST STATISTIC IS AT LEAST AS BIG AS IT IS IF THERE IS NO RELATIONSHIP (I.E., THE NULL IS TRUE)

The *p*-value in this case was shown in scientific notation, so Leslie converted it: $p = .0000000000002886$. Kiara suggested using $p < .05$ instead since the longer version of the *p*-value was difficult to read and took up a lot of space. Leslie interpreted this as indicating that the value of this *t*-statistic would happen with a probability of much less than 5% if the null hypothesis were true.

6.6.4 NHST STEPS 4 AND 5: INTERPRET THE PROBABILITY AND WRITE A CONCLUSION

In this case, the *t*-statistic was definitely in the rejection region, so there was sufficient evidence to reject the null hypothesis in favor of the alternate hypothesis. Even though the difference between the mean systolic blood pressure for males and females was small, it was statistically significant. The probability of this sample coming from a population where the means for males and females are equal is very low; it would happen about 0.00000000002886% of the time. The sample was therefore likely to be from a population where males and females had different mean systolic blood pressure.

Leslie summarized the results:

There was a statistically significant difference [$t(7143) = 7.31$; $p < .05$] in mean systolic blood pressure between males ($m = 122.18$) and females ($m = 118.97$) in the sample. The sample was taken from the U.S. population, indicating that males in the United States likely have a different mean systolic blood pressure than females in the United States. The difference between male and female mean systolic blood pressure was 3.21 in the sample; in the population this sample came from, the difference between male and female mean blood pressure was likely to be between 2.35 and 4.07 ($d = 3.21$; 95% CI: 2.35–4.07).

6.6.5 ACHIEVEMENT 3: CHECK YOUR UNDERSTANDING

Conduct the same independent-samples t-test comparing mean systolic blood pressure for males to females on the sample created in the previous section of people 65+ years old. Interpret your results.

6.7 Achievement 4: Comparing two related sample means with a dependent-samples t-test

Kiara mentioned that sometimes the means to compare would be related. This usually happens in one of two ways; either the same people are measured twice, or people in the sample are siblings or spouses or co-workers or have some other type of relationship. Leslie remembered this from learning about the assumptions of chi-squared. Kiara explained that it may seem strange to measure the same people twice, but often people are measured before and after some sort of intervention, and the measures are compared to see if they changed. Kiara wrote the test statistic in Equation (6.5) so she could refer to it while explaining.

$$t = \frac{m_d - 0}{\sqrt{\dfrac{s_d^2}{n_d}}} \tag{6.5}$$

In the dependent-samples t-test formula, Equation (6.5), the m_d is the *mean of the differences* between the related measures, the s_d^2 is the variance of the mean difference between the measures, and n_d is the sample size.

Kiara explained that the dependent-samples t-test worked a little differently from the independent-samples t-test. In this case, the formula uses the mean of the differences between the two related measures (m_d). For example, if Leslie's systolic blood pressure were measured to be 110 before she went to the dentist and 112 after she went to the dentist, the difference between the two measures would be 2. If Nancy were measured as having 115 before the dentist and 110 after, the difference between the two measures would be –5. In a study of blood pressure before and after going to the dentist, the numerator for the dependent-samples t-test would take the mean of those differences, 2 and –5, and subtract zero. The reason it would subtract zero is that zero is the mean difference if the measures of blood pressure were exactly the same before and after the dentist visit—this is the null hypothesis.

In the case of the systolic blood pressure measurement for NHANES, the measure was taken up to four times for each person to ensure that it was accurate. Kiara noted that the blood pressure numbers should be the same or very similar since they are from the same person and nothing in particular happened between the first and second measure to increase or decrease blood pressure. If they were measured accurately, there should not be much of a difference between the first and second systolic blood pressure measures.

Kiara suggested that they should look at some visuals and descriptive statistics before they conducted the t-test. Leslie nodded and took a look at the codebook to see what the variable names were for the measures of systolic blood pressure. She found that the second measure of systolic blood pressure was BPXSY2. To conduct the dependent-samples t-test, she thought renaming this variable so it would be easier to remember was a good start. Then she thought she would make the variable *d*, which is a variable of the differences between the first systolic blood pressure measure (`systolic`) and the second one (`BPXSY2`). She decided to call this new variable `diff.syst` for difference in systolic blood pressure.

```
# rename second systolic measure and create diff variable for
# difference between measure 1 and 2 for systolic BP
nhanes.2016.cleaned <- nhanes.2016 %>%
  mutate(RIAGENDR = recode_factor(.x = RIAGENDR,
                                  `1` = 'Male',
                                  `2` = 'Female')) %>%
  rename(sex = RIAGENDR) %>%
  rename(systolic = BPXSY1) %>%
  rename(systolic2 = BPXSY2) %>%
  mutate(diff.syst = systolic - systolic2)
```

Now that there was a variable, `diff.syst`, measuring the difference between the first and second systolic blood pressure measures, Leslie checked the descriptive statistics and visualized the distribution of the new *d* variable, `diff.syst`.

```
# mean of the differences
nhanes.2016.cleaned %>%
  drop_na(diff.syst) %>%
  summarize(m.diff = mean(x = diff.syst))
##       m.diff
## 1 0.5449937
```

The mean difference between the first and second systolic blood pressure measures was 0.54, which was not zero, but it was pretty small. On average, the systolic blood pressure measure showed a difference of 0.54 between the first measure and the second measure on the same person in the NHANES 2015–2016 data set. Leslie created a histogram to check out the distribution of the differences (Figure 6.10).

```
# histogram of the differences between first and second (Figure 6.10)
# blood pressure measures
nhanes.2016.cleaned %>%
  ggplot(aes(x = diff.syst)) +
  geom_histogram(fill = "#7463AC", color = "white") +
  theme_minimal() +
  labs(x = "Difference between SBP Measures 1 and 2",
       y = "Number of NHANES participants")
```

The distribution of differences looked close to normal and the center was near zero, but maybe not exactly zero. The mean difference was .54. If Measures 1 and 2 were exactly the same for each person,

FIGURE 6.10 Difference between Measures 1 and 2 for systolic blood pressure (mmHg) in 2015–2016 NHANES participants

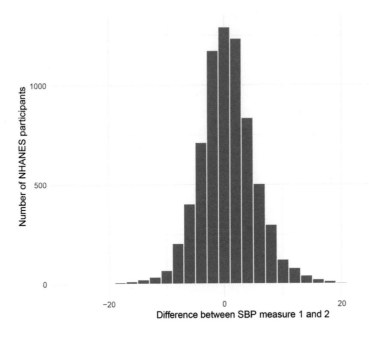

there would just be one long bar at 0 in the histogram and the mean difference would be zero. Using the NHST process, Leslie tested to see if the m_d of 0.54 was statistically significantly different from the zero she would expect to see if the first and second measures of systolic blood pressure had been exactly the same for each person.

6.7.1 NHST STEP 1: WRITE THE NULL AND ALTERNATE HYPOTHESES

H0: There is no difference between Measures 1 and 2 for systolic blood pressure.

HA: There is a difference between Measures 1 and 2 for systolic blood pressure.

6.7.2 NHST STEP 2: COMPUTE THE TEST STATISTIC

To substitute the mean, standard deviation, and sample size of `diff.syst` into Equation (6.5), the dependent-samples *t*-test statistic, Leslie needed to add variance and sample size to the descriptive statistics code.

```
# mean, var, and sample size of the difference variable
nhanes.2016.cleaned %>%
  drop_na(diff.syst) %>%
  summarize(m.sbp = mean(x = diff.syst),
            var.sbp = var(x = diff.syst),
            n = n())
##     m.sbp   var.sbp    n
## 1 0.5449937 23.99083 7101
```

Leslie noticed that the sample size was even smaller this time; it looked like 7,101 people had data for both measures available.

$$t = \frac{.5449937 - 0}{\sqrt{\dfrac{23.99083}{7101}}} = 9.38 \tag{6.6}$$

Kiara asked Leslie what she expected to find with a *t*-statistic as large as the one she computed with Equation (6.6). In light of the significant tests for the one-sample and independent-samples *t*-tests, Leslie thought this was likely to be a *statistically significant* result as well. Kiara suggested using the t.test() function again, but this time with the paired = TRUE argument since the default for the function is an independent-samples *t*-test and they were using a dependent-samples *t*-test. Leslie tried it:

```
# dependent-samples t-test for systolic measures 1 and 2
t.test(x = nhanes.2016.cleaned$systolic,
       y = nhanes.2016.cleaned$systolic2,
       paired = TRUE)
## Paired t-test
## data:  nhanes.2016.cleaned$systolic and nhanes.2016.cleaned$systolic2
## t = 9.3762, df = 7100, p-value < 2.2e-16
## alternative hypothesis: true difference in means is not equal to 0
## 95 percent confidence interval:
## 0.4310514 0.6589360
## sample estimates:
## mean of the differences
##              0.5449937
```

The test statistic produced by t.test() was consistent with the one Leslie calculated by hand. Using R is so much faster, but Leslie felt good knowing she computed the statistic correctly. She thought to herself that the *t*-test is just a clever use of means and standard deviations and sample sizes . . . there was no magic required!

6.7.3 NHST STEP 3: CALCULATE THE PROBABILITY THAT YOUR TEST STATISTIC IS AT LEAST AS BIG AS IT IS IF THERE IS NO RELATIONSHIP (I.E., THE NULL IS TRUE)

The *p*-value was shown in scientific notation as < 2.2e-16 which is well below .05. Just as Leslie suspected, the probability is very low of finding a mean difference between systolic and systolic2 of 0.54 if there were no difference between the measures in the population that the sample came from.

6.7.4 NHST STEPS 4 AND 5: INTERPRET THE PROBABILITY AND WRITE A CONCLUSION

The *t*-statistic has a low probability, so there was sufficient evidence to reject the null hypothesis in favor of the alternate hypothesis. Even though the mean difference between the first and second measures was small, it was statistically significant. The probability of the sample coming from a population where the first and second measures of blood pressure were equal was very low. This sample is likely to be from a population where systolic blood pressure is not consistent over time.

Leslie saw the confidence interval and asked Kiara if this was the range where the difference between the first and second measures is for the population. Kiara confirmed and added one more piece of information.

She said the difference statistic was calculated by subtracting the second measure of systolic blood pressure, `systolic2`, from the first measure, `systolic`, and the mean difference is positive. This indicated that the first measure of systolic blood pressure tended to be higher than the second measure in the sample.

Leslie summarized the interpretation:

> The mean difference between two measures of systolic blood pressure was statistically significantly different from zero [$t(7100) = 9.38$; $p < .05$]. The positive difference of 0.54 indicated that systolic blood pressure was significantly higher for the first measure compared to the second measure. While the mean difference in the sample was .54, the mean difference between the first and second measures in the population was likely between 0.43 and 0.66 ($m_d = 0.54$; 95% CI: 0.43–0.66).

Kiara wanted to bring up one last point. She explained to Leslie that the mean difference was quite small and did not seem to be reason to worry. While it was not zero, as it would be if the measures were completely consistent, it was .54 on average, which is not a large clinical difference (Lane et al., 2002). She continued to explain that this example and the small but significant differences for the one-sample and independent-samples *t*-tests demonstrated that results can be statistically significant but not *meaningful*.

Kiara suggested that they review Equations (6.1), (6.3), and (6.5) for the three *t*-statistics to look for reasons why the *t*-statistics were large, and therefore the results of these three *t*-tests were all significant even though the differences among the means were small.

$$t = \frac{m_x - \mu_x}{\frac{s_x}{\sqrt{n_x}}} \quad (6.1)$$

$$t = \frac{m_1 - m_2}{\sqrt{\frac{s_1^2}{n_1} + \frac{s_2^2}{n_2}}} \quad (6.3)$$

$$t = \frac{m_d - 0}{\sqrt{\frac{s_d^2}{n_d}}} \quad (6.5)$$

Leslie noted a lot of similarities. Things that would make the *t*-statistic larger across these formulas included larger differences between the means, smaller standard deviations, and larger sample size. Since the differences between the means were not all that big for any of the tests, and the standard deviations or variances were relatively large, Leslie thought the main reason for the *t*-statistics to be large enough to be statistically significant was the large sample size, *n*. Larger sample sizes in these three formulas resulted in smaller denominator values, which, in turn, resulted in larger *t*-statistics. Kiara agreed that that was probably the reason since the numerators were so small with .54, 3.21, and .54 all being statistically significant without really being all that big or important.

6.7.5 ACHIEVEMENT 4: CHECK YOUR UNDERSTANDING

Match each type of *t*-test to its description:

t-tests:
- One-sample
- Dependent-samples
- Independent-samples

Descriptions:
- Compares means of two unrelated groups
- Compares a single mean to a population or hypothesized value
- Compares two related means

6.8 Achievement 5: Computing and interpreting an effect size for significant *t*-tests

Leslie thought that the small differences between means being statistically significant suggested that reporting statistical significance might be misleading. She thought that, especially where differences between means were small, it would be useful to have something to report that was about the size of the difference or the strength of the relationship. Kiara explained that what she was looking for was the *effect size* for the *t*-test that is like the Cramér's *V*, phi, or odds ratio from the chi-squared test.

A difference in mean systolic blood pressure of .54 is statistically significant, but is it really a big enough difference to suggest that one group is different from the other in an important way? Kiara mentioned that some people have argued that effect sizes are even more important than *p*-values since *p*-values only report whether a difference or relationship from a sample is likely to be true in the population, while effect sizes provide information about the strength or size of a difference or relationship (Fritz, Morris, & Richler, 2012; Mays & Melnyk, 2009; Sullivan & Feinn, 2012). In addition, in analyses of large samples, *p*-values usually reach statistical significance, even for very small differences and very weak relationships (Sullivan & Feinn, 2012).

With the chi-squared test of independence, there were three effect sizes, Cramér's *V* (Section 5.10.1), φ (Section 5.10.5), and odds ratio (Section 5.10.6). For *t*-tests, the effect size statistic is *Cohen's d*. Cohen's *d* is computed when the test results are statistically significant and can be computed for each type of *t*-test using a slightly different formula. Before they examined the formulas, Kiara wanted to explain how the value of *d* was classified.

- Cohen's *d* = .2 to *d* < .5 is a *small* effect size

- Cohen's *d* = .5 to *d* < .8 is a *medium* effect size

- Cohen's *d* ≥ .8 is a *large* effect size

6.8.1 COHEN'S *d* FOR ONE-SAMPLE *t*-TESTS

The formula for Cohen's *d* for a one-sample *t*-test is shown in Equation (6.7) (Sullivan & Feinn, 2012).

$$d = \frac{m_x - \mu_x}{s_x} \tag{6.7}$$

Where m_x is the sample mean for *x*, μ_x is the hypothesized or population mean, and s_x is the sample standard deviation for *x*. This was a familiar equation to Leslie, so she asked how this is different from the calculation of *z*. Kiara agreed that this looked very familiar, including having the standard deviation in the denominator, but reminded Leslie that the numerator for *z* is different and referred her back to Section 4.7 as a refresher. Leslie looked back and found that the numerator for *z* included each individual observation value. She was satisfied that this was not the same as *z* and added the values from the one-sample *t*-test in Section 6.5 into the formula to calculate the effect size in Equation (6.8).

$$d = \frac{120.5 - 120}{18.62} = .027 \tag{6.8}$$

The effect size was less than .03, which was not even close to the small effect size value of .2. Nancy showed Leslie how to use R to get the value with the `cohensD()` function, which is available in the `lsr` package. She explained that for the one-sample test, there were two arguments to use: `x` = takes the variable name and `mu` = takes the hypothesized or population mean.

```
# Cohen's d effect size for one-sample t
lsr::cohensD(x = nhanes.2016.cleaned$systolic, mu = 120)
## [1] 0.02897354
```

Leslie noticed that there was a small difference between the hand calculation and the R calculation of *d*, which Kiara suggested was due to rounding error. Both the 120.5 and the 18.62 were rounded in the hand calculation, while R uses many digits in memory during all computations.

Leslie added the effect size to the interpretation of results from the one-sample *t*-test:

> The mean systolic blood pressure in a sample of 7,145 people was 120.54 (*sd* = 18.62). A one-sample *t*-test found this mean to be statistically significantly different from the hypothesized mean of 120 [$t(7144) = 2.45$; $p = 0.014$]. The sample likely came from a population with a mean systolic blood pressure not equal to 120. While the sample mean was statistically significantly different from 120, the difference was relatively small with a very small effect size (Cohen's *d* = .03).

6.8.2 COHEN'S *d* FOR INDEPENDENT-SAMPLES *t*-TESTS

The formula for Cohen's *d* for an independent-samples *t*-test is shown in Equation (6.9) (Salkind, 2010):

$$d = \frac{m_1 - m_2}{\sqrt{\dfrac{s_1^2 + s_2^2}{2}}} \tag{6.9}$$

where m_1 and m_2 are the sample means and s_1^2 and s_2^2 are the sample variances. Leslie used the formula to compute the effect size for the independent-samples *t*-test in Section 6.6.

```
# compare means of systolic by sex
nhanes.2016.cleaned %>%
  drop_na(systolic) %>%
  group_by(sex) %>%
  summarize(m.sbp = mean(systolic),
            var.sbp = var(systolic))
# A tibble: 2 x 3
```

## sex	m.sbp	var.sbp
## <fctr>	<dbl>	<dbl>
## Male	122.	329.
## Female	119.	358.

$$d = \frac{122 - 119}{\sqrt{\dfrac{329 + 358}{2}}} = .162 \tag{6.10}$$

The effect size from the calculations in Equation (6.10) was .162, which is close to the small effect size value of .2, but the effect of sex on systolic blood pressure is not quite even a small effect. Nancy showed Leslie how to use R to get the value, this time entering a formula (see Box 6.3) for x = and the data frame name for the `data` = argument. Because they were using the Welch's *t*-test that did not assume equal variances, Nancy added a `method` = "unequal" option to the code to account for possible unequal variances. Leslie double-checked and found the difference between the .162 calculated by hand and the R value of .173 was due to the rounding in the hand calculations.

```
# cohen's d effect size for indep sample t
lsr::cohensD(x = systolic ~ sex,
             data = nhanes.2016.cleaned,
             method = "unequal")
## [1] 0.1730045
```

Leslie added the effect size to the interpretation of results from the independent-samples *t*-test:

> There was a statistically significant difference [$t(7143) = 7.31; p < .05$] in the mean systolic blood pressure between males ($m = 122.18$) and females ($m = 118.97$) in the sample. The sample was taken from the U.S. population, indicating that males in the United States likely have a different mean systolic blood pressure than females in the United States. The difference between male and female mean systolic blood pressure was 3.21 in the sample; in the population this sample came from, the difference between male and female mean blood pressure was likely to be between 2.35 and 4.07 ($d = 3.21$; 95% CI: 2.35–4.07). The effect size for the relationship between sex and systolic blood pressure was small (Cohen's $d = .17$).

6.8.3 COHEN'S *d* FOR DEPENDENT-SAMPLES *t*-TESTS

The formula for Cohen's *d* for a dependent-samples *t*-test is shown in Equation (6.11):

$$d = \frac{m_d - 0}{s_d} \tag{6.11}$$

where m_d is the mean difference between the two measures—in this case, `systolic` and `systolic2`—and s_d is the standard deviation of the differences between the two measures. Leslie computed the effect size for the dependent-samples *t*-test in Section 6.7.

```
# var and sample size of the difference variable
nhanes.2016.cleaned %>%
  drop_na(diff.syst) %>%
  summarize(m.sbp = mean(x = diff.syst),
            sd.sbp = sd(x = diff.syst))
##       m.sbp    sd.sbp
## 1 0.5449937 4.898043
```

$$d = \frac{.5449937 - 0}{4.898043} = .111 \tag{6.12}$$

The effect size after the calculations in Equation (6.12) was .111, which was not quite up to the small effect size value of .2. Nancy showed Leslie how to use R to get this value, this time entering each blood pressure measure as a separate vector and adding a `method = "paired"` argument.

```
# cohen's d effect size for indep sample t
lsr::cohensD(x = nhanes.2016.cleaned$systolic,
             y = nhanes.2016.cleaned$systolic2,
             method = "paired")
## [1] 0.1112676
```

Leslie added the effect size to the interpretation of results from the one-sample *t*-test:

> The mean difference between two measures of systolic blood pressure was statistically significantly different from zero [$t(7100) = 9.38; p < .05$]. The positive difference of 0.54 indicated that systolic blood pressure was significantly higher for the first measure compared to the second measure.

While the mean difference in the sample was .54, the mean difference between the first and second measures in the population was likely between 0.43 and 0.66 (m_d = 0.54; 95% CI: 0.43–0.66). The effect size for the comparison of the two systolic blood pressure measures was very small (Cohen's d = .11).

Before they continued, Leslie wanted to mention one thing she had gotten confused about while learning Cohen's d. Between the tests being differences of means and the effect size being Cohen's d, there was a lot of use of "d" to refer to different things. Kiara agreed that this was confusing and suggested that Leslie just be very clear about what each measure is when reporting her results since this will not only help the audience, but also improve reproducibility.

6.9 Achievement 6: Examining and checking the underlying assumptions for using the *t*-test

Just like chi-squared, *t*-tests have to meet a few assumptions before they can be used. The first assumption for the *t*-test is that the data are normally distributed. For the one-sample *t*-test, the single variable being examined should be normally distributed. For the independent-samples *t*-test and the dependent-samples *t*-test, the data within each of the two groups should be normally distributed. There are several ways to assess normality. Visually, a histogram or a Q-Q plot is useful for identifying normal and non-normal data distribution. Statistically, a Shapiro-Wilk test can be used.

6.9.1 TESTING NORMALITY

For the one-sample *t*-test comparing systolic blood pressure to a hypothesized population mean of 120, the histogram to determine whether a *t*-test was appropriate would look like Figure 6.11.

FIGURE 6.11 Distribution of systolic blood pressure in mmHg for 2015–2016 NHANES participants

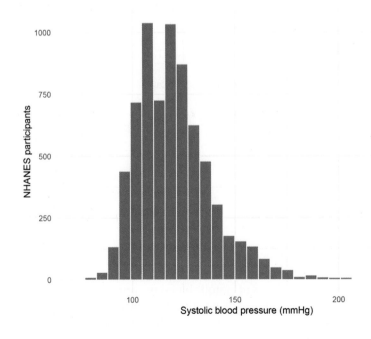

```
# graph systolic bp (Figure 6.11)
nhanes.2016.cleaned %>%
    ggplot(aes(x = systolic)) +
    geom_histogram(fill = "#7463AC", col = "white") +
    theme_minimal() +
    labs(x = "Systolic blood pressure (mmHg)",
         y = "NHANES participants")
```

The histogram does not look quite like a normal distribution. The data appear right-skewed, and it seems like there may be two peaks, which Kiara noted is called **bimodal**, for having two modes. Another way to visually check normality is with a **Q-Q plot**, or quantile-quantile plot. This plot is made up of points below which a certain percentage of the observations fall. On the *x*-axis are normally distributed values with a mean of 0 and a standard deviation of 1. On the *y*-axis are the observations from the data. If the data are normally distributed, the values will form a diagonal line through the graph.

Consistent with the right-skewed histogram, the higher observed values at the top of the graph are farther from the line representing normality. The visual evidence in Figure 6.12 is enough to state that the normality assumption is not met. However, if the graphs showed the data were closer to normal, computing skewness (Equation [2.2]) or kurtosis (Equation [2.5]), or using a statistical test for normality, would help to determine if the data were normally distributed.

Different statistical checks of normality are useful in different situations. The mean of a variable is sensitive to skew (Section 2.6.2.2), so checking for skewness is important when a statistical test relies on means (like *t*-tests). When the focus of a statistical test is on variance, it is a good idea to examine kurtosis (Section 2.6.4.1) because variance is sensitive to problems with kurtosis (e.g., a platykurtic or leptokurtic distribution).

FIGURE 6.12 Distribution of systolic blood pressure in mmHg for 2015–2016 NHANES participants

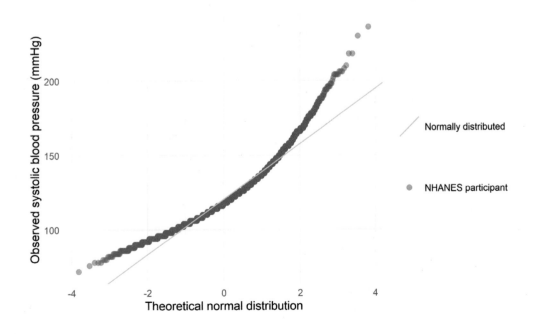

The *Shapiro-Wilk* test is an inferential test that tests the null hypothesis that the data are normally distributed. It is sensitive to even small deviations from normality and is not useful for sample sizes above 5,000 because it will *always* find non-normality. Given these limitations, Shapiro-Wilk is useful for testing normality in smaller samples when it is important that small deviations from normality are identified.

Given all of that information, Leslie decided that checking the skewness was a good idea before moving along to the other *t*-tests. She reviewed her notes and copied the code for computing skewness from Section 2.6.2.2.

```
# skewness of systolic bp
semTools::skew(object = nhanes.2016.cleaned$systolic)
##    skew (g1)          se          z          p
##   1.07037232  0.02897841  36.93689298  0.00000000
```

She reviewed the cutoffs for skewness that are problematic and found that *z* values outside the range –7 to 7 are problematic with large samples like this one. The *z* here is 36.94, so skew is definitely a problem! The data are not normal, and this assumption is failed.

Kiara explained that normality is checked for *each group* for the independent-samples *t*-test and dependent-samples *t*-test. Nancy advised Leslie that histograms could be shown together on the same *x*- and *y*-axes using different colors, or on separate plots. Leslie thought plotting them separately would be best to be able to see the shape clearly for each group. Nancy copied the ggplot() code

FIGURE 6.13 Distribution of systolic blood pressure in mmHg for 2015–2016 NHANES participants

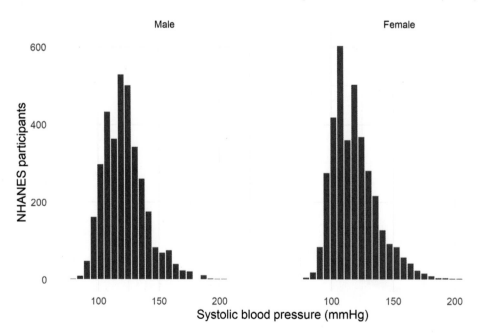

from earlier and added a `facet_grid()` option that plots each group as a "facet," with the facets identified by the sex variable. Nancy jumped in to add to the conversation about `facet_grid()`. She showed Leslie that `facet_grid(rows = vars(sex))` would put one category of sex *per row* while `facet_grid(cols = vars(sex))` will put one category of sex *per column*. Leslie used the per-column option this time (Figure 6.13).

```r
# graph systolic bp by sex (Figure 6.13)
nhanes.2016.cleaned %>%
  ggplot(aes(x = systolic)) +
  geom_histogram(fill = "#7463AC", col = "white") +
  facet_grid(cols = vars(sex)) +
  theme_minimal() +
  labs(x="Systolic blood pressure (mmHg)",
       y="NHANES participants")
```

Each of the two separate groups looked right-skewed, like the overall distribution. A Q-Q plot with facets might be able to confirm this (Figure 6.14).

```r
#graph systolic bp (Figure 6.14)
nhanes.2016.cleaned %>%
  drop_na(systolic) %>%
  ggplot(aes(sample = systolic)) +
  stat_qq(aes(color = "NHANES participant"), alpha = .6) +
  facet_grid(cols = vars(sex)) +
  geom_abline(aes(intercept = mean(x = systolic),
              slope = sd(x = systolic), linetype = "Normally distributed"),
              color = "gray", size = 1) +
  theme_minimal() +
  labs(x = "Theoretical normal distribution",
       y = "Observed systolic blood pressure (mmHg)")+
    scale_color_manual(values = "#7463AC", name = "") +
    scale_linetype_manual(values = 1, name = "")
```

The data within each group clearly failed the assumption of normal distribution. The skewness statistic could help to confirm this statistically for each of the two groups. Nancy showed Leslie that she could add the `semTools::skew()` code to the `summarize()` function to get the skew for each group. However, the `summarize()` function only prints a single number, so she would have to choose which statistic to print from `skew()`. Leslie looked at the previous use of `skew()` and decided to print the *z* since that is the statistic used to determine how much is too much skew. The *z* is the third statistic printed in the `skew()` output, so Leslie added [3] to print the *z*.

FIGURE 6.14 Distribution of systolic blood pressure in mmHg for 2015–2016 NHANES participants

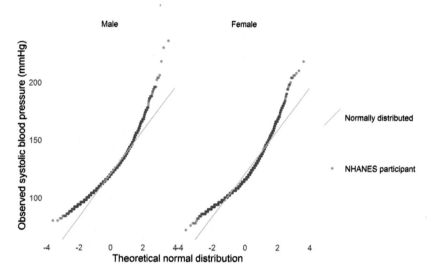

```
# statistical test of normality for systolic bp by sex
nhanes.2016.cleaned %>%
  drop_na(systolic) %>%
  group_by(sex) %>%
  summarize(z.skew = semTools::skew(object = systolic)[3])
```

sex	z.skew
<fctr>	<dbl>
Male	25.6
Female	27.6

The z values for skew of 25.6 for males and 27.6 for females were far above the acceptable range of −7 to 7 for this sample size, so both groups are skewed. The skew is likely to impact the means for the groups, so these data fail the assumption for normality for the independent-samples *t*-test. Leslie moved on to the final type of *t*-test.

Testing normality for the dependent-samples *t*-test is similar to the other *t*-tests. Use a graph and test for skewness of the `diff.syst` variable to see if the differences between the first and second measures are normally distributed.

```
# graph systolic difference between systolic and systolic2 (Figure 6.15)
nhanes.2016.cleaned %>%
  ggplot(aes(x = diff.syst)) +
  geom_histogram(fill = "#7463AC", col = "white") +
  theme_minimal() +
  labs(x = "Difference between measures of systolic blood pressure (mmHg)",
       y = "NHANES participants")
```

Leslie noted that the distribution in Figure 6.15 looked more normal than any of the previous ones. She tried a Q-Q plot to see if her observation would hold (Figure 6.16).

FIGURE 6.15 Distribution of differences in systolic blood pressure readings for 2015–2016 NHANES participants

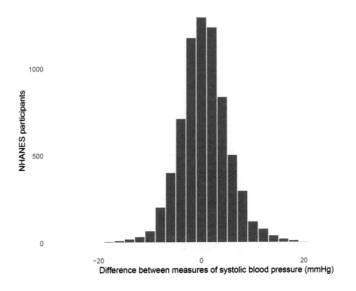

FIGURE 6.16 Distribution of differences in systolic blood pressure measures for 2015–2016 NHANES participants

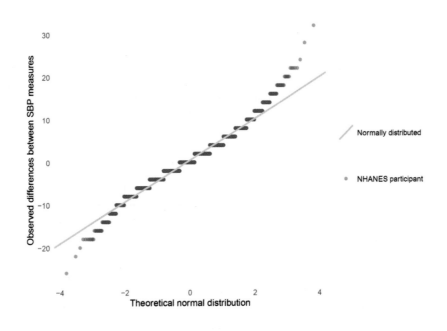

```
# Q-Q plot difference between systolic and systolic2 (Figure 6.16)
nhanes.2016.cleaned %>%
  drop_na(diff.syst) %>%
```

```
ggplot(aes(sample = diff.syst)) +
stat_qq(aes(color = "NHANES participant"), alpha = .6) +
geom_abline(aes(intercept = mean(x = diff.syst),
            slope = sd(x = diff.syst), linetype = "Normally distributed"),
            color = "gray", size = 1) +
theme_minimal() +
labs(x = "Theoretical normal distribution",
     y = "Observed differences between SBP measures")+
  scale_color_manual(values = "#7463AC", name = "") +
  scale_linetype_manual(values = 1, name = "")
```

Leslie was disappointed that the variable did not look normally distributed in this plot given the histogram, but she decided to try a statistical test of the variable to check one more time.

```
# statistical test of normality for difference variable
semTools::skew(object = nhanes.2016.cleaned$diff.syst)
##     skew (g1)           se            z            p
## 2.351789e-01 2.906805e-02 8.090632e+00 6.661338e-16
```

Despite the promising histogram, the Q-Q plot and *z* for skew of 8.09 suggest that the difference variable is not normally distributed. The `diff.syst` data failed this assumption.

Leslie noted that *none* of the *t*-tests met the normal distribution assumption! While failing this assumption would be enough of a reason to choose another test, Kiara explained that there is one additional assumption to test for the independent-samples *t*-test. The assumption is *homogeneity of variances*, or equal variances across groups. Not only do the data need to be normally distributed, but they should be equally spread out in each group. Nancy reminded Kiara that they had used the Welch's version of the *t*-test, which does not require homogeneity of variances. Kiara thought they should examine the assumption anyway since it would help Leslie if she ever needed to use the Student's *t*-test and it would help them choose an appropriate alternate test. Leslie reviewed Figure 6.13 and thought these data might actually meet the assumption.

Kiara explained that *Levene's test* is widely used to test the assumption of equal variances. The null hypothesis for Levene's test is that the variances are equal, while the alternate hypothesis is that the variances are not equal. A statistically significant Levene's test would mean rejecting the null hypothesis of equal variances and failing the assumption. Nancy wrote some code to test this assumption:

```
# equal variances for systolic by sex
car::leveneTest(y = systolic ~ sex, data = nhanes.2016.cleaned)
## Levene's Test for Homogeneity of Variance (center = median)
##          Df F value  Pr(>F)
## group     1   3.552 0.05952 .
##        7143
```

```
## ---
## Signif. codes:  0 '***' 0.001 '**' 0.01 '*' 0.05 '.' 0.1 ' ' 1
```

Kiara explained that the *p*-value in the output is shown in the column with the heading `Pr(>F)`. This Levene's test had a *p*-value of .06, which is not enough to reject the null hypothesis. Therefore, the assumption is met. The variances of systolic blood pressure for men and women are not statistically significantly different (*p* = .06), and the independent-samples *t*-test meets the assumption of homogeneity of variances.

Overall, none of the tests passed all assumptions. All of the tests failed the assumption of normal distribution.

Nancy summarized the assumptions for the tests to make sure Leslie had them all:

One-sample *t*-test assumptions
- Continuous variable
- Independent observations
- Normal distribution

Independent-samples *t*-test assumptions
- Continuous variable and two independent groups
- Independent observations
- Normal distribution in each group
- Equal variances for each group

Dependent-samples *t*-test assumptions
- Continuous variable and two dependent groups
- Independent observations
- Normal distribution of differences

Leslie asked Nancy to remind her what the difference was between independent observations and independent groups. Nancy explained that the independent observations assumption required that the people in the data not be related to one another in any important way. Things that might violate this assumption are having siblings or spouses in a data set or measuring the same person multiple times. Independent groups is the assumption that two groups are not related to one another. If some of the same people were in both groups, the two groups would not be independent.

Leslie wondered what to do now that none of the statistical tests passed the assumptions. Kiara explained that each test has a variation for when the assumptions are not met.

6.9.2 ACHIEVEMENT 6: CHECK YOUR UNDERSTANDING

Which independent-samples *t*-test assumption appears to be violated by the data in Figure 6.17?

- Continuous variable and two independent groups
- Independent observations
- Normal distribution in each group
- Equal variances for each group

FIGURE 6.17 Distribution of data violating a *t*-test assumption

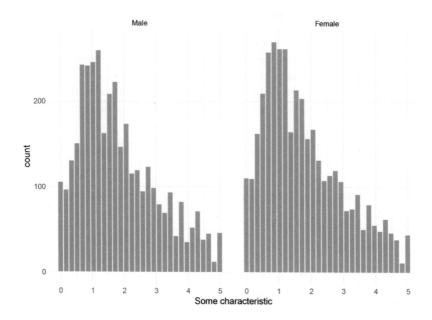

6.10 Achievement 7: Identifying and using alternate tests when *t*-test assumptions are not met

Nancy introduced Leslie to alternate tests she could use when assumptions are failed:

- one-sample *t*-test → sign test
- dependent-samples *t*-test → Wilcoxon Signed-Rank Test
- independent-samples *t*-test → Mann-Whitney *U* or Kolmogorov-Smirnoff

6.10.1 ALTERNATIVE TO ONE-SAMPLE *t*-TEST FAILING ASSUMPTIONS: THE SIGN TEST

When the data fail the assumption of normality for a one-sample *t*-test, the median could be examined rather than the mean, just like for descriptive statistics when the variable is not normally distributed. The *sign test* tests whether the median of a variable is equal to some hypothesized value. Before conducting a sign test, Leslie remembered that EDA is an important step and examined the median value of the systolic variable.

```
# examine median for systolic variable
median(x = nhanes.2016.cleaned$systolic, na.rm = TRUE)
## [1] 118
```

Now that she had a little information about the variable, Leslie put on her NHST hat and tried this new test.

6.10.1.1 NHST STEP 1: WRITE THE NULL AND ALTERNATE HYPOTHESES

H0: The median systolic blood pressure in the U.S. population is 120.

HA: The median systolic blood pressure in the U.S. population is not 120.

The median systolic blood pressure is 118. This is close but a little lower than the 120 hypothesized to be the median value. Nancy reminded Leslie and Kiara that the median value was exactly in the middle with the same number of observations above as below it. Leslie tested the median of 118 against the hypothesized median of 120.

6.10.1.2 NHST STEP 2: COMPUTE THE TEST STATISTIC

Leslie looks up the sign test and finds that it is conducted using the SIGN.test() function from the BSDA package. Nancy said Leslie would need to add the md = 120 argument to the code since the SIGN.test() can be used in other settings aside from one-sample median tests. The md = option in the SIGN.test() indicates the hypothesized value to test.

```
# compare observed median SBP to 120
BSDA::SIGN.test(x = nhanes.2016.cleaned$systolic, md = 120)
##
##  One-sample Sign-Test
##
## data:  nhanes.2016.cleaned$systolic
## s = 3004, p-value < 2.2e-16
## alternative hypothesis: true median is not equal to 120
## 95 percent confidence interval:
##  116 118
## sample estimates:
## median of x
##        118
##
## Achieved and Interpolated Confidence Intervals:
##
##                  Conf.Level L.E.pt U.E.pt
## Lower Achieved CI    0.9477    116    118
## Interpolated CI      0.9500    116    118
## Upper Achieved CI    0.9505    116    118
```

The test statistic for the Sign Test is s = 3004.

6.10.1.3 NHST STEP 3: CALCULATE THE PROBABILITY THAT YOUR TEST STATISTIC IS AT LEAST AS BIG AS IT IS IF THERE IS NO RELATIONSHIP (I.E., THE NULL IS TRUE)

The *p*-value is shown in scientific notation in the output as < 2.2e-16 which is well below .05.

6.10.1.4 NHST STEPS 4 AND 5: INTERPRET THE PROBABILITY AND WRITE A CONCLUSION

The probability is extremely low of finding a median systolic blood pressure of 118 in the sample if the population had a median systolic blood pressure of 120. Leslie noted that the output also includes a 95% confidence interval of 116 to 118. She asked Kiara if this meant that this sample likely came from a population where the median systolic blood pressure was between 116 and 118. Leslie confirmed that this was correct. The median in the sample is 118, and the median in the population that the sample came from is likely between 116 and 118. Leslie pulled all the information together and wrote the interpretation of results:

> The median systolic blood pressure for NHANES participants was 118. A sign test comparing the median to a hypothesized median of 120 had a statistically significant ($s = 3004$; $p < .05$) result. The sample with a median systolic blood pressure of 118 was unlikely to have come from a population with a median systolic blood pressure of 120. The 95% confidence interval indicates this sample likely came from a population where the median systolic blood pressure was between 116 and 118. This suggests that the median systolic blood pressure in the U.S. population is between 116 and 118.

Leslie asked about the list of confidence intervals at the end of the output. Kiara and Nancy said they had never used those intervals and suggested that Leslie could do some research on her own if she were interested.

6.10.2 ALTERNATIVE WHEN THE DEPENDENT-SAMPLES t-TEST FAILS ASSUMPTIONS: THE WILCOXON SIGNED-RANKS TEST

The *Wilcoxon signed-ranks test* is an alternative to the dependent-samples *t*-test when the continuous variable is not normally distributed. The Wilcoxon test determines if the differences between paired values of two related samples are symmetrical around zero. That is, instead of comparing the mean difference to zero, the test compares the distribution of the differences around zero. Leslie, Nancy, and Kiara went back and reviewed Figure 6.15 so they could examine how `diff.syst` was distributed around zero, and it appeared relatively evenly distributed.

Since the Wilcoxon signed-ranks test was similar yet different from the dependent-samples *t*-test, Kiara thought it was important to consider the way it worked. She and Leslie looked up the test and made a list of the steps used to compute the test statistic:

- Step 1: Find the differences between the two paired measures (Measure 1 – Measure 2)
- Step 2: Put the *absolute values* of the differences in order from smallest to largest and give each one a rank
- Step 3: Sum the ranks for all the *positive* differences
- Step 4: Sum the ranks for all the *negative* differences

Nancy explained that the test statistic for the Wilcoxon test is usually W, although it was sometimes reported as T and called the Wilcoxon T-test because that was how it was referred to in one famous statistics book. Leslie thought that was confusing. Nancy continued explaining that the test statistic, whatever it is called, is the smaller of the Step 3 and Step 4 values. If the sum of the ranks of all the *positive* differences is smaller, that sum is W. If the sum of the ranks of the *negative* values is smaller, that sum is W. The distribution of W is approximately normal when the sample size is more than 20 (Gravetter & Wallnau, 2009), which is much of the time. Because it approximates a normal distribution, a z-statistic is used to test whether the W is statistically significant. The z-statistic has the standard cutoff values of -1.96 and 1.96 for statistical significance ($\alpha = .05$; $p < .05$). Now that they had information about the test statistic, Leslie started the NHST process.

6.10.2.1 NHST STEP 1: WRITE THE NULL AND ALTERNATE HYPOTHESES

H0: The distribution of the difference between the systolic blood pressure measures taken at Time 1 and Time 2 in the U.S. population is symmetric around zero.

HA: The distribution of the difference between the systolic blood pressure measures taken at Time 1 and Time 2 in the U.S. population is not symmetric around zero.

6.10.2.2 NHST STEP 2: CALCULATE THE TEST STATISTIC

The `wilcox.test()` function in base R can be used to test this null hypothesis. Kiara reminded Leslie to include the `paired = TRUE` argument in the code. She explained that Frank Wilcoxon had come up with this test and another test in a single paper in 1945 (Wilcoxon, 1945), and using the `paired = TRUE` argument specifies which of the two tests R should conduct and report.

```
# test the distribution of SBP by time period
wilcox.test(x = nhanes.2016.cleaned$systolic,
            y = nhanes.2016.cleaned$systolic2,
            paired = TRUE)
##
##  Wilcoxon signed rank test with continuity correction
##
## data:  nhanes.2016.cleaned$systolic and nhanes.2016.cleaned$systolic2
## V = 9549959, p-value < 2.2e-16
## alternative hypothesis: true location shift is not equal to 0
```

Leslie pointed out that there was no *T* or *W* in this output. Instead, the output showed `V = 9549959`, which looks like it is the test statistic. Nancy had forgotten about this quirk. She took a deep breath and explained that the `V` statistic that R returns in the output is the sum of the *ranks of positive differences* rather than the *W*, which would have been the larger of the two sums, positive differences or negative differences. She said that `V` would be the same as *W* when the sum of the ranks of *positive* differences was highest, but different from *W* when the sum of the ranks for *negative* differences was highest. Nancy said the *p*-value is correct for the Wilcoxon signed-rank test and that they could easily calculate *W* if Leslie was interested. Leslie thought this sounded like a good challenge to take on by herself sometime before the next meeting. She added it to her list of things to practice.

6.10.2.3 NHST STEP 3: CALCULATE THE PROBABILITY THAT YOUR TEST STATISTIC IS AT LEAST AS BIG AS IT IS IF THERE IS NO RELATIONSHIP (I.E., THE NULL IS TRUE)

The *p*-value is shown in scientific notation in the output as `< 2.2e-16`, which is well below .05.

6.10.2.4 NHST STEPS 4 AND 5: INTERPRET THE PROBABILITY AND WRITE A CONCLUSION

The resulting output is similar to the output for many of the tests. Leslie wrote her interpretation:

We used a Wilcoxon signed-ranks test to determine whether the distribution of the difference in systolic blood pressure measured at Time 1 and Time 2 was symmetrical around zero. The resulting test statistic and p-value indicated that the sample likely came from a population where the differences were not symmetrical around zero ($p < .05$).

Leslie thought this was a lot of jargon and asked Nancy and Kiara if they had a more comprehensible way of interpreting the results. Kiara said that she typically would give the very technical version but then she would add a more practical interpretation, like this:

We used a Wilcoxon signed-ranks test to determine whether the distribution of the difference in systolic blood pressure measured at Time 1 and Time 2 was symmetrical around zero. The resulting test statistic and p-value indicated that the sample likely came from a population where the differences were not symmetrical around zero ($p < .05$). That is, we found a significant difference between the first and second blood pressure measures.

Kiara explained that she would probably also add that, although the distribution was not symmetrical around zero and the difference from symmetry is statistically significant, Figure 6.15 showed that the distribution was close to symmetrical and the differences between Measure 1 and Measure 2 were unlikely to be a major concern for the NHANES survey team.

Kiara noted that this test, and the next two tests they were going to review (the Mann-Whitney U test in Section 6.10.3 and the Kolmogorov-Smirnov test in Section 6.10.5), are often interpreted as testing for *equal medians*. While none of these tests examine medians directly, the ordering and ranking of values is similar to how medians are identified, so there is logic to this interpretation. However, if the distribution shape or spread (or both) are different, interpreting the results as comparing medians can be misleading. Kiara suggested that Leslie remember to conduct visual and descriptive analyses before (or with) these tests to make sure she is interpreting her results accurately. The Wilcoxon signed-ranks test could be accompanied by a histogram or boxplot comparing the groups to support or clarify the statistical results.

6.10.3 ALTERNATIVE WHEN THE INDEPENDENT-SAMPLES t-TEST NORMALITY ASSUMPTION FAILS: THE MANN-WHITNEY U TEST

The *Mann-Whitney U test* is an alternative to the independent-samples t-test when the continuous variable is not normally distributed. The U test also relaxes the variable type assumption and can be used for ordinal variables in addition to continuous variables. Similar to the Wilcoxon signed-rank test, the Mann-Whitney U test puts all the values for the continuous (or ordinal) variable in order, assigns each value a rank, and compares ranks across the two groups of the categorical variable (Gravetter & Wallnau, 2009). The test statistic is computed using the sums of the ranks for each group. The distribution for the test statistic approximates normality as long as the sample size is greater than 20; a z-score is used to determine the corresponding p-value.

Leslie almost knew the NHST by heart and used it to organize a Mann-Whitney U test of systolic blood pressure by sex.

6.10.3.1 STEP 1: WRITE THE NULL AND ALTERNATE HYPOTHESES

H0: There is no difference in ranked systolic blood pressure values for males and females in the U.S. population.

HA: There is a difference in ranked systolic blood pressure values for males and females in the U.S. population.

6.10.3.2 STEP 2: COMPUTE THE TEST STATISTIC

As if the similar process was not confusing enough, this test is also called the *Wilcoxon rank sum test*—which is not the same as the Wilcoxon signed-ranks test. This is the other test that Frank Wilcoxon explained in his 1945 paper (Wilcoxon, 1945). The same R function used in the previous test can be used here with two changes: use of `formula =` (Box 6.3) instead of `x =` and `y =`, and use of `paired = FALSE`.

```
# test the distribution of systolic by sex
u.syst.by.sex <- wilcox.test(formula =
                           nhanes.2016.cleaned$systolic ~
                           nhanes.2016.cleaned$sex,
                        paired = FALSE)
u.syst.by.sex
##
##  Wilcoxon rank sum test with continuity correction
##
## data:  nhanes.2016.cleaned$systolic by nhanes.2016.cleaned$sex
## W = 7186882, p-value < 2.2e-16
## alternative hypothesis: true location shift is not equal to 0
```

Leslie noticed that the output now showed a `W` like she was expecting for the previous test, and she suggested just leaving the test statistic out of the final interpretation for these tests to avoid confusion. Kiara didn't like this suggestion since it was bad for reproducibility, but she also agreed that the different test statistics for the two tests by Wilcoxon were confusing, so she hesitantly agreed this was OK.

6.3 Nancy's fancy code: Formulas in R

R uses the tilde, or ~, to separate the right-hand side and left-hand side of a formula. A formula typically contains one variable that is being explained or predicted by one or more other variables. For example, income and sex may aid in explaining smoking status, so a formula might be `smoking.status ~ income + sex`.

In a formula in R, the variable that is being explained is on the left-hand side of the formula, and the variables that are explaining are on the right-hand side of the formula. The tilde that separates the right and left sides of the formula can usually be read as "is dependent on" or "is explained by." For example, in the Mann-Whitney *U* test explained earlier, the formula in the parentheses is systolic blood pressure explained by sex.

```
# compare systolic blood pressure by sex
wilcox.test(formula = nhanes.2016.cleaned$systolic ~ nhanes.2016.
cleaned$sex)
```

There may be other ways of reading the ~, but for now, try these two choices. Use the help documentation by typing `?tilde` at the R prompt to learn more.

6.10.3.3 STEP 3: CALCULATE THE PROBABILITY THAT YOUR TEST STATISTIC IS AT LEAST AS BIG AS IT IS IF THERE IS NO RELATIONSHIP (I.E., THE NULL IS TRUE)

The p-value is shown in scientific notation in the output as $< 2.2e-16$, which is well below .05.

6.10.3.4 STEPS 4 AND 5: INTERPRET THE PROBABILITY AND WRITE A CONCLUSION

Leslie wrote the conclusion:

> A Mann-Whitney U test comparing systolic blood pressure for males and females in the United States found a statistically significant difference between the two groups ($p < .05$).

It seemed a little short for a conclusion. Leslie asked what else they might include. Kiara suggested including medians and IQR to demonstrate the difference between the groups, or referring the audience back to Figure 6.13 showing the distributions of blood pressure for the two groups. Kiara also explained that they could include effect size with this test.

6.10.4 EFFECT SIZE FOR MANN-WHITNEY *U*

Leslie had been curious as to whether these alternative tests had effect sizes. Kiara explained that one effect size that can be used with Mann-Whitney U is r (Fritz et al., 2012), which is computed using the z-statistic from the Mann-Whitney U test and dividing by the square root of the sample size, as shown in Equation (6.13).

$$r = \frac{z}{\sqrt{n}} \tag{6.13}$$

For the current analysis, the effect size for the comparison of male and female systolic blood pressure can be determined using the z from the U test. Unfortunately, the u.syst.by.sex object does not include the z-statistic used to determine the p-value. But fortunately, Nancy knew a super-secret way to get z-statistics from p-values in R! She introduced the team to qnorm(), which finds the z-statistic that corresponds to a given p-value. She added the p-value from u.syst.by.sex to the qnorm() function to get the z-statistic.

```
# use qnorm to find z from p-value
qnorm(p = u.syst.by.sex$p.value)
## [1] -9.206125
```

The z-statistic was negative and large. Because effect size is about the size or strength and not the direction (positive or negative) of a relationship, the absolute value can be used to get the effect size r in Equation (6.14) with the sample size of 7,145 computed in Section 6.5.

$$r = \frac{9.206125}{\sqrt{7145}} = .109 \tag{6.14}$$

Consistent with the effect size from the t-test comparing males and females (Section 6.8.2), this is a pretty small effect size, with r effects being classified as follows:

- $r = .1$ to $r < .3$ is small
- $r = .3$ to $r < .5$ is medium
- $r \geq .5$ is large

FIGURE 6.18 `wilcoxonR()` help documentation details section

Details

r is calculated as Z divided by square root of the total observations.

Currently, the function makes no provisions for NA values in the data. It is recommended that NAs be removed beforehand.

When the data in the first group are greater than in the second group, r is positive. When the data in the second group are greater than in the first group, r is negative. Be cautious with this interpretation, as R will alphabetize groups if g is not already a factor.

When r is close to extremes, or with small counts in some cells, the confidence intervals determined by this method may not be reliable, or the procedure may fail.

As usual, Nancy had some R code to use instead of the hand calculations, although she noted that the code is a little tricky this time because the value of *n* used in the calculations is the entire *n* without considering the missing values. Leslie asked how she knew this, and Nancy showed her the help documentation from the `wilcoxonR()` function that she planned to use. The documentation has a section with extra details about the test (Figure 6.18).

Leslie asked Nancy how they should deal with this. Nancy suggested that they create a new data frame without the NA values for systolic, and use the new data frame with the `wilcoxonR()` function to get the *r*. Leslie thought that sounded reasonable and worked with Nancy and the help documentation for `wilcoxonR()` to write the code.

```
# new data frame with no NA
nhanes.2016.cleaned.noNA <- nhanes.2016.cleaned %>%
  drop_na(systolic)

# use new data frame to get r
rcompanion::wilcoxonR(x = nhanes.2016.cleaned.noNA$systolic,
                      g = nhanes.2016.cleaned.noNA$sex)

##     r
## 0.11
```

The value was consistent with a rounded version of the results from the hand calculations, and they all breathed a sigh of relief. That was a tricky one! Leslie added some descriptive information and the effect size to the full interpretation:

A Mann-Whitney *U* test comparing systolic blood pressure for males and females in the United States found a statistically significant difference between the two groups ($p < .05$). Histograms demonstrated the differences, with notably more females with systolic blood pressure below 100 compared to males along with some other differences. The effect size was small, $r = .11$, indicating a weak but statistically significant relationship between sex and systolic blood pressure.

6.10.5 ALTERNATIVE WHEN THE INDEPENDENT-SAMPLES *t*-TEST VARIANCE ASSUMPTION FAILS: THE KOLMOGOROV-SMIRNOV TEST

The *Kolmogorov-Smirnov* (K-S) *test* is used when the variances in the two groups are unequal. When the variances are unequal, the homogeneity of variances assumption is not met, whether or not the normality assumption is met. The larger variance has a bigger influence on the size of the *t*-statistic, so one group is dominating the *t*-statistic calculations that use Equation (6.3). Leslie was confused. She thought the Welch's *t*-test they used was already accounting for unequal variances. Nancy confirmed this but added that the K-S test is another option when variances are unequal and is especially useful when variances are unequal *and* the normality assumption is not met.

The K-S test compares the distributions of the groups, and Leslie sensed it was time for the NHST again.

6.10.5.1 NHST STEP 1: WRITE THE NULL AND ALTERNATE HYPOTHESES

H0: The distribution of systolic blood pressure for males and females is the same in the U.S. population.

HA: The distribution of systolic blood pressure for males and females is not the same in the U.S. population.

6.10.5.2 NHST STEP 2: COMPUTE THE TEST STATISTIC

The `ks.test()` function is used to test the null hypothesis. Unfortunately, `ks.test()` takes two vectors as arguments, one vector for each group. A little additional data management is needed to separate the males and the females into different vectors. Nancy was excited because there were so many ways to do this and she could show the team something new from the **tidyverse** package. She explained that the `pull()` function is useful for getting a single variable out of a data frame as a stand-alone vector. With `pull()`, Nancy used the `var =` argument with the name of the variable to pull out into its own vector to demonstrate the process for Leslie and Kiara.

```
# get vectors for male and female systolic
males.systolic <- nhanes.2016.cleaned %>%
  filter(sex == "Male") %>%
  pull(var = systolic)


females.systolic <- nhanes.2016.cleaned %>%
  filter(sex == "Female") %>%
  pull(var = systolic)
```

Now that they had two vectors, `males.systolic` and `females.systolic`, Nancy compared them using `ks.test()`.

```
# conduct the test
ks.test(x = males.systolic,
        y = females.systolic)
##
##  Two-sample Kolmogorov-Smirnov test
##
## data:  males.systolic and females.systolic
## D = 0.11408, p-value < 2.2e-16
## alternative hypothesis: two-sided
```

6.10.5.3 STEP 3: CALCULATE THE PROBABILITY THAT YOUR TEST STATISTIC IS AT LEAST AS BIG AS IT IS IF THERE IS NO RELATIONSHIP (I.E., THE NULL IS TRUE)

The *p*-value is shown in scientific notation in the output as $< 2.2e-16$, which is well below .05.

6.10.5.4 STEPS 4 AND 5: INTERPRET THE PROBABILITY AND WRITE A CONCLUSION

The K-S test compared the distribution of systolic blood pressure for males and females in the United States and found a statistically significant difference between the two groups ($D = .11$; $p < .05$). The test statistic, D, is the maximum distance between the two empirical cumulative distribution functions (ECDFs), which are a special type of probability distribution showing the cumulative probability of the values of a variable. To examine the difference between the ECDFs for systolic blood pressure of males and females in the sample, Nancy graphed the two ECDF curves in Figure 6.19.

```
# ECDF for male and female SBP (Figure 6.19)
nhanes.2016.cleaned %>%
  ggplot(aes(x = systolic, color = sex)) +
  stat_ecdf(size = 1) +
  theme_minimal() +
  labs(x = "Systolic blood pressure (mmHg)",
       y = "Cumulative probability") +
  scale_color_manual(values = c("Male" = "gray", "Female" = "#7463AC"),
                     name = "Sex")
```

FIGURE 6.19 ECDF of systolic blood pressure in mmHg by sex for 2015–2016 NHANES participants

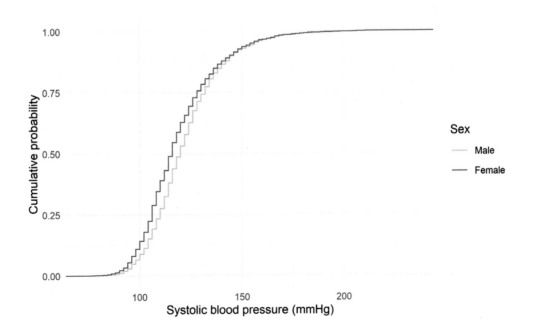

At the widest gap between these two curves, males and females were .11 apart, giving a test statistic of $D = .11$. The probability of getting a test statistic this large or larger is determined by examining the K-S probability distribution. In this case, the probability of .11 difference between the two was very tiny ($p < .05$) if the null hypothesis were true, so the difference between the distributions for males and females would be reported as statistically significant. Leslie rolled her eyes. Kiara explained that it is good to have some awareness of what statistical tests are actually doing, but that understanding the ECDF in depth is not important for the final reporting of the statistical test.

Leslie thought that sounded about right and asked if there was an effect size to consider for the K-S test. Kiara said that she read on a message board that the K-S D statistic could be used as an effect size in addition to using it for significance testing, but that she could not find any published papers or book chapters to confirm this, so she thought just using descriptive information and graphs would probably be the best approach. Leslie agreed and wrote the final interpretation:

> A K-S test comparing systolic blood pressure for males and females found a statistically significant difference between the two groups ($D = .11$; $p < .05$). This sample likely came from a population where the distribution of systolic blood pressure was different for males and females.

Nancy noticed they had finished all the food and drinks at their table and she was feeling ready to head home. Before they left, Leslie summarized what they had learned for the day. While the t-tests were great, she found the most interesting part of the day was seeing how very small differences can still be statistically significant. The .54 difference between the sample mean systolic blood pressure and the threshold for healthy systolic blood pressure was small, but it was statistically significant. The small gap between the distributions of male and female blood pressure in Figure 6.19 was also statistically significant. Even the small difference between the first and second measures of blood pressure was statistically significant. Leslie found this to be a big shift in her thinking. Instead of paying attention mostly to p-values in the future, she would use graphs and descriptive statistics to better understand her results. Statistically significant results are not necessarily large or important results. Kiara and Nancy thought this was a great takeaway lesson for the day, in addition to how to do the t-tests and their alternatives, of course.

"Anyone for a Guinness?" asked Leslie.

"No thanks," Kiara and Nancy said in unison.

"You're probably right," Leslie agreed. "It is getting late. I'll find us some space for next time," she said as she picked up her bag.

"Sounds great. I'll look for your email," said Kiara.

"What she said," Nancy gestured toward Kiara as she zipped up her bag.

Nancy headed toward the door as Kiara and Leslie packed up. "Are there any more statistical methods about beer? Or maybe about chips and salsa?" Leslie joked.

"I don't think so, but we can always search the Internet to find out!" Kiara said as they walked toward their cars.

6.10.6 ACHIEVEMENT 7: CHECK YOUR UNDERSTANDING

Which of the following is each alternative test for: one-sample t-test, independent-samples t-test, and dependent-samples t-test.

- K-S test
- Mann-Whitney U test
- Sign test
- Wilcoxon signed-rank test

/// 6.11 CHAPTER SUMMARY

6.11.1 Achievements unlocked in this chapter: Recap

Congratulations! Like Leslie, you've learned and practiced the following in this chapter.

6.11.1.1 Achievement 1 recap: Understanding the relationship between one categorical variable and one continuous variable using histograms, means, and standard deviations

Prior to conducting inferential statistical tests like chi-squared, it is useful to get some idea of the characteristics and relationships in your data. Descriptive statistics and graphs, or exploratory data analysis (EDA), can serve two purposes: It can help you better understand the people, things, or phenomena you are studying, and it can help you make an educated prediction about the likely results of a statistical test, which can help identify issues if (or when) the test is not properly conducted.

6.11.1.2 Achievement 2 recap: Comparing a sample mean to a population mean with a one-sample t-test

The t-test compares means to determine if one mean is statistically significantly different from another. There are three types of t-tests: one-sample, independent-samples, and dependent-samples. The one-sample t-test compares the mean of one variable to a hypothesized or population mean. Significant results indicate that the difference between the means likely reflects a difference in means from the population the samples came from.

6.11.1.3 Achievement 3 recap: Comparing two unrelated sample means with an independent-samples t-test

The independent-samples t-test compares means from two unrelated groups (e.g., males and females). Significant results indicate that the difference between the means likely reflects a difference in means from the population that was sampled.

6.11.1.4 Achievement 4 recap: Comparing two related sample means with a dependent-samples t-test

The dependent-samples t-test compares means from related groups (e.g., pre and post measures on the same person). Significant results indicate that the difference between the means likely reflects a difference in means from the population the samples came from.

6.11.1.5 Achievement 5 recap: Computing and interpreting an effect size for significant t-tests

Effect sizes can be used to show the strength of an association and are important for adding context to statistically significant findings.

6.11.1.6 Achievement 6 recap: Examining and checking the underlying assumptions for using the t-test

Statistical tests rely on underlying assumptions about the characteristics of the data. When these assumptions are not met, the results may not reflect the true relationships among the variables.

6.11.1.7 Achievement 7 recap: Identifying and using alternate tests when t-test assumptions are not met

When assumptions are not met for t-tests, there are several alternative tests that compare medians or distributions rather than means.

6.11.2 Chapter exercises

The coder and hacker exercises are an opportunity to apply the skills from this chapter to a new scenario or a new data set. The coder edition evaluates the application of the concepts and functions learned in this R-Team meeting to scenarios similar to those in the meeting. The hacker edition evaluates the use of the concepts and functions from this R-Team meeting in new scenarios, often going a step beyond what was explicitly explained.

The coder edition might be best for those who found some or all of the Check Your Understanding activities to be challenging or if they needed review before picking the correct responses to the multiple-choice questions. The hacker edition might be best if the Check Your Understanding activities were not too challenging and the multiple-choice questions were a breeze.

The multiple-choice questions and materials for the exercises are online at **edge.sagepub.com/harris1e**.

Q1: Which of the following tests would be used to test the mean of a continuous variable to a population mean?

a. One-sample t-test

b. Independent-samples t-test

c. Chi-squared t-test

d. Dependent-samples t-test

Q2: What is the primary purpose of the three t-tests?

a. Comparing means among groups

b. Comparing medians among groups

c. Examining the relationship between two categorical variables

d. Identifying normally distributed data

Q3: Which of the following assumptions does *not* apply to all three t-tests?

a. Independent observations

b. Normal distribution of continuous variable

c. Homogeneity of variances

d. Inclusion of one continuous variable

Q4: Which t-test would you use to compare mean BMI in sets of two brothers?

a. One-sample t-test

b. Independent-samples t-test

c. Chi-squared t-test

d. Dependent-samples t-test

Q5: When an independent-samples t-test does not meet the assumption of normality, what is an appropriate alternative test?

a. Sign test

b. Levene's test

c. Mann-Whitney U test

d. Dependent-samples t-test

6.11.2.1 Chapter exercises: Coder edition

Depending on your score in the knowledge check, choose either the coder or hacker edition of the chapter exercises. Use the NHANES data from this chapter and the appropriate tests to examine diastolic blood pressure for males and females.

1) Open the 2015–2016 NHANES data using the strategy shown in this chapter.

2) Clean the sex variable and the two diastolic blood pressure measurement variables so they have clear names, category labels, and missing value coding.

3) Use graphics and descriptive statistics to examine Measure 1 on its own and by participant sex (Achievement 1).

4) Use graphics and descriptive statistics to examine Measure 2 on its own (Achievement 1).

5) Based on the graphs and statistics from Questions 3 and 4, make predictions about what you would find when you compare the mean diastolic blood pressure from Measure 1 and Measure 2 (Achievement 1).

6) Based on the graphs and statistics from Questions 3 and 4, make predictions about what you would find when you compare the mean diastolic blood pressure from Measure 1 by sex (Achievement 1).

7) Select and use the appropriate t-test to compare Measure 1 for males and females, then interpret your results using the test statistics and p-value along with a graph showing the two groups. Check assumptions for this test. If the assumptions were not met, conduct and interpret the appropriate alternate test (Achievements 3–5).

8) Select and use the appropriate t-test to compare the means of Measure 1 and Measure 2, then interpret

your results using the test statistics and *p*-value. Check assumptions for this test. If the assumptions were not met, conduct and interpret the appropriate alternate test (Achievements 4, 6).

6.11.2.2 Chapter exercises: Hacker edition

Complete #1 through #8 of the coder edition, then complete the following:

9) Restrict the data to a subset of people under 50 years old. Using the appropriate test, compare their mean diastolic blood pressure to the normal threshold of 80. Interpret your results and check the test assumptions. If the test does not meet assumptions, conduct and interpret the appropriate alternate test (Achievements 2, 6, 7).

10) Restrict the data to a subset of people 50+ years old. Using the appropriate test, compare their mean diastolic blood pressure to the normal threshold of 80. Interpret your results and check the test assumptions. If the test does not meet assumptions, conduct and interpret the appropriate alternate test (Achievements 2, 6, 7).

6.11.2.3 Instructor note

Solutions to exercises can be found on the website for this book, along with ideas for gamification for those who want to take it further.

Visit **edge.sagepub.com/harris1e** to download the datasets, complete the chapter exercises, and watch R tutorial videos.

ANALYSIS OF VARIANCE

The R-Team and the
Technical Difficulties Problem

On her way to meet Nancy and Kiara, Leslie noticed her cell phone battery was dead. Again. She sighed and tucked it in her backpack until she could find a way to charge it. Meanwhile, on her walk to campus, she began to notice just how many people she passed were using cell phones.

When she arrived at the library study room she'd reserved, she saw Kiara had already arrived.

"Hey," said Leslie.

"Three minutes early," said Kiara. "A first."

"Very funny," Leslie said. For fun, she was going to double-check the time on her phone and see if Kiara was correct. Then she remembered her phone battery was dead.

"Wonder where Nancy is?" asked Kiara. "She's usually the early bird."

Leslie started to check her cell phone for a possible text from Nancy when she remembered, again, that her battery was dead.

"I think we can get started without her," Kiara said. "So, as we know from our previous meeting, the *t*-test and its alternatives worked great for comparing two groups, but what happens when there are three or more groups to compare? Today, we'll discuss *analysis of variance*, or ANOVA, which is the statistical method used for comparing means across three or more groups. Like the *t*-test, ANOVA has underlying assumptions to be met, and there are alternative methods to use when the assumptions are not met."

"What did I miss?" Nancy asked, entering the room. "And sorry I'm late. I was using a navigation app on my phone, and it took me the long way."

"No worries," said Kiara. "I was just introducing ANOVA to Leslie." She continued, "Similar to chi-squared, ANOVA is an omnibus test, which means a significant result indicates there is a difference between the means, but it is not useful in determining which means are different from each other."

Nancy jumped in and added, "And instead of using standardized residuals, ANOVA uses planned contrasts and post hoc tests to determine which means are statistically significantly different from one another. Instead of Cramér's *V* or odds ratios for chi-squared and Cohen's *d* for *t*-tests, η^2 and ω^2 are often reported as effect sizes for ANOVA."

"I'm ready to get started," said Leslie. "But first, does anyone have a phone charger to share?"

Laughing, Nancy handed hers to Leslie and said, "What would we all do without our phones?"

Then Nancy and Kiara shared the list of achievements for this meeting.

7.1 Achievements to unlock

- Achievement 1: Exploring the data using graphics and descriptive statistics
- Achievement 2: Understanding and conducting one-way ANOVA
- Achievement 3: Choosing and using post hoc tests and contrasts
- Achievement 4: Computing and interpreting effect sizes for ANOVA

⑤SAGE edge™

Visit **edge.sagepub .com/harris1e** to watch an R tutorial

- Achievement 5: Testing ANOVA assumptions

- Achievement 6: Choosing and using alternative tests when ANOVA assumptions are not met

- Achievement 7: Understanding and conducting two-way ANOVA

7.2 The technical difficulties problem

Leslie's dead cell phone battery started her thinking about her cell phone use and all the ways she looked at screens and used technology throughout the day. Certainly, she thought, it was very different from her life just 10 years earlier, when she rarely used a cell phone. She thought about the time she spent with her friends and how they all were using phones or at least had phones nearby during gatherings. Her colleagues at work spent most of their time in front of computer screens in addition to having cell phones on. She remembered talking to her friend Paige, who was majoring in communication. Paige was studying how phones and other new technologies are changing the way humans interact with each other and with the world.

Leslie asked Nancy and Kiara how much of their time awake each day they thought they spent looking at a screen or using technology. Both of them answered "a lot," maybe close to 60% or 70%. Nancy mentioned that one of her favorite forms of exercise is walking to play Pokémon GO, and Kiara described listening to podcasts whenever she had a spare moment and also playing app games like Tetris and Candy Crush. Leslie remembered being on vacation and the sheer panic and disconnectedness that she had felt when she thought she had lost her cell phone, only to find it 10 minutes later under the seat of the rideshare she was in (the one she had requested using her phone).

After this discussion, they started researching technology use and how it might be influencing culture and health and mental health. Leslie started looking up and reading some of the research Paige had mentioned about how text messaging had become common and tolerated in social situations while at the same time viewed as an interruption that can signal a lack of care by the texter for others who are present (Cahir & Lloyd, 2015). Kiara found some research linking cell phone use to college students having lower satisfaction with life (Lepp, Barkley, & Karpinski, 2014), lower test scores and grade point averages (Bjornsen & Archer, 2015; Lepp, Barkley, & Karpinski, 2015), and more sedentary behavior (Barkley & Lepp, 2016). She also found a couple of studies showing that cell phone use was associated with stress, sleep disorders, and depression symptoms among recent college graduates (Rosen, Carrier, Miller, Rokkum, & Ruiz, 2016; Thomée, Härenstam, & Hagberg, 2011).

Nancy started looking for some publicly available data on technology use and found a technology use variable in the General Social Survey (GSS). She used the Data Explorer on the GSS website (https://gssdataexplorer.norc.org/) to select variables and download a GSS data set with 2018 data that included the technology use variable and some demographic variables. The tech variable measured the percentage of time the survey participant estimated using technology at work each week. Kiara went ahead and loaded and summarized the data.

7.3 Data, codebook, and R packages for learning about ANOVA

Before they examined the data, Kiara made a list of all the data, documentation, and packages needed for learning ANOVA.

- Download the **gss2018.rda** data set from **edge.sagepub.com/harris1e**

- Access variable documentation (not a full codebook) on the GSS Data Explorer website at https://gssdataexplorer.norc.org/

- Install the following packages
  - **tidyverse**, by Hadley Wickham (https://www.rdocumentation.org/packages/tidyverse/)
  - **car**, by John Fox (https://www.rdocumentation.org/packages/car/)
  - *dunn.test*, by Alexis Dinno (https://www.rdocumentation.org/packages/dunn.test/)

7.4 Achievement 1: Exploring the data using graphics and descriptive statistics

Kiara went ahead and loaded and summarized the GSS data. Because Nancy had saved the data in an R data file with the file extension .rda, importing the data required only the `load()` command. The limitation of this, Nancy explained, was that the name of the data object resulting from `load()` was included in the .rda file, so assigning the data to a new object with a new name using `<-` would not work. The data object name would have to be changed separately if needed.

```
# load GSS rda file
load(file = "[data folder location]/data/gss2018.rda")
```

Looking under the Environment tab in R Studio, Leslie saw that Nancy was right; the data frame was automatically named `GSS` when Kiara used `load()`. Leslie thought it might be good to specify the year the data were collected by changing the data frame name to `gss.2018`. She asked Kiara if she could take over coding. Kiara agreed, and Leslie changed the name by assigning the data frame to a new object and then removing the old object with the `rm()` function.

```
# assign GSS to gss.2018
gss.2018 <- GSS

# remove GSS
rm(GSS)
```

7.4.1 DATA MANAGEMENT

Leslie opened the GSS Data Explorer website (https://gssdataexplorer.norc.org/) to determine how the variables of interest were coded. Much of the research they had reviewed was with younger adults who were in college or who were recent college graduates, which could be a unique group given their high level of education and rapid changes in technology and technology use during their lives. With this in mind, the R-Team decided to examine five variables: USETECH, HAPPY, SEX, AGE, and DEGREE. Leslie used `summary(object = gss.2018)` to take a first look at the data frame.

```
# examine the variables

summary(object = gss.2018)
##      YEAR            BALLOT          USETECH          HAPPY
## Min.    :2018    Min.    :1.000    Min.    : -1.00    Min.    :1.000
## 1st Qu.:2018    1st Qu.:1.000    1st Qu.: -1.00    1st Qu.:1.000
## Median :2018    Median :2.000    Median : 10.00    Median :2.000
## Mean    :2018    Mean    :2.002    Mean    : 48.09    Mean    :1.855
## 3rd Qu.:2018    3rd Qu.:3.000    3rd Qu.: 80.00    3rd Qu.:2.000
## Max.    :2018    Max.    :3.000    Max.    :999.00    Max.    :8.000
##      PARTYID         RINCOME          RACE             SEX
## Min.    :0.000    Min.    : 0.000    Min.    :1.000    Min.    :1.000
## 1st Qu.:1.000    1st Qu.: 0.000    1st Qu.:1.000    1st Qu.:1.000
## Median :3.000    Median : 9.000    Median :1.000    Median :2.000
## Mean    :2.968    Mean    : 7.509    Mean    :1.394    Mean    :1.552
## 3rd Qu.:5.000    3rd Qu.:12.000    3rd Qu.:2.000    3rd Qu.:2.000
## Max.    :9.000    Max.    :98.000    Max.    :3.000    Max.    :2.000
##      DEGREE           EDUC             AGE            MARITAL
## Min.    :0.000    Min.    : 0.00    Min.    :18.00    Min.    :1.00
## 1st Qu.:1.000    1st Qu.:12.00    1st Qu.:34.00    1st Qu.:1.00
## Median :1.000    Median :14.00    Median :48.00    Median :2.00
## Mean    :1.684    Mean    :13.84    Mean    :49.13    Mean    :2.67
## 3rd Qu.:3.000    3rd Qu.:16.00    3rd Qu.:63.00    3rd Qu.:5.00
## Max.    :4.000    Max.    :99.00    Max.    :99.00    Max.    :9.00
##      HRS2             HRS1           WRKSTAT           ID_
## Min.    :-1.00000    Min.    :-1.00    Min.    :1.000    Min.    : 1
## 1st Qu.:-1.00000    1st Qu.:-1.00    1st Qu.:1.000    1st Qu.: 588
## Median :-1.00000    Median :30.00    Median :2.000    Median :1176
## Mean    : 0.08017    Mean    :24.47    Mean    :2.963    Mean    :1175
## 3rd Qu.:-1.00000    3rd Qu.:40.00    3rd Qu.:5.000    3rd Qu.:1762
## Max.    :99.00000    Max.    :99.00    Max.    :9.000    Max.    :2348
##      UNHAPPY
## Min.    :0.000
## 1st Qu.:0.000
## Median :0.000
## Mean    :1.039
## 3rd Qu.:2.000
## Max.    :9.000
```

Leslie found that the USETECH variable had a minimum value of –1 and a maximum of 999. She opened the GSS Data Explorer again to look for the question used to get this variable and found the following:

During a typical week, about what percentage of your total time at work would you normally spend using different types of electronic technologies (such as computers, tablets, smart phones, cash registers, scanners, GPS devices, robotic devices, and so on)?

The responses should be between 0% and 100% of the time, so Leslie decided to recode values outside this range to be NA. In the GSS Data Explorer, she found how the variable was recorded. The Data Explorer showed that there were three values outside the logical range of 0 to 100. The three values were –1, 998, and 999 (Figure 7.1).

FIGURE 7.1 Screenshot of GSS Data Explorer 2018 USETECH variable values outside logical range

Source: https://gssdataexplorer.norc.org/variables/2840/vshow.

Using the `mutate()` command with `na_if()` from the **tidyverse** package, she recoded these two values. The `na_if()` function recodes specific values of a variable to NA for missing. In this case, Leslie made the USETECH variable NA if it had the value of –1, 998, or 999. The `na_if()` function takes two arguments, x = for the name of the variable to recode and y = for the value to change to NA.

```
# recode USETECH to valid range
library(package = "tidyverse")
gss.2018.cleaned <- gss.2018 %>%
  mutate(USETECH = na_if(x = USETECH, y = -1)) %>%
  mutate(USETECH = na_if(x = USETECH, y = 998)) %>%
  mutate(USETECH = na_if(x = USETECH, y = 999))

# check recoding
summary(object = gss.2018.cleaned$USETECH)
##    Min.  1st Qu.  Median    Mean  3rd Qu.    Max.   NA's
##    0.00    15.00   60.00   55.15    90.00  100.00    936
```

Leslie noticed the range was now 0.00 for the minimum and 100.00 for the maximum. She also noticed there were a lot of NA values for this variable.

The other variables of interest were AGE, DEGREE, SEX, and HAPPY. Leslie looked at the Data Explorer to find the AGE variable. She found three values for the AGE variable that were not ages in years:

- 89 = 89 or older
- 98 = "Don't know"
- 99 = "No answer"

She decided to leave the 89 code for 89 or older and recode the 98 and 99 responses to be NA. Instead of starting new data management code, she just added on to the existing code. She also decided that this might be a good time to select the five variables they were interested in so she wouldn't have to keep working with the larger data frame.

```r
# recode USETECH and AGE to valid ranges
gss.2018.cleaned <- gss.2018 %>%
  select(HAPPY, SEX, DEGREE, USETECH, AGE) %>%
  mutate(USETECH = na_if(x = USETECH, y = -1)) %>%
  mutate(USETECH = na_if(x = USETECH, y = 998)) %>%
  mutate(USETECH = na_if(x = USETECH, y = 999)) %>%
  mutate(AGE = na_if(x = AGE, y = 98)) %>%
  mutate(AGE = na_if(x = AGE, y = 99))

# check recoding
summary(object = gss.2018.cleaned)
##      HAPPY            SEX            DEGREE          USETECH
## Min.    :1.000   Min.    :1.000   Min.    :0.000   Min.    :  0.00
## 1st Qu.:1.000   1st Qu.:1.000   1st Qu.:1.000   1st Qu.: 15.00
## Median :2.000   Median :2.000   Median :1.000   Median : 60.00
## Mean    :1.855   Mean    :1.552   Mean    :1.684   Mean    : 55.15
## 3rd Qu.:2.000   3rd Qu.:2.000   3rd Qu.:3.000   3rd Qu.: 90.00
## Max.    :8.000   Max.    :2.000   Max.    :4.000   Max.    :100.00
##                                                    NA's    :936
##
##      AGE
## Min.    :18.00
## 1st Qu.:34.00
## Median :48.00
## Mean    :48.98
## 3rd Qu.:63.00
## Max.    :89.00
## NA's    :7
```

The three other variables, SEX, DEGREE, and HAPPY, are categorical variables. The codebook shows some categories that might be better coded as NA:

- DEGREE
  - 8 = "Don't know"
  - 9 = "No answer"
- HAPPY
  - 8 = "Don't know"
  - 9 = "No answer"
  - 0 = "Not applicable"

```
# recode variables of interest to valid ranges
gss.2018.cleaned <- gss.2018 %>%
    select(HAPPY, SEX, DEGREE, USETECH, AGE) %>%
    mutate(USETECH = na_if(x = USETECH, y = -1)) %>%
    mutate(USETECH = na_if(x = USETECH, y = 998)) %>%
    mutate(USETECH = na_if(x = USETECH, y = 999)) %>%
    mutate(AGE = na_if(x = AGE, y = 98)) %>%
    mutate(AGE = na_if(x = AGE, y = 99)) %>%
    mutate(DEGREE = na_if(x = DEGREE, y = 8)) %>%
    mutate(DEGREE = na_if(x = DEGREE, y = 9)) %>%
    mutate(HAPPY = na_if(x = HAPPY, y = 8)) %>%
    mutate(HAPPY = na_if(x = HAPPY, y = 9)) %>%
    mutate(HAPPY = na_if(x = HAPPY, y = 0))

# check recoding
summary(object = gss.2018.cleaned)
##      HAPPY           SEX           DEGREE          USETECH
## Min.   :1.000   Min.   :1.000   Min.   :0.000   Min.   :  0.00
## 1st Qu.:1.000   1st Qu.:1.000   1st Qu.:1.000   1st Qu.: 15.00
## Median :2.000   Median :2.000   Median :1.000   Median : 60.00
## Mean   :1.844   Mean   :1.552   Mean   :1.684   Mean   : 55.15
## 3rd Qu.:2.000   3rd Qu.:2.000   3rd Qu.:3.000   3rd Qu.: 90.00
## Max.   :3.000   Max.   :2.000   Max.   :4.000   Max.   :100.00
## NA's   :4                                       NA's   :936
##      AGE
## Min.   :18.00
## 1st Qu.:34.00
## Median :48.00
## Mean   :48.98
## 3rd Qu.:63.00
## Max.   :89.00
## NA's   : 7
```

The variables for analysis look like they all contain valid response options now, but every variable appears to be either numeric data type or integer data type. For DEGREE, HAPPY, and SEX, the data type should be factor. Leslie also preferred to have the category labels in her factors rather than just numbers. She reviewed the Data Explorer entry for the DEGREE variable (Figure 7.2) and the HAPPY variable (Figure 7.3) and added category labels to the data using factor() with mutate().

The factor() function has the x = argument for the name of the variable to change to a factor and the labels = argument to list the labels for each of the categories in the factor variable. Leslie made sure she listed the categories in the appropriate order for both of the variables.

FIGURE 7.2 Screenshot of GSS Data Explorer 2018 `DEGREE` variable

Survey Questions

Questions associated with this variable:
RESPONDENT'S DEGREE

Related Variables

educemp	billinged
engteach	colaff
colaffy	pubsch
homesch	cathsch
chrissch	denomsch
more...	

Year Availability

Available in 32 of 32 years total. Hover over a year to see ballot information.

72 73 74 75 76 77 78 80 82 83 84 85 86 87 88 89 90 91 93 94 96 98 00 02 04 06 08 10 12 14 16 18

Summary by Year   Showing Filtered Years ▾

Code	Label	2018
0	Lt high school	262
1	High school	1178
2	Junior college	196
3	Bachelor	465
4	Graduate	247
8	Don't know	0
9	No answer	0

FIGURE 7.3 Screenshot of GSS Data Explorer 2018 `HAPPY` variable

Survey Questions

Questions associated with this variable:
Taken all together, how would you say things are these days--would you say that you are very happy, pretty happy, or not too happy?

Related Variables

happy7	hapunhap
hapmar	abdefect
abnomore	abhlth
abpoor	abrape
absingle	abany
more...	

Year Availability

Available in 32 of 32 years total. Hover over a year to see ballot information.

72 73 74 75 76 77 78 80 82 83 84 85 86 87 88 89 90 91 93 94 96 98 00 02 04 06 08 10 12 14 16 18

Summary by Year   Showing Filtered Years ▾

Code	Label	2018
1	Very happy	701
2	Pretty happy	1307
3	Not too happy	336
8	Don't know	4
9	No answer	0
0	Not applicable	0

```
# recode variables of interest to valid ranges
gss.2018.cleaned <- gss.2018 %>%
  select(HAPPY, SEX, DEGREE, USETECH, AGE) %>%
  mutate(USETECH = na_if(x = USETECH, y = -1)) %>%
  mutate(USETECH = na_if(x = USETECH, y = 999)) %>%
  mutate(USETECH = na_if(x = USETECH, y = 998)) %>%
  mutate(AGE = na_if(x = AGE, y = 98)) %>%
  mutate(AGE = na_if(x = AGE, y = 99)) %>%
  mutate(DEGREE = na_if(x = DEGREE, y = 8)) %>%
  mutate(DEGREE = na_if(x = DEGREE, y = 9)) %>%
  mutate(HAPPY = na_if(x = HAPPY, y = 8)) %>%
  mutate(HAPPY = na_if(x = HAPPY, y = 9)) %>%
  mutate(HAPPY = na_if(x = HAPPY, y = 0)) %>%
  mutate(SEX = factor(x = SEX, labels = c("male","female"))) %>%
  mutate(DEGREE = factor(x = DEGREE, labels = c("< high school",
                                "high school", "junior college",
                                "bachelor", "graduate"))) %>%
  mutate(HAPPY = factor(x = HAPPY, labels = c("very happy",
                                "pretty happy",
                                "not too happy")))

# check recoding
summary(object = gss.2018.cleaned)
##         HAPPY            SEX             DEGREE            USETECH
## very happy   : 701   male  :1051   < high school : 262   Min.   :  0.00
## pretty happy :1304   female:1294   high school   :1175   1st Qu.: 15.00
## not too happy: 336                 junior college: 196   Median : 60.00
## NA's         :   4                 bachelor      : 465   Mean   : 55.15
##                                    graduate      : 247   3rd Qu.: 90.00
##                                                          Max.   :100.00
##                                                          NA's   :936

##      AGE
## Min.   :18.00
## 1st Qu.:34.00
## Median :48.00
## Mean   :48.98
## 3rd Qu.:63.00
## Max.   :89.00
## NA's   :  7
```

7.4.2 EXPLORATORY DATA ANALYSIS

Leslie thought their first research question for today could be, do people with higher educational degrees use technology at work more? They started with EDA and checked group means and standard deviations. To get the mean and standard deviation for each degree category, they used `group_by()` with `DEGREE` and then `summarize()` with the mean and standard deviation listed. At the last second, Leslie remembered to drop the `NA` with `drop_na()` so that `mean()` and `sd()` would work.

```
# mean and sd of USETECH by group
use.stats <- gss.2018.cleaned %>%
  drop_na(USETECH) %>%
  group_by(DEGREE) %>%
  summarize(m.techuse = mean(x = USETECH),
            sd.techuse = sd(x = USETECH))
use.stats

# A tibble: 5 x 3
## DEGREE              m.techuse      sd.techuse
## <fctr>                <dbl>          <dbl>

## < high school        24.78750       36.18543

## high school          49.61228       38.62908

## junior college       62.39453       35.22194

## bachelor             67.87346       32.05142

## graduate             68.69822       30.20457
```

Leslie and Kiara thought they might be right about tech use increasing with higher degree groups. The mean portion of time using tech at work was higher with each degree group. Leslie noticed that the standard deviations were quite large and, for the less than high school group, the standard deviation was larger than the mean. She remembered back to Section 2.6.4.1 and thought that a large spread could indicate that the distribution has a problem with kurtosis and might be platykurtic, with more observations in the tails than a normal distribution would have.

Nancy thought maybe a set of boxplots would provide more insight into how the data were distributed in each of the groups and how the groups compared to each other. She created Figure 7.4 to show the underlying data for the five groups. Leslie noticed she had used a different set of colors compared to their usual color scheme. Nancy said she didn't feel like picking out five different colors right now and so decided to use one of the palettes that came with the `scale_color_brewer()` function. She said there was a list of these palettes in the help documentation for `scale_color_brewer()`. Leslie liked the rainbow colors in the palette Nancy used and looked at the code to see what the palette was called. She saw "Spectral" as the palette name and wrote it down for later use.

```
# graph usetech (Figure 7.4)
gss.2018.cleaned %>%
  drop_na(USETECH) %>%
```

```
ggplot(aes(y = USETECH, x = DEGREE)) +
  geom_jitter(aes(color = DEGREE), alpha = .6) +
  geom_boxplot(aes(fill  = DEGREE), alpha = .4) +
  scale_fill_brewer(palette = "Spectral", guide = FALSE) +
  scale_color_brewer(palette = "Spectral", guide = FALSE) +
  theme_minimal() +
  labs(x = "Highest educational attainment",
       y = "Percent of time spent using technology")
```

Leslie noticed that a lot of people in the first two categories had selected 0% of their time at work is spent using technology. She also noted that for all but the first category, there were a lot of people who selected 100% of their time at work is spent using technology. Leslie asked Kiara about these observations and how they might influence the results. Kiara explained that there are terms for measures where people are at the very top or very bottom of the range. When there are a lot of observations at the very bottom of a range, this is called a *floor effect*, while a lot of observations at the top of a range is called a *ceiling effect*.

Leslie asked if they could still use ANOVA when there are floor and ceiling effects. Kiara said yes, but with some caution. She explained that when there are floor or ceiling effects, this often means that the variation in a measure is limited by its range. Since ANOVA is an analysis of *variance,* which examines central tendency and variation together, the limitations of floor and ceiling effects can result in not finding differences when there are differences.

Kiara added that one common reason for ceiling and floor effects is when the underlying measure has a wider range than what is measured. In the case of technology use, the range of 0% to 100% of the time is as wide as it can be, so the observations at the ceiling and floor of this measure are just reflecting very low and very high levels of technology use at work among many of the people in the sample.

FIGURE 7.4 Distribution of work time spent using technology by educational attainment

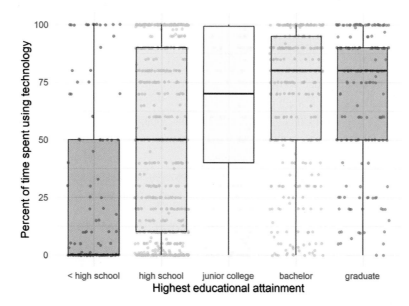

7.4.3 ACHIEVEMENT 1: CHECK YOUR UNDERSTANDING

Describe the different parts of a boxplot: the upper and lower bounds of the box, the middle line through the box, and the whiskers.

7.5 Achievement 2: Understanding and conducting one-way ANOVA

The *t*-tests were great for comparing two means, and Leslie wondered if they could just use the *t*-tests to compare all the means for the five DEGREE variable groups. She thought she could just do a *t*-test for each pair of means. This would result in *t*-tests to compare mean tech use for those with less than high school to high school, less than high school to junior college, and so on. Kiara explained that conducting multiple tests on the same variables is not a great idea given that each statistical test comes with some probability that what is going on in the sample is not a good representation of what is happening in the population.

For example, with the first independent-samples *t*-test from the prior chapter, the probability that the two group means were the same in the populations the samples came from was very small, but it was not zero (see Section 6.6.4). If the threshold for the *p*-value to indicate statistical significance is .05, there can be up to a 5% probability that rejecting the null hypothesis is an error. Rejecting the null hypothesis when it is true is called a *Type I error* (Box 7.1).

7.1 Leslie's stats stuff: Type I and Type II errors

Leslie summarized the four possible outcomes to a statistical test:

	In reality, the null hypothesis is . . .	
	True	False
Null hypothesis test		
Failed to reject	True	Type II error (β)
Rejected	Type I error (α)	True

A *Type II error*, also called β, occurs when there is a relationship but the study did not detect it. A Type I error, also called α, is when there is no relationship but the study detects one. The α for Type I error is also the threshold set for statistical significance. The threshold for statistical significance is the amount of uncertainty tolerated in concluding whether or not a result is statistically significant. If α is .05, this is a willingness to risk a 5% chance of making a Type I error of rejecting the null hypothesis when it should be retained. Increasing sample size and decreasing the threshold for statistical significance (α) can aid in decreasing Type I and II errors.

Type I and II errors are related to the concept of *statistical power*. The power of a statistical test is the probability that the results of the test are not a Type II error. Leslie asked if power could be described as rejecting the null hypothesis when it should be rejected. Kiara agreed that this is another way to think about it. Or, she explained, power is the probability of finding a relationship when there is a relationship.

With five groups in the degree variable, comparing each pair with a *t*-test (i.e., conducting *pairwise comparisons*) would result in 10 *t*-tests. If each *t*-test had a *p*-value threshold of .05 for statistical significance, the probability of at least one Type I error is fairly high. The formula for this probability of a Type I error when there are multiple comparisons is shown in Equation (7.1).

$$\alpha_f = 1 - (1 - \alpha_i)^c \tag{7.1}$$

Where α_f is the *familywise* Type I error rate, α_i is the individual alpha set as the statistical significance threshold, and c is the number of comparisons. The formula for computing c is $\dfrac{k(k-1)}{2}$, where k is the total number of groups.

For a five-group DEGREE variable with $\alpha = .05$ for each pairwise comparison, the familywise α_f would be the .40 computed in Equation (7.2).

$$\alpha_f = 1 - (1 - .05_i)^{10} = .40 \tag{7.2}$$

With 10 pairwise comparisons, the familywise α_f indicated there would be a 40% probability of making a Type I error. To control this error rate, and for efficiency, use a single ANOVA test instead of 10 *t*-tests. ANOVA is useful for testing whether three or more means are equal. It can be used with two means, but the *t*-test is preferable because it is more straightforward.

7.5.1 THE *F* TEST STATISTIC FOR ANOVA

To compare mean technology use time across the five degree categories, Nancy introduced Leslie to one of the ANOVA functions in R, oneway.test(). The oneway.test() function is in the stats library that loads with base R, so there are no new packages to install and load. The oneway.test() function has several arguments. The first argument is formula =, where the formula for testing would be entered. The formula for oneway.test() places the continuous variable first, then the tilde, then the categorical variable. The formula would be continuous ~ categorical. In this case, with the USETECH and DEGREE variables, the formula is USETECH ~ DEGREE.

After the formula, the data frame name is entered for the data = argument, and the final argument is var.equal =, which refers to one of the assumptions of ANOVA that Kiara assured Leslie they would discuss later (Section 7.9). For now, Kiara recommended using var.equal = TRUE. Based on these instructions, Leslie wrote the ANOVA code.

```
# mean tech use percent by degree groups
techuse.by.deg <- oneway.test(formula = USETECH ~ DEGREE,
                              data = gss.2018.cleaned,
                              var.equal = TRUE)
techuse.by.deg
##
##   One-way analysis of means
##
## data:  USETECH and DEGREE
## F = 43.304, num df = 4, denom df = 1404, p-value < 2.2e-16
```

The output showed a couple of familiar statistics and one new one, the *F*-statistic. The **F-*statistic*** is a ratio where the variation *between* the groups is compared to the variation *within* the groups. The

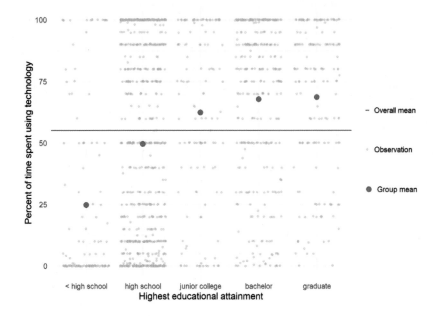

between-group variation is in the numerator to calculate F, while the within-group variation is in the denominator. Leslie was confused by this, so Kiara suggested modifying the boxplot to help think it through. Nancy removed the boxes and added a horizontal line across the entire plot to show the overall mean of USETECH. She also added points to show mean of USETECH for each group (Figure 7.5).

Leslie noticed that the group mean for the junior college group was higher than the overall mean. That is, the mean percentage of time people use technology in this group is higher than the overall mean percentage of time people use technology. For each group, the group mean does a better job than the overall mean of explaining tech use *for that group*. The difference between the group mean and the overall mean is *how much better* the group mean is at representing the data in the group. This difference is used to compute the numerator of the F-statistic in Equation (7.3):

$$F = \frac{\frac{\sum_{j=1}^{k} n_j (\bar{y}_j - \bar{y})^2}{k-1}}{\frac{\sum_{j=1}^{k} \sum_{i=1}^{n} (y_{ij} - \bar{y}_j)^2}{n-k}} \tag{7.3}$$

where y represents the continuous variable, n represents number of observations, k represents the number of groups, i stands for an observation, and j stands for a group. In the numerator, $\bar{y}_j$ is the mean of the continuous variable for each group, and $\bar{y}$ is the overall or ***grand mean*** of the continuous variable. Subtracting the grand mean from the group mean results in the difference between the group and the overall sample. The difference between the grand mean and the group mean can be positive or negative and so is squared for the sum to more accurately represent the total of the differences. This squared value is then multiplied by n_j or the number of people in the group and divided by $k - 1$, where k is the number of groups. This results in a numerator that quantifies the difference between the group means and grand mean for all the participants in the sample. Leslie asked if there was a difference between a mean denoted like m_x and a mean denoted like $\bar{x}$. Nancy said these are equivalent and that people tend to use

m_x because many word processing programs cannot easily add a line over a letter like $\bar{x}$. Nancy explained that she tends to use whichever version makes the equation she is working on easier to understand.

The denominator sums the squared difference between each individual observation y_{ij} and the mean of the individual's group, quantifying how far the individuals in the group are from the mean of the group. This is divided by the number of individuals in the whole sample minus the number of groups.

Thus, the numerator quantifies the variation between the group means and the grand mean, while the denominator quantifies the variation between the individual values and the group means. Equation (7.3) could be simplified to Equation (7.4).

$$F = \frac{between\text{-}group\ variability}{within\text{-}group\ variability} \tag{7.4}$$

Because the difference between the group means and the grand mean represents the variability that the group mean explains for the group, the numerator is also sometimes referred to as *explained variance*. The denominator sums the distances between the observations and their group mean, which is the variability that the group mean cannot explain. The denominator is sometimes called *unexplained variance*. The F-statistic, then, could be referred to as a ratio of explained to unexplained variance. That is, how much of the variability in the outcome does the model explain compared to how much it leaves unexplained? The larger the F-statistic, the more the model has explained compared to what it has left unexplained.

Leslie noticed that some observations are clearly closer to the overall mean than they are to the group mean for all of the groups. Kiara explained that this is true for some observations, but the differences between each observed value and the group mean added together will be a smaller number than the differences between each observed value and the overall mean.

True to the analysis of variance name, the F-statistic can also be represented as the ratio of the variance between the groups to the variance within the groups, as in Equation (7.5).

$$F = \frac{s_b^2}{s_w^2} \tag{7.5}$$

Once the F-statistic is computed, the probability of finding an F-statistic at least as big as the one computed is determined by the **F-*distribution***. Like n and p were the parameters for the binomial distribution, m and s were the parameters for the normal distribution, and df was the parameter for chi-squared, the F-distribution also has parameters that define its shape. For F, the parameters are the degrees of freedom for the numerator and the degrees of freedom for the denominator in Equation (7.3). These values are $df_{numerator} = k - 1$ and $df_{denominator} = n - k$, where k is the number of groups and n is the sample size.

Nancy mentioned that the F-distribution may remind Leslie of the chi-squared distribution since they are both right-skewed and do not go below zero. Nancy found a tutorial (https://rpubs.com/monoboy/f-test) with instructions for plotting examples of the F-distribution and made a graph so they could examine a few F-distributions to see how the df influenced its shape (Figure 7.6).

The shape of the F-distribution changed the most with the numerator degrees of freedom. The denominator changing from 25 to 2,000 made very little difference. Nancy clarified that even though the four lines were fairly close together, there was definitely a difference in the area under the curve in the right tail of the distribution.

The ANOVA comparing mean time using technology across categories of degree (`techuse.by.deg` object) had an F-statistic of 43.30 from a distribution with 4 and 1404 degrees of freedom. Nancy graphed the F-distribution for these degrees of freedom (Figure 7.7).

FIGURE 7.6 *F*-distribution examples

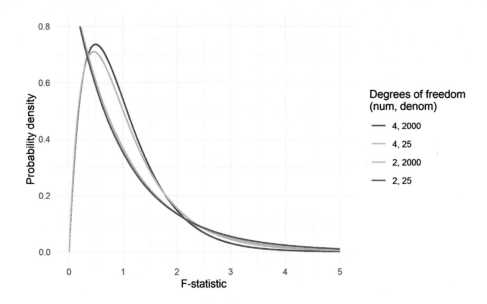

FIGURE 7.7 *F*-distribution for the technology use by degree ANOVA (*df* = 4 and 1404)

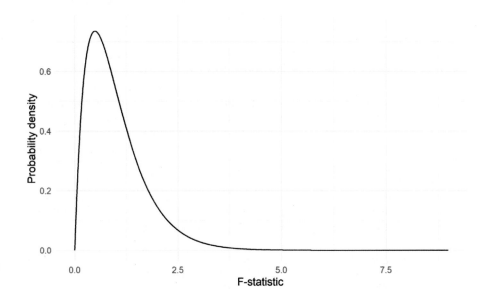

The *F*-distribution in Figure 7.7 suggested the *F*-statistic of 43.30 was far to the right in the tail of the distribution. The probability of an *F*-statistic this large or larger if the null were true was reported in the output as $< 2.2e-16$, which is $< .001$. With a *p*-value this tiny, the *F*-statistic would be considered statistically significant. Kiara suggested going through the steps of NHST to organize the analyses more clearly.

7.5.1.1 NHST FOR ANOVA

7.5.1.1.1 NHST Step 1: Write the null and alternate hypotheses

H0: The mean time spent on technology use is equal across degree groups.

HA: The mean time spent on technology use is not equal across degree groups.

7.5.1.1.2 NHST Step 2: Compute the test statistic   The *F*-statistic is 43.3.

```
# print the results of the ANOVA
techuse.by.deg
##
##   One-way analysis of means
##
## data:  USETECH and DEGREE
## F = 43.304, num df = 4, denom df = 1404, p-value < 2.2e-16
```

7.5.1.1.3 NHST Step 3: Calculate the probability that your test statistic is at least as big as it is if there is no relationship (i.e., the null is true)   The *p*-value is $< 2.2e-16$, which is very small. The value of an *F*-statistic being at least this large happens a tiny percentage of the time when the null hypothesis is true.

7.5.1.1.4 NHST Steps 4 and 5: Interpret the probability and write a conclusion   With a *p*-value $< .001$, the ANOVA indicates that there is likely a difference among the means of time spent using technology based on degree. With Kiara's guidance, Leslie wrote out the ANOVA interpretation:

The mean time spent on technology use was significantly different across degree groups [$F(4, 1404)$ = 43.3; $p < .05$], indicating that these groups likely came from a population with different mean time spent on technology use by educational attainment. The highest mean was the percent of time used for technology by those with graduate degrees. The lowest mean was the percent of time used for technology by those with less than a high school diploma.

7.5.2 ACHIEVEMENT 2: CHECK YOUR UNDERSTANDING

Analysis of variance, or ANOVA, is useful for which scenario?

- Comparing the means for three or more groups
- Comparing a single mean to a population or hypothesized value
- Transforming a categorical variable into a continuous variable
- Examining the relationship between two categorical variables

7.6 Achievement 3: Choosing and using post hoc tests and contrasts

Leslie asked Kiara if they could report that the graduate degree group had a significantly higher mean time spent using technology than did the other groups. Kiara explained that ANOVA is an omnibus test, which means it identifies whether there are any differences, but doesn't give any information about what is driving the significant results. Nancy reminded Leslie that another example of an omnibus test was the chi-squared test. While they used chi-squared to determine whether a relationship was statistically significant, they had to examine standardized residuals or an odds ratio to make any claims about what the relationship was. Nancy mentioned that there are two main ways to determine where significant differences among groups are following a significant omnibus test:

- Post hoc tests
- Planned contrasts

The two methods are both useful for examining differences among means. The distinction between post hoc tests and planned contrasts is that post hoc tests examine each pair of means to determine which means are the most different from each other and are therefore driving the statistically significant results, whereas planned contrasts compare specified subsets of means or groups of means. Leslie was confused by the planned contrasts idea. Kiara thought examples of post hoc tests and planned contrasts would clarify the difference.

7.6.1 POST HOC TESTS

7.6.1.1 BONFERRONI

There are several different types of post hoc tests, and one of the more commonly used is the Bonferroni post hoc test. The *Bonferroni post hoc test* is a pairwise test that conducts a *t*-test for each pair of means but adjusts the threshold for statistical significance to ensure that there is a small enough risk of Type I error.

Nancy slid the laptop over and wrote a line of code to conduct the Bonferroni post hoc tests with the `pairwise.t.test()` function. The function has several arguments, such as x = for the continuous variable; g = for the grouping or categorical variable; and the *p*-value adjustment, p.adj =, which can be set as bonf for Bonferroni.

```
# find differences in mean tech use by degree groups
bonf.tech.by.deg <- pairwise.t.test(x = gss.2018.cleaned$USETECH,
                                    g = gss.2018.cleaned$DEGREE,
                                    p.adj = "bonf")
bonf.tech.by.deg
## Pairwise comparisons using t tests with pooled SD

## data:  gss.2018.cleaned$USETECH and gss.2018.cleaned$DEGREE
```

```
##                       < high school   high school   junior college   bachelor
## high school     3.8e-11              -                -                  -
## junior college  2.8e-15         0.0022                -                  -
## bachelor        < 2e-16         8.0e-13           1.0000                  -
## graduate        < 2e-16         7.3e-09           1.0000             1.0000

## P value adjustment method: bonferroni
```

The output is different from previous statistical testing. Instead of a test statistic like t or F, the output is a matrix of p-values. While the calculation of the t-statistic for each pair of groups is the same as other independent-samples t-tests, the corresponding p-value is adjusted to correct for the multiple statistical tests that could lead to an inflated Type I error.

Specifically, the Bonferroni adjustment multiplies each p-value from each t-test by the overall number of t-tests conducted. Leslie remembered that there were 10 pairwise comparisons, so these p-values have been multiplied by 10. Higher p-values will not reach the threshold for statistical significance as often. Leslie noticed that a few of the resulting p-values were 1.0000. Kiara explained that the p-value cannot be over 1, so for p-values that are over 1 when adjusted by the multiplication, they are rounded to exactly 1.

The adjusted p-values for seven of the t-tests fall below .05 and so indicate that the difference in mean time using technology between two groups is statistically significant. There are significant differences in mean time between less than high school and all of the other groups ($p < .05$); likewise, there are significant differences in mean time using technology between high school and all other groups. There are no significant differences among the means of the three college groups. Kiara suggested that reporting the differences might be more meaningful with the actual means included. She reprinted the `use.stats` object.

```
# mean age by groups
use.stats
# A tibble: 5 x 3
## DEGREE            m.techuse     sd.techuse
## <fctr>                <dbl>          <dbl>

## < high school          24.8           36.2

## high school            49.6           38.6

## junior college         62.4           35.2

## bachelor               67.9           32.1

## graduate               68.7           30.2
```

Leslie summarized the statistically significant differences identified in the Bonferroni post hoc test:

Mean percentage of time using technology at work was statistically significantly ($p < .05$) *lower* for people with less educational attainment than a high school diploma ($m = 24.8$) compared to each of the other groups, where the mean percentage of time using technology ranged from 49.6 to 68.7.

7.6.1.2 TUKEY'S HONESTLY SIGNIFICANT DIFFERENCE

Kiara advised Leslie that the Bonferroni post hoc test is generally considered a very conservative post hoc test that only identifies the largest differences between means as statistically significant. This might be useful sometimes, but not always. When a less strict test will work, Kiara recommended using *Tukey's Honestly Significant Difference* (HSD) test. Tukey's HSD post hoc test is a modified *t*-test with the test statistic, *q*, calculated using Equation (7.6).

$$q = \frac{m_1 - m_2}{se} \qquad (7.6)$$

Kiara explained that the *q* test statistic formula is the same as some versions of *t*, but the *q*-distribution is different from the *t*-distribution, raising the critical value necessary to reach statistical significance. Even with the same test statistic, it is more difficult to reach statistical significance with a Tukey's HSD *q*-statistic compared to a *t*-test.

Unfortunately, Nancy explained, the `TukeyHSD()` function does not work well with the `oneway.test()` output from earlier, so the entire ANOVA model has to be reestimated. The `aov()` function works and takes similar arguments to the `oneway.test()` function, so nesting the `aov()` is one way to go. Leslie did not understand what Nancy meant by *nesting* the function. Nancy created a short demonstration of how the same process might work with nested compared to non-nested functions for Leslie to review later (Box 7.2). Nancy demonstrated the concept by showing the `aov()` function with two arguments, `formula =` and `data =`. She then explained that the `aov()` code was then entered in the parentheses of the `TukeyHSD()` function, like this:

```
# Tukey's post hoc test for tech.by.deg
tukey.tech.by.deg <- TukeyHSD(x = aov(formula = USETECH ~ DEGREE,
                                      data = gss.2018.cleaned))

tukey.tech.by.deg
##     Tukey multiple comparisons of means
##       95% family-wise confidence level
##
## Fit: aov(formula = USETECH ~ DEGREE, data = gss.2018.cleaned)
##
## $DEGREE
##                                    diff        lwr       upr      p adj
## high school-< high school     24.8247754  15.145211  34.50434  0.0000000
## junior college-< high school  37.6070312  25.201887  50.01218  0.0000000
## bachelor-< high school        43.0859568  32.653180  53.51873  0.0000000
## graduate-< high school        43.9107249  32.256416  55.56503  0.0000000
## junior college-high school    12.7822558   3.362603  22.20191  0.0020352
## bachelor-high school          18.2611813  11.651711  24.87065  0.0000000
## graduate-high school          19.0859494  10.679691  27.49221  0.0000000
## bachelor-junior college        5.4789255  -4.713166  15.67102  0.5833665
## graduate-junior college        6.3036936  -5.135659  17.74305  0.5592907
## graduate-bachelor              0.8247681  -8.438819  10.08835  0.9992282
```

7.2 Nancy's fancy code: Nested and non-nested code

Nancy explained that sometimes it was more efficient, although not always more clear, to nest R functions inside each other. Nested functions work from the inside to the outside, so if Function A is nested inside Function B, Function A will run first, and the results of Function A will be passed on to Function B. For example, there are nested and non-nested ways to compute `TukeyHSD()` after a significant ANOVA result.

7.2.1 Non-nested

```
# run the ANOVA and get a new object
anova.for.Tukey <- aov(formula = USETECH ~ DEGREE,
                       data = gss.2018.cleaned)

# use the newly created ANOVA object in TukeyHSD
tukey.tech.by.deg <- TukeyHSD(x = anova.for.Tukey)
tukey.tech.by.deg
##    Tukey multiple comparisons of means
##      95% family-wise confidence level

## Fit: aov(formula = USETECH ~ DEGREE, data = gss.2018.cleaned)

## $DEGREE
##                                diff        lwr      upr    p adj
## high school-< high school      24.8247754  15.145211 34.50434 0.0000000
## junior college-< high school   37.6070312  25.201887 50.01218 0.0000000
## bachelor-< high school         43.0859568  32.653180 53.51873 0.0000000
## graduate-< high school         43.9107249  32.256416 55.56503 0.0000000
## junior college-high school     12.7822558   3.362603 22.20191 0.0020352
## bachelor-high school           18.2611813  11.651711 24.87065 0.0000000
## graduate-high school           19.0859494  10.679691 27.49221 0.0000000
## bachelor-junior college         5.4789255  -4.713166 15.67102 0.5833665
## graduate-junior college         6.3036936  -5.135659 17.74305 0.5592907
## graduate-bachelor               0.8247681  -8.438819 10.08835 0.9992282
```

7.2.2 Nested

Put the ANOVA analysis inside the `TukeyHSD()` function to do the ANOVA first and then pass its results directly to `TukeyHSD()`.

(Continued)

(Continued)

```
# Tukey's post hoc test for tech.by.deg
tukey.tech.by.deg <- TukeyHSD(x = aov(formula = USETECH ~ DEGREE,
                                      data = gss.2018.cleaned))

tukey.tech.by.deg
##  Tukey multiple comparisons of means
##    95% family-wise confidence level

## Fit: aov(formula = USETECH ~ DEGREE, data = gss.2018.cleaned)

## $DEGREE
##                                  diff       lwr       upr      p adj
## high school-< high school    24.8247754 15.145211 34.50434 0.0000000
## junior college-< high school 37.6070312 25.201887 50.01218 0.0000000
## bachelor-< high school       43.0859568 32.653180 53.51873 0.0000000
## graduate-< high school       43.9107249 32.256416 55.56503 0.0000000
## junior college-high school   12.7822558  3.362603 22.20191 0.0020352
## bachelor-high school         18.2611813 11.651711 24.87065 0.0000000
## graduate-high school         19.0859494 10.679691 27.49221 0.0000000
## bachelor-junior college       5.4789255 -4.713166 15.67102 0.5833665
## graduate-junior college       6.3036936 -5.135659 17.74305 0.5592907
## graduate-bachelor             0.8247681 -8.438819 10.08835 0.9992282
```

The nested version is less code overall, but if the ANOVA object is useful for other reasons, the non-nested option may be more efficient. Both versions return the same results; it just depends on the purpose of the code which is more useful.

Comparing these results to the Bonferroni test results above, the means that were statistically significantly different with Bonferroni were also statistically significantly different with Tukey's HSD. However, the p-values were lower with Tukey's HSD. For example, the p-value for the comparison of bachelor to junior college was 1 with the Bonferroni post hoc test but 0.58 with Tukey's HSD. Two additional comparisons were significant with the Tukey's HSD; the high school mean was different from the means for bachelor and graduate.

Leslie asked about the columns in the Tukey's HSD output. Kiara explained that the first column called "diff" is the difference between the means in the sample, while the second and third columns, "lwr" and "upr," are the lower and upper bounds of a confidence interval around the "diff" value. For example, the difference in time spent on technology between participants who graduated high school and those with less than high school is 24.82% in the sample. In the population that this sample came from, the difference in time spent on technology is likely between 15.15% and 34.50%.

Leslie combined the F-test results and the Bonferroni post hoc results and wrote a single interpretation:

The mean time spent on technology use was significantly different across education groups [$F(4, 1404) = 43.3$; $p < .05$], indicating that these groups likely came from a population with different mean time spent on technology use depending on educational attainment. The highest mean was 68.7% of time used for technology for those with graduate degrees. The lowest mean was 24.8% of the time for those with less than a high school diploma. Mean percentage of time using technology was statistically significantly ($p < .05$) *lower* for people with less than a high school diploma ($m = 24.8$) compared to each of the other groups where the mean percentage of time using technology ranged from 49.6 to 68.7.

7.6.2 PLANNED COMPARISONS

Kiara enthusiastically explained that, rather than comparing every group to every other group, it might be more interesting to compare all the college groups as a whole to the other groups, or the two lowest groups to the two highest groups. Bonferroni and Tukey's HSD are not designed to group the groups together and compare these means, but this can be accomplished using planned comparisons. Kiara said that *planned comparisons* could be used to compare one mean to another mean, two means to one mean, or really any subset of means to any other subset of means.

Planned comparisons are computed by developing *contrasts* that specify which means to compare to which other means. For example, to compare all the college groups to the high school group, the contrast would omit the less than high school group and compare the mean for everyone in the high school group to the mean of the combined three college groups: junior college, bachelor, and graduate. Nancy printed the categories of DEGREE as a reminder.

```
# look at the levels of education variable
levels(x = gss.2018.cleaned$DEGREE)
## [1] "< high school"  "high school"  "junior college" "bachelor"  "graduate"
```

Kiara explained that the order of the factor variable is the exact order that should be used in the contrast, and there are a few rules to keep in mind:

- A contrast is a group of numbers used to group categories.

- The categories grouped together should all be represented by the same number in the contrast.

- The numbers in the contrast should all add to zero.

- Any category not included in the contrast should be represented by a zero.

Comparing the second level of the factor, high school, with the third, fourth, and fifth levels combined could be written as follows:

- 0 (do not include)

- 3 (high school)

- –1 (junior college)

- –1 (bachelor)

- –1 (graduate)

The three categories represented by –1 will be grouped together because they are all represented by the same number. Adding 0 + 3 + –1 + –1 + –1 is equal to zero. The first step is to enter the contrast into R as a vector. Nancy went ahead with the code.

```
# put the contrast in a vector
contrast1 <- c(0, 3, -1, -1, -1)
```

Kiara suggested they look in the Environment pane, where they saw the new `contrast1` vector in the list of values. The next step was to assign `contrast1` to the DEGREE variable using the `contrasts()` function and the `<-` to assign.

```
# link the contrast to the categorical variable using contrasts()
contrasts(x = gss.2018.cleaned$DEGREE) <- contrast1
```

Kiara explained they could use `str()` to examine the structure of DEGREE and see the contrast.

```
# view the structure of the DEGREE variable with contrast
str(object = gss.2018.cleaned$DEGREE)
## Factor w/ 5 levels "< high school",..: 3 2 4 4 5 4 2 2 1 2 ...
## - attr(*, "contrasts")= num [1:5, 1:4] 0 3 -1 -1 -1 ...
##   ..- attr(*, "dimnames")=List of 2
##   .. ..$ : chr [1:5] "< high school" "high school" "junior college"
## "bachelor" ...
##   .. ..$ : NULL
```

The second row of the `str()` output showed the contrast, which was one of the attributes of the DEGREE variable now. Kiara said they were ready to rerun the ANOVA using `aov()`. Once the model has been estimated, the model object can be entered into `summary.aov()` along with information about the contrast. Nancy thought it was easier to show the team than to explain the features of `summary.aov()`, so she wrote some code to demonstrate.

```
# re-run the model using aov()
techuse.by.deg.aov <- aov(formula = USETECH ~ DEGREE,
            data = gss.2018.cleaned)

# apply the contrasts to the anova object techuse.by.deg.aov
# give the contrast a good descriptive name of "high school vs. all
college"
tech.by.deg.contr <- summary.aov(object = techuse.by.deg.aov,
                        split = list(DEGREE = list("high
                        school vs. all college" = 1)))
```

```
tech.by.deg.contr
##                                          Df    Sum Sq  Mean Sq  F value  Pr(>F)
## DEGREE                                    4    221301   55325    43.30    < 2e-16 ***
## DEGREE: high school vs. all college       1     64411   64411    50.41    1.97e-12 ***
## Residuals                              1404   1793757    1278
## ---
## Signif. codes: 0 '***' 0.001 '**' 0.01 '*' 0.05 '.' 0.1 ' ' 1
## 936 observations deleted due to missingness
```

The output showed that mean technology use for those who finished high school was statistically significantly different from mean technology use for the three college groups combined [$F(1, 1404) =$ 50.41; $p < .001$].

Leslie was interested in looking at the means being compared with this contrast so she could understand more of what was happening. She decided to create a graph that showed the mean technology use time for the high school group and a combined mean technology use time for the three college groups. To create the graph, Leslie used `mutate()` on the `DEGREE` variable so it grouped the three college groups into a single group by recoding all three categories into one category called "all college." Leslie examined the means first.

```
# recode and compute the means for high school and college groups
gss.2018.cleaned %>%
  mutate(DEGREE = factor(x = DEGREE,
                  labels = c("< high school",
                  "high school", "all college",
                  "all college", "all college"))) %>%
  group_by(DEGREE) %>%
  summarize(m.techuse = mean(x = USETECH, na.rm = T),
            sd.techuse = sd(x = USETECH, na.rm = T))
# A tibble: 3 x 3
## DEGREE                 m.techuse        sd.techuse
## <fctr>                    <dbl>             <dbl>
## < high school          24.78750          36.18543
## high school            49.61228          38.62908
## all college            66.96860          32.28123
```

The difference between the mean technology use time for high school ($m = 49.61$) compared to all college groups combined ($m = 66.97$) is pretty large; Figure 7.8 might help to add more context.

```
# add filter and ggplot (Figure 7.8)
gss.2018.cleaned %>%
  mutate(DEGREE = factor(x = DEGREE, labels = c("< high school",
                                    "high school", "all college",
                                    "all college", "all
college"))) %>%
  filter(DEGREE == "high school" | DEGREE == "all college") %>%
  ggplot(aes(y = USETECH, x = DEGREE, fill = DEGREE, color = DEGREE)) +
  geom_boxplot(alpha = .4) +
  geom_jitter(alpha = .6) +
  scale_fill_manual(values = c("gray70", "#7463AC"), guide = FALSE) +
  scale_color_manual(values = c("gray70", "#7463AC"), guide = FALSE) +
  theme_minimal() +
  labs(x = "Educational attainment", y = "Percent of time spent using technology")
```

It was clear to Leslie that these means were different from each other. She thought the less than high school group was probably also different from the combined college groups. Nancy said they could test both those ideas together using planned comparisons by writing some fancy code.

```
# less than HS v. all college contrast
contrast2 <- c(3, 0, -1, -1, -1)

# bind the two contrasts together into a matrix
cons <- cbind(contrast1, contrast2)
# connect the matrix with the factor variable
contrasts(x = gss.2018.cleaned$DEGREE) <- cons

# estimate the ANOVA with contrasts
tech.by.deg.contr <- summary.aov(object = techuse.by.deg.aov,
                    split =
                  list(DEGREE =
                    list("high school vs. all college" = 1,
                         "<high school vs. all college" = 2)))
tech.by.deg.contr
```
```
##                                    Df   Sum Sq   Mean Sq  F value   Pr(>F)
## DEGREE                              4   221301    55325    43.30   < 2e-16  ***
##   DEGREE: high school vs. all college  1    64411    64411    50.41   1.97e-12 ***
##   DEGREE: < high school vs. all college  1    20188    20188    15.80   7.39e-05 ***
## Residuals                          1404  1793757    1278
## ---
## Signif. codes:  0 '***' 0.001 '**' 0.01 '*' 0.05 '.' 0.1 ' ' 1
## 936 observations deleted due to missingness
```

FIGURE 7.8 Distribution of time using technology at work by educational attainment for contrast

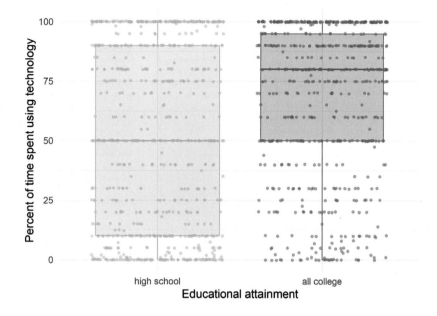

Leslie followed along with the coding and read the comments to be sure she understood the process. She noticed that Nancy first made the new contrast, `contrast2`, then combined it with `contrast1` using `cbind()` into a matrix called `cons`. Then Nancy assigned the two contrasts to `DEGREE` and put them into the `summary.aov()` function. Leslie decided to graph the data again to better understand both contrasts. There was a clear visual difference between the high school group and the all college combined group and also between the less than high school group and the all college combined group (Figure 7.9).

```
# recode to group the college groups
gss.2018.cleaned %>%
  mutate(DEGREE = factor(x = DEGREE,
                    labels = c("< high school",
                          "high school", "all college",
                          "all college", "all college"))) %>%
  ggplot(aes(y = USETECH, x = DEGREE)) +
  geom_boxplot(aes(fill    = DEGREE), alpha = .4) +
  geom_jitter(aes(color   = DEGREE), alpha = .6) +
  scale_fill_manual(values = c("gray70","#7463AC","dodgerblue2"),
                guide = FALSE) +
  scale_color_manual(values = c("gray70","#7463AC","dodgerblue2"),
                guide = FALSE) +
  theme_minimal() +
  labs(x = "Educational attainment",
      y = "Percent of time spent using technology")
```

FIGURE 7.9 Distribution of tech use at work by degree for contrast comparing all college groups combined to each of the other groups

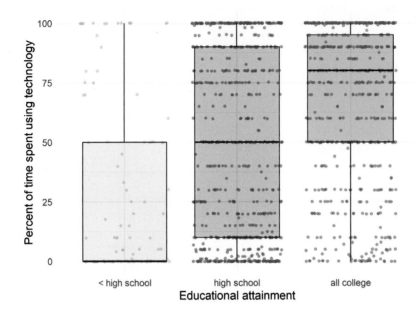

Leslie was interested in how many contrasts could be done and also how all these statistical comparisons might be inflating the Type I error that they discussed with the post hoc tests. Kiara explained that, in addition to each comparison comparing two things and each comparison adding to zero, the planned comparisons as a group should isolate each group (e.g., the high school group) *only one time*. This ensures that the contrasts are independent of each other since the variance for each group is only used by itself in a statistical comparison one time. Because each group is isolated one time, the total maximum number of contrasts allowable is one less than the number of groups. Leslie wanted to make sure she had this right and summarized the important characteristics of contrasts.

- Contrast values add to zero.
- Each contrast compares two groups.
- Each category is only isolated one time.
- The maximum number of contrasts is one less than the number of categories.

Kiara confirmed that these are the characteristics of contrasts. She explained that two things would ensure you are following all the rules:

1. Add up each contrast to make sure it adds to zero.
2. Multiply each value in each contrast with the corresponding values in the other contrasts and add up the products; this should also add to zero.

If each contrast adds to zero and the sum of the products across contrasts adds to zero, then the set of contrasts follows the rules for independence and can be used to understand differences among means and groups of means.

Leslie noticed that they didn't have a full set of contrasts that fit these criteria. So far they only had two contrasts. With five total degree groups, there should be four contrasts in the list. Leslie thought about the interesting comparisons they could do and came up with an idea for four comparisons:

- < high school versus high school and junior college
- high school versus all three college groups
- junior college versus bachelor's and graduate degrees (i.e., more college)
- bachelor's versus graduate degree

She created the set of four contrasts that corresponded to these ideas:

```
# contrasts for ANOVA of tech time by degree
c1 <- c(2, -1, -1,  0,  0)
c2 <- c(0,  3, -1, -1, -1)
c3 <- c(0,  0,  2, -1, -1)
c4 <- c(0,  0,  0, -1,  1)

# bind the contrasts into a matrix
conts <- cbind(c1, c2, c3, c4)

conts
##      c1 c2 c3 c4
## [1,]  2  0  0  0
## [2,] -1  3  0  0
## [3,] -1 -1  2  0
## [4,]  0 -1 -1 -1
## [5,]  0 -1 -1  1
```

Leslie looked at the matrix and noticed that her vectors were now columns rather than rows. She started to check the values. The first column was the first contrast. When she added up $2 + -1 + -1 + 0 + 0$, it equaled zero. She added up each of the other three columns and they were all equal to zero, so the first requirement was met. The second requirement was more complicated. She had to multiply each value across the four contrasts. The first value for the first contrast was 2, the first value of the second contrast was 0, the first value of the third contrast was 0, and the first value of the fourth contrast was also 0. Multiply $2 \times 0 \times 0 \times 0 = 0$. The product of the second set of values across the four contrasts is $-1 \times 3 \times 0 \times 0 = 0$. The product of the third set of values is $-1 \times -1 \times 2 \times 0 = 0$, and that of the fourth set of values is $0 \times -1 \times -1 \times -1 = 0$. Finally, the product across the fifth set of values in the contrasts is $0 \times -1 \times -1 \times 1 = 0$. Adding all these products together results in $0 + 0 + 0 + 0 + 0 = 0$, so the second requirement is met. The set of contrasts is independent and ready to use.

```
# connect the matrix with the factor variable
contrasts(x = gss.2018.cleaned$DEGREE) <- conts

# estimate the ANOVA with 4 independent contrasts
tech.by.deg.contr <-
```

```
summary.aov(object = techuse.by.deg.aov,
          split =
              list(DEGREE =
                  list("< high school vs. high school & jr college" = 1,
                      "high school vs. all college" = 2,
                      "jr college vs. bach or grad degree" = 3,
                      "bachelor's vs. graduate degree" = 4)))
tech.by.deg.contr
```

	Df	Sum Sq	Mean Sq	F value	Pr(>F)
DEGREE	4	221301	55325	43.30	< 2e-16 ***
DEGREE: < high school vs. high school & jr college	1	64411	64411	50.41	1.97e-12 ***
DEGREE: high school vs. all college	1	20188	20188	15.80	7.39e-05 ***
DEGREE: jr college vs. bach or grad degree	1	63902	63902	50.02	2.40e-12 ***
DEGREE: bachelor's vs. graduate degree	1	72800	72800	56.98	7.88e-14 ***
Residuals	1404	1793757	1278		

```
---
Signif. codes: 0 '***' 0.001 '**' 0.01 '*' 0.05 '.' 0.1 ' ' 1
936 observations deleted due to missingness
```

Leslie was excited that it worked! She wondered whether the *p*-values should be adjusted to account for the multiple testing. Kiara did some reading on this, and there did not seem to be consistent guidance, but since multiple statistical tests inflate the probability of a Type I error, she decided it was a good idea to apply some sort of correction. While this is not an option available in the `aov()` or `summary.aov()` commands, there is a `p.adjust()` command that adjusts *p*-values using one of several types of adjustments. Since Bonferroni was familiar and had been used in the post hoc pairwise comparisons, Kiara thought it was a good place to start.

The first argument in the `p.adjust()` command is `p =`, which takes a *p*-value or a vector of *p*-values. The second argument is `method =`, which is where to specify "bonferroni." Nancy gave it a try, entering the vector `Pr(>F)` from the `tech.by.deg.contr` object since this was the vector that held all the *p*-values.

```
# adjust p-values for multiple comparisons
adj.p.vals <- p.adjust(p = tech.by.deg.contr[[1]]$`Pr(>F)`,
                      method = "bonferroni")

adj.p.vals
                                    < high school vs. high school & jr college
                1.329994e-33                                     9.850341e-12
       high school vs. all college           jr college vs. bach or grad degree
                3.696043e-04                                     1.198280e-11
```

The adjusted *p*-values were still very small, so the conclusions about statistical significance did not change, even when using a conservative adjustment like Bonferroni.

Leslie wanted one last visualization showing all the different comparison groups. It took Nancy a few minutes given how complicated this was, but she came up with a nice set of graphs demonstrating the differences among the various groups. She decided to use a violin plot instead of a boxplot this time. Violin plots show the probability density of the data along the range of values and so might more clearly show some of the patterns in the data. Kiara suggested that the difference between violin plots and the boxplots is similar to the difference between a density plot and a histogram. The violin plot shows more subtle variations in the distribution of observations (Figure 7.10).

FIGURE 7.10 Visualizing the distribution of technology use at work by educational attainment for four planned comparisons

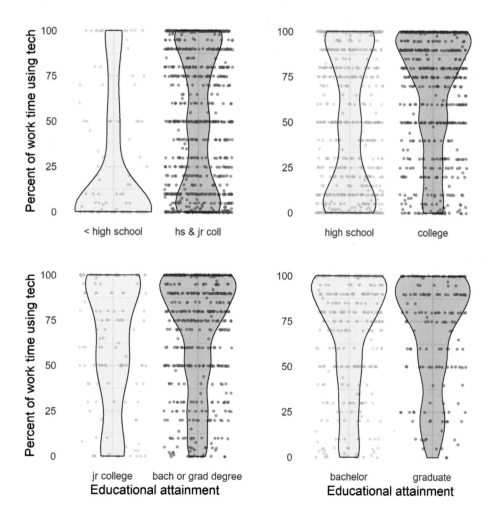

Leslie was still not convinced the bachelor's and graduate degree categories should be statistically significantly different, but the violin helped to show the differences in the distributions a little more. Leslie asked Kiara when it was most appropriate to use the post hoc tests that compare each pair of means and when it was more appropriate to do planned comparisons. Kiara explained that, when you have hypotheses ahead of time about which groups are different from one another, use planned comparisons. When you do not have hypotheses ahead of time about which means are different from each other, use post hoc tests if the ANOVA has a statistically significant *F*-statistic. Good research practices suggest that having hypotheses ahead of time is a stronger strategy unless the research is truly exploratory.

Leslie wanted to incorporate the means of the combined groups into the final interpretation with the planned comparisons. She turned to Nancy to help her write some code.

```
# contrast 1 statistics
gss.2018.cleaned %>%
  mutate(DEGREE = factor(DEGREE, labels = c("< high school",
                  "high school & jr coll", "high school & jr coll",
                  NA, NA))) %>%
  group_by(DEGREE) %>%
  summarise(m.techuse = mean(x = USETECH, na.rm = T),
          sd.techuse = sd(x = USETECH, na.rm = T))
## # A tibble: 3 x 3
##    DEGREE                   m.techuse  sd.techuse
##    <fct>                    <dbl>      <dbl>
## 1 < high school             24.8       36.2
## 2 high school & jr coll     51.7       38.4
## 3 <NA>                      68.2       31.4
# contrast 2 statistics
gss.2018.cleaned %>%
  mutate(DEGREE = factor(DEGREE, labels = c(NA,
                  "high school", "all college",
                  "all college", "all college"))) %>%
  group_by(DEGREE) %>%
  summarise(m.techuse = mean(x = USETECH, na.rm = T),
          sd.techuse = sd(x = USETECH, na.rm = T))
## # A tibble: 3 x 3
##    DEGREE          m.techuse  sd.techuse
##    <fct>           <dbl>      <dbl>
## 1 <NA>             24.8       36.2
## 2 high school      49.6       38.6
## 3 all college      67.0       32.3
# contrast 3 statistics
gss.2018.cleaned %>%
```

```
    mutate(DEGREE = factor(DEGREE, labels = c(NA,
                    NA, "jr college",
                    "bach or grad degree", "bach or grad degree"))) %>%
  group_by(DEGREE) %>%
  summarise(m.techuse = mean(x = USETECH, na.rm = T),
            sd.techuse = sd(x = USETECH, na.rm = T))
## # A tibble: 3 x 3
##    DEGREE              m.techuse  sd.techuse
##    <fct>                  <dbl>       <dbl>
## 1 <NA>                    45.8        39.3
## 2 jr college              62.4        35.2
## 3 bach or grad degree     68.2        31.4
# contrast 4 statistics
gss.2018.cleaned %>%
  mutate(DEGREE = factor(DEGREE, labels = c(NA,
                    NA, NA,
                    "bachelor", "graduate"))) %>%
  group_by(DEGREE) %>%
  summarise(m.techuse = mean(x = USETECH, na.rm = T),
            sd.techuse = sd(x = USETECH, na.rm = T))
## # A tibble: 3 x 3
##    DEGREE           m.techuse  sd.techuse
##    <fct>               <dbl>       <dbl>
## 1 <NA>                 48.1        39.1
## 2 bachelor             67.9        32.1
## 3 graduate             68.7        30.2
```

Leslie wrote a final interpretation:

The mean time spent on technology use at work was significantly different across educational attainment groups [$F(4, 1404) = 43.3$; $p < .05$], indicating these groups likely came from populations with different mean time spent on technology use. The highest mean was percent of time used for technology for those with graduate degrees. The lowest mean was percent of time for those with less than a high school diploma. A set of planned comparisons found that the mean time spent using technology was statistically significantly ($p < .05$) lower for (a) those with < high school education ($m = 24.8$) compared to those with high school or junior college ($m = 51.7$), (b) those with a high school education ($m = 49.61$) compared to those with all college groups combined ($m = 67.0$), (c) those with a junior college degree ($m = 62.4$) compared to those with a bachelor's or graduate degree ($m = 68.2$), and (d) those with a bachelor's degree ($m = 67.9$) compared to those with a graduate degree ($m = 68.7$). Overall, the patterns show statistically significant increases in time spent using technology at work for those with more education.

7.6.3 ACHIEVEMENT 3: CHECK YOUR UNDERSTANDING

Why is a post hoc or planned comparison test useful after a statistically significant ANOVA result?

- There is no other way to know what the means are for each group.
- They confirm whether or not your ANOVA is statistically significant.
- Post hoc and planned comparison tests help identify which groups' means are different from each other.
- Post hoc and planned comparison tests ensure that both variables have minimal missing data for ANOVA

Create a different set of planned comparisons that follows the contrast rules, write and run the code, and interpret your results.

7.7 Achievement 4: Computing and interpreting effect sizes for ANOVA

After learning about Cramér's V for chi-squared (Section 5.10.1) and Cohen's d for t-tests (Section 6.8), Leslie asked Kiara what the effect sizes were for ANOVA. Kiara explained that *eta-squared* (η^2) is the proportion of variability in the continuous outcome variable that is explained by the groups and is the commonly used effect size for ANOVA (Fritz & Morris, 2018). Nancy was not so sure! She recently read a paper (Skidmore & Thompson, 2013) that recommended *omega-squared* (ω^2) instead. Eta-squared has a known positive bias and is used widely possibly because it is easily available in some statistical software programs (Skidmore & Thompson, 2013). The omega-squared effect size has the same general meaning, is adjusted to account for the positive bias, and is more stable when assumptions are not completely met. Kiara wrote out the formula for omega-squared in Equation (7.7) to help her explain to Leslie how it works (Skidmore & Thompson, 2013).

$$\omega^2 = \frac{F-1}{F + \dfrac{n-k+1}{k-1}} \tag{7.7}$$

In Equation (7.7), n is the number of observations and k is the number of groups. The F is from the ANOVA results.

Nancy jumped in with some R code to compute the omega-squared for the technology use analyses. First, she explained that the two functions they have used so far, `oneway.test()` and `aov()`, do not compute omega-squared as part of the output. However, there are R packages that do compute it. Even so, Nancy recommended sticking with `aov()` and using the output from `aov()` to compute omega-squared. She showed the team how to do this by first examining the output from the earlier `aov()`.

```
# ANOVA model from earlier
summary(object = techuse.by.deg.aov)
##                Df    Sum Sq   Mean Sq   F value   Pr(>F)
## DEGREE          4    221301     55325      43.3   <2e-16 ***
## Residuals    1404   1793757      1278
```

```
## ---
## Signif. codes: 0 '***' 0.001 '**' 0.01 '*' 0.05 '.' 0.1 ' ' 1
## 936 observations deleted due to missingness
```

Everything they needed to compute omega-squared was in the output, so they used Equation (7.8) to compute the value.

$$\omega^2 = \frac{F-1}{F+\dfrac{n-k+1}{k-1}} = \frac{43.3-1}{43.3+\dfrac{1409-5+1}{5-1}} = .107 \tag{7.8}$$

Kiara was a little uneasy with Nancy's solution here and asked, for the sake of reproducibility, if there was any way to do this calculation directly in R without retyping the numbers. Nancy said there was, but it required some fancy coding to access certain values in the output. Kiara thought that sounded better than typing out the values, so she and Nancy worked on a set of instructions for Leslie to use for reproducible calculations of the omega-squared effect size if she was so inclined (Box 7.3).

7.3 Kiara's reproducibility resource: Accessing elements of a list

Kiara wanted to demonstrate how working with R code is going to be more precise and therefore easier to reproduce than copying results and doing the math by hand, even if working by hand does seem more efficient sometimes. She computed the ω^2 for the ANOVA by hand and with R. To do this math in R from the `aov()` object `techuse.by.deg.aov`, some fancy code was needed to access the list that is created with `summary()`. The object created by `summary()` is a list.

```
# create a summary object
summ.tech.anova <- summary(object = techuse.by.deg.aov)
```

Looking at the list in the Environment pane, there are several entries in the list (Figure 7.11).

FIGURE 7.11 List object of summ.tech.anova containing the output from summary(object = techuse.by.deg.aov)

```
⊙ summ.tech.anova          List of 1
   :Classes 'anova' and 'data.frame': 2 obs. of 5 variables:
   ..$ Df : num [1:2] 4 1404
   ..$ Sum Sq : num [1:2] 221301 1793757
   ..$ Mean Sq: num [1:2] 55325 1278
   ..$ F value: num [1:2] 43.3 NA
   ..$ Pr(>F) : num [1:2] 2.66e-34 NA
   - attr(*, "class")= chr [1:2] "summary.aov" "listof"
   - attr(*, "na.action")= 'omit' Named int [1:936] 2 5 6 13 15 17 18 22 26 28 ...
   ..- attr(*, "names")= chr [1:936] "2" "5" "6" "13" ...
```

(Continued)

(Continued)

To access the parts of the list, square brackets `[]` are used. Accessing a single element of the list requires double square brackets `[[]]` with the position of the element inside. For the full `summ.tech.anova` object, use the following:

```
# access first item in the summ.tech.anova list
summ.tech.anova[[1]]
##               Df    Sum Sq Mean Sq  F value      Pr(>F)
## DEGREE         4    221301   55325   43.304  < 2.2e-16 ***
## Residuals   1404   1793757    1278
## ---
## Signif. codes: 0 '***' 0.001 '**' 0.01 '*' 0.05 '.' 0.1 ' ' 1
```

To get a single number from this first list element, first check what the class of the element is, since lists and data frames require different use of brackets to access different parts.

```
# determine the class of the first element in the summ.tech.anova
# list
class(x = summ.tech.anova[[1]])
## [1] "anova"     "data.frame"
```

The first element is two classes, `anova` and `data.frame`. To access individual numbers or groups of numbers from a data frame, use the single square brackets `[]`. Inside single square brackets, put the position of the number you need with *row first and column second*. For example, to get the *F*-statistic value from the data frame that is the first element of the `summ.tech.anova` list, use row 1 and column 4.

```
# access the entry in the first row and 4th column
# of the first item in the summ.tech.anova list
summ.tech.anova[[1]][1, 4]
## [1] 43.30381
```

The code `summ.tech.anova[[1]][1, 4]` returned the *F*-statistic from the `summ.tech.anova` object. This strategy could be used to compute the ω^2 using code instead of retyping numbers. Equation (7.8) can be used to compute ω^2 by hand by substituting in values from `summ.tech.anova`.

$$\omega^2 = \frac{F-1}{F+\dfrac{n-k+1}{k-1}} = \frac{43.3-1}{43.3+\dfrac{1409-5+1}{5-1}} = .107 \tag{7.8}$$

The degrees of freedom for DEGREE are $k - 1$, and the degrees of freedom for the residuals are $n - k$. These two values can be used to compute k and n in R.

```
# compute omega using R code
k.om <- summ.tech.anova[[1]][1, 1] + 1
n.om <- summ.tech.anova[[1]][2, 1] + summ.tech.anova[[1]][1, 1] + 1
omega.sq <- (summ.tech.anova[[1]][1, 4])/(summ.tech.anova[[1]][1, 4]
+ (n.om - k.om + 1)/(k.om - 1))
omega.sq
## [1] 0.1097539
```

The ω^2 from R is slightly larger due to the rounding of the F-statistic in the hand calculations.

The final thing Leslie wanted to know was the cutoffs for small, medium, and large effect size. Were they the same as for the other effect sizes? Kiara said that unfortunately they were not. Here are the commonly used cutoffs for omega-squared effect size:

- $\omega^2 = .01$ to $\omega^2 < .06$ is a small effect
- $\omega^2 = .06$ to $\omega^2 < .14$ is a medium effect
- $\omega^2 \geq .14$ is a large effect

In this case, the effect size was medium. There was a medium-strength relationship between educational attainment and time spent using technology. Leslie copied her interpretation from above and added effect size:

The mean time spent on technology use at work was significantly different across educational attainment groups [$F(4, 1404) = 43.3$; $p < .05$], indicating these groups likely came from populations with different mean time spent on technology use. The highest mean was percent of time used for technology for those with graduate degrees. The lowest mean was percent of time for those with less than a high school diploma. A set of planned comparisons found that the mean time spent using technology was statistically significantly ($p < .05$) lower for (a) those with < high school education ($m = 24.8$) compared to those with high school or junior college ($m = 51.7$), (b) those with a high school education ($m = 49.61$) compared to those with all college groups combined ($m = 67.0$), (c) those with a junior college degree ($m = 62.4$) compared to those with a bachelor's or graduate degree ($m = 68.2$), and (d) those with a bachelor's degree ($m = 67.9$) compared to those with a graduate degree ($m = 68.7$). Overall, the patterns show statistically significant increases in time spent using technology at work for those with more education. The strength of the relationship between degree and time using technology at work was medium ($\omega^2 = .11$).

7.7.1 ACHIEVEMENT 4: CHECK YOUR UNDERSTANDING

Explain the difference between the statistical significance of a relationship and the effect size of a relationship.

7.8 Achievement 5: Testing ANOVA assumptions

The assumptions for ANOVA are having a continuous outcome and independent groups, independent observations, an outcome that is normally distributed within groups, and equal variance of the outcome within groups. Leslie checked normality first. There are several ways to assess normality. Visually, a histogram, density plot, or Q-Q plot can be used to identify normal and non-normal data distribution. Statistically, a Shapiro-Wilk test can be used.

7.8.1 TESTING NORMALITY

Leslie decided to start with density plots (Figure 7.12) and used the same colors they used for the box-plots at the beginning.

```
# graph tech use by degree (Figure 7.12)
gss.2018.cleaned %>%
  drop_na(USETECH) %>%
  ggplot(aes(x = USETECH)) +
  geom_density(aes(fill = DEGREE)) +
  facet_wrap(facets = vars(DEGREE), nrow = 2) +
  scale_fill_brewer(palette = "Spectral", guide = FALSE) +
  theme_minimal() +
  labs(x = "Percent of time using tech",
       y = "Probability density")
```

FIGURE 7.12 Distribution of technology use at work by educational attainment categories

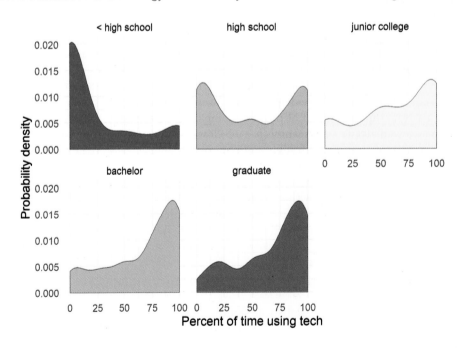

Based on the density plots, none of the groups looked normally distributed. While Leslie was making density plots, Nancy put together some Q-Q plots to confirm (Figure 7.13). The yellow was not showing up well, but Nancy wasn't sure it made much difference in this case.

```r
# graph tech use by degree (Figure 7.13)
gss.2018.cleaned %>%
  drop_na(USETECH) %>%
  ggplot(aes(sample = USETECH)) +
  geom_abline(aes(intercept = mean(USETECH), slope = sd(USETECH),
              linetype = "Normally distributed"),
              color = "gray60", size = 1) +
  stat_qq(aes(color = DEGREE)) +
  scale_color_brewer(palette = "Spectral", guide = FALSE) +
  scale_linetype_manual(values = 1, name = "") +
  labs(x = "Theoretical normal distribution",
       y = "Observed values of percent time using tech") +
  theme_minimal() +
  facet_wrap(facets = vars(DEGREE), nrow = 2)
```

Leslie noted that none of the groups appeared to be normally distributed based on either type of plot. She also noticed that the floor and ceiling values appeared to be driving some of the non-normality. The Shapiro-Wilk test did not seem necessary in this case given the big deviations from normality in

FIGURE 7.13 Distribution of time spent on technology use by educational attainment

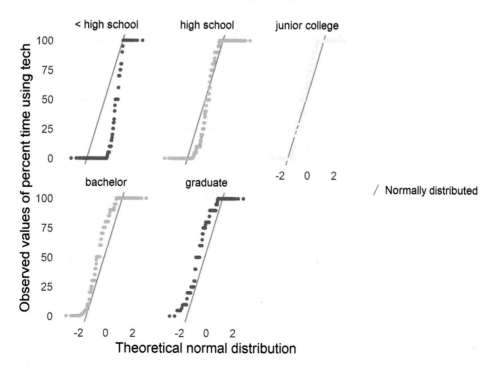

the histograms and Q-Q plots, but Nancy suggested that they try it just to confirm. Leslie reminded herself that the Shapiro-Wilk test was testing the null hypothesis that the data are normally distributed. Nancy remembered that she had trouble before with using this test for multiple groups. She tried something new with the R code, which was to use the usual `summarize()` after `group_by()` but just to print the *p*-value for the Shapiro-Wilk tests.

```
# statistical test of normality for groups
gss.2018.cleaned %>%
  drop_na(USETECH) %>%
  group_by(DEGREE) %>%
  summarize(shapiro.pval = shapiro.test(x = USETECH)$p.value)

# A tibble: 5 x 2

## DEGREE            shapiro.pval
## <fctr>                   <dbl>

## < high school         1.83e-14

## high school           5.99e-24

## junior college        2.92e- 9

## bachelor              1.22e-16

## graduate              4.34e-11
```

Based on the *p*-values, all five of the Shapiro-Wilk tests were statistically significant, indicating that the null hypothesis for this test (i.e., the data are normally distributed) was rejected in each group. The team felt they had plenty of evidence that the data were not normally distributed; this assumption is failed.

7.8.2 HOMOGENEITY OF VARIANCES ASSUMPTION

Another assumption for ANOVA is homogeneity of variances, or equal variances across groups. The data need to be not only normally distributed, but also spread out equally in each group. Leslie reviewed the graphs and thought this might actually be an easier assumption to meet.

Nancy mentioned that Levene's test is widely used to test the assumption of equal variances. The null hypothesis is that the variances are equal, while the alternate is that at least two of the variances are different. The `leveneTest()` function can be used to conduct the Levene's test.

```
# equal variances for USETECH by DEGREE
car::leveneTest(y = USETECH ~ DEGREE, data = gss.2018.cleaned, center = mean)
## Levene's Test for Homogeneity of Variance (center = mean)
```

```
##            Df  F value     Pr(>F)
## group       4    18.312  1.121e-14 ***
##          1404
## ---
## Signif. codes:  0 '***' 0.001 '**' 0.01 '*' 0.05 '.' 0.1 ' ' 1
```

The *p*-value for the Levene's test suggests rejecting the null hypothesis; the variances of USETECH are statistically significantly different across groups ($p < .05$). The ANOVA fails the assumption of homogeneity of variances.

7.8.3 ANOVA ASSUMPTIONS RECAP

Nancy summarized the assumptions for ANOVA to ensure Leslie remembered them all:

- Continuous variable and independent groups
- Independent observations
- Normal distribution in each group
- Equal variances for each group

Leslie confirmed again with Nancy what the difference was between independent observations and independent groups. Nancy reminded her that the assumption of independent observations requires that the people in your data are not related to one another in any important way. Things that might violate this assumption are having siblings or spouses in a data set together or measuring the same person multiple times. The assumption of independent groups is the requirement that the groups are not related to one another. If two groups had some of the same people in them or if one group was comprised of the neighbors of the people in another group, the two groups would not be independent. Leslie and Nancy agreed that the ANOVA met the continuous variable and independent groups assumptions and the independent observations assumption.

Leslie expressed some disappointment that ANOVA failed its assumptions, although she was getting used to it after the *t*-test meeting. Kiara explained that, like with the *t*-tests, there are alternate statistical tests available when ANOVA assumptions are not met.

7.8.4 ACHIEVEMENT 5: CHECK YOUR UNDERSTANDING

Which ANOVA assumption(s) appear(s) to be violated by the data in Figure 7.14?

- Continuous variable and independent groups
- Independent observations
- Normal distribution in each group
- Equal variances for each group

FIGURE 7.14 Distribution of technology use data violating an ANOVA assumption

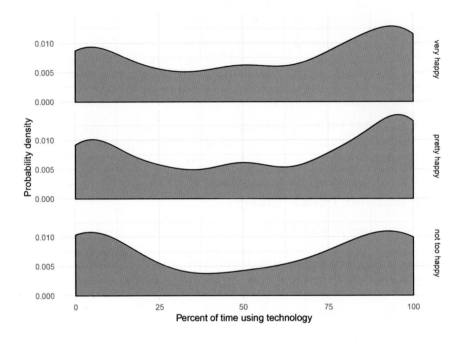

7.9 Achievement 6: Choosing and using alternative tests when ANOVA assumptions are not met

Kiara explained to Leslie that the two main assumptions for ANOVA, normality and homogeneity of variances, suggest different alternatives when each assumption is not met and that they would review a few of the more commonly used alternatives (Lix, Keselman, & Keselman, 1996).

7.9.1 CALCULATING AN ALTERNATE *F*-STATISTIC FOR FAILING THE HOMOGENEITY ASSUMPTION

The first option Kiara suggested is for when the normality assumption is met but the homogeneity of variances assumption fails. In this situation, the standard approach is to use ANOVA but compute an alternate *F*-statistic that does not rely on equal variances. Two alternate *F*-statistics are widely used for this purpose:

- Brown-Forsythe
- Welch's

7.9.1.1 BROWN-FORSYTHE *F*-STATISTIC

The *Brown-Forsythe* approach to calculating *F* starts with a transformation of the continuous variable from its measured values to values that represent the distance each observation is from the median of the variable. Had the normality assumption been met for the ANOVA comparing the percentage of work time using technology across educational attainment groups, the technology use variable might be transformed as in Equation (7.9).

$$t_{ij} = \left| y_{ij} - median_{y_j} \right|$$ (7.9)

In this equation, y_{ij} is each observation i in group j, $median_{y_j}$ is the median of group j, and enclosing the equation in $|$ is for absolute value.

The alternate F-statistic is then computed as in Equation (7.10) using the same F formula but with the means computed from the transformed t_{ij} of the technology use variable rather than from the raw values of the continuous variable.

$$F_{BF} = \frac{\dfrac{\sum_{j=1}^{k} n_j (\bar{t}_j - \bar{t})^2}{k-1}}{\dfrac{\sum_{j=1}^{k}\sum_{i=1}^{n}(t_{ij} - \bar{t}_j)^2}{n-k}}$$ (7.10)

While there are R packages that can be used to compute the Brown-Forsythe directly, another option is to transform the outcome variable and use the `aov()` command used for ANOVA. Nancy showed the team how to create the transformed version of the USETECH variable using `abs()` to get the absolute value of the difference between each value of USETECH and the median of USETECH, making sure to remove the NA in the `median()` function so it works.

```
# add new variable to data management
gss.2018.cleaned <- gss.2018 %>%
  mutate(USETECH = na_if(x = USETECH, y = -1)) %>%
  mutate(USETECH = na_if(x = USETECH, y = 999)) %>%
  mutate(USETECH = na_if(x = USETECH, y = 998)) %>%
  mutate(AGE = na_if(x = AGE, y = 98)) %>%
  mutate(AGE = na_if(x = AGE, y = 99)) %>%
  mutate(DEGREE = na_if(x = DEGREE, y = 8)) %>%
  mutate(DEGREE = na_if(x = DEGREE, y = 9)) %>%
  mutate(HAPPY = na_if(x = HAPPY, y = 8)) %>%
  mutate(HAPPY = na_if(x = HAPPY, y = 9)) %>%
  mutate(HAPPY = na_if(x = HAPPY, y = 0)) %>%
  mutate(SEX = factor(SEX, labels = c("male","female"))) %>%
  mutate(DEGREE = factor(x = DEGREE, labels = c("< high school",
                                "high school", "junior college",
                                "bachelor", "graduate"))) %>%
  mutate(HAPPY = factor(x = HAPPY, labels = c("very happy",
                                "pretty happy",
                                "not too happy"))) %>%
  group_by(DEGREE) %>%
  mutate(usetech.tran = abs(USETECH - median(USETECH, na.rm = TRUE)))
```

```
# check new variable
summary(object = gss.2018.cleaned$usetech.tran)
##    Min. 1st Qu.  Median   Mean 3rd Qu.    Max.   NA's
##    0.00   10.00   30.00  30.22   50.00  100.00    936
```

Leslie copied the `oneway.test()` from earlier, changed USETECH to use the `usetech.tran` trans-formed variable instead, and started the NHST process.

7.9.1.2 NHST STEP 1: WRITE THE NULL AND ALTERNATE HYPOTHESES

The null and alternate hypotheses are as follows:

H0: The mean value of the transformed technology use variable is the same across educational attainment groups.

HA: The mean value of the transformed technology use variable is not the same across educational attainment groups.

7.9.1.3 NHST STEP 2: COMPUTE THE TEST STATISTIC

```
# brown-forsythe anova
usetech.t.by.degree <- oneway.test(formula = usetech.tran ~ DEGREE,
                                   data = gss.2018.cleaned)
usetech.t.by.degree
##
##   One-way analysis of means (not assuming equal variances)
##
## data:  usetech.tran and DEGREE
## F = 19.747, num df = 4.00, denom df = 364.77, p-value = 9.965e-15
```

7.9.1.4 NHST STEP 3: CALCULATE THE PROBABILITY THAT YOUR TEST STATISTIC IS AT LEAST AS BIG AS IT IS IF THERE IS NO RELATIONSHIP (I.E., THE NULL IS TRUE)

The *p*-value in this case is much less than .05. The value of an F_{BF}-statistic being this large or larger hap-pens a tiny percentage of the time when the null hypothesis is true.

7.9.1.5 NHST STEPS 4 AND 5: INTERPRET THE PROBABILITY AND WRITE A CONCLUSION

Leslie wrote her conclusion:

The results show a statistically significant difference of the means of the transformed technology use variable by educational attainment group [$F_{BF}(4, 364.77) = 19.747$; $p < .05$].

Leslie was interested in how the transformed data used in these calculations looked. She decided to compute the descriptive statistics and examine a graph of the transformed variable to better understand the results.

```
# means of transformed variable
usetech.t.stats <- gss.2018.cleaned %>%
  drop_na(usetech.tran) %>%
  group_by(DEGREE) %>%
  summarise(m.usetech.tran = mean(x = usetech.tran),
            sd.usetech.tran = sd(x = usetech.tran))
usetech.t.stats
## # A tibble: 5 x 3
##    DEGREE           m.usetech.tran  sd.usetech.tran
##    <fct>                <dbl>            <dbl>
## 1 < high school         24.8             36.2
## 2 high school           35.1             16.1
## 3 junior college        30.1             19.7
## 4 bachelor              25.5             22.9
## 5 graduate              24.1             21.4
```

The mean of the transformed USETECH variable, usetech.tran, which consisted of differences between the original values and the median value of USETECH, was 35.1 for the high school group and 30.1 for the junior college group. The rest of the means were smaller. The transformation made the differences among the means somewhat smaller. Figure 7.15 shows the differences across the groups.

```
# graph transformed USETECH variable (Figure 7.15)
gss.2018.cleaned %>%
  drop_na(usetech.tran) %>%
  ggplot(aes(y = usetech.tran, x = DEGREE)) +
  geom_jitter(aes(color = DEGREE), alpha = .6) +
  geom_boxplot(aes(fill = DEGREE), alpha = .4) +
  scale_fill_brewer(palette = "Spectral", guide = FALSE) +
  scale_color_brewer(palette = "Spectral", guide = FALSE) +
  theme_minimal() +
  labs(x = "Educational attainment",
       y = "Distance to median of tech use time for group")
```

Leslie noticed that the transformation had reduced the differences between the junior college, bachelor, and graduate categories, with the boxplots showing nearly the same median values for the groups of the transformed variable. Kiara reminded Leslie that they have another option when an ANOVA assumption fails. The Welch's variation on computing the F-statistic is also useful when the assumption of homogeneity of variances is not met.

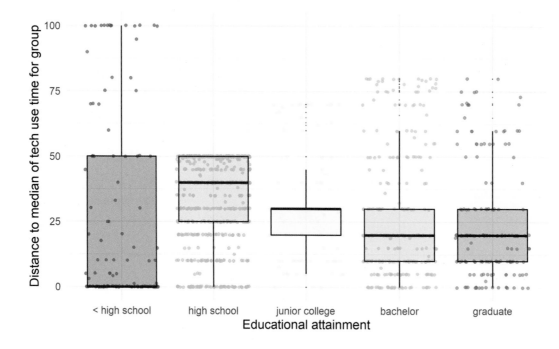

FIGURE 7.15 Transformed time at work using technology by educational attainment

7.9.1.6 WELCH'S *F*-STATISTIC

While Leslie was working on the Brown-Forsythe test, Kiara looked up some additional information on the *Welch's F-statistic* (Field, 2013). Rather than use a transformed outcome variable, the main idea behind the Welch's *F*-statistic is to use weights in the calculation of the group means and overall mean (also known as the grand mean). The weight is computed as shown in Equation (7.11) for each group to account for the different variances across groups (Field, 2013):

$$w_j = \frac{n_j}{s_j^2} \tag{7.11}$$

where n_j is the sample size in group j and s_j^2 is the variance in group j. The grand mean is computed using the weight and the weighted mean for each of the groups, like in Equation (7.12),

$$\overline{y}_{welch} = \frac{\sum_{j=1}^{k} w_j \overline{y}_j}{\sum_{j=1}^{k} w_j}, \tag{7.12}$$

where w_j is the weight for group j and $\overline{y}_j$ is the mean of the continuous variable for group j. The $\sum_{j=1}^{k}$ is the sum of each group from the first group, $j = 1$, to the last group, $j = k$. The grand mean for Welch's *F*-statistic was then used in the final computation of the Welch's *F*-statistic, which, Kiara warned everyone, gets a little complex (Field, 2013). In fact, she decided just to type it out and send it to Leslie and Nancy in case they wanted to look at it later (Box 7.4), since it did not seem like a good use of time to try and use it to compute the *F* by hand. Nancy explained that the `oneway.test()` command computes Welch's *F*-statistic when the option `var.equal =` is set to be false. Leslie got her NHST started.

7.4 Kiara's reproducibility resource: The gigantic Welch's *F*-statistic equation

Kiara typed out the Welch's *F* equation from Field (2013) in case Nancy or Leslie wanted to review it, but given its length, she thought that learning R was a better use of their time. In this formula, *k* represents the number of groups, *j* represents a group, and *n* represents number of individuals.

$$
F_{Welch} = \frac{\dfrac{\sum \dfrac{n_j}{s_j^2} \left(\bar{y}_j - \dfrac{\sum \dfrac{n_j}{s_j^2} y_j}{\sum \dfrac{n_j}{s_j^2}} \right)^2}{r-1}}{1 + \dfrac{2}{3} \left(\dfrac{3 \sum \left(1 - \dfrac{\dfrac{n_j}{s_j^2}}{\sum \dfrac{n_j}{s_j^2}} \right)^2}{\dfrac{n_j - 1}{k^2 - 1}} \right) (k-2)}
$$

7.9.1.7 NHST STEP 1: WRITE THE NULL AND ALTERNATE HYPOTHESES

The null and alternate hypotheses are as follows:

H0: Time spent using technology is the same across educational attainment groups.

HA: Time spent using technology is not the same across educational attainment groups.

7.9.1.8 NHST STEP 2: COMPUTE THE TEST STATISTIC

```
# welch test for unequal variances
welch.usetech.by.degree <- oneway.test(formula = USETECH ~ DEGREE,
          data = gss.2018.cleaned,
          var.equal = FALSE)
welch.usetech.by.degree
```

```
##
##  One-way analysis of means (not assuming equal variances)
##
## data: USETECH and DEGREE
## F = 46.06, num df = 4.00, denom df = 400.31, p-value < 2.2e-16
```

7.9.1.9 NHST STEP 3: CALCULATE THE PROBABILITY THAT YOUR TEST STATISTIC IS AT LEAST AS BIG AS IT IS IF THERE IS NO RELATIONSHIP (I.E., THE NULL IS TRUE)

The p-value in this case is $<$ 2.2e-16, which is much less than .05. The value of an F_w-statistic being this large or larger happens a tiny amount of the time when the null hypothesis is true.

7.9.1.10 NHST STEPS 4 AND 5: INTERPRET THE PROBABILITY AND WRITE A CONCLUSION

The results show a statistically significant difference in the mean of the USETECH variable by degree group $[F_w(4, 400.31) = 46.06; p < .05]$. Leslie noticed that the F-statistic was a little larger and the degrees of freedom for the denominator was a smaller number compared to the original ANOVA. Kiara showed her Equation (7.13) and explained that the weighting was also used in the calculation of the denominator degrees of freedom (Field, 2013).

$$df_{denom} = \cfrac{1}{\cfrac{3\sum_{j=1}^{k}\left(1 - \cfrac{w_j}{\sum_{j=1}^{k}w_j}\right)^2}{n_j - 1}} \tag{7.13}$$

With fewer degrees of freedom, the F-statistic has to be a larger number to reach statistical significance. Nancy made a graph so they could examine a few F-distributions to see how this works (Figure 7.16).

Leslie reviewed the graph and noticed that, while different, the distributions do not seem to be *very* different. Nancy noted that although it is true that there isn't much difference between the distributions, the area under the curves is what matters for the p-value cutoff. When the line is just slightly closer to the x-axis, this changes things quickly for the area under the curve. The thresholds for statistical significance ($p < .05$) for these three lines are 2.38 for the 2000 degrees of freedom, 2.76 for the 25 degrees of freedom, and 3.48 for the 10 degrees of freedom. Nancy reminded Leslie that the numerator degrees of freedom had a bigger impact on the significance threshold. For example, an ANOVA with 2 degrees of freedom and the same 2000 degrees of freedom in the denominator would have a threshold for ($p < .05$) significance of 3.00 instead of 2.38 for the 4 and 2000 threshold.

Leslie asked if the omega-squared could be used to determine effect size for Welch's F and the Brown-Forsythe F. Kiara had not seen any resources that explicitly showed this as an option, but an article by Skidmore and Thompson (2013) suggested it may be biased, especially when groups being compared are different sizes and the homogeneity of variances assumption fails. At this point, Kiara suggested using descriptive statistics and graphs to demonstrate differences until the statistical theory catches up. Or, Nancy said, Leslie could develop the "L" effect size! Leslie rolled her eyes and smiled. "I'm probably not quite ready for that yet. Give me another meeting or two," she said.

FIGURE 7.16 *F*-distributions with 4 degrees of freedom in the numerator

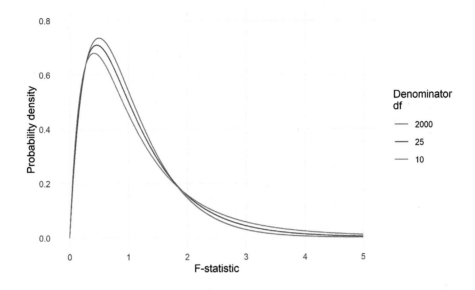

7.9.2 THE KRUSKAL-WALLIS TEST FOR FAILING THE NORMALITY ASSUMPTION

The *Kruskal-Wallis test* is used to compare three or more groups when the normal distribution assumption fails for ANOVA (Feir-Walsh & Toothaker, 1974; Van Hecke, 2012). Like several of the tests used when the outcome is not normally distributed for a *t*-test, the Kruskal-Wallis (K-W) test compares ranks among groups. Specifically, the observations are put in order by size, and each is assigned a rank. The mean rank for each group is then computed and used to calculate the K-W test statistic, *H*, as shown in Equation (7.14).

$$H = \frac{12}{n(n+1)} \sum_{j=1}^{k} n_j \left(\bar{r}_j - \frac{n+1}{2} \right)^2 \qquad (7.14)$$

In this formula, *n* is the overall sample size, n_j is the sample size for group *j*, and $\bar{r}_j$ is the mean rank for group *j*. Almost out of habit, Leslie started writing the NHST steps for the K-W alternative to ANOVA.

7.9.2.1 NHST STEP 1: WRITE THE NULL AND ALTERNATE HYPOTHESES

H0: The mean rank of technology use is the same across educational attainment groups.

HA: The mean rank of technology use is not the same across educational attainment groups.

7.9.2.2 NHST STEP 2: COMPUTE THE TEST STATISTIC

```
# compare usetech by degree
kw.usetech.by.degree <- kruskal.test(formula = USETECH ~ DEGREE,
                                     data = gss.2018.cleaned)
```

```
kw.usetech.by.degree
##
##  Kruskal-Wallis rank sum test
##
## data:  USETECH by DEGREE
## Kruskal-Wallis chi-squared = 142.21, df = 4, p-value < 2.2e-16
```

Nancy explained that the distribution of the H statistic is approximately a chi-squared distribution, so the R output lists "chi-squared" instead of H.

7.9.2.3 NHST STEP 3: CALCULATE THE PROBABILITY THAT YOUR TEST STATISTIC IS AT LEAST AS BIG AS IT IS IF THERE IS NO RELATIONSHIP (I.E., THE NULL IS TRUE)

The p-value is $< 2.2\text{e-}16$, which, as usual, is very tiny. The value of an H-statistic being this large or larger happens a tiny percentage of the time when the null hypothesis is true.

7.9.2.4 NHST STEPS 4 AND 5: INTERPRET THE PROBABILITY AND WRITE A CONCLUSION

The conclusion is that there is a difference in the mean rank for technology use by degree group [$H(4) = 142.21$; $p < .05$]. Like the ANOVA results, the K-W test identifies whether there is a difference somewhere among the means, but it does not identify which groups are different from one another. A post hoc test like Bonferroni or Tukey's HSD could help. For K-W, the ***Dunn's post hoc test*** of multiple comparisons is useful for identifying which groups are statistically significantly different from which other groups.

7.9.2.5 DUNN'S POST HOC TEST FOR KRUSKAL-WALLIS

The Dunn's test function, dunn.test(), is in the **dunn.test** package and requires that a method be selected for adjusting the p-value to account for the multiple comparisons. Nancy suggested Bonferroni, since that is one of the methods commonly used with ANOVA. She showed Leslie that the dunn.test() function takes three arguments: The x = argument is the continuous variable, the g = argument is for the groups, and the method = argument is the p-value adjustment method.

```
# post hoc test for usetech by degree
dunn.usetech.by.degree <-  dunn.test::dunn.test(x = gss.2018.cleaned$USETECH,
                                                g = gss.2018.cleaned$DEGREE,
                                                method = "bonferroni")
##   Kruskal-Wallis rank sum test
##
## data: x and group
## Kruskal-Wallis chi-squared = 142.2141, df = 4, p-value = 0
##
##
##                     Comparison of x by group
##                           (Bonferroni)
```

```
## Col Mean-|
## Row Mean |    < high s    bachelor     graduate     high sch
## ---------+-------------------------------------------------------
## bachelor |   -10.43723
##          |      0.0000*
##          |
## graduate |   -9.495755    -0.191842
##          |      0.0000*      1.0000
##          |
## high sch |   -6.834568     6.465520     5.294962
##          |      0.0000*      0.0000*      0.0000*
##          |
## junior c |   -7.755300     1.244464     1.264131    -3.190136
##          |      0.0000*      1.0000       1.0000       0.0071*
##
## alpha = 0.05
## Reject Ho if p <= alpha/2
```

The Dunn's test is a rank-sum test just like the Mann-Whitney U and can be interpreted in the same way. In this case, it appears that there is no difference in technology use for graduate versus bachelor, junior college versus bachelor, or junior college versus graduate. All other pairings have statistically significant differences between the mean ranks. The table shows a z-statistic for each pair computed for the difference in the mean ranks for the pair. Below the z-statistic is a p-value associated with the z-statistic. The p-value is adjusted using a Bonferroni adjustment, which means it was multiplied by the number of comparisons. In this case, the number of comparisons was $\dfrac{5(5-1)}{2} = 10$.

Leslie thought it would be good to visualize the differences in order to better understand the results. Nancy knew some code that would recode a variable into a rank variable. Leslie saw she had used an argument for this variable that was new, `na.last = "keep"`. Nancy explained that the default for `rank()` is to give the NA values a rank; since it makes more sense to leave them as NA, she added the "keep" option to the argument so that the code would keep NA as NA. She showed Leslie the help documentation where she found this information after noticing that the NA values had been given ranks in an earlier project.

```
# add new variable to data management
gss.2018.cleaned <- gss.2018 %>%
  mutate(USETECH = na_if(x = USETECH, y = -1)) %>%
  mutate(USETECH = na_if(x = USETECH, y = 999)) %>%
  mutate(USETECH = na_if(x = USETECH, y = 998)) %>%
  mutate(AGE = na_if(x = AGE, y = 98)) %>%
  mutate(AGE = na_if(x = AGE, y = 99)) %>%
  mutate(DEGREE = na_if(x = DEGREE, y = 8)) %>%
```

```
    mutate(DEGREE = na_if(x = DEGREE, y = 9)) %>%
    mutate(HAPPY = na_if(x = HAPPY, y = 8)) %>%
    mutate(HAPPY = na_if(x = HAPPY, y = 9)) %>%
    mutate(HAPPY = na_if(x = HAPPY, y = 0)) %>%
    mutate(SEX = factor(SEX, labels = c("male","female"))) %>%
    mutate(DEGREE = factor(x = DEGREE, labels = c("< high school",
                                        "high school", "junior college",
                                        "bachelor", "graduate"))) %>%
    mutate(HAPPY = factor(x = HAPPY, labels = c("very happy",
                                        "pretty happy",
                                        "not too happy"))) %>%
    mutate(usetech.rank = rank(x = USETECH, na.last = "keep")) %>%
    group_by(DEGREE) %>%
    mutate(usetech.t = abs(x = USETECH - median(USETECH, na.rm = TRUE)))
# check new variable
summary(object = gss.2018.cleaned$usetech.rank)
##    Min.  1st Qu.   Median    Mean 3rd Qu.     Max.    NA's
##    88.5    357.5    699.5   705.0  1019.0   1272.0     936
```

The new variable was ready, and Leslie created a graph to examine the five groups (Figure 7.17).

```
# graph the ranks (Figure 7.17)
gss.2018.cleaned %>%
  ggplot(aes(y = usetech.rank, x = DEGREE)) +
  geom_jitter(aes(color = DEGREE), alpha = .6) +
  geom_boxplot(aes(fill = DEGREE), alpha = .4) +
  scale_fill_brewer(palette = "Spectral", guide = FALSE) +
  scale_color_brewer(palette = "Spectral", guide = FALSE) +
  theme_minimal() +
  labs(x = "Educational attainment", y = "Ranks of work time using technology")
```

Leslie noticed that the plot clearly demonstrated the significant differences seen in the post hoc tests. The three college groups were very similar to one another, and there were differences among the other groups.

7.9.2.6 EFFECT SIZE FOR KRUSKAL-WALLIS

Leslie asked if there was also an effect size to report with the Kruskal-Wallis H. Kiara explained that eta-squared works for Kruskal-Wallis (Cohen, 2008). She wrote out Equation (7.15) for computing eta-squared for H.

$$\eta^2_H = \frac{H - k + 1}{n - k} \tag{7.15}$$

FIGURE 7.17 Ranks of percentage of time using technology at work by educational attainment groups

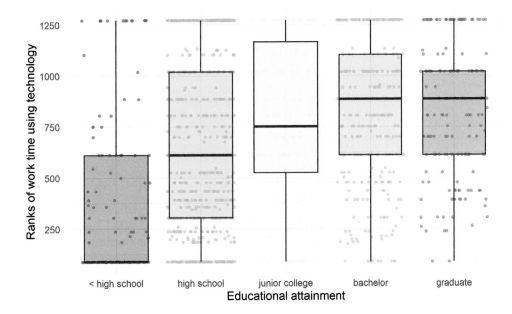

To use the eta-squared formula for the effect size of the Kruskal-Wallis test of technology use time by educational attainment, the H test statistic, k groups, and n number of observations are needed. The H is 142.21, there are 5 educational attainment groups, and there are 936 NA values out of the 2,345 observations in the data frame, so $n = 2,345 - 936 = 1,409$. Leslie entered these into Equation (7.16) to compute eta-squared.

$$\eta_H^2 = \frac{142.21 - 5 + 1}{1409 - 5} = .098 \tag{7.16}$$

The cutoff values are the same as for the omega-squared:

- $\eta^2 = .01$ to $\eta^2 < .06$ is a small effect
- $\eta^2 = .06$ to $\eta^2 < .14$ is a medium effect
- $\eta^2 \geq .14$ is a large effect

In this case, consistent with the original ANOVA results, the eta-squared effect size for the Kruskal-Wallis test is medium. There is a medium-strength relationship between educational attainment and percentage of time spent using technology at work. Leslie wrote her interpretation:

A Kruskal-Wallis test found a statistically significant difference in technology use time at work across educational attainment groups ($H = 142.21$; $p < .05$). Based on a Dunn's post hoc test, those with less than a high school education had statistically significantly lower mean ranked technology use time than all of the other groups ($p < .05$), and people with a bachelor's degree, a graduate degree, or a junior college degree had significantly higher mean ranks than those with a high school diploma. There were no statistically significant differences among the three college groups. There was a medium effect size for the relationship between educational attainment and ranked values of technology use time ($\eta^2 = .098$).

7.9.3 ACHIEVEMENT 6: CHECK YOUR UNDERSTANDING

Next to each test, put the ANOVA assumption violation it addresses:

- Brown-Forsyth
- Welch's
- Kruskal-Wallis

7.10 Achievement 7: Understanding and conducting two-way ANOVA

One-way ANOVA is useful when there is a single categorical variable (with 3+ categories) and the means of a continuous variable being compared across the categories. What happens when there are two categorical variables that may both be useful in explaining a continuous outcome? For example, Leslie had read that technology use varies by sex. Could they answer a research question that asked whether technology use at work varied by educational attainment *and* sex? Kiara said they could use two-way ANOVA. *Two-way ANOVA* is useful for situations where means are compared across the categories of two variables.

7.10.1 EXPLORATORY DATA ANALYSIS FOR TWO-WAY ANOVA

The boxplots for technology use by degree showed an increase in the percentage of time using technology for those with higher educational attainment. Leslie suggested looking at the use of technology by sex with a boxplot (Figure 7.18).

```
# graph usetech by sex (Figure 7.18)
gss.2018.cleaned %>%
  ggplot(aes(y = USETECH, x = SEX)) +
  geom_jitter(aes(color = SEX), alpha = .4) +
  geom_boxplot(aes(fill  = SEX), alpha = .6) +
  scale_fill_manual(values = c("gray70", "#7463AC"), guide = FALSE) +
  scale_color_manual(values = c("gray70", "#7463AC"), guide = FALSE) +
  theme_minimal() +
  labs(x = "Sex", y = "Percent of work time using technology")
```

It appeared that sex did have some relationship to time spent on technology use. Nancy explained that two-way ANOVA could be used to determine if educational attainment and sex both have relationships with technology use by themselves and whether they *interact* to explain technology use. That is, does technology use differ by educational attainment differently for males compared to females? She suggested examining a boxplot with both categorical variables to help understand the relationship (Figure 7.19).

FIGURE 7.18 Distribution of percentage of time spent using technology at work by sex

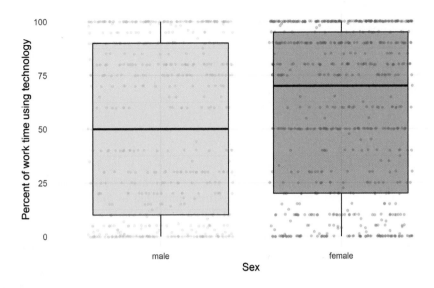

FIGURE 7.19 Distribution of percentage of time spent using technology at work by educational attainment and sex

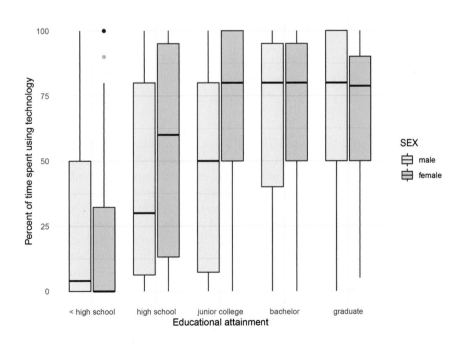

```
# graph usetech by degree and sex (Figure 7.19)
gss.2018.cleaned %>%
    ggplot(aes(y = USETECH, x = DEGREE)) +
    geom_boxplot(aes(fill = SEX), alpha = .4) +
    scale_fill_manual(values = c("gray70", "#7463AC")) +
    theme_minimal() +
    labs(x = "Educational attainment",
        y = "Percent of work time using technology")
```

Leslie noticed that there was a different pattern of technology use for males and females. Females with less than a high school degree were using technology a lower percentage of the time than males in this group. However, females use technology more of the time compared to the males in the high school group and for the junior college group. Males and females seem to have relatively equal time spent with technology once a bachelor or graduate degree is earned.

Nancy explained that this pattern of differences is consistent with an interaction. She suggested that they look at a traditional *means plot* to visualize the idea of an interaction. Although line graphs are ideally not used to display means by groups, they do aid in understanding what an interaction looks like. Nancy wrote some code to graph the possible interaction (Figure 7.20).

```
# means plots graph (Figure 7.20)
gss.2018.cleaned %>%
    ggplot(aes(y = USETECH, x = DEGREE, color = SEX)) +
    stat_summary(fun.y = mean, geom="point", size = 3) +
    stat_summary(fun.y = mean, geom="line", aes(group = SEX), size = 1) +
    scale_color_manual(values = c("gray70", "#7463AC")) +
    theme_minimal() +
    labs(x = "Educational attainment",
        y = "Percent of time spent using technology") +
    ylim(0, 100)
```

Kiara said that when the lines in means plots like this one are parallel, it indicates that there is no interaction between the two categorical variables. She explained that parallel lines show that the mean of the continuous variable is consistently higher or lower for certain groups compared to others. When the means plot shows lines that cross or diverge, this indicates that there is an interaction between the categorical variables. The mean of the continuous variable is different at different levels of one categorical variable depending on the value of the other categorical variable. For example, mean technology use is lower for females compared to males for the lowest and highest educational attainment categories, but female technology use is higher than male technology use for the three other categories of educational attainment. The two variables are working together to influence the value of technology use.

Given this interaction and the differences seen in technology use by DEGREE and by SEX, Kiara suggested that the two-way ANOVA would likely find significant relationships for DEGREE, SEX, and the interaction between the two. Leslie thought this sounded logical and started the NHST process to test it. She wanted to examine the group means before estimating the ANOVA, but now she had two different grouping variables. Nancy explained that group_by() will still work; just put both grouping variables in the parentheses.

FIGURE 7.20 Means plot of technology use at work by educational attainment and sex

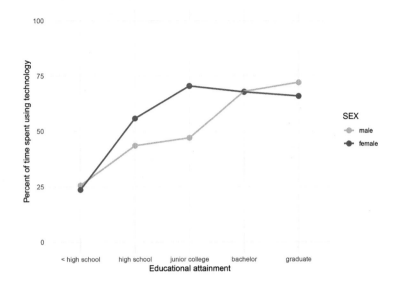

```
# means by degree and sex
use.stats.2 <- gss.2018.cleaned %>%
  group_by(DEGREE, SEX) %>%
  drop_na(USETECH) %>%
  summarize(m.techuse = mean(USETECH),
            sd.techuse = sd(USETECH))
use.stats.2
## # A tibble: 10 x 4
## # Groups:   DEGREE [5]
##    DEGREE         SEX       m.techuse   sd.techuse
##    <fct>          <fct>        <dbl>        <dbl>
##  1 < high school  male          25.7         35.4
##  2 < high school  female        23.7         37.5
##  3 high school    male          43.5         37.8
##  4 high school    female        55.9         38.6
##  5 junior college male          47.0         36.8
##  6 junior college female        70.4         31.7
##  7 bachelor       male          68.0         33.1
##  8 bachelor       female        67.7         31.2
##  9 graduate       male          72.1         29.2
## 10 graduate       female        65.9         30.9
```

Leslie reviewed the means and found that the most striking difference among the means for males and females is in junior college, when males spend a mean of 47.0% of their time on technology while females spend a mean of 70.4% of their time. Within each education group, the other means for males and females are much closer. Leslie started the NHST process.

7.10.2 TWO-WAY ANOVA NHST

7.10.2.1 NHST STEP 1: WRITE THE NULL AND ALTERNATE HYPOTHESES

H0: The mean time using technology at work is the same across groups of degree and sex.

HA: The mean time using technology at work is not the same across the groups.

7.10.2.2 NHST STEP 2: COMPUTE THE TEST STATISTIC

Kiara stepped in to help Leslie. She explained that the interaction term was included in the ANOVA command `aov()` by multiplying the two categorical variables. Leslie started to write `formula = USETECH ~ DEGREE + SEX + DEGREE*SEX` in the `aov()` command. Kiara said that the terms for `DEGREE` and `SEX` are not needed if there is an interaction. The `aov()` command will include these terms, which are called *main effects*, for any variables included in an interaction.

Leslie understood and modified the code to conduct the two-way ANOVA.

```
# two-way ANOVA technology use by degree and sex
techuse.by.deg.sex <- aov(formula = USETECH ~ DEGREE * SEX,
                          data = gss.2018.cleaned)
summary(object = techuse.by.deg.sex)
##                Df    Sum Sq   Mean Sq    F value     Pr(>F)
## DEGREE          4    221301     55325     44.209     < 2e-16 ***
## SEX             1     16473     16473     13.163     0.000296 ***
## DEGREE:SEX      4     26510      6627      5.296     0.000311 ***
## Residuals    1399   1750775      1251
## ---
## Signif. codes:  0 '***' 0.001 '**' 0.01 '*' 0.05 '.' 0.1 ' ' 1
## 936 observations deleted due to missingness
```

Leslie noticed that there are three *F*-statistics for this ANOVA: one for each of the two individual variables (the *main effects*), and one for the interaction term. Nancy explained that a main effect is the relationship between only one of the independent variables and the dependent variable; that is, they ignore the impact of any additional independent variables or interaction effects. When the interaction term is statistically significant, it is interpreted first and the main effects are only interpreted if a main effect variable influences the outcome alone. Nancy clarified by asking Leslie if she could say anything about the influence of SEX on USETECH without mentioning DEGREE after looking at Figure 7.20. Leslie tried, but males did not always have higher nor lower technology use; technology use for males and females was different by DEGREE. Nancy explained that this meant there was no main effect of SEX in this case. Leslie asked if there were cases when the main effect was reported. Nancy explained that there were ways in which two variables could interact with a main effect present; for example, if tech use had started lower for females than males but increased consistently and statistically significantly for both males and females as educational attainment increased, this would be a main effect of DEGREE. Leslie looked a the plot and saw tech use drop slightly for females in the bachelor and graduate categories, so this main effect was not present either; only the interaction would be reported this time.

7.10.2.3 NHST STEP 3: CALCULATE THE PROBABILITY THAT YOUR TEST STATISTIC IS AT LEAST AS BIG AS IT IS IF THERE IS NO RELATIONSHIP (I.E., THE NULL IS TRUE)

The p-value in this case was .000311. This is a very tiny p-value, and so the value of an F-statistic being as large or larger than the F-statistic for the interaction term happens a tiny percentage of the time when the null hypothesis is true.

7.10.2.4 NHST STEPS 4 AND 5: INTERPRET THE PROBABILITY AND WRITE A CONCLUSION

Leslie wrote the full interpretation:

> There was a statistically significant interaction between degree and sex on mean percent of work time spent using technology [$F(4, 1399) = 5.3$; $p < .001$]. The highest mean was 72.1% of time used for technology for males with graduate degrees. The lowest mean was 23.7% of the time for females with less than a high school diploma. The interaction between degree and sex shows that time spent on technology use increases more quickly for females, with both males and females eventually having high tech use in the top two educational attainment groups.

7.10.3 POST HOC TEST FOR TWO-WAY ANOVA

After a little searching, Leslie was disappointed to find that the Bonferroni post hoc test is not available in R for two-way ANOVA, but she did find that the Tukey's HSD test still works. She wrote a single line of code to determine which groups have statistically significantly different mean technology use.

```
# Tukey's HSD post hoc test
TukeyHSD(x = techuse.by.deg.sex)
##   Tukey multiple comparisons of means
##     95% family-wise confidence level
##
## Fit: aov(formula = USETECH ~ DEGREE * SEX, data = gss.2018.cleaned)
##
## $DEGREE
##                                 diff        lwr        upr     p adj
## high school-< high school      24.8247754 15.244768 34.404783 0.0000000
## junior college-< high school   37.6070312 25.329478 49.884584 0.0000000
## bachelor-< high school         43.0859568 32.760484 53.411429 0.0000000
## graduate-< high school         43.9107249 32.376284 55.445165 0.0000000
## junior college-high school     12.7822558  3.459487 22.105024 0.0017563
## bachelor-high school           18.2611813 11.719691 24.802671 0.0000000
## graduate-high school           19.0859494 10.766152 27.405746 0.0000000
## bachelor-junior college         5.4789255 -4.608337 15.566188 0.5733923
## graduate-junior college         6.3036936 -5.018002 17.625389 0.5490670
```

```
## graduate-bachelor               0.8247681  -8.343540  9.993076 0.9991960
##
## $SEX
##                   diff      lwr       upr      p adj
## female-male    6.80899 3.108699 10.50928 0.0003174
##
## $`DEGREE:SEX`
##                                                      diff          lwr
## high school:male-< high school:male            17.8132060    2.7275183
## junior college:male-< high school:male         21.3181818   -0.4992077
## bachelor:male-< high school:male               42.3151914   25.7902764
## graduate:male-< high school:male               46.3538961   27.5496712
## < high school:female-< high school:male        -2.0378788  -22.6075109
## high school:female-< high school:male          30.1500000   15.0344692
## junior college:female-< high school:male       44.7418831   26.3028236
## bachelor:female-< high school:male             42.0396406   25.8082011
## graduate:female-< high school:male             40.1813241   22.0984520
## junior college:male-high school:male            3.5049758  -14.4610385
## bachelor:male-high school:male                 24.5019854   13.5542915
## graduate:male-high school:male                 28.5406901   14.3851943
## < high school:female-high school:male         -19.8510848  -36.2793820
## high school:female-high school:male            12.3367940    3.6616307
## junior college:female-high school:male         26.9286771   13.2619985
## bachelor:female-high school:male               24.2264346   13.7269673
## graduate:female-high school:male               22.3681181    9.1859540
## bachelor:male-junior college:male              20.9970096    1.8065820
## graduate:male-junior college:male              25.0357143    3.8508477
## < high school:female-junior college:male      -23.3560606  -46.1224714
## high school:female-junior college:male          8.8318182   -9.1592621
## junior college:female-junior college:male      23.4237013    2.5622868
## bachelor:female-junior college:male            20.7214588    1.7831557
## graduate:female-junior college:male            18.8631423   -1.6841193
## graduate:male-bachelor:male                     4.0387047  -11.6416301
## < high school:female-bachelor:male            -44.3530702  -62.1121183
## high school:female-bachelor:male              -12.1651914  -23.1539720
## junior college:female-bachelor:male             2.4266917  -12.8138117
## bachelor:female-bachelor:male                  -0.2755508  -12.7548798
## graduate:female-bachelor:male                  -2.1338673  -16.9414427
## < high school:female-graduate:male            -48.3917749  -68.2892584
```

```
## high school:female-graduate:male              -16.2038961 -30.3911918
## junior college:female-graduate:male            -1.6120130 -19.2981376
## bachelor:female-graduate:male                  -4.3142555 -19.6849976
## graduate:female-graduate:male                  -6.1725720 -23.4870269
## high school:female-< high school:female        32.1878788  15.7321731
## junior college:female-< high school:female     46.7797619  27.2270154
## bachelor:female-< high school:female           44.0775194  26.5912218
## graduate:female-< high school:female           42.2192029  23.0019908
## junior college:female-high school:female       14.5918831   0.8922699
## bachelor:female-high school:female             11.8896406   1.3473395
## graduate:female-high school:female             10.0313241  -3.1849820
## bachelor:female-junior college:female          -2.7022425 -17.6240305
## graduate:female-junior college:female          -4.5605590 -21.4777217
## graduate:female-bachelor:female                -1.8583165 -16.3376501
##                                                        upr       p adj
## high school:male-< high school:male             32.8988937   0.0072699
## junior college:male-< high school:male          43.1355713   0.0619111
## bachelor:male-< high school:male                58.8401064   0.0000000
## graduate:male-< high school:male                65.1581210   0.0000000
## < high school:female-< high school:male         18.5317533   0.9999995
## high school:female-< high school:male           45.2655308   0.0000000
## junior college:female-< high school:male        63.1809427   0.0000000
## bachelor:female-< high school:male              58.2710800   0.0000000
## graduate:female-< high school:male              58.2641962   0.0000000
## junior college:male-high school:male            21.4709901   0.9998264
## bachelor:male-high school:male                  35.4496792   0.0000000
## graduate:male-high school:male                  42.6961858   0.0000000
## < high school:female-high school:male           -3.4227876   0.0052315
## high school:female-high school:male             21.0119573   0.0003049
## junior college:female-high school:male          40.5953557   0.0000000
## bachelor:female-high school:male                34.7259018   0.0000000
## graduate:female-high school:male                35.5502821   0.0000039
## bachelor:male-junior college:male               40.1874372   0.0192892
## graduate:male-junior college:male               46.2205808   0.0071871
## < high school:female-junior college:male        -0.5896498   0.0389231
## high school:female-junior college:male          26.8228985   0.8690307
## junior college:female-junior college:male       44.2851158   0.0141081
## bachelor:female-junior college:male             39.6597618   0.0192858
## graduate:female-junior college:male             39.4104039   0.1039186
```

```
## graduate:male-bachelor:male                          19.7190396      0.9983501
## < high school:female-bachelor:male                   -26.5940220      0.0000000
## high school:female-bachelor:male                      -1.1764108      0.0167764
## junior college:female-bachelor:male                   17.6671952      0.9999688
## bachelor:female-bachelor:male                         12.2037783      1.0000000
## graduate:female-bachelor:male                         12.6737082      0.9999867
## < high school:female-graduate:male                   -28.4942914      0.0000000
## high school:female-graduate:male                      -2.0166004      0.0113631
## junior college:female-graduate:male                   16.0741116      0.9999998
## bachelor:female-graduate:male                         11.0564866      0.9967894
## graduate:female-graduate:male                         11.1418829      0.9816675
## high school:female-< high school:female               48.6435845      0.0000000
## junior college:female-< high school:female            66.3325084      0.0000000
## bachelor:female-< high school:female                  61.5638170      0.0000000
## graduate:female-< high school:female                  61.4364150      0.0000000
## junior college:female-high school:female              28.2914963      0.0261888
## bachelor:female-high school:female                    22.4319416      0.0133486
## graduate:female-high school:female                    23.2476303      0.3233313
## bachelor:female-junior college:female                 12.2195454      0.9999069
## graduate:female-junior college:female                 12.3566037      0.9976459
## graduate:female-bachelor:female                       12.6210171      0.9999951
```

Kiara explained that the output is showing one comparison per row. The first section under $DEGREE was comparing groups of DEGREE to each other. The second section under $SEX was comparing males and females to each other. The third section was the interaction, comparing groups of DEGREE*SEX with each other. For example, the first row in this last section is high school:male-< high school:male, which compares high school male to < high school male. The numbers that follow are the difference between the means (diff = 17.81), the confidence interval around the difference (95% CI: 2.73 to 32.90), and the *p*-value for the difference between the means ($p = 0.007$). This indicates that there is a statistically significant ($p < .05$) difference of 17.81 between the mean percentage time of technology use for males with less than high school compared to males with high school *in the sample*, and that the difference between the means of these two groups is likely somewhere between 2.73 and 32.90 in the population this sample came from.

Leslie found that there were so many groups with significant differences that she suggested it would be more useful to just include the boxplot from the exploratory analysis or the means plot and a paragraph about any interesting overall patterns in the comparisons. Kiara and Nancy agreed. Leslie found that there were significant differences between males and females in the high school and junior college groups, but that males and females were not significantly different across the other educational groups. Overall, it appeared that males and females in higher education groups spent more time using technology than those with less education, and that high school- and junior college-educated females spent more time using technology than males with these same education levels. This was demonstrated quite clearly by Figure 7.20.

7.10.4 TWO-WAY ANOVA ASSUMPTIONS

Kiara mentioned that the assumptions of homogeneity of variances and normality were also applicable in two-way ANOVA. She explained that normality would be a little trickier to test by looking at each group since there are five degree groups, two sex groups, and 10 degree-by-sex groups (e.g., male and < high school). Instead of checking normality one group at a time when there are a large number of groups in an ANOVA model, this assumption can be checked by examining the *residuals*. The residuals are the distances between the value of the outcome for each person and the value of the group mean for that person. When the residuals are normally distributed, this indicates that the values in each group are normally distributed around the group mean.

7.10.4.1 TESTING THE NORMALITY ASSUMPTION

Leslie looked at the `techuse.by.deg.sex` object in the Environment pane and saw the residuals. She used a Shapiro-Wilk test to check the normality of the residuals statistically and then plotted the residuals for a visual assessment.

```
# statistical test of normality for groups
shapiro.test(x = techuse.by.deg.sex$residuals)

##

##   Shapiro-Wilk normality test

##

## data:  techuse.by.deg.sex$residuals
## W = 0.95984, p-value < 2.2e-16
```

Leslie reminded herself that the null hypothesis for the Shapiro-Wilk test is that the distribution is normal. By rejecting this null hypothesis with a tiny *p*-value, the assumption is failed. So, this test shows that the residuals fail the normality assumption. Leslie graphed the residuals to confirm. She found that the `ggplot()` command did not work with the ANOVA object, so she converted the residuals to a new data frame first and then graphed them (Figure 7.21).

```
# make a data frame
tech.deg.sex <- data.frame(techuse.by.deg.sex$residuals)

# plot the residuals (Figure 7.21)
tech.deg.sex %>%
  ggplot(aes(x = techuse.by.deg.sex.residuals)) +
  geom_histogram(fill = "#7463AC", col = "white") +
  theme_minimal() +
  labs(x = "Residuals", y = "Number of observations")
```

FIGURE 7.21 Distribution of residuals from ANOVA explaining tech use at work based on educational attainment and sex

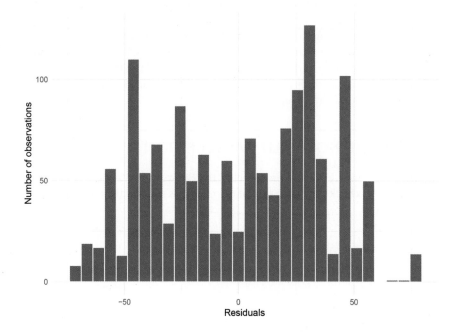

The residuals did not appear to be normally distributed. Instead, Leslie noticed, they seemed bimodal, with some large residuals at the lower end and some at the upper end of the range. This indicated that some observations were quite far below or above the group mean value for their group. Leslie found this was consistent with the boxplots showing quite a few people who reported 0% or 100% of their time using technology at work. This was also consistent with the tests of normality from the one-way ANOVA.

7.10.4.2 TESTING THE HOMOGENEITY OF VARIANCES ASSUMPTION

Leslie remembered that the `leveneTest()` function could be used to test the null hypothesis that the variances are equal, and she used `car::` to open the package just to test this assumption.

```
# Levene test for ANOVA
car::leveneTest(y = USETECH ~ DEGREE*SEX, center = mean,
                data = gss.2018.cleaned)
## Levene's Test for Homogeneity of Variance (center = mean)
##         Df    F value      Pr(>F)
## group    9     8.5912    1.289e-12 ***
##       1399
## ---
## Signif. codes:  0 '***' 0.001 '**' 0.01 '*' 0.05 '.' 0.1 ' ' 1
```

Leslie saw that the results were statistically significant so the null hypothesis was rejected. The equal variances assumption was not met. The two-way ANOVA had failed its assumptions.

7.10.5 ALTERNATIVES WHEN TWO-WAY ANOVA ASSUMPTIONS FAIL

Kiara had recently read a book that suggested using a Friedman test when two-way ANOVA assumptions fail (MacFarland & Yates, 2016). Nancy and Leslie thought this sounded good, and Nancy looked up the code to conduct the test. She found the Friedman test can be conducted using `friedman.test()` on a set of means for each group in a summary data format rather than raw data. Nancy enjoyed a challenge and went to work creating a new data frame of summary data from the USETECH, DEGREE, and SEX variables.

```
# Friedman two-way ANOVA for ranked data
# R command requires summary data
agg.gss.2018 <- gss.2018.cleaned %>%
  drop_na(USETECH) %>%
  group_by(DEGREE, SEX) %>%
  summarize(m.usetech = mean(x = USETECH))
agg.gss.2018
## # A tibble: 10 x 3
## # Groups:  DEGREE [5]
##     DEGREE          SEX       m.usetech
##     <fct>           <fct>        <dbl>
##  1 < high school    male          25.7
##  2 < high school    female        23.7
##  3 high school      male          43.5
##  4 high school      female        55.9
##  5 junior college   male          47.0
##  6 junior college   female        70.4
##  7 bachelor         male          68.0
##  8 bachelor         female        67.7
##  9 graduate         male          72.1
## 10 graduate         female        65.9
```

Now that she had a new data frame with summary data in it, she looked at the help documentation to find the format for using `friedman.test()` and tried it with the `agg.gss.2018` summary data she had just created.

```
# Friedman test
tech.by.deg.sex.f <- friedman.test(formula = m.usetech ~ DEGREE | SEX,
                                   data = agg.gss.2018)
tech.by.deg.sex.f
##
##  Friedman rank sum test
```

```
## 
## data: m.usetech and DEGREE and SEX
## Friedman chi-squared = 6.4, df = 4, p-value = 0.1712
```

The team was surprised that the Friedman test found no statistically significant difference in technology use by degree and sex [$\chi^2(4) = 6.4$; $p = 0.17$]. Given the means plots and boxplots developed in the exploratory data analysis for two-way ANOVA, this seemed like an unusual result. Kiara did a little digging and found a number of manuscripts suggesting that the Friedman test is not a great option for addressing failed assumptions (Harwell & Serlin, 1994; Zimmerman & Zumbo, 1993).

Instead of using Friedman, another suggested method is to compute the ranks of the outcome variable and conduct the two-way ANOVA on the ranked outcome variable. Luckily, Leslie had computed the ranks of USETECH for the Dunn's test earlier and tried out the two-way ANOVA code with the transformed outcome variable.

```
# two-way ANOVA ranked technology use by degree and sex
techuse.by.deg.sex.t <- aov(formula = usetech.rank ~ DEGREE * SEX,
                            data = gss.2018.cleaned)
summary(object = techuse.by.deg.sex.t)
##                Df      Sum Sq    Mean Sq    F value     Pr(>F)
## DEGREE          4    23270305    5817576      40.26    < 2e-16 ***
## SEX             1     1849104    1849104      12.80   0.000359 ***
## DEGREE:SEX      4     3120976     780244       5.40   0.000258 ***
## Residuals    1399   202148767     144495
## ---
## Signif. codes: 0 '***' 0.001 '**' 0.01 '*' 0.05 '.' 0.1 ' ' 1
## 936 observations deleted due to missingness
```

Nancy made plots of the ranks to add context to the results (Figure 7.22).

The plots showed difference from one educational attainment group to another and between males and females. Leslie wrote her interpretation of the ranked outcome ANOVA:

A two-way ANOVA with ranked technology time use as the outcome found a statistically significant interaction between degree and sex ($p < .05$). The overall pattern of results indicates that males and females with less than a high school education use technology the least, while those with higher educational attainment use technology the most. Males and females differ a lot in use of technology for those with a junior college degree, with females having a junior college degree having the highest use of technology of all females.

Kiara mentioned that another strategy she had seen used when two-way ANOVA assumptions were not met was a Box-Cox transformation on the outcome variable. She remembered that the Box-Cox power transformations were developed to reduce the non-normality of residuals, so they might be useful here. The original paper by Box and Cox explains the transformations (Box & Cox, 1964), and there are numerous tutorials on the use of them. Nancy suggested that they could try other data transformations as well for future tests when assumptions are failed.

FIGURE 7.22 Ranks of percentage of time spent using technology by educational attainment and sex

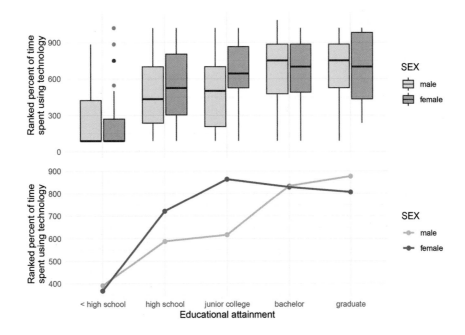

Leslie was glad to be done with another day. She thought she would find a lot of uses for ANOVA since comparing means of different groups seemed like a common research strategy. She found it interesting to see the differences in technology use at work by educational attainment and sex. She had not been expecting the big differences in percentage of time spent using technology at work for males and females in the high school and junior college groups. She also felt that the differences among educational attainment groups overall were bigger than she would have imagined. Nancy thought that it might be due to who they tend to interact with in their lives. Since the R-Team members are all college educated, their friends and colleagues were mostly college educated, so most people they know would be in the same place for percentage of time spent using technology at work.

Leslie was finished with the day and her phone was fully charged at last. It was time to reconnect with the world. Her friend Amy had sent her a podcast to listen to called *Follow the Data*. She got out her earbuds, plugged them in, and clicked on the podcast app.

"See you later, alligators!" she said loudly to Nancy and Kiara, who were deep in conversation about something.

Nancy and Kiara looked up and waved as Leslie started to walk away.

"See you next time!" Kiara said.

"Bye!" said Nancy.

7.10.6 ACHIEVEMENT 7: CHECK YOUR UNDERSTANDING

List the assumptions for one-way and two-way ANOVA and describe at least one way to test each assumption.

7.11.1 Achievements unlocked in this chapter: Recap

Congratulations! Like Leslie, you've learned and practiced the following in this chapter.

7.11.1.1 Achievement 1 recap: Exploring the data using graphics and descriptive statistics

Prior to conducting inferential statistical tests like χ^2, it is useful to get some idea of the characteristics and relationships in your data. Descriptive statistics and graphs are useful for understanding who is in the data set and what their characteristics are.

7.11.1.2 Achievement 2 recap: Understanding and conducting one-way ANOVA

One-way ANOVA compares the means of multiple groups, usually three or more. Significant results indicate that the differences among the means likely reflect differences in means from the populations the samples came from. One-way ANOVA is an omnibus test (like χ^2), identifying significant relationships but providing no measure of the strength of the association between variables.

7.11.1.3 Achievement 3 recap: Choosing and using post hoc tests and contrasts

Following a significant ANOVA result, planned comparisons or a post hoc test like Bonferroni or Tukey's HSD can identify significant differences between pairs of means. Planned comparisons are typically used when there are hypothesized differences among the groups, while post hoc tests are used when there are no specific hypotheses about differences among group means.

7.11.1.4 Achievement 4: Computing and interpreting effect sizes for ANOVA

The two most common types of effect sizes for ANOVA are η^2 and ω^2. Eta-squared is the proportion of variance explained by the model relative to the total variance. However, ω^2 is generally recommended over η^2 because it gets at the same idea but is less biased than η^2. The cutoffs for the ω^2 effect size are as follows:

- $\omega^2 = .01$ to $\omega^2 < .06$ is a small effect
- $\omega^2 = .06$ to $\omega^2 < .14$ is a medium effect
- $\omega^2 \geq .14$ is a large effect

7.11.1.5 Achievement 5 recap: Testing ANOVA assumptions

Statistical tests rely on underlying assumptions about the characteristics of the data. When these assumptions are not met, the results may not reflect the true relationships among the variables. For ANOVA, four assumptions need to be met: (a) continuous variable and independent groups, (b) independent observations, (c) normal distribution in each group, and (d) equal variances for each group.

7.11.1.6 Achievement 6 recap: Choosing and using alternative tests when ANOVA assumptions are not met

When assumptions are not met for ANOVA, there are alternative tests that account for the data not meeting assumptions. When the homogeneity of variances assumption is not met, two alternative F-statistics are good options: Brown-Forsythe and Welch's. When the normality assumption is not met, the Kruskal-Wallis test is an alternative test that compares the mean ranks across groups.

7.11.1.7 Achievement 7 recap: Understanding and conducting two-way ANOVA

Two-way ANOVA is useful for comparing means across groups of two categorical variables for main effects and as an interaction. This type of statistical model can answer questions like how time using technology varies by educational attainment, sex, and the interaction of educational attainment and sex. Assumption checking and post hoc tests apply in two-way ANOVA just like in one-way ANOVA.

7.11.2 Chapter exercises

The coder and hacker exercises are an opportunity to apply the skills from this chapter to a new scenario or a new data set. The coder edition evaluates the application of the concepts and commands learned in this R-Team meeting to scenarios similar to those in the meeting. The hacker edition evaluates the use of the concepts and commands from this R-Team meeting in new scenarios, often going a step beyond what was explicitly explained.

The coder edition might be best for those who found some or all of the Check Your Understanding activities to be challenging or if they needed review before picking the correct responses to the multiple-choice questions. The hacker edition might be best if the Check Your Understanding activities were not too challenging and the multiple-choice questions were a breeze.

The multiple-choice questions and materials for the exercises are online at **edge.sagepub.com/harris1e**.

Q1: What is the primary purpose of ANOVA?

a. Comparing means across three or more groups

b. Comparing medians across three or more groups

c. Examining the relationship between two categorical variables

d. Identifying normally distributed data

Q2: Which of the following assumptions does *not* apply to ANOVA?

a. Independent observations

b. Normal distribution of continuous variable

c. Homogeneity of variances

d. Inclusion of one bivariate variable

Q3: How many pairwise comparisons would there be for an ANOVA with four groups?

a. 16

b. 4

c. 12

d. 6

Q4: Apply a Bonferroni adjustment to a *p*-value of .01 if the analyses included six pairwise comparisons. If the threshold for statistical significance were .05, would the adjusted *p*-value be significant?

a. Yes

b. No

Q5: In which situation would you use planned comparisons?

a. After a significant ANOVA to compare each pair of means

b. Instead of an ANOVA when the data did not meet the normality assumption

c. When you have to choose between two categorical variables

d. When you conduct an ANOVA and have hypotheses about which sets of means are different from one another

7.11.2.1 Chapter exercises: Coder edition

Use the data from this chapter and the appropriate tests to examine technology use by marital status.

1) Open the data using the strategy shown in this chapter.

2) Clean the marital status, sex, and tech use variables so they have clear variable names, category labels, and missing value coding.

3) Use graphics and descriptive statistics to examine tech use on its own, by sex, and by marital status (Achievement 1).

4) Based on the graphs and statistics from Question 3, make a prediction about what you would find when you compare tech use across groups by marital status and by sex (Achievement 1).

5) Conduct the appropriate test to compare mean time using tech across marital status groups. If the *F*-statistic is significant, use a post hoc test to determine which means are statistically significantly different from each other. Interpret your results (Achievements 2 and 3).

6) Check assumptions for the ANOVA and conduct an appropriate alternate analysis if it does not pass assumptions. Interpret your results (Achievements 5 and 6).

7) Conduct a two-way ANOVA with time using technology by sex and marital status. Interpret results and check assumptions (Achievement 7).

7.11.2.2 Chapter exercises: Hacker edition

Complete the coder edition and also do the following:

8) Use the graphics in Question 3 to hypothesize which marital status groups have different tech use means. Write planned comparisons instead to test your hypotheses and conduct an appropriate planned

comparison analysis instead of post hoc tests in Question 5.

9) Conduct and interpret post hoc tests for the two-way ANOVA developed in Question 7.

7.11.2.3 Instructor note

Solutions to exercises can be found on the website for this book, along with ideas for gamification for those who want to take it further.

Visit **edge.sagepub.com/harris1e** to download the datasets, complete the chapter exercises, and watch R tutorial videos.

8

CORRELATION COEFFICIENTS

The R-Team and the Clean Water Conundrum

It had been a month since the last R-Team meeting because Nancy had been traveling, and Leslie was anxious to continue learning about R. They had all agreed to meet at their favorite café.

Nancy and Leslie walked in at the same time. They saw that Kiara, early as always, had snagged the best booth.

"Hello, R-Team," Kiara said.

"Hey," said Leslie.

"Hujambo," Nancy said. "That's Swahili for 'hello.'"

"Nice!" said Kiara.

"How was your trip to Tanzania?" Leslie asked.

"It was amazing!" Nancy enthused. "Going to Serengeti National Park and later seeing Mount Kilimanjaro in the distance were everything I'd imagined. Also, there is a group building an R community in the city of Dar es Salaam (https://twitter.com/daR_users), which is on the coast of the Indian Ocean. I connected to the organizers through Twitter and at the end of my trip was lucky enough to meet a few of the people involved. I really enjoyed learning about what they are doing."

"Very cool," said Leslie.

"Tell us more later," said Kiara. "For now, let's get down to some local R learning right here." Then Kiara summarized: "So far, we've discussed chi-squared and its alternatives, *t*-tests and their alternatives, and ANOVA and its alternatives."

"Right," Nancy said. "These methods are useful for when you encounter a question that can be answered by examining the relationship between two categorical variables (chi-squared) or between a continuous variable and one or two categorical variables (*t*-tests, ANOVA). The goodness-of-fit chi-squared and the one-sample *t*-test are versions of these tests for comparing one continuous variable or one categorical variable to a hypothesized or population value."

"Today, we will be adding the correlation coefficient to the list," said Kiara. "The *correlation coefficient* is used to examine the relationship between two continuous variables. It has assumptions to meet and alternatives when assumptions aren't met, just like the other tests we've learned."

"I didn't realize we'd covered so much already!" Leslie exclaimed. Then she pointed out some patterns she noticed that were emerging for an analysis plan that works across all the statistical tests:

- Import and clean the data (e.g., check missing values, add labels to categories, rename variables for easier use).

- Conduct descriptive and visual exploratory data analysis to get familiar with the data.

- Choose the test that fits the data and your research question.

- Check the assumptions to make sure the test is appropriate.

$SAGE edge™

Visit **edge.sagepub.com/harris1e** to watch an R tutorial

- Use the NHST process to conduct the test or an alternative test if assumptions are not met.
- If test results find a statistically significant relationship, follow up with post hoc tests, effect size calculations, or other strategies for better understanding the relationship.

"Excellent plan," Kiara said. "Let's keep it in mind for organizing our next few meetings."

"Great," Leslie answered. "Now, who wants some of my fries?"

Nancy was ready to get started on correlation and had already created a list of achievements.

8.1 Achievements to unlock

- Achievement 1: Exploring the data using graphics and descriptive statistics
- Achievement 2: Computing and interpreting Pearson's *r* correlation coefficient
- Achievement 3: Conducting an inferential statistical test for Pearson's *r* correlation coefficient
- Achievement 4: Examining effect size for Pearson's *r* with the coefficient of determination
- Achievement 5: Checking assumptions for Pearson's *r* correlation analyses
- Achievement 6: Transforming the variables as an alternative when Pearson's *r* correlation assumptions are not met
- Achievement 7: Using Spearman's rho as an alternative when Pearson's *r* correlation assumptions are not met
- Achievement 8: Introducing partial correlations

8.2 The clean water conundrum

On one of Nancy's day trips in Tanzania, she had seen firsthand what she had been reading about: the lack of access to clean water and sanitation and how this impacts people living in poverty, poor women and girls in particular (Thompson, Folifac, & Gaskin, 2011; Warrington & Kiragu, 2012). Specifically, women and girls tend to be responsible for collecting water for their families, often walking long distances in unsafe areas and carrying heavy loads (Devnarain & Matthias, 2011; Thompson et al., 2011). In some cultures, lack of access to sanitation facilities also means that women can only defecate after dark, which can be physically uncomfortable and/or put them at greater risk for harassment and assault. In many places in the world, including parts of Tanzania (Frisone, 2017), the lack of sanitation facilities can keep girls out of school when they are menstruating (Sommer, 2010). Nancy was interested in exploring this problem further, and Leslie and Kiara came right on board.

Nancy shared a graph she had started working on when she was on the plane home. She used data from a few different sources to examine the relationship between the percentage of people in a country with water access and the percentage of school-aged girls who are in school (Figure 8.1).

Nancy and Kiara asked Leslie to describe what she was seeing in the graph. Leslie saw that the percent of people with basic access to water ranged from just below 20% to 100%, and the percent of females in school ranged from around 30% to 100%. She noticed that the percentage of females in school increased

FIGURE 8.1 Relationship between percentage of females in school and percentage of citizens with basic water access in countries worldwide

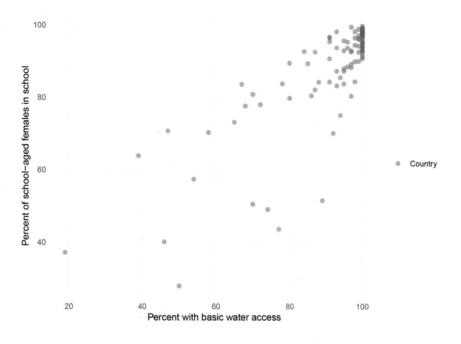

Sources: UNESCO Institute for Statistics (n.d.), WHO (n.d.).

as the percentage of people with access to water in a country increased. She also saw a bunch of values at the top (or ceiling) value of the water access variable, but no problem with ceiling values for the percentage of females in school variable.

Nancy explained that the pattern in the graph could indicate that there is a relationship, or correlation, between water access and percentage of females in school. Specifically, she said, if one goes up as the other one goes up, the relationship between the two could be a *positive correlation*. Leslie asked if there was such a thing as a negative correlation. Nancy showed her the relationship between the percentage of females in school and the percentage of people living on less than $1 per day (Figure 8.2).

Nancy explained that the data for Figures 8.1 and 8.2 came from the World Health Organization (WHO) and the UNESCO Institute for Statistics. The WHO data on access to basic or safe sanitation and basic or safe water was in the Global Health Observatory data repository (WHO, n.d.).

Leslie noticed that the pattern of points goes in a different direction, from the top left to the bottom right. As the percentage of people living on less than $1 per day increases, the percentage of females in school decreases. As the values of one variable go up, the values of the other go down. This time, fewer points appear to be located at the ceiling or floor values. Nancy explained that this shows a negative relationship, or *negative correlation*, between the two variables.

Leslie asked if there is such thing as a correlation that is neither positive nor negative. Nancy explained that correlations are either positive or negative. A correlation of zero would suggest that there is no relationship or no correlation between two variables (Mukaka, 2012).

FIGURE 8.2 Relationship between percentage of people living on less than $1 per day and percentage of females in school in countries worldwide

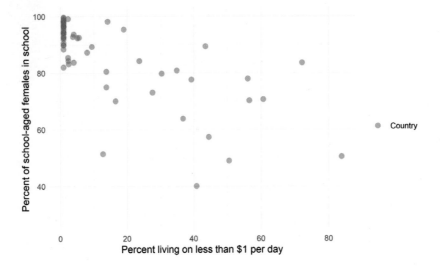

Sources: UNESCO Institute for Statistics (n.d.), WHO (n.d.).

Kiara reviewed Nancy's data sources and found that the way the data were posted online was not easy to manage or import directly into R quickly. Nancy had spent quite a bit of time downloading and merging the two data sources and thought she would share them so the team could spend their time on correlation rather than data importing and management. She saved the code and sent it to Leslie to review later (Box 8.1). She then shared the clean data with the team so they could get started.

8.1 Nancy's fancy code: Bringing in and merging original data from websites

The data for this chapter were imported from the World Health Organization (WHO) and UNESCO Institute for Statistics websites. Nancy found the water data on the WHO website and copied the URL for importing. There were a lot of variables, so she would not use `summary()` yet to check the data, but instead checked it by clicking on the name of the data frame in the Environment tab in the upper right pane to view the data.

```
# import water data from WHO website

library(package = "tidyverse")

water <- read_csv("http://apps.who.int/gho/athena/data/GHO/WSH_
WATER_SAFELY_MANAGED,WSH_WATER_BASIC?filter=COUNTRY:*;RESIDENCEAREA
```

```
TYPE:*&x-sideaxis=COUNTRY&x-topaxis=YEAR;GHO;RESIDENCEAREATYPE&profi
le=crosstable&format=csv")
```

In viewing the data from this import, Nancy noticed that the first two rows were not data but looked like row headings.

Nancy checked the WHO website and limited the data to the first column with the country names (x1), the 2015 column with the total percentage of people using at least basic drinking water services (2015_2), and the seventh column with the total percentage of people using safely managed drinking water services (2015_5). She used select() to limit the data to these three columns. To keep only the rows of data from row 3 to the end of the data, she used slice().

```
# limit data to 2015 basic and safe water
water.cleaned <- water %>%
select(X1, '2015_2', '2015_5') %>%
   slice(3:n()) %>%
   rename(country = 'X1', perc.basic2015water = '2015_2',
          perc.safe2015water = '2015_5')
```

She reviewed the water.cleaned data frame and found a very clean data frame with three variables: country, perc.basic2015water, and perc.safe2015water. She moved on to the sanitation data source and noticed it resembled the water data; she used her experience from the water data source to write some efficient importing code.

```
# get sanitation data
sanitation <- read_csv("http://apps.who.int/gho/athena/data/GHO/
WSH_SANITATION_SAFELY_MANAGED,WSH_SANITATION_BASIC?filter=COUNTRY:*;
RESIDENCEAREATYPE:*&x-sideaxis=COUNTRY&x-topaxis=YEAR;GHO;RESIDENCE
AREATYPE&profile=crosstable&format=csv")

# limit to 2015
# name the variables consistent with water data
sanitation.cleaned <- sanitation %>%
select(X1, '2015_2', '2015_5') %>%
   slice(3:n()) %>%
   rename(country = 'X1', perc.basic2015sani = '2015_2',
          perc.safe2015sani = '2015_5')
```

(Continued)

(Continued)

Nancy noticed that poverty data are also available in the WHO data repository. She downloaded population characteristics including median age for residents of each country along with the percentage of people living on $1 per day or less. She found several countries with < 2.0 as the entry for the percentage of people living on $1 or less per day. Because the value is not precise and the less than symbol cannot be included in a numeric variable type for analysis, Nancy decided to replace these values with 1 as the percentage of people living on less than $1 per day. Although this is not perfect, the entry of < 2.0 indicates these countries have between 0% and 1.99% of people living at this level of poverty, so 1.0 would be a reasonable replacement.

Nancy was a little uneasy with this but decided that she would explain exactly what she did if they ended up using these data outside their meeting. She thought about what Kiara would say and knew that there would be no way to reproduce her results unless the data management choices were clear.

```
# get population data
pop <- read_csv("[data folder location]/data/2015-who-income-data-
ch8.csv", skip = 1)

# add variable names and recode
# change to numeric
pop.cleaned <- pop %>%
  rename(country = "Country", med.age = "2013",
                  perc.1dollar = "2007-2013") %>%
  mutate(perc.1dollar = as.numeric(recode(perc.1dollar,
                                  `&lt;2.0` = "1")))
```

Next, Nancy needed the UNESCO data for the percentage of males and females who complete primary and secondary school. She found the data on the UNESCO Institute for Statistics website under the Education menu with the heading "Out-of-school rate for children, adolescents, and youth of primary and secondary school age." Nancy explained that there was no way to download it directly into R from the website, so Leslie downloaded and saved the Excel spreadsheet to her computer. To import an Excel spreadsheet, she used `read_xl()` from the **readxl** package.

```
# bring in education data
educ <- readxl::read_excel(path = "[data folder location]/data/2015-
outOfSchoolRate-primarySecondary-ch8.xlsx", skip = 4)
```

```
# examine the education data
View(x = educ)
```

Leslie noticed that the second column was blank, the variable names were not useful, and the last five rows looked like notes instead of values. She decided to remove the second column and the last five rows and add better variable names. Nancy used `slice()` to select rows to keep. To keep rows 1 to 280, use `slice(1:280)`.

```
# remove second column and rename the variables
educ.cleaned <- educ %>%
  select(-...2) %>%
  slice(1:280) %>%
  rename(country = "Country", perc.in.school = "...3",
  female.in.school = "...4", male.in.school = "...5")
```

In viewing the data in the Environment, Nancy noticed that the percentage variables were saved as character variables. This was because the missing data are stored as ".." instead of true NA values. To change the three percentage variables to numeric, she first replaced the ".." as NA, and added the `as.numeric()` function to the data management. Nancy knew that the data were percentages out-of-school and subtracted the percentage of females out-of-school from 100 to get a percentage of in-school females, males, and total.

```
# change variable types and recode
educ.cleaned <- educ %>%
  select(-...2) %>%
  slice(1:280) %>%
  rename(country = "Country", perc.in.school = "...3",
  female.in.school = "...4", male.in.school = "...5") %>%
  na_if("..") %>%
  mutate(perc.in.school = 100 - as.numeric(perc.in.school)) %>%
  mutate(female.in.school = 100 - as.numeric(female.in.school)) %>%
  mutate(male.in.school = 100 - as.numeric(male.in.school))
```

Nancy used `summary()` to review the data and determined that they were ready to merge with the water and sanitation data.

```
# review data
summary(object = educ.cleaned)
```

She used the `merge()` function to make one data frame from the `educ.cleaned`, `pop.cleaned`, `sanitation.cleaned`, and `water.cleaned` objects.

(Continued)

(Continued)

```
# merge population, sanitation, water data frames by country
# merge the data frames
water.educ <- educ.cleaned %>%
  merge(pop.cleaned) %>%
  merge(sanitation.cleaned) %>%
  merge(water.cleaned)
```

The resulting data frame contained 182 observations and 10 variables. Before she saved the file for use by the R-Team, Nancy restricted the data to countries that had reported education data for 2015 by dropping NA for the school variables: perc.in.school, female.in.school, and male.in.school. This left a sample of 97 countries. She used the write.csv() function to save the new data in the data folder, adding row.names = FALSE so that the row names would not be included as a new variable.

```
# remove observations with na for school variables
water.educ <- water.educ %>%
  drop_na(perc.in.school) %>%
  drop_na(female.in.school) %>%
  drop_na(male.in.school)

# save as a csv
write.csv(x = water.educ, file = "[data folder location]/data/water_
educ.csv", row.names = FALSE)
```

8.3 Data and R packages for learning about correlation

Before they examined the data, Kiara made a list of all the data and packages needed for learning about correlation.

- Two options for accessing the data
  - Download the **water_educ_2015_who_unesco_ch8.csv** and **2015-outOfSchoolRate-primarySecondary-ch8.xlsx** data sets from **edge.sagepub.com/harris1e**
  - Follow the instructions in Box 8.1 to import and clean the data directly from the original Internet sources. Please note that the WHO makes small corrections to past data occasionally, so use of data imported based on Box 8.1 instructions may result in minor differences in results throughout the chapter. To match chapter results exactly, use the data provided at **edge.sagepub.com/harris1e**.

- Install the following R packages if not already installed
  - ○ **tidyverse**, by Hadley Wickham (https://www.rdocumentation.org/packages/tidyverse/)
  - ○ **readxl**, by Jennifer Bryan (https://www.rdocumentation.org/packages/readxl/)
  - ○ *lmtest*, by Achim Zeileis (https://www.rdocumentation.org/packages/lmtest/)
  - ○ **rcompanion**, by Salvatore Mangiafico (https://www.rdocumentation.org/packages/rcompanion/)
  - ○ *ppcor*, by Seongho Kim (https://www.rdocumentation.org/packages/ppcor/)

8.4 Achievement 1: Exploring the data using graphics and descriptive statistics

Leslie imported the data and used summary() to see what was in the data frame.

```
# import the water data
water.educ <- read.csv(file = "[data folder location]/data/water_educ_2015_
who_unesco_ch8.csv")

# examine the data. Please note that due to occasional updates to online
# WHO data, if you are using data imported as instructed in
# Box 8.1, your results may vary slightly from those shown.
summary(object = water.educ)
##                    country        med.age          perc.1dollar
##   Albania             : 1    Min.    :15.00    Min.    : 1.00
##   Antigua and Barbuda : 1    1st Qu.:22.50     1st Qu.: 1.00
##   Argentina           : 1    Median :29.70     Median : 1.65
##   Australia           : 1    Mean    :30.33    Mean    :13.63
##   Azerbaijan          : 1    3rd Qu.:39.00     3rd Qu.:17.12
##   Bahrain             : 1    Max.    :45.90    Max.    :83.80
##   (Other)             :91                      NA's    :33
##   perc.basic2015sani  perc.safe2015sani  perc.basic2015water
##   Min.    : 7.00      Min.    : 9.00     Min.    : 19.00
##   1st Qu.: 73.00      1st Qu.: 61.25     1st Qu.: 88.75
##   Median : 93.00      Median : 76.50     Median : 97.00
##   Mean    : 79.73     Mean    : 71.50    Mean    : 90.16
##   3rd Qu.: 99.00      3rd Qu.: 93.00     3rd Qu.:100.00
##   Max.    :100.00     Max.    :100.00    Max.    :100.00
##                       NA's    : 47       NA's    : 1
##   perc.safe2015water  perc.in.school  female.in.school  male.in.school
##   Min.    : 11.00     Min.    :33.32  Min.    :27.86    Min.    :38.66
##   1st Qu.: 73.75      1st Qu.:83.24   1st Qu.:83.70     1st Qu.:82.68
```

```
##   Median  : 94.00    Median :92.02   Median :92.72    Median :91.50
##   Mean    : 83.38    Mean   :87.02   Mean   :87.06    Mean   :87.00
##   3rd Qu.: 98.00    3rd Qu.:95.81   3rd Qu.:96.61    3rd Qu.:95.57
##   Max.    :100.00    Max.   :99.44   Max.   :99.65    Max.   :99.36
##   NA's    :45
```

Since there was not a single codebook for these merged data sources, Kiara wrote out the definitions of the variables.

- country: the name of the country
- med.age: the median age of the citizens in the country
- perc.1dollar: percentage of citizens living on $1 per day or less
- perc.basic2015sani: percentage of citizens with basic sanitation access
- perc.safe2015sani: percentage of citizens with safe sanitation access
- perc.basic2015water: percentage of citizens with basic water access
- perc.safe2015water: percentage of citizens with safe water access
- perc.in.school: percentage of school-age people in primary and secondary school
- female.in.school: percentage of female school-age people in primary and secondary school
- male.in.school: percentage of male school-age people in primary and secondary school

The data were all from 2015. Leslie noticed that the data frame in the Environment pane showed 97 countries and 10 variables. Except for country, all of the variables appeared to be numeric. Leslie computed the mean and standard deviation for the two variables of interest, female.in.school and perc.basic2015water.

```
# open the tidyverse
library(package = "tidyverse")

# descriptive statistics for females in school and water access
water.educ %>%
  drop_na(female.in.school) %>%
  drop_na(perc.basic2015water) %>%
  summarize(m.f.educ = mean(x = female.in.school),
            sd.f.educ = sd(x = female.in.school),
            m.bas.water = mean(x = perc.basic2015water),
            sd.bas.water = sd(x = perc.basic2015water))
##    m.f.educ sd.f.educ m.bas.water sd.bas.water
## 1 87.01123   15.1695    90.15625     15.81693
```

The mean percent of school-aged females in school was 87.06 (sd = 15.1), and the mean percent of citizens who had basic access to water was 90.16 (sd = 15.82). These means appeared high to Leslie, and after looking at the scatterplots, she was already thinking that the variables may be left-skewed.

8.4.1 MAKE A SCATTERPLOT TO EXAMINE THE RELATIONSHIP

Leslie used `ggplot()` to re-create one of Nancy's graphs. She asked Nancy about adding percent signs to the axes, so Nancy introduced her to some new layers for `ggplot()`. The `scale_x_continuous()` and `scale_y_continuous()` layers with the `label =` argument can be used to change the scale on the *x*-axis and *y*-axis so that it shows percentages. To use these scales, Nancy showed Leslie that she needed to divide the percent variables by 100 in the `aes()` function in order to get a decimal version of the percentages for use with the `labels = scales::percent` option (Figure 8.3).

```
# explore plot of female education and water access (Figure 8.3)
water.educ %>%
  ggplot(aes(y = female.in.school/100, x = perc.basic2015water/100)) +
  geom_point(aes(color = "Country"), size = 2, alpha = .6) +
  theme_minimal() +
  labs(y = "Percent of school-aged females in school",
       x = "Percent with basic water access") +
  scale_color_manual(values = "#7463AC", name = "") +
  scale_x_continuous(labels = scales::percent) +
  scale_y_continuous(labels = scales::percent)
```

Figure 8.3 demonstrated that the relationship between percentage with access to basic water and percentage of females in school is positive. That is, as the percentage with basic water access went up, so did the percentage of females in school.

FIGURE 8.3 Relationship of percentage of females in school and percentage of citizens with basic water access in countries worldwide

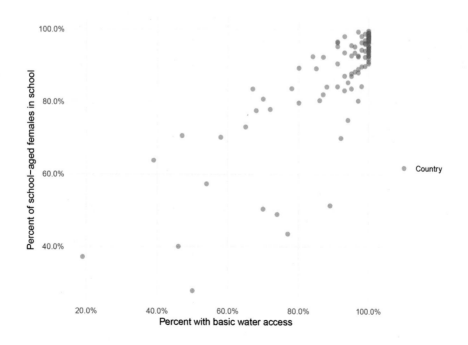

8.4.2 ACHIEVEMENT 1: CHECK YOUR UNDERSTANDING

Which of the following is correct? A positive correlation between two variables occurs when

    a. one variable increases when the other increases.

    b. one variable increases when the other decreases.

    c. a good result is obtained after some treatment or intervention.

8.5 Achievement 2: Computing and interpreting Pearson's *r* correlation coefficient

8.5.1 COMPUTING AND INTERPRETING THE COVARIANCE BETWEEN TWO VARIABLES

Nancy said they were ready to start computing the correlation statistic now. She explained that the relationship between two variables can be checked in a few different ways. One method for measuring this relationship is *covariance*, which quantifies whether two variables vary together (co-vary) using Equation (8.1).

$$cov_{xy} = \frac{\sum_{i=1}^{n}(x_i - m_x)(y_i - m_y)}{n - 1} \tag{8.1}$$

Leslie examined Equation (8.1). She saw the summation from the first observation in the data, $i = 1$, to the last observation in the data set, n. The sum is of the product of the difference between each individual observation value for the first variable x_i and the mean of that variable m_x, and the same thing for the second variable, y. The numerator essentially adds up how far each observation is away from the mean values of the two variables being examined, so this ends up being a very large number quantifying how far away all the observations are from the mean values. The denominator divides this by the Bessel correction (Section 4.8.5) of $n - 1$, which is close to the sample size and essentially finds the average deviation from the means for each observation.

If the numerator is positive, the covariance will be positive, representing a positive relationship between two variables. This happens when many of the observations have x and y values that are either both higher than the mean, or both lower than the mean. When x_i and y_i are *both* greater than m_x and m_y, respectively, the contribution of that observation to the numerator of Equation (8.1) is a positive amount. Likewise, when x_i and y_i are both less than m_x and m_y, respectively, the contribution of that observation to the numerator of Equation (8.1) is also a positive amount because multiplying two negatives results in a positive. Nancy thought a visual might help here and revised the graph to show the means of x and y and highlight the points that were either above or below m_x and m_y. Leslie noticed that there were a lot more points above m_x and m_y than below in Figure 8.4, which was consistent with the positive value of the covariance. The observations with x and y values both above or below the means contribute positive amounts to the sum in the numerator, while the other observations contributed negative amounts to the sum in the numerator. Since there were so many more positive contributing data points in the figure, the sum was positive and the covariance was positive.

Likewise, if there were more negative values contributed to the numerator, the covariance is likely to be negative like in Figure 8.5.

FIGURE 8.4 Relationship of percentage of females in school and percentage of citizens with basic water access in countries worldwide

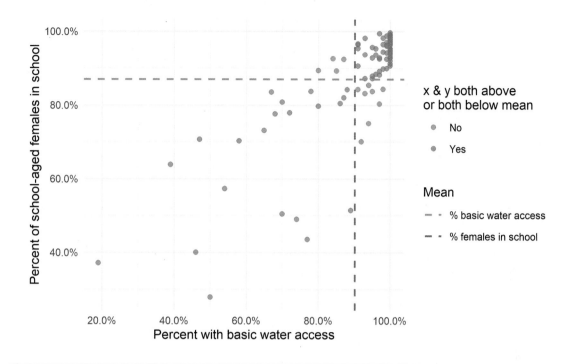

FIGURE 8.5 Relationship of percentage of females in school and percentage of people living on less than $1 per day in countries worldwide

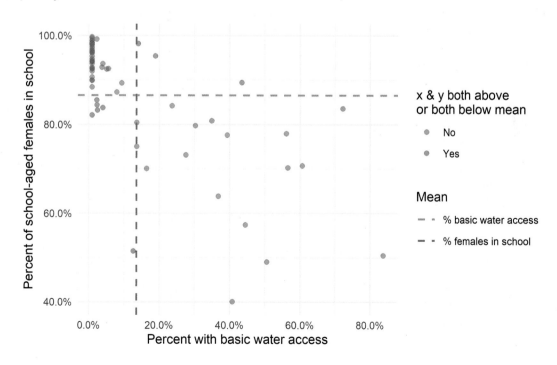

Females in school and basic water access appeared to have a positive relationship while poverty and females in school had a negative relationship; the covariance can help quantify it. Note that the covariance function is like the `mean()` function in that it cannot handle `NA` values. In the **tidyverse** style, using `drop_na()` for the variables used to compute covariance is one way to ensure that no missing values are included in the calculations. However, each `drop_na()` will drop all the observations with missing values for that variable. Since there were three variables to consider for these two correlations, `perc.basic2015water`, `perc.1dollar`, and `female.in.school`, Nancy thought this might be trouble.

Nancy explained that it was important to think through how the missing values were being handled before they wrote the final code. To think it through, Nancy suggested they examine different ways to compute the covariance in order to understand the missing data treatment. First, she demonstrated using `use = complete` as an argument for each `cov()` function, which worked to drop any missing values for either of the variables involved in the covariance.

```r
# covariance of females in school, poverty, and
# percentage with basic access to drinking water
water.educ %>%
  summarize(cov.females.water = cov(x = perc.basic2015water,
                                    y = female.in.school,
                                    use = "complete"),
            cov.females.pov = cov(x = perc.1dollar,
                                  y = female.in.school,
                                  use = "complete"))
##   cov.females.water cov.females.pov
## 1           194.027       -203.1335
```

Second, she used the `drop_na()` for all three variables first and then used `cov()` without the `use = "complete"` option.

```r
# covariance of females in school, poverty, and
# percentage with basic access to drinking water
water.educ %>%
  drop_na(female.in.school) %>%
  drop_na(perc.basic2015water) %>%
  drop_na(perc.1dollar) %>%
  summarize(cov.females.water = cov(x = perc.basic2015water,
                                    y = female.in.school),
            cov.females.pov = cov(x = perc.1dollar,
                                  y = female.in.school))
##   cov.females.water cov.females.pov
## 1          162.2263       -203.1335
```

Leslie was puzzled by the result and asked Nancy why the covariances were different. Nancy explained that the `drop_na()` function dropped the NA for *all three variables* before computing the two covariances for the second coding option. The calculations using `use = "complete"` dropped the NA only from the two variables *in that specific calculation*. The version with the `drop_na()` is dropping some observations that could be used in each of the `cov()` calculations. Nancy suggested they try the `drop_na()` method, but use it in two separate code chunks instead.

```
# covariance of females in school and
# percentage with basic access to drinking water
water.educ %>%
  drop_na(female.in.school) %>%
  drop_na(perc.basic2015water) %>%
  summarize(cov.females.water = cov(x = perc.basic2015water,
                                    y = female.in.school))
##    cov.females.water
## 1           194.027
```

Leslie compared this to the results from the `use = "complete"` option and noticed that it was the same as both of the previous coding options. The strategy mattered for the covariance between `female.in.school` and `perc.basic2015water` but not for the covariance between `perc.1dollar` and `female.in.school`.

```
# covariance of poverty and
# percentage of females in school
water.educ %>%
  drop_na(perc.1dollar) %>%
  drop_na(female.in.school) %>%
  summarize(cov.females.pov = cov(x = perc.1dollar,
                                  y = female.in.school))
##    cov.females.pov
## 1        -203.1335
```

This was also consistent with the first code using `use = "complete"`. These results made Leslie realize, again, how important it was to think through how to treat the data, especially when there are missing values.

Now that they agreed on an appropriate way to compute covariance, Kiara interpreted the results. She explained that the covariance does not have an intuitive inherent meaning; it is not a percentage or a sum or a difference. In fact, the size of the covariance depends largely on the size of what is measured. For example, something measured in millions might have a covariance in the millions or hundreds of thousands. The value of the covariance indicates whether there is a relationship at all and the direction of the relationship—that is, whether the relationship is positive or negative. In this case, a nonzero value indicates that there is some relationship. The positive value indicates the relationship is positive. Leslie was not impressed, but Kiara explained that the covariance is not reported very often to quantify the relationship between two continuous variables. Instead, the covariance is *standardized* by dividing it by the standard deviations of the two variables involved (Falk & Well, 1997). The result is called the correlation coefficient and is referred to as *r*. "Like R?" said Leslie, amused. "Yep," Kiara confirmed.

8.5.2 COMPUTING THE PEARSON'S *R* CORRELATION BETWEEN TWO VARIABLES

Kiara wrote out the equation for the *r* correlation coefficient in Equation (8.2).

$$r_{xy} = \frac{cov_{xy}}{s_x s_y} \tag{8.2}$$

Kiara explained that this correlation coefficient is called *Pearson's* **r** after Karl Pearson, who used an idea from Francis Galton and a mathematical formula from Auguste Bravais to develop one of the more commonly used statistics (Stanton, 2001; Zou, Tuncali, & Silverman, 2003). Pearson's *r* can range from −1 (a perfect negative relationship) to 0 (no relationship) to 1 (a perfect positive relationship) (Falk & Well, 1997; Garner, 2010).

Leslie noticed that her book called Pearson's *r* something else, the Pearson's *product-moment* correlation coefficient. Kiara said she had seen this before and looked it up to see if she could figure out the meaning of product-moment. In her reading, she found that *moment* was another term for the mean, and a *product-moment* was a term for the mean of some products (Garner, 2010). Leslie noticed that Equation (8.2) did not seem to show the mean of some products. Kiara thought she might know why. The formula for *r* can be organized in many different ways, one of which is as the mean of the summed products of *z*-scores (Section 4.7) from *x* and *y*. Kiara wrote out the alternate version of the *r* calculation in Equation (8.3). This equation fits better with the product-moment language.

$$r_{xy} = \frac{\sum_{i=1}^{n} z_x z_y}{n-1} \tag{8.3}$$

This made more sense to Leslie in terms of using the product-moment terminology because it is the product of the *z*-scores. Kiara said they could show with some algebra how Equation (8.2) and Equation (8.3) are equivalent, but Leslie was satisfied with believing Kiara. Leslie did comment that saying *Pearson's product-moment correlation coefficient* instead of *r* or *correlation* feels borderline silly. Kiara and Nancy agreed.

8.5.3 INTERPRETING THE DIRECTION OF THE PEARSON'S PRODUCT-MOMENT CORRELATION COEFFICIENT, *R*

Leslie wrote out her current understanding of how Pearson's product-moment correlation coefficient values work.

- *Negative correlations* occur when one variable goes up and the other goes down (Figure 8.4).

- *No correlation* happens when there is no discernable pattern in how two variables vary.

- *Positive correlations* occur when one variable goes up, and the other one also goes up (or when one goes down, the other one does too); both variables move together in the same direction (Figure 8.5).

Nancy created a simple visual to solidify the concept for the team (Figure 8.6).

FIGURE 8.6 Examples of negative correlation, no correlation, and positive correlation between two variables

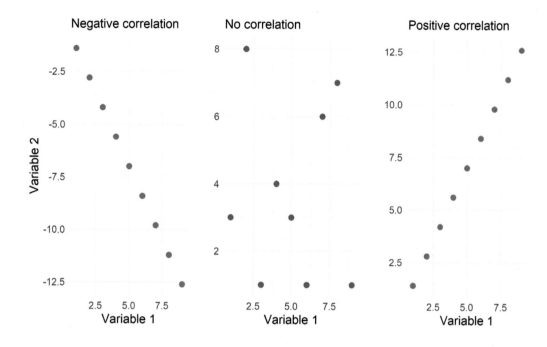

Nancy suggested that adding a line to Figures 8.4 and 8.5 to capture the relationship would be useful for better understanding. Leslie copied the code for these two graphs and added a `geom_smooth()` layer to add a line showing the relationship between female education and water access.

As she coded, Nancy explained that the `geom_smooth()` layer requires a few arguments to get a useful line. The first argument is `method =`, which is the method used for drawing the line. In this case, Nancy told Leslie to use the `lm` method, with `lm` standing for linear model. Leslie looked confused, and Kiara explained that they had not yet covered linear models and it would become clearer next time they met. While that was unsatisfying for Leslie, adding the line did seem to clarify that the relationship between female education and water access was positive (Figure 8.7). Nancy wanted to point out that the legend was getting more complicated, with two different types of symbols, points, and lines. She said that the legend was generated from attributes included in the `aes()` argument and that different symbols can be generated by using different attributes. In this case, Nancy used the `color =` attribute for the points and the `linetype =` attribute for the lines. Leslie was curious how this worked so Nancy wrote her some instructions (Box 8.2).

```
# explore plot of female education and water access (Figure 8.7)
water.educ %>%
  ggplot(aes(y = female.in.school/100, x = perc.basic2015water/100)) +
  geom_smooth(method = "lm", se = FALSE, aes(linetype = "Fit line"),
              color = "gray60") +
  geom_point(size = 2, aes(color = "Country"), alpha = .6) +
  theme_minimal() +
  labs(y = "Percent of school-aged females in school",
```

```
        x = "Percent with basic water access") +
    scale_x_continuous(labels = scales::percent) +
    scale_y_continuous(labels = scales::percent) +
    scale_color_manual(values = "#7463AC", name = "") +
    scale_linetype_manual(values = 1, name = "")
```

Nancy was excited to start working on the correlation coefficient code and to show a new function. She computed *r* using `cor()`. Like `cov()`, the `cor()` function uses complete data, so the missing values need to be removed or addressed somehow. Nancy chose to remove the observations with missing values by using the `use = "complete"` option in `cor()`.

```
# correlation between water access and female education
water.educ %>%
    summarize(cor.females.water = cor(x = perc.basic2015water,
                                      y = female.in.school,
                                      use = "complete"))

##    cor.females.water
## 1          0.8086651
```

FIGURE 8.7 Relationship of percentage of females in school and percentage of citizens with basic water access in countries worldwide

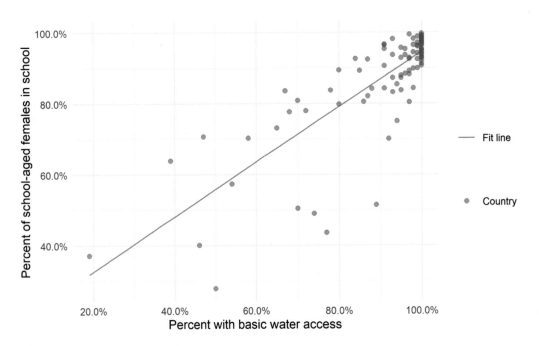

Some figures are more complicated than others, and it is useful to have a complete legend to be able to distinguish the different parts. The only things that show up in the legend are those things that are added to the graph inside of aesthetics, `aes()`. For example, color can be added to this graph without using aesthetics, but it would not be included in the legend (Figure 8.8).

```
# explore plot of female education and water access (Figure 8.8)
water.educ %>%
  ggplot(aes(y = female.in.school/100,
             x = perc.basic2015water/100)) +
  geom_smooth(method = "lm", se = FALSE, color = "gray60") +
  geom_point(size = 2, color = "#7463AC", alpha = .6) +
  theme_minimal() +
  labs(y = "Percent of school-aged females in school",
       x = "Percent with basic water access") +
  scale_x_continuous(labels = scales::percent) +
  scale_y_continuous(labels = scales::percent)
```

FIGURE 8.8 Relationship of percentage of females in school and percentage of citizens with basic water access in countries worldwide

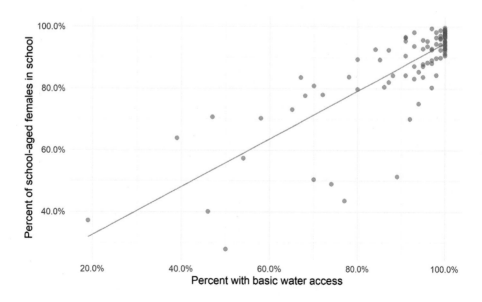

(Continued)

(Continued)

FIGURE 8.9 Relationship of percentage of females in school and percentage of citizens with basic water access in countries worldwide

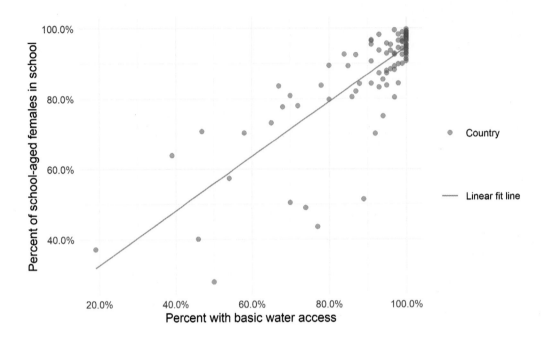

The same graph using the same colors for the same graph elements but with a legend explaining what the colors represent is possible if attributes of the layer are included in `aes()` functions (Figure 8.9).

```
# explore plot of female education and water (Figure 8.9)
water.educ %>%
  ggplot(aes(y = female.in.school/100,
             x = perc.basic2015water/100)) +
  geom_smooth(method = "lm", se = FALSE,
              aes(color = "Linear fit line")) +
  geom_point(aes(size = "Country"), color = "#7463AC",
             alpha = .6) +
  theme_minimal() +
  labs(y = "Percent of school-aged females in school",
       x = "Percent with basic water access") +
  scale_x_continuous(labels = scales::percent) +
```

```
scale_y_continuous(labels = scales::percent) +
scale_color_manual(values = "gray60", name = "") +
scale_size_manual(values = 2, name = "")
```

The two `aes()` functions used for this graph are `aes(size = "Country")` and `aes(linetype = "Linear fit line")`. To get two different symbols, two different attributes were used within the `aes()`. For example, Figure 8.10 has `color =` for both the points and the line within `aes()` and so they are both included in the legend with the same merged symbol. Contrast that with Figure 8.9, where the line has a line symbol and the points have a point symbol. Figure 8.10 looks the same as Figure 8.9 except for the legend, which shows the point and line symbol merged together rather than the point symbol for the points and the line symbol for the lines.

FIGURE 8.10 Relationship of percentage of females in school and percentage of citizens with basic water access in countries worldwide

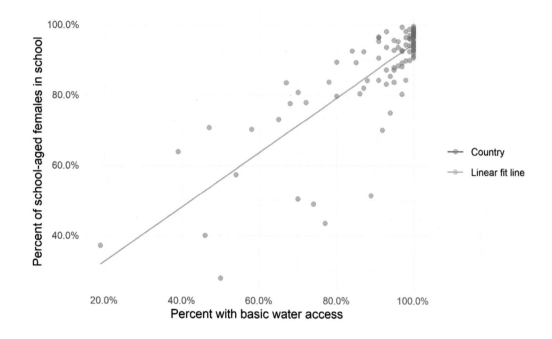

```
# explore plot of female education and water (Figure 8.10)
water.educ %>%
  ggplot(aes(y = female.in.school/100,
             x = perc.basic2015water/100)) +
```

(Continued)

(Continued)

```
geom_smooth(method = "lm", se = FALSE,
            aes(color = "Linear fit line")) +
geom_point(aes(color = "Country"), size = 2, alpha = .6) +
theme_minimal() +
labs(y = "Percent of school-aged females in school",
     x = "Percent with basic water access") +
scale_x_continuous(labels = scales::percent) +
scale_y_continuous(labels = scales::percent) +
scale_color_manual(values = c("#7463AC", "gray60"), name = "")
```

She found a positive correlation of 0.81, which was consistent with Figure 8.7. Leslie wrote a draft of an interpretation based on what she had learned so far about r:

> The Pearson's product-moment correlation coefficient demonstrated that the percentage of females in school is positively correlated with the percentage of citizens with basic access to drinking water ($r = 0.81$). Essentially, as access to water goes up, the percentage of females in school also increases in countries.

Kiara agreed and smiled at Leslie's use of the full name of r.

8.5.4 INTERPRETING THE STRENGTH OF THE PEARSON'S PRODUCT-MOMENT CORRELATION COEFFICIENT

Kiara said that not only is r positive, but it also shows a very strong relationship. While there are minor disagreements in the thresholds (Mukaka, 2012; Zou et al., 2003), Kiara explained that most values describing the strength of r are similar to the following (Zou et al., 2003):

- $r = -1.0$ is perfectly negative
- $r = -.8$ is strongly negative
- $r = -.5$ is moderately negative
- $r = -.2$ is weakly negative
- $r = 0$ is no relationship
- $r = .2$ is weakly positive
- $r = .5$ is moderately positive
- $r = .8$ is strongly positive
- $r = 1.0$ is perfectly positive

To make sure she understood, Leslie graphed the correlation between poverty and percent of females in school (Figure 8.11).

FIGURE 8.11 Relationship of percentage of citizens living on less than $1 per day and the percent of school-aged females in school in countries worldwide

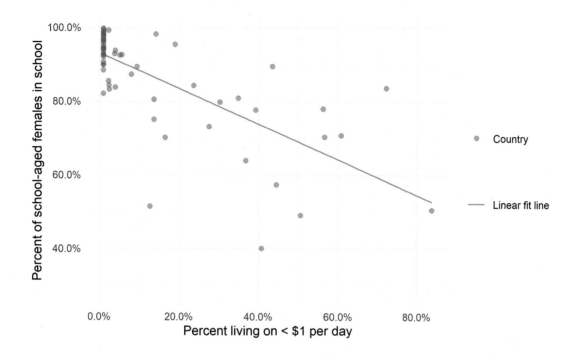

Then she worked with Nancy to add the poverty variable to the correlation code she had created earlier.

```
# correlations between water access, poverty, and female education
water.educ %>%
    summarize(cor.females.water = cor(x = perc.basic2015water,
                                      y = female.in.school,
                                      use = "complete"),
              cor.females.pov = cor(x = perc.1dollar,
                                    y = female.in.school,
                                    use = "complete"))
##   cor.females.water cor.females.pov
## 1        0.8086651      -0.7144238
```

Leslie said that Figure 8.11 and the correlation coefficient of −0.71 consistently showed a moderate to strong negative relationship between poverty and females in school. That is, as poverty goes up, females in school goes down. Kiara agreed with this interpretation.

8.5.5 ACHIEVEMENT 2: CHECK YOUR UNDERSTANDING

Graph and calculate the correlation between percentage of females in school, `female.in.school`, and basic sanitation measured by the `perc.basic2015sani` variable. Interpret your results.

8.6 Achievement 3: Conducting an inferential statistical test for Pearson's *r* correlation coefficient

The correlation coefficients and plots indicated that, for this sample of countries, percentage of females in school was positively correlated with basic water access and negatively correlated with poverty. Leslie wondered if this relationship held for all countries. Kiara explained that there is an inferential statistical test that can be used to determine if the correlation coefficient in the sample is statistically significant. Leslie got out her NHST notes and began.

8.6.1 NHST STEP 1: WRITING THE NULL AND ALTERNATE HYPOTHESES

H0: There is no relationship between the two variables ($r = 0$).

HA: There is a relationship between the two variables ($r \neq 0$).

8.6.2 NHST STEP 2: COMPUTING THE TEST STATISTIC

Kiara explained that the null hypothesis is tested using a *t*-statistic comparing the correlation coefficient of *r* to a hypothesized value of zero, like the one-sample *t*-test (Section 6.5) (Puth, Neuhäuser, & Ruxton, 2014). Equation (8.4) shows the one-sample *t*-test *t*-statistic formula where m_x is the mean of *x* and se_{m_x} is the standard error of the mean of *x*.

$$t = \frac{m_x - 0}{se_{m_x}} \tag{8.4}$$

Kiara reminded Leslie that they were not actually working with means, but instead comparing the correlation of r_{xy} to zero. She rewrote the equation so it was appropriate to compute the *t*-statistic to test the correlation coefficient instead (Equation 8.5).

$$t = \frac{r_{xy}}{se_{r_{xy}}} \tag{8.5}$$

Kiara explained that there were multiple ways to compute the standard error for a correlation coefficient. She wrote one option in Equation (8.6).

$$se_{r_{xy}} = \sqrt{\frac{1 - r_{xy}^2}{n - 2}} \tag{8.6}$$

Kiara substituted the formula for $se_{r_{xy}}$ into the *t*-statistic formula to get Equation (8.7).

$$t = \frac{r_{xy}}{\sqrt{\dfrac{1 - r_{xy}^2}{n - 2}}} \tag{8.7}$$

Finally, she simplified Equation (8.7) to get the final version, Equation (8.8), that they would use to compute the *t*-statistic for the significance test of *r*.

$$t = \frac{r_{xy}\sqrt{n - 2}}{\sqrt{1 - r_{xy}^2}} \tag{8.8}$$

Use of this formula requires r_{xy} and n. The correlation between water access and females in school is 0.81, but it is unclear what the value of n is for this correlation. While the overall data frame has 97 observations, some of these have missing values. To find the n for the correlation between `perc.basic2015water` and `female.in.school`, Nancy suggested using `drop_na()` and adding `n()` to `summarize()` to count the number of cases after dropping the missing `NA` values. Leslie gave this a try with the `drop_na()` function and the functions for creating subsets from previous chapters.

```
# correlation between water access and female education
water.educ %>%
  drop_na(perc.basic2015water) %>%
  drop_na(female.in.school) %>%
  summarize(cor.females.water = cor(x = perc.basic2015water,
                                    y = female.in.school),
            samp.n = n())
##    cor.females.water samp.n
## 1          0.8086651     96
```

Leslie saw that there were 96 observations. She substituted the value of `cor.females.water`, or r, and `samp.n`, or n, into Equation (8.8) to compute the test statistic in Equation (8.9).

$$t = \frac{r_{xy}\sqrt{n-2}}{\sqrt{1-r_{xy}^2}} = \frac{.81\sqrt{96-2}}{\sqrt{1-(.81)^2}} = 13.39 \tag{8.9}$$

The t-statistic was 13.39. Nancy scooted her laptop over to show Leslie how to compute the t-statistic with code using `cor.test()` with the two variables as the two arguments.

```
# test for correlation coefficient
cor.test(x = water.educ$perc.basic2015water,
         y = water.educ$female.in.school)
##
##   Pearson's product-moment correlation
##
## data:  water.educ$perc.basic2015water and water.educ$female.in.school
## t = 13.328, df = 94, p-value < 2.2e-16
## alternative hypothesis: true correlation is not equal to 0
## 95 percent confidence interval:
##   0.7258599 0.8683663
## sample estimates:
##        cor
## 0.8086651
```

Leslie noticed that the t-statistic she computed by hand in Equation (8.9) was close but not the same as the t-statistic that R computed. Nancy reassured her that this was due to rounding the value of r in her calculation to two decimal places while R uses a lot more decimal places during calculation. Leslie calculated it again using more decimal places and found that Nancy was correct. She was relieved. Kiara added that this is one thing that can influence reproducibility. If people compute values by hand, rounding can make a difference!

8.6.3 NHST STEP 3: CALCULATE THE PROBABILITY THAT YOUR TEST STATISTIC IS AT LEAST AS BIG AS IT IS IF THERE IS NO RELATIONSHIP (I.E., THE NULL IS TRUE)

Although `cor.test()` prints out a *p*-value, Leslie decided to examine the probability distribution used to convert the test statistic into a *p*-value and to remind herself what the *p*-value means. Nancy was happy to oblige and graphed a *t*-distribution with 94 degrees of freedom. Leslie could not figure out why it was 94 degrees of freedom when there were 96 observations used to compute the correlation. She thought she remembered that the one-sample *t*-test had $n - 1$ degrees of freedom (Section 6.5) and so $n - 1$ would be 95 degrees of freedom. Kiara reminded her that the one-sample *t*-test they used in Section 6.5 tested the mean of *one* variable against a hypothesized or population mean. This *t*-statistic was for a different situation where there were *two* variables involved, even though the *r* is a single statistic. With two variables involved, 2 is subtracted from the sample size.

Leslie found that the *t*-distribution in Figure 8.12 was not very useful in this situation since there was almost no area left under the curve, even at a value of $t = 5$, so there would not be anything to see at $t = 13.33$. She thought at least it was consistent with the very tiny *p*-value from the `cor.test()` output.

8.6.4 NHST STEPS 4 AND 5: INTERPRET THE PROBABILITY AND WRITE A CONCLUSION

The *p*-value was very tiny, well under .05. This *p*-value is the probability that the very strong positive relationship ($r = .81$) observed between percentage of females in school and percentage with basic water access would have happened if the null were true. It is extremely unlikely that this correlation would happen in the sample if there were not a very strong positive correlation between females in school and access to water in the population that this sample came from.

Leslie noticed that the output included a 95% confidence interval. Kiara explained that this was the confidence interval around *r*, so the value of *r* in the sample is .81, and the likely value of *r* in the population that this sample came from is somewhere between .73 and .87.

Leslie wrote her final interpretation with this in mind:

> The percentage of people who have basic access to water is statistically significantly, positively, and very strongly correlated with the percentage of primary- and secondary-age females in school in a country [$r = .81$; $t(94) = 13.33$; $p < .05$]. As the percentage of people living with basic access to water goes up, the percentage of females in school also goes up. While the correlation is .81 in the sample, it is likely between .73 and .87 in the population (95% CI: .73–.87).

Before they moved on, Nancy wanted to mention one of her favorite statisticians, Florence Nightingale David. She told Leslie that (fun fact) Florence Nightingale David was named after her parents' friend, the more famous Florence Nightingale, who developed modern nursing. More importantly, David was involved in making correlation analyses more accessible to researchers. She developed tables of correlation coefficients in 1938 to aid researchers in using this statistical tool before R was available (long before computers were invented!) (David, 1938). Although they were vastly outnumbered by the males in the field, many women like David played key roles in the development of current statistical practice.

FIGURE 8.12 *t-distribution with 94 degrees of freedom*

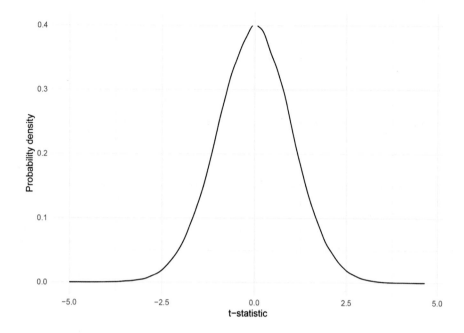

Nancy explained that the more famous Florence Nightingale also contributed to statistical theory with her pioneering graph called a *coxcomb* or *rose diagram*, which is similar to a pie chart but with multiple layers (Brasseur, 2005). Leslie was intrigued and made a note on her calendar to look up rose diagrams after they finished with correlation.

8.6.5 ACHIEVEMENT 3: CHECK YOUR UNDERSTANDING

Use `cor.test()` to examine the relationship between females in school and poverty (percentage living on less than $1 per day). Which of the following is true about the correlation?

  a. Negative, statistically significant

  b. Negative, statistically nonsignificant

  c. Positive, statistically significant

  d. Positive, statistically nonsignificant

8.7 Achievement 4: Examining effect size for Pearson's *r* with the coefficient of determination

Leslie wondered if the correlation coefficient was considered its own effect size since it measures the strength of the relationship. Kiara said this is true, but there was also another value that was easy to calculate and that had a more direct interpretation to use as an effect size with *r*. She introduced Leslie to the *coefficient of determination*, which is the percentage of the variance in one variable that is shared, or explained, by the other variable.

Leslie was going to need some more information before this made sense. Kiara thought they should start by looking at the equation for the coefficient of determination. Before they did that, Kiara told Leslie that the notation for the coefficient of determination is r^2.

8.7.1 CALCULATING THE COEFFICIENT OF DETERMINATION

There are several ways to compute the coefficient of determination. For a Pearson's r correlation coefficient, the coefficient of determination can be computed by squaring the correlation coefficient as in Equation (8.10).

$$r_{xy}^2 = \left(\frac{cov_{xy}}{s_x s_y} \right)^2 \tag{8.10}$$

Leslie understood the concept of squaring, but not the reason behind why this captures how much variance these two variables share. Nancy thought maybe a little R code could help.

8.7.2 USING R TO CALCULATE THE COEFFICIENT OF DETERMINATION

Kiara explained that the coefficient of determination is often referred to just as **r-squared** and reported as r^2 or more commonly, R^2. Nancy said there was no specific R function, that she knew of, for computing the coefficient of determination directly from the data, but there were many options for computing it from the output of a correlation analysis. The most straightforward way might be to use `cor()` and square the result, but it is also possible to use `cor.test()` and square the correlation from the output of this procedure. Leslie was curious about the second method, so Kiara decided to demonstrate (Box 8.3) and calculate the coefficient of determination from the r for the relationship between females in school and basic water access. The value was then assigned to an object name. To see the structure of the new object, Kiara used `str()`.

```
# conduct the correlation analysis
# assign the results to an object
cor.Fem.Educ.Water <- cor.test(x = water.educ$perc.basic2015water,
                               y = water.educ$female.in.school)

# explore the object
str(object = cor.Fem.Educ.Water)
## List of 9
##  $ statistic  : Named num 13.3
##   ..- attr(*, "names")= chr "t"
##  $ parameter  : Named int 94
##   ..- attr(*, "names")= chr "df"
##  $ p.value    : num 2.21e-23
##  $ estimate   : Named num 0.809
##   ..- attr(*, "names")= chr "cor"
##  $ null.value : Named num 0
```

```
##    ..- attr(*, "names")= chr "correlation"
##  $ alternative: chr "two.sided"
##  $ method     : chr "Pearson's product-moment correlation"
##  $ data.name  : chr "water.educ$perc.basic2015water and water.
educ$female.in.school"
##  $ conf.int   : num [1:2] 0.726 0.868
##    ..- attr(*, "conf.level")= num 0.95
##  - attr(*, "class")= chr "htest"
```

Leslie saw that the `cor.Fem.Educ.Water` object was a list with nine entries. She looked at the object and found an entry called `estimate`, which appeared to be the correlation coefficient. Kiara then showed her how to use the `estimate` from the `cor.Fem.Educ.Water` object and square it to get the r^2 for this correlation.

```
# square the correlation coefficient
r.squared <- cor.Fem.Educ.Water$estimate^2
r.squared
##        cor
## 0.6539392
```

FIGURE 8.13 Visualizing percentage of shared variance

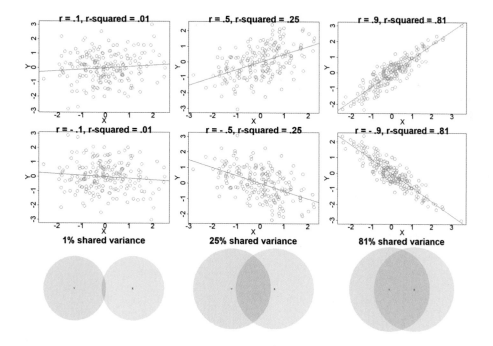

The result can be multiplied by 100 to find that `female.in.school` and `perc.basic2015water` have 65.39% shared variance. Leslie understood how this was computed, but the concept of shared variance was still fuzzy. Kiara thought a visual representation might be useful to explain what it means. Nancy did some fancy coding and created scatterplots and corresponding *Venn diagrams*. Venn diagrams are useful for showing overlap among variables and correlations with different amounts of shared variance (Figure 8.13).

Leslie examined the scatterplots and Venn diagrams. The first column had weak positive and negative correlations. The points were spread out without much pattern. The fit line that went through the points

8.3 Kiara's reproducibility resource: Using objects in R

Kiara sensed another opportunity to teach Leslie about reproducibility when Nancy started explaining how to use objects to improve precision. She thought of a situation where the coefficient of determination was needed for a report about the correlation between access to water and access to sanitation. There were two options: (a) conduct the correlation and use the number from the correlation to compute the coefficient of determination by hand using the numbers in the output, or (b) assign the correlation results to an object and use the object to compute the coefficient.

8.3.1 Conduct without objects

```
# correlation of sanitation and water access
cor.test(x = water.educ$perc.basic2015sani,
         y = water.educ$perc.basic2015water)
##
##  Pearson's product-moment correlation
##
## data:  water.educ$perc.basic2015sani and water.educ$perc.
basic2015water
## t = 19.249, df = 94, p-value < 2.2e-16
## alternative hypothesis: true correlation is not equal to 0
## 95 percent confidence interval:
##  0.8436881 0.9275162
## sample estimates:
##       cor
## 0.8931071
# compute coefficient of determination
.89^2
## [1] 0.7921
```

8.3.2 Conduct with objects

```
# correlation of sanitation and water access
cor.sani.water <- cor.test(x = water.educ$perc.basic2015sani,
                           y = water.educ$perc.basic2015water)
cor.sani.water
##
## Pearson's product-moment correlation
##
## data:  water.educ$perc.basic2015sani and water.educ$perc.
basic2015water
## t = 19.249, df = 94, p-value < 2.2e-16
## alternative hypothesis: true correlation is not equal to 0
## 95 percent confidence interval:
##   0.8436881 0.9275162
## sample estimates:
##       cor
## 0.8931071
# coefficient of determination for
# sanitation and water access
cod <- cor.sani.water$estimate^2
cod
##       cor
## 0.7976403
```

Kiara wrote that, while the difference was small in this case, it was still a difference. Without knowing exactly how the correlation was rounded to compute the coefficient of determination, even differences this small hinder reproducibility. In addition, a small difference can change the statistical significance of a result, which might influence a policy, program, or funding decision. In other cases, a small difference can contribute to big differences if additional analyses are conducted using a hand-calculated version of a statistic. When possible, using the tools and strategies available in R to get the reported statistic is highly recommended.

was slightly slanted up for the first graph and slightly down for the second one. The Venn diagram in the first column showed just a small amount of overlap.

The second column shows moderate *correlations* of .5 and −.5 along with 25% shared variance. The difference is pretty clear between the first column and this column. The points clearly show a pattern with a positive relationship between *x* and *y* in the top graph and a negative relationship in the graph below that. The Venn diagram shows more overlap between the two. The third column shows strong positive and negative relationships with a more pronounced slope of the line, points close to the line, and a large amount of shared variance.

Altogether, the graphs suggest that shared variance is related to the strength of the relationship between x and y. If y tends to change with x, they are varying together. The more this occurs, the more the graph looks like one of the ones in the third column on the right. Leslie thought she understood. Kiara informed her that this idea will continue to come up in future chapters, so there will be additional examples and ways of thinking about variance and shared variance.

8.7.3 ACHIEVEMENT 4: CHECK YOUR UNDERSTANDING

What is the coefficient of determination for the relationship between females in school and basic sanitation access?

    a.   0.69

    b.   0.83

    c.   14.45

    d.   0.75

8.8 Achievement 5: Checking assumptions for Pearson's r correlation analyses

Leslie asked if there were assumptions for the Pearson's product-moment correlation coefficient like there are for the other statistical tests. Kiara rolled her eyes at Leslie's use of the full name for r and explained that correlation coefficients rely on several assumptions:

- Observations are independent.

- Both variables are continuous.

- Both variables are normally distributed.

- The relationship between the two variables is *linear* (*linearity*).

- The variance is constant with the points distributed equally around the line (*homoscedasticity*).

Leslie thought she could probably check these all on her own already with some graphs. Nancy wanted to discuss the independent observations assumptions before they started looking at graphs. Meeting this assumption relies on each observation being unrelated to the other observations. Nancy made the point that countries that are geographically close to each other, or that are in the same geographic region, may be more likely to share characteristics and therefore fail this assumption. Kiara thought education seemed like a characteristic that might be similar within geographic regions, so countries within those regions would not be independent. Kiara was also skeptical that the countries in the sample were truly representative of all the countries in the world. The countries in the analysis were those reporting data on the variables of interest, rather than a random sample of countries. Countries reporting data may be different from countries missing data. For example, they may have better computing infrastructure and more human and financial resources to afford to collect, store, and report data. Leslie and Nancy agreed that these data did not seem to meet the independence assumption or represent all countries.

After talking with the R-Team about using ANOVA and correlation with percentage variables, Leslie wondered what the other options were. She did a little searching online and discovered a few strategies that were recommended, but nothing stood out as the *one best way* to model a variable that is a percentage. A couple of the papers suggested that percentage variables are problematic for statistical models that have the purpose of *predicting* values of the outcome because predictions can fall outside the range of 0 to 100 (Ferrari & Cribari-Neto, 2004). Some of the things she found she had heard of, like logistic regression (Zhao, Chen, & Schaffner, 2001), transforming the variable, and recoding the variable into a categorical variable. She also found something called beta regression (Cribari-Neto & Zeileis, 2010; Ferrari & Cribari-Neto, 2004; Schmid et al., 2013), which was new to her. She asked Nancy and Kiara about it and texted a couple of her classmates; two people had heard of it but nobody had used it. Leslie did some more reading and made a short list of strategies and resources that are options for dealing with percentage data.

- Logistic regression (Zhao et al., 2001)

- Beta regression (Cribari-Neto & Zeileis, 2010; Ferrari & Cribari-Neto, 2004; Schmid et al., 2013)

- Transforming the percentage

- Recoding the variable to categorical and using a nonparametric method like chi-squared

Each of these methods has strengths and weaknesses, and each could be useful for certain situations.

Even so, Leslie still wanted to check the remaining assumptions for practice. She started by checking the assumptions for the correlation between percentage of females in school and percentage of citizens with basic water access. Although percentages are limited by a floor and ceiling, within the range of 0 to 100, they can take any value along the continuum. Both variables are continuous, so the continuous variables assumption is met. Kiara and Leslie had been having a side conversation about variables that show percentages, and Leslie wrote some notes on methods for examining percentage variables (Box 8.4).

8.8.1 CHECKING THE NORMALITY ASSUMPTION

Leslie started by using histograms to check the normality assumption. She dropped the missing values from the two variables in the analysis so that the histogram contained only the observations that contributed to the correlation coefficient. Kiara and Nancy were impressed! Leslie smiled. She had been paying attention.

```
# check normality of female.in.school variable (Figure 8.14)
water.educ %>%
  drop_na(female.in.school) %>%
  drop_na(perc.basic2015water) %>%
  ggplot(aes(x = female.in.school)) +
  geom_histogram(fill = "#7463AC", col = "white") +
  theme_minimal() +
  labs(x = "Percent of school-aged females in school",
       y = "Number of countries")
```

The values of the `female.in.school` variable do not appear to be normally distributed. Instead, the distribution is very left- or negatively skewed, where there are values that create a longer tail to the left of the histogram (Figure 8.14). Leslie decided to try a Q-Q plot to confirm this conclusion (Figure 8.15).

```
# Q-Q plot of female.in.school variable to check normality (Figure 8.15)
water.educ %>%
  drop_na(female.in.school) %>%
  drop_na(perc.basic2015water) %>%
  ggplot(aes(sample = female.in.school)) +
  stat_qq(aes(color = "Country"), alpha = .6) +
  geom_abline(aes(intercept = mean(female.in.school),
                  slope = sd(female.in.school),
                  linetype = "Normally distributed"),
              color = "gray60", size = 1) +
  theme_minimal() +
  labs(x = "Theoretical normal distribution",
       y = "Observed values of percent of\nschool-aged females in school") +
  ylim(0,100) +
  scale_linetype_manual(values = 1, name = "") +
  scale_color_manual(values = "#7463AC", name = "")
```

Leslie noticed that the points deviated from the line the most at the extremes. In the lower left corner of the graph, there were countries well below 50% for percentage of females in school. Likewise, there were countries where nearly 100% of school-aged females were in school in the top right portion of the graph—they were more than two standard deviations above the mean, as shown by being above 2 on the *x*-axis. These deviations from normal are consistent with the histogram, which shows countries at both extremes.

She concluded that the normality assumption was violated for `female.in.school`, but thought it might be OK for `perc.basic2015water`. It was not (Figures 8.16 and 8.17).

FIGURE 8.14 Distribution of percentage of school-aged females in school

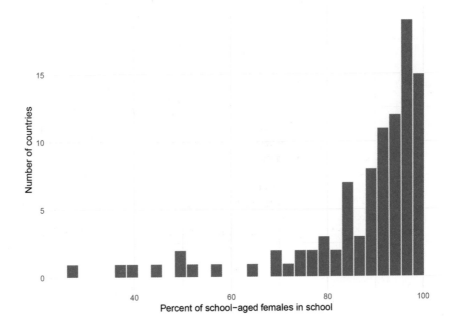

Source: UNESCO Institute for Statistics (n.d.).

FIGURE 8.15 Distribution of percentage of school-aged females in school

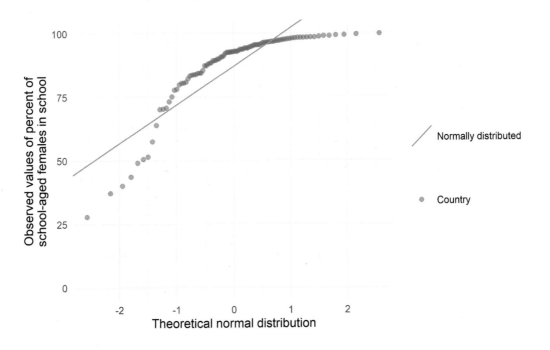

Source: UNESCO Institute for Statistics (n.d.).

```
# check normality of water access variable (Figure 8.16)
water.educ %>%
  drop_na(female.in.school) %>%
  drop_na(perc.basic2015water) %>%
  ggplot(aes(x = perc.basic2015water)) +
  geom_histogram(fill = "#7463AC", col = "white") +
  theme_minimal() +
  labs(x = "Percent with basic water access",
       y = "Number of countries")
```

```
# Q-Q plot of water access variable to check normality (Figure 8.17)
water.educ %>%
  drop_na(female.in.school) %>%
  drop_na(perc.basic2015water) %>%
  ggplot(aes(sample = perc.basic2015water)) +
  stat_qq(aes(color = "Country"), alpha = .6) +
  geom_abline(aes(intercept = mean(x = perc.basic2015water),
                  slope = sd(x = perc.basic2015water),
                  linetype = "Normally distributed"),
              color = "gray60", size = 1) +
  theme_minimal() +
  labs(x = "Theoretical normal distribution",
       y = "Observed values of percent of people\nwith basic water access") +
  ylim(0,100) +
  scale_linetype_manual(values = 1, name = "") +
  scale_color_manual(values = "#7463AC", name = "")
```

FIGURE 8.16 Distribution of the percentage of citizens with basic water access (WHO, n.d.)

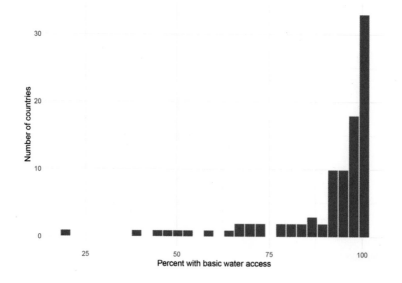

FIGURE 8.17 Distribution of percentage of citizens with basic water access (WHO, n.d.)

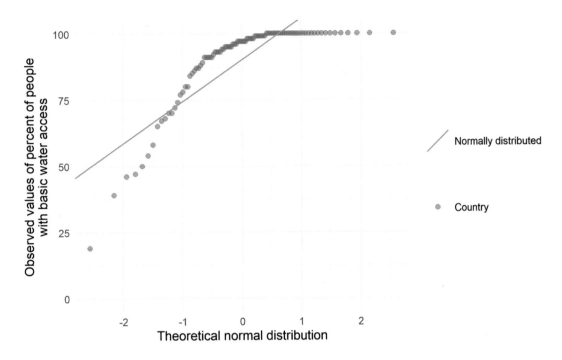

Leslie was surprised by how non-normal the water access variable appeared. The histogram showed a distribution that was extremely left-skewed, and the Q-Q plot confirmed the lack of normality, with most of the points being quite far from the line representing a normal distribution. The data had failed the normality assumption. Leslie concluded that the data had failed the normality assumption spectacularly. Through all of this coding and discussion, she had forgotten why they were removing the NA values for both variables in each of the histograms, since each histogram plotted only one variable. Nancy reminded her that the correlation analysis had dropped any observations missing from either variable. The observations included in the assumption checking should be the same as those analyzed in the correlation analysis. For this reason, they should remove the NA for both variables before testing each assumption.

8.8.2 CHECKING THE LINEARITY ASSUMPTION

The linearity assumption requires that the relationship between the two variables falls along a line. The assumption is met if a scatterplot of the two variables shows that the relationship falls along a line. Figure 8.7 suggests that this assumption is met. When graphed, the points fell generally along the straight line without any major issues. If it is difficult to tell, a *Loess curve* can be added to confirm linearity.

A Loess curve shows the relationship between the two variables without constraining the line to be straight like the linear model `method = lm` option does. Nancy wrote some code to show Figure 8.7 with an added Loess curve in a second `geom_smooth()` layer (Figure 8.18). The Loess curve shows some minor deviation from linear at the lower percentages, but overall the relationship seems close to linear. This assumption appears to be met.

```
# female education and water graph with linear fit line and Loess curve (Figure 8.18)
water.educ %>%
```

```
ggplot(aes(y = female.in.school/100, x = perc.basic2015water/100)) +
geom_point(aes(size = "Country"), color = "#7463AC", alpha = .6) +
geom_smooth(aes(color = "Linear fit line"), method = "lm", se = FALSE) +
geom_smooth(aes(color = "Loess curve"), se = FALSE) +
theme_minimal() +
labs(y = "Percent of school-aged females in school",
     x = "Percent with basic access to water") +
scale_x_continuous(labels = scales::percent) +
scale_y_continuous(labels = scales::percent) +
scale_color_manual(values = c("gray60", "deeppink"), name= "") +
scale_size_manual(values = 2, name = "")
```

Leslie looked at the code that Nancy had written to create Figure 8.18 and noticed a couple of new things. In the two `geom_smooth()` layers, Nancy had added aesthetics with `aes()` and, inside the aesthetics, she added a `color` = argument, but the value she gave the argument was the type of line and not an actual color. The actual color for the lines was in the `scale_color_manual()` layer at the very bottom of the code. Nancy explained that she wanted to make sure she was able to add a legend to clarify which line was the Loess curve and which was the linear fit line. Only things that are in `aes()` can be added to a legend in `ggplot()`, so putting the color inside `aes()` was for this purpose. The reason for using the

FIGURE 8.18 Relationship of percentage of females in school and percentage of citizens with basic water access in countries worldwide

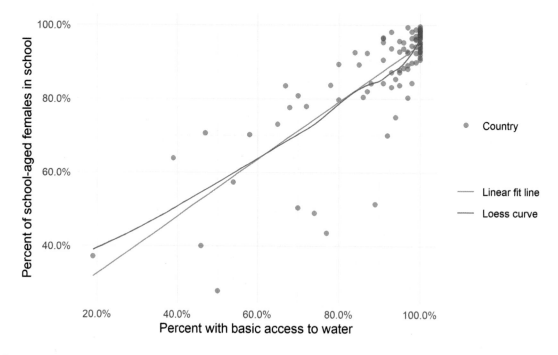

Sources: UNESCO Institute for Statistics (n.d.), WHO (n.d.).

name of the line instead of the actual color with the `color =` argument was so that the name of the line would appear in the legend.

This made sense, but Leslie thought it was yet another thing she would not remember. Nancy saw the look on her face and let her know that looking up things online frequently while coding in R is common. There is no way to remember all the code tricks. Nancy assured her that she would get to know some code really well once she has used it a lot, but other things she might have to look up every single time. This is one of the drawbacks of R being open source and extremely flexible. There is a lot to remember, and it does not all follow the same patterns. Kiara added that it's OK to forget things because there are several ways to remind yourself, such as the History pane in the upper right (next to Environment), the help tab in the lower right for documentation on particular functions, and all the online resources available with a quick search.

Leslie went back to thinking about the lines in Figure 8.18. She asked what a nonlinear relationship might look like, and Nancy simulated some data to show possible shapes for relationships that do not fall along a straight line (Figure 8.19).

Both of these plots show that there is some relationship between x and y, but the relationship is not linear. The relationships fall along curves instead of along straight lines.

8.8.3 CHECKING THE HOMOSCEDASTICITY ASSUMPTION

The final assumption is the equal distribution of points around the line, which is often called the assumption of homoscedasticity. Nancy added some lines around the data points in Figure 8.7 to get Figure 8.20. She explained to Leslie that the funnel shape of the data indicated that the points were not evenly spread around the line from right to left. On the left of the graph they were more spread out than on the right, where they were very close to the line. This indicates the data do not meet this assumption.

FIGURE 8.19 Nonlinear relationship examples

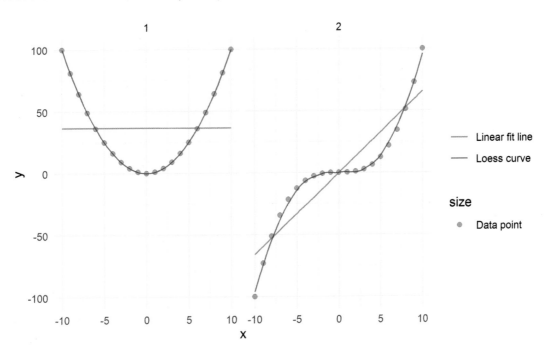

FIGURE 8.20 Relationship of percentage of females in school and percentage of citizens with basic water access in countries worldwide

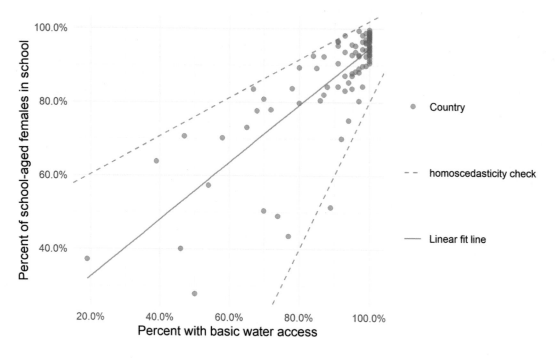

Sources: UNESCO Institute for Statistics (n.d.), WHO (n.d.).

Although typically graphs are used to check this assumption, Kiara suggested that it might be worth mentioning a statistical test that is sometimes used to check whether the difference in spread from one end to the other is statistically significant. She explained that the ***Breusch-Pagan test*** could be used to test the null hypothesis that the variance is constant around the line. The Breusch-Pagan test relies on the chi-squared distribution, and the `bptest()` function can be found in the **lmtest** package.

```
# Breusch-Pagan test for constant variance
testVar <- lmtest::bptest(formula = water.educ$female.in.school ~
                          water.educ$perc.basic2015water)

testVar

##

##   studentized Breusch-Pagan test

##

## data:  water.educ$female.in.school ~ water.educ$perc.basic2015water
## BP = 12.368, df = 1, p-value = 0.0004368
```

The Breusch-Pagan test statistic has a low *p*-value (BP = 12.37; $p = 0.0004$), indicating that the null hypothesis that the variance is constant would be rejected. When the null hypothesis that the variance is constant is rejected, the assumption of constant variance is not met. Leslie thought this was consistent with the graph, given the difference in spread around the line at the lower and higher ends of the graph (Figure 8.20).

8.8.4 INTERPRETING THE ASSUMPTION CHECKING RESULTS

In all, the correlation analysis for females in school and basic water access met two of the four assumptions. It failed the assumption of normally distributed variables and the assumption of homoscedasticity, but it met the variable type assumption and the linearity assumption. Kiara explained that there are a few options for what they could do with these results: (a) report the results and explain that the analysis does not meet assumptions, so that it is unclear if what is happening in the sample is a good reflection of what is happening in the population; (b) transform the two variables to try and meet the assumptions for Pearson's r and conduct the analysis again; and (c) choose a different type of analysis with assumptions that can be met by these data.

8.8.5 ACHIEVEMENT 5: CHECK YOUR UNDERSTANDING

Use the `cor.test()` function to examine the relationship between living on less than $1 per day and females in school. Test the assumptions. Check all the assumptions that were *met*.

a. Observations are independent.

b. Both variables are continuous.

c. Both variables are normally distributed.

d. The relationship between the two variables is linear (linearity).

e. The variance is constant with the points distributed equally around the line (*homoscedasticity*).

8.9 Achievement 6: Transforming the variables as an alternative when Pearson's *r* correlation assumptions are not met

Kiara explained that one of the ways to deal with data that do not meet assumptions for Pearson's r is to use a data transformation and examine the relationship between the transformed variables. There are two types of transformations:

- *Linear transformations* keep existing linear relationships between variables, often by multiplying or dividing one or both of the variables by some amount.

- *Nonlinear transformations* increase (or decrease) the linear relationship between two variables by applying an exponent (i.e., *power transformation*) or other function to one or both of the variables.

Different transformations are appropriate in different settings. Kiara explained that, for variables that are percentages or proportions, a *logit transformation* or *arcsine transformation* is often used to account for the floor and ceiling effects (Osborne, 2002). The logit transformation uses Equation (8.11) to make percentage data more normally distributed.

$$y_{logit} = log\left(\frac{y}{1-y}\right) \tag{8.11}$$

In Equation (8.11), y is a percent ranging from 0 to 1. The arcsine transformation is also used to normalize percentage or proportion data by using Equation (8.12) to transform the variable y.

$$y_{arcsine} = arcsin\left(\sqrt{y}\right) \tag{8.12}$$

Kiara looked up the arcsine function; she thought she remembered this word from a trigonometry class she took as a teenager. She found that it is the inverse of the sine function, which was not all that helpful, but she decided she would go back and read more about it later.

Leslie looked up information on both of these transformations and found an article that was critical of the arcsine transformation (Warton & Hui, 2011), so she asked if they could try the logit transformation first. Nancy wrote some code to transform the two variables with the logit and arcsine transformations to examine both before they chose. After looking up the function for arcsine, which is `asin()`, Nancy used `mutate()` to add new transformed variables to the data frame, `logit.female.school`, `logit.perc.basic.water`, `arcsin.female.school`, and `arcsin.perc.basic.water`.

```
# create new variables
water.educ.new <- water.educ %>%
  mutate(logit.female.school = log(x = (female.in.school/100)/(1-female.
in.school/100))) %>%
  mutate(logit.perc.basic.water = log(x = (perc.basic2015water/100)/(1-
perc.basic2015water/100))) %>%
  mutate(arcsin.female.school = asin(x = sqrt(female.in.school/100))) %>%
  mutate(arcsin.perc.basic.water = asin(x = sqrt(perc.basic2015water/100)))

# check the data
summary(water.educ.new)
##                      country       med.age        perc.1dollar
##   Albania                : 1   Min.   :15.00   Min.   : 1.00
##   Antigua and Barbuda: 1       1st Qu.:22.50   1st Qu.: 1.00
##   Argentina              : 1   Median :29.70   Median : 1.65
##   Australia              : 1   Mean   :30.33   Mean   :13.63
##   Azerbaijan             : 1   3rd Qu.:39.00   3rd Qu.:17.12
##   Bahrain                : 1   Max.   :45.90   Max.   :83.80
##   (Other)                :91                   NA's   :33
##   perc.basic2015sani  perc.safe2015sani  perc.basic2015water
##   Min.   :  7.00      Min.   :  9.00     Min.   : 19.00
##   1st Qu.: 73.00      1st Qu.: 61.25     1st Qu.: 88.75
##   Median : 93.00      Median : 76.50     Median : 97.00
##   Mean   : 79.73      Mean   : 71.50     Mean   : 90.16
##   3rd Qu.: 99.00      3rd Qu.: 93.00     3rd Qu.:100.00
##   Max.   :100.00      Max.   :100.00     Max.   :100.00
##                       NA's   :47         NA's   : 1
##   perc.safe2015water  perc.in.school  female.in.school  male.in.school
##   Min.   : 11.00      Min.   :33.32   Min.   :27.86     Min.   :38.66
##   1st Qu.: 73.75      1st Qu.:83.24   1st Qu.:83.70     1st Qu.:82.68
##   Median : 94.00      Median :92.02   Median :92.72     Median :91.50
##   Mean   : 83.38      Mean   :87.02   Mean   :87.06     Mean   :87.00
```

```
## 3rd Qu.: 98.00      3rd Qu.:95.81  3rd Qu.:96.61    3rd Qu.:95.57
## Max.    :100.00      Max.    :99.44 Max.    :99.65   Max.    :99.36
## NA's    :45
## logit.female.school logit.perc.basic.water arcsin.female.school
## Min.    :-0.9513     Min.    :-1.450        Min.    :0.5561
## 1st Qu.: 1.6359      1st Qu.: 2.066         1st Qu.:1.1552
## Median : 2.5440      Median : 3.476         Median :1.2975
## Mean   : 2.4625      Mean    :   Inf        Mean    :1.2431
## 3rd Qu.: 3.3510      3rd Qu.:   Inf         3rd Qu.:1.3857
## Max.   : 5.6624      Max.    :   Inf        Max.    :1.5119
##                      NA's    :1
## arcsin.perc.basic.water
## Min.    :0.451
## 1st Qu.:1.229
## Median :1.397
## Mean    :1.341
## 3rd Qu.:1.571
## Max.    :1.571
## NA's    :1
```

There was something strange about the `logit.perc.basic.water` variable in the `summary()` output. It had a mean value of `Inf`. Kiara remembered that the logit function has a denominator that is $1 - y$, so when y is 1 for 100%, the denominator is zero and it is impossible to divide by zero. Leslie suggested that they subtract a very small amount from the variable before transforming, but Kiara thought this was a bad idea. Once transformed, even a very tiny amount of subtracted value could make a big difference with the logit transformation. Instead, Kiara suggested they try a folded power transformation, shown in Equation (8.13), from the set of transformations suggested by Tukey (1977). "The same Tukey of HSD fame?" asked Leslie. "Yep," Kiara replied. "Good observation."

$$y_{folded.power} = y^{\frac{1}{p}} - (1-y)^{\frac{1}{p}} \qquad (8.13)$$

Kiara explained that the p in the formula is for the power to raise it to. Leslie asked how they would know what value of p to use. Nancy thought she had seen this somewhere before and searched the help documentation in RStudio for "Tukey." She found the **rcompanion** package, which could be used to choose the value of p. Nancy followed the help documentation and wrote some code to find p for each variable.

```
# use Tukey transformation to get power for transforming
# female in school variable to more normal distribution
p.female <- rcompanion::transformTukey(x = water.educ$female.in.school,
                    plotit = FALSE,
                    quiet = TRUE,
                    returnLambda = TRUE)

p.female
```

```
## lambda
##   8.85
# use Tukey transformation to get power for transforming
# basic 2015 water variable to more normal distribution
p.water <- rcompanion::transformTukey(x = water.educ$perc.basic2015water,
                    plotit = FALSE,
                    quiet = TRUE,
                    returnLambda = TRUE)
p.water
## lambda
##  9.975
```

It looked like the best value for *p*, which is called lambda (λ) by the package, was 8.85 for the `female.in.school` variable and 9.975 for the `perc.basic2015water` variable. Nancy edited the transformation code to remove the logit transformation and add the folded power transformations.

```
# create new transformation variables
water.educ.new <- water.educ %>%
  mutate(arcsin.female.school = asin(x = sqrt(female.in.school/100))) %>%
  mutate(arcsin.perc.basic.water = asin(x =
                        sqrt(perc.basic2015water/100))) %>%
  mutate(folded.p.female.school = (female.in.school/100)^(1/p.female) -
(1-female.in.school/100)^(1/p.female)) %>%
  mutate(folded.p.basic.water = (perc.basic2015water/100)^(1/p.water) - (1-
perc.basic2015water/100)^(1/p.water))

# check the data
summary(water.educ.new)
##                        country      med.age        perc.1dollar
##  Albania               : 1   Min.   :15.00   Min.   : 1.00
##  Antigua and Barbuda: 1      1st Qu.:22.50   1st Qu.: 1.00
##  Argentina             : 1   Median :29.70   Median : 1.65
##  Australia             : 1   Mean   :30.33   Mean   :13.63
##  Azerbaijan            : 1   3rd Qu.:39.00   3rd Qu.:17.12
##  Bahrain               : 1   Max.   :45.90   Max.   :83.80
##  (Other)               :91                   NA's   :33
##  perc.basic2015sani  perc.safe2015sani  perc.basic2015water
##  Min.   :  7.00      Min.   :  9.00     Min.   : 19.00
##  1st Qu.: 73.00      1st Qu.: 61.25     1st Qu.: 88.75
##  Median : 93.00      Median : 76.50     Median : 97.00
```

```
##   Mean   : 79.73      Mean   : 71.50      Mean   : 90.16
##   3rd Qu.: 99.00      3rd Qu.: 93.00      3rd Qu.:100.00
##   Max.   :100.00      Max.   :100.00      Max.   :100.00
##                       NA's   :47          NA's   :1
##   perc.safe2015water perc.in.school  female.in.school male.in.school
##   Min.   : 11.00      Min.   :33.32   Min.   :27.86    Min.   :38.66
##   1st Qu.: 73.75      1st Qu.:83.24   1st Qu.:83.70    1st Qu.:82.68
##   Median : 94.00      Median :92.02   Median :92.72    Median :91.50
##   Mean   : 83.38      Mean   :87.02   Mean   :87.06    Mean   :87.00
##   3rd Qu.: 98.00      3rd Qu.:95.81   3rd Qu.:96.61    3rd Qu.:95.57
##   Max.   :100.00      Max.   :99.44   Max.   :99.65    Max.   :99.36
##   NA's   :45
##   arcsin.female.school arcsin.perc.basic.water folded.p.female.school
##   Min.   :0.5561       Min.   :0.451           Min.   :-0.09822
##   1st Qu.:1.1552       1st Qu.:1.229           1st Qu.: 0.16540
##   Median :1.2975       Median :1.397           Median : 0.24771
##   Mean   :1.2431       Mean   :1.341           Mean   : 0.23292
##   3rd Qu.:1.3857       3rd Qu.:1.571           3rd Qu.: 0.31398
##   Max.   :1.5119       Max.   :1.571           Max.   : 0.47243
##                        NA's   :1
##   folded.p.basic.water
##   Min.   :-0.1325
##   1st Qu.: 0.1849
##   Median : 0.2933
##   Mean   : 0.4761
##   3rd Qu.: 1.0000
##   Max.   : 1.0000
##   NA's   :1
```

Leslie thought the next step would be to check the assumption of normality to see how the transformations worked. She created a couple of graphs, starting with the arcsine transformation (Figure 8.21).

```
# histogram of arcsin females in school (Figure 8.21)
water.educ.new %>%
  ggplot(aes(x = arcsin.female.school)) +
  geom_histogram(fill = "#7463AC", color = "white") +
  theme_minimal() +
  labs(x = "Arcsine transformation of females in school",
      y = "Number of countries")
```

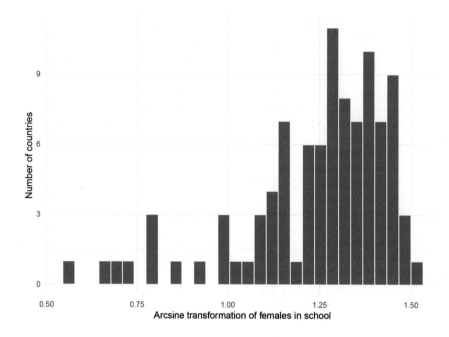

Source: UNESCO Institute for Statistics (n.d.).

That looked more normally distributed, but still left skewed. She tried the folded power transformation variable next (Figure 8.22).

```
# histogram of folded power transf females in school (Figure 8.22)
water.educ.new %>%
  ggplot(aes(x = folded.p.female.school)) +
  geom_histogram(fill = "#7463AC", color = "white") +
  theme_minimal() +
  labs(x = "Folded power transformation of females in school",
       y = "Number of countries")
```

This looked much better to everyone. It was not perfectly normal, but it was pretty close with a little left skew still. Leslie graphed the histogram of water access next (Figure 8.23).

```
# histogram of arcsine of water variable (Figure 8.23)
water.educ.new %>%
  ggplot(aes(x = arcsin.perc.basic.water)) +
  geom_histogram(fill = "#7463AC", color = "white") +
  theme_minimal() +
  labs(x = "Arcsine transformed basic water access", y = "Number of countries")
```

FIGURE 8.22 Distribution of folded power transformed percentage of females in school

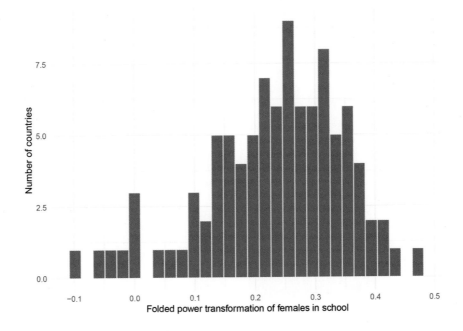

Source: UNESCO Institute for Statistics (n.d.).

FIGURE 8.23 Distribution of arcsine transformed basic water access

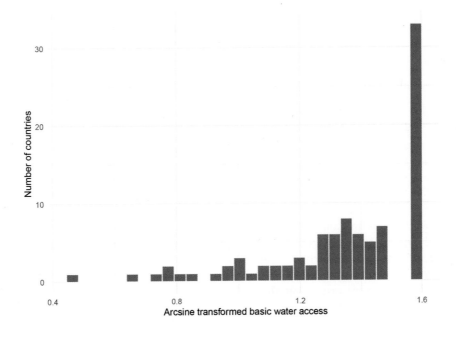

Source: WHO (n.d.).

FIGURE 8.24 Distribution of folded power transformed percentage of basic water access

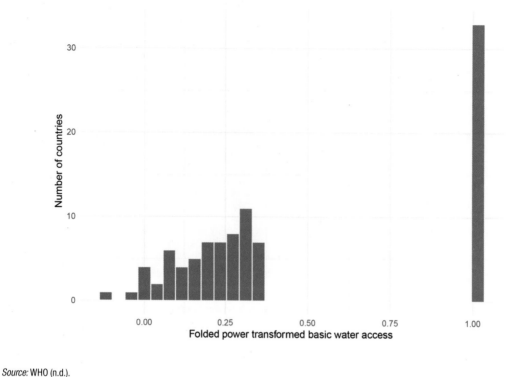

Source: WHO (n.d.).

Figure 8.23 looked terrible. It was not much better than the original variable, or maybe it was worse. Leslie hoped the folded power would work better when she graphed Figure 8.24.

```
# histogram of folded power transformed water variable (Figure 8.24)
water.educ.new %>%
  ggplot(aes(x = folded.p.basic.water)) +
  geom_histogram(fill = "#7463AC", color = "white") +
  theme_minimal() +
  labs(x = "Folded power transformed basic water access",
       y = "Number of countries")
```

The folded power transformation for water access was also terrible (Figure 8.24). Kiara suggested that this variable might actually be one that works better by recoding it into categories. Since so many countries have 100% access, the variable could be binary, with 100% access in one category and less than 100% access in another category. That sounded reasonable to the team, but Leslie wanted to practice the NHST with transformed variables. She thought the folded power transformations were probably best given that they did well for the females in school variable. Kiara explained that Leslie could use the same NHST process for the transformed variables as for the original variables, so Leslie got started.

8.9.1 NHST STEP 1: WRITE THE NULL AND ALTERNATE HYPOTHESES

H0: There is no correlation between the transformed values of percentage of females in school and percentage of citizens with basic water access ($r = 0$).

HA: There is a correlation between the transformed values of percentage of females in school and percentage of citizens with basic water access ($r \neq 0$).

8.9.2 NHST STEP 2: COMPUTE THE TEST STATISTIC

The cor.test() function is then used with the transformed variables.

```
# correlation test for transformed variables
cor.test(water.educ.new$folded.p.female.school,
        water.educ.new$folded.p.basic.water)
##
##   Pearson's product-moment correlation
##
## data:  water.educ.new$folded.p.female.school and water.educ.
new$folded.p.basic.water
## t = 8.8212, df = 94, p-value = 5.893e-14
## alternative hypothesis: true correlation is not equal to 0
## 95 percent confidence interval:
##  0.5461788 0.7696207
## sample estimates:
##       cor
## 0.6729733
```

The test statistic is $t = 8.82$ for the correlation of $r = .67$ between the two transformed variables.

8.9.3 NHST STEP 3: CALCULATE THE PROBABILITY THAT YOUR TEST STATISTIC IS AT LEAST AS BIG AS IT IS IF THERE IS NO RELATIONSHIP (I.E., THE NULL IS TRUE)

The *p*-value shown in the output of cor.test() is very tiny. The probability that the *t*-statistic would be 8.82 or larger if there were no relationship is very tiny, nearly zero.

8.9.4 NHST STEPS 4 AND 5: INTERPRET THE PROBABILITY AND WRITE A CONCLUSION

With a very tiny *p*-value, Leslie rejected the null hypothesis. There was a statistically significant relationship between the transformed variables for percentage of females in school and percentage of citizens with basic water access in a country. The relationship was positive and moderate to strong ($r = .67$). As the percentage of citizens with basic water access goes up, the percentage of females in school also goes up. The correlation is .67 in the sample, and the 95% confidence interval shows that it is likely between .55 and .77 in the sampled population.

8.9.5 TESTING ASSUMPTIONS FOR PEARSON'S *r* BETWEEN THE TRANSFORMED VARIABLES

They knew the independence of observations assumption was not met. Nancy wrote out the four other assumptions to examine with the transformed variables:

- Both variables are continuous.

- Both variables are normally distributed.

- The relationship between the two variables is *linear* (linearity).

- The variance is constant with the points distributed equally around the line (homoscedasticity).

The continuous variables assumption is met; the transformations resulted in continuous variables. The assumption of normal distributions was *not* met based on the left-skewed histogram of the transformed water variable examined during data transformation. To test the remaining assumptions, Leslie made a scatterplot with the Loess curve and the linear model line to check linearity and homoscedasticity (Figure 8.25).

```
# explore plot of transformed females in school and basic water
# with linear fit line and Loess curve (Figure 8.25)
water.educ.new %>%
  ggplot(aes(y = folded.p.female.school, x = folded.p.basic.water)) +
  geom_smooth(aes(color = "linear fit line"), method = "lm", se = FALSE) +
  geom_smooth(aes(color = "Loess curve"), se = FALSE) +
  geom_point(aes(size = "Country"), color = "#7463AC", alpha = .6) +
  theme_minimal() +
  labs(y = "Power transformed percent of females in school",
      x = "Power transformed percent with basic water access") +
  scale_color_manual(name="Type of fit line",
                    values=c("gray60", "deeppink")) +
  scale_size_manual(values = 2)
```

The plot shows a pretty terrible deviation from linearity, which looks like it is mostly due to all the countries with 100% basic water access. The homoscedasticity looked a little strange, so Leslie decided to use Breusch-Pagan (BP) to determine if this spread is considered equal around the line. She reminded herself that the BP test is testing the null hypothesis that the variance is constant around the line.

```
# testing for homoscedasticity
bp.test.trans <- lmtest::bptest(formula = water.educ.new$folded.p.female.
school ~ water.educ.new$folded.p.basic.water)
bp.test.trans
##
##  studentized Breusch-Pagan test
```

```
##
## data: water.educ.new$folded.p.female.school ~ water.educ.
new$folded.p.basic.water
## BP = 6.3816, df = 1, p-value = 0.01153
```

With a *p*-value of .01, the null hypothesis is rejected and the assumption fails. The data transformation worked to mostly address the problem of normality for the females in school variable, but the transformed data were not better for linearity or homoscedasticity. Leslie wrote her conclusion:

> There was a statistically significant, positive, and strong ($r = .67$; $t = 8.82$; $p < .05$; 95% CI: .55–.77) relationship between the transformed variables for percentage of females in school and percentage of citizens with basic water access in a sample of countries. As the percentage of citizens with basic water access increases, so does the percentage of school-age females in school. The data failed several of the assumptions for *r* and so these results should not be generalized outside the sample.

Kiara wanted to add one more caveat to the analyses. She explained that although transformations may work to meet assumptions in some cases, transformations also make interpretation more complicated. Because the relationship is now between the transformed values, the interpretation is now with respect to the transformed values and not the original data (Osborne, 2002). When possible, she recommended using the original untransformed data. Nancy clarified that the conclusion Leslie wrote included a *p*-value and a confidence interval, both of which are for generalizing from a sample to a population. She reminded Leslie that these values could be omitted from the results since the analysis is not reliable when the assumptions are failed.

FIGURE 8.25 Transformed females in school and basic water access variables

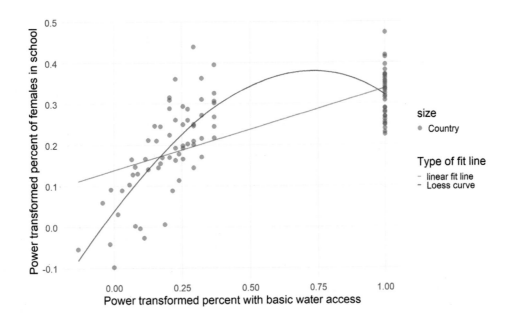

Sources: UNESCO Institute for Statistics (n.d.), WHO (n.d.).

8.9.6 ACHIEVEMENT 6: CHECK YOUR UNDERSTANDING

Use the Tukey method to transform the poverty variable, `perc.1dollar`, and check normality for the transformed variable.

8.10 Achievement 7: Using Spearman's rho as an alternative when Pearson's *r* correlation assumptions are not met

---

Kiara said that there are other correlation statistics that do not have the same strict assumptions as Pearson's *r*. Given the difficulty of meeting the assumptions, she suggested using a different statistic. The most commonly used alternative to the Pearson's *r* correlation coefficient is the *Spearman's rho* rank correlation coefficient. Technically, Kiara said, using Spearman's rho is just using another transformation, but instead of computing the arcsine or raising the variables to a power, the values of the variables are transformed into ranks, like with some of the alternatives to the *t*-tests. The values of the variables are ranked from lowest to highest, and the calculations for correlation are conducted using the ranks instead of the raw values for the variables.

8.10.1 COMPUTING SPEARMAN'S RHO CORRELATION COEFFICIENT

Nancy repeated that Spearman's rho (ρ) was computed by ranking each value for each variable from lowest to highest and then computing the extent to which the two variable ranks are the same. Leslie remembered that most of the time, the Greek letters like rho are used to represent the population and there is some other way to represent the sample. Kiara said rho is usually denoted "rho" or "r_s." Leslie liked r_s, so they decided to use this notation for the correlation in the sample.

Kiara explained that r_s for females in school and basic water access would be computed by first ranking the values of percentage of females in school from lowest to highest and then ranking the values of basic water access from lowest to highest. Then, once the ranks were assigned, Kiara wrote Equation (8.14) to show how the r_s correlation coefficient is computed:

$$\rho = \frac{6\sum d^2}{n(n^2 - 1)},$$ (8.14)

where

- *d* is the difference between the ranks of the two variables
- *n* is the number of observations

Leslie prepared her NHST for the new analysis.

8.10.2 NHST STEP 1: WRITE THE NULL AND ALTERNATE HYPOTHESES

H0: There is no correlation between the percentage of females in school and the percentage of citizens with basic water access ($\rho = 0$).

HA: There is a correlation between the percentage of females in school and the percentage of citizens with basic water access ($\rho \neq 0$).

8.10.3 NHST STEP 2: COMPUTE THE TEST STATISTIC

Using the `cor.test()` function, Nancy showed Kiara and Leslie how to test the null hypothesis of no correlation between females in school and basic water access by adding `method = "spearman"` as one of the options.

```
# spearman correlation females in school and water access
spear.fem.water <- cor.test(x = water.educ$perc.basic2015water,
                            y = water.educ$female.in.school,
                            method = "spearman")
spear.fem.water
##
##  Spearman's rank correlation rho
##
## data:  water.educ$perc.basic2015water and water.educ$female.in.school
## S = 34050, p-value < 2.2e-16
## alternative hypothesis: true rho is not equal to 0
## sample estimates:
##        rho
## 0.7690601
```

While Pearson's r between females in school and basic water access was 0.81, r_s was slightly lower at 0.77.

Instead of a t-statistic, the output for r_s reports the S test statistic. Kiara wrote out Equation (8.15), which shows how S is computed (Best & Roberts, 1975).

$$S = \left(n^3 - n\right)\frac{1 - r_s}{6},$$

(8.15)

where r_s is the Spearman's correlation coefficient and n is the sample size. The p-value in the output of the `cor.test()` function is not from the S test statistic, said Kiara. Instead, it is determined by computing an approximation of the t-statistic and degrees of freedom. Kiara wrote out Equation (8.16) to show how this special approximation of the t-statistic is computed (Best & Roberts, 1975).

$$t_s = r_s\sqrt{\frac{n-2}{1-r_s^2}}$$

(8.16)

While it is not included in the output from R, the t-statistic can be computed easily by using R as a calculator.

```
# compute the sample size
# drop rows with NA
water.educ.new %>%
  drop_na(perc.basic2015water) %>%
```

```
  drop_na(female.in.school) %>%
  summarize(n = n(),
            t.spear = spear.fem.water$estimate*sqrt((n()-2)/(1-spear.fem.
water$estimate^2)))
##    n t.spear
## 1 96 11.6655
```

Leslie was confused by the `spear.fem.water$estimate` part of the code. Kiara reminded her that `$` can be used to access parts of objects, just like `$` can be used to access columns of a data frame. The Spearman's rho code from earlier had produced a list of nine things that could be explored and used in reporting and in other calculations. The dollar sign operator can be used to refer to items in a list in the same way it is used to refer to variables in a data frame. Leslie printed the summary of the list to take a look.

```
# print the list from the Spearman's analysis
summary(object = spear.fem.water)
##              Length Class  Mode
## statistic    1      -none- numeric
## parameter    0      -none- NULL
## p.value      1      -none- numeric
## estimate     1      -none- numeric
## null.value   1      -none- numeric
## alternative  1      -none- character
## method       1      -none- character
## data.name    1      -none- character
```

Kiara showed Leslie she could access any of these items in the list using the name of the object, `spear.fem.water`, followed by `$` and then the name of the element she wanted to access. For example, to access the `statistic` from `spear.fem.water`, Leslie could use the following code:

```
# access the statistic
spear.fem.water$statistic
## S
## 34049.77
```

Kiara suggested Leslie spend a little time examining the objects created from analyses and referred her back to Box 8.2.

8.10.4 NHST STEP 3: CALCULATE THE PROBABILITY THAT YOUR TEST STATISTIC IS AT LEAST AS BIG AS IT IS IF THERE IS NO RELATIONSHIP (I.E., THE NULL IS TRUE)

In this case, t is 11.67 with 94 degrees of freedom ($n = 96$). A quick plot of the t-distribution with 94 degrees of freedom revealed that the probability of a t-statistic this big or bigger would be very tiny if

FIGURE 8.26 *t*-distribution with 94 degrees of freedom

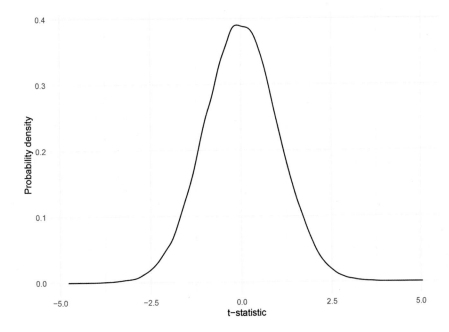

the null hypothesis were true. The *p*-value of < 2.2e-16 in the output for the Spearman analysis makes sense (Figure 8.26).

8.10.5 NHST STEPS 4 AND 5: INTERPRET THE PROBABILITY AND WRITE A CONCLUSION

Given the very small area under the curve of the *t*-distribution that would be at 11.67 or a higher value for 94 degrees of freedom, the tiny *p*-value makes sense and indicates that the null hypothesis is rejected.

Leslie interpreted the results:

> There was a statistically significant positive correlation between basic access to water and females in school (r_s = 0.77; p < .001). As the percentage of the population with basic access to water increases, so does the percentage of females in school.

8.10.6 ASSUMPTION CHECKING FOR SPEARMAN'S RHO

Nancy explained that the independence of observations assumption is still required and was still a problem. Kiara looked up the other assumptions for r_s and found just two:

- The variables must be at least ordinal or even closer to continuous.
- The relationship between the two variables must be monotonic.

The first assumption was met; the two variables were continuous. Kiara asked Nancy to help her demonstrate the monotonic assumption with some graphing.

8.10.7 CHECKING THE MONOTONIC ASSUMPTION

A *monotonic* relationship is a relationship that goes in only one direction. Leslie asked how this differs from the linear relationship. Kiara clarified that the relationship does not have to follow a straight line; it can curve as long as it is always heading in the same direction. Nancy created examples to demonstrate (Figure 8.27).

Leslie understood the assumption after this visual. For the females in school and basic water access analysis, she reviewed Figure 8.18 to see if the relationship met the monotonic assumption. The Loess curve in Figure 8.18 only goes up, which demonstrates that the relationship between females in school and basic water access meets the monotonic assumption. The values of females in school consistently go up while the values of basic access to water go up. The relationship does not change direction. Kiara noted that the r_s met more assumptions than Pearson's r with the original data or with the transformed variables. Even so, Leslie reminded her that the independent observation assumption failed, so any reporting should stick to descriptive statistics about the sample and not generalize to the population. Kiara wrote a final interpretation of the relationship:

> There was a positive correlation between basic access to water and females in school ($r_s = 0.77$). As the percentage of the population with basic access to water increases, so does the percentage of females in school.

Leslie asked Kiara if a test had ever met assumptions in all of their meetings. "Maybe," Kiara laughed. "Didn't we meet assumptions during our chi-squared meeting?" she asked.

That sounded right to Leslie, but certainly there had been a lot of failing assumptions.

8.10.8 ACHIEVEMENT 7: CHECK YOUR UNDERSTANDING

Use the `cor.test()` function with the `method = "spearman"` option to examine the relationship between living on less than $1 per day and females in school. Check the assumptions and interpret your results.

FIGURE 8.27 Monotonic relationship examples

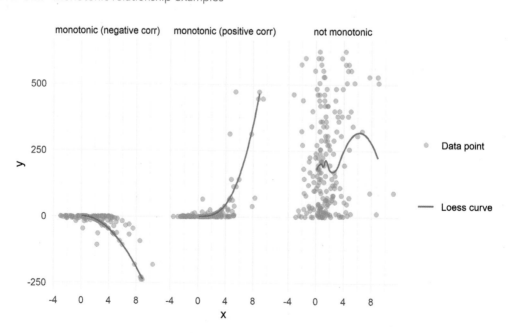

8.11 Achievement 8: Introducing partial correlations

Kiara thought they were nearly done for the day and wanted to introduce one additional topic. Specifically, she was concerned that females in school and basic water access might both be related to poverty, and that poverty might be the reason both of these variables increase at the same time. Basically, Kiara thought that poverty was the reason for the shared variance between these two variables. She thought that countries with higher poverty had fewer females in school and lower percentages of people with basic water access. She explained that there is a method called *partial correlation* for examining how multiple variables share variance with each other. Kiara was interested in how much overlap there was between females in school and basic water access after accounting for poverty.

Nancy thought it might be useful to think about partial correlation in terms of the shared variance like in Figure 8.13. She created a Venn diagram with three variables that overlap (Figure 8.28). There are two ways the variables overlap in Figure 8.28. There are places where just two of the variables overlap (X and Y overlap, X and Z overlap, Y and Z overlap), and there is the space where X and Y and Z all overlap in the center of the diagram. The overlap between just two colors is the partial correlation between the two variables. It is the extent to which they vary in the same way after accounting for how they are both related to the third variable involved.

8.11.1 COMPUTING PEARSON'S *r* PARTIAL CORRELATIONS

Nancy was aware of an R package for examining partial correlations called **ppcor**. Using the function for partial correlation (pcor()) and for the partial correlation statistical test (pcor.test())

FIGURE 8.28 Visualizing partial correlation for three variables

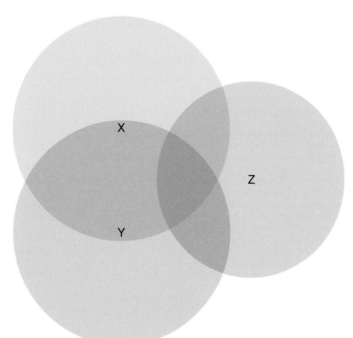

requires having a small data frame that consists only of the variables involved in the correlation with no missing data. Nancy created this data frame containing the females in school, basic water access, and poverty variables.

```
# create a data frame with only females in school
# poverty and water access
water.educ.small <- water.educ.new %>%
  select(female.in.school, perc.basic2015water, perc.1dollar) %>%
  drop_na()

# check the new data
summary(water.educ.small)
##   female.in.school perc.basic2015water  perc.1dollar
##   Min.   :40.05    Min.   : 39.00       Min.   : 1.00
##   1st Qu.:81.74    1st Qu.: 85.75       1st Qu.: 1.00
##   Median :92.45    Median : 95.50       Median : 1.65
##   Mean   :86.52    Mean   : 88.88       Mean   :13.63
##   3rd Qu.:96.28    3rd Qu.:100.00       3rd Qu.:17.12
##   Max.   :99.65    Max.   :100.00       Max.   :83.80
```

Once the small data frame was ready, Nancy checked the Pearson's r correlations among the variables.

```
# examine the bivariate correlations
water.educ.small %>%
  summarize(corr.fem.water = cor(x = perc.basic2015water,
                                 y = female.in.school),
            corr.fem.pov = cor(x = perc.1dollar, y = female.in.school),
            corr.water.pov = cor(x = perc.basic2015water,
                                 y = perc.1dollar))
##   corr.fem.water corr.fem.pov corr.water.pov
## 1      0.7650656   -0.7144238     -0.8320895
```

The three correlations were all strong. Nancy used pcor() to determine how they were interrelated.

```
# conduct partial Pearson correlation
educ.water.poverty <- ppcor::pcor(x = water.educ.small, method = "pearson")
educ.water.poverty
## $estimate
##                     female.in.school perc.basic2015water perc.1dollar
```

```
## female.in.school            1.0000000          0.4395917   -0.2178859
## perc.basic2015water         0.4395917          1.0000000   -0.6336436
## perc.1dollar               -0.2178859         -0.6336436    1.0000000
##
## $p.value
##                     female.in.school perc.basic2015water perc.1dollar
## female.in.school        0.0000000000        3.125684e-04 8.626064e-02
## perc.basic2015water     0.0003125684        0.000000e+00 2.490386e-08
## perc.1dollar            0.0862606413        2.490386e-08 0.000000e+00
##
## $statistic
##                     female.in.school perc.basic2015water perc.1dollar
## female.in.school            0.000000            3.822455    -1.743636
## perc.basic2015water         3.822455            0.000000    -6.397046
## perc.1dollar               -1.743636           -6.397046     0.000000
##
## $n
## [1] 64
##
## $gp
## [1] 1
##
## $method
## [1] "pearson"
```

The original Pearson correlation from the cor.Fem.Educ.Water object between females in school and basic water access in these data was $r = 0.81$. Once all the missing values were removed from the data, the correlation between females in school and basic water access dropped to .77. Looking at the first section of the output from pcor() under the $estimate subheading, it shows the partial correlations between all three of the variables. The partial correlation between females in school and basic water access is $r_{partial} = .44$. So, after accounting for poverty, the relationship between females in school and basic water access is a moderate .44. Nancy thought a visual might help, so she entered the correlations into the Venn diagram code to make a diagram that shows the relationships from this analysis (Figure 8.29).

There is quite a bit of overlap among all the variables. The $r_{partial} = .44$ is the section of Figure 8.26 where the *female.school* circle and the *basic.water* circle overlap but there is no overlap from the *less.than.dollar* circle. The unique variance in basic water access that is shared with females in school is the overlap between those two circles. This is the partial correlation.

To get the percentage of shared variance, this coefficient of determination r^2 could be computed and reported as a percentage. The squared value of .44 is .194, so 19.4% of the variance in percentage of females in school is shared with the percentage who have basic access to water.

FIGURE 8.29 Visualizing partial correlations between females in school, basic water access, and living on less than $1 per day

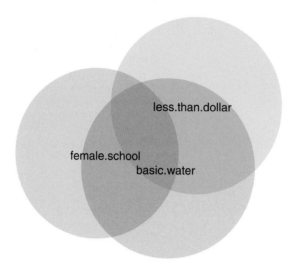

Sources: UNESCO Institute for Statistics (n.d.), WHO (n.d.).

8.11.2 COMPUTING SPEARMAN'S RHO PARTIAL CORRELATIONS

Leslie reminded Kiara that the data do not meet the assumptions for the Pearson's *r* correlation. She explained that the assumptions that applied to the two variables for a Pearson's *r* correlation would apply to all three variables for a partial Pearson's *r* correlation. Each variable would be continuous and normally distributed, each pair of variables would demonstrate linearity, and each pair would have to have constant variances (homoscedasticity). Since she already knew that several assumptions were not met, Leslie computed the Spearman correlation, which was more appropriate in this case. The Spearman assumption of monotonic relationship would apply to each pair of variables. Kiara changed the `method= "spearman"` argument in the `pcor()` function for r_s.

```
# conduct partial correlation with Spearman
educ.water.poverty.spear <- ppcor::pcor(x = water.educ.small, method =
"spearman")
educ.water.poverty.spear
## $estimate
##                      female.in.school perc.basic2015water perc.1dollar
## female.in.school          1.0000000            0.4305931   -0.2841782
## perc.basic2015water       0.4305931            1.0000000   -0.5977239
## perc.1dollar             -0.2841782           -0.5977239    1.0000000
##
##
## $p.value
##                      female.in.school perc.basic2015water perc.1dollar
```

```
## female.in.school        0.0000000000        4.272781e-04 2.399667e-02
## perc.basic2015water     0.0004272781        0.000000e+00 2.312820e-07
## perc.1dollar            0.0239966731        2.312820e-07 0.000000e+00
##
## $statistic
##                        female.in.school perc.basic2015water perc.1dollar
## female.in.school              0.000000            3.726169    -2.314944
## perc.basic2015water           3.726169            0.000000    -5.823078
## perc.1dollar                 -2.314944           -5.823078     0.000000
##
## $n
## [1] 64
##
## $gp
## [1] 1
##
## $method
## [1] "spearman"
```

The original r_s between females in school and basic water access was 0.77, but the partial Spearman's r_s correlation between females in school and basic water access after accounting for poverty was .43. Including poverty reduced the magnitude of the correlation by nearly half.

8.11.3 SIGNIFICANCE TESTING FOR PARTIAL CORRELATIONS

Like the r and r_s correlations, the partial correlations can be tested for statistical significance using a t-test. The t-statistic for each partial correlation is shown in the output from pcor(). The second chunk of numbers are the p-values and the third chunk of numbers are the t-test test statistics. Leslie skipped over NHST this time and used the output to write her interpretation of the partial correlation between females in school and basic water access, accounting for poverty:

> The partial correlation between percentage of females in school and the percentage of citizens who have basic water access was moderate, positive, and statistically significant ($r_{s\cdot partial} = 0.43$; $t = 3.73$; $p < .05$). Even after poverty is accounted for, increased basic water access was moderately, positively, and significantly associated with an increased percentage of females in school.

8.11.4 CHECKING ASSUMPTIONS FOR PARTIAL CORRELATIONS

Kiara reminded Leslie that she needed to check the assumptions before reporting these results. They already knew the data failed the independent observations assumption. The variables all met the assumption of being at least ordinal, and Leslie already checked for a monotonic relationship between females in school and percentage with basic water. She checked the monotonic assumption for females in school with poverty (Figure 8.30) and for percentage with basic water and poverty (Figure 8.31).

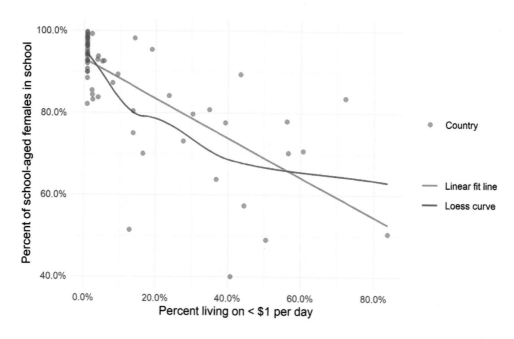

FIGURE 8.30 Relationship of percentage of females in school and percentage of citizens living on less than $1 per day in countries worldwide

Sources: UNESCO Institute for Statistics (n.d.), WHO (n.d.).

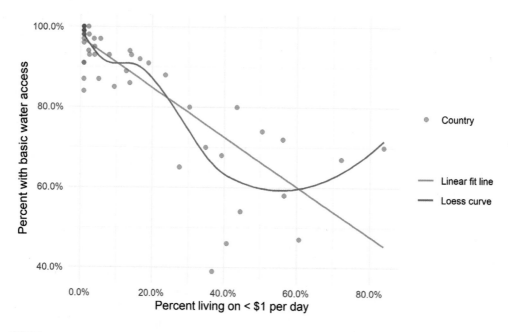

FIGURE 8.31 Relationship of percentage with basic water access and percentage of citizens living on less than $1 per day in countries worldwide

Sources: UNESCO Institute for Statistics (n.d.), WHO (n.d.).

```
# check monotonic of plot of females in school and poverty (Figure 8.30)
water.educ.small %>%
  ggplot(aes(y = female.in.school/100, x = perc.1dollar/100)) +
  geom_smooth(aes(color = "Linear fit line"), method = "lm", se = FALSE) +
  geom_smooth(aes(color = "Loess curve"), se = FALSE) +
  geom_point(aes(size = "Country"), color = "#7463AC", alpha = .6) +
  theme_minimal() +
  labs(y = "Percent of school-aged females in school",
       x = "Percent living on < $1 per day") +
  scale_x_continuous(labels = scales::percent) +
  scale_y_continuous(labels = scales::percent) +
  scale_color_manual(name="", values = c("gray60", "deeppink")) +
  scale_size_manual(name="", values = 2)
```

The Loess curve in Figure 8.30 goes just one direction, down. The monotonic assumption is met.

```
# check monotonic assumption for water access and poverty (Figure 8.31)
water.educ.small %>%
  ggplot(aes(x = perc.1dollar/100, y = perc.basic2015water/100)) +
  geom_smooth(aes(color = "Linear fit line"), method = "lm", se = FALSE) +
  geom_smooth(aes(color = "Loess curve"), se = FALSE) +
  geom_point(aes(size = "Country"), color = "#7463AC", alpha = .6) +
  theme_minimal() +
  labs( x = "Percent living on < $1 per day",
        y = "Percent with basic water access") +
  scale_x_continuous(labels = scales::percent) +
  scale_y_continuous(labels = scales::percent) +
  scale_color_manual(name = "", values = c("gray60", "deeppink")) +
  scale_size_manual(name = "", values = 2)
```

Leslie was disappointed when she saw that the Loess curve went both down and up for the relationship between poverty and water access. Figure 8.31 showed that the analyses did not meet the monotonic assumption for the poverty variable and the basic water access variable. The results could still be reported, but without meeting the assumptions for the statistical test, interpreting the statistical significance was a problem.

8.11.5 INTERPRETING RESULTS WHEN ASSUMPTIONS ARE NOT MET

When assumptions are not met, there are a few possible strategies. Kiara recommended two strategies: interpreting the results for the sample only, and recoding one of the variables to be categorical and using a different type of analysis. She reminded Leslie that the partial correlation interpretation should change since the assumption was not met. Leslie rewrote the interpretation:

The partial correlation between the percentage of females in school and the percentage of citizens who have basic water access was moderate and positive ($r_{s \cdot partial} = 0.43$). Even after poverty is accounted for, increased basic water access was moderately and positively associated with an increased percentage of females in school. The assumptions were not met, so it is not clear that the partial correlation from the sample of countries can be generalized to the population of all countries.

Kiara suggested that the poverty variable might also be recoded into ordinal categories. The ordinal variable could then be used in place of the original version of the variable and the r_s analysis could be conducted again. Nancy and Leslie thought this was a great idea, but with the independent observations assumptions failed, it wouldn't make any difference for reporting statistical significance and generalizing results, so they thought they might as well stop for the day.

Leslie thought back to their initial conversations from this meeting. She had learned that basic access to water had a strong positive correlation with the percentage of school-aged females in school, and that this correlation persisted with moderate strength even after poverty was accounted for. This suggested that the number of females in school would increase with improving water access. Nancy mentioned that the Water, Sanitation, and Hygiene (WASH) Promotion in Temeke Primary Schools program that she had heard about in Tanzania (Frisone, 2017) had added more latrines, handwashing, safe drinking water tanks, and separate facilities for girls. This sounded promising to Leslie, and she made a note to read more. In addition to learning about water access and its relationship to educating girls, Leslie had learned more than she ever wanted to know about conducting and interpreting Pearson's and Spearman's correlation analyses. Nancy was satisfied with their work but continued to be unsatisfied with the lack of sanitation and clean water for many girls and women around the world.

The R-Team packed up their laptops, paid for their fries, and waved across the parking lot as they got into their separate cars to head home.

/// 8.12 CHAPTER SUMMARY

8.12.1 Achievements unlocked in this chapter: Recap

Congratulations! Like Leslie, you've learned and practiced the following in this chapter.

8.12.1.1 Achievement 1 recap: Exploring the data using graphics and descriptive statistics

Prior to conducting a correlation analysis, it is useful to examine how the two variables are related to one another visually. In the case of correlation analyses, the best visual to use is a scatterplot. The scatterplot shows whether the relationship appears to be linear, how strong it might be, and whether it looks like a positive or negative relationship.

8.12.1.2 Achievement 2 recap: Computing and interpreting Pearson's r correlation coefficient

The Pearson's r correlation coefficient is used to examine the relationship between two continuous variables. To use Pearson's r, the two variables must be normally distributed, have a linear relationship to each other, and have constant variance throughout the linear relationship.

Pearson correlation coefficients range from −1 to 1, where values below zero represent negative relationships where one variable goes down when the other goes up. Values above zero represent positive relationships where one variable goes up as the other goes up, or one variable goes down as the other goes down.

8.12.1.3 Achievement 3 recap: Conducting an inferential statistical test for Pearson's r correlation coefficient

A *t*-statistic comparing the Pearson's *r* to zero determines whether the correlation coefficient is statistically significantly different from zero.

8.12.1.4 Achievement 4 recap: Examining effect size for Pearson's *r* with the coefficient of determination

The coefficient of determination is an alternate effect size computed by squaring the correlation coefficient. The coefficient of determination, or r^2, is interpreted as the amount of shared variance the two variables have.

8.12.1.5 Achievement 5 recap: Checking assumptions for Pearson's *r* correlation analyses

Statistical tests rely on underlying assumptions about the characteristics of the data. When these assumptions are not met, the results may not reflect the true relationships among the variables. The variable type can be checked by examining the two variables to be sure they are continuous. Histograms and Q-Q plots can be used to determine if the variables are normally distributed. A scatterplot with a Loess curve is useful for examining linearity. Finally, a scatterplot and Breusch-Pagan test can aid in identifying problems with constant variance.

8.12.1.6 Achievement 6 recap: Transforming the variables as an alternative when Pearson's *r* correlation assumptions are not met

One of the methods that can be useful when the data do not meet the assumptions for Pearson's *r* is to transform the variables. The type of transformation depends on the characteristics of the data. For percentages and proportions, using a logit transformation or folded power transformation can be useful. One caution of transforming variables for analysis is that the interpretation of results is no longer as straightforward.

8.12.1.7 Achievement 7 recap: Using Spearman's rho as an alternative when Pearson's *r* correlation assumptions are not met

When assumptions are not met for Pearson's *r*, the Spearman's rho correlation coefficient can be used instead.

This correlation coefficient requires that the data are measured at the ordinal, interval, or ratio level. The second assumption is that the relationship is monotonic, which means that it is either consistently positive or consistently negative. Spearman's rho does not assume normally distributed variables, constant variance, or linearity. The interpretation of the direction (positive or negative) and strength of r_s is consistent with the interpretation of the direction and strength of the Pearson's *r* correlation coefficient.

8.12.1.8 Achievement 8 recap: Introducing partial correlations

Some correlations may be influenced by additional variables. Partial correlation analyses account for the influence of other variables and quantify the shared variance unique to the two variables of interest. Partial correlations can use Pearson or Spearman methods depending on whether the data meet the assumptions for these tests.

8.12.2 Chapter exercises

The coder and hacker exercises are an opportunity to apply the skills from this chapter to a new scenario or a new data set. The coder edition evaluates the application of the concepts and functions learned in this R-Team meeting to scenarios similar to those in the meeting. The hacker edition evaluates the use of the concepts and functions from this R-Team meeting in new scenarios, often going a step beyond what was explicitly explained.

The coder edition might be best for those who found some or all of the Check Your Understanding activities to be challenging or if they needed review before picking the correct responses to the multiple-choice questions. The hacker edition might be best if the Check Your Understanding activities were not too challenging and the multiple-choice questions were a breeze.

The multiple-choice questions and materials for the exercises are online at **edge.sagepub.com/harris1e**.

Q1: Which of the following is not an assumption for the Pearson's correlation analysis?

a. Normally distributed variables

b. Monotonic relationship

c. Linear relationship

d. Constant variance

e. Continuous variables

Q2: What is the primary purpose of Pearson's and Spearman's correlation coefficients?

a. Examining the relationship between two noncategorical variables

b. Identifying deviations from normality for continuous variables

c. Examining the relationship between two categorical variables

d. Comparing means across groups

Q3: Which of the following would be considered a very strong negative correlation?

a. .89

b. −.09

c. −.89

d. .09

Q4: What percentage of the variance is shared if two variables are correlated at .4?

a. 40%

b. 4%

c. 8%

d. 16%

Q5: Which test is used to determine whether a correlation coefficient is statistically significant?

a. Paired samples t-test

b. Chi-squared test

c. One-sample t-test

d. P-value

8.12.2.1 Chapter exercises: Coder edition

Depending on your score in the knowledge check, choose either the coder or hacker edition of the chapter exercises. Use the data from this chapter and the appropriate tests to examine males and females in school and basic water access.

1) Import the `water.educ` data frame as shown in this chapter.

2) Make a table of descriptive statistics for all the variables in the data frame except for country. Be sure to use appropriate statistics for each variable.

3) Use a graph to examine the relationship between `male.in.school` and `female.in.school` (Achievement 1).

4) Use a graph to examine the relationship between `male.in.school` and `perc.basic2015water` (Achievement 1).

5) Based on the graphs from Questions 3 and 4, make predictions about what you would find when you conduct Pearson correlation analyses for `male.in.school` and `female.in.school` and for `male.in.school` and `perc.basic2015 water` (Achievement 1).

6) Conduct a Pearson's r correlation analysis for each pair of variables. Interpret each r statistic in terms of direction, size, and significance (Achievements 2 and 3).

7) Compute and interpret the coefficient of determination for each pair of variables (Achievement 4).

8) Check assumptions for the Pearson's r for each pair of variables (Achievement 5).

9) If assumptions are not met for the Pearson's r, conduct and interpret a Spearman's correlation analysis, including assumption testing (Achievement 7).

10) Conduct the appropriate partial correlation (Pearson or Spearman) examining the relationship between `male.in.school` and `perc.basic2015water` accounting for `perc.1dollar`. Check any assumptions not previously checked and interpret your results accordingly (Achievement 8).

11) Write a paragraph explaining what you found and how it compares to the correlation analyses for females in school and water access.

8.12.2.2 Chapter exercises: Hacker edition

Complete #1 through #9 of the coder edition; then complete the following:

10) Create a new variable by recoding the `perc.1dollar` variable into 10 categories: 0 to < 10, 10 to < 20, 20 to < 30, and so on. The new variable should have a logical name and clear labels.

11) Conduct the partial correlation between females in school and basic water access accounting for poverty by including this new variable. Use the appropriate

kind of partial correlation (Pearson's or Spearman's) given the variable type for the new variable.

12) Check assumptions and interpret your results (Achievement 8).

13) Write a paragraph explaining what you found and how the results differed (or did not differ) once you were

using the new ordinal version of the poverty variable (Achievement 8).

8.12.2.3 Instructor note

Solutions to exercises can be found on the website for this book, along with ideas for gamification for those who want to take it further.

Visit **edge.sagepub.com/harris1e** to download the datasets, complete the chapter exercises, and watch R tutorial videos.

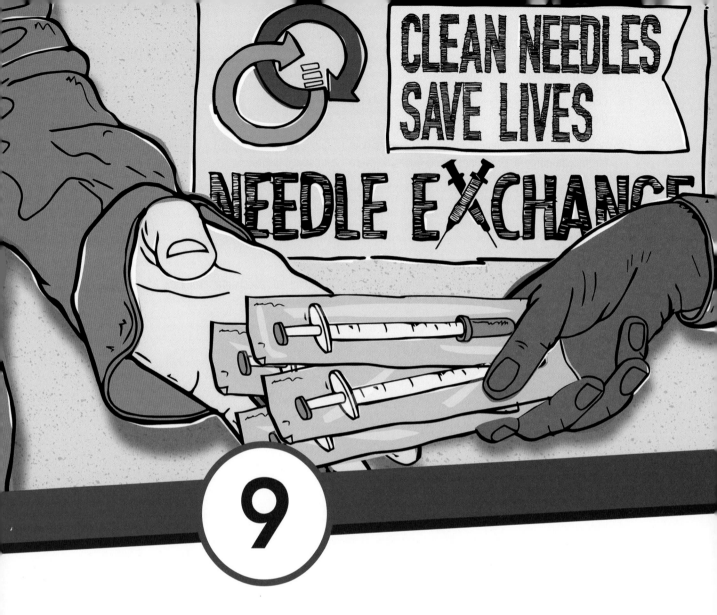

9

LINEAR REGRESSION

The R-Team and the Needle Exchange Examination

Nancy offered to host the next meeting of the R-Team at her house. After the meeting, she offered to share an episode of the 1980s hit TV show *The A-Team*. Kiara and Leslie thought that sounded like fun.

Kiara and Leslie carpooled and were relieved to finally pull up in front of Nancy's place.

"Sorry we're late, Nancy!" Kiara said.

"Wow, we underestimated just how far your place was from the city," Leslie said. "It's nice to see some pretty scenery, but I think it must be tough for you to have to drive so far for everything."

"It just takes planning, organization, and a love for driving," Nancy said. "That's me in a nutshell."

Kiara couldn't contain her enthusiasm any longer. "Finally, we are moving on to linear models, which, aside from descriptive statistics and graphs, are some of the most useful methods across many fields. Linear models are useful because they allow people to use multiple variables to explain or predict the values of an outcome such as voter fraud, getting screened for breast cancer, systolic blood pressure, technology use, and many other things. The outcome can be explained or predicted not just by one other variable like sex, race, income, or education; instead, linear models allow multiple variables to be combined to explain or predict something."

Leslie said, "This makes me think of the two-way ANOVA [Section 7.11], where sex and education together were useful in understanding technology use and also how poverty influences the relationship between females in school and basic water access when discussing partial correlations [Section 8.11]."

"Exactly!" Nancy exclaimed, "but I did want to mention that *t*-tests and ANOVA are technically linear models; they are just special cases with limitations. The linear models we start on today are useful in many different situations."

Kiara continued, "Linear models are really flexible. Linear models can be simple—with just one variable explaining an outcome—or complex—using 3, 4, 5, or even 10 variables to explain an outcome. Also, the variables explaining an outcome in a linear model are not limited to just categorical, as in two-way ANOVA, or just continuous, as in the partial correlation example. They can be most variable types."

"They sound very useful," Leslie said.

"And widely used in published research," Nancy added.

Kiara had already compiled a list of achievements for the day.

9.1 Achievements to unlock

- Achievement 1: Using exploratory data analysis to learn about the data before developing a linear regression model

- Achievement 2: Exploring the statistical model for a line

- Achievement 3: Computing the slope and intercept in a simple linear regression

- Achievement 4: Slope interpretation and significance (b_1, p-value, CI)

- Achievement 5: Model significance and model fit

- Achievement 6: Checking assumptions and conducting diagnostics

- Achievement 7: Adding variables to the model and using transformation

9.2 The needle exchange examination

Nancy told Leslie and Kiara that yesterday she had caught up with her neighbor, Bryan, who had just returned from a trip to Seattle. Bryan had mentioned that he was surprised to learn about an outbreak of human immunodeficiency virus (HIV) in the homeless population in Seattle (Golden et al., 2019). Nancy thought she'd heard of this happening in other cities as well. She looked online and found that the Indiana HIV Outbreak Investigation Team had reported on the same thing several years earlier (Peters et al., 2016). In this instance, there was an outbreak of HIV primarily among persons who inject drugs. Nancy also found a press release from the Massachusetts Department of Public Health describing a cluster of HIV cases in another group of people who either inject drugs, have experienced homelessness, or both (Scales, 2018). While new HIV cases have been declining in the United States, Nancy found a related study reporting that Hepatitis C rates have been increasing rapidly starting in 2010, with young people in nonurban areas having the highest increases and needle-sharing being a major factor (Canary et al., 2017). The study reported that those infected with Hepatitis C mostly lived more than 10 miles from a needle exchange program (Canary et al., 2017). Other infectious diseases were also on the rise, with increases related to drug use (Edelman et al., 2019; Schranz, Fleischauer, Chu, Wu, & Rosen, 2019).

Nancy shared some of the press releases and papers about these outbreaks. Kiara found that one of the strategies mentioned for protecting people who inject drugs from infectious disease is to provide clean needles. This strategy does not address the injection drug use problem, but it can prevent transmission of disease among injection drug users (Teshale et al., 2019). Clean needles are distributed by syringe services programs (SSPs), which can also provide a number of other related services including overdose prevention, referrals for substance use treatment, and infectious disease testing (Teshale et al., 2019). In her search for more information on the benefits and downsides to SSPs, Leslie found an article about needle litter, or used syringes left improperly in public places, something she had never considered before (Tookes et al., 2012). Apparently, one city with needle exchange programs was compared to a city without needle exchange programs, and the city without the programs had substantially more used syringes discarded in public places (Tookes et al., 2012). Another study found a reduction in syringe litter in one city when they looked at the volume before versus after a needle exchange program was opened (Wood et al., 2004).

Nancy was surprised to learn that needle exchange programs are illegal in many U.S. states. She found that opposition to these programs may come from the opinion that providing free needles to drug addicts promotes drug use (Goodlatte, Armey, & Tiahrt, 1999) or that these programs are an inadequate way to address the connection between injection drug use and infectious disease spread (Rogers & Osborn, 1993). She also discovered some evidence of speculation that needle exchange programs increased the spread of HIV for injection drug users (Schechter et al., 1999), but an evaluation of this hypothesis did not provide supporting evidence. The majority of studies Nancy reviewed suggested that needle exchange programs provided some benefit to their communities (Teshale et al., 2019).

Leslie was especially interested in the study Nancy mentioned about the young people in rural areas having a large increase in Hepatitis C, and that many of the infected lived far from the nearest needle exchange (Canary et al., 2017). Having lived mostly in bigger cities, Leslie had not considered how far some people must have to travel for health services, especially for services that are specialized, such as needle exchanges. After the commute to Nancy's today, she had already been thinking about the issue of having to travel. Online she found the amfAR (American Foundation for AIDS Research) website, which includes a database related to HIV including information on HIV prevalence, opioid prescriptions and other drug-related variables, and several variables related to health services. Leslie was happy to find a distance-to-syringe-services-program variable among the health services data sources (https://opioid.amfar.org/). The variable is at the county level and measures how many miles it is from a county to the nearest syringe services program.

Leslie shared her discovery with the R-Team, and they decided that this sounded like a good research question to explore with linear regression. They discussed it for a few minutes and looked through the database Leslie had found. Unfortunately, many of the more interesting variables were not available for much of the nation, and many of them were only at the state level. Given these limitations, they decided to examine whether the distance to a syringe program could be explained by whether a county is urban or rural, what percentage of the county residents have insurance (as a measure of both access to health care and socioeconomic status [SES]), HIV prevalence, and the number of people with opioid prescriptions. The amfAR database does not have a variable for rural or urban status, which Leslie thought was really important, so she searched for one and found a variable that classifies all counties as metro or nonmetro on the U.S. Department of Agriculture Economic Research Services website (https://www.ers.usda.gov/data-products/county-typology-codes/). Finally, they were ready to get started.

9.3 Data, codebook, and R packages for linear regression practice

Before they examined the data, Kiara made a list of all the data, documentation, and packages for learning linear regression they could download and install:

- Two options for accessing the data
  - Download the clean data set **dist_ssp_amfar_ch9.csv** from **edge.sagepub.com/harris1e**
  - Follow the instructions in Box 9.1 to import, merge, and clean the data from multiple files or from the original online source
- Two options for accessing the codebook
  - Download the codebook file **opioid_county_codebook.xlsx** from **edge.sagepub.com/harris1e**
  - Use the online codebook from the amfAR Opioid & Health Indicators Database website (https://opioid.amfar.org/)
- Install the following R packages if not already installed:
  - **tidyverse**, by Hadley Wickham (https://www.rdocumentation.org/packages/tidyverse/)
  - **tableone** (Yoshida, n.d.)
  - **lmtest**, by Achim Zeileis (https://www.rdocumentation.org/packages/lmtest/)
  - **broom**, by David Robinson and Alex Hayes (https://cran.r-project.org/web/packages/broom/index.html)
  - **car**, by John Fox (https://www.rdocumentation.org/packages/car/)

9.4 Achievement 1: Using exploratory data analysis to learn about the data before developing a linear regression model

As usual, Nancy wanted to jump right into the modeling, but Kiara slowed her down. Before they could examine relationships between variables, they needed to do data importing, data management, and data exploration first.

9.4.1 IMPORTING AND MERGING DATA SOURCES

The data were available in comma separated values files on the amfAR website in the Opioid & Health Indicators Database (https://opioid.amfar.org/) and on the U.S. Department of Agriculture Economic Research Services website (https://www.ers.usda.gov/data-products/county-typology-codes/). To keep the team moving along, Kiara downloaded, cleaned, and merged the data sources (Box 9.1). Nancy suggested that they take a sample of 500 counties to work with since they wanted to practice inferential statistics, so Kiara selected 500 counties. Leslie looked back at Section 4.8.2 to remind herself why they would take a sample instead of using the entire population. She found that inferential statistics are used to infer what is going on in a population based on characteristics and relationships in a sample. While she was looking this up, Nancy had already loaded the data that Kiara had cleaned and sampled into R.

```
# distance to syringe program data
dist.ssp <- read.csv(file = "[data folder location]/data/dist_ssp_amfar_ch9.csv")

# summary
summary(object = dist.ssp)
##                    county      STATEABBREVIATION      dist_SSP
## jackson county   :  5    TX     : 50        Min.   :  0.00
## jefferson county :  5    GA     : 30        1st Qu.: 35.12
## lincoln county   :  5    KS     : 21        Median : 75.94
## washington county:  5    NC     : 21        Mean   :107.74
## benton county    :  4    TN     : 21        3rd Qu.:163.83
## decatur county   :  4    KY     : 19        Max.   :510.00
## (Other)          :472    (Other):338
## HIVprevalence      opioid_RxRate       pctunins          metro
## Min.   :  -1.00   Min.   :  0.20   Min.   : 3.00    metro    :226
## 1st Qu.:  52.98   1st Qu.: 45.12   1st Qu.: 8.60    non-metro:274
## Median : 101.15   Median : 62.40   Median :11.70
## Mean   : 165.75   Mean   : 68.33   Mean   :12.18
## 3rd Qu.: 210.35   3rd Qu.: 89.95   3rd Qu.:15.00
## Max.   :2150.70   Max.   :345.10   Max.   :35.90
##
```

Leslie looked through the variables and the codebook and determined that the variables had the following meanings:

- `county`: the county name
- `STATEABBREVIATION`: the two-letter abbreviation for the state the county is in
- `dist_SSP`: distance in miles to the nearest syringe services program
- `HIVprevalence`: people age 13 and older living with diagnosed HIV per 100,000
- `opioid_RxRate`: number of opioid prescriptions per 100 people
- `pctunins`: percentage of the civilian noninstitutionalized population with no health insurance coverage
- `metro`: county is either nonmetro, which includes open countryside, rural towns, or smaller cities with up to 49,999 people, or metro

9.1 Kiara's reproducibility resource: Merging data from multiple csv files

In order to make the data frame for today, Kiara downloaded several comma separated values files from amfAR (https://opioid.amfar.org/) and merged them by the state and county they were in. Some of the files had data from multiple years, so Kiara chose the most recent year. To practice data merging and cleaning, download the raw data in csv format directly from the amfAR Opioid & Health Indicators Database (https://opioid.amfar.org/) or go to **edge.sagepub.com/harris1e** and download:

- **opioid_dist_to_needle_exchange_2018.csv**
- **hiv_prevalence_amfar_ch9.csv**
- **opioid_script_rate_amfar_ch9.csv**
- **percent_unins_amfar_2016_ch9.csv**
- **metro_nonmetro_usda_ers_2015_ch9.csv**

Kiara started by importing all the data sets.

```
# read in all the data
op.dist <- read.csv(file = "[data folder location]/data/opioid_dist_
to_needle_exchange_2018.csv")

hiv.prev <- read.csv(file = "[data folder location]/data/hiv_
prevalence_amfar_ch9.csv")

op.scripts <- read.csv(file = "[data folder location]/data/opioid_
script_rate_amfar_ch9.csv")

unins <- read.csv(file = "[data folder location]/data/percent_unins_
amfar_2016_ch9.csv")

metro <- read.csv(file = "[data folder location]/data/metro_nonmetro_
usda_ers_2015_ch9.csv")
```

(Continued)

(Continued)

Once the data were all imported into R, Kiara opened and checked each file to make sure that the county and state variables she would use to merge the files together were named the exact same thing for every file. For each file she did the following:

- Changed the name of the county variable to `county`

- Changed the `county` variable to a character variable

- Changed the names of the counties saved in the `county` variable to all lowercase

- Changed the name of the variable of interest from `VALUE` in most of the files to whatever it was named in the codebook (e.g., `dist_SSP` or `HIVprevalence`)

- Limited each file to the `county` variable, the `STATEABBREVIATION` variable, and the variable of interest from each file

```
# open tidyverse
library(package = "tidyverse")

# clean distance variable
op.dist <- op.dist %>%
  rename(county = COUNTY) %>%
  mutate(county = tolower(x = as.character(x = county))) %>%
  rename(dist_SSP = VALUE) %>%
  select(county, dist_SSP, STATEABBREVIATION)
# clean HIV prevalence variable
hiv.prev <- hiv.prev %>%
  filter(YEAR == 2016) %>%
  rename(county = COUNTY) %>%
  mutate(county = tolower(x = as.character(x = county))) %>%
  rename(HIVprevalence = VALUE) %>%
  select(county, HIVprevalence, STATEABBREVIATION)
# clean opioid prescriptions variable
op.scripts <- op.scripts %>%
  filter(YEAR == 2017) %>%
  rename(county = COUNTY) %>%
  mutate(county = tolower(x = as.character(x = county))) %>%
  rename(opioid_RxRate = VALUE) %>%
  select(county, opioid_RxRate, STATEABBREVIATION)
# clean percent uninsured variable
```

```
unins <- unins %>%
  filter(YEAR == 2016) %>%
  rename(county = COUNTY) %>%
  rename(pctunins = VALUE) %>%
  mutate(county = tolower(x = as.character(x = county))) %>%
  select(county, pctunins, STATEABBREVIATION)
# clean metro status variable
metro <- metro %>%
  rename(metro = Metro.nonmetro.status..2013.0.Nonmetro.1.Metro) %>%
  mutate(metro = as.factor(recode(metro, `0` = "non-metro", `1` =
"metro"))) %>%
  rename(county = County_name) %>%
  rename(STATEABBREVIATION = State) %>%
  mutate(county = tolower(x = as.character(x = county))) %>%
  select(county, metro, STATEABBREVIATION)
```

Once the data were cleaned and managed, Kiara used `merge()` to combine the data frames based on variables that are named the same across the data sets, in this case `county` and `STATEABBREVIATION`. The state variable is needed because many counties are named the same but are in different states.

```
# merge the data frames
dist.data <- op.dist %>%
  merge(x = hiv.prev) %>%
  merge(x = op.scripts) %>%
  merge(x = unins) %>%
  merge(x = metro)

# summary of data
summary(object = dist.data)
```

The `dist.data` object includes all the counties in the United States, so it is a population. Samples are used for the purposes of modeling, so Kiara took a sample of 500 counties to practice modeling with and saved the data for use. Before she took the sample, she checked to confirm, yet again, that she was using a recent version of R since the versions before 3.6.0 had a different **set.seed**() algorithm (see Box 4.2). She was using R-3.6.0 and went ahead with the sampling.

(Continued)

(Continued)

```
# sample 500 counties
set.seed(seed = 42)
dist.data.samp <- dist.data %>%
  drop_na(HIVprevalence) %>%
  drop_na(opioid_RxRate) %>%
  sample_n(size = 500, replace = FALSE)

# check sample
summary(object = dist.data.samp)

# save data
write.csv(x = dist.data.samp, file = "[data folder location]/data/
dist_ssp_amfar_ch9.csv", row.names = FALSE)
```

9.4.2 CHECKING THE DESCRIPTIVE STATISTICS

Leslie noticed that there was a value of –1 for the minimum of HIVprevalence, and she looked at the website to see if this was a code for a missing value since –1 would not make sense as the number of HIV cases per 100,000 people in a county. Although it was not included in the codebook online, she decided it made more sense as a missing value and wrote the code to fix it before they began. Nancy and Kiara agreed that this sounded reasonable.

```
# open tidyverse
library(package = "tidyverse")

# recoding -1 to NA for HIVprevalence
dist.ssp <- dist.ssp %>%
  mutate(HIVprevalence = na_if(x = HIVprevalence, y = -1))

# check recoding
summary(object = dist.ssp)
```

```
##                 county       STATEABBREVIATION      dist_SSP
##   jackson county    : 5     TX       : 50       Min.    :  0.00
##   jefferson county  : 5     GA       : 30       1st Qu.: 35.12
##   lincoln county    : 5     KS       : 21       Median : 75.94
##   washington county : 5     NC       : 21       Mean    :107.74
##   benton county     : 4     TN       : 21       3rd Qu.:163.83
```

```
##  decatur county  :  4    KY     : 19      Max.   :510.00
##  (Other)          :472   (Other):338
##  HIVprevalence      opioid_RxRate        pctunins          metro
##  Min.   :   14.4   Min.   :   0.20   Min.   : 3.00   metro    :226
##  1st Qu.:   72.3   1st Qu.: 45.12   1st Qu.: 8.60   non-metro:274
##  Median :  119.0   Median : 62.40   Median :11.70
##  Mean   :  192.9   Mean   : 68.33   Mean   :12.18
##  3rd Qu.:  227.5   3rd Qu.: 89.95   3rd Qu.:15.00
##  Max.   : 2150.7   Max.   :345.10   Max.   :35.90
##  NA's   :   70
```

The values looked better and Leslie moved on to descriptive statistics. She thought `CreateTableOne()` from the **tableone** package was the easiest way to get descriptive statistics for all the variables of interest, so she started with that. Nancy reminded her that the state and county are in the data set and probably do not need to be in the descriptive statistics table. Leslie added a vector of the variables she would like in the table to `CreateTableOne()`.

```
# descriptive statistics for syringe data
tableone::CreateTableOne(data = dist.ssp,
                         vars = c('dist_SSP', 'HIVprevalence',
                                  'opioid_RxRate', 'pctunins',
                                  'metro'))

##
##                              Overall
##   n                            500
##   dist_SSP (mean (SD))       107.74 (94.23)
##   HIVprevalence (mean (SD))  192.89 (213.35)
##   opioid_RxRate (mean (SD))   68.33 (36.81)
##   pctunins (mean (SD))        12.18 (4.97)
##   metro = non-metro (%)        274 (54.8)
```

Leslie looked through the results and noticed that the `HIVprevalence` variable had a standard deviation much higher than its mean. She remembered that this might indicate a problem with kurtosis (see Section 2.6.4.1), which means the variable may not be normally distributed and the median would be better. She decided to use a histogram to check the distribution (Figure 9.1).

```
# check distribution of HIV prevalence (Figure 9.1)
dist.ssp %>%
  ggplot(aes(x = HIVprevalence)) +
  geom_histogram(fill = "#7463AC", color = "white") +
  labs(x = "HIV cases per 100,000 people", y = "Number of counties") +
  theme_minimal()
```

FIGURE 9.1 Distribution of HIV prevalence in 500 counties

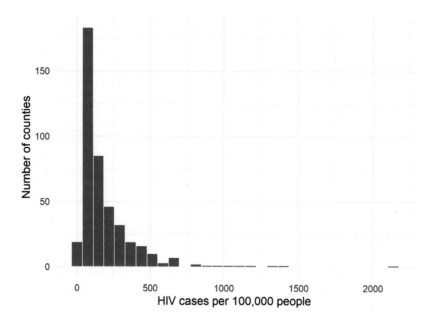

Source: https://opioid.amfar.org.

Leslie found that `HIVprevalence` was right-skewed, so the median would be a better option than the mean (Section 2.6.2). She revised the table to show the median and IQR instead of the mean and standard deviation for `HIVprevalence`.

```
# descriptive statistics for syringe data
syringe.desc <- tableone::CreateTableOne(data = dist.ssp,
                                         vars = c('dist_SSP',
                                                  'HIVprevalence',
                                                  'opioid_RxRate',
                                                  'pctunins',
                                                  'metro'))
print(x = syringe.desc, nonnormal = c("HIVprevalence"))
##
##                                  Overall
##   n                                500
##   dist_SSP (mean (SD))           107.74 (94.23)
##   HIVprevalence (median [IQR])   118.95 [72.30, 227.47]
##   opioid_RxRate (mean (SD))       68.33 (36.81)
##   pctunins (mean (SD))            12.18 (4.97)
##   metro = non-metro (%)          274 (54.8)
```

Leslie asked Kiara if they should check the other continuous variables to see about distributions. Kiara said that they might not need to check them all, so they could probably skip it for now.

9.4.3 USING A SCATTERPLOT TO EXPLORE THE RELATIONSHIP

Kiara explained that, while the descriptive statistics were a good place to start getting to know the data, linear regression is about examining relationships among variables. Specifically, linear regression is used to examine how one or more variables can predict or explain some continuous outcome variable. The research question to address with linear regression could be: How can being uninsured, metro or nonmetro status, HIV prevalence, and number of opioid prescriptions predict or explain distance to the nearest syringe program at the county level?

Kiara and Leslie decided to start by examining whether the distance to a syringe program could be explained or predicted by percentage of county residents without insurance. Kiara suggested they start by making a graph of the relationship. Leslie remembered how relationships between two continuous variables are often examined using a scatterplot (Section 3.6.4). Using what she knew about `ggplot()` from prior R-Team meetings, she created a scatterplot of distance to syringe program and percentage of uninsured people (Figure 9.2). Kiara explained that she should put the variable they were interested in explaining, also known as the outcome variable or the dependent variable, on the *y*-axis and the predictor or independent variable on the *x*-axis. In this case, they were explaining distance to syringe program, so `dist_SSP` was on the *y*-axis and `pctunins` was on the *x*-axis. Graphs used to explore bivariate relationships before a linear model should have the outcome on the *y*-axis.

```
# percent without health insurance and distance to needle exchange (Figure 9.2)
dist.ssp %>%
  ggplot(aes(x = pctunins, y = dist_SSP)) +
  geom_point(aes(size = "County"), color = "#7463AC", alpha = .6) +
  theme_minimal() +
  labs(x = "Percent uninsured", y = "Miles to syringe program") +
  scale_size_manual(values = 2, name = "")
```

The plot showed that, as percentage without health insurance went up, so did distance to the nearest syringe program. That is, counties with a higher percentage of uninsured people were farther from the nearest needle exchange. Leslie remembered the correlation coefficients from Section 8.5 and concluded that these two variables had a positive correlation.

Kiara suggested that Leslie use a `geom_smooth()` layer to add a line to the plot and get a better understanding of the relationship between the variables. Leslie used `geom_smooth()` to add the line. As she reviewed the help documentation for `geom_smooth()`, she was reminded that the `method = "lm"` argument added a line to the plot that represents the linear model for the relationship between the variables. Since they were working toward conducting a linear regression analysis, she used this option to update the plot showing a linear fit line, which Nancy explained is the linear regression line between the two variables in the model (Figure 9.3). The graph was getting more complicated, so Leslie added the line to the legend to clarify what the line represents. Nancy reminded Leslie about Box 8.2, which shows this can be done using aesthetics within `geom_point()` and `geom_smooth()`. Nancy reminded Leslie about the RStudio cheat sheet of aesthetics she used to remember which aesthetics can be used with each type of geom_ (https://

FIGURE 9.2 Relationship between percentage without health insurance and distance in miles to the nearest syringe services program in 500 counties

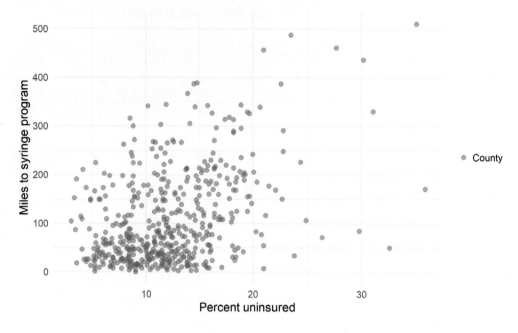

Source: https://opioid.amfar.org.

www.rstudio.com/wp-content/uploads/2015/03/ggplot2-cheatsheet.pdf) and created another example for Leslie in Box 9.2.

```
# percent without health insurance and distance to needle exchange (Figure 9.3)
dist.ssp %>%
    ggplot(aes(x = pctunins, y = dist_SSP)) +
    geom_point(aes(size = "County"), color = "#7463AC", alpha = .6) +
    geom_smooth(aes(linetype = "Linear fit line"), method = "lm",
                se = FALSE, color = "gray60") +
    theme_minimal() +
    labs(x = "Percent uninsured", y = "Miles to syringe program") +
    scale_size_manual(values = 2, name = "") +
    scale_linetype_manual(values = 1, name = "")
```

In Figure 9.3, the line goes up from left to right, demonstrating a positive relationship between percentage uninsured and distance to a syringe program. As the percentage of uninsured people in a county increases, so does the distance to the nearest syringe program. Leslie was right in her assessment that the relationship between percentage uninsured and distance to syringe program was a positive correlation.

FIGURE 9.3 Relationship between percentage without health insurance and distance in miles to the nearest syringe services program in 500 counties

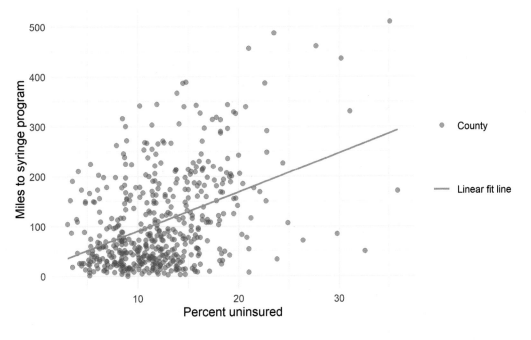

Source: https://opioid.amfar.org.

9.2 Nancy's fancy code: More aesthetics for customizing figure legends

Nancy reviewed the cheat sheet (https://www.rstudio.com/wp-content/uploads/2015/03/ggplot2-cheatsheet.pdf), which showed that `geom_point()` could use the following inside `aes()`:

- x
- y
- alpha
- color
- fill

(Continued)

(Continued)

- shape
- size

She also listed the attributes that could be inside the `geom_smooth() aes()`:

- x
- y
- alpha
- color
- fill
- linetype
- size
- weight

Nancy wanted to show Leslie a few examples to demonstrate how it works. She started by modifying the code from Figure 9.3. First, she changed `size` to `shape` in the `aes()`, from `geom_point(aes(size = "County")` to `geom_point(aes(shape = "County")`.

For this change, not only did the `aes()` have to be modified, but the `scale_size_manual()` layer had to change to match the `aes()`. Instead of `scale_size_manual()`, it was now `scale_shape_manual()`.

Within the `scale_size_manual()`, or whatever `scale_ _manual` it is, the `values =` argument is filled with values specific to the attribute. For `scale_size_manual()`, the `values =` argument specifies the size of the points or line or whatever is linked. For the `scale_shape_manual()`, the `values =` argument is the number referring to one of the shapes available. Nancy found the shape numbers on the second page of the cheat sheet. She decided to try square data points, which were `shape = 0`. Nancy edited the graph to show Leslie the use of `shape` instead of `size` in the `aes()` (Figure 9.4).

```
# percent without health insurance and distance to needle exchange
# (Figure 9.4)
dist.ssp %>%
  ggplot(aes(x = pctunins, y = dist_SSP)) +
  geom_point(aes(shape = "County"), color = "#7463AC", alpha = .6) +
  geom_smooth(aes(linetype = "Linear fit line"), method = "lm",
              se = FALSE, color = "gray60") +
  theme_minimal() +
  labs(x = "Percent uninsured", y = "Miles to syringe program") +
```

```
scale_shape_manual(values = 0, name = "") +
scale_linetype_manual(values = 1, name = "")
```

FIGURE 9.4 Relationship between percentage without health insurance and distance in miles to the nearest syringe services program in 500 counties

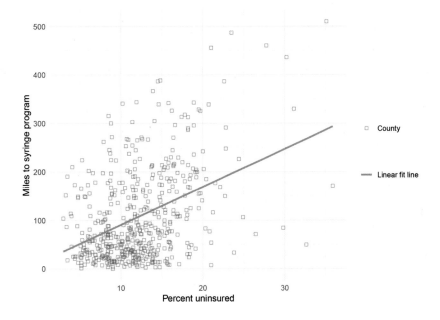

Source: https://opioid.amfar.org.

Nancy thought she should try replacing the `linetype =` attribute for the `geom_smooth()` `aes()` to show Leslie how that one worked as well. She decided to use `size =` instead of `linetype =`. She also wanted to try another shape since the squares were so fun. She replaced the `shape = 0` with `shape = 17` for triangles and replaced `linetype` with `size` in the `aes()` and in the `scale_linetype_manual()` (Figure 9.5).

```
# percent without health insurance and distance to needle exchange
# (Figure 9.5)
dist.ssp %>%
  ggplot(aes(x = pctunins, y = dist_SSP)) +
  geom_point(aes(shape = "County"), color = "#7463AC", alpha = .6) +
  geom_smooth(aes(size = "Linear fit line"), method = "lm",
              se = FALSE, color = "gray60") +
```

(Continued)

(Continued)

```
theme_minimal() +
labs(x = "Percent uninsured", y = "Miles to syringe program") +
scale_shape_manual(values = 17, name = "") +
scale_size_manual(values = 1, name = "")
```

FIGURE 9.5 Relationship between percentage without health insurance and distance in miles to the nearest syringe services program in 500 counties

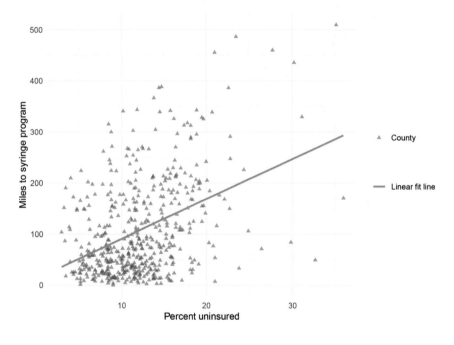

Source: https://opioid.amfar.org.

Nancy thought that would be enough examples for Leslie to understand the process.

9.4.4 USING A CORRELATION COEFFICIENT TO EXPLORE THE RELATIONSHIP

Kiara suggested Leslie could confirm her idea about this being a positive correlation even more using `cor()`. Leslie reviewed Section 8.6 to remind herself how to do this and wrote the function.

```
# correlation between percent uninsured and distance
dist.ssp %>%
  summarize(cor.dist.uninsur = cor(x = dist_SSP,
                                   y = pctunins),
            samp.n = n())
##   cor.dist.uninsur samp.n
## 1        0.4126744    500
```

The correlation coefficient was positive ($r = 0.41$). Leslie thought the strength was moderate but just to be sure, she looked back again to Section 8.5.4 and found that the threshold for moderate strength is $r = .5$, so this correlation is between weak and moderate. Kiara summarized what they knew so far about the relationship between percentage uninsured and the distance to a syringe exchange for the counties:

- The mean distance from a county to the nearest syringe program is 107.74 miles with a standard deviation of 94.23.

- The mean percent of county residents without insurance is 12.18% with a standard deviation of 4.97.

- The relationship between the percentage of uninsured residents and distance to syringe program is weak to moderate and positive; counties with a higher percentage of uninsured are farther from syringe programs ($r = 0.41$).

9.4.5 EXPLORING THE DATA BY COMPARING MEANS ACROSS GROUPS

Kiara suggested they examine the other bivariate relationships between distance to syringe program and opioid prescriptions (`opioid_RxRate`), HIV prevalence (`HIVprevalence`), and metro or non-metro status (`metro`).

```
# bivariate relationships with distance to SSP
dist.ssp %>%
  summarize(cor.rx.rate = cor(x = dist_SSP, y = opioid_RxRate),
            cor.hiv = cor(x = dist_SSP, y = HIVprevalence, use =
                            "complete"),
            cor.unins = cor(x = dist_SSP, y = pctunins))
##   cor.rx.rate     cor.hiv cor.unins
## 1 -0.09979404 -0.02397473 0.4126744
```

Leslie found that the correlations were weak and negative for `dist_SSP` with `opioid_RxRate` and `HIVprevalence`. She remembered that `HIVprevalence` was not normally distributed and so Spearman's rho, or r_s, might be better (Section 8.10). She revised the code.

```
# bivariate relationships with distance to SSP
dist.ssp %>%
  summarize(cor.rx.rate = cor(x = dist_SSP, y = opioid_RxRate),
            cor.s.hiv = cor(x = dist_SSP, y = HIVprevalence,
                            method = "spearman", use = "complete"),
            cor.unins = cor(x = dist_SSP, y = pctunins))
##   cor.rx.rate  cor.s.hiv cor.unins
## 1 -0.09979404 0.08553823 0.4126744
```

She noticed that a small change made a pretty big difference in the correlation between `dist_SSP` and `HIVprevalence`! It was still weak, but it was now positive, r_s = .09, indicating that distance to syringe programs increases as HIV prevalence increases in a county.

Next, Leslie checked the mean distance to a syringe program for metro and nonmetro counties.

```
# metro and distance to SSP
dist.ssp %>%
  group_by(metro) %>%
  summarize(m.dist = mean(x = dist_SSP))
## # A tibble: 2 x 2
##   metro     m.dist
##   <fct>      <dbl>
## 1 metro       85.0
## 2 non-metro  126.
```

She found that there is a notably higher mean distance in miles to a syringe program in nonmetro counties ($m_{nonmetro}$ = 126 miles) compared to metro counties (m_{metro} = 85.0 miles).

9.4.6 EXPLORING THE DATA WITH BOXPLOTS

Leslie was interested in learning more about the difference in `dist_SSP` for metro and nonmetro counties since the difference in the mean distance was large. Nancy thought a boxplot would work well since they were comparing a continuous variable across two groups (Section 3.6.3). She added a scatterplot behind the boxplot so that they could see not only the boxplot but also the raw data. Leslie remembered this trick from Figure 3.53 and Figure 7.4. Even though she looked back at those two figures, Leslie could not remember what `alpha = .4` and `alpha = .6` were for the two `geom_` layers. Nancy reminded her that `alpha =` in this context was used to measure how transparent the colors in the graph are. The values for `alpha =` range from 0, which is completely transparent, to 1, which is the full color. Numbers in between 0 and 1 are partially transparent versions of the color. Nancy preferred making the data points for `geom_jitter()` a little darker than the fill color for the boxes, but she suggested that Leslie try different values for the alphas to find a style she preferred. Leslie tried a few values and preferred darker data points with lighter fill for the boxes (Figure 9.6).

```
# metro and distance to SSP (Figure 9.6)
dist.ssp %>%
  ggplot(aes(x = metro, y = dist_SSP, fill = metro)) +
  geom_jitter(aes(color = metro), alpha = .6) +
  geom_boxplot(aes(fill = metro), alpha = .4) +
  labs(x = "Type of county",
       y = "Distance to nearest syringe program") +
  scale_fill_manual(values = c("#78A678", "#7463AC"), guide = FALSE) +
  scale_color_manual(values = c("#78A678", "#7463AC"), guide = FALSE) +
  theme_minimal()
```

Kiara asked Nancy if they should try a violin plot instead. Nancy replaced `geom_boxplot()` with `geom_violin()` and they reviewed the results (Figure 9.7).

FIGURE 9.6 Distance in miles to nearest syringe programs by metro or nonmetro status for 500 counties

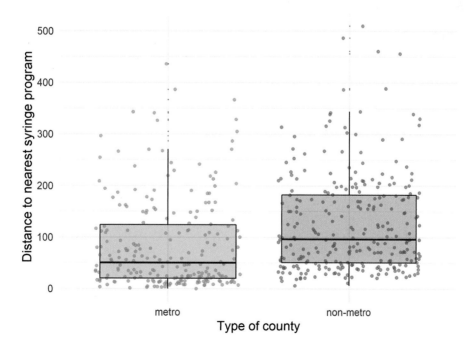

Source: https://opioid.amfar.org.

```
# metro and distance to SSP (Figure 9.7)
dist.ssp %>%
  ggplot(aes(x = metro, y = dist_SSP, fill = metro)) +
  geom_jitter(aes(color = metro), alpha = .8) +
  geom_violin(aes(fill = metro), alpha = .4) +
  labs(x = "Type of county",
       y = "Distance to nearest syringe program") +
  scale_fill_manual(values = c("#78A678", "#7463AC"), guide = FALSE) +
  scale_color_manual(values = c("#78A678", "#7463AC"), guide = FALSE) +
  theme_minimal()
```

Nancy reminded Leslie that the shape of the "violin" shows the distribution of the data within each group. In this case, the data were skewed toward the higher numbers, which (if the graph were rotated sideways) is a right skew or positive skew. Leslie thought this was easier to interpret quickly compared to the boxplot. Kiara agreed but mentioned that they do lose some information, such as the value of the median and the boundaries of the IQR, when they use this strategy. Nancy thought she might be able to add the boxplot to the violin plot so they could keep all the information. She added the boxplot and tried rotating the graph with `coord_flip()` to see if they could make the right skew more intuitive. She changed some of the colors so that everything was visible (Figure 9.8).

FIGURE 9.7 Distance in miles to nearest syringe programs by metro or nonmetro status for 500 counties

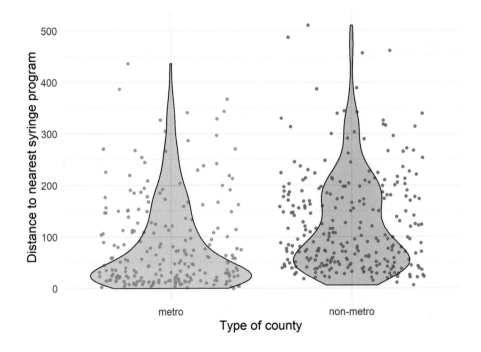

Source: https://opioid.amfar.org.

```
# metro and distance to SSP (Figure 9.8)
dist.ssp %>%
  ggplot(aes(x = metro, y = dist_SSP, fill = metro)) +
  geom_violin(aes(color = metro), fill = "white", alpha = .8) +
  geom_boxplot(aes(fill = metro, color = metro), width = .2, alpha = .3) +
  geom_jitter(aes(color = metro), alpha = .4) +
  labs(x = "Type of county",
       y = "Miles to syringe program") +
  scale_fill_manual(values = c("#78A678", "#7463AC"), guide = FALSE) +
  scale_color_manual(values = c("#78A678", "#7463AC"), guide = FALSE) +
  theme_minimal() +
  coord_flip()
```

Leslie asked Nancy to explain her code a little since they did not usually use *three* types of `geom_` layered together. Nancy told Leslie that each new layer of `ggplot()` built upon the previous layers. She said she chose to put the `geom_violin()` as the first layer since the outline of the violin is important. She decided that, rather than filling it by metro versus nonmetro county, she would fill the violin plot with the color white so that everything else on top of it would be easier to see. She then added the `geom_boxplot()` as the next layer, but changed the width of the boxes in the boxplot with the `width = .2` option so that the boxes would fit inside the violin outline. Finally, she included the data points with `geom_jitter()`.

FIGURE 9.8 Distance in miles to nearest syringe programs by metro or nonmetro status for 500 counties

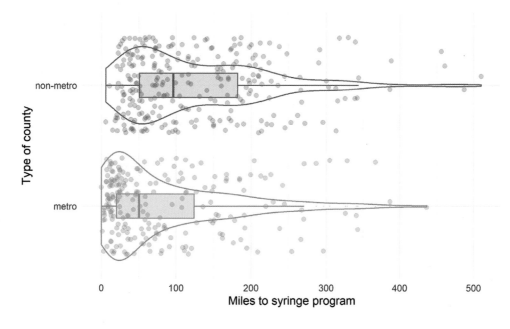

Source: https://opioid.amfar.org.

After finalizing the `geom_` layers, she added `coord_flip()` to flip the axes to better show the right skew. Nancy suggested that when Leslie had some free time, she could play with this code a little.

They all preferred Figure 9.8 to the other options because the skew was clear and the boxplot provided the median and IQR.

9.4.7 ACHIEVEMENT 1: CHECK YOUR UNDERSTANDING

Import the data and check the distributions of `opioid_RxRate` and `pctunins`. Are the variables normally distributed? If not, what changes might Leslie make to the descriptive statistics and correlations to account for the non-normal data?

Copy the code for Figure 9.8 and switch the order of the `geom_violin()`, `geom_boxplot()`, and `geom_jitter()` layers to see what happens. Explain what you find.

9.5 Achievement 2: Exploring the statistical model for a line

9.5.1 THE EQUATION FOR A LINE

Leslie was familiar with simple linear regression modeling. She knew that linear models use the concept of a line to explain and predict things about relationships among variables. To build and use linear models, it was useful to think about Equation (9.1):

$$y = mx + b, \tag{9.1}$$

where

- m is the slope of the line
- b is the **y-intercept** of the line, or the value of y when $x = 0$
- x and y are the coordinates of each point along the line

In statistics, the intercept is often represented by c or b_0, and the slope is often represented by b_1. Rewriting the equation for a line with these options would look like Equation (9.2) or Equation (9.3).

$$y = b_0 + b_1 x \tag{9.2}$$

$$y = c + b_1 x \tag{9.3}$$

Leslie remembered that occasionally she had seen a β rather than a b, but typically, Greek letters were used for *population* values, so when working with samples the lowercase b is more appropriate. Kiara added that occasionally she has seen a b^*, which meant that the variable had been standardized, or transformed into z-scores, before the regression model was estimated.

9.5.2 USING THE EQUATION FOR A LINE

Kiara and Leslie discussed how the equation for a line was useful in two ways: to *explain* values of the outcome (y) and to *predict* values of the outcome (y). Kiara suggested they review how the linear model works with a simple example. She wrote down the equation for the line with a slope of 2 and a y-intercept of 3 for an example in Equation (9.4).

$$y = 3 + 2x \tag{9.4}$$

Kiara made up a scenario where this model predicts the number of gallons of clean drinking water per person per week needed to survive. In this example, x would be the number of weeks and y would represent the gallons of water needed to survive. Consider a person who hears from their landlord that there is a major repair needed with the pipes and the water supply in the building will not be safe for drinking for up to 4 weeks. Based on the equation, how many gallons of drinking water would be needed to survive?

Leslie started by rewriting the equation using the names of the variables of interest to clarify the meaning in Equation (9.5).

$$gallons = 3 + 2 \times weeks \tag{9.5}$$

She then substituted the value of 4, for the 4 weeks without drinking water, into Equation (9.6).

$$gallons = 3 + 2 \times 4 \tag{9.6}$$

Keeping in mind the order of operations (Box 9.3), Leslie solved the right-hand side of the equation, giving her the number of gallons of drinking water she would need for 4 weeks:

$$gallons = 11$$

9.3 Leslie's stats stuff: Order of operations

Leslie remembered back to algebra class and how they had to learn the order for solving equations, known as **PEMDAS**. There were several mnemonic devices used to help remember; the one she learned in her class was

- Please
- Excuse
- My
- Dear
- Aunt
- Sally

which represents the **order of operations**, or the order in which to solve an equation:

- Parentheses
- Exponents
- Multiplication
- Division

(Continued)

(Continued)

- Addition

- Subtraction

For any set of calculations, do what is inside parentheses first, followed by any exponents, then multiplication, division, addition, and subtraction. Kiara reminded Leslie that multiplication and division should be together as a single level; neither had priority over the other. The same thing applies to addition and subtraction, she said. Leslie remembered that Kiara was correct and revised the order:

- Parentheses

- Exponents

- Multiplication and Division

- Addition and Subtraction

Leslie explained that any number could be substituted in for x to predict how many gallons of water (y) would be needed. The values of x (weeks) and y (gallons) would together produce a line with a y-intercept of 3 and a slope of 2. Nancy made a graph to demonstrate this idea (Figure 9.9).

```r
# make a vector called weeks that has the values 1 through 12 in it
weeks <- 1:12

# use the regression model to make a vector called gallons with
# weeks as the values
gallons <- 3 + 2 * weeks

# make a data frame of weeks and gallons
water <- data.frame(weeks, gallons)

# Make a plot (Figure 9.9)
water %>%
  ggplot(aes(x = weeks, y = gallons)) +
  geom_line(aes(linetype = "Linear model \ngallons=3+2*weeks"),
            color = "gray60", size = 1) +
  geom_point(aes(color = "Observation"), size = 4, alpha = .6) +
  theme_minimal() +
  labs(x = "Weeks", y = "Gallons of water needed") +
  scale_linetype_manual(values = 2, name = "") +
  scale_color_manual(values = "#7463AC", name = "")
```

Nancy explained that, using different values for x (weeks), they could find the corresponding values for y (gallons) by using Equation (9.5). These pairs of x and y values could then be used to draw a straight line through the points.

FIGURE 9.9 Example of linear model with gallons of water needed as an outcome and weeks as a predictor

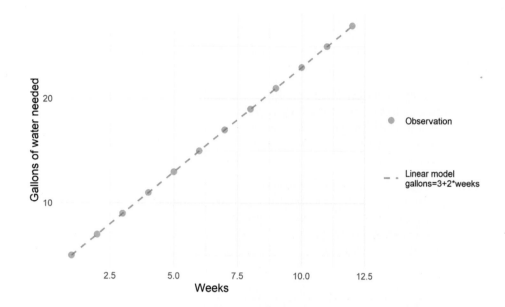

Kiara thought it might be good to review some additional terminology before they started modeling with data. She explained that each part of the model could be referred to in several ways:

- The y variable on the left-hand side of the equation is called the *dependent* or *outcome* variable.

- The x variable(s) on the right-hand side of the equation is/are called the *independent* or *predictor* variable(s).

The equation can be rewritten with these terms (Equation 9.7).

$$outcome = b_0 + b_1 \times predictor \qquad (9.7)$$

In the water example, `weeks` was the predictor variable and `gallons` was the outcome variable.

9.5.3 THE DISTINCTION BETWEEN DETERMINISTIC AND STOCHASTIC

Kiara had one more term to add to the discussion before they got started. She suggested the relationships between y and x in all of the equations presented so far are *deterministic*. A deterministic equation, or model, has one precise value for y for each value of x. This is true for some relationships. For example, many people have heard of the equation from physics $e = mc^2$. In this equation, e represents energy, m represents mass, and c represents the speed of light. The laws of physics dictate that this equation will give an exact value for energy given a specific mass traveling at the speed of light squared.

Kiara explained that relationships measured in social science are typically not deterministic; rather, they are *stochastic*. That is, it is unusual to be able to predict or explain something exactly. Most of the time, there is some variability that cannot be fully explained or predicted. This unexplained variability is represented by an error term that is added to the equation, as shown in Equation (9.8).

$$outcome = b_0 + b_1 \times predictor + error \qquad\qquad (9.8)$$

For example, it is unlikely that every human would drink exactly 11 gallons of water over a period of 4 weeks. If a person is larger or smaller or active or inactive, or if it is summer or winter, they may need to drink a different amount of water. The error term in Equation (9.8) accounts for the variability in the data that cannot be fully explained or quantified. Equation (9.8) is the theoretical *simple linear regression* equation or model.

Instead of the deterministic model of gallons of water in Figure 9.9 and Equation (9.5), the relationship between weeks and gallons of water needed by a human is bound to look more like Figure 9.10. Notice that the observations are mostly near the line but not exactly on the line. The line is still the same equation, but now the observations do not lie perfectly along the line. The distance between the line representing the linear model and each observation is the *residual*.

Leslie wanted to be sure she understood. She looked at the observations and saw that, at the 4-week mark, rather than drinking exactly 11 gallons of water like Equation (9.5) would have predicted, the person actually drank about 13 gallons. While Equation (9.5) does a good job explaining how much clean drinking water per week a person needs to survive, it isn't perfect. Kiara reiterated that this is true for nearly all data in the social sciences. There will be variability that cannot be completely explained by a model.

9.5.4 ACHIEVEMENT 2: CHECK YOUR UNDERSTANDING

Write out the equation for a line where income is the outcome and years of education is the predictor. Write out an explanation of each part of the model.

FIGURE 9.10 Example of a linear model with gallons of water needed as an outcome and weeks as a predictor

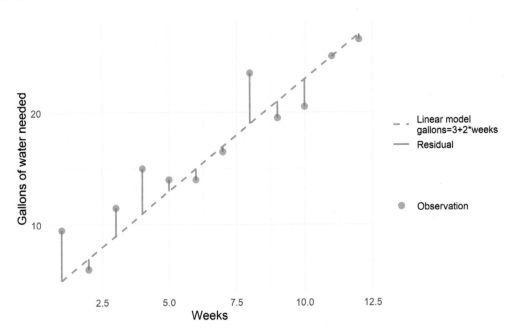

9.6 Achievement 3: Computing the slope and intercept in a simple linear regression

Kiara explained that, for simple linear regression, *simple* does not mean *easy*; instead, it is the term used for a regression model with one predictor. For example, Kiara suggested that a simple linear regression model could be used to examine the relationship between the percentage of people without health insurance and the distance to a syringe program for a county. She thought lack of insurance was related to socioeconomic status and that counties with poorer residents were likely to be farther from health resources like needle exchange programs. To understand this relationship between one predictor and an outcome, she would use a simple linear regression model.

9.6.1 SAMPLING FROM A DATA FRAME

Kiara explained that, like the *t*-test and chi-squared, linear regression is appropriate for examining relationships in a sample to understand what is happening in the population sampled.

9.6.2 EXPLORING THE RELATIONSHIP WITH A SCATTERPLOT

Leslie looked back at Figure 9.3, which contained the `geom_smooth()` layer with the `method = "lm"` option. The line was the simple linear regression line that they would be estimating and interpreting for the relationship between percentage of people without health insurance and distance to a syringe program for a county.

9.6.3 COMPUTING THE SLOPE OF THE LINE

Leslie wrote Equation (9.9) for the line with the independent variable x being the percentage of uninsured people in a county and the outcome variable y being the distance in miles to a needle exchange program.

$$distance = b_0 + b_1 \times uninsured \tag{9.9}$$

The formula to compute the slope, which is b_1 in Equation (9.9), uses the difference between the x and y for each observation and the overall mean values of x and y (Equation [9.10]).

$$b_1 = \frac{\sum_{i=1}^{n}(x_i - m_x)(y_i - m_y)}{\sum_{i=1}^{n}(x_i - m_x)^2} \tag{9.10}$$

In Equation (9.10),

- i is an individual observation, in this case a county
- n is the sample size, in this case 500
- x_i is the value of `pctunins` for i
- m_x is the mean value of `pctunins` for the sample
- y_i is the value of `dist_SSP` for i
- m_y is the mean value of `dist_SSP` for the sample

- Σ is the symbol for sum
- b_1 is the slope

Kiara explained that the slope formula in Equation (9.10) was adding up the product of differences between the observed values and mean value of percentage uninsured (`pctunins`) and the observed values and mean value of distance to syringe program (`dist_SSP`) for each of the 500 counties. This value was divided by the summed squared differences between the observed and mean values of `pctunins` for each county.

Once the slope is computed, the intercept can be computed by putting the slope and the values of m_x and m_y into the equation for the line with x and y replaced by m_x and m_y, $m_y = b_0 + b_1 * m_x$, and solving it for b_0, which is the y-intercept.

Because this method of computing the slope and intercept relies on the squared differences and works to minimize the residuals overall, it is often called *ordinary least squares* or OLS regression.

Leslie was distracted by the calculations for the slope; she saw the means in the formula for b_1 and immediately thought that they were going to have to check for normal distributions.

9.6.4 ESTIMATING THE LINEAR REGRESSION MODEL IN R

Kiara stated that if the electricity went off, the slope and intercept of a line could still be calculated by hand using the OLS method without too much trouble, depending on the sample size. Leslie was glad to have electricity and for R to do the work for her, and she asked Nancy which function worked best to find the equation for the line. Nancy introduced the `lm()` function. Leslie recognized the abbreviation `lm` from plotting a line through the scatterplot. Nancy reminded her that the `lm` stands for *linear model*.

Leslie looked up the help documentation for the `lm()` function and found that it takes two arguments, `formula =` and `data =`. There is also an `na.action =` option that Nancy recommended in order to deal with missing values even though these data do not have any. The `formula =` argument is where to enter the regression model of interest, in this case `dist_SSP` explained by `pctunins`. The `data =` argument is the same as usual in requiring the name of the data frame for analysis. The `na.action =` argument is used to specify treatment of missing values, and `na.exclude` is the option for excluding observations with missing values. Nancy mentioned that the output for the `lm()` code is best viewed using `summary()`. Leslie used `lm()` and filled in the arguments to find the slope and the intercept of the regression line shown in Figure 9.3.

```
# linear regression of distance to syringe program by percent uninsured
dist.by.unins <- lm(formula = dist_SSP ~ pctunins,
              data = dist.ssp, na.action = na.exclude)
summary(object = dist.by.unins)
##
## Call:
## lm(formula = dist_SSP ~ pctunins, data = dist.ssp, na.action =
## na.exclude)
##
## Residuals:
```

```
##      Min      1Q  Median      3Q      Max
## -217.71  -60.86  -21.61   47.73   290.77
##
## Coefficients:
##              Estimate Std. Error t value Pr(>|t|)
## (Intercept)  12.4798    10.1757   1.226    0.221
## pctunins      7.8190     0.7734  10.110   <2e-16 ***
## ---
## Signif. codes:  0 '***' 0.001 '**' 0.01 '*' 0.05 '.' 0.1 ' ' 1
##
## Residual standard error: 85.91 on 498 degrees of freedom
## Multiple R-squared:  0.1703, Adjusted R-squared:  0.1686
## F-statistic: 102.2 on 1 and 498 DF,  p-value: < 2.2e-16
```

9.6.5 NAVIGATING THE LINEAR REGRESSION OUTPUT

Leslie was a little shocked by how much the output showed. She expected just the slope and y-intercept. She found what she believed to be a y-intercept of 12.48. Kiara confirmed that she was correct and reminded Leslie that the y-intercept is the value of y when x is zero. The model would predict that a county with 0% of people being uninsured would have a distance to the nearest syringe program of 12.48 miles. The slope is 7.82. The *slope* is the change in y for every one-unit change in x. If the percent uninsured goes up by 1% in a county, the distance in miles to a syringe program would change by 7.82. Leslie used this information to write out Equation (9.11), the regression equation for this model.

$$distance = 12.48 + 7.82 \times uninsured \tag{9.11}$$

Leslie used the regression model to predict distance to syringe program for a county with 10% of the residents uninsured in Equation (9.12).

$$distance = 12.48 + 7.82 \times 10 \tag{9.12}$$

Based on the linear regression model, a county with 10% of people uninsured would be 90.68 miles from the nearest syringe program. Leslie noticed that the error term was no longer included in the model. Nancy explained that once a model is estimated, the error term is no longer included when writing out the model.

9.6.6 UNDERSTANDING RESIDUALS

The linear fit line in Figure 9.3 was based on the values of the intercept and slope that were the best at minimizing the distances between all the points and the regression line. These distances are called residuals and are the leftover information that the regression line does not explain. Nancy had learned to graph residuals using an online tutorial (Jackson, 2016) and modified some of the instructions to come up with Figure 9.10 and Figure 9.11. The tutorial demonstrated how to add a layer with `geom_segment()` that created line segments between each observed value (the dots) and the value predicted by the linear regression line. Before they looked at residuals for the model of `dist_SSP`, Kiara thought Leslie could use a little more information given how important residuals are to regression modeling.

Kiara asked Nancy to use her tutorial skills to create four graphs based on the water example so they could compare them side by side. The first graph was the deterministic graph. The second was one where the total of the differences between observed and predicted are minimized so that, overall, the predicted y (i.e., $\hat{y}$) values are closest to the actual observed y values (this is OLS regression). The third was what happens if the slope of the fit line does *not* minimize the residuals. The fourth was what happens if there is a slope of zero, representing no relationship at all between the two variables (Figure 9.11).

The top left graph in Figure 9.11 is the ideal since it would predict every observation perfectly, but this is not realistic in most research where there are many potential sources of variability. In the remaining three graphs, all the points stayed in the same place, but each line was different. The graph on the top right in Figure 9.11 is the best of the nondeterministic fit lines because it minimizes the residual differences between the values predicted by the regression line and the observed values. Kiara explained that this is how OLS works. OLS minimizes those distances captured in Figure 9.11 by the solid vertical lines—it minimizes the *residuals*.

Now that they had looked at a less messy example, Nancy graphed Figure 9.12, which showed the messy distance to needle exchange data and the model from Equation (9.12) and the residuals.

Leslie saw that the vertical lines in Figure 9.12 showed the residuals.

FIGURE 9.11 Examples of data and fit lines with residuals

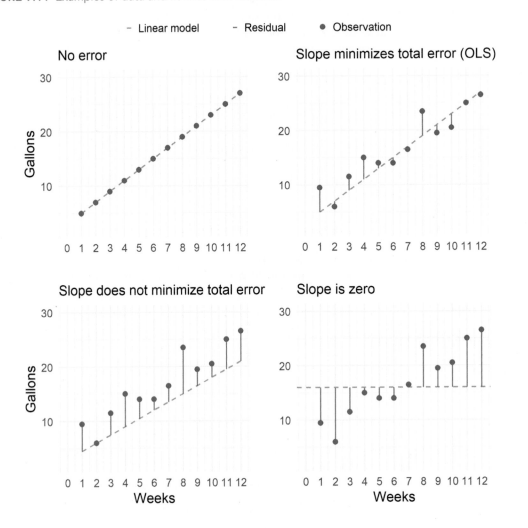

FIGURE 9.12 Relationship between percentage without health insurance and distance to nearest syringe program in 500 counties with residuals

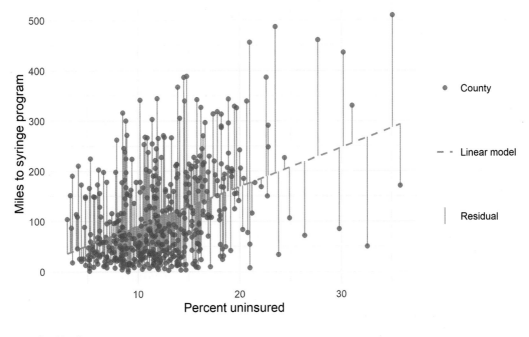

Source: https://opioid.amfar.org.

9.6.7 ACHIEVEMENT 3: CHECK YOUR UNDERSTANDING

Pick a county from the data frame and enter its observed value for percentage uninsured into the regression equation like in Equation (9.12). Compute the distance to the nearest syringe program that is predicted by this model. Compare the predicted distance to the actual distance for the county.

9.7 Achievement 4: Slope interpretation and significance (b_1, *p*-value, CI)

In addition to writing the regression model, there are three things to interpret when reporting the results of a linear regression analysis: model fit, model significance, and slope value and significance. Kiara suggested they start with slope value and significance.

9.7.1 INTERPRETING THE VALUE OF THE SLOPE

Kiara wanted to start examining the slope by demonstrating how the slope and the value of the predictor work together to explain or predict the outcome. As shown in the regression model, the value of the independent variable, percentage uninsured, would be substituted into the equation and multiplied by the slope in order to predict the value of the outcome for a county. In this case, the value of the slope is 7.82. For every additional 1% uninsured in a county, the distance to the nearest syringe program goes up by 7.82 miles. Consider a county with 10% of people uninsured. Using the regression model, the distance to syringe program would be predicted as follows:

- distance to syringe program = 12.48 + 7.82 × uninsured
- distance to syringe program = 12.48 + 7.82 × 10
- distance to syringe program = 90.68

Another county with 11% uninsured would have a predicted distance to syringe program as follows:

- distance to syringe program = 12.48 + 7.82 × uninsured
- distance to syringe program = 12.48 + 7.82 × 11
- distance to syringe program = 98.50

Because the slope is 7.82, the distance to the nearest syringe program increases by 7.82 miles for each 1% increase in people without insurance.

9.7.2 INTERPRETING THE STATISTICAL SIGNIFICANCE OF THE SLOPE

Leslie noticed that the output for the linear model included a *p*-value for the slope and a *p*-value for the intercept. She asked Nancy about the *p*-value. Nancy explained that the statistical significance of the slope in linear regression is tested using a *Wald test*, which is like a one-sample *t*-test where the hypothesized value of the slope is zero. To get the *p*-value from the regression model of distance to syringe program, the slope of 12.48 was compared to a hypothesized value of zero using the Wald test. The null hypothesis is *The slope of the line is equal to zero.* Leslie stopped Nancy there so that they could use NHST to organize.

9.7.2.1 NHST STEP 1: WRITE THE NULL AND ALTERNATE HYPOTHESES

H0: The slope of the line is equal to zero.

HA: The slope of the line is not equal to zero.

9.7.2.2 NHST STEP 2: COMPUTE THE TEST STATISTIC

The test statistic for the Wald test in OLS regression is the *t*-statistic. The formula to get *t* is shown in Equation (9.13). Note that the formula is the same as the formula for the one-sample *t*-test from Equation (6.1), but with the slope of the regression model instead of the mean.

$$t = \frac{b_1 - 0}{se_{b_1}} \tag{9.13}$$

The formula can be used by substituting in the slope and standard error from the model output as in Equation (9.14).

$$t = \frac{7.82 - 0}{.77} = 10.16 \tag{9.14}$$

The *t*-statistic can also be found in the model output. Leslie noticed that their computed *t*-statistic was slightly larger than the one R calculated. Nancy thought that the difference was due to rounding.

R keeps a lot of digits after the decimal point for all the calculations, and when they limited the number of digits after the decimal to two, this resulted in a small difference.

```
##
## Call:
## lm(formula = dist_SSP ~ pctunins, data = dist.ssp, na.action =
na.exclude)
##
## Residuals:
##     Min      1Q  Median      3Q     Max
## -217.71  -60.86  -21.61   47.73  290.77
##
## Coefficients:
##              Estimate Std. Error t value Pr(>|t|)
## (Intercept)   12.4798    10.1757   1.226    0.221
## pctunins       7.8190     0.7734  10.110   <2e-16 ***
## ---
## Signif. codes:  0 '***' 0.001 '**' 0.01 '*' 0.05 '.' 0.1 ' ' 1
##
## Residual standard error: 85.91 on 498 degrees of freedom
## Multiple R-squared: 0.1703, Adjusted R-squared: 0.1686
## F-statistic: 102.2 on 1 and 498 DF,  p-value: < 2.2e-16
```

9.7.2.3 NHST STEP 3: CALCULATE THE PROBABILITY THAT YOUR TEST STATISTIC IS AT LEAST AS BIG AS IT IS IF THERE IS NO RELATIONSHIP (I.E., THE NULL IS TRUE)

Leslie found the p-value of $< 2e-16$ for the slope in the output.

9.7.2.4 NHST STEPS 4 AND 5: INTERPRET THE PROBABILITY AND WRITE A CONCLUSION

The small p-value suggests a tiny chance that the t-statistic for the slope would be as big as it is (or bigger) if the null hypothesis were true. The null hypothesis is rejected in favor of the alternate hypothesis that the slope is not equal to zero. Kiara said this is often reported as the slope being statistically significantly different from zero. Leslie wrote an interpretation of what she knew about the slope so far:

The percentage of uninsured residents in a county is a statistically significant predictor of the distance to the nearest syringe program ($b = 7.82$; $p < .05$) in our sample. For every 1% increase in uninsured residents in a county, the predicted distance to the nearest syringe program increases by 7.82 miles.

9.7.3 COMPUTING CONFIDENCE INTERVALS FOR THE SLOPE AND INTERCEPT

Leslie asked Kiara if they would also be reporting confidence intervals for slopes. Kiara said that this was a great idea, and they could compute confidence intervals using the standard error of the slope from the regression output and a *z*-score of 1.96, like when they first examined confidence intervals in Section 4.9. Nancy explained that they did not have to compute the confidence intervals by hand; they could use the `confint()` function with the `dist.by.unins` linear regression model object they had made.

```
# confidence interval for regression parameters
ci.dist.by.unins <- confint(object = dist.by.unins)
ci.dist.by.unins
##                    2.5 %    97.5 %
## (Intercept)  -7.512773  32.472391
## pctunins      6.299493   9.338435
```

The output for `confint()` gives the confidence interval for the intercept and the slope. Leslie asked whether they should be paying attention to the intercept more. Kiara explained that the intercept was often reported but not interpreted because it did not usually contribute much to answering the research question. This made sense to Leslie. She added the confidence interval to her interpretation of the slope.

> The percentage of uninsured residents in a county is a statistically significant predictor of the distance to the nearest syringe program ($b = 7.82$; $p < .05$). For every 1% increase in uninsured residents in a county, the predicted distance to the nearest syringe program increases by 7.82 miles. The value of the slope in the sample is 7.82, and the value of the slope is likely between 6.30 and 9.34 in the population that the sample came from (95% CI: 6.30–9.34). With every 1% increase in uninsured residents in a county, the nearest syringe program is between 6.30 and 9.34 more miles away. These results suggest that counties with a larger percentage of uninsured are farther from this resource, which may exacerbate existing health disparities.

9.7.4 USING THE MODEL TO MAKE PREDICTIONS

Nancy suggested that they look at *predicted values*, which are the values of *y* predicted by the model for a given value of *x*. The regression line is essentially the line made of the predicted values based on the regression model. Predicted values of *y* are called *y*-hat and denoted $\hat{y}$. Nancy knew that `predict()` can be used to find the predicted values for all observations, or for a specific value of the independent variable. For example, for a county with 10% uninsured, `predict()` can be used to get the predicted value and the confidence interval around it for distance to nearest syringe program. The `predict()` function takes three arguments. First, the `object =` argument takes the linear regression model object, which the team had named `dist.by.unins`. The second argument is the name of a data frame with the observed value(s) of *x* in it. In this case, instead of predicting values from the larger `dist.ssp` data frame, Nancy created a tiny data frame with a single value of *x* in it, like this: `data.frame(pctunins = 10)`. Finally, the `interval =` argument uses "confidence" to get the confidence interval around each prediction. Nancy wrote the code and ran it for the team.

```
# use predict to find predicted value of distance for 10% uninsured
pred.dist.ssp <- predict(object = dist.by.unins,
                         newdata = data.frame(pctunins = 10),
                         interval = "confidence")
pred.dist.ssp
##       fit      lwr      upr
## 1 90.66945 82.42356 98.91534
```

The predicted distance to a syringe program from a county with 10% of people uninsured is 90.67 miles with a confidence interval for the prediction (sometimes called a prediction interval) of 82.42 to 98.92 miles. The confidence interval shows where the population value of the statistic likely lies. In this case, the likely true distance to a syringe program from a county where 10% of people are uninsured is between 82.42 and 98.92 miles. Remembering that her long trip to get to Nancy's for this meeting was not even half as far as the lower end of the confidence interval, Leslie thought this was ridiculously far to travel for a syringe exchange, especially for people who are already struggling with addiction and in need of this service.

Nancy agreed and wanted to show Leslie how the predict() function predicts $\hat{y}$ for all the observed values of x in the data. These predicted values can help determine how well the model fits the data. Since they are using the data that were used to create the model, there is no need to add the newdata = argument this time, so Nancy told Leslie to just include the linear regression object dist.by.unins and the argument to get confidence intervals with the predicted values. Nancy cautioned Leslie that there were 500 observations in this data frame, so printing the predicted values would result in 500 rows of output. Leslie decided to use head() just to print out the first six rows so that she could see a few of the predicted values.

```
# use predict to find predicted value for all observed x
pred.dist.ssp.all <- predict(object = dist.by.unins,
                             interval = "confidence")
# print out the first six predicted values and CI
head(x = pred.dist.ssp.all)
##       fit       lwr       upr
## 1  52.35653  39.20985  65.50321
## 2 157.13064 144.92001 169.34128
## 3 136.80134 127.37402 146.22865
## 4 109.43496 101.87889 116.99103
## 5 157.91254 145.58211 170.24297
## 6 128.20048 119.66871 136.73224
```

9.7.5 ACHIEVEMENT 4: CHECK YOUR UNDERSTANDING

Based on the linear model, how much closer to a syringe program is a county with 2% of people uninsured compared to a county with 12% of people uninsured?

9.8 Achievement 5: Model significance and model fit

Leslie noticed that there was another *p*-value toward the bottom of the output for the linear regression that was not for the intercept or the slope. Kiara explained that this *p*-value was from a test statistic that measures how much better the regression line is at getting close to the data points compared to the mean value of the outcome. Essentially, are the predicted values shown by the regression line in Figure 9.13 better than the mean value of the distance to the syringe program at capturing the relationship between `pctunins` and `dist_SSP`?

Kiara explained that, like the *t*-statistic is the test statistic for a *t*-test comparing two means, the *F*-statistic is the test statistic for linear regression comparing the regression line to the mean. Leslie remembered the *F*-statistic from ANOVA and asked if this was the same *F*. Kiara confirmed that this is the same *F* with the same *F*-distribution and explained that ANOVA is actually a special type of linear model where all the predictors are categorical.

FIGURE 9.13 Relationship between percentage without health insurance and distance to needle exchange in 500 counties

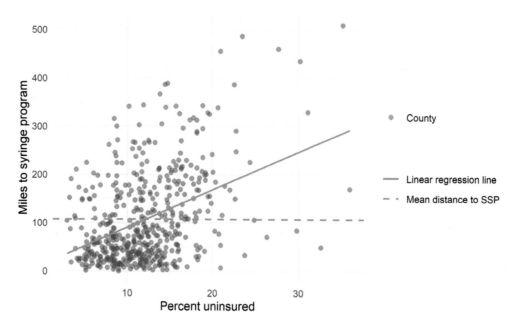

Source: https://opioid.amfar.org.

The *F*-statistic is used to determine whether the line showing the regression model is better overall at getting close to the data points than the line showing the mean of the outcome. Kiara thought it might be useful to visualize this with two separate plots, so Nancy graphed the observations and the regression and mean lines (Figure 9.14).

Kiara admitted that it was a little difficult to see for counties with a low percentage of uninsured individuals on the left in Figure 9.14, but she showed Leslie that on the right side, the dotted lines between the observed data points and the linear regression line in the top plot were mostly shorter than the dotted lines between the observed points and mean line in the bottom plot. The *F*-statistic is essentially comparing these amounts, the difference between observed and predicted and the difference between observed and the mean.

9.8.1 UNDERSTANDING THE *F*-STATISTIC

The *F*-statistic is a ratio of explained information (in the numerator) to unexplained information (in the denominator). If a model explains more than it leaves unexplained, the numerator is larger and the *F*-statistic is greater than 1. *F*-statistics that are much greater than 1 are explaining much more of the variation in the outcome than they leave unexplained. Large *F*-statistics are more likely to be statistically significant. Kiara wrote out how the *F*-statistic is computed for the linear regression in Equation (9.15).

FIGURE 9.14 Distance from observed to regression line (residuals) and from observed to mean line for miles to nearest syringe program by percentage uninsured in a county

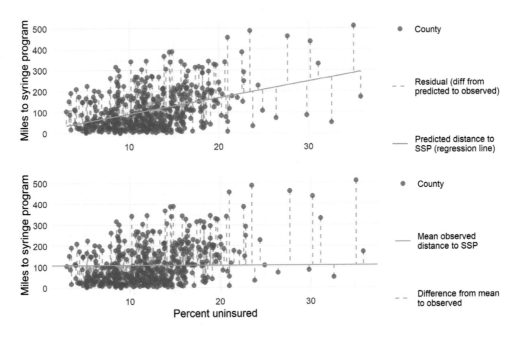

Source: https://opioid.amfar.org.

$$F = \frac{\dfrac{\sum_{i=1}^{n}(\hat{y}_i - m_y)^2}{p-1}}{\dfrac{\sum_{i=1}^{n}(y_i - \hat{y}_i)^2}{n-p}}$$ (9.15)

Leslie noticed that the equation was similar but not exactly the same as Equation (7.3) from the ANOVA chapter. Kiara explained that Equation (9.15) could be used for both situations, while Equation (7.3) is just useful in situations when there are groups from categorical predictors being compared since it uses *group means* in the calculation. Kiara explained the different parts of this F equation:

- i is an individual observation, in this case a county
- n is the sample size, or total number of counties
- p is the number of parameters in the model; the slope and intercept are parameters
- y_i is the observed outcome of distance to syringe program for county i
- $\hat{y}_i$ is the predicted value of distance to syringe program for county i
- m_y is the mean of the observed outcomes of distance to syringe program

Kiara pointed out that the numerator of F was how much the predicted values differ from the mean observed value on average. This is divided by how much the predicted values differ from the actual observed values on average. Kiara repeated that the F-statistic is how much a predicted value differs from the mean value on average—which is explained variance, or how much better (or worse) the prediction is than the mean at explaining the outcome—divided by how much an observed value differs from the predicted value on average, which is the residual information or unexplained variance. Sometimes, these are referred to in similar terminology to ANOVA: the numerator is the $MS_{regression}$ (where MS stands for *mean square*) divided by the $MS_{residual}$.

Nancy noted that the F-statistic is always positive due to the squaring of the terms in the numerator and denominator. As a result, the F-distribution starts at zero (when the regression line is exactly the same as the mean) and goes to the right. The shape of the F-distribution depends on the number of parameters in the statistical model and the sample size, which determine two degrees of freedom values. Nancy graphed a few different versions with different numbers of parameters and sample sizes (Figure 9.15). She reminded Leslie and Kiara that the F-statistic is usually written with two degrees of freedom (df) numbers that influence the shape of the distribution. The first number in the parentheses after the F is the degrees of freedom for the numerator. This value is one less than the number of parameters in the model, $p - 1$. The second number in the parentheses after an F-statistic is the degrees of freedom for the denominator, or $n - p$.

The more the model explains the variation in the outcome, the larger the F-statistic gets. Like t-statistics and chi-squared statistics, larger values of F-statistics are less likely to occur when there is no relationship between the variables. Leslie asked about graphing the F-distribution from the linear regression model, and she printed out the regression results again to review the F-statistic.

FIGURE 9.15 Examples of the distribution of probability density for *F*

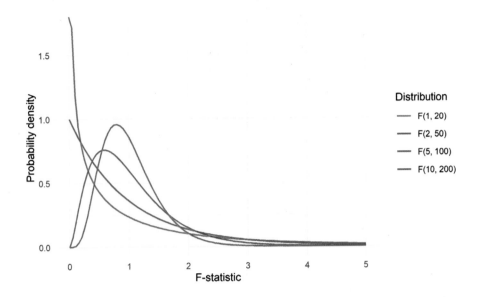

```
## 
## Call:
## lm(formula = dist_SSP ~ pctunins, data = dist.ssp, na.action =
## na.exclude)
## 
## Residuals:
##     Min      1Q  Median      3Q     Max
## -217.71  -60.86  -21.61   47.73  290.77
## 
## Coefficients:
##             Estimate Std. Error t value Pr(>|t|)
## (Intercept) 12.4798    10.1757   1.226    0.221
## pctunins     7.8190     0.7734  10.110   <2e-16 ***
## ---
## Signif. codes: 0 '***' 0.001 '**' 0.01 '*' 0.05 '.' 0.1 ' ' 1
## 
## Residual standard error: 85.91 on 498 degrees of freedom
## Multiple R-squared:  0.1703, Adjusted R-squared:  0.1686
## F-statistic: 102.2 on 1 and 498 DF,  p-value: < 2.2e-16
```

FIGURE 9.16 F-distribution with 1 and 498 degrees of freedom for model of distance to syringe program by uninsured

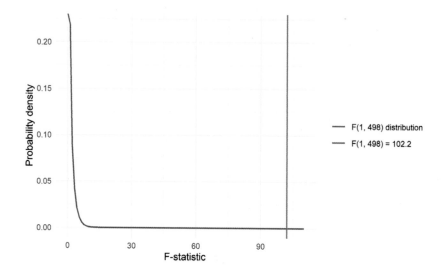

Nancy knew the numerator degrees of freedom were $p - 1$, and since there are two parameters, the intercept and the slope ($p = 2$), the numerator degrees of freedom were $2 - 1 = 1$. For the denominator, the sample size and number of parameters were used to determine the denominator degrees of freedom ($n - p$). Here, the denominator degrees of freedom were $500 - 2 = 498$. Leslie verified that these degrees of freedom $F(1, 498)$ align with the output of the linear model `dist.by.unins`. Nancy used the code from above and plotted the F-distribution for the model (Figure 9.16).

Just like with the t-statistic and chi-squared, the probability of an F-statistic this large or larger if the null is true is the area under the F-distribution curve starting at the vertical line ($F = 102.2$) and going right. There is really very little space under the curve from $F = 102.2$ to the right, which is consistent with the tiny p-value ($p < .001$). Leslie interpreted this as nearly a 0% chance that an F-statistic this large or larger would occur under the null hypothesis that there is no relationship between percentage uninsured and distance to syringe program. Essentially, the F-statistic and the associated p-value suggest a statistically significant relationship between percentage uninsured and distance to syringe program at the county level.

Leslie summarized the model significance process they went through with NHST.

9.8.1.1 NHST STEP 1: WRITE THE NULL AND ALTERNATE HYPOTHESES

H0: A model including percentage uninsured in a county is no better at explaining the distance to syringe programs than a baseline model of the mean value of distance.

HA: A model including percentage uninsured in a county is better at explaining the distance to syringe programs than a baseline model of the mean value of distance.

9.8.1.2 NHST STEP 2: COMPUTE THE TEST STATISTIC

The test statistic for this model is F and its value is $F(1, 498) = 102.2$.

9.8.1.3 NHST STEP 3: CALCULATE THE PROBABILITY THAT YOUR TEST STATISTIC IS AT LEAST AS BIG AS IT IS IF THERE IS NO RELATIONSHIP (I.E., THE NULL IS TRUE)

There is a tiny probability ($p < .001$) of an F as big as 102.2 or bigger if the null hypothesis were true.

9.8.1.4 NHST STEPS 4 AND 5: INTERPRET THE PROBABILITY AND WRITE A CONCLUSION

Given the tiny p-value, Leslie rejected the null hypothesis in favor of the alternate hypothesis that percentage uninsured is helpful in explaining distance to syringe programs from a county.

While it felt a little repetitive, Leslie still found it useful to go through the NHST process in order to solidify her understanding of what they were testing and why they were rejecting or retaining the null hypothesis.

9.8.2 UNDERSTANDING THE R^2 MEASURE OF MODEL FIT

Kiara suggested that they review one additional piece of information before writing a complete interpretation of the model. The measure that tells how well the model fits is the R^2 or R-squared. The R^2 is computed by squaring the value of the correlation between the observed distance to syringe programs in the 500 counties and the values of distance to syringe programs predicted for the 500 counties by the model. When the model predicts values that are close to the observed values, the correlation is high and the R^2 is high.

The R^2 is the amount of variation in the outcome that the model explains and is reported as a measure of *model fit*. For the relationship between uninsured percentage and distance to syringe program, the R^2 is 0.1703. To get the percentage of variance explained by the model, multiply by 100, so 17.03% of the variation in distance to syringe programs is explained by the percentage of uninsured people living in a county. Kiara explained that simply subtracting R^2 from 1 ($1 - R^2$) and multiplying by 100 for a percent will give the percent of variance *not* explained by the model (here, 82.97%).

Leslie saw another R^2 labeled *adjusted R-squared*—or R^2_{adj}—in the output. Kiara explained that the value of R^2 tends to increase with each additional variable added to the model, whether the variable actually improves the model or not. The R^2_{adj} penalizes the value of R^2 a small amount for each additional variable added to the model to ensure that the R^2_{adj} only increases when the additional predictors explain a notable amount of the variation in the outcome. Essentially, Kiara explained, the R^2_{adj} keeps analysts from just adding all the variables they have in order to get the highest possible value for model fit. The R^2_{adj} is more commonly reported than the R^2.

9.8.3 REPORTING LINEAR REGRESSION RESULTS

Now that they had been through the process, Kiara summarized the things that should be reported following any simple linear regression analysis:

- An interpretation of the value of the slope (b)
- The significance of the slope (t and p, confidence intervals)

- The significance of the model (F and p)
- Model fit (R^2 or R^2_{adj})

Nancy printed the model results again to use for writing the interpretation.

```
##
## Call:
## lm(formula = dist_SSP ~ pctunins, data = dist.ssp, na.action =
na.exclude)
##
## Residuals:
##      Min      1Q  Median      3Q     Max
## -217.71  -60.86  -21.61   47.73  290.77
##
## Coefficients:
##             Estimate Std. Error t value Pr(>|t|)
## (Intercept) 12.4798    10.1757   1.226    0.221
## pctunins     7.8190     0.7734  10.110   <2e-16 ***
## ---
## Signif. codes:  0 '***' 0.001 '**' 0.01 '*' 0.05 '.' 0.1 ' ' 1
##
## Residual standard error: 85.91 on 498 degrees of freedom
## Multiple R-squared:  0.1703, Adjusted R-squared:  0.1686
## F-statistic: 102.2 on 1 and 498 DF,  p-value: < 2.2e-16
```

Kiara wrote the model interpretation:

A simple linear regression analysis found that the percentage of uninsured residents in a county is a statistically significant predictor of the distance to the nearest syringe program ($b = 7.82$; $p < .001$). For every 1% increase in uninsured residents, the predicted distance to the nearest syringe program increases by 7.82 miles. The value of the slope is likely between 6.30 and 9.34 in the population that the sample came from (95% CI: 6.30–9.34). With every 1% increase in uninsured residents in a county, there is likely a 6.30- to 9.34-mile increase to the nearest syringe program. The model was statistically significantly better than the baseline model (the mean of the distance to syringe program) at explaining distance to syringe program [$F(1, 498) = 102.2$; $p < .001$] and explained 16.86% of the variance in the outcome ($R^2_{adj} = .1686$). These results suggest that counties with lower insurance rates are farther from this resource, which may exacerbate existing health disparities.

9.8.4 ACHIEVEMENT 5: CHECK YOUR UNDERSTANDING

Instead of `pctunins`, create a model using `lm()` with the predictor of `opioid_RxRate` and the outcome of `dist_SSP`. Find and interpret the model significance and model fit.

9.9 Achievement 6: Checking assumptions and conducting diagnostics

9.9.1 ASSUMPTIONS OF SIMPLE LINEAR REGRESSION

The calculations underlying the simple linear regression model of `dist_SSP ~ pctunins` are based on several assumptions about the data used in the model:

- Observations are independent.
- The outcome is continuous.
- The relationship between the two variables is linear (linearity).
- The variance is constant with the points distributed equally around the line (homoscedasticity).
- The residuals are independent.
- The residuals are normally distributed.

9.9.2 CHECKING THE INDEPENDENT OBSERVATIONS ASSUMPTION

The R-Team discussed the independent observations assumption for a few minutes. While the data had been collected in a reasonable way, one could argue that counties in the same state were not really independent because, like siblings in the same household, they may have the same characteristics and therefore may not vary as much from each other as truly independent areas would. This assumption is often seen as a possible problem for geographic data, Kiara commented, and researchers are increasingly using methods that account for geographic proximity in situations like this one. They decided that this assumption was not met.

9.9.3 CHECKING THE CONTINUOUS OUTCOME ASSUMPTION

The distance to a syringe program is measured in miles and can take any value of zero or higher. This assumption is met.

9.9.4 CHECKING THE LINEARITY ASSUMPTION

The linearity assumption is met if a scatterplot of the two variables shows a relationship that falls along a line. The earlier plot showing purple points and a straight line drawn through them suggests that this assumption may be met. When graphed, the points fall generally on the straight line. However, unlike the graph of basic water access and females in school in Figure 8.18, the data points seem to not follow the line as well in Figure 9.17. Using a Loess curve, the relationship between the two variables is shown without constraining the line to be straight. In this case, a Loess curve shows deviation from a linear relationship, especially at lower values of the predictor, percent uninsured.

```
# percent without health insurance and distance to needle exchange (Figure 9.17)
dist.ssp %>%
  ggplot(aes(x = pctunins, y = dist_SSP)) +
```

```
geom_point(aes(size = "County"), color = "#7463AC", alpha = .6) +
geom_smooth(aes(color = "Linear fit line"), method = "lm", se = FALSE) +
geom_smooth(aes(color = "Loess curve"), se = FALSE) +
theme_minimal() +
labs(y = "Miles to syringe program", x = "Percent uninsured") +
scale_color_manual(values = c("gray60", "deeppink"), name = "") +
scale_size_manual(values = 2, name = "")
```

The Loess curve does not fit well at the lower values of uninsured, but starting around 7% or 8%, the Loess curve stays pretty close to the regression line. Nancy did not think this would be good enough to meet linearity and suggested that this assumption failed.

9.9.5 CHECKING THE HOMOSCEDASTICITY ASSUMPTION

Kiara explained that the assumption of homoscedasticity requires the data points to be evenly distributed around the regression line. Nancy interjected that, for simple linear regression, this assumption is checked the same way as it was checked for the correlation analysis in their previous meeting (Section 8.8.3). Specifically, Nancy explained, a scatterplot where all the points were relatively evenly spread out around the line would be one way to check the assumption. In Figure 9.17, the points seem closer to the line on the far left and then are more spread out around the line at the higher values of percentage uninsured. It appears this assumption is not met.

FIGURE 9.17 Relationship between percentage without health insurance and distance to nearest syringe program in 500 counties

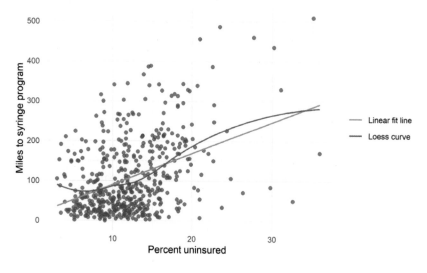

Source: https://opioid.amfar.org.

Kiara reminded Leslie that the Breusch-Pagan test was another way to check the assumption. Breusch-Pagan can be used to statistically test the null hypothesis that the variance is constant. The `bptest()` function takes a `formula =` argument, which can be the regression model written out, `dist.ssp$dist_SSP ~ dist.ssp$pctunins`, or it can be the name of the regression object, `dist.by.unins`. Leslie used the model name since she had not done that before.

```
# testing for equal variance
const.var.test <- lmtest::bptest(formula = dist.by.unins)
const.var.test
##
##  studentized Breusch-Pagan test
##
## data:  dist.by.unins
## BP = 46.18, df = 1, p-value = 1.078e-11
```

The Breusch-Pagan test statistic has a tiny p-value (BP = 46.18; $p < .001$), indicating that the null hypothesis of constant variance would be rejected. This is consistent with the scatterplot showing higher variance on the right-hand side of Figure 9.17.

Kiara also remembered that plotting the predicted values versus the residuals is another way of examining this constant error variance assumption and asked Nancy to make a graph to examine

FIGURE 9.18 Predicted values and residuals from linear regression model of distance to syringe program by percentage uninsured in a county

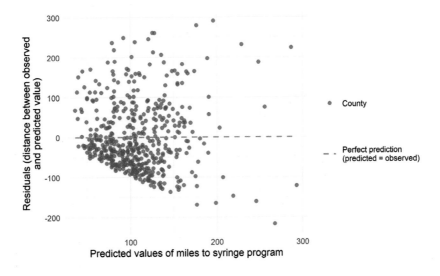

Source: https://opioid.amfar.org.

it (Figure 9.18). If there was a pattern in a scatterplot of residuals and predicted values, this would indicate that the model was better at some kinds of predictions than others, suggesting bias.

In Figure 9.18, a dashed line is shown to indicate no relationship between the fitted (or predicted) values and the residuals, which would be the ideal situation to meet the assumption. This line is a helpful reference point for looking at these types of graphs. For the homoscedasticity assumption to be met, the points should be roughly evenly distributed around the dashed line with no clear patterns. It should look like a cloud or random points on the graph with no distinguishable patterns. In this plot, there is a clear pattern. It looks like a fan or a cone on the lower left. While the points look more cloud-like above the dotted line and on the right side of the graph, the fan effect is still there on the left side of the graph. This is consistent with Figure 9.17 and with the Breusch-Pagan test. This confirms that the homoscedasticity assumption is not met.

9.9.6 TESTING THE INDEPENDENCE OF RESIDUALS ASSUMPTION

Kiara explained that the remaining assumptions are about residuals and reminded Leslie that residuals are the distances between each data point and the regression line. Conceptually, residuals are the variation in the outcome that the regression line does not explain.

The first assumption for residuals is that they are independent or unrelated to each other. Residuals that are independent do not follow a pattern. Kiara explained that a pattern in the residuals suggests that the regression model is doing better for certain types of observations and worse for others.

She introduced the *Durbin-Watson* test, which can be used to determine whether the model violates the assumption of independent residuals. The null hypothesis for the Durbin-Watson test is that the residuals are independent. The alternative hypothesis is that the residuals are not independent. A Durbin-Watson or D-W statistic of 2 indicates perfectly independent residuals.

There are a few R packages that contain a Durbin-Watson test function. Nancy suggested using `dwtest()` from the **lmtest** package that they used for the Breusch-Pagan test. Nancy wrote the code.

```
# test independence of residuals
lmtest::dwtest(formula = dist.by.unins)
##
## 	Durbin-Watson test
##
## data:  dist.by.unins
## DW = 2.0103, p-value = 0.5449
## alternative hypothesis: true autocorrelation is greater than 0
```

The D-W statistic was near 2 and the p-value was high, so Leslie concluded that the null hypothesis was retained. Since the null hypothesis was that the residuals were independent, she found that this assumption was met.

9.9.7 TESTING THE NORMALITY OF RESIDUALS ASSUMPTION

The last assumption to check is normality of residuals. Kiara explained that normally distributed residuals indicate that the regression line is far above a few points, far below a few others, and relatively near most of the points. If the residuals are skewed, that would mean that the regression line does a better job at explaining either the higher values of the outcome or the lower values of the outcome.

Leslie checked normality using a histogram and Q-Q plot (Figures 9.19 and 9.20). Nancy let her know that the `dist.by.unins` model object includes residuals to use in the plot and that they can be piped into `ggplot()` by first using the `data.frame()` function.

```
# check residual plot of uninsured percent and distance to syringe program
# (Figure 9.19)
data.frame(dist.by.unins$residuals) %>%
  ggplot(aes(x = dist.by.unins.residuals)) +
  geom_histogram(fill = "#7463AC", col = "white") +
  theme_minimal() +
  labs(x = "Residual (distance between observed and predicted\nmiles to
            syringe program)",
       y = "Number of counties")
```

```
# check residual plot of uninsured percent and distance to syringe program
# (Figure 9.20)
data.frame(dist.by.unins$residuals) %>%
  ggplot(aes(sample = dist.by.unins.residuals)) +
  geom_abline(aes(intercept = mean(x = dist.by.unins.residuals),
                  slope = sd(x = dist.by.unins.residuals),
                  linetype = "Normally distributed"),
              color = "gray60", size = 1) +
  stat_qq(aes(size = "County"), color = "#7463AC", alpha = .6) +
  theme_minimal() +
  labs(x = "Theoretical normal distribution",
       y = "Observed residuals (distance between observed and\npredicted
            miles to syringe program)") +
  scale_size_manual(values = 1, name = "") +
  scale_linetype_manual(values = 1, name = "")
```

Both graphs suggest some non-normality in the distribution of residuals. The histogram suggests the residuals are right-skewed. The Q-Q plot suggests the residuals are different from the values you'd expect from a normal distribution.

9.9.8 INTERPRETING THE RESULTS OF THE ASSUMPTION CHECKING

Leslie noted that the linear regression analysis met some assumptions and failed some assumptions. The assumptions it met were continuous outcome variable and independence of residuals. The assumptions it failed were independence of observations, linearity, homoscedasticity, and normally distributed

FIGURE 9.19 Distribution of residuals for model of uninsured percentage and distance to syringe program for 500 counties

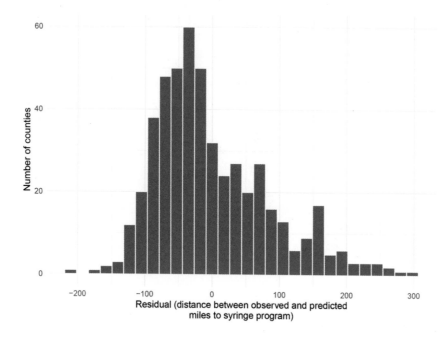

Source: https://opioid.amfar.org.

FIGURE 9.20 Distribution of residuals for model of uninsured percentage and distance to nearest syringe program for 500 counties

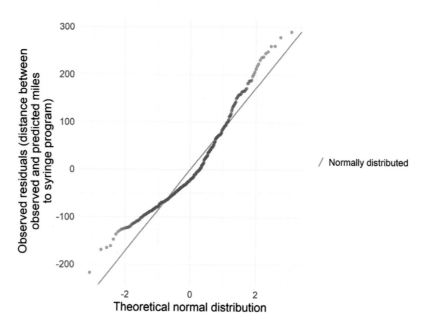

Source: https://opioid.amfar.org.

residuals. Because it does not meet all the assumptions, Leslie knew that the model was considered biased and should be interpreted with caution. Specifically, the results of a biased model are not usually considered generalizable to the population.

Leslie suggested they transform the variables like they did in Section 8.9, but Kiara said there was one more step before they were done with the regression modeling process.

9.9.9 USING MODEL DIAGNOSTICS TO FIND OUTLIERS AND INFLUENTIAL VALUES

Kiara explained that they were not quite done checking model quality. In addition to testing assumptions, she said that model *diagnostics* are useful for determining whether there are any observations that are outliers or influential observations that may be having some impact on the model. An *outlier* is an observation with unusual values. A *regression outlier* has an unusual value of the outcome given its value(s) of predictor(s). An *influential observation* changes the slope of the regression line.

There are several measures to help identify outliers and influential observations: *standardized residuals*, *df-betas*, *Cook's distance*, and *leverage*. One good strategy for identifying the truly problematic observations is to identify those observations that are outliers or influential observations on two or more of these four measures.

9.9.9.1 USING STANDARDIZED RESIDUALS TO FIND OUTLIERS

Kiara said that standardized residuals are *z*-scores for the residual values. Leslie reminded herself that the residuals are the distances between the observed and predicted values of the outcome and that *z*-scores over 1.96 or below −1.96 (often rounded to 2) are 1.96 standard deviations or more away from the mean of the measure (Section 4.7). Nancy mentioned that standardized residuals could be computed using the `rstandard()` function on the model object and then added to the data frame as a new variable. She created a new variable containing standardized residuals and named it `standardres`. Nancy thought having the predicted values would help here, so she added those to the data frame, too.

```
# add standardized residuals and predicted values to data frame
dist.ssp.diag <- dist.ssp %>%
  mutate(standardres = rstandard(model = dist.by.unins)) %>%
  mutate(predicted = predict(object = dist.by.unins))
```

Once the standardized residuals were added to the data, the counties with high standardized residuals could be examined. After adding standardized residuals to the data frame, Nancy suggested that Leslie find the counties with large standardized residuals by examining the subset of counties where the absolute value (`abs()`) of the residuals is greater than 2. Nancy showed Leslie how to use the `filter()` function and the absolute value function `abs()` to choose the observations with standard deviations above 1.96 or below −1.96. She decided to print just the information she needed to examine the counties that were outliers and used `select()` to select the relevant information: the two variables in the model, the name of the county and the state it is in, and the predicted values and standardized residuals.

```
# get a subset of counties with large standardized residuals
dist.ssp.diag %>%
  filter(abs(x = standardres) > 1.96) %>%
```

```
select(county, STATEABBREVIATION, dist_SSP, pctunins,
       predicted, standardres)
```

##	county	STATEABBREVIATION	dist_SSP	pctunins	predicted
## 1	webb county	TX	436.00	30.2	248.61252
## 2	garfield county	NE	300.00	8.8	81.28669
## 3	starr county	TX	510.00	35.1	286.92545
## 4	meade county	SD	267.67	10.7	96.14272
## 5	wyandotte county	KS	7.25	21.0	176.67806
## 6	coryell county	TX	341.10	10.2	92.23324
## 7	brazos county	TX	304.86	14.1	122.72720
## 8	harlan county	NE	266.20	10.9	97.70652
## 9	pawnee county	KS	262.00	7.9	74.24963
## 10	dewitt county	TX	388.50	14.8	128.20048
## 11	jim wells county	TX	456.00	21.0	176.67806
## 12	lampasas county	TX	326.33	16.2	139.14703
## 13	kennebec county	ME	315.54	8.5	78.94100
## 14	lincoln county	ME	302.92	11.4	101.61600
## 15	gonzales county	TX	386.50	22.6	189.18840
## 16	kiowa county	KS	271.67	8.9	82.06859
## 17	lee county	TX	339.40	14.6	126.63668
## 18	guadalupe county	TX	386.71	14.5	125.85479
## 19	waldo county	ME	343.94	11.9	105.52548
## 20	brooks county	TX	487.00	23.5	196.22547
## 21	comal county	TX	366.71	13.9	121.16341
## 22	burnet county	TX	342.00	15.8	136.01944
## 23	gaines county	TX	49.67	32.6	267.37804
## 24	falls county	TX	343.00	18.9	160.25823
## 25	duval county	TX	460.60	27.7	229.06511
## 26	caledonia county	VT	224.29	5.3	53.92032

##	standardres
## 1	2.212638
## 2	2.549455
## 3	2.656332
## 4	1.998675
## 5	-1.980297
## 6	2.900057
## 7	2.122380
## 8	1.963281
## 9	2.189146

```
## 10     3.033642
## 11     3.264751
## 12     2.182334
## 13     2.758179
## 14     2.345489
## 15     2.309108
## 16     2.210049
## 17     2.479533
## 18     3.039935
## 19     2.777821
## 20     3.405620
## 21     2.861252
## 22     2.401193
## 23    -2.580601
## 24     2.133069
## 25     2.724416
## 26     1.988839
```

Leslie found that 26 counties out of the 500 in the sample had large standardized residuals. Scrolling through the 26 counties, Leslie found that 24 of the 26 had distances to syringe programs that were farther away than predicted, with only two that were closer than predicted. A majority of the counties were in Texas (abbreviated TX), including one where the exchange was closer than predicted. It made sense that things would be farther away in Texas because it is a very large state. As Leslie noted the numerous counties from Texas, Nancy joked, "Well, they say everything is bigger in Texas!"

Texas was also one of 19 states in the United States where syringe exchange programs were not legal (https://opioid.amfar.org/). Two counties were in Nebraska (abbreviated NE) and three were in Kansas (abbreviated KS), also states with policies against syringe exchanges; however, three of the counties were in Maine (abbreviated ME), where exchanges are legal. Nancy said there were a few other measures of outlying and influential values to consider.

9.9.9.2 USING df-BETAS TO FIND INFLUENTIAL VALUES

Nancy explained that the next measure, df-beta, removes each observation from the data frame, conducts the analysis again, and compares the intercept and slope for the model with and without the observation. Observations with high df-beta values, usually with a cutoff of greater than 2, may be influencing the model. Using the same strategy as with the standardized residuals, Leslie identified counties with high df-betas. Nancy reminded her that the df-betas are different for slope and intercept, so she would have to create subsets and choose the part of the `dist.by.unins` object with the intercept and slope separately. Nancy helped her out with the coding to do this since it was a little tricky. She showed Leslie that the intercept could be accessed from the `dist.by.unins` model object by using the `[]` to make a subset of the first column from the object, and the slope could be accessed by making a subset of the second column.

```
# get dfbetas and add to data frame
# there will be one new variable per parameter
dist.ssp.diag <- dist.ssp %>%
  mutate(standardres = rstandard(model = dist.by.unins)) %>%
  mutate(dfbeta.intercept = dfbeta(model = dist.by.unins)[ , 1]) %>%
  mutate(dfbeta.slope = dfbeta(model = dist.by.unins)[ , 2])%>%
  mutate(predicted = predict(object = dist.by.unins))
# get subset of states with dfbetas > 2 for intercept and slope
dist.ssp.diag %>%
  filter(abs(x = dfbeta.intercept) > 2 | abs(x = dfbeta.slope) > 2) %>%
  select(county, STATEABBREVIATION, dist_SSP, pctunins, predicted,
         dfbeta.intercept, dfbeta.slope)
##              county STATEABBREVIATION dist_SSP pctunins predicted
## 1      webb county                TX   436.00     30.2  248.6125
## 2     starr county                TX   510.00     35.1  286.9254
## 3    hendry county                FL    84.33     29.8  245.4849
## 4  presidio county                TX   170.67     35.9  293.1806
## 5    brooks county                TX   487.00     23.5  196.2255
## 6    gaines county                TX    49.67     32.6  267.3780
## 7     duval county                TX   460.60     27.7  229.0651
##   dfbeta.intercept dfbeta.slope
## 1        -3.044345    0.2815289
## 2        -4.815209    0.4335469
## 3         2.549641   -0.2364609
## 4         2.754456   -0.2471943
## 5        -2.700398    0.2699724
## 6         4.099327   -0.3735266
## 7        -3.151451    0.2975064
```

Leslie reviewed the `dfbeta.intercept` variable, which showed the high df-betas for the intercept. She found that the df-betas for the intercept showed seven counties, six of them in Texas and one in Florida. She also reviewed the column for `dfbeta.slope`. None of the df-betas for the slope were greater than 2 or less than –2.

9.9.9.3 USING COOK'S DISTANCE TO FIND INFLUENTIAL VALUES

Leslie asked Nancy about the next measure of influence, Cook's distance. Nancy said it is often shortened to Cook's D and is computed in a very similar way to the df-beta. That is, each observation is removed and the model is re-estimated without it. Cook's D then combines the differences between the models with and without an observation for all the parameters together instead of one at a time like the df-betas. Nancy explained that cutoff for a high Cook's D value is usually $4/n$. Leslie tried writing the code for computing and examining the Cook's D values.

FIGURE 9.21 Miles to nearest syringe program based on percentage uninsured and metro status for 500 counties

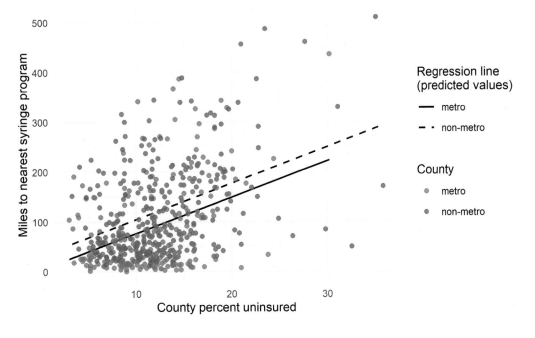

Source: https://opioid.amfar.org.

9.10.1.2 USING THE MULTIPLE REGRESSION MODEL

Leslie was a little confused, so Kiara showed her the regression model:

- distance to syringe program = 3.42 + 7.3 × percent uninsured + 28.05 × non-metro

Then she substituted in values for an example county with 10% uninsured in a *nonmetro* area:

- distance to syringe program = 3.42 + 7.3 × 10 + 28.05 × 1
- distance to syringe program = 104.48

She also substituted in the values for an example county with 10% uninsured in a *metro* area:

- distance to syringe program = 3.42 + 7.3 × 10 + 28.05 × 0
- distance to syringe program = 76.43

Kiara explained that a person in a county with 10% uninsured in a metro area would have to travel 28.05 fewer miles to a syringe program given the coefficient for `metro` in the model. Leslie looked at Figure 9.21 and noticed that the two lines looked about 28 miles apart, which was consistent with the interpretation of the `metro` coefficient. Kiara wanted to build the model a little more before they finished up. Since syringe exchanges are arguably important for HIV prevention, Kiara thought they should also add HIV prevalence to the model.

9.10.2 ADDING MORE VARIABLES TO THE MODEL

Before they added variables to the model, Kiara wanted to check the distributions for all the continuous variables and transform them if they were not normally distributed. She thought normalizing any non-normal variables could help to meet more of the model assumptions. She suggested they review Section 8.9 before beginning. Everyone took a few minutes to read through that section, and then they got started.

9.10.2.1 CHECKING THE DISTRIBUTION OF THE CONTINUOUS VARIABLES

The model would include three continuous variables, dist_SSP, pctunins, and HIVprevalence. Earlier in the day, they had checked HIVprevalence and found that it was right-skewed (Figure 9.1), so Kiara wrote the code to check the other two.

```
# check normality of distance variable (Figure 9.22)
dist.ssp %>%
  ggplot(aes(x = dist_SSP)) +
  geom_histogram(fill = "#7463AC", color = "white") +
  theme_minimal() +
  labs(x = "Miles to syringe program",
       y = "Number of counties")
```

FIGURE 9.22 Distribution of distance to syringe program in 500 counties

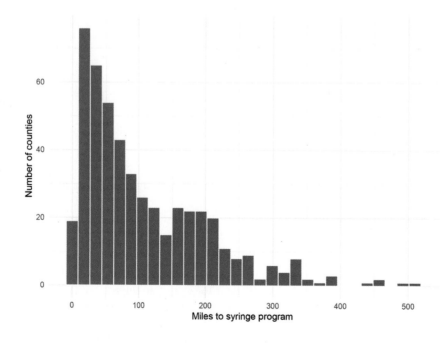

Source: https://opioid.amfar.org.

Figure 9.22 does not look normally distributed. The distribution is skewed to the right. Kiara checked the distribution of percentage uninsured.

```
# check normality of uninsured variable (Figure 9.23)
dist.ssp %>%
  ggplot(aes(x = pctunins)) +
  geom_histogram(fill = "#7463AC", color = "white") +
  theme_minimal() +
  labs(x = "Percent uninsured",
       y = "Number of counties")
```

Figure 9.23 looked close to normal, with a few counties that had high percentages of uninsured residents making the tail on the right-hand side of the distribution longer than it would be in a perfectly normal distribution.

FIGURE 9.23 Distribution of percentage uninsured in 500 counties

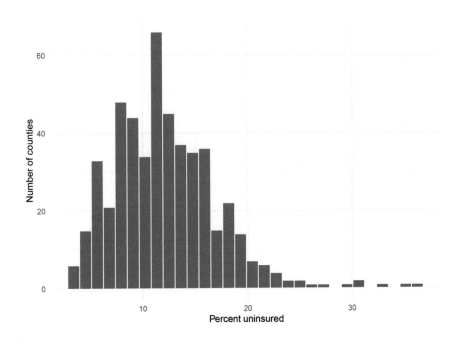

Source: https://opioid.amfar.org.

Leslie wanted to double-check Kiara's histograms with some Q-Q plots to see how far these two variables were from being normally distributed (Figures 9.24 and 9.25).

```
# Q-Q plot of distance variable to check normality (Figure 9.24)
dist.ssp %>%
  ggplot(aes(sample = dist_SSP)) +
```

```
  stat_qq(aes(color = "County"), alpha = .8) +
  geom_abline(aes(intercept = mean(x = dist_SSP), slope = sd(x = dist_SSP),
                  linetype = "Normally distributed"),
                  color = "gray60", size = 1) +
  theme_minimal() +
  labs(x = "Theoretical normal distribution",
       y = "Observed miles to syringe program") +
  scale_color_manual(values = "#7463AC", name = "") +
  scale_linetype_manual(values = 1, name = "")
```

FIGURE 9.24 Distribution of distance to nearest syringe program in 500 counties

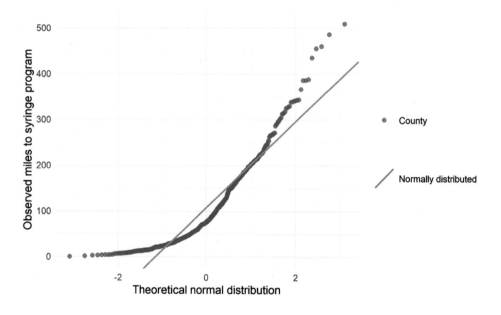

Source: https://opioid.amfar.org.

```
# Q-Q plot of uninsured variable to check normality (Figure 9.25)
dist.ssp %>%
  ggplot(aes(sample = pctunins)) +
  stat_qq(aes(color = "County"), alpha = .8) +
  geom_abline(aes(intercept = mean(x = pctunins),
                  slope = sd(x = pctunins), linetype = "Normally distributed"),
                  size = 1, color = "gray60") +
  theme_minimal() +
  labs(x = "Theoretical normal distribution",
```

```
        y = "Observed percent uninsured") +
  scale_color_manual(values = "#7463AC", name = "") +
  scale_linetype_manual(values = 1, name = "")
```

The Q-Q plots showed some deviation from normality, but they were not nearly as non-normal as the plot of water access from the previous meeting (Figure 8.17). Overall, the plots showed `pctunins` to be relatively normally distributed (Figure 9.25), while `dist_SSP` and `HIVprevalence` were right-skewed (Figures 9.24 and 9.1).

FIGURE 9.25 Distribution of percentage uninsured in 500 counties

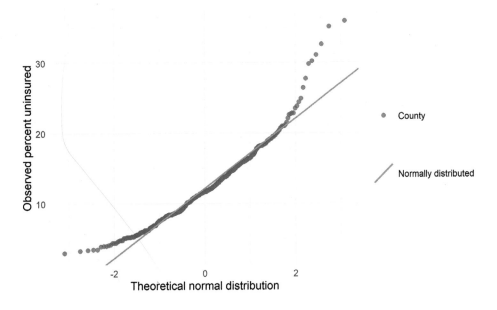

Source: https://opioid.amfar.org.

9.10.2.2 IDENTIFYING A TRANSFORMATION FOR THE DISTANCE AND HIV PREVALENCE VARIABLES

Both of the non-normal variables were right-skewed, so Kiara looked online to remind herself which transformations work best to make right-skewed data more normal. She found that square root, cube root, reciprocal, and log transformations are all recommended for right-skewed data (Field, 2013). Leslie remembered some of the transformation process from Section 8.9 and wanted to give the coding a try. Nancy slid the laptop over to her and Leslie wrote some code to plot the transformations of `dist_SSP` and `HIVprevalence` (Figure 9.26).

```
# histograms of square root of dist_SSP (Figure 9.26)
# cube root
cube.root.dist <- dist.ssp %>%
```

```
  ggplot(aes(x = (dist_SSP)^(1/3))) +
  geom_histogram(fill = "#7463AC", col = "white") +
  labs(x = "Cube root of distance", y = "Number of counties") +
  theme_minimal()
# square root
sq.root.dist <- dist.ssp %>%
  ggplot(aes(x = sqrt(x = dist_SSP))) +
  geom_histogram(fill = "#7463AC", col = "white") +
  labs(x = "Square root of distance", y = "")+
  theme_minimal()
# inverse
inverse.dist <- dist.ssp %>%
  ggplot(aes(x = 1/dist_SSP)) +
  geom_histogram(fill = "#7463AC", col = "white") +
  labs(x = "Inverse of distance", y = "Number of counties")+
  theme_minimal()
# log
log.dist <- dist.ssp %>%
  ggplot(aes(x = log(x = dist_SSP))) +
  geom_histogram(fill = "#7463AC", col = "white") +
  labs(x = "Log of distance", y = "")+
  theme_minimal()

# view options for transformation
gridExtra::grid.arrange(cube.root.dist, sq.root.dist,
                        inverse.dist, log.dist)
```

Leslie thought the cube root looked the closest to normally distributed of all the transformation options (Figure 9.26). She reused her code to check which transformation worked best for HIVprevalence (Figure 9.27).

```
# histograms of transformed HIVprevalence (Figure 9.27)
# cube root
cube.root.hiv <- dist.ssp %>%
  ggplot(aes(x = (HIVprevalence)^(1/3))) +
  geom_histogram(fill = "#7463AC", col = "white") +
  labs(x = "Cube root of HIV prevalence", y = "Number of counties")+
  theme_minimal()
# square root
sq.root.hiv <- dist.ssp %>%
  ggplot(aes(x = sqrt(x = HIVprevalence))) +
```

```
  geom_histogram(fill = "#7463AC", col = "white") +
  labs(x = "Square root of HIV prevalence", y = "")+
  theme_minimal()
# inverse
inverse.hiv <- dist.ssp %>%
  ggplot(aes(x = 1/HIVprevalence)) +
  geom_histogram(fill = "#7463AC", col = "white") +
  labs(x = "Inverse of HIV prevalence", y = "Number of counties")+
  theme_minimal()
# log
log.hiv <- dist.ssp %>%
  ggplot(aes(x = log(x = HIVprevalence))) +
  geom_histogram(fill = "#7463AC", col = "white") +
  labs(x = "Log of HIV prevalence", y = "") +
  theme_minimal()

# view options for transformation
gridExtra::grid.arrange(cube.root.hiv, sq.root.hiv,
                        inverse.hiv, log.hiv)
```

FIGURE 9.26 Distribution of transformed distance to syringe program in 2018 for 500 counties

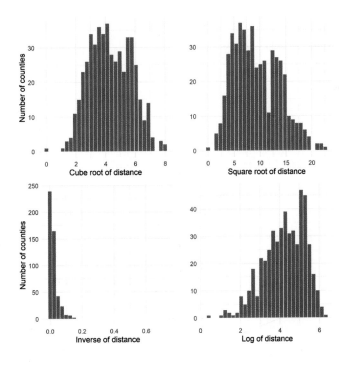

FIGURE 9.27 Distribution of transformed HIV prevalence for 500 counties

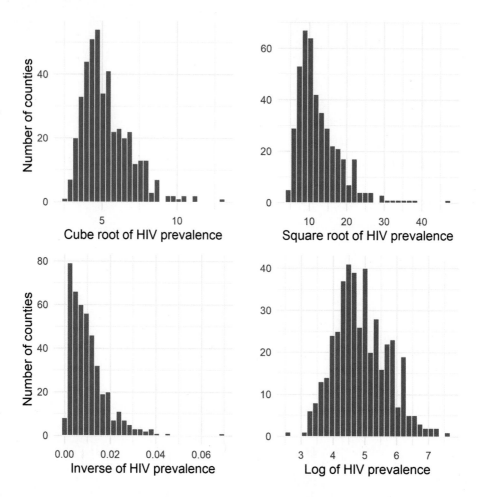

Source: https://opioid.amfar.org.

The log of HIV prevalence looked the most normally distributed of the options. Leslie suggested they use the cube root of `dist_SSP` for the outcome and the log of `HIVprevalence` as a predictor. Kiara thought this sounded good, although the interpretation of the results would be tricky. Nancy added the transformations directly into the `lm()` function code for the larger model.

```
# linear regression of distance by percent uninsured, HIV prevalence,
# metro status
dist.full.model <- lm(formula = (dist_SSP)^(1/3) ~ pctunins +
                   log(x = HIVprevalence) + metro,
                   data = dist.ssp,
                   na.action = na.exclude)
```

```
summary(object = dist.full.model)

##
## Call:
## lm(formula = (dist_SSP)^(1/3) ~ pctunins + log(x = HIVprevalence) +
##     metro, data = dist.ssp, na.action = na.exclude)
##
## Residuals:
##     Min      1Q  Median      3Q     Max
## -3.2624 -0.8959 -0.0745  0.8032  3.1967
##
## Coefficients:
##                         Estimate Std. Error t value Pr(>|t|)
## (Intercept)              3.03570    0.38448   7.896 2.48e-14 ***
## pctunins                 0.11269    0.01220   9.237  < 2e-16 ***
## log(x = HIVprevalence)  -0.06529    0.07729  -0.845 0.398691
## metronon-metro           0.48808    0.12763   3.824 0.000151 ***
## ---
## Signif. codes:  0 '***' 0.001 '**' 0.01 '*' 0.05 '.' 0.1 ' ' 1
##
## Residual standard error: 1.214 on 426 degrees of freedom
##   (70 observations deleted due to missingness)
## Multiple R-squared:  0.2372, Adjusted R-squared:  0.2318
## F-statistic: 44.16 on 3 and 426 DF,  p-value: < 2.2e-16
```

Leslie reported that the model was statistically significant, with an F-statistic of $F(3, 426) = 44.16$ and a p-value of $< .001$. The $R^2_{adj} = .2318$ indicated that 23.18% of the variation in distance to syringe program is accounted for by this model that has HIV prevalence, percentage uninsured, and metro status in it. This is higher than the R^2_{adj} from the previous two models. Finally, Leslie saw that the coefficient for pctunins was .1127, so for every additional 1% uninsured in a county, the *cube root* of the distance to a syringe program is expected to change by .1127. The positive and significant coefficient of .48808 for metronon-metro in the output suggests that nonmetro areas are farther from syringe programs. The log of HIV prevalence was not statistically significantly associated with distance to syringe program.

Leslie noticed that the denominator degrees of freedom value was now 426, which was a lot lower than the 498 from the simple linear regression model they first estimated. Nancy reminded her that HIV prevalence had some missing values, so these observations would have been dropped from the model. Leslie nodded her head yes. There were so many things to think about in building a regression model!

9.10.3 NO MULTICOLLINEARITY ASSUMPTION FOR MULTIPLE REGRESSION

Since they were nearly finished with linear regression modeling, Kiara stopped Leslie for a short detour to tell her about one additional assumption to be checked when there are multiple predictor variables in a model. There are multiple predictors in `dist.full.model`, so they should check this additional assumption.

Kiara explained that, in addition to the assumptions checked with the simple linear regression model, when a model has more than one predictor, there is an assumption of no perfect multicollinearity. The assumption list for multiple linear regression includes the following:

- Observations are independent.
- The outcome is continuous.
- The relationship between the outcome and each continuous predictor is linear (linearity).
- The variance is constant with the points distributed equally around the line (homoscedasticity).
- The residuals are independent.
- The residuals are normally distributed.
- There is no perfect multicollinearity.

Multicollinearity occurs when predictors are linearly related, or strongly correlated, to each other. When two or more variables are linearly related to one another, the standard errors for their coefficients will be large and statistical significance will be impacted. This can be a problem for model estimation, so variables that are linearly related to each other should not be in a model together. Leslie wondered why they didn't check this assumption for the model with metro and uninsured in it, since that model also had multiple predictors. Kiara said that since metro was a binary variable, it was unlikely there was a problem with it being linearly related to the percent uninsured.

9.10.3.1 USING CORRELATION TO CHECK MULTICOLLINEARITY

Kiara explained that there are several ways to check for multicollinearity. The first is to examine correlations between variables in a model before estimating the model. In this case, `pctunins` and the transformed `log(x = HIVprevalence)` are continuous. The correlation between these can be computed using the `cor()` function. The `cor()` function works with complete data, so Kiara removed the `NA` from the transformed `HIVprevalence` variable before computing the correlation.

```
# correlations among continuous variables in the full model
dist.ssp %>%
  mutate(log.HIVprev = log(x = HIVprevalence)) %>%
  drop_na(log.HIVprev) %>%
  summarize(cor.hiv.unins = cor(x = log.HIVprev, y = pctunins))
##   cor.hiv.unins
## 1     0.2444709
```

The result was a weak correlation of .24 between percent uninsured and the transformed value of `HIVprevalence`. If the absolute value of the correlation coefficient is .7 or higher, this would indicate a relatively strong correlation with a large amount of shared variance between the two variables and therefore a problem with multicollinearity. The correlation is weak, so there is no problem with multicollinearity. The assumption is met.

9.10.3.2 USING VARIANCE INFLATION FACTORS TO CHECK MULTICOLLINEARITY

Correlation coefficients can miss more complex problems with multicollinearity where, for example, one variable is linearly related to a combination of other variables. The way to identify these more complex problems with multicollinearity is through the use of *variance inflation factor* (VIF) statistics. The VIF statistics are calculated by running a separate regression model for each of the predictors where the predictor is the outcome and everything else stays in the model as a predictor. With this model, for example, the VIF for the `pctunins` variable would be computed by running this model:

```
pctunins = log(x = HIVprevalence) + metro
```

The R^2 from this linear regression model would be used to determine the VIF by substituting it into Equation (9.16).

$$VIF_{pctunins} = \frac{1}{1-R^2} \tag{9.16}$$

The result will be 1 if there is no shared variance at all. If there is any shared variance, the VIF will be greater than 1. If the VIF is large, this indicates that `pctunins` shares a lot of variance with the `metro` and `log(x = HIVprevalence)` variables. A VIF of 2.5, for example, would indicate that the R^2 was .60 and so 60% of the variation in `pctunins` was explained by `metro` and `log(x = HIVprevalence)`. Kiara noted that an R^2 of .60 translated to an r of about .77 (the square root of .60 is .77), which is a little higher than the cutoff of .7 often used when correlation coefficients are calculated for checking multicollinearity. While there is no consistent cutoff recommended for the size of a VIF that indicates too much multicollinearity, 2.5 is often used.

Kiara showed Leslie the `vif()` function to check VIF values for the model above.

```
# VIF for model with poverty
car::vif(mod = dist.full.model)
##            pctunins       log(x = HIVprevalence)        metro
##            1.165165                 1.207491          1.186400
```

The VIF values are small, especially given that the lower limit of the VIF is 1. This confirmed no problem with multicollinearity with this model. The model meets the assumption of no perfect multicollinearity. Kiara explained to Leslie that the rest of the assumption checking and diagnostics are conducted and interpreted in the same way as they were for the simple linear regression model.

Leslie was interested in checking some of the other assumptions since they now had transformed variables in the model. She knew they had already discussed independent observations and the outcome was still continuous. After checking the multicollinearity assumption, the assumptions left to check were linearity, homoscedasticity, independence of residuals, and normality of residuals. Leslie started with linearity.

9.10.4 CHECKING LINEARITY FOR MULTIPLE REGRESSION

Linearity is checked for each of the continuous predictors in a *multiple regression*. Leslie borrowed the code from Figure 9.17 and modified it to check each of the predictors for a linear relationship with the outcome, which is now the cube root of dist_SSP.

```
# log of HIV prevalence and cube root of distance to needle exchange
# (Figure 9.28)
dist.ssp %>%
  ggplot(aes(x = log(x = HIVprevalence), y = (dist_SSP)^(1/3))) +
  geom_point(aes(size = "County"), color = "#7463AC", alpha = .6) +
  geom_smooth(aes(color = "Linear fit line"), method = "lm", se = FALSE) +
  geom_smooth(aes(color = "Loess curve"), se = FALSE) +
  theme_minimal() +
  labs(y = "Cube root of miles to syringe program",
       x = "Log of HIV prevalence") +
  scale_color_manual(values = c("gray60", "deeppink"), name = "") +
  scale_size_manual(values = 2, name = "")
```

The log of HIV prevalence is not linearly related to the cube root of distance (Figure 9.28) since the Loess curve is far from the linear fit line, especially on the right side of the graph.

```
# percent uninsured and cube root of distance to needle exchange (Figure 9.29)
dist.ssp %>%
  ggplot(aes(x = pctunins, y = (dist_SSP)^(1/3))) +
  geom_point(aes(size = "County"), color = "#7463AC", alpha = .6) +
  geom_smooth(aes(color = "Linear fit line"), method = "lm", se = FALSE) +
  geom_smooth(aes(color = "Loess curve"), se = FALSE) +
  theme_minimal() +
  labs(y = "Cube root of miles to syringe program",
       x = "Percent uninsured") +
  scale_color_manual(values = c("gray60", "deeppink"), name = "") +
  scale_size_manual(values = 2, name = "")
```

Figure 9.29 was closer to linear. There was a relatively linear and positive relationship with some deviation from linearity at the lowest and highest values of percentage uninsured. Given the nonlinearity of Figure 9.28 and the borderline linearity of Figure 9.29, Leslie concluded that this assumption was not met.

FIGURE 9.28 Relationship between the log of HIV prevalence and transformed distance to nearest syringe program in 500 counties

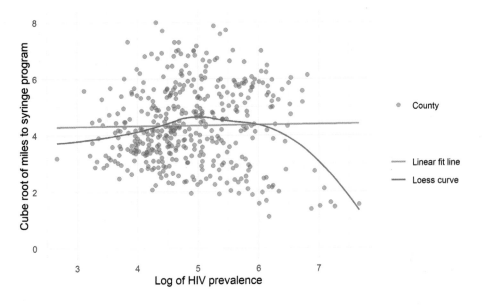

FIGURE 9.29 Relationship between percentage uninsured and transformed distance to nearest syringe program in 500 counties

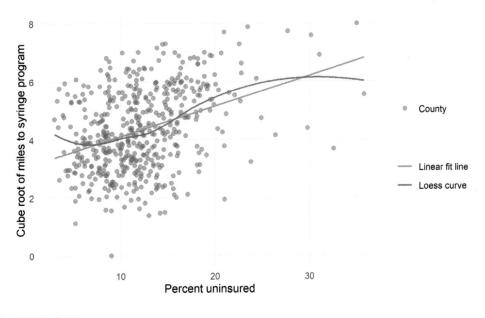

9.10.5 CHECKING THE HOMOSCEDASTICITY ASSUMPTION FOR MULTIPLE REGRESSION

Leslie remembered that the Breusch-Pagan test could be used to test the null hypothesis that the variance is constant, and wrote the code.

```
# testing for equal variance
const.var.test.full <- lmtest::bptest(formula = dist.full.model)
const.var.test.full
##
##  studentized Breusch-Pagan test
##
## data:  dist.full.model
## BP = 36.288, df = 3, p-value = 6.51e-08
```

The Breusch-Pagan test statistic has a tiny p-value associated with it (BP = 36.29; $p < .001$), indicating that the null hypothesis would be rejected. Leslie concluded that the assumption of constant variance was not met.

9.10.6 TESTING THE INDEPENDENCE OF RESIDUALS ASSUMPTION

Leslie used the Durbin-Watson test for the null hypothesis that the residuals are independent.

```
# test independence of residuals
lmtest::dwtest(formula = dist.full.model)
##
##  Durbin-Watson test
##
## data:  dist.full.model
## DW = 1.9631, p-value = 0.3494
## alternative hypothesis: true autocorrelation is greater than 0
```

The D-W statistic was near 2 and the p-value was high, so Leslie concluded that the null hypothesis was retained. Since the null hypothesis was that the residuals are independent, she found that this assumption was met.

9.10.7 TESTING THE NORMALITY OF RESIDUALS ASSUMPTION

The last assumption to check is normality of residuals.

```
# check residual plot of percent uninsured and distance to syringe program
# (Figure 9.30)
data.frame(dist.full.model$residuals) %>%
  ggplot(aes(x = dist.full.model.residuals)) +
```

```
geom_histogram(fill = "#7463AC", col = "white") +
theme_minimal() +
labs(x = "Residual (difference between observed and predicted values)",
     y = "Number of counties")
```

FIGURE 9.30 Distribution of residuals for model explaining distance to syringe program for 500 counties

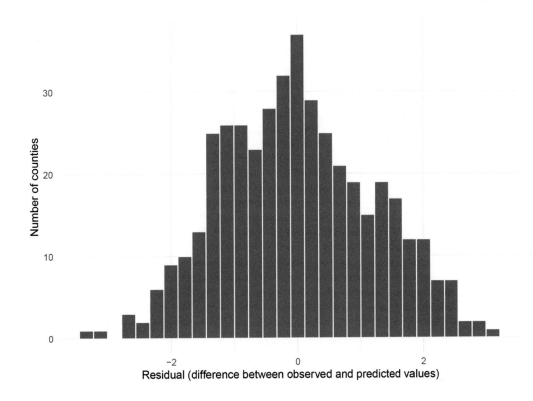

Source: https://opioid.amfar.org.

```
# check residual plot of percent uninsured and distance to syringe program
# (Figure 9.31)
data.frame(dist.full.model$residuals) %>%
  ggplot(aes(sample = dist.full.model.residuals)) +
  geom_abline(aes(intercept = mean(x = dist.full.model.residuals),
                  slope = sd(x = dist.full.model.residuals),
                  linetype = "Normally distributed"),
                  color = "gray60", size = 1) +
  stat_qq(aes(size = "County"), color = "#7463AC", alpha = .6) +
  theme_minimal() +
```

```
labs(x = "Theoretical normal distribution",
     y = "Observed residuals") +
  scale_size_manual(values = 1, name = "") +
  scale_linetype_manual(values = 1, name = "")
```

Figures 9.30 and 9.31 suggest the distribution of residuals is pretty close to normal. The assumption appears to be met.

After adding the `HIVprevalence` variable and transforming the outcome and the `HIVprevalence` variable, Leslie found several reasons why the larger model was not great. First, the `HIVprevalence` variable was not statistically significant. Second, the model failed the assumptions of linearity and homoscedasticity. There were some good changes, however. The model fit statistic (R^2_{adj}) was higher than for the previous models, and the normality of residuals assumption was met.

9.10.8 USING THE PARTIAL-*F* TEST TO CHOOSE A MODEL

Now that the R-Team had estimated three models (`dist.by.unins`, `dist.by.unins.metro`, and `dist.full.model`), Leslie was not sure which one she would choose to report if she were writing a paper or a policy brief about syringe programs. The HIV variable was not a significant predictor in the full model, and all three models failed one or more of the assumptions.

Kiara explained that there were a few things to think about in selecting a model before thinking about how it performed. First, the model should address the research question of interest. Second,

---

FIGURE 9.31 Distribution of residuals for model explaining distance to syringe program for 500 counties

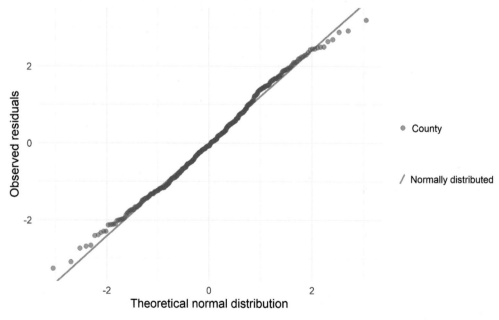

Source: https://opioid.amfar.org.

---

the model should include variables—if any—that have been demonstrated important in the past to help explain the outcome. For example, a statistical model explaining lung cancer should include smoking status since smoking has been demonstrated by many studies to have a strong relationship to lung cancer.

After answering the research question and including available variables that were demonstrably important in the past, choosing a model can still be complicated. One tool for choosing between two linear regression models is a statistical test called the Partial-F test. The ***Partial-F test*** compares the fit of two nested models to determine if the additional variables in the larger model improve the model fit enough to warrant keeping the variables and interpreting the more complex model. The Partial-F test can be conducted by hand using the Partial-F equation, shown in Equations (9.17) and (9.18):

$$F_{partial} = \frac{\dfrac{R^2_{full} - R^2_{reduced}}{q}}{\dfrac{1 - R^2_{full}}{n - p}} \tag{9.17}$$

where

- R^2_{full} is the R^2 for the larger model
- $R^2_{reduced}$ is the R^2 for the smaller nested model
- n is the sample size
- q is the difference in the number of parameters for the two models
- p is the number of parameters in the larger model

The $F_{partial}$ statistic has q and $n - p$ degrees of freedom. To compare the `dist.by.unins` model with the `dist.by.unins.metro` model, substitute their values into the equation and compute as in Equation (9.18).

```
## 
## Call:
## lm(formula = dist_SSP ~ pctunins, data = dist.ssp, na.action =
## na.exclude)
## 
## Residuals:
##     Min      1Q  Median      3Q     Max
## -217.71  -60.86  -21.61   47.73  290.77
## 
## Coefficients:
##              Estimate Std. Error t value Pr(>|t|)
## (Intercept)   12.4798    10.1757   1.226    0.221
## pctunins       7.8190     0.7734  10.110   <2e-16 ***
## ---
## Signif. codes:  0 '***' 0.001 '**' 0.01 '*' 0.05 '.' 0.1 ' ' 1
```

```
##
## Residual standard error: 85.91 on 498 degrees of freedom
## Multiple R-squared:  0.1703, Adjusted R-squared:  0.1686
## F-statistic: 102.2 on 1 and 498 DF,  p-value: < 2.2e-16
##
## Call:
## lm(formula = dist_SSP ~ pctunins + metro, data = dist.ssp)
##
## Residuals:
##     Min      1Q  Median      3Q     Max
## -219.80  -60.07  -18.76   48.33  283.96
##
## Coefficients:
##                 Estimate Std. Error t value Pr(>|t|)
## (Intercept)       3.4240    10.3621   0.330 0.741212
## pctunins          7.3005     0.7775   9.389  < 2e-16 ***
## metronon-metro   28.0525     7.7615   3.614 0.000332 ***
## ---
## Signif. codes:  0 '***' 0.001 '**' 0.01 '*' 0.05 '.' 0.1 ' ' 1
##
## Residual standard error: 84.89 on 497 degrees of freedom
## Multiple R-squared:  0.1915, Adjusted R-squared:  0.1883
## F-statistic: 58.88 on 2 and 497 DF,  p-value: < 2.2e-16
```

$$F_{partial} = \frac{\dfrac{.19 - .17}{1}}{\dfrac{1 - .19}{500 - 3}} = 12.29 \tag{9.18}$$

Nancy said there was a way to do this using R code instead of by hand using the `anova()` function. Enter the name of the smaller model first and then the larger model, and the function will compare the two models using a Partial-*F* test. Leslie decided that the largest model with the transformed variables did not seem worth checking since it did not seem better than the previous models and it had the transformations, which made it difficult to interpret. Instead, she compared the simple linear model `dist.by.unins` to the model that added the `metro` variable, `dist.by.unins.metro`.

```
# partial F test for dist.by.unins and dist.by.unins.metro
anova(object = dist.by.unins, dist.by.unins.metro)
## Analysis of Variance Table
##
## Model 1: dist_SSP ~ pctunins
## Model 2: dist_SSP ~ pctunins + metro
```

```
##     Res.Df      RSS Df Sum of Sq       F     Pr(>F)
## 1     498 3675855
## 2     497 3581712  1       94143 13.063 0.0003318 ***
## ---
## Signif. codes:  0 '***' 0.001 '**' 0.01 '*' 0.05 '.' 0.1 ' ' 1
```

The Partial-F was 13.06 and the p-value was .0003. Leslie saw that the number was a little different but fairly close, so it was likely the rounding that was the culprit. She added a couple more decimal places to the R^2 values to her calculation in Equation (9.18) and found an answer of 13.03 instead. Leslie thought this might be a good place to use NHST to understand this result. Kiara helped her walk through the steps.

9.10.8.1 NHST STEP 1: WRITE THE NULL AND ALTERNATE HYPOTHESES

H0: The larger model is no better than the smaller model at explaining the outcome.

HA: The larger model is better than the smaller model at explaining the outcome.

9.10.8.2 NHST STEP 2: COMPUTE THE TEST STATISTIC

The Partial-F is 13.06 with 1 and 497 degrees of freedom.

9.10.8.3 NHST STEP 3: CALCULATE THE PROBABILITY THAT YOUR TEST STATISTIC IS AT LEAST AS BIG AS IT IS IF THERE IS NO RELATIONSHIP (I.E., THE NULL IS TRUE)

The p-value is very small (p = .0003), so the probability is tiny that the test statistic would be this big or bigger if the null hypothesis were true.

9.10.8.4 NHST STEPS 4 AND 5: INTERPRET THE PROBABILITY AND WRITE A CONCLUSION

The null hypothesis is rejected. Leslie retained the alternate hypothesis that the larger model is better than the smaller model at explaining the outcome. This suggests that the model with percent uninsured and metro status was a better model for reporting than the simple linear model.

Leslie was about to write the final interpretation of the model when Kiara reminded her that she also needed to check the assumptions and diagnostics. Leslie knew this was correct, but she was tired of working. She promised to finalize the model before their next meeting. She wrote the interpretation of the model so far, pending assumption checking and diagnostics. To write an accurate interpretation, Leslie printed the model output again.

```
##
## Call:
## lm(formula = dist_SSP ~ pctunins + metro, data = dist.ssp)
##
```

```
## Residuals:
##     Min      1Q  Median      3Q     Max
## -219.80  -60.07  -18.76   48.33  283.96
##
## Coefficients:
##                 Estimate Std. Error t value Pr(>|t|)
## (Intercept)       3.4240    10.3621   0.330 0.741212
## pctunins          7.3005     0.7775   9.389  < 2e-16 ***
## metronon-metro   28.0525     7.7615   3.614 0.000332 ***
## ---
## Signif. codes:  0 '***' 0.001 '**' 0.01 '*' 0.05 '.' 0.1 ' ' 1
##
## Residual standard error: 84.89 on 497 degrees of freedom
## Multiple R-squared:  0.1915, Adjusted R-squared:  0.1883
## F-statistic: 58.88 on 2 and 497 DF,  p-value: < 2.2e-16
##                      2.5 %      97.5 %
## (Intercept)     -16.934973  23.782947
## pctunins          5.772859   8.828114
## metronon-metro   12.803152  43.301754
```

A linear regression model including percent uninsured and metro status of a county to explain distance in miles to the nearest syringe program was statistically significantly better than a baseline model at explaining the outcome [$F(2, 497) = 58.88$]. The model explained 18.83% of the variation in distance to syringe programs ($R^2_{adj} = .1883$). Percent uninsured was a statistically significant predictor of distance to the nearest syringe program ($b = 7.30$; $t = 9.39$; $p < .001$). In the sample, for every additional 1% uninsured people in a county, the distance to the nearest syringe program is 7.30 miles farther. The 95% confidence interval for the coefficient suggested that a 1% increase in uninsured in a county was associated with a 5.77- to 8.83-mile increase in distance to the nearest syringe program. Metro status was also a significant predictor of distance to a syringe program ($b = 28.05$; $t = 7.76$; $p = .0003$). Nonmetro counties are 28.05 miles farther than metro counties to the nearest syringe exchange in the sample and are 12.80 to 43.30 miles farther than metro counties from syringe programs in the population. Overall, the results suggest that more rural counties and counties that are poorer are farther from this health service, potentially exacerbating existing health disparities.

Leslie felt she had learned a lot about syringe programs from the exploration with linear regression. Although she had not yet checked assumptions to finalize her chosen model, she knew that, at least in the sample, people in nonmetro areas were farther from syringe programs and people in counties with higher percentages of uninsured residents were also farther from syringe programs. Both of these findings suggested a disparity in health-related services for low-income and less urban communities. In the model with HIV prevalence, there had been no association with distance to syringe exchange, which was surprising, and Leslie was interested in exploring this relationship further given that HIV and intravenous drug use are commonly seen together. Leslie had not previously thought about disparities in preventive health services and how they might impact poorer and less urban communities, but it was now something she was interested in working to better understand and address.

Kiara and Nancy agreed with Leslie's conclusions and thought working on the assumptions for next time was a good idea. Then Kiara grabbed the TV remote, and Nancy started popping popcorn. Leslie put her feet up. It was time for the R-Team to take a break and watch *The A-Team*.

9.10.9 ACHIEVEMENT 7: CHECK YOUR UNDERSTANDING

Write out the NHST process for model significance and for the significance of one of the predictors for the model `dist.full.model`.

/// 9.11 CHAPTER SUMMARY

9.11.1 Achievements unlocked in this chapter: Recap

Congratulations! Like Leslie, you've learned and practiced the following in this chapter.

9.11.1.1 Achievement 1 recap: Using exploratory data analysis to learn about the data before developing a linear regression model

Prior to conducting a regression analysis, it is useful to examine how the two variables are related to one another using correlation analysis and a scatterplot for continuous predictors and comparing means and boxplots for categorical predictors. These exploratory data analysis tools provide some early indication of whether the relationship appears to be linear, how strong it might be, and whether it looks like a positive or negative relationship.

9.11.1.2 Achievement 2 recap: Exploring the statistical model for a line

A linear regression model is based on the equation for a line, which can be written in multiple ways.

9.11.1.3 Achievement 3 recap: Computing the slope and intercept in a simple linear regression

The slope and the intercept for the regression line are computed using the `lm()` function.

9.11.1.4 Achievement 4 recap: Slope interpretation and significance (b_1, p-value, CI)

The value of the slope indicates how much the outcome goes up or down with a one-unit increase in the predictor variable. The p-value for the slope is the result of a Wald test comparing the slope to zero using a *t*-statistic; if the p-value is below some threshold (usually .05), the slope is considered statistically significantly different from zero.

The confidence interval for the slope indicates where the slope likely lies in the population.

9.11.1.5 Achievement 5 recap: Model significance and model fit

The R^2 is interpreted as the percentage of variance in the outcome that is explained by the model. The R^2_{adj} penalizes the R^2 for each variable in the model, resulting in a lower value that is considered a more accurate reflection of how well the model explains the variability in the outcome.

Overall model significance is determined using the *F*-statistic, which is a ratio of explained variance to unexplained variance. When the *F*-statistic is large, that indicates there is more explained variance relative to unexplained, and the model is likely reflecting a true relationship.

9.11.1.6 Achievement 6 recap: Checking assumptions and conducting diagnostics

Statistical tests rely on underlying assumptions about the characteristics of the data. When these assumptions are not met, the results may not reflect the true relationships among the variables. The variable type can be checked by examining the outcome variable to be sure it is continuous. A scatterplot with a Loess curve is useful for examining linearity. A scatterplot and a Breusch-Pagan test can aid in identifying problems with constant error variance. Residual independence is tested using the Durbin-Watson statistic, and residual normality can be examined with the histogram and Q-Q plot. Outliers and influential values can be identified using standardized residuals, df-betas, Cook's *D*, and leverage values. Observations that are identified as problematic by more than one measure should be examined and, if the data appear unreliable for the observation, the observation can be fixed or dropped before re-estimating and testing the model.

9.11.1.7 Achievement 7 recap: Adding variables to the model and using transformation

Continuous and categorical variables can be added to a regression model. Categorical variables added to a model will influence the y-intercept, while continuous variables will influence the slope. If multiple variables are in the model, there is an additional assumption of no perfect multicollinearity, which can be checked with correlation coefficients or VIF statistics.

9.11.2 Chapter exercises

The coder and hacker exercises are an opportunity to apply the skills from this chapter to a new scenario or a new data set. The coder edition evaluates the application of the concepts and functions learned in this R-Team meeting to scenarios similar to those in the meeting. The hacker edition evaluates the use of the concepts and functions from this R-Team meeting in new scenarios, often going a step beyond what was explicitly explained.

The coder edition might be best for those who found some or all of the Check Your Understanding activities to be challenging or if they needed review before picking the correct responses to the multiple-choice questions. The hacker edition might be best if the Check Your Understanding activities were not too challenging and the multiple-choice questions were a breeze.

The multiple-choice questions and materials for the exercises are online at **edge.sagepub.com/harris1e**.

Q1: Which of the following is not an assumption for simple linear regression?
   a. Independence of observations
   b. No perfect multicollinearity
   c. Linear relationship
   d. Constant variance
   e. Normally distributed residuals

Q2: Continuous predictors influence the _____ of the regression line, while categorical predictors influence the _____.
   a. slope, intercept
   b. intercept, slope
   c. R^2, p-value
   d. p-value, R^2

Q3: Which of the following is true about the adjusted R^2?
   a. It is usually larger than the R^2.
   b. It is only used when there is just one predictor.
   c. It is usually smaller than the R^2.
   d. It is used to determine whether residuals are normally distributed.

Q4: Significance for the coefficients (b) is determined by
   a. an F-test.
   b. an R^2 test.
   c. a correlation coefficient.
   d. a t-test.

Q5: The R^2 is the squared correlation of which two values?
   a. y and the predicted values of y
   b. y and each continuous x
   c. b and t
   d. b and se

9.11.2.1 Chapter exercises: Coder edition

Depending on your score on the knowledge check, choose either the coder or hacker edition of the chapter exercises. Use the data from this chapter and the appropriate tests to examine number of opioid prescriptions and distance to syringe program.

1) Import the cleaned data set **dist_ssp_amfar_ch9.csv** from **edge.sagepub.com/harris1e**.

2) Create a model with number of opioid prescriptions per 100 people as the predictor variable and the distance to syringe program variable transformed using a cube root transformation as the outcome variable (Achievements 3 and 7).

3) Check the model assumptions (Achievement 6).

4) Interpret the model results (Achievements 4 and 5).

5) Add the metro variable to the model (Achievement 7).

6) Interpret the model results (Achievements 3 and 7).

7) Compare the larger and smaller models using the Partial-F test (Achievement 7).

8) Interpret and report the results of the Partial-F test (Achievement 7).

9.11.2.2 Chapter exercises: Hacker edition

Complete #1 of the coder edition; then complete the following:

2) Check the distribution of the opioid prescription variable.

3) Try at least three transformations to transfer the opioid prescription variable to a more normally distributed variable; choose the transformation that works the best to normalize the variable (Achievement 7).

4) Create a model with percent uninsured as the predictor variable and the distance to syringe program variable transformed using a cube root transformation as the outcome variable (Achievements 3 and 7).

5) Check the model assumptions (Achievement 6).

6) Interpret the model results (Achievements 4 and 7).

7) Add the transformed opioid prescription variable and the metro variable to the model (Achievement 7).

8) Interpret the model results (Achievement 7).

9) Compare the larger and smaller models using the Partial-F test (Achievement 7).

10) Interpret and report the results of the Partial-F test (Achievement 7).

9.11.2.3 Instructor note

Solutions to exercises can be found on the website for this book, along with ideas for gamification for those who want to take it further.

Visit **edge.sagepub.com/harris1e** to download the datasets, complete the chapter exercises, and watch R tutorial videos.

BINARY LOGISTIC REGRESSION

The R-Team and the Perplexing Libraries Problem

"It's pretty amazing," Nancy said. "So far, the R-Team has learned about descriptive and visual data analysis, probability distributions, several tests for comparing means and percentages, and linear regression for predicting or explaining a continuous outcome."

Leslie put her feet up on the table in the library conference room. "Feels good," she said.

Kiara explained, "And the form of the linear regression model with the outcome variable on the left-hand side of the equation and the predictors or independent variables on the right-hand side is a common format. Many of the concepts from linear regression will transfer to other models that predict or explain other types of outcome variables."

"Like a binary variable," Nancy interjected.

"Isn't that one of the more common types of outcome variables in the social sciences?" Leslie asked.

"Very good," said Kiara, smiling at her. "Binary variables record information about whether or not a patient has had a breast cancer screening, whether or not a person owns a gun, whether or not someone voted in the last election, whether or not a state has an opioid policy, and many other measures."

Nancy explained, "The regression model that is useful for predicting or explaining a binary variable is binary logistic regression. Binary logistic regression uses a form similar to linear regression, and the methods for developing and using the model are consistent with the linear regression model. Because the outcome is not continuous, the assumptions and some of the interpretations are different, though."

"How should we get started, Leslie?" asked Kiara.

Leslie grinned and answered, "I know it by heart: import and clean the data, perform exploratory data analysis, develop and interpret a logistic model, and check model assumptions."

"Nailed it," said Nancy, giving her a high five.

Kiara was looking forward to exploring one of her favorite methods and created a list of achievements to work on.

10.1 Achievements to unlock

- Achievement 1: Using exploratory data analysis before developing a logistic regression model
- Achievement 2: Understanding the binary logistic regression statistical model
- Achievement 3: Estimating a simple logistic regression model and interpreting predictor significance and interpretation
- Achievement 4: Computing and interpreting two measures of model fit
- Achievement 5: Estimating a larger logistic regression model with categorical and continuous predictors
- Achievement 6: Interpreting the results of a larger logistic regression model
- Achievement 7: Checking logistic regression assumptions and using diagnostics to identify outliers and influential values

- Achievement 8: Using the model to predict probabilities for observations that are outside the data set

- Achievement 9: Adding and interpreting interaction terms in logistic regression

- Achievement 10: Using the likelihood ratio test to compare two nested logistic regression models

10.2 The perplexing libraries problem

Kiara had recently become interested in the concept of the digital divide. She explained to the group that the digital divide started in the 1970s but the term was not widely used until the 1990s when it was adopted to describe the gap between households with Internet access and households without Internet access. When she read the Wikipedia page about the digital divide in the United States, she learned that the current definition is broader and includes both *limited access* to information and communication technologies (ICT) and *a deficit in the ability to use information* gained through access to ICTs. The article stated that people were more likely to fall into this digital divide if they were poor, a racial minority, had limited education, had a disability, or lived in an area with low population density ("Digital Divide in the United States," n.d.).

Kiara explained that the consequences of being on the disadvantaged side of the digital divide often exacerbated other problems. One example of this is related to finding employment. In 2015, a report from the Pew Research Center found that 54% of Americans went online in their most recent job search to look for information about jobs, 45% had applied online for a job, and 79% overall used some online resource in their most recent job search (Smith, 2015). She went on to explain that not only does searching for work rely on access to technology, but a large percentage of the available jobs rely on having experience with technology (Andreason et al., 2018).

Nancy mentioned that one place where Internet access is publicly available is in libraries. Almost 100% of libraries were connected to the Internet by 2004, and 98.9% of those libraries offer public access to the Internet (Jaeger, Bertot, McClure, & Langa, 2006). As of 2016, 48% of people reported using the library in the past year, and 29% of library users reported using computers, WiFi, or the Internet at the library (Horrigan, 2016). While this was promising, Nancy found that some of the characteristics associated with being on the disadvantaged side of the digital divide were also associated with a lack of library use, including lower income, being a racial or ethnic minority, fewer years of education, and living in a nonurban (presumably lower population density) area (Horrigan, 2016). She also found that the evidence was inconsistent about the association of age, sex, marital status, and socioeconomic status with library use (Sin, 2011). The most consistent research finding has been that education level influences library use (Sin, 2011).

Kiara suggested they build a logistic regression model where the outcome is library use and the predictors are the factors related to the digital divide and library use. She thought they could explore some of the characteristics identified in past research and answer the research question "Which characteristics are associated with library use?" Nancy found a data source on the Pew Research Center website from a survey about library use and demographics in 2016.

10.3 Data, codebook, and R packages for logistic regression practice

Before they examined the data, Kiara made a list of all the data, documentation, and R packages needed for learning logistic regression.

- Two options for accessing the data
  - o Download the cleaned data set **pew_libraries_2016_cleaned_ch10.csv** from **edge.sage pub.com/harris1e**
  - o Follow the instructions in Box 10.1 to import and clean **pew_libraries_2016_ch10.csv** from **edge.sagepub.com/harris1e** or download from the original Internet data source and clean
- Two options for accessing the codebook
  - o Download the **pew_libraries_2016_codebook_ch10.docx** codebook file from **edge.sage pub.com/harris1e**
  - o Use the version that comes with the raw data file from Pew Research Center (https://www .pewinternet.org/dataset/march-2016-libraries/)
- Install the following R packages if not already installed
  - o **tidyverse**, by Hadley Wickham (https://www.rdocumentation.org/packages/tidyverse/)
  - o *odds.n.ends*, by Jenine Harris (https://www.rdocumentation.org/packages/odds.n.ends/)
  - o **car**, by John Fox (https://www.rdocumentation.org/packages/car/)
  - o **lmtest**, by Achim Zeileis (https://www.rdocumentation.org/packages/lmtest/)
  - o **tableone** (Yoshida, n.d.)

10.4 Achievement 1: Using exploratory data analysis before developing a logistic regression model

Before Nancy or Kiara even said a word, Leslie knew what came first—exploratory data analysis. She started by importing the library data. Kiara took one look and realized how much recoding there was to do. She thought it might be better to just work one-on-one with Leslie for a few minutes and bring Nancy back in once they had the data recoded in a reproducible way. Kiara and Leslie worked together to recode the raw data into a clean data set (Box 10.1). They saved the cleaned data in the file **pew_ libraries_2016_cleaned_ch10.csv** and imported it to start working.

```
# import the libraries cleaned file
libraries.cleaned <- read.csv(file = "[data folder location]/data/pew_libraries_
2016_cleaned_ch10.csv")

# check the data
summary(object = libraries.cleaned)
##       age            sex            parent          disabled     uses.lib
##   Min.   :16.00   female:768   not parent:1205   no  :1340   no :809
##   1st Qu.:33.00   male  :833   parent    : 391   yes : 253   yes:792
##   Median :51.00                NA's      :   5   NA's:   8
##   Mean   :49.31
##   3rd Qu.:64.00
##   Max.   :95.00
```

```
##  NA's    :30
##     ses                     raceth                         educ
##  high   : 158   Hispanic          : 194   < HS                 :171
##  low    : 246   Non-Hispanic Black: 170   Four-year degree or more:658
##  medium :1197   Non-Hispanic White:1097   HS to 2-year degree    :772
##                 NA's              : 140
##
##
##
##      rurality
##  rural   :879
##  suburban:355
##  urban   :353
##  NA's    : 14
##
##
##
```

After an exhausting data-cleaning process, Leslie was re-energized by the awesomeness of her clean data set.

10.1 Kiara's reproducibility resource: Cleaning the library data

Kiara saved **pew_libraries_2016_ch10.csv** from **edge.sagepub.com/ harris1e** and opened the codebook (Section 10.3) so she could work on recoding it for analyses. Kiara thought she could also save the data directly from the "Libraries 2016" survey by Pew Research Center if she wanted to try that, but decided to start with the data she already had. She saved the URL of the raw data for some other time and showed it to Leslie: https://www.pewinternet.org/dataset/march-2016-libraries/.

```
# bring in the data
libraries <- read.csv(file = "[data folder location]/data/pew_libraries_
2016_ch10.csv")
```

The data set was quite enormous, with 135 observations and 135 variables. Kiara and Leslie looked at the codebook for the data source. They found several of the variables associated in the past with library use from their research. They decided to include the following potential predictors in the data set for analyses:

- `libusea`: visited a public library
- `age`: age in years
- `sex`: biological sex
- `par`: is the participant a parent
- `disa`: lives with a disability
- `inc`: income of the participant household
- `race3m1`, `race3m2`, `race3m3`: race of participant
- `educ2`: education level of participant
- `live1`: rurality of participant
- `hh1`: how many people live in the household
- `hisp`: Hispanic ethnicity

Leslie examined the codebook and came up with a management plan for the data so that missing values were properly coded and categories were labeled for easier interpretation. She thought a subset of variables would work well so that the data source would not be so overwhelming. She started by limiting the data set to the 13 variables they decided on.

```
# open the tidyverse
library(package = "tidyverse")

# subset library data set to variables of interest
libraries.cleaned <- libraries %>%
  select(libusea, age, sex, par, disa, inc, race3m1,
         race3m2, race3m3, educ2, live1, hh1, hisp)

# check the new data frame
summary(object = libraries.cleaned)
##     libusea            age              sex              par
##  Min.   :1.000   Min.   :16.00   Min.   :1.00   Min.   :1.000
##  1st Qu.:1.000   1st Qu.:34.00   1st Qu.:1.00   1st Qu.:2.000
##  Median :2.000   Median :52.00   Median :1.00   Median :2.000
##  Mean   :1.685   Mean   :50.24   Mean   :1.48   Mean   :1.778
##  3rd Qu.:2.000   3rd Qu.:64.00   3rd Qu.:2.00   3rd Qu.:2.000
##  Max.   :3.000   Max.   :99.00   Max.   :2.00   Max.   :9.000
##
```

(Continued)

(Continued)

```
##      disa              inc            race3m1            race3m2
##  Min.   :1.000   Min.   : 1.00   Min.   :1.000   Min.   :1.000
##  1st Qu.:2.000   1st Qu.: 4.00   1st Qu.:1.000   1st Qu.:2.000
##  Median :2.000   Median : 6.00   Median :1.000   Median :3.000
##  Mean   :1.875   Mean   :16.74   Mean   :1.736   Mean   :3.271
##  3rd Qu.:2.000   3rd Qu.: 8.00   3rd Qu.:1.000   3rd Qu.:5.000
##  Max.   :9.000   Max.   :99.00   Max.   :9.000   Max.   :5.000
##                                                  NA's   :1553
##      race3m3           educ2            live1              hh1
##  Min.   :1.000   Min.   : 1.000   Min.   :1.000   Min.   : 1.000
##  1st Qu.:2.000   1st Qu.: 3.000   1st Qu.:2.000   1st Qu.: 2.000
##  Median :5.000   Median : 5.000   Median :3.000   Median : 2.000
##  Mean   :3.571   Mean   : 5.288   Mean   :2.558   Mean   : 3.736
##  3rd Qu.:5.000   3rd Qu.: 6.000   3rd Qu.:3.000   3rd Qu.: 4.000
##  Max.   :5.000   Max.   :99.000   Max.   :9.000   Max.   :99.000
##  NA's   :1594
##        hisp
##  Min.   :1.000
##  1st Qu.:2.000
##  Median :2.000
##  Mean   :1.934
##  3rd Qu.:2.000
##  Max.   :9.000
##
```

Now that the data frame was a more manageable size, Leslie started the process of recoding to make sure the missing values were treated logically, the variables were a reasonable data type, and labels were added to the categories for any categorical variables. She started by looking in the codebook and finding the `age` variable. The `age` variable was measured in years except for three of the values:

- 97 = 97 or older
- 98 = Don't know
- 99 = Refused

```
# add age data management
libraries.cleaned <- libraries %>%
```

```
    select(libusea, age, sex, par, disa, inc, race3m1,
           race3m2, race3m3, educ2, live1, hh1, hisp) %>%
  mutate(age = na_if(x = age, y = 98))%>%
  mutate(age = na_if(x = age, y = 99))

# check the recoding
summary(object = libraries.cleaned$age)
##    Min. 1st Qu.  Median    Mean 3rd Qu.    Max.    NA's
##   16.00   33.00   51.00   49.31   64.00   95.00      30
```

Next, Leslie looked at the `sex` variable, which was recorded with 1 representing male and 2 representing female. The parent variable, `par`, was coded with 1 representing parent and 2 representing nonparent. The `disa` variable was recorded with 1 representing disability and 2 representing no disability. Leslie added labels and checked her work for these three variables:

```
# recode sex, parent, disabled
libraries.cleaned <- libraries %>%
  select(libusea, age, sex, par, disa, inc, race3m1,
         race3m2, race3m3, educ2, live1, hh1, hisp) %>%
  mutate(age = na_if(x = age, y = 98)) %>%
  mutate(age = na_if(x = age, y = 99)) %>%
  mutate(sex = recode(.x = sex, `1` = "male", `2` = "female")) %>%
  mutate(parent = recode(.x = par, `1` = "parent",
                         `2` = "not parent")) %>%
  mutate(disabled = recode(.x = disa, `1` = "yes", `2` = "no"))

# check the recoding
summary(object = libraries.cleaned)
##     libusea            age            sex                 par
##  Min.   :1.000   Min.   :16.00   Length:1601        Min.   :1.000
##  1st Qu.:1.000   1st Qu.:33.00   Class :character   1st Qu.:2.000
##  Median :2.000   Median :51.00   Mode  :character   Median :2.000
##  Mean   :1.685   Mean   :49.31                      Mean   :1.778
##  3rd Qu.:2.000   3rd Qu.:64.00                      3rd Qu.:2.000
##  Max.   :3.000   Max.   :95.00                      Max.   :9.000
##                  NA's   :30
##     disa            inc            race3m1         race3m2
##  Min.   :1.000   Min.   : 1.00   Min.   :1.000   Min.   :1.000
```

(Continued)

(Continued)

```
## 1st Qu.:2.000      1st Qu.: 4.00     1st Qu.:1.000      1st Qu.:2.000
## Median :2.000      Median : 6.00     Median :1.000      Median :3.000
## Mean   :1.875      Mean   :16.74     Mean   :1.736      Mean   :3.271
## 3rd Qu.:2.000      3rd Qu.: 8.00     3rd Qu.:1.000      3rd Qu.:5.000
## Max.   :9.000      Max.   :99.00     Max.   :9.000      Max.   :5.000
##                                                         NA's   :1553
##      race3m3           educ2             live1             hh1
## Min.   :1.000      Min.   : 1.000    Min.   :1.000      Min.   : 1.000
## 1st Qu.:2.000      1st Qu.: 3.000    1st Qu.:2.000      1st Qu.: 2.000
## Median :5.000      Median : 5.000    Median :3.000      Median : 2.000
## Mean   :3.571      Mean   : 5.288    Mean   :2.558      Mean   : 3.736
## 3rd Qu.:5.000      3rd Qu.: 6.000    3rd Qu.:3.000      3rd Qu.: 4.000
## Max.   :5.000      Max.   :99.000    Max.   :9.000      Max.   :99.000
## NA's   :1594
##      hisp              parent            disabled
## Min.   :1.000      Length :1601      Length:1601
## 1st Qu.:2.000      Class  :character Class :character
## Median :2.000      Mode   :character Mode  :character
## Mean   :1.934
## 3rd Qu.:2.000
## Max.   :9.000
```

Leslie noticed that the three variables she recoded had now changed to character data types. She mentioned this to Kiara, who said there are a few ways to recode something into a factor data type. One way is to use `recode_factor()` instead of `recode()`, and another way is to add `factor()` in front of the `recode()`. The second way was more consistent with the rest of the recoding they would be doing, so Kiara suggested adding this. The codebook showed that the library use variable, `libusea`, consists of responses to the question "Have you personally ever visited a public library or used a public library bookmobile in person?" with the following response options:

- Yes, have done this in the past 12 months (`libusea` = 1)
- Yes, but not in the past 12 months (`libusea` = 2)
- No, have never done this (`libusea` = 3)

Binary logistic regression is used in the situation where the outcome variable has two categories. Leslie decided to recode the `libusea` variable so that it had two categories, `yes` for library use in the past 12 months and `no` for the other two groups. She also added `factor()` in front of the `recode()` for the four variables.

```
# recode library use variable
libraries.cleaned <- libraries %>%
  select(libusea, age, sex, par, disa, inc, race3m1,
         race3m2, race3m3, educ2, live1, hh1, hisp) %>%
  mutate(age = na_if(x = age, y = 98)) %>%
  mutate(age = na_if(x = age, y = 99)) %>%
  mutate(sex = factor(recode(.x = sex,
                                 `1` = "male",
                                 `2` = "female"))) %>%
  mutate(parent = factor(recode(.x = par,
                                 `1` = "parent",
                                 `2` = "not parent"))) %>%
  mutate(disabled = factor(recode(.x = disa,
                                 `1` = "yes",
                                 `2` = "no"))) %>%
  mutate(uses.lib = factor(recode(.x = libusea,
                                 `1` = "yes",
                                 `2` = "no",
                                 `3` = "no")))

# check the recoding
summary(object = libraries.cleaned$uses.lib)
## no  yes
## 809 792
```

The income variable was tricky to recode. Leslie and Kiara reviewed the income categories from the codebook (Figure 10.1).

FIGURE 10.1 Screenshot of income variable in Pew Research Center 2016 library use survey codebook

INC   Last year -- that is in 2015 -- what was your total family income from all sources, before taxes? Just stop me when I get to the right category... **[READ]** {Master INC2}

1	Less than $10,000
2	10 to under $20,000
3	20 to under $30,000
4	30 to under $40,000
5	40 to under $50,000
6	50 to under $75,000
7	75 to under $100,000
8	100 to under $150,000
9	$150,000 or more
98	**(VOL.)** Don't know
99	**(VOL.)** Refused

(Continued)

(Continued)

Leslie decided to use the U.S. Census Bureau 2017 poverty thresholds and the income (`inc`) and people living in household (`hh1`) variables to create a variable indicating socioeconomic status. Leslie coded people at or below the poverty threshold for the number of people living in the household as low socioeconomic status (SES). Consistent with the Census Bureau, Leslie also coded households above poverty and below $150,000 to be medium SES, and households at or above $150,000 in income to be high SES. To be consistent with the categories available for income, Leslie rounded the thresholds to the nearest $10,000.

```r
# subset library data set eight variables of interest
libraries.cleaned <- libraries %>%
  select(libusea, age, sex, par, disa, inc, race3m1,
         race3m2, race3m3, educ2, live1, hh1, hisp) %>%
  mutate(age = na_if(x = age, y = 98)) %>%
  mutate(age = na_if(x = age, y = 99)) %>%
  mutate(sex = factor(x = recode(.x = sex,
                                 `1` = "male",
                                 `2` = "female"))) %>%
  mutate(parent = factor(x = recode(.x = par,
                                    `1` = "parent",
                                    `2` = "not parent"))) %>%
  mutate(disabled = factor(x = recode(.x = disa,
                                      `1` = "yes",
                                      `2` = "no"))) %>%
  mutate(uses.lib = factor(x = recode(.x = libusea,
                                      `1` = "yes",
                                      `2` = "no",
                                      `3` = "no"))) %>%
  mutate(ses = factor(x = if_else(condition = hh1 == 1 & inc == 1 |
                        hh1 == 2 & inc <= 2 |
                        hh1 == 3 & inc <= 2 |
                        hh1 == 4 & inc <= 3 |
                        hh1 == 5 & inc <= 3 |
                        hh1 == 6 & inc <= 4 |
                        hh1 == 7 & inc <= 4 |
                        hh1 == 8 & inc <= 5 ,
                        true = "low",
                        false = if_else(condition = inc == 9,
```

```
                                         true = "high",
                                         false = "medium")))) 

# check recoding for SES
summary(object = libraries.cleaned$ses)
##    high    low medium
##     158    246   1197
```

The race and ethnicity questions allow multiple answers, so recoding the race-ethnicity data was complicated. First, the `hisp` variable was coded as follows:

- 1 = Hispanic, Latino, or Spanish origin
- 2 = Not Hispanic, Latino, or Spanish origin

The three race variables (`race3m1`, `race3m2`, and `race3m3`) allow the participants to choose as many as possible from the following:

- 1 = White (e.g., Caucasian, European, Irish, Italian, Arab, Middle Eastern)
- 2 = Black or African-American (e.g., Negro, Kenyan, Nigerian, Haitian)
- 3 = Asian or Asian-American (e.g., Asian Indian, Chinese, Filipino, Vietnamese, or other Asian origin groups)
- 4 = Some other race (SPECIFY) [IF NEEDED: What race or races is that?]
- 5 = Native American/American Indian/Alaska Native
- 6 = Pacific Islander/Native Hawaiian
- 7 = Hispanic/Latino (e.g., Mexican, Puerto Rican, Cuban)
- 8 = Don't know
- 9 = Refused (e.g., non-race answers like American, Human, purple)

Leslie decided to recode into four groups:

- Hispanic
- Non-Hispanic Black
- Non-Hispanic White
- Non-Hispanic Other or Mixed

```
# add race recoding
libraries.cleaned <- libraries %>%
```

(Continued)

(Continued)

```
    select(libusea, age, sex, par, disa, inc, race3m1,
           race3m2, race3m3, educ2, live1, hh1, hisp) %>%
  mutate(age = na_if(x = age, y = 98)) %>%
  mutate(age = na_if(x = age, y = 99)) %>%
  mutate(sex = factor(x = recode(.x = sex,
                                 `1` = "male",
                                 `2` = "female"))) %>%
  mutate(parent = factor(x = recode(.x = par,
                                    `1` = "parent",
                                    `2` = "not parent"))) %>%
  mutate(disabled = factor(x = recode(.x = disa,
                                      `1` = "yes",
                                      `2` = "no"))) %>%
  mutate(uses.lib = factor(x = recode(.x = libusea,
                                      `1` = "yes",
                                      `2` = "no",
                                      `3` = "no"))) %>%
  mutate(ses = factor(x = if_else(condition = hh1 == 1 & inc == 1 |
                                  hh1 == 2 & inc <= 2 |
                                  hh1 == 3 & inc <= 2 |
                                  hh1 == 4 & inc <= 3 |
                                  hh1 == 5 & inc <= 3 |
                                  hh1 == 6 & inc <= 4 |
                                  hh1 == 7 & inc <= 4 |
                                  hh1 == 8 & inc <= 5 ,
                                  true = "low",
                                  false = if_else(condition = inc == 9,
                                                  true = "high",
                                                  false = "medium")))) %>%
  mutate(raceth = factor(x = if_else(condition = hisp == 2 &
                                     race3m1 == 2 &
                                     is.na(x = race3m2),
                           true = "Non-Hispanic Black",
                           false = if_else(condition = hisp == 2 &
                           race3m1 == 1 & is.na(x = race3m2),
                           true = "Non-Hispanic White",
                           false = if_else(condition = hisp == 1 |
```

```
                              race3m1 == 7 |
                              race3m2 == 7 |
                              race3m3 == 7,
                              true = "Hispanic",
                              false = "Non-Hisp Other or Mixed")))))
# check recoding for raceth
summary(object = libraries.cleaned$raceth)
##            Hispanic Non-Hisp Other or Mixed Non-Hispanic Black
##                 194                       7               170
##    Non-Hispanic White                   NA's
##                1097                    133
```

Given that there were just seven people in the Non-Hispanic Other or Mixed category, Kiara suggested they recode this category to be missing. Having few people in a category can make estimates from a regression model unstable since they are based on information from such a small group.

```
# recode other and mixed to NA
libraries.cleaned <- libraries %>%
  select(libusea, age, sex, par, disa, inc, race3m1,
         race3m2, race3m3, educ2, live1, hh1, hisp) %>%
  mutate(age = na_if(x = age, y = 98)) %>%
  mutate(age = na_if(x = age, y = 99)) %>%
  mutate(sex = factor(x = recode(.x = sex,
                  `1` = "male",
                  `2` = "female"))) %>%
  mutate(parent = factor(x = recode(.x = par,
                    `1` = "parent",
                    `2` = "not parent"))) %>%
  mutate(disabled = factor(x = recode(.x = disa,
                    `1` = "yes",
                    `2` = "no"))) %>%
  mutate(uses.lib = factor(x = recode(.x = libusea,
                    `1` = "yes",
                    `2` = "no",
                    `3` = "no"))) %>%
  mutate(ses = factor(x = if_else(condition = hh1 == 1 & inc == 1 |
                          hh1 == 2 & inc <= 2 |
                          hh1 == 3 & inc <= 2 |
                          hh1 == 4 & inc <= 3 |
```

(Continued)

```
                                    hh1 == 5 & inc <= 3 |
                                    hh1 == 6 & inc <= 4 |
                                    hh1 == 7 & inc <= 4 |
                                    hh1 == 8 & inc <= 5 ,
                              true = "low",
                              false = if_else(condition = inc == 9,
                                          true = "high",
                                          false = "medium")))) %>%
  mutate(raceth = factor(x = if_else(condition = hisp == 2 &
                              race3m1 == 2 &
                              is.na(race3m2),
                    true = "Non-Hispanic Black",
                    false = if_else(condition = hisp == 2 &
                    race3m1 == 1 & is.na(x = race3m2),
                    true = "Non-Hispanic White",
                    false = if_else(condition = hisp == 1 |
                    race3m1 == 7 |
                    race3m2 == 7 |
                    race3m3 == 7,
                    true = "Hispanic",
                    false = NA_character_)))))
# check recoding for raceth
summary(object = libraries.cleaned$raceth)
##          Hispanic Non-Hispanic Black Non-Hispanic White
##               194                170               1097
##             NA's
##              140
```

Leslie was already ready to be done with R for the day and they hadn't even started their main work. Kiara cheered her on; there were only two variables left to recode, the education variable and the urban and rural residence variable. Leslie looked in the codebook and finished up the recoding and cleaning. The education variable had eight categories ranging from less than high school through a postgraduate or professional degree. Leslie decided to create three categories: less than high school, high school through two-year degree, and four-year degree or more. She went with the urban, suburban, and rural categories for the live1 recoding. Finally, Leslie decided to clean up the final data set so that it just had the variables she needed. She did this by using select().

```
# complete cleaning
libraries.cleaned <- libraries %>%
  select(libusea, age, sex, par, disa, inc, race3m1,
         race3m2, race3m3, educ2, live1, hh1, hisp) %>%
  mutate(age = na_if(x = age, y = 98)) %>%
  mutate(age = na_if(x = age, y = 99)) %>%
  mutate(sex = factor(x = recode(.x = sex,
                                 `1` = "male",
                                 `2` = "female"))) %>%
  mutate(parent = factor(x = recode(.x = par,
                                    `1` = "parent",
                                    `2` = "not parent"))) %>%
  mutate(disabled = factor(x = recode(.x = disa,
                                      `1` = "yes",
                                      `2` = "no"))) %>%
  mutate(uses.lib = factor(x = recode(.x = libusea,
                                      `1` = "yes",
                                      `2` = "no",
                                      `3` = "no"))) %>%
  mutate(ses = factor(x = if_else(condition = hh1 == 1 & inc == 1 |
                                    hh1 == 2 & inc <= 2 |
                                    hh1 == 3 & inc <= 2 |
                                    hh1 == 4 & inc <= 3 |
                                    hh1 == 5 & inc <= 3 |
                                    hh1 == 6 & inc <= 4 |
                                    hh1 == 7 & inc <= 4 |
                                    hh1 == 8 & inc <= 5 ,
                                  true = "low",
                                  false = if_else(condition = inc == 9,
                                                  true = "high",
                                                  false = "medium")))) %>%
  mutate(raceth = factor(x = if_else(condition = hisp == 2 &
                                       race3m1 == 2 &
                                       is.na(race3m2),
                                     true = "Non-Hispanic Black",
                                     false = if_else(condition = hisp == 2 &
```

```
                          race3m1 == 1 & is.na(x = race3m2),
                          true = "Non-Hispanic White",
                          false = if_else(condition = hisp == 1 |
                          race3m1 == 7 |
                          race3m2 == 7 |
                          race3m3 == 7,
                          true = "Hispanic",
                          false = NA_character_ ))))) %>%
  mutate(educ = factor(x = if_else(condition = libraries$educ2 < 3,
              true = "< HS",
              false = if_else(condition = libraries$educ2 < 6,
              true = "HS to 2-year degree",
              false = "Four-year degree or more")))) %>%
  mutate(rurality = factor(x = if_else(condition =
                                    libraries$live1 == 1,
              true = "urban",
              false = if_else(condition = libraries$live1 == 2,
              true = "suburban",
              false = if_else(condition = libraries$live1 < 8,
              true = "rural",
              false = NA_character_ ))))) %>%
  select(-c(libusea, par, disa, inc, race3m1, race3m2,
           race3m3, educ2, live1, hh1, hisp))
# check recoding
summary(object = libraries.cleaned)
      age            sex           parent        disabled    uses.lib
Min.   :16.00  female:768  not parent:1205  no  :1340  no :809
1st Qu.:33.00  male  :833  parent    : 391  yes : 253  yes:792
Median :51.00              NA's      :   5  NA's:   8
Mean   :49.31
3rd Qu.:64.00
Max.   :95.00
NA's   :30
```

```
       ses                    raceth                      educ
   high  : 158   Hispanic          : 194   < HS                    :171
   low   : 246   Non-Hispanic Black: 170   Four-year degree or more:658
   medium:1197   Non-Hispanic White:1097   HS to 2-year degree     :772
                 NA's              : 140

        rurality
   rural   :879
   suburban:355
   urban   :353
   NA's    : 14
```

Finally, Leslie used the `write.csv()` function to save the cleaned data file to the data folder on her laptop.

```
# write to a new csv file
write.csv(x = libraries.cleaned,
          file = "data/pew_libraries_2016_cleaned_ch10.csv",
          row.names = FALSE)
```

10.4.1 EXPLORATORY DATA ANALYSIS

Leslie started to look back through the earlier R notes and was reminded of the **tableone** package for examining descriptive statistics for multiple variables at the same time (Section 2.5.3). Kiara thought this was a great idea. They looked at the data set and saw that all the variables except for age were categorical, so the descriptive statistics would be frequencies and percentages. For age, the appropriate descriptive statistics would be either mean and standard deviation or median and IQR (Section 2.6.2) depending on whether or not the variable was normally distributed. Leslie made a density plot to check (Figure 10.2).

```
# open tidyverse
library(package = "tidyverse")

# examine the distribution of age (Figure 10.2)
libraries.cleaned %>%
  ggplot(aes(x = age)) +
  geom_density(fill = "#7463AC", alpha = .6) +
  theme_minimal() +
  labs(y = "Probability density", x = "Age in years")
```

FIGURE 10.2 The distribution of age in the 2016 Pew Research Center library use data set

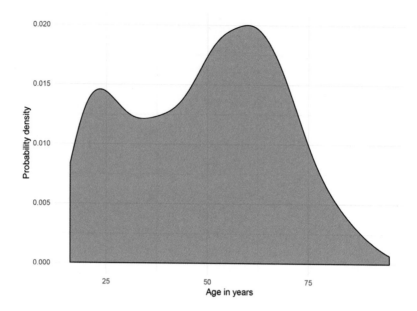

This did not look very normal to Leslie. The others agreed. Leslie looked at the help documentation for `CreateTableOne()` to remember how to specify a non-normal variable. She found that she could add `nonnormal = 'age'` to the `print()` function to show median and IQR for `age` since it was not normally distributed. While she was working on the `print()` function, she decided to add `showAll-Levels = TRUE` to be able to see all the categories for the categorical variables.

```
# open tableone package
library(package = "tableone")

# get a table of descriptive statistics
table.desc <- CreateTableOne(data = libraries.cleaned)
print(table.desc,
      nonnormal = 'age',
      showAllLevels = TRUE)
##
##                      level                 Overall
##    n                                        1601
##    age (median [IQR])                       51.00 [33.00, 64.00]
##    sex (%)          female                    768 (48.0)
##                     male                      833 (52.0)
##    parent (%)       not parent               1205 (75.5)
##                     parent                    391 (24.5)
##    disabled (%)     no                       1340 (84.1)
##                     yes                       253 (15.9)
```

```
## uses.lib (%)        no                      809 (50.5)
##                      yes                     792 (49.5)
##    ses (%)           high                    158 ( 9.9)
##                      low                     246 (15.4)
##                      medium                 1197 (74.8)
##    raceth (%)        Hispanic                194 (13.3)
##                      Non-Hispanic Black      170 (11.6)
##                      Non-Hispanic White     1097 (75.1)
##    educ (%)          < HS                    171 (10.7)
##                      Four-year degree or more 658 (41.1)
##                      HS to 2-year degree     772 (48.2)
##    rurality (%)      rural                   879 (55.4)
##                      suburban                355 (22.4)
##                      urban                   353 (22.2)
```

Nancy had an idea to make this table even more useful before they started logistic regression to explore the predictors of library use. One of the strategies used in some fields to develop a logistic regression model is to start with *bivariate* inferential tests for each of the potential predictors. Predictors that show a statistically significant relationship with the outcome are then entered into a larger model to see how they all work together to predict or explain the outcome of interest. Kiara liked the idea of bivariate analyses, but wasn't sure she liked this modeling strategy. It sounded to her a lot like a *questionable research practice* that could threaten research quality and reproducibility (Banks et al., 2016). Questionable research practices (QRPs) are strategies, like dropping (or adding) observations, that researchers use that introduce bias, typically in pursuit of statistical significance. Nancy argued that using bivariate analyses is not always a QRP and is a good strategy for exploratory research. However, since there was a lot of other research on library use already, she agreed their work wasn't exploratory and they should use bivariate analyses as information but not for developing the statistical model.

After this discussion, they decided to make a plan for what they would use in their statistical model before finishing the exploratory data analyses. Based on prior research that Nancy had described, they decided that age, sex, race-ethnicity, income, education, and rurality were important characteristics. Leslie thought that being a parent was a logical predictor of library use, and Nancy was interested in disabilities and library use. Kiara noted that they had selected all of the variables in their data set as predictors for the model.

Rather than conducting separate bivariate statistical tests for each of these variables and library use, Nancy suggested they take advantage of the built-in statistical testing in the **tableone** package. She explained that the `CreateTableOne()` function can be used to create a table with descriptive statistics *and* bivariate statistical test results for any or all of the variables in a data frame.

The outcome of interest was library use, which is a categorical variable with two categories. Examining the relationship between this categorical variable and each of the other variables in the data set requires statistical tests to examine (a) the relationship between two categorical variables, and (b) the relationship between one categorical variable and a non-normally distributed continuous variable (`age`).

Leslie remembered that chi-squared was useful for examining whether there was a statistically significant relationship between two categorical variables (Section 5.6). She had to look up the test for examining the relationship between one categorical variable (with two categories) and one non-normal continuous one. She found the Mann-Whitney *U* test works for this (Section 6.10.3), so they would use *U* to examine the relationship between the numeric variable `age` and the outcome variable `uses.lib`. Nancy thought it was good to know which tests were being used, but `CreateTableOne()` automatically uses the appropriate test based on the data types.

Leslie read the documentation for the package and noted that two functions are needed to show the statistical test results, `CreateTableOne()` and `print()`. The `CreateTableOne()` function takes arguments for `data` = to identify the data frame and `vars` = to identify the variables to include (if this is left out, all the variables in the data frame are included). To make the table with columns representing the categories of a variable like `uses.lib`, the `strata` = argument can be used, which will show descriptive statistics for each variable for each category of the factor specified. In this case, using `strata` = `uses.lib` will result in descriptive statistics for the yes and no values of the `uses.lib` variable.

In addition, when the `strata` = argument is used, the table shows the *p*-value association with a bivariate statistical test that is conducted as appropriate given the data types in the table. For variables in the table that are factor data types, this is chi-squared. For variables that are numeric data types, the test is one-way ANOVA, which is equivalent to an independent-samples *t*-test when the means are compared across two groups (instead of three or more).

In the second function, `print()`, there are a number of options for changing the table. One is to specify if any of the numeric variables do not meet the normality assumption for ANOVA; this is done with the `nonnormal` = option with the name of the variable that does not meet the normality assumption, like this: `nonnormal` = `'age'`. When non-normal is specified for a variable, the median and IQR are printed in the table and the Kruskal-Wallis test is used in lieu of ANOVA. Kruskal-Wallis is equivalent to the Mann-Whitney *U* test when there are two groups. Another useful option for printing is to use `showAllLevels` = `TRUE` in order to show all the categories for the factor variables. If this option is left out, one reference category will be omitted for each categorical variable in the table. Leslie finished writing the code and ran it.

```
# get a table of descriptive statistics with bivariate tests
table.desc <- CreateTableOne(data = libraries.cleaned,
                    strata = 'uses.lib',
                    vars = c("age", "sex", "parent", "disabled",
                        "ses", "raceth", "educ", "rurality"))
print(table.desc,
     nonnormal = 'age',
     showAllLevels = TRUE)
##                       Stratified by uses.lib
##                       level                 no
##     n                                       809
##     age (median [IQR])                      53.00 [35.00, 65.00]
##     sex (%)           female                330 (40.8)
##                       male                  479 (59.2)
##     parent (%)        not parent            639 (79.1)
##                       parent                169 (20.9)
##     disabled (%)      no                    661 (82.0)
##                       yes                   145 (18.0)
```

```
## ses (%)           high                             67 ( 8.3)
## 
## 
## 
## 
## 
## 
## 
## 
## 
## 
## 
## 
## 
## 
## 
## 
## 
## 
## 
## 
## 
## 
## 
## 
## 
## 
## 
## 
## 
## 
## 
## 
## 
## 
## 
## 
## 
## 
## 
## 
## 
## 
## 
## 
## 
## 
## 
## 
## 
## 
## 
## 
## 
## 
## 
## 
## 
## 
## 
## 
```

## ses (%)	high	67 (8.3)	
##	low	130 (16.1)	
##	medium	612 (75.6)	
## raceth (%)	Hispanic	111 (14.9)	
##	Non-Hispanic Black	79 (10.6)	
##	Non-Hispanic White	557 (74.6)	
## educ (%)	< HS	102 (12.6)	
##	Four-year degree or more	276 (34.1)	
##	HS to 2-year degree	431 (53.3)	
## rurality (%)	rural	478 (59.7)	
##	suburban	159 (19.9)	
##	urban	164 (20.5)	

```
##                   Stratified by uses.lib
##                    yes                     p       test
## n                  792
## age (median [IQR]) 49.00 [31.00, 62.00]  0.001 nonnorm
## sex (%)            438 (55.3)           <0.001
##                    354 (44.7)
## parent (%)         566 (71.8)            0.001
##                    222 (28.2)
## disabled (%)       679 (86.3)            0.024
##                    108 (13.7)
## ses (%)             91 (11.5)            0.088
##                    116 (14.6)
##                    585 (73.9)
## raceth (%)          83 (11.6)            0.110
##                     91 (12.7)
##                    540 (75.6)
## educ (%)            69 ( 8.7)           <0.001
##                    382 (48.2)
##                    341 (43.1)
## rurality (%)       401 (51.0)            0.002
##                    196 (24.9)
##                    189 (24.0)
```

The R-Team found that SES and race were not statistically significantly associated with library use ($p > .05$), but all the other variables that they had selected based on reviewing prior research were statistically significantly associated with library use.

Although it was a great option for making a table quickly, the output from the `CreateTableOne()` function was missing standardized residuals for better understanding the significant chi-squared results for the relationships between library use and all of the factor variables. Kiara recommended that Leslie examine the frequencies and percentages in the table to identify some possible categories that may be driving the significant results for the bivariate tests. Leslie noted that of those who use the library, 55.3% are female, while of those who do not use the library, 59.2% are male. Among library users, 48.2% have a four-year degree or more, while among library nonusers, 34.1% have a four-year degree or more. Library users tend to be female and have higher education than nonusers. Leslie also saw that the library users were younger, with a lower median age (med = 49 years) compared to library nonusers (med = 53 years).

10.4.2 ACHIEVEMENT 1: CHECK YOUR UNDERSTANDING

Review the table created with the `CreateTableOne()` function and examine the patterns of library use and nonuse by parental status, race, SES, disability, and rurality. Who are the library users? Who are the nonusers in these groups?

Use the chi-squared process from Section 5.9 to get standardized residuals for each of the significant associations. Which groups have significantly higher or lower frequencies than expected based on the residuals?

10.5 Achievement 2: Understanding the binary logistic regression statistical model

Kiara explained that binary logistic regression follows a similar format and process as linear regression, but the outcome or dependent variable is *binary* (e.g., library use, smoking status, voting) (Stoltzfus, 2011). Because the outcome is binary, or categorical consisting of two categories, the model predicts the probability that a person is in one of the categories. For example, a logistic regression might predict the probability that someone is or is not a smoker, is or is not incarcerated, does or does not vote, or any other outcome with two categories. In this case, Leslie was interested in predicting what is associated with whether or not someone uses the library. After checking the recoding, Leslie knew that 49.47% of people in the sample use the library. She had also learned about some of the characteristics of library users compared to nonusers. The next step was to determine how individual characteristics (e.g., sex, age, education) work together to predict library use.

10.5.1 THE STATISTICAL FORM OF THE MODEL

Because the outcome variable was binary, the linear regression model would not work since it requires a continuous outcome. However, the linear regression statistical model can be transformed using the *logit transformation* in order to be useful for modeling binary outcomes. Kiara wrote out the statistical model for the logistic model in Equation (10.1).

$$p(y) = \frac{1}{1 + e^{-(b_0 + b_1 x_1 + b_2 x_2)}} \tag{10.1}$$

Leslie was not quite following it, so Kiara explained each part:

- y is the binary outcome variable (e.g., library use)
- $p(y)$ is the probability of the outcome (e.g., probability of library use)
- b_0 is the y-intercept
- x_1 and x_2 are predictors of the outcome (e.g., age, rurality)
- b_1 and b_2 are the coefficients for x_1 and x_2

10.5.2 THE LOGISTIC FUNCTION

Kiara suggested that examining a graph of the logistic function might help. The logistic function has a sigmoid shape that stretches from $-\infty$ to ∞ on the x-axis and from 0 to 1 on the y-axis. She explained to Leslie that the function can take any value along the x-axis and give the corresponding value between 0 and 1 on the y-axis. Nancy made a graph of the logistic function (Figure 10.3).

The logistic function is defined in Equation (10.2) (Peng, Kuk, & Ingersoll, 2002).

$$\sigma(t) = \frac{e^t}{1 + e^t} \qquad (10.2)$$

Equation (10.2) can be simplified to Equation (10.3).

$$\sigma(t) = \frac{1}{1 + e^{-t}} \qquad (10.3)$$

In Equations 10.2 and 10.3, t is the value along the x-axis of the function and $\sigma(t)$ is the value of y for a specific value of t, or the probability of y given t. In the case of logistic regression, the value of t will be the *right-hand side* of the regression model, which looks something like $\beta_0 + \beta_1 x$, where x is an independent variable, β_1 is the coefficient (rather than slope) for that variable, and β_0 is the constant (rather than y-intercept). Substituting this regression model for t in the logistic function gives Equation (10.4).

$$p(y) = \frac{1}{1 + e^{-(\beta_0 + \beta_1 x)}} \qquad (10.4)$$

Kiara explained that this is useful because it returns a probability of the outcome happening for any value of an independent predictor or set of independent predictors. To visualize how it works, she asked Nancy to add some example data points (i.e., observations) representing the values of a binary outcome variable to the logistic graph (Figure 10.4).

FIGURE 10.3 Shape of logistic function

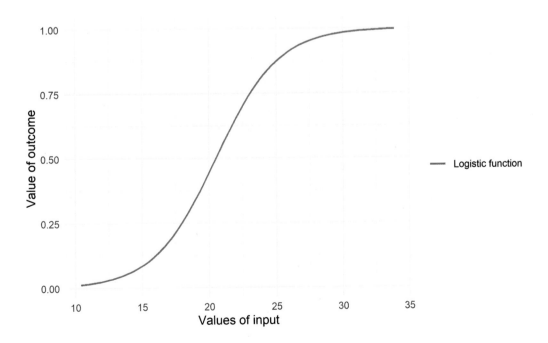

FIGURE 10.4 Example of logistic function with data points

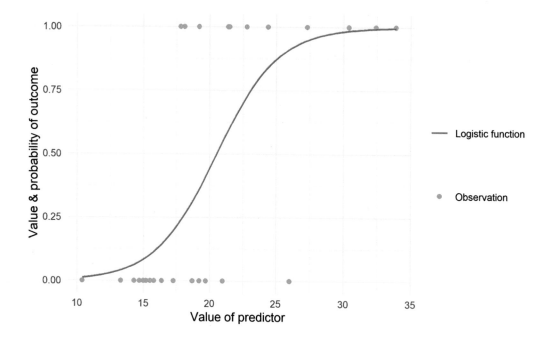

By starting at 20 on the *x*-axis, Kiara traced a straight line up to the logistic function curve, and from there she looked to the *y*-axis for a value. She found that for a value of *x* = 20 in these data, the model would predict a probability of *y* around .44 or 44% (Figure 10.5).

Leslie asked if this were a model predicting library use from age, would it predict a 44% probability of library use for a 20-year-old? Kiara nodded yes. She then mentioned that, since 44% is lower than a 50% probability of the value of *y*, the model is predicting that the 20-year-old does not have the outcome. So, if the outcome is library use, the logistic model would predict this 20-year-old was not a library user.

Nancy had been listening and added that, while finding the predicted probability of having the outcome (e.g., using the library) is interesting, it is not as useful when there are multiple variables in the model. At that point, knowing the influence of each variable on the probability of having the outcome would be better. This would be similar to having the coefficients in linear regression that allow interpretation of how much the value of the outcome changes with each increase or decrease in the value of a predictor.

With transformation of the outcome variable, there is no direct interpretation for how the value of the coefficient of each predictor is related to the value of the outcome. Luckily, said Nancy, someone figured this out already, and there is a way to transform the model results to get a more interpretable value to describe the relationship between each independent variable and the outcome.

First, the logistic model can be transformed to show odds on the left-hand side of the equal sign. Odds are related to probability as shown in Equation (10.5).

$$odds = \frac{probability}{1 - probability} \tag{10.5}$$

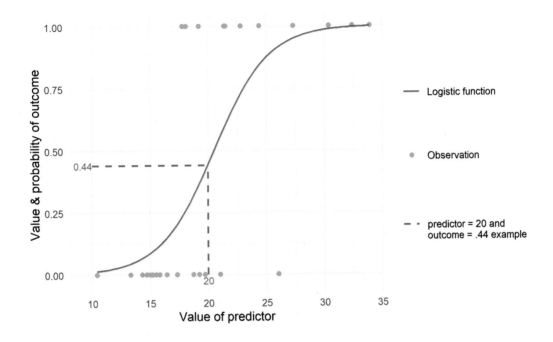

Substituting the logistic model from Equation (10.1) into Equation (10.5) results in Equation (10.6).

$$odds = \frac{\dfrac{1}{1+e^{-(\beta_0+\beta_1 x)}}}{1-\dfrac{1}{1+e^{-(\beta_0+\beta_1 x)}}} \tag{10.6}$$

Equation (10.6) simplifies to Equation (10.7).

$$odds = e^{\beta_0+\beta_1 x} \tag{10.7}$$

Once β_0 and β_1 are estimated, which would make them b_0 and b_1 since they are sample statistics rather than population statistics, this equation can be used to determine the odds of the outcome for a given value of the independent variable x. To be equivalent to the interpretation of the coefficients in linear regression, however, there is one more step. That is, what is the *increase or decrease* in the odds of the outcome with a one-unit increase in x? To the delight of Leslie, it was going to take a little more math to determine the odds ratio, and she wrote Equation (10.8) to show this math.

$$OR = \frac{e^{b_0+b_1(x+1)}}{e^{b_0+b_1 x}} = e^{b_1} \tag{10.8}$$

Equation (10.8) shows that for every one-unit increase in the independent variable x, the odds of the outcome increase or decrease by e^{b_1}. Taking e to the power of b_1 is referred to as *exponentiating* b_1. After a model is estimated, the analyst will usually exponentiate the b value(s) in order to report odds ratios describing the relationships between each predictor and the outcome.

10.5.3 ACHIEVEMENT 2: CHECK YOUR UNDERSTANDING

In your own words, write out a statement that explains the different components of the logistic regression statistical model in Equation (10.4), repeated here:

$$p(y) = \frac{1}{1 + e^{-(\beta_0 + \beta_1 x)}} \tag{10.4}$$

> # 10.6 Achievement 3: Estimating a simple logistic regression model and interpreting predictor significance and interpretation

Leslie was ready and started the NHST process. Kiara suggested they start with a simple logistic regression with age as the only predictor of library use. Leslie agreed and began to write the null and alternate hypotheses. She wanted to know if they could use the logistic formula to write out the model before they started. Kiara agreed and reminded Leslie that Greek letters like β are usually representing population statistics and are usually replaced with letters from the Latin alphabet like b for statistics from sample data. Leslie wrote out the model in Equation (10.9).

$$p(uses.lib) = \frac{1}{1 + e^{-(b_0 + b_1 age)}} \tag{10.9}$$

She replaced y with the name of the outcome variable, `uses.lib`, and x with the name of the predictor variable, `age`.

10.6.1 NHST

10.6.1.1 NHST STEP 1: WRITE THE NULL AND ALTERNATE HYPOTHESES

The null and alternate hypotheses are similar to those in linear regression. For this logistic regression analysis, the outcome is library use and 49.5% of people in the data set use the library. Without any other information, it is slightly more likely that a person selected from the data frame is *not* a library user. This is the *baseline* value. By using information like age, sex, and education, the logistic model may be better able to predict the probability of library use for a given person from the data set. This suggests a null hypothesis to test for the logistic model.

> H0: The model is no better than the baseline at predicting library use.

> HA: The model is better than the baseline at predicting library use.

10.6.1.2 NHST STEP 2: COMPUTE THE TEST STATISTIC

The *generalized linear model* or `glm()` function can be used to estimate a binary logistic regression model. The model is generalized because it starts with the basic linear model and generalizes to other situations. The `glm()` function takes several arguments. Before estimating the model, it is important to understand how R is interpreting the order of the categories in the outcome variable. The `glm()` function will treat the first category as the reference group (the group *without* the outcome) and the second category as the group *with* the outcome. To see the order of `uses.lib`, use `levels()` to show the two levels in order.

```
# checking the order of the outcome variable categories
levels(x = libraries.cleaned$uses.lib)
## [1] "no" "yes"
```

Leslie noticed that the first category is "no" and the second is "yes." This means the model will be predicting the "yes" category of library use. This made sense to Leslie, but Kiara wanted to be sure Leslie knew how to reorder the levels in case she ever encountered a variable with a level order that did not make sense for the analysis. Nancy knew how to change the reference group using mutate() and relevel(). She wrote the code to demonstrate even though they did not need it this time.

```
# make no the reference group
libraries.cleaned <- libraries.cleaned %>%
  mutate(uses.lib = relevel(x = uses.lib, ref = "no"))

# check the re-ordering
levels(x = libraries.cleaned$uses.lib)
## [1] "no" "yes"
```

With all the descriptive and bivariate tests done and a confirmation of the correct coding for their outcome variable, it was time for a logistic model. First, the formula was entered into the glm() function with the outcome variable uses.lib on the left side of the ~ and the predictor age on the right. After the formula, the data source and the family or model type were entered. Leslie asked what the family = argument referred to. Kiara explained that, since there are different sorts of generalized linear models that are appropriate for different types of outcome variables, the family = argument is used to specify which type of model to estimate.

```
# estimate the library use model and print results
lib.model.small <- glm(formula = uses.lib ~ age,
                       data = libraries.cleaned,
                       family = binomial("logit"))
summary(object = lib.model.small)
##
## Call:
## glm(formula = uses.lib ~ age, family = binomial("logit"), data =
## libraries.cleaned)
##
## Deviance Residuals:
##    Min      1Q  Median      3Q     Max
## -1.291  -1.150  -1.027   1.190   1.363
##
## Coefficients:
##              Estimate Std. Error z value Pr(>|z|)
```

```
## (Intercept)   0.403785    0.142194    2.840  0.00452 **
## age           -0.008838    0.002697   -3.277  0.00105 **
## ---
## Signif. codes:  0 '***' 0.001 '**' 0.01 '*' 0.05 '.' 0.1 ' ' 1
##
## (Dispersion parameter for binomial family taken to be 1)
##
##     Null deviance: 2177.5 on 1570 degrees of freedom
## Residual deviance: 2166.7 on 1569 degrees of freedom
##   (30 observations deleted due to missingness)
## AIC: 2170.7
##
## Number of Fisher Scoring iterations: 3
```

Leslie did not know how to interpret the output, but she did notice that the term "odds ratio" did not show up anywhere. Kiara explained that the output from `glm()` contains information about the significance of the predictors, but is missing several pieces of information for reporting results, such as the odds ratios, model significance, and model fit. To get this information, Nancy suggested they use the `odds.n.ends()` function from the **odds.n.ends** package to get this information.

```
# open odds.n.ends
library(package = "odds.n.ends")

# get model fit, model significance, odds ratios
odds.n.ends(x = lib.model.small)
## $`Logistic regression model significance`
## Chi-squared         d.f.              p
##     10.815        1.000          0.001
##
## $`Contingency tables (model fit): percent predicted`
##                   Percent observed
## Percent predicted          1          0        Sum
##                1   0.2151496  0.1896881  0.4048377
##                0   0.2768937  0.3182686  0.5951623
##              Sum  0.4920433  0.5079567  1.0000000
##
## $`Contingency tables (model fit): frequency predicted`
##                  Number observed
## Number predicted   1    0   Sum
##                1  338  298  636
```

```
##                    0    435  500  935
##                  Sum  773  798 1571
##
## $`Predictor odds ratios and 95% CI`
##                     OR      2.5 %      97.5 %
## (Intercept) 1.497482 1.1339164 1.9804811
## age         0.991201 0.9859589 0.9964415
##
## $`Model sensitivity`
## [1] 0.4372574
##
## $`Model specificity`
## [1] 0.6265664
```

Leslie wanted to know more about the measures of significance and fit in the `odds.n.ends()` output. Nancy explained that the chi-squared statistic in logistic regression is computed by finding the difference between how well the model fits the data when it has no predictors in it (the null model) and how well it fits with all the predictors in it. A model with no predictors in it is a baseline or null model and just consists of the percentage of people with the outcome. In this case, it is the percentage of people who use the library. Looking at the model fit table, the percentage of people who were observed with a value of 1, indicating they use the library, was 773 out of 1571, or 49.2%. Without any other information, we would predict that each person has a 49.2% probability of being a library user.

If a person in the data set was a library user, their probability would be 100% chance, or 1 on a scale of 0 to 1, of being a library user. The predicted probability would be .492, which translates to a 49.2% probability of being a library user. The difference between the actual value of library use, 1, and the observed probability of library use would be 1 − .492 = .508. The predicted probability is .508 away from the correct observed value.

If a person in the data was a library nonuser, the predicted probability from the null model would still be .492, but the observed value would be 0. The difference between observed and predicted in this case is 0 − .492 = −.492.

Finding these differences between observed values (0s and 1s) and the predicted values (percentages), squaring each difference, and adding up all the squared differences from each person in the data set results in a value called the *deviance*. The deviance is a measure of how well the model fits the data. If the differences between the observed values and the predicted values are small, the deviance is small and the model is doing well at fitting the data. A smaller deviance is an indicator of a better fitting model. "I thought about becoming a model," Kiara said, "until I learned that, on average, statisticians earn higher salaries!" Leslie and Nancy paused and then laughed at Kiara's joke attempt.

"Not to mention you get to advance science and policy," Nancy added, with a wink.

After the deviance is computed for the null model, or the model without predictors, it is computed for the model with predictors in it. In this case, the deviance is predicted for the model with age only as a predictor. If age is useful in making the model a better predictor of library use than the null model is, the deviance would be smaller for the model with age in it than it is for the null or baseline model.

The difference between the deviance for the null model and the deviance for a model with predictors in it has a chi-squared distribution and is used to determine whether the full model is doing a statistically significantly better job at predicting the observed values than the null model. In the `summary()` results from the model above, you will find the null deviance of 2177.5 and the "residual" or model deviance of 2166.7. The difference between the two is 10.8, which you see at the top of the output from the `odds.n.ends()` function as the model chi-squared.

10.6.1.3 NHST STEP 3: CALCULATE THE PROBABILITY THAT YOUR TEST STATISTIC IS AT LEAST AS BIG AS IT IS IF THERE IS NO RELATIONSHIP (I.E., THE NULL IS TRUE)

Once she knew a little more, Leslie was ready to report and interpret the model significance. She remembered that the chi-squared distribution shows the probability of getting a chi-squared test statistic as large (or larger) than the one computed if the null hypothesis were true. In this case, the sample size is 1601 for the libraries data frame, but the `odds.n.ends()` output shows 1571 observations in the model fit contingency table. She reviewed the data and found this was due to missing values in the outcome and predictor variables; the model only used cases with complete data for all variables in the model.

The `odds.n.ends()` output also shows the model chi-squared of 10.815 with the corresponding degrees of freedom of 1 and a p-value of .001. Visualizing a chi-squared distribution for an n of 1571 and 1 degree of freedom made it clear why the p-value was so small. Nancy graphed the probability of the chi-squared distribution with 1 degree of freedom (Figure 10.6) to show that the probability that the chi-squared would be 10.815 or higher—if the null hypothesis were true—is the area under the curve from 10.815 to the right. Leslie saw that this was barely any area at all, which was consistent with the tiny p-value.

FIGURE 10.6 Chi-squared distribution with $df = 1$ and $n = 1571$

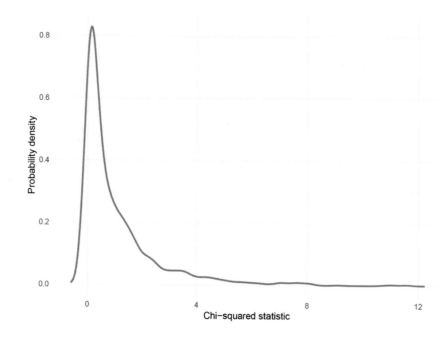

10.6.1.4 NHST STEPS 4 AND 5: INTERPRET THE PROBABILITY AND WRITE A CONCLUSION

Leslie interpreted the results:

The chi-squared test statistic for a logistic regression model with age predicting library use had a p-value of .001. This p-value indicates there is a .1% chance of a chi-squared statistic this large or larger if the null hypothesis were true. The null hypothesis is therefore rejected in favor of the alternate hypothesis that the model is better than the baseline at predicting library use. A logistic regression model including age was statistically significantly better than a null model at predicting library use [$\chi^2(1) = 10.82; p = .001$].

10.6.2 INTERPRETING PREDICTOR SIGNIFICANCE

The next thing to look at was predictor significance and interpretation. Leslie noticed that the `summary()` and `odds.n.ends()` output both included values and significance statistics for the age predictor. The `odds.n.ends()` output included odds ratios, which Kiara said are easier to interpret; because the outcome is transformed by the logistic function, the coefficients from `summary()` are not easy to interpret directly.

10.6.3 COMPUTING ODDS RATIOS

Leslie used the `odds.n.ends()` function again to review the odds ratios.

```
# checking model results again
odds.n.ends(x = lib.model.small)
## $`Logistic regression model significance`
## Chi-squared          d.f.              p
##        10.815        1.000          0.001
##
## $`Contingency tables (model fit): percent predicted`
##                    Percent observed
## Percent predicted          1          0        Sum
##               1    0.2151496  0.1896881  0.4048377
##               0    0.2768937  0.3182686  0.5951623
##             Sum  0.4920433  0.5079567  1.0000000
##
## $`Contingency tables (model fit): frequency predicted`
##                  Number observed
## Number predicted     1     0   Sum
##               1    338   298   636
##               0    435   500   935
##             Sum    773   798  1571
##
```

```
## $`Predictor odds ratios and 95% CI`
##                    OR      2.5 %     97.5 %
## (Intercept) 1.497482 1.1339164 1.9804811
## age         0.991201 0.9859589 0.9964415
##
## $`Model sensitivity`
## [1] 0.4372574
##
## $`Model specificity`
## [1] 0.6265664
```

10.6.4 ODDS RATIO SIGNIFICANCE

Nancy reminded Leslie that the interpretation of an odds ratio is the increase (or decrease) in odds with a one-unit increase in the predictor. For example, the age variable has an odds ratio of .99. This could be interpreted as, "The odds of library use decrease by 1% for every 1-year increase in age." Leslie thought this sounded familiar, but she could not remember why it was 1%. Kiara explained that the 1% comes from subtracting the odds ratio of .99 from 1 and multiplying by 100 to convert it to a percent, which is one strategy for making the odds ratio easier to interpret when it is below 1. She clarified that it would be just as correct, although a little more difficult to understand, to conclude, "The odds of library use are .99 times as high with every 1-year increase in age." Kiara explained that in order to make the interpretation clearer, subtracting the value of smaller odds ratios from 1 and treating the result as a percentage decrease in odds is preferred.

Leslie asked what they would do about the significance of the odds ratios. Kiara explained that the significance of an odds ratio is determined by its confidence interval. Just like the other confidence intervals they had discussed, the confidence interval for the odds ratio shows where the population value of the odds ratio likely lies. A confidence interval that includes 1 indicates that the true or population value of the relationship could have an odds ratio of 1. The interpretation of an odds ratio of 1 is that the odds are 1 times higher or 1 times as high for a one-unit increase in x. This is essentially the same odds. When the confidence interval includes 1, the odds of the outcome are not statistically significantly different with a change in the independent variable.

10.6.5 INTERPRETING SIGNIFICANT ODDS RATIOS

The odds ratio for the age variable is less than 1, and the confidence interval does not include 1. Thus, the interpretation of this odds ratio would be as follows: The odds of library use are 1% lower for every 1-year increase in age (OR = .99; 95% CI: .986–.996).

10.6.6 USING NHST TO ORGANIZE THE SIGNIFICANCE TESTING OF ODDS RATIOS

Kiara thought it might be useful to be a little more formal about the significance testing for the predictors in the model. Leslie started the NHST process with Kiara's help.

10.6.6.1 NHST STEP 1: WRITE THE NULL AND ALTERNATE HYPOTHESES

H0: Library use is not associated with age.

HA: Library use is associated with age.

10.6.6.2 NHST STEP 2: COMPUTE THE TEST STATISTIC

For each predictor, Kiara explained that there were two possible test statistics to use to determine statistical significance. The `summary()` function following a `glm()` function includes a z-statistic comparing the coefficient estimate to zero. Leslie looked back at her notes about z-statistics and was reminded that the z-statistic computed in previous meetings was used to measure how many standard deviations away a value is from a mean. This one seems to be computed using the standard error rather than the standard deviation, however, and Leslie looked perplexed. Kiara noticed and explained that, for logistic regression, the coefficient divided by the standard error follows a z-distribution. She said that this z-statistic is the test statistic for the Wald test, which has the same purpose (but follows a different distribution) as the Wald test from their linear regression meeting (Section 9.7.2). Leslie remembered that the purpose of the Wald test was to determine whether the coefficient in a model was statistically significantly different from zero. In the case of the age variable, dividing the estimate of –0.009 by its standard error of .003 gives a z-statistic of –3.28, which is well beyond the boundary of –1.96 for statistical significance when α is set at .05.

```
##
## Call:
## glm(formula = uses.lib ~ age, family = binomial("logit"), data =
libraries.cleaned)
##
## Deviance Residuals:
##     Min       1Q   Median       3Q      Max
## -1.291   -1.150   -1.027    1.190    1.363
##
## Coefficients:
##               Estimate Std. Error z value Pr(>|z|)
## (Intercept)   0.403785   0.142194   2.840  0.00452 **
## age          -0.008838   0.002697  -3.277  0.00105 **
## ---
## Signif. codes:  0 '***' 0.001 '**' 0.01 '*' 0.05 '.' 0.1 ' ' 1
##
## (Dispersion parameter for binomial family taken to be 1)
##
##     Null deviance: 2177.5 on 1570 degrees of freedom
## Residual deviance: 2166.7 on 1569 degrees of freedom
##   (30 observations deleted due to missingness)
## AIC: 2170.7
##
## Number of Fisher Scoring iterations: 3
```

As a reminder, Kiara explained that the z-distribution is a normal distribution with a mean of 0 and a standard deviation of 1. Nancy graphed a z-distribution to visualize how often a z-score of –3.28 or larger would happen if there were no relationship between age and library use in a sample of 1571 observations (Figure 10.7).

FIGURE 10.7 z-distribution for sample size of 1571

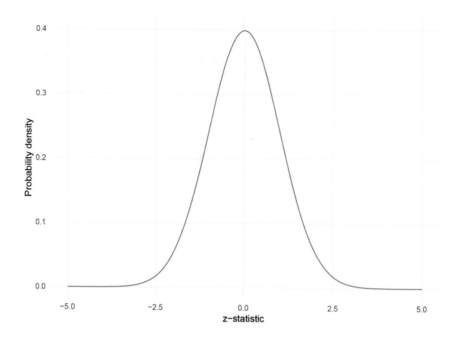

10.6.6.3 NHST STEP 3: CALCULATE THE PROBABILITY THAT YOUR TEST STATISTIC IS AT LEAST AS BIG AS IT IS IF THERE IS NO RELATIONSHIP (I.E., THE NULL IS TRUE)

The area under the curve to the left of the test statistic is the percentage of the time you would get a z-statistic of −3.28 or more extreme under the null hypothesis of no relationship between age and library use. Given this area is very small, the p-value of .00105 in the output from `summary(object = lib.model.small)` makes sense. There is a .105% probability that this sample came from a population where there was no relationship between age and library use. Thus, there is a statistically significant relationship between age and library use ($z = -3.28$; $p = .001$).

Kiara explained that the other way to determine statistical significance of predictors is to examine the confidence intervals around the odds ratios like they did in Section 10.6.3.

10.6.6.4 NHST STEPS 4 AND 5: INTERPRET THE PROBABILITY AND WRITE A CONCLUSION

The odds ratio for age is .99 with a 95% CI of .986–.996. The confidence interval shows the range where the odds ratio likely is in the population. Because the confidence interval does not include 1, this indicates that the odds ratio is statistically significantly different from 1. The interpretation would be as follows: The null hypothesis of no relationship between library use and age is rejected. The odds of library use are 1% lower for every 1-year increase in age in the sample (OR = .99; 95% CI: .986–.996). The 95% confidence interval indicates that the odds of library use are .4%–1.4% lower with each 1-year increase in age in the population that the sample came from.

10.6.7 ACHIEVEMENT 3: CHECK YOUR UNDERSTANDING

Use the code below to estimate a simple logistic model with sex as the only predictor model. Review the output to find and interpret model significance for a model including sex as a predictor of library use.

```
# simple logistic with sex predicting library use
lib.by.sex <- glm(formula = uses.lib ~ sex,
                  data = libraries.cleaned,
                  family = binomial("logit"))
odds.n.ends(x = lib.by.sex)
## $`Logistic regression model significance`
## Chi-squared         d.f.              p
##     33.886         1.000          0.000
##
## $`Contingency tables (model fit): percent predicted`
##                       Percent observed
## Percent predicted          1          0        Sum
##               1    0.2735790  0.2061212  0.4797002
##               0    0.2211118  0.2991880  0.5202998
##             Sum  0.4946908  0.5053092  1.0000000
##
## $`Contingency tables (model fit): frequency predicted`
##                     Number observed
## Number predicted     1     0   Sum
##               1    438   330   768
##               0    354   479   833
##             Sum   792   809  1601
##
## $`Predictor odds ratios and 95% CI`
##                     OR      2.5 %      97.5 %
## (Intercept) 1.3272727  1.1510520  1.5319401
## sexmale      0.5568107  0.4564639  0.6785707
##
## $`Model sensitivity`
## [1] 0.5530303
##
## $`Model specificity`
## [1] 0.592089
```

10.7 Achievement 4: Computing and interpreting two measures of model fit

Leslie remembered that, for linear regression, the R^2 statistic measured how well the model fit the observed data by measuring how much of the variability in the outcome was explained by the model. Kiara explained that the concept of variance is appropriate for continuous but not categorical variables, so a different measure of model fit is needed. She explained that there are several to choose from including the *percent correctly predicted* which is sometimes referred to as the *count* R^2.

10.7.1 PERCENT CORRECTLY PREDICTED OR COUNT R^2

Kiara explained that the percent correctly predicted by the model was computed using the predicted probabilities, or fitted values, for each of the observations and comparing these probabilities to the true value of the outcome. For example, if a person in the data set were predicted to have a 56% chance of library use, this would be transformed into a "yes" or "1" value of the outcome and then compared to the person's actual library use. If the predicted value and the true value matched, this would be considered a correct prediction.

Likewise, if the predicted probability for library use was less than 50%, the person would be considered to be a "no" or "0" for library use. Comparing this to the true value for that person would indicate whether the model was correct or incorrect. The total number of people the model gets correct out of the total number of people in the data analyzed is the *percent correctly predicted* or *count* R^2.

The `odds.n.ends()` function includes a table showing how many observations were correctly predicted in each category of the outcome. These values can be used to determine the overall percent correctly predicted.

```
## $`Logistic regression model significance`
## Chi-squared        d.f.            p
##      10.815        1.000        0.001
##
## $`Contingency tables (model fit): percent predicted`
##                 Percent observed
## Percent predicted       1         0        Sum
##             1   0.2151496 0.1896881 0.4048377
##             0   0.2768937 0.3182686 0.5951623
##           Sum 0.4920433 0.5079567 1.0000000
##
## $`Contingency tables (model fit): frequency predicted`
##                 Number observed
## Number predicted   1    0  Sum
##             1    338  298  636
##             0    435  500  935
##           Sum    773  798 1571
##
## $`Predictor odds ratios and 95% CI`
##                   OR     2.5 %     97.5 %
## (Intercept) 1.497482 1.1339164 1.9804811
## age         0.991201 0.9859589 0.9964415
##
## $`Model sensitivity`
```

```
## [1] 0.4372574
##
## $`Model specificity`
## [1] 0.6265664
```

Leslie saw that the model correctly predicted 338 of those who used the library and 500 of those who did not use the library. She computed the overall percent correctly predicted of 838/1571 or 53%. Kiara wrote out Equation (10.10) for the count R^2 or R^2_{count}.

$$R^2_{count} = \frac{n_{correct}}{n_{total}} \tag{10.10}$$

One alternative to the percent correctly predicted is the *adjusted count* R^2, which adjusts the count R^2 for the number of people in the largest of the two categories of the outcome (Hardin & Hilbe, 2007) as in Equation (10.11). The argument behind this adjustment is that a null model, or a model with no predictors, could get a good percent correctly predicted just by predicting everyone was in the outcome category that had the bigger percentage of people in it.

$$R^2_{count.adj} = \frac{n_{correct} - n_{most.common.outcome}}{n_{total} - n_{most.common.outcome}} \tag{10.11}$$

For the library use data, the most common category is library nonuse (or 0), with 798 of the 1571 participants with complete data for the model. Without knowing anything about library use, you could predict everyone in the data set was a nonuser and be right $\frac{798}{1571}$ or 50.8% of the time. Using the age predictor, the model is right $\frac{338 + 500}{1571}$ or 53% of the time. While this is not a huge increase, it did classify 40 additional people correctly compared to using the percentages in the outcome categories with no other information.

Nancy explained that interpreting this statistic is pretty straightforward and could go something like this: The model using age to predict library use was correct 53% of the time (Count R^2 = .53).

The adjusted count R^2 would be $\frac{338 + 500 - 798}{1571 - 798}$ or .05. The interpretation could then be written as follows: There were 5% more correct predictions by the age model than by the baseline (Adjusted Count R^2 = .05).

Both of these interpretations of fit are correct. It is up to the analyst to decide which they prefer or which may make more sense for their audience. Nancy mentioned that there are other fit statistics that are sometimes reported with logistic models called pseudo-R^2. These generally try to quantify the reduction in lack of fit between a null and full model. While they are reported relatively frequently, Nancy preferred the count and adjusted count R^2 because of their clear interpretations.

10.7.2 SENSITIVITY AND SPECIFICITY

Leslie was interested in the last two values in the `odds.n.ends()` output. Kiara explained that sometimes it is useful to know whether the model is better at predicting people with the outcome or people without the outcome. The measures used for these two concepts are sensitivity and specificity. *Sensitivity* determines the percentage of the 1s or "yes" values the model got correct, while *specificity* computes the percentage of 0s or "no" values the model got correct. In this case, the sensitivity is 43.7% while the specificity is 62.7%. The model was better at predicting the no values than the yes values. These percentages could also be computed from the frequency table in the output: The model predicted 500 of the 798 people in the 0 category correctly (62.7%) and 338 of the 773 in the 1 category correctly (43.7%).

10.7.3 ACHIEVEMENT 4: CHECK YOUR UNDERSTANDING

Compute and interpret the count R^2 and adjusted count R^2 values for the model with sex as the only predictor.

10.8 Achievement 5: Estimating a larger logistic regression model with categorical and continuous predictors

Now that she had worked through the different parts of model development and interpretation, Leslie was ready to estimate and interpret the model with all the predictors. First she wrote out the model in Equation (10.12).

$$p\left(uses.lib\right)=\frac{1}{1+e^{-(b_0+b_1 \cdot age+b_2 \cdot sex+b_3 \cdot educ+b_4 \cdot parent+b_5 \cdot disabled+b_6 \cdot rurality+b_7 \cdot raceth+b_8 \cdot ses)}} \tag{10.12}$$

Kiara reviewed the model and it looked good. Leslie started by using the `glm()` function and followed the steps she used in the simple linear regression analysis. Instead of using `summary()`, she went right to `odds.n.ends()`.

```
# estimate the library use model and print results
lib.model <- glm(formula = uses.lib ~ age + sex + educ + parent +
                    disabled + rurality + raceth + ses,
                data = libraries.cleaned,
                na.action = na.exclude,
                family = binomial("logit"))
odds.n.ends(x = lib.model)
## $`Logistic regression model significance`
## Chi-squared          d.f.              p
##       94.736        12.000          0.000
##
## $`Contingency tables (model fit): percent predicted`
##
##                 Percent observed
## Percent predicted         1          0        Sum
##              1    0.2648914  0.1744919  0.4393833
##              0    0.2228451  0.3377715  0.5606167
##            Sum  0.4877365  0.5122635  1.0000000
##
```

```
## $`Contingency tables (model fit): frequency predicted`
##                Number observed
## Number predicted   1    0  Sum
##               1   378  249  627
##               0   318  482  800
##             Sum   696  731 1427
##
## $`Predictor odds ratios and 95% CI`
##                              OR      2.5 %     97.5 %
## (Intercept)              1.3180091 0.6778733 2.5644803
## age                      0.9899123 0.9835415 0.9962814
## sexmale                  0.4891734 0.3921079 0.6091430
## educFour-year degree or more 1.9040694 1.2584331 2.8953329
## educHS to 2-year degree  1.1475517 0.7808490 1.6947789
## parentparent             1.2652862 0.9710624 1.6500243
## disabledyes              0.8003756 0.5836481 1.0949054
## ruralitysuburban         1.1899804 0.9019925 1.5704210
## ruralityurban            1.2300055 0.9281956 1.6307183
## racethNon-Hispanic Black 1.5539262 1.0018330 2.4167032
## racethNon-Hispanic White 1.3152888 0.9312650 1.8632329
## seslow                   0.9323567 0.5720558 1.5162449
## sesmedium                0.8471423 0.5747503 1.2441896
##
## $`Model sensitivity`
## [1] 0.5431034
##
## $`Model specificity`
## [1] 0.6593707
```

10.8.1 NHST STEP 1: WRITE THE NULL AND ALTERNATE HYPOTHESES

Kiara suggested they try writing the hypotheses in a more specific way. The null and alternate hypotheses used for the first model would be fine here, but it is also nice to explicitly state what is being tested.

H0: A model containing age, sex, education, parent status, disability status, rurality, SES, and race-ethnicity is no better than the baseline at explaining library use.

HA: A model containing age, sex, education, parent status, disability status, rurality, SES, and race-ethnicity is better than the baseline at explaining library use.

FIGURE 10.8 Chi-squared distribution with *n* = 1427 and *df* = 12

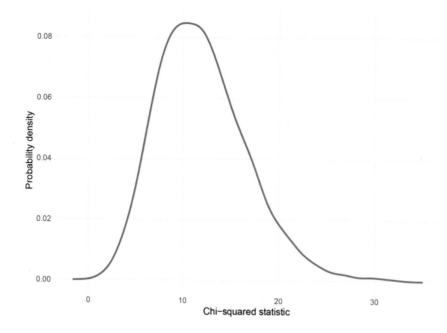

10.8.2 NHST STEP 2: COMPUTE THE TEST STATISTIC

The chi-squared test statistic of 94.74 was computed by the `odds.n.ends()` function.

10.8.3 NHST STEP 3: CALCULATE THE PROBABILITY THAT YOUR TEST STATISTIC IS AT LEAST AS BIG AS IT IS IF THERE IS NO RELATIONSHIP (I.E., THE NULL IS TRUE)

The `odds.n.ends()` output also shows the model chi-squared of 94.74 with the corresponding degrees of freedom of 12 and a very small *p*-value. Visualizing a chi-squared distribution with 12 degrees of freedom makes it clear why the *p*-value is so small (Figure 10.8). The probability that the chi-squared would be 94.74 if the full model were no better than the null model is shown as the area under the curve to the right starting at 94.74.

10.8.4 NHST STEPS 4 AND 5: INTERPRET THE PROBABILITY AND WRITE A CONCLUSION

With a very tiny probability of getting a chi-squared of 94.74 or larger if the null were true, the null hypothesis is rejected. Leslie wrote the conclusion:

> A logistic regression model containing age, sex, education, parental status, disability status, SES, race-ethnicity, and rurality was statistically significantly better than the baseline probability at predicting library use [$\chi^2(12) = 94.74$; $p < .001$].

10.8.5 ACHIEVEMENT 5: CHECK YOUR UNDERSTANDING

Rerun the model without the parent and SES predictors. Find and interpret model significance.

10.9 Achievement 6: Interpreting the results of a larger logistic regression model

The `summary()` and `odds.n.ends()` output both include values and significance statistics for the predictors. The `odds.n.ends()` output includes odds ratios, which are easier to interpret given the form of the logistic function used in computing the results.

10.9.1 COMPUTING ODDS RATIOS

```
# run the odds.n.ends code again
odds.n.ends(x = lib.model)
## $`Logistic regression model significance`
## Chi-squared        d.f.            p
##      94.736      12.000        0.000
##
## $`Contingency tables (model fit): percent predicted`
##                   Percent observed
## Percent predicted          1         0        Sum
##               1    0.2648914 0.1744919 0.4393833
##               0    0.2228451 0.3377715 0.5606167
##             Sum    0.4877365 0.5122635 1.0000000
##
## $`Contingency tables (model fit): frequency predicted`
##                 Number observed
## Number predicted    1    0  Sum
##               1    378  249  627
##               0    318  482  800
##             Sum    696  731 1427
##
## $`Predictor odds ratios and 95% CI`
##                                       OR      2.5 %     97.5 %
## (Intercept)                    1.3180091 0.6778733 2.5644803
## age                            0.9899123 0.9835415 0.9962814
## sexmale                        0.4891734 0.3921079 0.6091430
## educFour-year degree or more   1.9040694 1.2584331 2.8953329
## educHS to 2-year degree        1.1475517 0.7808490 1.6947789
## parentparent                   1.2652862 0.9710624 1.6500243
## disabledyes                    0.8003756 0.5836481 1.0949054
## ruralitysuburban               1.1899804 0.9019925 1.5704210
## ruralityurban                  1.2300055 0.9281956 1.6307183
```

```
## racethNon-Hispanic Black        1.5539262 1.0018330 2.4167032

## racethNon-Hispanic White        1.3152888 0.9312650 1.8632329

## seslow                          0.9323567 0.5720558 1.5162449

## sesmedium                       0.8471423 0.5747503 1.2441896

##

## $`Model sensitivity`

## [1] 0.5431034

##

## $`Model specificity`

## [1] 0.6593707
```

10.9.2 ODDS RATIO STATISTICAL SIGNIFICANCE

Leslie summarized what she remembered about the significance of odds ratios from the simple logistic models. The statistical significance of an odds ratio is determined by the range of its confidence interval. The confidence interval shows where the true or population value of the odds ratio likely lies. A confidence interval that includes 1 indicates that the true or population value of the relationship could be 1. The interpretation of an odds ratio of 1 is that the odds are 1 times higher or 1 times as high for a change in the predictor. This is essentially the same odds. When the confidence interval includes 1, the odds ratio could be 1 and this indicates it is not statistically significantly different from 1.

10.9.3 INTERPRETING ODDS RATIOS

Odds ratios greater than 1 indicate an increase in the odds of the outcome with a one-unit increase in a numeric variable or in comparison with the reference group for a factor variable. If the odds ratio is greater than 1 *and* the confidence interval does not include 1, the odds ratio suggests a statistically significant increase in the odds of the outcome.

Leslie noticed that there were several factor type variables in this larger model. Some of them had two categories and some had more than two categories. Since they had only interpreted the age variable as a predictor in the simple logistic model, Leslie was not sure what to do. It didn't seem to make sense to interpret them as having a "one-unit change."

Kiara explained that factor variables with two categories were interpreted with respect to the reference group, or the group not shown in the output. Since the factor variables can only change by going from one group to the other, instead of the odds ratio being for a one-unit change in the predictor, it is the change in the odds of the outcome when moving from the reference group to the other group. For the sex variable, male is the group shown in the output, so Kiara interpreted the odds ratio for sex as "Males have 51% lower odds of library use compared to females." She showed Leslie that the 51% came from subtracting the odds ratio of .489 from 1 (1 − .49 = .51) and multiplying by 100.

For factor variables with more than two categories, Kiara explained, each odds ratio is interpreted with respect to the reference group for that variable. For educ, the group not shown is the < HS group, indicating that it is the reference group. The odds ratio for the Four-year degree or more group is 1.90, so the interpretation would be that individuals with a four-year degree or more have 1.90 times higher odds of library use compared to people with less than a high school education.

This was a lot of information for Leslie to keep in her brain. Kiara suggested she start with identifying everything that was statistically significant. Leslie made a list of the odds ratios where the confidence interval did not include 1:

- `age` (OR = .99; 95% CI: .984–.996)

- `sexmale` (OR = .49; 95% CI: .39–.61)

- `educFour year degree or more` (OR = 1.90; 95% CI: 1.26–2.90)

- `racethNon-Hispanic Black` (OR = 1.55; 95% CI: 1.002–2.417)

10.9.3.1 INTERPRETING SIGNIFICANT ODDS RATIOS GREATER THAN 1

There were two significant predictors with odds ratios greater than 1: People with a four-year degree or more education had 1.90 times higher odds of library use compared to people with less than a high school education (OR = 1.90; 95% CI: 1.26–2.90), and people who were non-Hispanic Black had 1.55 times higher odds of library use compared to people who were Hispanic (OR = 1.55; 95% CI: 1.002–2.417).

10.9.3.2 INTERPRETING NON-SIGNIFICANT ODDS RATIOS GREATER THAN 1

Some odds ratios greater than 1 were nonsignificant. For example, the odds ratios for urban and suburban are greater than 1, but both of these odds ratios have confidence intervals that include 1. For suburban, the confidence interval is .90 to 1.57 (see odds ratio table in `odds.n.ends()` output). For urban, the confidence interval is .93 to 1.63. When the confidence interval includes 1, it is possible that the true value of the odds ratio is 1, so the values would be reported without the interpretation of higher odds: The odds of library use were not statistically significantly different for urban residents compared to rural residents (OR = 1.23; 95% CI: .93–1.63).

10.9.3.3 INTERPRETING SIGNIFICANT ODDS RATIOS LESS THAN 1

The age variable and male sex both show significant odds ratios lower than 1. For age, the odds of library use are 1% lower for every 1-year increase in a person's age (OR = .99; 95% CI: .984–.996). For male sex, the reference group is female and the odds ratio is .49. Subtracting 1 – .49 results in .51, so the odds of library use are 51% lower for males compared to females (OR = .49; 95% CI: .39–.61).

10.9.3.4 INTERPRETING NONSIGNIFICANT ODDS RATIOS LESS THAN 1

The low-SES category had a nonsignificant odds ratio of .93 (95% CI: .57–1.52). The interpretation would be as follows: The odds of library use are not statistically significantly different for those with low SES compared to those in the reference group of high SES (OR = .93; 95% CI: .57–1.52).

10.9.3.5 USING NHST TO ORGANIZE ODDS RATIO INTERPRETATION

The NHST process can be used to organize the reporting of odds ratios, such as that for sex and library use.

10.9.3.5.1 NHST Step 1: Write the null and alternate hypotheses

H0: There is no relationship between sex and library use.

HA: There is a relationship between sex and library use.

10.9.3.5.2 NHST Step 2: Compute the test statistic The odds ratio is the test statistic, OR = .49.

The confidence interval shows the probable range of the true or population value of an odds ratio, 95% CI: .39–.61.

The odds of library use are 51% lower for males than for females (OR = .49; 95% CI: .39–.61).

10.9.4 COMPUTE AND INTERPRET MODEL FIT

The model correctly predicted 378 of the 696 who use the library and 482 of the 731 who do not use the library. Overall, it was correct for $\dfrac{860}{1427}$ of the observations, or 60.3% of the time (count $R^2 = .603$). It was better at classifying those who do not use the library (specificity = 65.9%) than those who use the library (sensitivity = 54.3%). Leslie preferred the adjusted count R^2 and used the output to compute $R^2_{adj.count} = \dfrac{860 - 731}{1427 - 731} = .185$, which indicated that the model predicted 18.5% more of the observations correctly than a baseline model would have. Leslie noticed that there were fewer observations in this model compared to the smaller model, `lib.model.small`. Kiara explained that there were missing values for some of the variables, and observations with missing values on any of the variables in the model were not included, resulting in a smaller sample size for this model.

10.9.5 ACHIEVEMENT 6: CHECK YOUR UNDERSTANDING

Which of the following would be the most appropriate interpretation if the relationship between age in years and library use had an odds ratio of .56 with a 95% confidence interval of .34 to 1.23:

- The odds of library use are 44% lower for each 1-year increase in age (OR = .56; 95% CI: .34–1.23).

- There is no statistically significant association between age and library use (OR = .56; 95% CI: .34–1.23).

- The odds of library use are 56% lower for each 1-year increase in age (OR = .56; 95% CI: .34–1.23).

- There is no statistically significant association between age and library use (OR = .44; 95% CI: .34–1.23).

10.10 Achievement 7: Checking logistic regression assumptions and using diagnostics to identify outliers and influential values

Leslie was excited to be finished with the analyses! Kiara reminded her that it is important to check the assumptions of every model. There are three assumptions for logistic regression: independence of observations, linearity, and no perfect multicollinearity. Kiara introduced the *generalized variance inflation factor* (GVIF) to check for multicollinearity. The GVIF is similar to the VIF used for linear regression, but modified to account for the categorical outcome. She said linearity could be checked by graphing the log-odds of the outcome against each continuous predictor to see if the relationship is linear (i.e., falling along a line).

In addition, as with linear regression, diagnostics can aid in identifying whether there are outliers and influential observations that may be problematic. The same statistics are used in logistic as in linear regression to identify outliers and influential observations.

10.10.1 ASSUMPTION: INDEPENDENCE OF OBSERVATIONS

Kiara reminded Leslie that independence of observations is about whether there are observations in the data that are dependent on each other. For example, siblings, close friends, or spouses are more likely to share some behaviors or characteristics than unrelated people and would therefore influence the amount of variation in the data and violate the independence of observations assumption. The Pew Research Center conducted a phone survey where they selected a single person in a randomly selected household. This data collection strategy is likely to result in independent observations. The assumption is met.

10.10.2 ASSUMPTION: LINEARITY

In linear regression, the linearity assumption is checked by examining the relationship between each continuous predictor and the outcome variable. For logistic regression, the outcome variable is binary, so its relationship with another variable will never be linear. Instead of plotting the relationship of the outcome with each continuous predictor, linearity is tested by plotting the log-odds of the predicted probabilities for the outcome against each of the continuous predictors in the model.

By examining the relationship between the predicted probabilities and a continuous predictor, the graph for checking linearity shows whether the predictions are equally accurate along the range of values of the predictor. For example, are the predicted values equally accurate for people of a younger age compared to people of an older age? Kiara helped Leslie compute the log-odds, or logit, of the predicted values by showing her that the predicted probabilities are stored in the model object in R. She pointed out the model in the Environment pane and clicked on the small arrow to the left of the model name. All the information stored in the model was shown, and Kiara pointed out the item that says `fitted.values`, which contains the predicted probabilities for each observation in the data frame. Nancy noticed they were ready for some code and showed Leslie how to compute the log odds from the `fitted.values` and use it in a graph (Figure 10.9).

```
# make a variable of the log-odds of the predicted values
logit.use <- log(x = lib.model$fitted.values/(1-lib.model$fitted.values))

# make a small data frame with the log-odds variable and the age predictor
linearity.data <- data.frame(logit.use, age = lib.model$model$age)

# create a plot (Figure 10.9)
linearity.data %>%
  ggplot(aes(x = age, y = logit.use))+
  geom_point(aes(size = "Observation"), color = "gray60", alpha = .6) +
  geom_smooth(se = FALSE, aes(color = "Loess curve")) +
  geom_smooth(method = lm, se = FALSE, aes(color = "linear")) +
  theme_minimal() +
  labs(x = "Age in years",
       y = "Log-odds of library use predicted probability") +
  scale_color_manual(name = "Type of fit line",
                     values = c("dodgerblue2", "deeppink")) +
  scale_size_manual(values = 1.5, name = "")
```

The graph shows the Loess curve close to the linear fit line with the exception of the youngest ages. In this case, the linear fit line represents a linear relationship and the Loess curve represents the actual

FIGURE 10.9 Checking linearity of the age variable for the model of library use

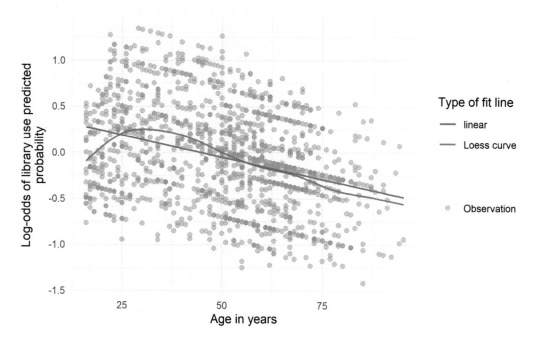

Source: https://www.pewinternet.org/dataset/march-2016-libraries.

relationship. It is up to the analyst to determine whether the actual relationship is close enough to linear to meet this assumption. If the assumption is not met, this variable might be removed from analysis, transformed, or recoded. Nancy mentioned that she had heard about spline regression as one way to deal with problems of linearity in linear and logistic regression. Kiara suggested that it might be worth considering that the data frame includes people as young as 16 years old; it is possible that there are different predictors of library use before adulthood and restricting the age range of the data frame to adults over 18 could be another option for addressing this deviation from linearity in the youngest survey participants.

10.10.3 ASSUMPTION: NO PERFECT MULTICOLLINEARITY

The GVIF is similar to the VIF in linear regression. It examines how well each predictor variable in the model is explained by the group of other predictor variables. If a predictor is well explained by the others, it is redundant and unnecessary. For the GVIF, often a threshold of $GVIF^{\frac{1}{2*Df}} < 2.5$ is used as a cutoff, with values of 2.5 or higher indicating a failed multicollinearity assumption. The **car** package is used, and the same `vif()` function that was used for the linear model can be used here.

```
# compute GVIF
car::vif(mod = lib.model)
##               GVIF Df GVIF^(1/(2*Df))
## age       1.254322  1        1.119965
## sex       1.051221  1        1.025291
## educ      1.309506  2        1.069737
```

```
## parent    1.101618  1          1.049580
## disabled  1.153173  1          1.073859
## rurality  1.118617  2          1.028420
## raceth    1.212126  2          1.049269
## ses       1.249162  2          1.057194
```

None of the values in the right-hand column have a value of 2.5 or higher, so there is no discernable problem with multicollinearity.

Overall, the assumption checking revealed a possible problem with age as a predictor, mostly at the youngest ages. The other assumptions were met. It might be useful to restrict the age variable to adults or to transform the age variable.

10.10.4 MODEL DIAGNOSTICS

In addition to checking assumptions, Kiara reminded Leslie about model diagnostics for determining whether there are any observations that are having an unusual impact on the model. Leslie looked through her notes and remembered that an outlier is an observation with unusual values, regression outliers have unusual values of the outcome given the value(s) of predictor(s), and influential observations change the regression coefficients. Kiara explained that the same measures from linear regression can be used to help identify outliers and influential values.

10.10.4.1 USING STANDARDIZED RESIDUALS TO FIND OUTLIERS

Leslie looked back to the previous meeting (Section 9.9.10) and reminded herself that residuals are the distances between the predicted value of the outcome and the true value of the outcome for each person or observation in the data set. These values are standardized by computing z-scores for each one so that they follow a z-distribution. Z-scores that are greater than 1.96 or less than –1.96 are about two standard deviations or more away from the mean of a measure. In this case, they are more than two standard deviations away from the mean residual value. Very large values of standardized residuals can indicate that the predicted value for an observation is far from the true value for that observation, indicating that an examination of that observation could be useful.

Standardized residuals are computed using the `rstandard()` function and can be added to the data frame. Nancy introduced the `max()` function, which returns the maximum value from an object. In this case, she had it return the maximum value of the standardized residuals variable she added to the `libraries.cleaned` data frame. She explained to Kiara and Leslie that `max()` does not like `NA` values, so before using this function, she dropped the `NA` values from the new `standardized` variable.

```
# get standardized residuals and add to data frame
libraries.cleaned <- libraries.cleaned %>%
  mutate(standardized = rstandard(model = lib.model))

# check the residuals for large values > 2
libraries.cleaned %>%
  drop_na(standardized) %>%
  summarize(max.resid = max(abs(x = standardized)))
##   max.resid
## 1  1.816214
```

FIGURE 10.10 Standardized residuals for library use model

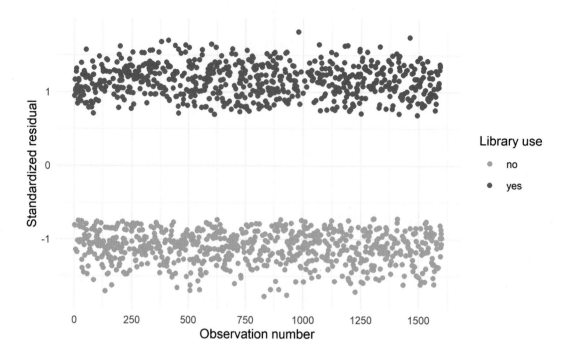

The maximum absolute value of any standardized residual was less than 1.96, so the standardized residuals did not reveal any outliers. A graph of the standardized residuals confirms they were all close to 1 for those who used the library and close to –1 for those who did not (Figure 10.10). Most predicted probabilities were about one standard deviation above or below the mean predicted probability.

10.10.4.2 USING df-BETAS TO FIND INFLUENTIAL VALUES

Next, Leslie used the df-betas to find influential values. Kiara reminded Leslie that the df-beta removes each observation from the data frame, conducts the analysis again, and compares the results with the existing model. Observations with high df-betas (more than 2) may be influencing the model, causing large differences in the intercept or coefficients. Leslie remembered that df-betas were computed for the intercept and each variable in the model, so there could be several lines of code to write to get the df-beta for each variable. Kiara thought she had seen something in the **car** package that might help. She checked the documentation and found a function that would compute not only the df-betas but also Cook's Distance and leverage, the other measures they were planning to use.

Kiara explained to Leslie and Nancy that the `influence.measures()` function in the **car** package results in a list of five things: a data frame containing the values of df-beta, df-fit, the covariance ratio, Cook's Distance, and leverage (called hat). The data frame containing these values is the first thing in the list and is named `infmat`.

Nancy was excited to try a new function and typed `influence.measures()` with the `model = lib.model` argument. To get a general idea of what is in the data frame of influence statistics, she printed a summary of the `infmat` list entry.

```
# get influence statistics
influence.lib.mod <- influence.measures(model = lib.model)

# summarize data frame with dfbetas, cooks, leverage
summary(object = influence.lib.mod$infmat)
##      dfb.1_                dfb.age               dfb.sxml
##  Min.   :-0.1051922   Min.   :-0.0767940   Min.   :-0.039027
##  1st Qu.:-0.0129510   1st Qu.:-0.0160893   1st Qu.:-0.023107
##  Median : 0.0000000   Median : 0.0000000   Median :-0.015882
##  Mean   : 0.0001392   Mean   :-0.0005355   Mean   :-0.001121
##  3rd Qu.: 0.0125725   3rd Qu.: 0.0142736   3rd Qu.: 0.024395
##  Max.   : 0.1142539   Max.   : 0.0825243   Max.   : 0.055434
##
##     dfb.edom              dfb.et2d              dfb.prnt
##  Min.   :-0.1161072   Min.   :-0.1179326   Min.   :-0.073641
##  1st Qu.:-0.0106307   1st Qu.:-0.0069438   1st Qu.:-0.013862
##  Median : 0.0000000   Median : 0.0000000   Median : 0.000000
##  Mean   : 0.0005464   Mean   : 0.0001351   Mean   : 0.000333
##  3rd Qu.: 0.0113543   3rd Qu.: 0.0068441   3rd Qu.: 0.014662
##  Max.   : 0.0967673   Max.   : 0.0949315   Max.   : 0.069974
##
##     dfb.dsbl              dfb.rrltys             dfb.rrltyr
##  Min.   :-0.079962    Min.   :-0.0733540   Min.   :-0.0742958
##  1st Qu.:-0.011309    1st Qu.:-0.0152557   1st Qu.:-0.0150995
##  Median : 0.000000    Median : 0.0000000   Median : 0.0000000
##  Mean   :-0.000256    Mean   : 0.0002054   Mean   : 0.0002627
##  3rd Qu.: 0.009065    3rd Qu.: 0.0139402   3rd Qu.: 0.0147617
##  Max.   : 0.089810    Max.   : 0.0741895   Max.   : 0.0714801
##
##     dfb.rN-B              dfb.rN-W              dfb.sslw
##  Min.   :-0.0843655   Min.   :-0.1059933   Min.   :-9.111e-02
##  1st Qu.:-0.0023347   1st Qu.:-0.0079223   1st Qu.:-9.360e-03
##  Median : 0.0000000   Median : 0.0000000   Median : 0.000e+00
##  Mean   : 0.0003143   Mean   : 0.0002498   Mean   :-2.919e-05
##  3rd Qu.: 0.0025706   3rd Qu.: 0.0083564   3rd Qu.: 8.515e-03
##  Max.   : 0.0847660   Max.   : 0.0939644   Max.   : 9.547e-02
##
##     dfb.ssmd              dffit                cov.r
##  Min.   :-0.1118319   Min.   :-0.17302    Min.   :0.9952
##  1st Qu.:-0.0062815   1st Qu.:-0.09024    1st Qu.:1.0035
```

```
##  Median : 0.0000000    Median :-0.04160    Median :1.0079
##  Mean    :-0.0001344   Mean    :-0.00026   Mean    :1.0082
##  3rd Qu.: 0.0073985    3rd Qu.: 0.08853    3rd Qu.:1.0127
##  Max.    : 0.1113670   Max.    : 0.18890   Max.    :1.0250
##                        NA's    :174
##       cook.d              hat
##  Min.   :0.00011    Min.   :0.000000
##  1st Qu.:0.00032    1st Qu.:0.004505
##  Median :0.00057    Median :0.007261
##  Mean   :0.00071    Mean   :0.008120
##  3rd Qu.:0.00093    3rd Qu.:0.011625
##  Max.   :0.00353    Max.   :0.022682
##  NA's   :174
```

The output entries starting with dfb. are the df-betas. A quick look through the summary shows that none of the variables had df-betas larger than 2, so, by the df-beta measure, there were no influential observations.

10.10.4.3 USING COOK'S DISTANCE TO FIND INFLUENTIAL VALUES

Kiara reminded Leslie that the next measure of influence, Cook's Distance, is computed in a similar way to df-beta—each observation is removed and the model is re-estimated without it. Cook's D then combines the differences between the models with and without an observation for all the parameters together instead of one at a time like the df-betas. A high Cook's D would indicate that removing the observation made a big difference and therefore it might be considered influential.

Kiara explained that cutoff for a high Cook's D value is usually $4/n$, the same as in linear regression. With 1427 observations used in this model, Leslie determined that a Cook's D greater than 0.0028 will be problematic. It looked like there might be a few observations that fit this description, so Leslie wanted to determine which observations they were to take a closer look. Kiara suggested taking a subset of the cook.d column from the data frame and including only values greater than the cutoff. Creating the subset is complicated this time because the data frame with the numbers is one of the entries in a list. To make the process a little clearer, Leslie decided to save the data frame object outside the list and then take the subset.

```
# save the data frame
influence.lib <- data.frame(influence.lib.mod$infmat)

# observations with high Cook's D
influence.lib %>%
  filter(cook.d > 4/1427)
##          dfb.1_      dfb.age     dfb.sxml     dfb.edom     dfb.et2d
## 1 -0.089968791 0.06811733  0.05291068 -0.01482971 -0.003299788
## 2  0.030721307 0.06698698 -0.02050929 -0.09820409 -0.108857230
```

```
## 3    0.002832481 0.08252428    0.04199633 -0.09143730 -0.105390995
## 4    0.010410729 0.02204048    0.04365804 -0.02292003  0.001809933
## 5    0.014767212 0.05758856    0.05008263 -0.10059417 -0.106892895
## 6   -0.028273550 0.02666186    0.04253825  0.08914222  0.090112886
##          dfb.prnt      dfb.dsbl    dfb.rrltys   dfb.rrltyr      dfb.rN.B
## 1    0.0396513933 -0.004729808   0.021942935 -0.05627540 -0.004880216
## 2    0.0007253862  0.040622780  -0.011490805 -0.02882916  0.080510047
## 3   -0.0109348717 -0.055368373  -0.010223876 -0.02738762  0.084766010
## 4   -0.0558308631  0.009065273   0.004802848 -0.05369690 -0.076283416
## 5    0.0025424537  0.056500556  -0.015055642 -0.01620049  0.010835404
## 6   -0.0516576254  0.027851495  -0.073218857 -0.00850814 -0.027064355
##          dfb.rN.W      dfb.sslw      dfb.ssmd        dffit       cov.r        cook.d
## 1   -0.027773586  0.090412815  0.1094683737  -0.1621125  1.0010074  0.003005208
## 2    0.002088386 -0.032365340 -0.0027014760   0.1821590  1.0154358  0.002976640
## 3    0.014049614  0.046463660  0.0008830421   0.1889008  1.0116403  0.003526649
## 4   -0.010206138 -0.001115642 -0.0225046580  -0.1505078  0.9968121  0.002804872
## 5    0.023317516 -0.019984909  0.0023303909   0.1591076  0.9965610  0.003265925
## 6   -0.061144528 -0.049016898 -0.0091338373  -0.1730234  1.0109954  0.002815924
##              hat
## 1   0.011863095
## 2   0.020492118
## 3   0.019068983
## 4   0.009432757
## 5   0.010104224
## 6   0.017260236
```

Counting the rows in the output, it looked like there were six observations with Cook's D values that indicated some possible influence.

10.10.4.4 USING LEVERAGE TO FIND INFLUENTIAL VALUES

The last measure to look at, said Kiara, was leverage. Leslie looked back to the linear regression meeting notes and read that leverage is the influence that the observed value of the outcome has on the predicted value of the outcome (Section 9.9.10). Leverage values range between 0 and 1. To determine which leverage values indicate influential observations, a cutoff of $\frac{2p}{n}$ is often used. In this case, the cutoff is $\frac{2 \times 13}{1427} = 0.01822004$.

```
# observations with high Leverage
influence.lib %>%
  filter(hat > 2*13/1427)
```

```
##        dfb.1_         dfb.age       dfb.sxml        dfb.edom       dfb.et2d
## 1    0.079409735   0.0107229420  -0.029561280    0.0256295349    0.012018677
## 2   -0.039393366  -0.0111769006   0.019748087    0.0678941555    0.076642077
## 3   -0.021281313   0.0355064851   0.019975575   -0.0510898854   -0.056242988
## 4   -0.077183444   0.0747610090   0.030241098    0.0684679590    0.075757975
## 5   -0.057559813  -0.0546836579   0.022616742    0.0032325745   -0.015737131
## 6    0.030721307   0.0669869812  -0.020509287   -0.0982040887   -0.108857230
## 7   -0.075334091  -0.0315274353   0.028120064   -0.0002796066   -0.020493355
## 8    0.002832481   0.0825242803   0.041996330   -0.0914372961   -0.105390995
## 9   -0.064404816   0.0724579739   0.032636544    0.0779878220    0.081721885
## 10  -0.043733703  -0.0282909252   0.026113782    0.0552817155    0.060915809
## 11  -0.007933519   0.0074388525  -0.025201833    0.0747049069    0.082239779
## 12   0.113851646  -0.0482938681   0.009886817   -0.1040377858   -0.092205139
## 13   0.114253911  -0.0500992106  -0.039027114    0.0114532114    0.030828106
## 14   0.088979266  -0.0571907986  -0.029043295   -0.0533142870   -0.060535476
## 15  -0.057081828   0.0385513346  -0.015179454    0.0695940439    0.076713580
## 16  -0.105192184   0.0434533648  -0.010624333    0.0796089184    0.074498752
## 17   0.016686793  -0.0001542193  -0.032652813   -0.0342428624   -0.041261763
## 18  -0.006217131  -0.0369797409  -0.023031106    0.0514096277    0.059701670
## 19   0.013608403   0.0179440943  -0.018420778   -0.0618904933   -0.073746667
## 20  -0.046791253  -0.0180548436  -0.016379164    0.0022119838   -0.023422114
## 21   0.052888090  -0.0382704755   0.015710952   -0.0914872762   -0.094461508
## 22   0.024073297   0.0237156904   0.018064796   -0.0202586089    0.006708797
## 23   0.078249796  -0.0767939980  -0.030571010   -0.0685378389   -0.075895835
## 24  -0.027265449   0.0097291843   0.023393897    0.0632945231    0.076790413
## 25  -0.009500767   0.0028145055  -0.030160945    0.0466623616    0.058572741
## 26   0.021156764   0.0355210972  -0.015542577   -0.0478802228   -0.056735740
## 27  -0.023227863  -0.0611043749   0.017768081    0.0533243480    0.059060692
## 28  -0.029604373  -0.0354893552  -0.023325706   -0.0050421592    0.008307609
## 29  -0.033384871   0.0202845524   0.050883340    0.0482285670    0.059091166
## 30   0.049665794  -0.0366789970   0.024687559   -0.0667682765   -0.081555201
## 31  -0.094056078   0.0328195924  -0.018051777   -0.0360578859   -0.019654713
## 32   0.052888090  -0.0382704755   0.015710952   -0.0914872762   -0.094461508
## 33   0.059409943   0.0336899299   0.027100934    0.0271196781    0.014316122
## 34   0.113851646  -0.0482938681   0.009886817   -0.1040377858   -0.092205139
## 35  -0.017319665   0.0314987910   0.026128315    0.0687906960    0.075633096
##        dfb.prnt        dfb.dsbl      dfb.rrltys      dfb.rrltyr       dfb.rN.B
## 1   -0.0276165743  -0.0053793873  -0.031866578   -0.032531470    -0.05213104
## 2    0.0084991997  -0.0394554769   0.011846209    0.025201726    -0.06199058
## 3   -0.0396104127  -0.0735276930   0.016396348    0.033046807     0.06101559
## 4    0.0253078179  -0.0680813961   0.020099367    0.024400593    -0.01715561
## 5    0.0117278826   0.0199864314   0.018930110    0.020963944     0.04936099
```

```
## 6    0.0007253862   0.0406227796  -0.011490805  -0.028829165   0.08051005
## 7    0.0195253827   0.0151432412   0.023198571   0.025762421   0.05264427
## 8   -0.0109348717  -0.0553683726  -0.010223876  -0.027387621   0.08476601
## 9    0.0200033200  -0.0688695988  -0.001033099  -0.053609020  -0.01997295
## 10   0.0196211052   0.0355778942  -0.058441837   0.007916966   0.03884489
## 11  -0.0478107775   0.0261223081  -0.007280239  -0.052024824  -0.08436554
## 12  -0.0353871279  -0.0032494340   0.043632374  -0.002659650   0.02182784
## 13  -0.0398241744   0.0039678774  -0.031327207  -0.034975919  -0.05059823
## 14  -0.0263771967   0.0675210840  -0.001523604   0.036584757  -0.04088620
## 15   0.0269509362   0.0105715434   0.019235194   0.028656647  -0.06718146
## 16   0.0309226842   0.0023613425   0.027936592   0.020084509  -0.01664272
## 17  -0.0396188580  -0.0540012345  -0.003871475  -0.035276494   0.04788413
## 18   0.0088250189   0.0294472996   0.006822026   0.016867443  -0.04956707
## 19  -0.0078573682   0.0343647803   0.011224063   0.044213490   0.07090551
## 20  -0.0350948374  -0.0003046082  -0.037624214   0.005734283   0.04838014
## 21  -0.0293920007  -0.0140280489   0.054623685  -0.012516700   0.08266419
## 22   0.0491354422  -0.0093688250  -0.005709968   0.049261060   0.05888826
## 23  -0.0258171439   0.0687856227  -0.020332489  -0.024672399   0.01732181
## 24   0.0153620763  -0.0442894959  -0.009702604  -0.045192553  -0.07857442
## 25  -0.0395363993  -0.0464015099   0.010512825   0.022863228  -0.06065991
## 26   0.0597446867   0.0447890199   0.011782313   0.050277566  -0.04413748
## 27   0.0064860459   0.0435601853  -0.010788069  -0.043153226   0.03733043
## 28   0.0186709819   0.0125927554   0.014809362  -0.043479112  -0.05923715
## 29   0.0636047817   0.0755257430   0.007465150   0.054402071  -0.07228202
## 30  -0.0355371242  -0.0231089438  -0.018516987  -0.035118484   0.08153756
## 31   0.0419510043  -0.0121728541   0.041520899   0.040895958   0.05661182
## 32  -0.0293920007  -0.0140280489   0.054623685  -0.012516700   0.08266419
## 33  -0.0248721357  -0.0055185507  -0.018099683   0.040928969  -0.06470003
## 34  -0.0353871279  -0.0032494340   0.043632374  -0.002659650   0.02182784
## 35  -0.0598941520  -0.0609699591  -0.010846440  -0.066052397  -0.02139160
##        dfb.rN.W     dfb.sslw      dfb.ssmd       dffit    cov.r        cook.d
## 1   -0.078580215  -0.06515218  -0.0787955395   0.1255463 1.020245  0.0010758274
## 2   -0.006707985   0.02812380   0.0032862354  -0.1265721 1.020932  0.0010887619
## 3    0.067357818  -0.02971106   0.0045910206  -0.1466448 1.017510  0.0016361698
## 4   -0.036097537   0.03431203   0.0060364795  -0.1404703 1.018254  0.0014533752
## 5    0.072619037   0.06583699   0.0786046859  -0.1273418 1.025043  0.0010607027
## 6    0.002088386  -0.03236534  -0.0027014760   0.1821590 1.015436  0.0029766402
## 7    0.075895203   0.07521835   0.0871975544  -0.1300789 1.021683  0.0011537247
## 8    0.014049614   0.04646366   0.0008830421   0.1889008 1.011640  0.0035266488
## 9   -0.051414949   0.03480796   0.0041308932  -0.1577528 1.018326  0.0019476491
```

```
## 10   0.050730320 -0.03689925 -0.0035219296 -0.1351858 1.019214 0.0013049298
## 11  -0.044835596 -0.03607562 -0.0062882084 -0.1613738 1.019343 0.0020351644
## 12   0.040525104 -0.09111270 -0.0964751142  0.1666143 1.021365 0.0021506931
## 13  -0.068281884 -0.08730533 -0.0939044531  0.1411342 1.022946 0.0013890760
## 14  -0.044990025 -0.03822783 -0.0035786915  0.1505135 1.019018 0.0017110303
## 15  -0.016079239  0.02173913 -0.0026349465 -0.1254146 1.020499 0.0010700203
## 16  -0.031253240  0.08212058  0.0856328848 -0.1340068 1.023581 0.0012158268
## 17   0.045327488 -0.03042063 -0.0020579336 -0.1161294 1.021710 0.0008789675
## 18  -0.009548633 -0.02573747 -0.0001569230 -0.1049441 1.022391 0.0006891087
## 19   0.027632442  0.02074460 -0.0075190685  0.1448717 1.020103 0.0015322179
## 20   0.064291200  0.06173702  0.0710163541 -0.1253606 1.021141 0.0010613592
## 21   0.021309148 -0.01669700  0.0115039847  0.1592530 1.019444 0.0019643495
## 22   0.008153057 -0.07794336 -0.0867134514  0.1468969 1.021134 0.0015662201
## 23   0.036482604 -0.03463995 -0.0061191251  0.1419996 1.018420 0.0014898731
## 24  -0.033905189 -0.01948330  0.0091301764 -0.1564394 1.017805 0.0019207770
## 25  -0.020882028 -0.02078610  0.0005576394 -0.1282944 1.023379 0.0010966122
## 26  -0.041731480  0.02699902 -0.0008666398  0.1521154 1.018495 0.0017704092
## 27   0.042435928 -0.03126015  0.0005370276 -0.1287519 1.021510 0.0011275188
## 28   0.006909687  0.07051869  0.0882891520 -0.1503856 1.017193 0.0017522163
## 29  -0.070079667  0.04733124  0.0037217683  0.1738857 1.012952 0.0027474811
## 30   0.027235066  0.02995312 -0.0028500063  0.1559980 1.017171 0.0019249873
## 31   0.081082098  0.07142185  0.0843648193 -0.1390828 1.019492 0.0013950101
## 32   0.021309148 -0.01669700  0.0115039847  0.1592530 1.019444 0.0019643495
## 33  -0.085678757 -0.07090008 -0.0893892090  0.1528936 1.016503 0.0018469586
## 34   0.040525104 -0.09111270 -0.0964751142  0.1666143 1.021365 0.0021506931
## 35  -0.066562056 -0.02878936  0.0032450846 -0.1712747 1.016190 0.0024936647
##            hat
## 1   0.01840580
## 2   0.01896105
## 3   0.01848798
## 4   0.01840156
## 5   0.02194186
## 6   0.02049212
## 7   0.01977174
## 8   0.01906898
## 9   0.01998386
## 10  0.01855190
## 11  0.02093788
## 12  0.02268194
```

```
## 13 0.02156559
## 14 0.01977308
## 15 0.01856697
## 16 0.02142212
## 17 0.01863681
## 18 0.01823362
## 19 0.01997471
## 20 0.01900247
## 21 0.02081350
## 22 0.02082705
## 23 0.01864169
## 24 0.01954697
## 25 0.02081459
## 26 0.01958616
## 27 0.01954146
## 28 0.01863020
## 29 0.01836331
## 30 0.01912239
## 31 0.01907325
## 32 0.02081350
## 33 0.01844156
## 34 0.02268194
## 35 0.01992819
```

Thirty-five observations had high leverage. It was hard to tell from this output if any of the observations were outlying or influential by more than one metric. Leslie suggested writing code that would look for problem `hat` and `cook.d` values together. She tried writing it herself with Nancy looking over her shoulder, ready to help.

```
# observations with high leverage and Cook's D
influence.lib %>%
  filter(hat > 2*13/1427 & cook.d > 4/1427)
##         dfb.1_     dfb.age    dfb.sxml     dfb.edom     dfb.et2d      dfb.prnt
## 1 0.030721307 0.06698698 -0.02050929 -0.09820409 -0.1088572  0.0007253862
## 2 0.002832481 0.08252428  0.04199633 -0.09143730 -0.1053910 -0.0109348717
##       dfb.dsbl   dfb.rrltys   dfb.rrltyr     dfb.rN.B     dfb.rN.W      dfb.sslw
## 1  0.04062278 -0.01149080 -0.02882916 0.08051005 0.002088386 -0.03236534
## 2 -0.05536837 -0.01022388 -0.02738762 0.08476601 0.014049614  0.04646366
##        dfb.ssmd       dffit     cov.r      cook.d         hat
## 1 -0.0027014760 0.1821590 1.015436 0.002976640 0.02049212
## 2  0.0008830421 0.1889008 1.011640 0.003526649 0.01906898
```

It looked like two of the observations were problematic by more than one measure, which was a small number for such a large data set. To review these two cases, Nancy suggested she merge the `influence .lib` object with the `libraries.cleaned` data frame. Unfortunately, there was no variable to use for the merge, so Nancy added the observation numbers for each row to each of the data frames and used the observation numbers to merge. Nancy thought it might be helpful to add the predicted probabilities to the data frame as well to compare to the observed values. She used `predict()` to add these values. The use of `predict()` with a logistic model will predict the probability of the outcome when the argument `type = "response"` is included. Once the data frames were merged and the predicted probabilities added, Nancy filtered the two cases so they could review to see if there was anything suspicious.

```r
# make row names as a variable
influence.lib <- influence.lib %>%
  rownames_to_column()

# merge data frame with diagnostic stats
libraries.cleaned.diag <- libraries.cleaned %>%
  rownames_to_column() %>%
  merge(x = influence.lib, by = 'rowname') %>%
  mutate(pred.prob = predict(object = lib.model, type = "response"))

# find mean predicted probability
libraries.cleaned.diag %>%
  summarize(mean.predicted = mean(x = pred.prob, na.rm = TRUE))
##   mean.predicted
## 1      0.4877365
```

The mean predicted probability was .49, which may be useful to know in looking at the possible outliers. Nancy filtered the outliers and selected relevant variables from the model and fit statistics to review.

```r
# review influential observations
libraries.cleaned.diag %>%
 filter(hat > 2*13/1427 & cook.d > 4/1427) %>%
 select(rowname, age, sex, educ, parent, disabled,
        rurality, uses.lib, raceth, ses, hat, cook.d, pred.prob)
##   rowname age    sex educ     parent disabled rurality uses.lib
## 1     204  91 female < HS not parent      yes    rural      yes
## 2     329  76   male < HS not parent       no    rural      yes
##
##                 raceth    ses        hat   cook.d pred.prob
## 1 Non-Hispanic Black medium 0.02049212 0.002976640  0.453502
## 2 Non-Hispanic Black    low 0.01906898 0.003526649  0.625088
```

The observations did not seem unusual or like data entry errors. Both of the observations were at the higher end of the age range, and both were library users. Because there do not appear to be any data entry errors or strange values, the observations should stay in the data frame.

10.10.5 ACHIEVEMENT 7: CHECK YOUR UNDERSTANDING

Which of the following are logistic regression model assumptions?

- Independence of observations
- Cook's Distance
- Standardized residuals
- Linearity

10.11 Achievement 8: Using the model to predict probabilities for observations that are outside the data set

Logistic regression models are useful not only for examining relationships between predictors and binary outcomes, but also for predicting probabilities for hypothetical or new cases that are not in the data frame. Leslie found this interesting and wanted to try predicting the probability of library use for her brother and her parents. Her brother is 35 years old, is male, has a four-year degree, is not a parent, has low socioeconomic status, is non-Hispanic white, and lives in a rural area. Her parents are 65 and 68 years old, are female and male, are non-Hispanic White, have medium SES, have four-year degrees, are parents (clearly), and live in a rural area. None of the three are disabled.

Nancy showed her how to make a small new data frame that included the data for her brother and parents and demonstrated use of the `predict()` function to predict their probabilities of library use.

```
# make a new data frame containing the observations of interest
examp.data <- data.frame(age = c(35, 65, 68),
                sex = c("male", "female", "male"),
                educ = c("Four-year degree or more",
                        "Four-year degree or more",
                        "Four-year degree or more"),
                disabled = c("no", "no", "no"),
                parent = c("not parent", "parent", "parent"),
                rurality = c("rural", "rural", "rural"),
                raceth = c("Non-Hispanic White",
                        "Non-Hispanic White",
                        "Non-Hispanic White"),
                ses = c("low", "medium", "medium"))

# use the new data frame to predict
```

```
predictions <- predict(object = lib.model, newdata = examp.data,
                       type = "response")
predictions
##         1         2         3
## 0.5135547 0.6466977 0.4648331
```

The model predicted that Leslie's brother had a 51.4% probability of library use, her mom had a 64.7% probability of library use, and her dad had a 46.5% probability of library use. Leslie noticed that her dad and brother had very similar probabilities, while her mom was much more likely to be a library user. The differences in the data between her dad and brother are age, parent status, and socioeconomic status. The only difference between her parents is between female and male. She looked back at the odds ratios and saw that the odds of library use are 51% lower for males compared to females, so that must be what made the difference from 64.7% for mom and 46.5% for dad!

10.11.1 ACHIEVEMENT 8: CHECK YOUR UNDERSTANDING

Create a small data frame that includes your personal characteristics and those of two relatives or friends. Predict the probability of library use for the people in your small data frame. Does it seem correct? Do you want to go to the library now? There are a lot of good books there!

10.12 Achievement 9: Adding and interpreting interaction terms in logistic regression

Leslie started thinking about when she used to go to the library as a kid. She remembered it was always her mom who took her to the library, and she wondered if sex and parent status might work together to influence the odds of library use. Nancy thought that was an interesting question that could be answered by adding an interaction term to the model. An interaction term examines how two (or more) variables might work together to influence an outcome. Visualizing this idea might be the most useful way to start exploring it (Figure 10.11).

```
# the relationship between parent status and library use (Figure 10.11)
libraries.cleaned %>%
  drop_na(parent) %>%
  ggplot(aes(x = parent, fill = factor(uses.lib))) +
  geom_bar(position = "dodge") +
  theme_minimal() +
  labs(x = "Parent status", y = "Number of participants") +
  scale_fill_manual(values = c("#7463AC", "gray"),
                    name = "Library use")
```

It looks like there are more parents who are library users than there are parents who are nonusers, while fewer nonparents are users than nonusers of the library. What is the relationship by sex?

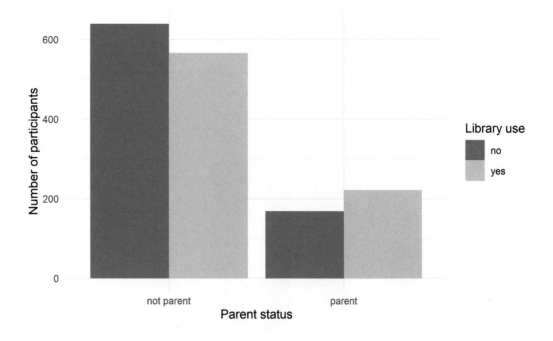

```
# library use by sex (Figure 10.12)
libraries.cleaned %>%
  drop_na(parent) %>%
  ggplot(aes(x = sex, fill = factor(uses.lib))) +
  geom_bar(position = "dodge") +
  theme_minimal() +
  labs(x = "Sex", y = "Number of participants") +
  scale_fill_manual(values = c("#7463AC", "gray"),
                    name = "Library use")
```

Males are more likely to be nonusers of the library than to be users, while females are more likely to be users of the library than nonusers (Figure 10.12). What happens if we look at sex and parent status together? Does being a parent change library use for males and females?

```
# the relationship among sex, parent status, and library use (Figure 10.13)
libraries.cleaned %>%
  drop_na(parent) %>%
  ggplot(aes(x = parent, fill = factor(uses.lib))) +
  geom_bar(position = "dodge") +
  theme_minimal() +
```

```
    labs(x = "Parent status", y = "Number of participants") +

    scale_fill_manual(values = c("#7463AC", "gray"),

                          name = "Library use") +

    facet_grid("sex")
```

FIGURE 10.12 Library use by sex from 2016 Pew Research Center survey

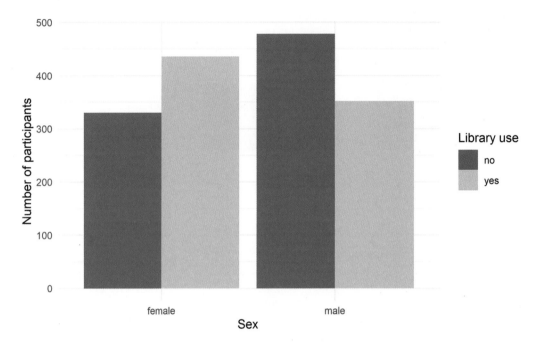

It does look like there is a difference between males and females who are parents and nonparents (Figure 10.13). For females, both parents and nonparents are more often library users than they are nonusers. For males, nonparents are not library users, and parents are almost equally library users and nonusers. This suggests that sex and parental status *interact* to influence library use. That is, the two characteristics work together to influence the outcome.

This possible interaction between sex and parental status can be included in the logistic regression model by adding a term, + sex*parent, to the formula. Kiara explained that, when an interaction is included in a model, it is customary to also include the interacting variables separately. In a model with interaction terms, the terms that are not part of the interaction are called *main effects*. Leslie remembered the distinction between main effects and interaction terms from ANOVA and added the interaction term to the model, leaving all the main effects as they were. She started by writing out Equation (10.13) first to make sure she remembered what she was testing.

$$p\left(uses.lib\right)=\frac{1}{1+e^{-\left(b_0+b_1\cdot age+b_2\cdot sex+b_3\cdot educ+b_4\cdot parent+b_5\cdot disabled+b_6\cdot rurality+b_7\cdot raceth+b_8\cdot ses+b_9\cdot sex\cdot parent\right)}} \tag{10.13}$$

Now that she had the model in mind, she used glm() to estimate it.

FIGURE 10.13 Library use by sex and parent status from 2016 Pew Research Center survey

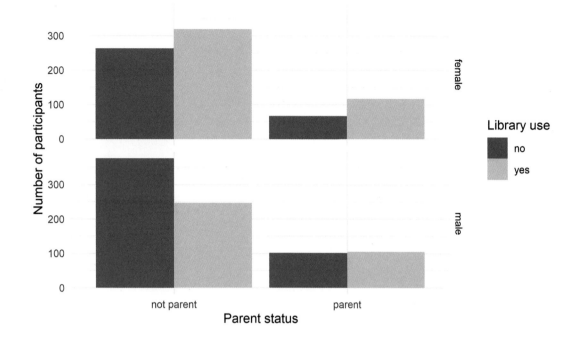

```
# estimate the library use model and print results
lib.model.int <- glm(formula = uses.lib ~ age + sex + educ + parent +
                    disabled + rurality + ses + raceth + sex*parent,
            data = libraries.cleaned,
            family = binomial("logit"))
odds.n.ends(x = lib.model.int)
## $`Logistic regression model significance`
## Chi-squared        d.f.              p
##      96.296     13.000         0.000
##
## $`Contingency tables (model fit): percent predicted`
##                  Percent observed
## Percent predicted          1          0      Sum
##              1    0.2683952 0.1850035 0.4533987
##              0    0.2193413 0.3272600 0.5466013
##            Sum  0.4877365 0.5122635 1.0000000
##
## $`Contingency tables (model fit): frequency predicted`
##                  Number observed
## Number predicted     1      0    Sum
```

```
##              1    383  264  647
##              0    313  467  780
##            Sum  696  731 1427
##
## $`Predictor odds ratios and 95% CI`
##                                  OR      2.5 %     97.5 %
## (Intercept)                1.3896208 0.7106390 2.7205274
## age                        0.9894621 0.9830350 0.9958813
## sexmale                    0.4518131 0.3500795 0.5816044
## educFour-year degree or more 1.9341335 1.2770482 2.9441143
## educHS to 2-year degree    1.1558031 0.7862126 1.7074900
## parentparent               1.0553800 0.7182384 1.5579958
## disabledyes                0.7939236 0.5785547 1.0867415
## ruralitysuburban           1.1796693 0.8937225 1.5575559
## ruralityurban              1.2198083 0.9199887 1.6180430
## seslow                     0.9509862 0.5828701 1.5483108
## sesmedium                  0.8534710 0.5788626 1.2539095
## racethNon-Hispanic Black   1.5599911 1.0060581 2.4253682
## racethNon-Hispanic White   1.3110430 0.9283916 1.8568026
## sexmale:parentparent       1.3855389 0.8300643 2.3074929
##
## $`Model sensitivity`
## [1] 0.5502874
##
## $`Model specificity`
## [1] 0.6388509
```

To organize her work, Leslie used the NHST process.

10.12.1 NHST

10.12.1.1 NHST STEP 1: WRITE THE NULL AND ALTERNATE HYPOTHESES

H0: A model containing age, sex, education, parent status, disability status, rurality, SES, race-ethnicity, and an interaction between sex and parent status is not useful in explaining library use.

HA: A model containing age, sex, education, parent status, disability status, rurality, SES, race-ethnicity, and an interaction between sex and parent status is useful in explaining library use.

10.12.1.2 NHST STEP 2: COMPUTE THE TEST STATISTIC

The test statistic is $\chi^2 = 96.30$ with 13 degrees of freedom.

10.12.1.3 NHST STEP 3: CALCULATE THE PROBABILITY THAT YOUR TEST STATISTIC IS AT LEAST AS BIG AS IT IS IF THERE IS NO RELATIONSHIP (I.E., THE NULL IS TRUE)

The *p*-value is less than .001.

10.12.1.4 NHST STEPS 4 AND 5: INTERPRET THE PROBABILITY AND WRITE A CONCLUSION

The null hypothesis is rejected. The model including age, sex, education, parent status, disability status, rurality, SES, race-ethnicity, and an interaction between sex and parent status is useful in explaining library use [$\chi^2(13)$ = 96.30; *p* < .001].

10.12.2 COMPUTE AND INTERPRET ODDS RATIOS

Age, sex, having a four-year degree or more, and non-Hispanic Black race-ethnicity were statistically significant predictors of library use. For every 1-year increase in age, the odds of library use decreased by 1% (OR = .99; 95% CI: .983–.996). Males have 55% lower odds of library use compared to females (OR = .45; 95% CI: .35–.58) and those with a four-year degree have 1.93 times higher odds of library use compared to those with less than a high school education (OR = 1.93; 95% CI: 1.28–2.94). Finally, non-Hispanic Black participants had 1.56 times higher odds of library use compared to Hispanic participants (OR = 1.56; 95% CI: 1.01–2.43). Disability status, SES, disabled status, and rurality were not significantly associated with library use, and those with a high school to 2-year degree had no higher nor lower odds of library use than those with less education. Likewise, non-Hispanic White participants had no higher nor lower odds of library use compared to Hispanic participants. There was no statistically significant interaction between sex and parent status on the odds of library use.

10.12.3 COMPUTE AND INTERPRET MODEL FIT

The model correctly predicted 383 of 696 library users and 467 of 731 library nonusers. Overall, the model correctly predicted 850 of 1427 observations (59.6%); the model was more specific (63.9%) than sensitive (55.0%), indicating that it was better at classifying library nonusers than library users.

10.12.4 CHECK ASSUMPTIONS

10.12.4.1 INDEPENDENCE OF OBSERVATIONS

The data source is the same as for the previous analyses; this assumption is met.

10.12.4.2 NO MULTICOLLINEARITY

```
# compute GVIF
car::vif(mod = lib.model.int)
##              GVIF Df GVIF^(1/(2*Df))
## age      1.272824  1        1.128195
## sex      1.394525  1        1.180900
```

```
## educ        1.317568   2           1.071379
## parent      2.373418   1           1.540590
## disabled    1.155785   1           1.075074
## rurality    1.122362   2           1.029279
## ses         1.255048   2           1.058437
## raceth      1.214412   2           1.049764
## sex:parent  2.570189   1           1.603181
```

None of the values in the right-hand column were greater than 2.5, so this assumption is met.

10.12.4.3 LINEARITY

```
# make a variable of the log-odds of the outcome
logit.use.int <- log(lib.model.int$fitted.values/(1-lib.model.int$fitted.
values))

# make a small data frame with the log-odds variable and the age predictor
linearity.data.int <- data.frame(logit.use.int, age.int = lib.model.
int$model$age)

# create a plot (Figure 10.14)
linearity.data.int %>%
  ggplot(aes(x = age.int, y = logit.use.int))+
  geom_point(aes(size = "Observation"), color = "gray", alpha = .6) +
  geom_smooth(se = FALSE, aes(color = "Loess curve")) +
  geom_smooth(method = lm, se = FALSE, aes(color = "linear model")) +
  scale_color_manual(name = "Type of fit line",
                     values = c("dodgerblue2", "deeppink")) +
  scale_size_manual(values = 1.5, name = "") +
  theme_minimal() +
  labs(x = "Age in years",
       y = "Log-odds of library use predicted probability")
```

The linearity concerns are similar to those in Figure 10.9. There is a large deviation from linearity at the younger end of the age range, and some more minor deviations throughout (Figure 10.14).

Given that the interaction term was not statistically significant and the model violated the linearity assumption, it seems preferable to report the previous model without the interaction term as the final model. However, there is a statistical test that can be used to determine whether a larger model is statistically significantly better than a smaller model. The test is called the *likelihood ratio test*.

10.12.5 ACHIEVEMENT 9: CHECK YOUR UNDERSTANDING

List and define the three assumptions for a logistic regression model.

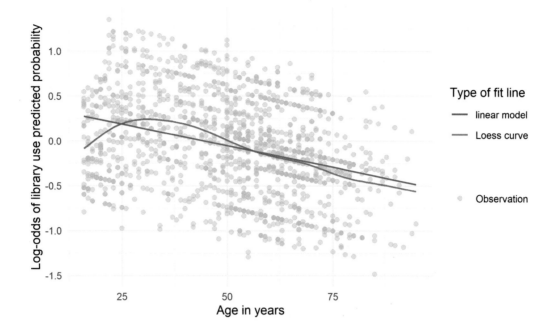

10.13 Achievement 10: Using the likelihood ratio test to compare two nested logistic regression models

Kiara explained that the likelihood ratio (LR) test compares two nested models where one model includes a subset of the variables in the other model. For example, the simple logistic regression model with age as the only predictor could be compared statistically to any of the larger models because they all have the age variable in them. The small model is nested in each of the larger models. In addition, the larger model without the interaction could be compared to the model with the interaction term. Models where the variables of one are completely different from the variables of the other cannot be compared with this test.

The idea behind the LR test is to determine if the additional variables in a model make the model *better enough* to warrant the complexity of adding more variables to the model. The **lmtest** package has the `lrtest()` function, which can be used to compare two nested models. The LR test computes the difference between the log-likelihoods for the two models and multiplies this by 2; the result has a chi-squared distribution.

10.13.1 USING NHST TO ORGANIZE AND CONDUCT AN LR TEST

Leslie went through the steps of NHST for the LR test with a little help from Nancy on using `lrtest()`.

10.13.1.1 NHST STEP 1: WRITE THE NULL AND ALTERNATE HYPOTHESES

H0: The larger model with the interaction term is no better at explaining library use compared to the model without the interaction term.

HA: The interaction term model is better than the smaller model at explaining library use.

10.13.1.2 NHST STEP 2: COMPUTE THE TEST STATISTIC

Nancy showed Leslie how to use `lrtest()`. The two arguments for the test are the two models to compare. It does not matter which model is listed as the first argument and which is listed second. Nancy added the small model first and the larger model with the interaction term second.

```
# compare models with and without interaction term
lmtest::lrtest(object = lib.model, lib.model.int)
## Likelihood ratio test
##
## Model 1: uses.lib ~ age + sex + educ + parent + disabled + rurality +
##      raceth + ses
## Model 2: uses.lib ~ age + sex + educ + parent + disabled + rurality +
##       ses + raceth + sex * parent
##   #Df LogLik Df Chisq   Pr(>Chisq)
## 1  13 -941.32
## 2  14 -940.54  1 1.5599      0.2117
```

The output from `lrtest()` shows the test statistic is $\chi^2 = 1.56$.

10.13.1.3 NHST STEP 3: CALCULATE THE PROBABILITY THAT YOUR TEST STATISTIC IS AT LEAST AS BIG AS IT IS IF THERE IS NO RELATIONSHIP (I.E., THE NULL IS TRUE)

Leslie saw that the probability of the test statistic was included in the output from the `lrtest()` function. The test statistic of $\chi^2 = 1.56$ had a p-value of .21.

10.13.1.4 NHST STEPS 4 AND 5: INTERPRET THE PROBABILITY AND WRITE A CONCLUSION

The null hypothesis was retained; the model with the interaction term was no different in explaining library use from the model without the interaction term ($\chi^2 = 1.56$; $p = .21$).

When the larger model is not statistically significantly better, then use of the smaller model to aid in interpretation is preferred. The more complex a model becomes, the more difficult it is to interpret. Generally speaking, parsimony is preferable. However, there are exceptions to this, such as when the larger model has variables in it that have been consistently related to the outcome in other research or are important to understanding the outcome for some other reason.

10.13.2 COMPLETE INTERPRETATION OF FINAL MODEL

Leslie put everything together to create a paragraph to report the final logistic regression results:

A logistic regression model with age, sex, education, parent status, socioeconomic status, race-ethnicity, and disability status was statistically significantly better than a baseline model at explaining library use [$\chi^2(12) = 94.74$; $p < .001$]. A likelihood ratio test comparing this model to a model that also included an interaction between sex and parent status showed that the larger model was not statistically significantly better than the smaller model [$\chi^2(1) = 1.56$; $p = .21$], so the smaller model was retained. The odds of library use were 51% lower for males compared to females (OR = .49; 95% CI: .39–.61). The odds of library use were 1.90 times higher for those with a four-year degree compared to those with less than a high school education (OR = 1.90; 95% CI: 1.26–2.90). The odds of library use are 1.55 times higher for non-Hispanic Black participants compared to Hispanic participants (OR = 1.55; 95% CI: 1.002–2.42). The odds of library use are 1% lower for every 1-year increase in a person's age (OR = .99; 95% CI: .984–.996). The odds of library use are not statistically significantly different for urban or suburban residents compared to rural residents, for parents compared to non-parents, for non-Hispanic Whites compared to Hispanics, or for people with low or medium SES compared to high SES. Assumption checking revealed a possible problem with the linearity of the age predictor, especially at the youngest ages. The other assumptions were met. Diagnostics found two problematic outlying or influential observations, but the observations did not appear to be data entry mistakes or much different from the rest of the sample in any way.

Leslie wondered aloud if there was any good way to visually demonstrate the results. As usual, Nancy had a code suggestion for that and showed Leslie how to make *forest plots* for future reporting of odds ratios (Box 10.2).

10.2 Nancy's fancy code: Forest plots for odds ratios and confidence intervals

Visualizing odds ratios is a great way to show the relationships between the predictors and the outcome. Using the odds ratio table from the `odds.n.ends()` output, Nancy showed Leslie how this might work (Figure 10.15).

```
# get odds ratio table from lib.model
odds.lib.mod <- data.frame(odds.n.ends(x = lib.model)[4])

# make row names a variable
odds.lib.mod$var <- row.names(x = odds.lib.mod)

# change variable names for easier use
names(x = odds.lib.mod) <- c("OR", "lower", "upper", "variable")

# forest plot of odds ratios from lib.model (Figure 10.15)
odds.lib.mod %>%
  ggplot(aes(x = variable, y = OR, ymin = lower, ymax = upper)) +
    geom_pointrange(color = "#7463AC") +
    geom_hline(yintercept = 1, lty = 2,
               color = "deeppink", size = 1) +
    coord_flip() +
```

(Continued)

(Continued)

```
     labs(x = "Variable from library use model",
          y = "Odds ratio (95% CI)") +

     theme_minimal()
```

The vertical line makes it clear which of the odds ratios have confidence intervals that cross over and which do not. Odds ratios with confidence intervals that fall completely on the right side of the dotted line show statistically significant increased odds of the outcome for the group shown compared to the reference group. Odds ratios with confidence intervals on the left side of the dotted line show decreased odds of the outcome compared to the reference group.

Leslie thought this was a great way to show significant increases and decreases in odds, but was a little concerned about the odds ratios below 1 since the range is limited compared to odds ratios above 1. That is, the confidence interval is bounded so that it has to be between 0 and 1, while odds ratios above 1 can be between 1 and ∞. Odds ratios and confidence intervals for decreased odds are going to seem more narrow, even if the decrease is relatively large. Nancy explained that they can transform the axis so that the odds ratios and confidence intervals below 1 are on a scale where the relative increase or decrease in odds is represented more consistently.

FIGURE 10.15 Association between demographic characteristics and library use from Pew Research Center 2016 library use survey

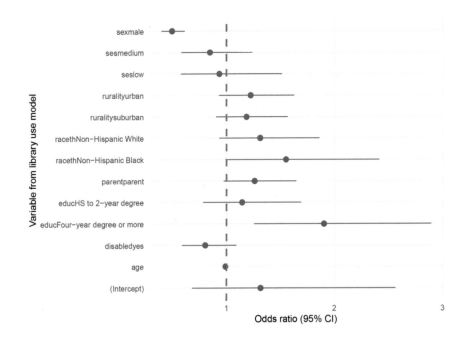

Leslie asked Nancy if they could clean up the names of the variables shown on the *y*-axis while they were working on the graph formatting. Nancy said this could be done in two ways. The first way was to recode the variable in the data frame and either overwrite the existing values or make a new variable with the recoded values. The second way was to recode directly in the graph, which would not change anything in the data frame. Leslie decided to change the data frame by adding a new variable called `clean.varnames` with updated values (Figure 10.16).

```r
# clean variable names for graph
odds.lib.mod.cleaned <- odds.lib.mod %>%
  mutate(variable = recode(.x = variable,
        "sexmale" = "Male",
        "ruralityurban" = "Urban residence",
        "ruralitysuburban" = "Suburban residence",
        "parentparent" = "Parent",
        "educHS to 2-year degree" = "HS to 2-year degree",
        "educFour-year degree or more" = "Four-year degree or more",
        "disabledyes" = "Disabled",
        "age" = "Age",
        "seslow" = "Low socioeconomic status",
        "sesmedium" = "Medium socioeconomic status",
        "racethNon-Hispanic White" = "Non-Hispanic white",
        "racethNon-Hispanic Black" = "Non-Hispanic black",
        "(Intercept)" = "Intercept"))

# modify graph to include clean variable names (Figure 10.16)
# change scale of y-axis (flipped) to log scale for visualization
odds.lib.mod.cleaned %>%
  ggplot(aes(x = variable, y = OR, ymin = lower, ymax = upper)) +
  geom_pointrange(color = "#7463AC") +
  geom_hline(yintercept = 1, lty = 2, color = "deeppink", size = 1) +
  scale_y_log10(breaks = c(0.1, 0.2, 0.5, 1.0, 2.0, 5.0, 10),
                minor_breaks = NULL)+
  coord_flip() +
  labs(x = "Variable from library use model", y = "Odds ratio (95% CI)") +
  theme_minimal()
```

(Continued)

(Continued)

FIGURE 10.16 Association between demographic characteristics and library use from Pew Research Center 2016 library use survey

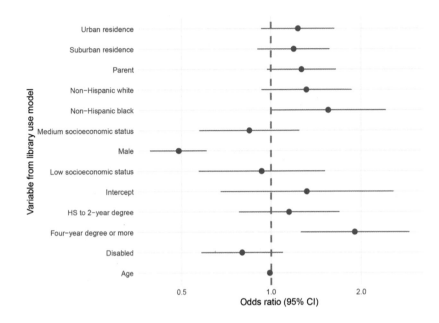

Leslie preferred this version with the clean variable names and the log scale for the *y*-axis, which seemed to show the decreased odds on a much more even scale with the increased odds. She wondered if there was a way to order the variables by the value of the odds ratio to see if that would make it faster to determine the strongest predictors both above and below 1. Nancy reminded her that she could order by the odds ratio using the `reorder()` option within the `ggplot()` function. Leslie also thought including the intercept was not necessary. She tried deleting the intercept and reordering the variables by the value of the odds ratio (Figure 10.17).

```
# reorder the variable names by odds ratio size (Figure 10.17)
odds.lib.mod.cleaned %>%
  ggplot(aes(x = reorder(variable, OR), y = OR, ymin = lower,
             ymax = upper)) +
  geom_pointrange(color = "#7463AC") +
  geom_hline(yintercept = 1, lty = 2, color = "deeppink", size = 1) +
  scale_y_log10(breaks = c(0.1, 0.2, 0.5, 1.0, 2.0, 5.0, 10),
                minor_breaks = NULL)+
  coord_flip() +
  labs(x = "Variable from library use model", y = "Odds ratio (95% CI)") +
  theme_minimal()
```

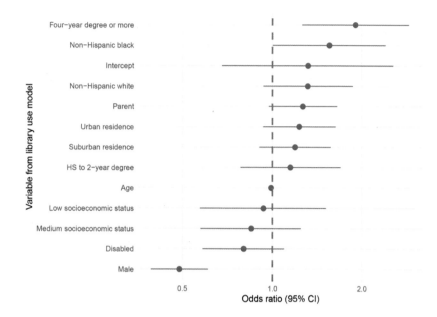

FIGURE 10.17 Association between demographic characteristics and library use from Pew Research Center 2016 library use survey

It was now clear that a high level of education was associated with the largest increases in the odds of library use compared to its reference group, and being male was associated with the biggest decrease in odds of library use compared to being female.

Leslie went back to her notes from the beginning and compared what they found to what they had learned from the literature about library use. Prior descriptive research had found that lower income, racial or ethnic minority status, lower educational attainment, and living in a nonurban area were related to lower library use (Horrigan, 2016). In contrast, past evidence was inconsistent about the relationship of age, sex, marital status, and socioeconomic status with library use (Sin, 2011). The one consistent finding was that education level influenced library use (Sin, 2011). Leslie found their work to confirm education as a predictor of library use, and they could add to the discussion in the research about the relationship of age and sex with library use, although they might need to transform the age variable to address the linearity issue. Leslie wondered if any different recoding choices (Box 10.2) would have made any difference for the final model. Overall, Leslie was satisfied with their work and glad to know more about library use and logistic regression.

"Excellent work today," Kiara said, beaming.

Leslie started pulling things out of her backpack and throwing them on the table.

"What are you doing?" Nancy asked.

"I just remembered I have two library books in here, and they're overdue!" Leslie exclaimed.

This cracked them all up, and they headed out the door together.

10.13.3 ACHIEVEMENT 10: CHECK YOUR UNDERSTANDING

Use the LR test to compare `lib.model.small` to `lib.model`. Note that the small model includes more observations than the larger model, and the LR test requires the same observations for both models. Create a new data frame with no missing values and re-estimate the small model before conducting the LR test. Interpret the results.

/// 10.14 CHAPTER SUMMARY

10.14.1 Achievements unlocked in this chapter: Recap

Congratulations! Like Leslie, you've learned and practiced the following in this chapter.

10.14.1.1 Achievement 1 recap: Using exploratory data analysis before developing a logistic regression model

Prior to conducting a logistic regression analysis, it is useful to examine how the predictor variables are related to the outcome variable using t-tests for comparing the means by group of continuous predictors and chi-squared for examining frequencies and percentages by group for categorical variables. Creating a table of descriptive and bivariate inferential test results for all the possible variables that might be included in a logistic regression model is one way to understand existing relationships and to help select variables for the model.

10.14.1.2 Achievement 2 recap: Understanding the binary logistic regression statistical model

The statistical form of the binary logistic regression model is shown in Equation (10.1).

$$p(y) = \frac{1}{1 + e^{-(b_0 + b_1 x_1 + b_2 x_2)}} \qquad (10.1)$$

where

- y is the binary outcome variable (e.g., library use)

- $p(y)$ is the probability of the outcome (e.g., probability of library use)

- b_0 is the constant

- x_1 and x_2 are predictors of the outcome (e.g., age, rurality)

- b_1 and b_2 are the coefficients for x_1 and x_2

10.14.1.3 Achievement 3 recap: Estimating a simple logistic regression model and interpreting predictor significance and interpretation

The coefficients and coefficient standard errors for predictors are transformed to produce odds ratios and confidence intervals representing the relationships between the predictor and the outcome variable. Odds ratios with confidence intervals not including 1 indicate the odds of the outcome are statistically significantly different for one group compared to another. Odds ratios with confidence intervals that do include 1 are considered nonsignificant; there is no statistically significant difference in odds of the outcome from one group to another. Significant odds ratios above 1 indicate an increase in the odds of the outcome, while significant odds ratios below 1 indicate decreased odds of the outcome. The Wald test with a z-statistic as the test statistic can also be used to determine predictor significance.

10.14.1.4 Achievement 4 recap: Computing and interpreting two measures of model fit

The percentage of observations that are correctly classified into an outcome category is one measure of model fit that is easy to compute and interpret. This measure is called the count R^2. Adjusting the count R^2 to account for the baseline frequencies results in another measure of fit that quantifies how much better the model is at predicting the value of the outcome than the baseline was; this is the adjusted count R^2.

10.14.1.5 Achievement 5 recap: Estimating a larger logistic regression model with categorical and continuous predictors

Like linear regression models, logistic regression models can handle multiple predictor variables of many types.

10.14.1.6 Achievement 6 recap: Interpreting the results of a larger logistic regression model

The interpretation of larger models is the same as for the simple logistic regression model, although there will be additional odds ratios and confidence intervals to report.

10.14.1.7 Achievement 7 recap: Checking logistic regression assumptions and using diagnostics to identify outliers and influential values

Binary logistic regression has three assumptions: independent observations, linearity, and no perfect multicollinearity. The assumptions can be checked using the same tools used in linear regression.

Outliers and influential values can be identified using standardized residuals, df-betas, Cook's *D*, and leverage statistics. The `lmtest` package has a function that will produce many of these metrics. Large values for two or more of these measures suggest an observation could be an outlier or influential value.

10.14.1.8 Achievement 8 recap: Using the model to predict probabilities for observations that are outside the data set

The logistic regression model can be used to predict probabilities for future observations or for observations outside of the data set.

10.14.1.9 Achievement 9 recap: Adding and interpreting interaction terms in logistic regression

Sometimes, variables work together to influence the odds of the outcome. When this is suspected, an interaction term can be added to the model to check whether the variables interact to increase or decrease the odds. The resulting odds ratio(s) and confidence interval(s) are interpreted in the same way as odds ratio(s) and confidence interval(s) for the main effects.

10.14.1.10 Achievement 10 recap: Using the likelihood ratio test to compare two nested logistic regression models

The likelihood ratio (LR) test can be used to determine if one model is statistically significantly better than another nested model at explaining the outcome. To use the LR test, the larger of the two models must contain all the variables that are in the smaller model.

10.14.2 Chapter exercises

The coder and hacker exercises are an opportunity to apply the skills from this chapter to a new scenario or a new data set. The coder edition evaluates the application of the concepts and functions learned in this R-Team meeting to scenarios similar to those in the meeting. The hacker edition evaluates the use of the concepts and functions from this R-Team meeting in new scenarios, often going a step beyond what was explicitly explained.

The coder edition might be best for those who found some or all of the Check Your Understanding activities to be challenging or if they needed review before picking the correct responses to the multiple-choice questions. The hacker edition might be best if the Check Your Understanding activities were not too challenging and the multiple-choice questions were a breeze.

The multiple-choice questions and materials for the exercises are online at **edge.sagepub.com/harris1e**.

Q1: Which of the following is not an assumption for binary logistic regression?

a. Normally distributed variables

b. No multicollinearity

c. Linearity

d. Independence of observations

Q2: A significant odds ratio of 2.5 for BMI as a continuous predictor of heart disease in a binary logistic model would indicate which of the following?

a. The odds of heart disease increase 2.5% for every 1-point increase in BMI.

b. Those with heart disease have 2.5 times higher odds of having an increasing BMI compared to those without heart disease.

c. The odds of heart disease are 2.5 times higher for every 1-point increase in BMI.

d. There are 2.5 times as many people with heart disease as without among those with higher BMI.

Q3: A confidence interval indicates a significant odds ratio when

a. it includes 1.

b. it includes 0.

c. it does not include 1.

d. it does not include 0.

Q4: For a categorical predictor in a logistic regression model, what is the group that other groups are compared to called?

a. Null group

b. Independent group

c. Standard group

d. Reference group

Q5: Computing the percent correctly predicted by the model is one way to determine

a. model fit.

b. model significance.

c. predictor significance.

d. if assumptions are met.

10.14.2.1 Chapter exercises: Coder edition

Use the data from this chapter and the appropriate tests to examine additional predictors of library use.

1. Import the library data that have not been cleaned from this chapter: **pew_libraries_2016_ch10.csv**

2. Create a small library data frame that contains variables for age, sex, parental status, education, library use, and registered to vote (`reg`).

3. Follow the strategies in Box 10.2 to clean the variables in the small data frame. Write new code to clean the `reg` variable. The `reg` variable has the options listed below; recode 8 and 9 to be NA and make sure the other three categories have logical names:

   - 1 - You are absolutely certain that you are registered to vote at your current address

   - 2 - You are probably registered, but there is a chance your registration has lapsed

   - 3 - You are not registered to vote at your current address

   - 8 - Don't know

   - 9 - Refused

4. Use `CreateTableOne()` to create a table showing the bivariate relationships between library use and all of the variables in the data frame (Achievement 1).

5. Write out the statistical form of the model explaining library use by age, sex, parental status, and education (Achievement 2).

6. Use `glm()` to run the model corresponding to the formula you wrote out and `odds.n.ends()` to get model significance, model fit, and odds ratios with confidence intervals (Achievement 5).

7. Discuss model significance and model fit (Achievement 6).

8. Interpret the model odds ratios and confidence intervals (Achievement 6).

9. Check the assumptions and conduct diagnostics. Interpret what you find, including examining any observations that appear problematic during diagnostics (Achievement 7).

10. Add the voting variable to the model, run the model, interpret results, and compare the two models using the likelihood ratio test (Achievement 10).

11. Decide which model is preferable, and explain why you selected the model (Achievement 10).

10.14.2.2 Chapter exercises: Hacker edition

Complete #1 and #2 from the coder edition and create a subset of the data so that the observations are removed when age is under 18 years old. Complete #3–#9 using *all* variables to explain library use, including voting. After estimating and interpreting the model, add an interaction between sex and voting to the model. Compare the model with and without the new interaction term using the likelihood ratio test. Based on the results of the LR test, choose a final model. Report and interpret model significance, model fit, and the odds ratios and confidence intervals for the predictors. Write at least one sentence explaining what you found (Achievements 5–7, 8, and 10).

10.14.2.3 Instructor note

Solutions to exercises can be found on the website for this book, along with ideas for gamification for those who want to take it further.

Visit **edge.sagepub.com/harris1e** to download the datasets, complete the chapter exercises, and watch R tutorial videos.

MULTINOMIAL AND ORDINAL LOGISTIC REGRESSION

The R-Team and the
Diversity Dilemma in STEM

It was a gorgeous day, so Leslie suggested they meet at one of the outside tables on campus.

When Leslie arrived, a little late as usual, Nancy reached into her bag. She carefully removed an old-looking book and placed it on the table in front of Kiara and Leslie.

"What's that?" asked Kiara.

"Hope you don't have an overdue library book," Leslie said, grinning.

"Ha! And nope," Nancy answered. "This book's mine, and it's important to me."

Leslie read the title: "*Tables of the Correlation Coefficient*, by Florence Nightingale David."

"Florence Nightingale David is such an inspiration!" Nancy explained. "There just aren't enough women in STEM fields, especially in technology, engineering, and math. I'm sorry to say that holds true for when this book was published back in 1954 and for right now."

"So sad and so true," Kiara agreed.

"At least the R-Team is doing something in the STEM field," Leslie said.

"Also true," said Nancy. "We started with descriptive statistics and graphs, then learned several methods used mostly for examining relationships between two variables, and finally explored linear and logistic regression for explaining or predicting a continuous or binary outcome. While this seems like a lot, there are many more statistical methods that are useful in different situations."

"That's why we'd like to introduce two additional regression models to use for outcome variables that are ordinal or nominal data types," Kiara said. "Friendly reminder: Ordinal variables are categorical with categories that have an order. Some variables are inherently ordinal, such as variables measured on a Likert scale (e.g., strongly disagree, disagree, agree, strongly agree), while other ordinal variables have some underlying concept, like age or education, that could have been measured in a different way. Nominal variables are categorical as well, but the categories do not have a logical order. Commonly used nominal variables include marital status and religious affiliation."

"I get it," said Leslie. "Even though the models are new, the model form will be familiar and the analysis process will remain the same with cleaning data, performing exploratory data analysis, estimating and interpreting the model, and checking its assumptions."

"We've taught you so well," Nancy said as she wrote down the list of achievements for the meeting.

11.1 Achievements to unlock

- Achievement 1: Using exploratory data analysis for multinomial logistic regression
- Achievement 2: Estimating and interpreting a multinomial logistic regression model
- Achievement 3: Checking assumptions for multinomial logistic regression
- Achievement 4: Using exploratory data analysis for ordinal logistic regression
- Achievement 5: Estimating and interpreting an ordinal logistic regression model
- Achievement 6: Checking assumptions for ordinal logistic regression

$SAGE edge™

Visit **edge.sagepub .com/harris1e** to watch an R tutorial

11.2 The diversity dilemma in STEM

Leslie was super excited about all her new R skills and was starting to think about her career path. She had read a lot about the lack of diversity in the science, technology, engineering, and math (*STEM*) fields and specifically about the lack of women (Dasgupta & Stout, 2014; Johnson, 2011; Kahn & Ginther, 2017). She had noted three main reasons cited for fewer women in STEM: beliefs about natural ability (Blickenstaff, 2005), societal and cultural norms (Keller, 2007; Spencer, Steele, & Quinn, 1999), and institutional barriers (Blickenstaff, 2005). One thing that appeared to encourage women in STEM is the visibility of other women in STEM careers (Blickenstaff, 2005; Herrmann et al., 2016). Leslie was excited about the opportunity to contribute to increasing diversity and to be a role model for other women. However, she was also hesitant to go into a field where she would not be valued or where it would be difficult to advance. She asked Nancy and Kiara if they could examine diversity in STEM careers for their last R meeting. She was particularly interested in how many women go into computer science, math, and engineering, and how satisfied they are with their careers compared with women who go into other fields. Nancy reminded Leslie that the percentage of women college graduates in computer science and math jobs had actually decreased in the past 15 years, so it might be worth examining age as one of the predictors of job satisfaction. Kiara thought this was a great idea, since having age and sex in the model would allow the team to discuss both continuous and categorical predictors.

Leslie was still staring at Nancy. She could not believe that there were fewer women college graduates in computer science and math jobs now compared to 15 years ago. Nancy downloaded several years of data from the National Science Foundation's National Survey of College Graduates (https://ncses-data.nsf.gov/datadownload/). She imported the data and put together a graph that showed that the percentage of women in these jobs has decreased, and the gap between the percentage of women and men with computer science and math jobs has increased (Figure 11.1).

FIGURE 11.1 Percentage of male and female college graduates with a job in computer science or math

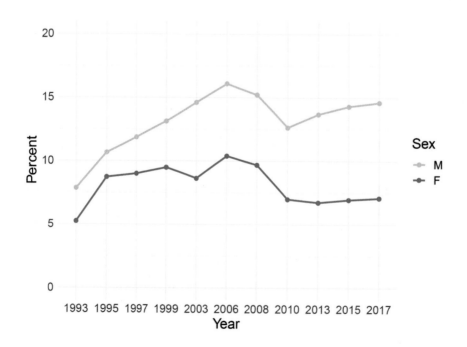

The only other variable to examine before beginning analyses was the `age` variable. Leslie looked at the variables in the Environment tab of the upper right-hand pane. She noticed that the `age` variable shown was an integer data type. While this works for most things, R treats integer data types differently from numeric data types in some situations. Kiara suggested recoding the `age` variable to be numeric. While they were working on this last data management task, Kiara suggested they drop the original variables that were no longer needed since there were new recoded versions of them: `n2ocprmg`, `satadv`, `satsal`, `satsoc`, and `gender`. Leslie used select to drop these variables.

```
# recode and rename
stem.cleaned <- stem %>%
   select(n2ocprmg, satadv, satsal, satsoc, gender, age) %>%
   mutate(job.cat = recode(.x = n2ocprmg,
                           "1" = "CS, Math, Eng",
                           "2" = "Other Sciences",
                           "3" = "Other Sciences",
                           "4" = "Other Sciences",
                           "5" = "CS, Math, Eng",
                           "6" = NA_character_,
                           "7" = "Nonscience",
                           "8" = NA_character_)) %>%
   mutate(satis.advance = RecSatis(x = satadv)) %>%
   mutate(satis.salary = RecSatis(x = satsal)) %>%
   mutate(satis.contrib = RecSatis(x = satsoc)) %>%
   mutate(sex = recode(.x = gender, "M" = "Male", "F"= "Female")) %>%
   mutate(sex = fct_relevel(.f = sex, c("Male", "Female"))) %>%
   mutate(age = as.numeric(x = age)) %>%
   select(-n2ocprmg, -satadv, -satsal, -satsoc, -gender)

# check a summary
summary(object = stem.cleaned)
```

Kiara and Leslie agreed that the `stem.cleaned` data frame was ready for analyses.

11.3 Data, codebook, and R packages for multinomial and ordinal regression practice

Before they examined the data, Kiara made a list of all the data, documentation, and packages needed for learning ordinal and nominal regression:

- Three options for accessing the data
  - Download and save the original SAS file **stem-nsf-2017-ch11.xpt** from **edge.sagepub.com/harris1e** and run the code in the first code chunk to clean the data
  - Download and save the original SAS file **stem-nsf-2017-ch11.xpt** from **edge.sagepub.com/harris1e** and follow the steps in Box 11.1 to clean the data
  - Download and save the original 2017 National Survey of College Graduates data from the National Science Foundation's SESTAT Data Tool (https://ncsesdata.nsf.gov/datadownload/) and follow Box 11.1 to clean the data
- Two options for accessing the codebook
  - Download the **stem-nsf-2017-ch11-codebook.pdf** from **edge.sagepub.com/harris1e**
  - Use the version that comes when downloading the raw data file from the National Science Foundation's SESTAT Data Tool (https://ncsesdata.nsf.gov/datadownload/)
- Install the following R packages if not already installed
  - **tidyverse**, by Hadley Wickham (https://www.rdocumentation.org/packages/tidyverse/)
  - **Hmisc**, by Frank Harrell Jr. (https://www.rdocumentation.org/packages/Hmisc/)
  - **nnet**, by Brian Ripley (https://www.rdocumentation.org/packages/nnet/)
  - **mlogit**, by Yves Croissant (https://www.rdocumentation.org/packages/mlogit/)
  - **MASS**, by Brian Ripley (https://www.rdocumentation.org/packages/MASS/)
  - **ordinal**, by Rune Haubo Bojesen Christensen (https://www.rdocumentation.org/packages/ordinal/)

11.4 Achievement 1: Using exploratory data analysis for multinomial logistic regression

After working with Kiara (Box 11.1), Leslie shared the data-importing management code they had developed so that Nancy could review it. Nancy noticed they had written a function to recode the satisfaction variables and had used a few new tools in the recoding. Leslie explained that the function was useful because they had to recode three satisfaction variables and that they had described all the data cleaning decisions in Box 11.1 if she wanted to review it more closely later.

Nancy highlighted the code and ran it to import and clean the data.

```
# import the STEM career data
stem <- Hmisc::sasxport.get(file = "[data folder location]/data/stem-nsf-
2017-ch11.xpt")
# function to recode the satisfaction variables
RecSatis <- function(x){
  return(recode(x,
              "1" = "Very satisfied",
              "2" = "Somewhat satisfied",
              "3" = "Somewhat dissatisfied",
              "4" = "Very dissatisfied",
              "L" = NA_character_))
```

```
}

# open tidyverse
library(package = "tidyverse")

# recode and rename variables
stem.cleaned <- stem %>%
  select(n2ocprmg, satadv, satsal, satsoc, gender, age) %>%
  mutate(job.cat = recode(.x = n2ocprmg,
                          "1" = "CS, Math, Eng",
                          "2" = "Other Sciences",
                          "3" = "Other Sciences",
                          "4" = "Other Sciences",
                          "5" = "CS, Math, Eng",
                          "6" = NA_character_,
                          "7" = "Nonscience",
                          "8" = NA_character_)) %>%
  mutate(satis.advance = RecSatis(x = satadv)) %>%
  mutate(satis.salary = RecSatis(x = satsal)) %>%
  mutate(satis.contrib = RecSatis(x = satsoc)) %>%
  mutate(sex = recode(.x = gender, "M" = "Male", "F" = "Female")) %>%
  mutate(sex = fct_relevel(.f = sex, c("Male", "Female"))) %>%
  mutate(age = as.numeric(age)) %>%
  select(-n2ocprmg, -satadv, -satsal, -satsoc, -gender)

# check a summary
summary(object = stem.cleaned)
##       age              job.cat                    satis.advance
##  Min.   :20.00   CS, Math, Eng :17223   Very satisfied        :16980
##  1st Qu.:32.00   Other Sciences: 7642   Somewhat satisfied    :30443
##  Median :44.00   Nonscience    :31043   Somewhat dissatisfied:15632
##  Mean   :45.53   NA's          :27764   Very dissatisfied     : 6576
##  3rd Qu.:58.00                          NA's                  :14041
##  Max.   :75.00
##              satis.salary                satis.contrib
##  Very satisfied        :21073   Very satisfied        :35124
##  Somewhat satisfied    :34453   Somewhat satisfied    :25341
##  Somewhat dissatisfied : 9854   Somewhat dissatisfied : 6774
##  Very dissatisfied     : 4251   Very dissatisfied     : 2392
##  NA's                  :14041   NA's                  :14041
##
```

```
##       sex
## Male   :45470
## Female:38202
##
##
##
##
```

Leslie explained to Nancy that she and Kiara had renamed the variables and she would need to know the original variable names to look them up in the codebook. Leslie thought it might be easier to just create a small codebook list for the variables in the cleaned data frame.

- job.cat: Job category of current job
  - n2ocprmg was the original variable name
  - Recoded into three categories:
    - CS, Math, Eng = Computer science, math, and engineering fields
    - Other sciences = Other science fields
    - Nonscience = Not a science field
- satis.advance: Satisfaction with advancement opportunity
  - satadv was the original variable name
  - 4-point Likert scale from 4 = *very dissatisfied* to 1 = *very satisfied*
- satis.salary: Satisfaction with salary
  - satsal was the original variable name
  - 4-point Likert scale from 4 = *very dissatisfied* to 1 = *very satisfied*
- satis.contrib: Satisfaction with contribution to society
  - satsoc was the original variable name
  - 4-point Likert scale from 4 = *very dissatisfied* to 1 = *very satisfied*
- sex
  - gender was the original variable name
  - Two categories: Female, Male
- age: Age in years, not recoded or renamed

Leslie's laptop was running really slowly with the sample of more than 80,000 people in the NSF data. Nancy suggested that they take a sample and use it to practice the analyses. Kiara recommended that they sample 500 people from each of the three job categories, and Nancy agreed this would be a good idea. Leslie was interested in how this would be done since they had not taken samples like this before. Nancy wrote a set of instructions for Leslie to review when she had some time (Box 11.2) and wrote some code to sample 500 cases from each of the three job types. Before she took the sample, Nancy and Leslie checked to make sure they had installed a recent version of R since the versions before 3.6.0 had a different set.seed() algorithm (see Box 4.2). They both had R-3.6.0 and so went ahead with the sampling.

```
# set a seed value to take a sample
set.seed(seed = 143)

# take a sample of 1500 cases
# 500 from each job.cat category
stem.samp <- stem.cleaned %>%
  drop_na(job.cat) %>%
  group_by(job.cat) %>%
  sample_n(size = 500)

# check work
summary(object = stem.samp)
##       age                    job.cat              satis.advance
##  Min.   :23.00   CS, Math, Eng :500   Very satisfied      :342
##  1st Qu.:32.00   Other Sciences:500   Somewhat satisfied  :646
##  Median :40.00   Nonscience    :500   Somewhat dissatisfied:361
##  Mean   :42.89                        Very dissatisfied   :151
##  3rd Qu.:54.00
##  Max.   :75.00
##                 satis.salary                satis.contrib         sex
##  Very satisfied      :420   Very satisfied      :732   Male  :911
##  Somewhat satisfied  :763   Somewhat satisfied  :570   Female:589
##  Somewhat dissatisfied:225   Somewhat dissatisfied:154
##  Very dissatisfied   : 92   Very dissatisfied   : 44
##
##
```

11.2 Nancy's clever code: Taking a random sample by group

Taking random samples from data can be a useful strategy when data sets are very large. Models can be developed on smaller samples and confirmed on larger data sets. Sometimes, it is important to have enough people in some group or groups within your sample, so random sampling *by group* is needed. As usual in R, there are many ways to take random samples by group. One way uses the **tidyverse** and allows for random samples by group through the use of the group_by() and sample_n() functions.

(Continued)

(Continued)

For example, taking a sample of 200 from each of the categories of `job.cat` in the `stem .small` data frame could be accomplished with a few lines of code:

```
# set a seed
set.seed(seed = 143)

# take 200 from each job.cat
stem.samp.200 <- stem.cleaned %>%
  group_by(job.cat) %>%
  sample_n(size = 200)
summary(object = stem.samp.200)
##      age                    job.cat                  satis.advance
##  Min.   :23.00   CS, Math, Eng :200   Very satisfied        :153
##  1st Qu.:32.00   Other Sciences:200   Somewhat satisfied    :299
##  Median :44.00   Nonscience    :200   Somewhat dissatisfied:167
##  Mean   :45.34   NA's          :200   Very dissatisfied    : 77
##  3rd Qu.:57.00                        NA's                  :104
##  Max.   :75.00
##
##              satis.salary            satis.contrib      sex
##  Very satisfied        :200   Very satisfied      :358   Male  :438
##  Somewhat satisfied    :339   Somewhat satisfied  :242   Female:362
##  Somewhat dissatisfied:107   Somewhat dissatisfied: 69
##  Very dissatisfied    : 50   Very dissatisfied    : 27
##  NA's                  :104   NA's                :104
##
```

Note that this process has included NA as one of the groups of `job.cat`. There are a few ways to remove this as a group. One way is to use the subset function to limit the data frame being piped to `group_by()` so that it does not include the NA values of `job.cat`:

```
# take 200 from each job.cat
# subset first to remove NA from job.cat
set.seed(seed = 143)
stem.samp.200.noNA <- stem.cleaned %>%
  drop_na(job.cat) %>%
  group_by(job.cat) %>%
  sample_n(size = 200)
summary(object = stem.samp.200.noNA)
```

```
##       age                 job.cat                  satis.advance
## Min.   :23.00   CS, Math, Eng :200   Very satisfied       :131
## 1st Qu.:32.00   Other Sciences:200   Somewhat satisfied :253
## Median :42.00   Nonscience    :200   Somewhat dissatisfied:150
## Mean   :43.68                        Very dissatisfied  : 66
## 3rd Qu.:55.00
## Max.   :74.00
##               satis.salary          satis.contrib       sex
## Very satisfied       :176   Very satisfied       :295   Male  :348
## Somewhat satisfied :291     Somewhat satisfied :215     Female:252
## Somewhat dissatisfied: 89   Somewhat dissatisfied: 64
## Very dissatisfied  : 44     Very dissatisfied  : 26
##
##
```

If the goal is to take a percentage from each category, the same structure can be used with `sample_frac()` instead of `sample_n()`. For example, here is the code for taking 10% from each group:

```
# sample 10% of each job.cat group
set.seed(seed = 143)
stem.samp.perc <- stem.cleaned %>%
  drop_na(job.cat) %>%
  group_by(job.cat) %>%
  sample_frac(size = .1)
summary(object = stem.samp.perc)
##       age                 job.cat                  satis.advance
## Min.   :23.00   CS, Math, Eng :1722   Very satisfied       :1372
## 1st Qu.:32.00   Other Sciences: 764   Somewhat satisfied :2402
## Median :42.00   Nonscience    :3104   Somewhat dissatisfied:1280
## Mean   :43.54                         Very dissatisfied  : 536
## 3rd Qu.:54.00
## Max.   :75.00
##               satis.salary           satis.contrib       sex
## Very satisfied       :1660   Very satisfied       :2634   Male  :3252
## Somewhat satisfied :2785     Somewhat satisfied :2150     Female:2338
## Somewhat dissatisfied: 779   Somewhat dissatisfied: 590
## Very dissatisfied  : 366     Very dissatisfied  : 216
##
##
```

FIGURE 11.3 Job type by sex among 1,500 college graduates in 2017

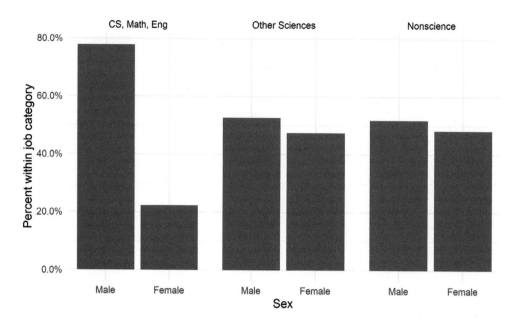

11.4.1 VISUALIZING EMPLOYMENT IN COMPUTER SCIENCE, MATH, AND ENGINEERING BY SEX AND AGE

Leslie started with a few plots to get a better idea of the data. She was interested in how sex and age are related to employment in the computer science, mathematics, and engineering fields, so she started with some bivariate graphs. First, she used all her `ggplot()` tricks to examine the distribution of sex across job types (Figure 11.3).

```
# plotting distribution of sex within job type (Figure 11.3)
stem.samp %>%
  ggplot(aes(x = sex, group = job.cat, y = ..prop..)) +
  geom_bar(fill = "#7463AC") +
  theme_minimal() +
  labs(y = "Percent within job category", x = "Sex") +
  facet_grid(cols = vars(job.cat)) +
  scale_y_continuous(labels = scales::percent)
```

Figure 11.3 showed that computer science, math, and engineering have about a third as many females as males, other sciences and nonscience were slightly more male than female. While this was interesting, Leslie also wanted to know, out of all females, what percentage chose each job type. She revised her `ggplot()` code so that `job.cat` was the grouping variable (Figure 11.4).

```
# plotting distribution of job type by sex (Figure 11.4)
stem.samp %>%
```

```
ggplot(aes(x = job.cat, y = ..prop.., group = sex)) +
geom_bar(fill = "#7463AC") +
theme_minimal() +
labs(y = "Percent within sex category", x = "Job category") +
facet_grid(cols = vars(sex)) +
scale_y_continuous(labels = scales::percent)
```

Figure 11.4 showed computer science, math, and engineering jobs were the least common for females while this category was the largest for males.

Leslie then examined the distribution of age across the three fields (Figure 11.5).

```
# plotting distribution of job type and age (Figure 11.5)
stem.samp %>%
  ggplot(aes(y = age, x = job.cat)) +
  geom_jitter(aes(color = job.cat), alpha = .6) +
  geom_boxplot(aes(fill = job.cat), alpha = .4) +
  scale_fill_manual(values = c("dodgerblue2","#7463AC", "gray40"),
                    guide = FALSE) +
  scale_color_manual(values = c("dodgerblue2","#7463AC", "gray40"),
                     guide = FALSE) +
  theme_minimal() + labs(x = "Job type", y = "Age in years")
```

FIGURE 11.4 Sex and job type among 1,500 college graduates in 2017

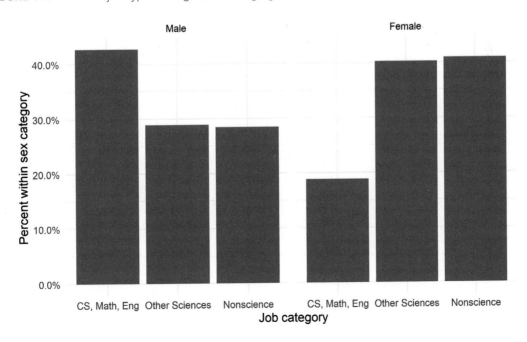

FIGURE 11.5 Job type by age among 1,500 college graduates in 2017

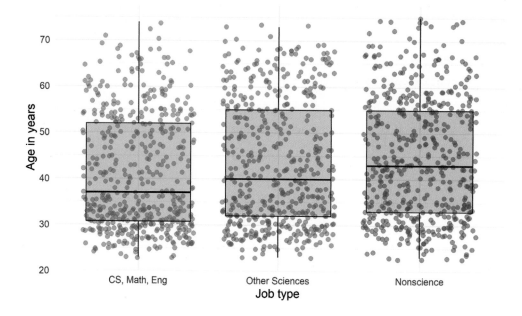

While the age range for all the data appeared similar across the three job types, the computer science, math, and engineering field employed the youngest people on average. Leslie wondered if the distribution of age varied by sex. That is, is the difference in age distribution across job types the same for male and female employees, or are there more young men in the computer science, math, and engineering fields, as research might suggest? She edited the graph to check (Figure 11.6).

FIGURE 11.6 Job type by age and sex among 1,500 college graduates in 2017

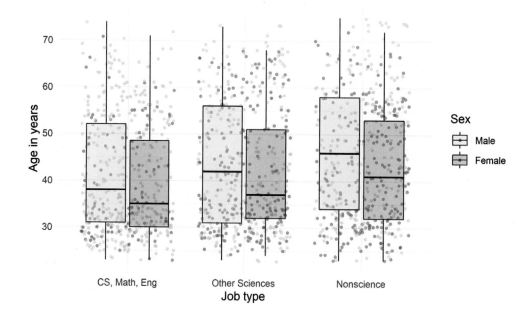

```
# plotting distribution of job type, age, and sex (Figure 11.6)
stem.samp %>%
  ggplot(aes(y = age, x = job.cat, fill = sex)) +
  geom_jitter(aes(color = sex), alpha = .6) +
  geom_boxplot(aes (fill = sex), alpha = .4) +
  scale_fill_manual(values = c("gray", "#7463AC"), name = "Sex") +
  scale_color_manual(values = c("gray", "#7463AC"), guide = FALSE) +
  theme_minimal() +
  labs(x = "Job type", y = "Age in years")
```

In all three fields, the distribution of age showed that males have an older median age than females, and in the two science fields, the range of age is wider for males than females. Leslie wanted to see the graphs by sex to get a better picture of what was going on (Figure 11.7).

```
# plotting distribution of job type, sex, and age (Figure 11.7)
stem.samp %>%
  ggplot(aes(y = age, x = job.cat)) +
  geom_jitter(aes(color = sex), alpha = .6) +
  geom_boxplot(aes (fill = sex), alpha = .4) +
  scale_fill_manual(values = c("gray", "#7463AC"), guide = FALSE) +
  scale_color_manual(values = c("gray", "#7463AC"), guide = FALSE) +
  theme_minimal() + labs(x = "Job type", y = "Age in years") +
  facet_grid(cols = vars(sex))
```

FIGURE 11.7 Job type by age and sex among 1,500 college graduates in 2017

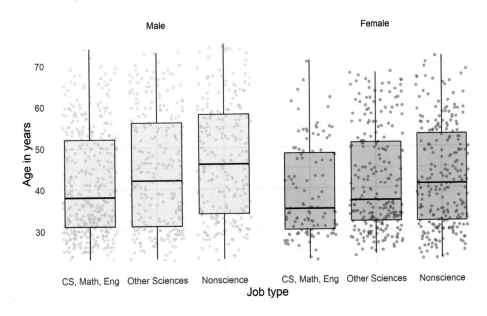

Figure 11.7 revealed a little different picture, with the lowest median age for females in computer science, math, and engineering and higher in other sciences and nonscience. The age distribution for males showed a similar pattern across the three job types. Computer science, math, and engineering has the youngest median age for both sexes.

11.4.2 CHECKING BIVARIATE STATISTICAL ASSOCIATIONS BETWEEN JOB TYPE, SEX, AND AGE

In addition to visualizing potential differences by sex, Leslie remembered that `CreateTableOne()` could be used to explore bivariate associations. For associations between two categorical variables in the table, the *p*-value is for a chi-squared test. For the continuous variable of age, Leslie checked a histogram to see whether it was normally distributed (Figure 11.8),

```
# plotting distribution of age (Figure 11.8)
stem.samp %>%
  ggplot(aes(x = age)) +
  geom_histogram(fill = "#7463AC", color = "white") +
  theme_minimal() +
  labs(x = "Age in years", y = "Number of observations") +
  facet_grid(cols = vars(job.cat))
```

The histograms were not normally distributed for any of the three groups. Leslie added `nonnormal = 'age'` to the `print()` function for `CreateTableOne()` so that the bivariate test was the Kruskal-Wallis

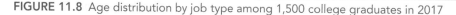

FIGURE 11.8 Age distribution by job type among 1,500 college graduates in 2017

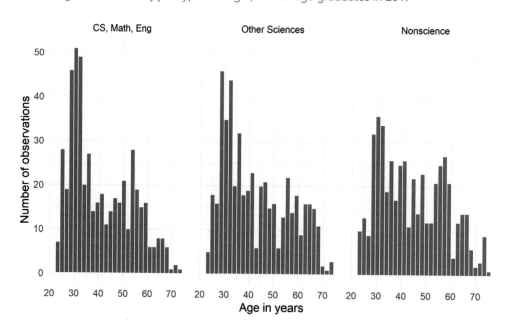

test (Section 7.9.2) comparing age across the three groups instead of ANOVA, which requires a normal distribution to compare means across groups (Section 7.8.3).

```
# open tableone package
library(package = "tableone")

# make a table of statistics to examine job.cat
table.desc <- CreateTableOne(data = stem.samp, strata = 'job.cat',
                vars = c('sex', 'age'))
print(table.desc, showAllLevels = TRUE, nonnormal = 'age')
##                  Stratified by job.cat
##                  level   CS, Math, Eng    Other Sciences    Nonscience        p        test
##    n                     500              500               500
##    sex (%)        Male    389 (77.8)       263 (52.6)        259 (51.8)       <0.001
##                   Female  111 (22.2)       237 (47.4)        241 (48.2)
##    age (median [IQR])     37.00 [30.75, 52.00] 40.00 [32.00, 55.00] 43.00 [33.00, 55.00] <0.001  nonnorm
```

The visual differences in the graphs corresponded to statistically significant differences from the chi-squared and Kruskal-Wallis tests. The median age for college graduates in computer science, math, or engineering was 3 years lower than the median age in other sciences and 6 years younger than the median age in nonscience careers. Computer science, math, and engineering has more than three times as many males as females.

11.4.3 ACHIEVEMENT 1: CHECK YOUR UNDERSTANDING

Review the table created in the previous step and complete a more detailed summary of the statistics in this table. Include the frequencies, percentages, medians, and ranges. Be sure to interpret the percentages correctly—they are tricky!

11.5 Achievement 2: Estimating and interpreting a multinomial logistic regression model

Leslie started to think about a model using sex and age to predict job type. Since job type is a nominal variable, she would use multinomial logistic regression. She wanted to add an interaction term since there were some clearly different patterns in job type by age for males and females. She made her plan to examine the three things that are important to report with every model:

- Model significance: Is the model significantly better than some baseline at explaining the outcome?

- Model fit: How well does the model capture the relationships in the underlying data?

- Predictor values and significance: What is the size, direction, and significance of the relationship between each predictor and the outcome?

Kiara reminded her to check the assumptions once she was done with the multinomial logistic regression model. Nancy asked Leslie if she wanted to check the reference groups for the two categorical variables before they began. It would be easier to interpret the results if the reference groups were consistent with what they were interested in. Leslie thought this was a great idea and remembered that `levels()` could be used to see which group was the reference group.

```
# get reference groups for job.cat and sex
levels(x = stem.samp$job.cat)
## [1] "CS, Math, Eng" "Other Sciences" "Nonscience"
levels(x = stem.samp$sex)
## [1] "Male" "Female"
```

The reference group for `job.cat` was CS, Math, Eng, which Leslie thought made sense, and the reference group for `sex` was Male, which was also good. Nancy reminded her that she could always use `relevel` if needed to change a reference group.

They were now ready to start with the modeling. Kiara suggested they start by examining model significance.

11.5.1 MULTINOMIAL MODEL SIGNIFICANCE

Leslie started the NHST process to organize her work.

11.5.1.1 NHST STEP 1: WRITE THE NULL AND ALTERNATE HYPOTHESES

H0: A multinomial model including sex and age is not useful in explaining or predicting job type for college graduates.

HA: A multinomial model including sex and age is useful in explaining or predicting job type for college graduates.

11.5.1.2 NHST STEP 2: COMPUTE THE TEST STATISTIC

Kiara introduced Leslie to the `multinom()` function from the **nnet** package, one of several functions that can be used to estimate a multinomial model. Like the `lm()` and `glm()` functions for linear and logistic regression, the `multinom()` function requires a formula for the statistical model and the name of the data frame where the variables are.

Kiara had been looking at the help documentation and noticed that there was an option for the function that saves the data used in the model as part of the model object, which can be useful for examining the results afterwards. For example, in the binary logistic regression model, the underlying data were needed in order to check some of the assumptions (Section 10.10.2). She suggested that Leslie add the `model = TRUE` argument. Leslie wrote the code to estimate the model predicting `job.cat` using `age`, `sex`, and the interaction `age*sex`.

```
# load the nnet package
library(package = "nnet")

# estimate the model and print its summary
job.type.mod <- multinom(formula = job.cat ~ age + sex + age*sex,
```

```
                        data = stem.samp,
                        model = TRUE)

summary(object = job.type.mod)
## Call:
## multinom(formula = job.cat ~ age + sex + age * sex, data = stem.samp,
##      model = TRUE)
##
## Coefficients:
##                   (Intercept)          age sexFemale age:sexFemale
## Other Sciences     -1.108879 0.01671124   1.190186   5.013094e-05
## Nonscience         -1.659125 0.02846208   1.521268  -6.082880e-03
##
## Std. Errors:
##                   (Intercept)          age sexFemale age:sexFemale
## Other Sciences     0.2724993 0.006032186 0.4968062     0.01166812
## Nonscience         0.2803308 0.006040267 0.5010979     0.01162522
##
## Residual Deviance: 3171.072
## AIC: 3187.072
```

This output looked weird to Leslie, since she was used to seeing the predictors along the left-hand side with their coefficients and *p*-values or with odds ratios and confidence intervals in the columns. Instead, the predictors were the column headings and the categories of the outcome were along the left-hand side. Kiara said they would review this more in a minute, but first they needed to figure out the test statistic to see if the model was statistically significant.

Leslie noticed that the `summary()` function for `multinom()` did not include a test statistic, and Kiara explained that the test statistic for multinomial regression can be computed from two pieces of information. Similar to logistic regression, model significance is determined based on a chi-squared statistic found by taking the difference between the null deviance and the residual deviance (see logistic regression Section 10.6.1.2). The deviance is a measure of how well the model fits the data. If the differences between the observed values and predicted values are small, the deviance is small and the model is doing well. A smaller deviance is an indicator of a better fitting model.

The null deviance is computed for the null model, which is the model without predictors. In this case, the null deviance is not printed in the summary information, and a look at the model object in the Environment pane finds no null deviance entry. To get the null deviance in order to compute model significance, Kiara suggested estimating a model with no predictors in it. Nancy had done this before and showed Leslie some code to get a null model. The only thing that was different from the full model was that the formula was `job.cat ~ 1` rather than `job.cat = age + sex + age*sex`.

```
# multinomial null model
job.type.mod.null <- multinom(formula = job.cat ~ 1,
                        data = stem.samp,
                        model = TRUE)
```

```
summary(object = job.type.mod.null)
## Call:
## multinom(formula = job.cat ~ 1, data = stem.samp, model = TRUE)
##
## Coefficients:
##                    (Intercept)
## Other Sciences -1.081690e-12
## Nonscience       2.222222e-12
##
## Std. Errors:
##                    (Intercept)
## Other Sciences 0.06324555
## Nonscience     0.06324555
##
## Residual Deviance: 3295.837
## AIC: 3299.837
```

In the `summary()` results from the null model, Leslie found the deviance of 3295.84, but it was labeled Residual Deviance. Since this model has no predictors, it is a null model, and the deviance shown is the null deviance. The residual deviance from the model with age, sex, and age*sex in it is 3171.07. Once Leslie had the null and residual deviance for the null model and the full model, she knew that it was just a matter of finding the difference between the two. The difference value follows a chi-squared distribution and can be used with the degrees of freedom to find a *p*-value for model significance.

```
# get the job model chi-squared
job.chisq <- job.type.mod.null$deviance - job.type.mod$deviance
```

To determine the *p*-value from a chi-squared, Leslie also needed the degrees of freedom, which corresponds to the number of parameters in the model. She could count this quickly since each parameter has a coefficient in the output. Kiara suggested they try to use code so the work would be reproducible and could be used with other models in the future. They spent some time figuring out how to count the parameters in the null and full models. After examining the model object in the Environment pane and the summary output, they determined that counting the number of coefficients printed with the `summary()` function was the easiest way. Nancy suggested the `length()` function to count the number of entries that were coefficients in the summary output and it worked well. Subtracting the length of the null model from the full model gave the difference in the number of parameters between the two, which was the degrees of freedom number she needed.

```
# get the degrees of freedom for chi-squared
job.df <- length(x = summary(object = job.type.mod)$coefficients) - length(x
= summary(object = job.type.mod.null)$coefficients)
```

Finally, Leslie used the `pchisq()` function to determine the *p*-value. This function takes a chi-squared value and a degrees of freedom value and returns the *p*-value. Nancy reminded her to add the `lower .tail = FALSE` option to this function since larger values of the chi-squared distribution indicate bigger differences in fit between the null and full models and larger values are in the upper tail only (or right-side tail). The lower tail of the chi-squared distribution is not useful in this case (it is not used very often) to determine statistical significance. A chi-squared statistic would be in the lower tail of the distribution if there were no difference or very little difference between observed and expected values (see Section 5.5) or between the null and full models. Kiara suggested they discuss one- and two-tailed tests just to be clear about why this is a one-tailed test (Box 11.3).

11.3 Leslie's stats stuff: One-tailed versus two-tailed tests

Some probability distributions, like the chi-squared distribution and the *F*-distribution, have only positive values with a right-hand tail that extends theoretically to positive ∞. Figure 11.9 is one example of a chi-squared distribution, and Figure 11.10 is one example of an *F*-distribution.

The chi-squared statistic is larger when the observed frequencies are much different from what was expected during a chi-squared test. Likewise, when group means are very different from one another in an ANOVA, the *F*-statistic is larger. Larger values of chi-squared and *F* are in the right-hand tail of the chi-squared and *F*-distributions. Values on the left of the chi-squared or *F*-distribution would happen when there was little

FIGURE 11.9 Example of a chi-squared distribution

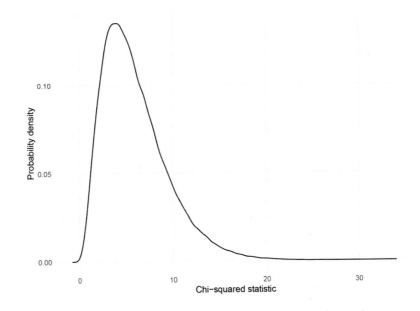

(Continued)

(Continued)

FIGURE 11.10 Example of an *F*-distribution

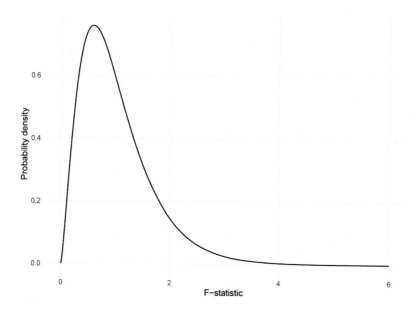

difference between observed and expected or among the groups being compared. To use the chi-squared and *F*-distributions to determine whether the difference is large enough that it is unlikely to have happened by chance, the values that represent large enough differences to be deemed statistically significant are in the right-hand tail. Thus, as they are typically used, many of the tests that rely on these distributions are one-tailed tests with statistical significance determined by where the test statistic is in the right-hand tail.

Statistical tests that rely on one tail of a distribution typically have a threshold value somewhere in the tail. The threshold usually marks the point on the distribution where 5% of the area under the curve is to the right. Statistical tests using one-tailed distributions have test statistics where larger values tend to indicate statistical significance.

There are also two-tailed distributions like the *t*-distribution (Figure 11.11).

Distributions like *t* are used in two ways: to conduct either one- or two-tailed statistical tests. The two-tailed test sets two thresholds, one on the right-hand side of the distribution and one on the left-hand side of the distribution. The area under the curve that is to the right of the right-hand-side threshold and the area under the curve that is to the left of the left-hand-side threshold are added together to reach whatever the threshold is, usually 5% of the total area under the curve (if alpha is set at .05). An alpha of .05 would be achieved by having a threshold on either side of the curve where there was 2.5% of the area under the curve past

FIGURE 11.11 Example of a *t*-distribution

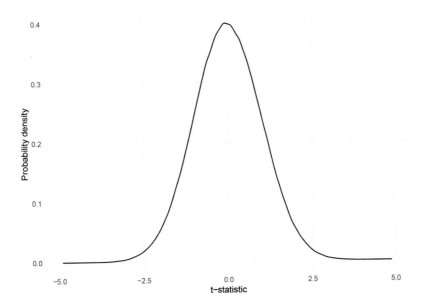

the threshold on each side of the curve. An example of a null and alternate hypothesis for a two-tailed *t*-test would be as follows:

H0: Mean 1 is equal to Mean 2 ($m_1 = m_2$).

HA: Mean 1 is not equal to Mean 2 ($m_1 \neq m_2$).

There is no language in this test that specifies whether "not equal" is due to Mean 1 being *greater than* or *less than* Mean 2. The *t*-test could result in a positive difference if Mean 1 is greater than Mean 2 or a negative difference if Mean 1 is less than Mean 2. Either of these differences could be past the threshold for statistical significance in a two-tailed test (Figure 11.12).

For a *t*-statistic to be in the rejection region, it would have to be in the shaded region in either tail.

To use the distribution for a one-tailed test, the threshold would be set differently. If, for example, the hypotheses above stated

H0: Mean 1 is greater than Mean 2 ($m_1 > m_2$).

HA: Mean 1 is not greater than Mean 2 ($m_1 \not> m_2$).

the threshold would be set only in the upper tail of the *t*-distribution and the area under the curve to the right of the threshold would contain 5% of the distribution rather than the 2.5% on each side (Figure 11.13). Because the threshold is not as far to the right as it would be in a two-tailed test, a *t*-statistic for a one-tailed *t*-test could be smaller in magnitude and still reach statistical significance.

(Continued)

(Continued)

FIGURE 11.12 Rejection region in a two-tailed test

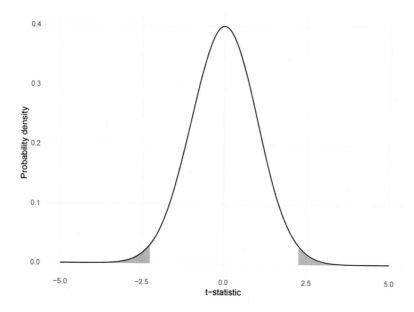

FIGURE 11.13 Rejection region in a one-tailed test

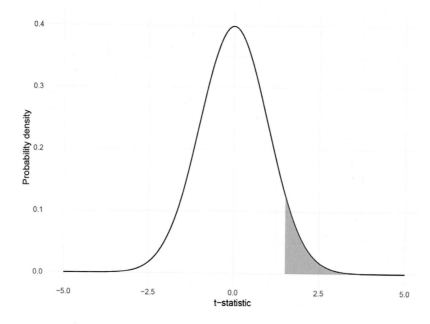

To be in the rejection region in this distribution, the *t*-statistic would have to be a positive value greater than 1.5.

Nancy and Leslie worked together to finish the code.

```
# get the p-value for chi-squared
job.p <- pchisq(q = job.chisq, df = job.df, lower.tail = FALSE)

# put together into a vector and round to 3 decimal places
modelsig <- round(x = c(job.chisq, job.df, job.p), 3)

# add names to the vector
names(x = modelsig) <- c("Chi-squared", "df", "p")

# print the vector
modelsig
## Chi-squared          df            p
##     124.765       6.000        0.000
```

The test statistic is a chi-squared of 124.77 with 6 degrees of freedom.

11.5.1.3 NHST STEP 3: CALCULATE THE PROBABILITY THAT YOUR TEST STATISTIC IS AT LEAST AS BIG AS IT IS IF THERE IS NO RELATIONSHIP (I.E., THE NULL IS TRUE)

The probability computed for the chi-squared was < .001. Leslie had started to notice that she had gained some intuition for when a test statistic is going to have a small p-value. Just thinking about the chi-squared distribution and how far to the right a value of 124.77 would be on the graph, it was getting more obvious to her when a chi-squared value is so large that the corresponding p-value will be small.

11.5.1.4 NHST STEPS 4 AND 5: INTERPRET THE PROBABILITY AND WRITE A CONCLUSION

Leslie rejected the null hypothesis and concluded that a model including age, sex, and age*sex explained job type statistically significantly better [$\chi^2(6) = 124.77$; $p < .001$] than a null model with no predictors.

11.5.2 MULTINOMIAL MODEL FIT

Leslie asked if percent correctly predicted would be a good measure of fit for the multinomial model given that it is a lot like a binary logistic regression model, just with more categories for the outcome. Kiara agreed, and they discussed how to find this value since there are three possible categories of job type and each person could be predicted into each category based on the model. Kiara noticed that there was a fitted.values entry in the model object and asked Leslie to print the first few lines so they could examine what these values are.

```
# print first six rows of fitted values
head(x = job.type.mod$fitted.values)
##   CS, Math, Eng Other Sciences Nonscience
## 1     0.4029162      0.2964827  0.3006010
```

```
## 2          0.1540909       0.4063450 0.4395641
## 3          0.3599802       0.3027778 0.3372420
## 4          0.3339452       0.3053575 0.3606973
## 5          0.1235340       0.4050756 0.4713904
## 6          0.4193110       0.2934594 0.2872296
```

Leslie looked over the values and noted that they were the predicted probability for each person to be in each of the three job type groups. The first person on the list had a 40.3% probability of being in computer science, math, or engineering. The first person also had 29.6% and 30.1% chances of being in other sciences and nonscience, respectively. It would make sense that the largest probability would be the category that each person would be predicted into, so this first person would be predicted to be in a computer science, math, or engineering job.

Kiara thought they could use the same count R^2 strategy from the binary logistic models (see Section 10.7) to check the model fit. Specifically, she compared which job type had the highest probability based on the model with the observed job type that the person actually had. Luckily, Nancy knew the `predict()` function could be used to extract predicted values from the model object. Leslie was curious how that worked, so Nancy showed her, but she did not want to print out all 1,500 people, so she used the `head()` function to print the predicted job type for the first six observations.

```
# predict job type
head(x = predict(object = job.type.mod))
## [1] Nonscience      Other Sciences Nonscience      Other Sciences
## [5] CS, Math, Eng Nonscience
## Levels: CS, Math, Eng Other Sciences Nonscience
```

The use of `predict()` resulted in the first person being predicted as a nonscience job, the second person as other science, and so on. This was consistent with what they saw in the predicted probabilities list from printing the `fitted.values` above.

Leslie used `predict()` to make a table with the observed values of job type in the rows and the predicted values of job type for the columns.

```
# observed vs. predicted category for each observation
fit.n <- table(observed = job.type.mod$model$job.cat,
               predicted = predict(object = job.type.mod))
fit.n
##                 predicted
## observed        CS, Math, Eng Other Sciences Nonscience
##    CS, Math, Eng           342             66         92
##    Other Sciences          206            129        165
##    Nonscience              201            112        187
```

Leslie noticed that the correct predictions were listed in the diagonal of the `fit.n` table she had just made. It looked like 342 of the people with computer science, math, or engineering jobs were predicted correctly to be in this category. Just 129 of the other sciences were correctly predicted and 187 of the nonscience were correctly predicted. Since the sample they were working with had 500 people from each job type, these do not seem like high numbers of correct predictions. Leslie computed some percentages to check the specific values.

```
# observed vs. predicted category for each observation
fit.perc <- prop.table(table(observed = job.type.mod$model$job.cat,
                             predicted = predict(object = job.type.mod)),
                       margin = 1)

fit.perc
##                    predicted
## observed      CS, Math, Eng Other Sciences Nonscience
##   CS, Math, Eng       0.684          0.132      0.184
##   Other Sciences      0.412          0.258      0.330
##   Nonscience          0.402          0.224      0.374
```

The model was best at predicting the computer science, math, or engineering job type, with 68.4% of the observations in this category correctly predicted. The nonscience job type was predicted with 37.4% accuracy, and other sciences was predicted with 25.8% accuracy. Overall, the model predicted job type correctly for 658 out of 1,500 observations (43.9%). Given that the sample included 500 people from each job type, without any other information, we would guess that everyone was in a single category and would be right for 500, or 33.3%, of the observations. Although the overall correctness was low, it was higher than this baseline probability of correctly classifying observations by job type.

11.5.3 MULTINOMIAL MODEL PREDICTOR INTERPRETATION

So far, Leslie knew that the model was statistically significantly better than baseline at explaining job type and that the predictions from the model were better than a baseline percentage would be. She also knew that the prediction was best for computer science, math, and engineering. The next thing she wanted to examine was the predictor fit and significance.

11.5.3.1 PREDICTOR SIGNIFICANCE

The `summary()` output did not include any indication of whether or not each predictor (age, sex, age*sex) was statistically significantly associated with job type. To get statistical significance and more interpretable values, Kiara suggested that Leslie compute odds ratios and 95% confidence intervals around the odds ratios. Leslie had no idea how to even start this process. Kiara reminded her that the coefficients can be exponentiated to get the odds ratios. Leslie was still confused, so Nancy wrote some code using `coef()` to get the coefficients from the model and `exp()` to exponentiate them. She explained that this was what was behind the `odds.n.ends()` function when it was computing the odds ratios for binary logistic regression.

```
# get odds ratios
exp(x = coef(object = job.type.mod))
```

```
##                 (Intercept)      age sexFemale age:sexFemale
## Other Sciences    0.3299285 1.016852  3.287693     1.0000501
## Nonscience        0.1903055 1.028871  4.578025     0.9939356
```

Leslie still did not like this output format. It made much more sense to her with the `lm()` and `glm()` output that had the predictors on the left-hand side. Nancy said there was an R function for that! The `t()` function transposes a matrix, so the rows and columns would be exchanged but the information in the matrix would stay the same. Nancy showed Leslie how to do it.

```
# get odds ratios and transpose
t(x = exp(x = coef(object = job.type.mod)))
##              Other Sciences Nonscience
## (Intercept)       0.3299285  0.1903055
## age               1.0168517  1.0288710
## sexFemale         3.2876930  4.5780248
## age:sexFemale     1.0000501  0.9939356
```

Leslie found this much easier to read. Before she tried interpreting the odds ratios, she had to remind herself what all the reference groups were since it gets more complicated with this type of regression. Not only do the predictors have reference groups, but the outcome variable also has a reference group. The reference group for the outcome variable is computer science, math, or engineering. Leslie knew this was true because it was missing from the list of categories in the columns and because it was first when they examined the levels. Each odds ratio is the odds of being in the job type shown in the column compared to being in the computer science, math, or engineering job type. Leslie tried interpreting an odds ratio before they worked on getting confidence intervals, which seemed like it was going to be difficult.

> For every year older a person gets, the odds of having a career in other sciences is 1.02 times higher compared to the odds of being in computer science, math, or engineering.

Kiara thought this was a good start but that they really needed confidence intervals before they spent too much time interpreting. Nancy was ready with the `confint()` function to get the confidence intervals.

```
# confidence intervals for odds ratios
exp(x = confint(object = job.type.mod))
## , , Other Sciences
##
##
##                     2.5 %     97.5 %
## (Intercept)     0.1934052 0.5628228
## age             1.0049003 1.0289451
## sexFemale       1.2416783 8.7050932
## age:sexFemale   0.9774394 1.0231839
##
##
## , , Nonscience
##
```

```
##                       2.5 %    97.5 %
## (Intercept)      0.1098584  0.3296623
## age              1.0167623  1.0411239
## sexFemale        1.7145211 12.2240033
## age:sexFemale    0.9715448  1.0168424
```

Leslie reviewed the confidence intervals and found that age and Female sex were statistically significant predictors of job category but that the interaction between the two was not statistically significant. Kiara asked her to explain her finding, and Leslie pointed out that age and Female sex both had 95% confidence intervals that did not include 1 for both the nonscience and other sciences categories of the outcome.

Leslie wondered if there was a way to put the odds ratios and the confidence intervals together in one set of output to make it easier to read everything. Always ready for an R coding challenge, Nancy gave it a try for the other sciences category using square brackets to create a subset of the objects. For the odds ratio object, she just wanted the first row (which was the first column once transformed), and for the confidence intervals, she wanted the first set of confidence intervals. The square brackets for the odds ratios just have rows and columns, like this [rows, columns], while the confidence interval brackets need rows, columns, and list entry, like this [rows, columns, list]. Nancy reminded Leslie that, whenever one of the spots in the square brackets is left blank, this indicates *all* the rows or *all* the columns. She wrote some code to get the other sciences group.

```
# get odds ratios for other sciences from the model object
oddsrat.other.sci <- t(x = exp(x = coef(object = job.type.mod)))[ , 1]

# get CI for other sciences
confint.other.sci <- exp(x = confint(object = job.type.mod))[ , 1:2, 1]

# put into a data frame and print
other.sci <- data.frame(OR.other = oddsrat.other.sci,
                        CI.other = confint.other.sci)

other.sci
##                  OR.other CI.other.2.5.. CI.other.97.5..
## (Intercept)     0.3299285     0.1934052       0.5628228
## age             1.0168517     1.0049003       1.0289451
## sexFemale       3.2876930     1.2416783       8.7050932
## age:sexFemale   1.0000501     0.9774394       1.0231839
```

Leslie thought she understood and made a data frame for the nonscience job category.

```
# get odds ratios for nonscience
oddsrat.non.sci <- t(x = exp(x = coef(object = job.type.mod)))[ , 2]

# get CI for nonscience
confint.non.sci <- exp(x = confint(object = job.type.mod))[ , 1:2, 2]
```

```
# put into a data frame and print
non.sci <- data.frame(OR.non = oddsrat.non.sci,
                      CI.non = confint.non.sci)
non.sci
##                     OR.non CI.non.2.5.. CI.non.97.5..
## (Intercept)     0.1903055    0.1098584     0.3296623
## age             1.0288710    1.0167623     1.0411239
## sexFemale       4.5780248    1.7145211    12.2240033
## age:sexFemale   0.9939356    0.9715448     1.0168424
```

Nancy put the two data frames together to have everything at once.

```
# all together
or.ci <- data.frame(other.sci, non.sci)
or.ci
##                  OR.other CI.other.2.5.. CI.other.97.5..    OR.non
## (Intercept)     0.3299285      0.1934052       0.5628228 0.1903055
## age             1.0168517      1.0049003       1.0289451 1.0288710
## sexFemale       3.2876930      1.2416783       8.7050932 4.5780248
## age:sexFemale   1.0000501      0.9774394       1.0231839 0.9939356
##                CI.non.2.5.. CI.non.97.5..
## (Intercept)       0.1098584     0.3296623
## age               1.0167623     1.0411239
## sexFemale         1.7145211    12.2240033
## age:sexFemale     0.9715448     1.0168424
```

11.5.3.2 PREDICTOR INTERPRETATION

The new or.ci data frame shows several significant odds ratios. The first three columns of numbers are the odds ratios and confidence intervals for the job type of other sciences, while columns 4 through 6 are for the nonscience job type. Leslie tried her hand at interpreting the odds ratios and confidence intervals. Kiara reminded her that the outcome variable with multiple categories now had a reference group. In this case, the reference group is computer science, math, or engineering job type. The odds ratios are interpreted with respect to this reference group. This works OK for the continuous variable of age but gets a little tricky for the categorical variable of sex, where there are now two reference groups to consider. Leslie thought about it and then wrote the following:

The age row starts with the odds ratio of 1.02 with confidence interval 1.00–1.03. For every 1-year increase in age, the odds of being in an other sciences job are 1.02 times higher than being in a computer science, math, or engineering job (95% CI: 1.00–1.03). Likewise, for every 1-year increase in age, the odds of being in a nonscience job are 1.03 times higher than being in a computer science, math, or engineering job (95% CI: 1.02–1.04).

Compared to males, the odds of females being in an other sciences job are 3.29 times higher than being in a computer science, math, or engineering job (95% CI: 1.24–8.71). Also, compared to males, females have 4.58 times higher odds of being in nonscience jobs compared to computer science, math, or engineering jobs (95% CI: 1.71–12.22).

The interaction between age and sex was not statistically significant for either other sciences jobs or nonscience jobs compared to computer science, math, or engineering jobs.

This looked good to Kiara. Overall, it seems that females had higher odds than males of being in other sciences or nonscience compared to being in computer science, math, or engineering. Likewise, the older someone gets, the more likely they are to work in other sciences or nonscience compared to computer science, math, or engineering. It seems that, overall, computer science, math, or engineering job types are most likely to be held by males and people who are younger.

11.5.4 ACHIEVEMENT 2: CHECK YOUR UNDERSTANDING

Pick two of the statistically significant odds ratios in the model to interpret without looking at Leslie's interpretation. When you are finished, compare your interpretation with Leslie's interpretation.

11.6 Achievement 3: Checking assumptions for multinomial logistic regression

There are two assumptions to meet for multinomial logistic regression: independence of observations and the *independence of irrelevant alternatives* (IIA) assumption.

11.6.1 INDEPENDENCE OF OBSERVATIONS

Nancy reminded Leslie that the independence of observations assumption requires that the observations in the data be independent of each other. Data sets that include spouses, siblings, neighbors, or multiple observations on the same people would not meet this assumption. Since these data are from a random sample of college graduates, this assumption is met.

11.6.2 INDEPENDENCE OF IRRELEVANT ALTERNATIVES ASSUMPTION

Nancy had to look this one up. She found that this assumption required that the categories of the outcome be independent of one another. For example, the relative probability of having a job in the computer science, math, or engineering field compared to the other science field cannot depend on the existence of nonscience jobs. This assumption can be tested by taking a subset of the data that includes two of the outcome categories and estimating binary logistic regression models with the same predictors. These model results can then be compared with the multinomial model results to see if the relationship is consistent.

Kiara read that the test used for this assumption is the Hausman-McFadden test, which has the following null and alternate hypotheses:

H0: The IIA assumption is met.

HA: The IIA assumption is not met.

Leslie found that this test can be conducted using the `hmftest()` function in the **mlogit** package. The `hmftest()` function requires two things: the full multinomial model and a second model estimated on a subset of the data that includes only some of the outcome variable categories. In this case, the subset could include the computer science, math, or engineering and nonscience outcome categories.

Unfortunately, Leslie determined that the multinomial model objects saved from the `multinom()` function were not in the same format as the multinomial objects from the **mlogit** package. She looked up the documentation for the **mlogit** package and found that it required reshaping the data before estimating the models. After several minutes of trial and error, she determined that the `mlogit.data()` function works to reshape the data with two options: the shape of the data, `shape = "wide"`, and the name of the outcome variable, `choice = "job.cat"`. Leslie created the reshaped data and estimated the model again using `mlogit()`.

```
# load the mlogit package
library(package = "mlogit")

# reshape data to use with the mlogit function
stem.samp.4mlog <- mlogit.data(data = stem.samp,
                               choice = "job.cat",
                               shape = "wide")

# estimate the model and print its summary
mlogit.job <- mlogit(formula = job.cat ~ 0 | age + sex + age*sex,
                     data = stem.samp.4mlog)
summary(object = mlogit.job)
##
## Call:
## mlogit(formula = job.cat ~ 0 | age + sex + age * sex, data = stem.
samp.4mlog,
##       method = "nr")
##
## Frequencies of alternatives:
##   CS, Math, Eng     Nonscience Other Sciences
##         0.33333        0.33333        0.33333
##
## nr method
## 4 iterations, 0h:0m:0s
## g'(-H)^-1g = 3.03E-07
## successive function values within tolerance limits
##
## Coefficients :
##                             Estimate Std. Error z-value  Pr(>|z|)
## Nonscience:(intercept)      -1.6591e+00 2.8033e-01 -5.9184 3.250e-09 ***
## Other Sciences:(intercept)  -1.1089e+00 2.7250e-01 -4.0693 4.716e-05 ***
```

```
## Nonscience:age                        2.8462e-02 6.0403e-03  4.7121 2.452e-06 ***
## Other Sciences:age                     1.6711e-02 6.0322e-03  2.7703 0.005600 **
## Nonscience:sexFemale                   1.5212e+00 5.0110e-01  3.0358 0.002399 **
## Other Sciences:sexFemale              1.1902e+00 4.9681e-01  2.3956 0.016592 *
## Nonscience:age:sexFemale             -6.0824e-03 1.1625e-02 -0.5232 0.600830
## Other Sciences:age:sexFemale          5.0832e-05 1.1668e-02  0.0044 0.996524
## ---
## Signif. codes:  0 '***' 0.001 '**' 0.01 '*' 0.05 '.' 0.1 ' ' 1
##
## Log-Likelihood: -1585.5
## McFadden R^2:  0.037855
## Likelihood ratio test : chisq = 124.76 (p.value = < 2.22e-16)
```

She was pretty happy to see the same model coefficients, and it was extra satisfying to see the same chi-squared statistic. Next, she estimated the model with a subset of data including only two of the three outcome choices listed in the `alt.subset` = argument.

```
# estimate the model with two outcome categories and print its summary
mlogit.job.alt <- mlogit(formula = job.cat ~ 0 | age + sex + age*sex,
                         data = stem.samp.4mlog,
                         alt.subset = c("CS, Math, Eng", "Nonscience"))
summary(object = mlogit.job.alt)
##
## Call:
## mlogit(formula = job.cat ~ 0 | age + sex + age * sex, data = stem.
samp.4mlog,
##      alt.subset = c("CS, Math, Eng", "Nonscience"), method = "nr")
##
## Frequencies of alternatives:
## CS, Math, Eng    Nonscience
##          0.5           0.5
##
## nr method
## 3 iterations, 0h:0m:0s
## g'(-H)^-1g = 0.000204
## gradient close to zero
##
## Coefficients :
##                         Estimate Std. Error z-value Pr(>|z|)
## Nonscience:(intercept)  -1.6914715  0.2849648 -5.9357 2.926e-09 ***
```

```
## Nonscience:age                0.0291976   0.0061498    4.7478 2.057e-06 ***
## Nonscience:sexFemale          1.5384978   0.5068185    3.0356 0.002401 **
## Nonscience:age:sexFemale     -0.0064503   0.0117627   -0.5484 0.583441
## ---
## Signif. codes:  0 '***' 0.001 '**' 0.01 '*' 0.05 '.' 0.1 ' ' 1
##
## Log-Likelihood: -641.19
## McFadden R^2:   0.074965
## Likelihood ratio test : chisq = 103.92 (p.value = < 2.22e-16)
```

Now that the full model, `mlogit.job`, and the partial model, `mlogit.job.alt`, had been estimated using the `mlogit()` function, they could be entered into the Hausman-McFadden test function, `hmftest()`. Leslie reminded herself that they were testing the null hypothesis that the IIA assumption is met. Rejecting the null hypothesis would mean the assumption fails, but if the *p*-value is greater than .05, the assumption is met.

```
# hmftest
hmftest(x = mlogit.job, z = mlogit.job.alt)
##
##   Hausman-McFadden test
##
## data:  stem.samp.4mlog
## chisq = 0.4851, df = 4, p-value = 0.9749
## alternative hypothesis: IIA is rejected
```

The *p*-value was .97, which is much higher than .05, so the null hypothesis is retained and the IIA assumption is met. Leslie was curious to compare the larger and smaller models to get a better idea of why this is the case. She examined the output and noted that the coefficients and *p*-values were nearly (but not perfectly) identical, which suggested that the existence of the other science job type did not influence the probability of choosing computer science, math, or engineering compared to nonscience.

11.6.3 FULL INTERPRETATION OF MODEL RESULTS

A multinomial logistic regression including age, sex, and the interaction between age and sex was statistically significantly better at predicting job type than a null model with no predictors [$\chi^2(6) = 124.77$; $p < .001$]. The model met its assumptions and correctly predicted the job type for 43.9% of observations. For every 1-year increase in age, the odds of being in an other sciences job are 1.02 times higher than being in a computer science, math, or engineering job (95% CI: 1.00–1.03). Likewise, for every 1-year increase in age, the odds of being in a nonscience job are 1.03 times higher than being in a computer science, math, or engineering job (95% CI: 1.02–1.04). Compared to males, the odds of females being in an other sciences job are 3.29 times higher than being in a computer science, math, or engineering job (95% CI: 1.24–8.71). Also, compared to males, females have 4.58 times higher odds of being in nonscience jobs compared to computer science, math, or engineering jobs (95% CI: 1.71–12.22). The interaction between age and sex was not a statistically significant indicator of job type.

11.6.4 ACHIEVEMENT 3: CHECK YOUR UNDERSTANDING

Remove the interaction term from the model and rerun it. Interpret the results and compare them to the full model results.

11.7 Achievement 4: Using exploratory data analysis for ordinal logistic regression

Leslie felt like she had learned a little about who chooses the different job types from the multinomial model, but the analysis so far had not really given her much new information to make a choice about a career in data science. She thought that it might help to know more about whether those women who do choose data science careers are satisfied with their choice. The R-Team discussed how to think about job satisfaction for a few minutes. Leslie explained that she was not as interested in comparing satisfaction of women to the satisfaction of men with computer science, math, or engineering. She was more interested in understanding whether job satisfaction differs for women across the three job types. Kiara suggested they take a sample of female participants from the original data frame so that they would have a larger number in the sample than using the females from the subset of 1,500. She also suggested that since there were very few people (relatively speaking) in the dissatisfied categories when they looked at the summary in the beginning, they could take 250 people from each category of one of the satisfaction variables to ensure they had enough people in the dissatisfied categories. Leslie thought this sounded good and suggested starting with the satisfaction with salary, so they used `satis.salary` to choose the sample.

```
# sample of 1,000 females
set.seed(seed = 143)
stem.samp.f<- stem.cleaned %>%
  drop_na(job.cat) %>%
  filter(sex == "Female") %>%
  group_by(satis.salary) %>%
  sample_n(size = 250) %>%
  ungroup()

# check work
summary(object = stem.samp.f)
##       age                   job.cat                satis.advance
##  Min.   :23.00   CS, Math, Eng :149   Very satisfied       :206
##  1st Qu.:31.00   Other Sciences:162   Somewhat satisfied   :375
##  Median :39.00   Nonscience    :689   Somewhat dissatisfied:241
##  Mean   :41.58                        Very dissatisfied    :178
##  3rd Qu.:51.00
##  Max.   :75.00
##                satis.salary            satis.contrib            sex
##  Very satisfied     :250   Very satisfied     :511   Male  :   0
##  Somewhat satisfied :250   Somewhat satisfied :330   Female:1000
```

```
##   Somewhat dissatisfied:250    Somewhat dissatisfied:107
##   Very dissatisfied    :250    Very dissatisfied    : 52
##
##
```

Leslie noticed a function in Nancy's code she had never seen before, `ungroup()`. Nancy said she was working on some code the week before and had trouble with some of her analyses after using `group_by()` with sampling because it added an attribute to the variable for R to treat it as a grouping variable for the sample. The `ungroup()` function removed this attribute. Leslie made a note to herself to try `ungroup()` with `group_by()` when she had trouble with analysis after using `group_by()`. The team reviewed the data and saw that the data were distributed pretty well across all the categories for the satisfaction variables, so this seemed like a good sample to work with.

11.7.1 VISUALIZING SATISFACTION WITH SALARY BY JOB TYPE AND AGE

There were several options for graphing the proportion of female college graduates in each job type that were satisfied or dissatisfied. One was to use a stacked bar graph where each bar represents all of the observations in the category. Leslie was not sure how to do this since none of her bar graphs in the past had represented 100% of each group. Kiara showed her the `position = "fill"` option for the `geom_bar()` layer and suggested that Leslie pick colors in the same family to visually display the ordered characteristic of the variable. Leslie added the position option and chose the purple palette from the color brewer website to differentiate the groups. She also decided that the way the color filled the categories looked backwards, with the darkest color on the left and the lightest on the right; to fix this, Nancy showed her how to add the `direction = -1` option to the `scale_fill_brewer()` function so that the purples go from lightest to darkest from left to right (Figure 11.14).

FIGURE 11.14 Satisfaction with salary by job type for 1,000 female college graduates

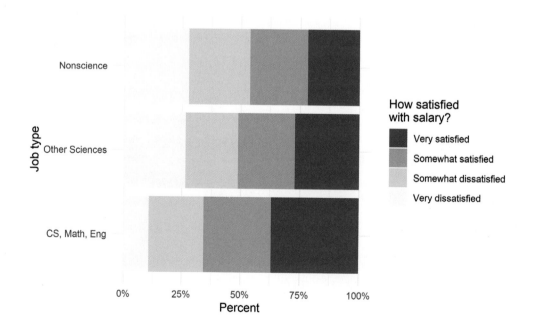

```
# job satisfaction in job type (Figure 11.14)
stem.samp.f %>%
  ggplot(aes(x = job.cat, fill = satis.salary)) +
  geom_bar(position = "fill") + coord_flip() +
  theme_minimal() + labs(x = "Job type", y = "Percent") +
  scale_fill_brewer(name = "How satisfied\nwith salary?",
                    palette = "Purples",
                    direction = -1) +
  scale_y_continuous(labels = scales::percent)
```

The bar plot shows that college-educated females in computer science, math, or engineering had the highest total percentage of very or somewhat satisfied with their salary. More than half of the non-science group was not satisfied. Leslie was curious whether these patterns held when age was considered. She created a boxplot to see what it looked like (Figure 11.15).

```
# job satisfaction by age (Figure 11.15)
stem.samp.f %>%
ggplot(aes(y = age, x = job.cat, fill = satis.salary)) +
  geom_jitter(aes(color = satis.salary), alpha = .6) +
  geom_boxplot(aes (fill = satis.salary), alpha = .4) +
  scale_fill_brewer(name = "How satisfied\nwith salary?",
                    palette = "Purples",
                    direction = -1) +
  scale_color_brewer(name = "How satisfied\nwith salary?",
                     palette = "Purples",
                     direction = -1) +
  theme_minimal() + labs(x = "Job type", y = "Age in years")
```

The very satisfied groups had much higher median age for nonscience jobs. There was not much of a pattern for median age across the satisfaction groups overall.

Leslie found all this information to be interesting, but she still didn't feel like she had the full picture. She moved on to some bivariate statistical tests before developing her models.

11.7.2 BIVARIATE STATISTICAL TESTS TO EXAMINE JOB SATISFACTION BY JOB TYPE AND AGE

While chi-squared and Kruskal-Wallis were useful for examining the relationships among sex, age, and job category, the satisfaction measures were a different variable type and may need to be treated differently. Specifically, the categories of satisfaction are in a logical order, similar to how the values of a continuous variable go in order from smallest to largest, so this variable is ordinal. The underlying concept or idea for an ordinal variable may be more like a continuous variable than it is like a nominal

FIGURE 11.15 Satisfaction with salary by age for 1,000 female college graduates

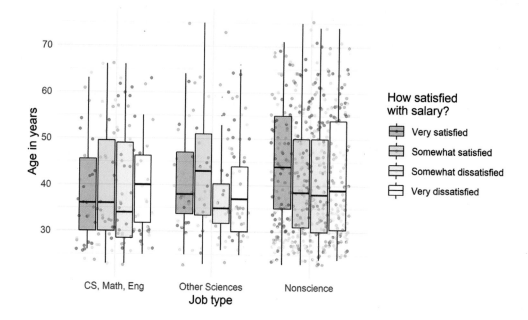

variable. Nancy explained that the Kruskal-Wallis test *can* be used to examine the relationship between an ordinal variable and a nominal variable that has more than two categories.

Leslie looked back to her notes on *t*-tests, ANOVA, and correlation and reminded herself that the code for the Kruskal-Wallis test is `kruskal.test()` and the code for Spearman's rho is `cor.test()` with `method = "spearman"` specified as part of the argument. She looked through the help documentation for `cor.test()` and noticed that the ordinal variable would have to be converted to either a numeric data type or an interval data type. She was a little worried that converting the four categories to numeric or integer would change the order of the categories, which would not be great for analysis. She wanted to recode it so that the values went from least satisfaction having the lowest value to the most satisfaction having the highest value. Nancy let her know that the `ordered()` function could be used to specify an order to categories of factor data type variables so that any subsequent transformations or uses of that variable would follow the given order.

Leslie looked up the help documentation for the `ordered()` function. She wanted to make sure the order of a recoded satisfaction variable maintained the order of satisfaction levels. She wrote a short function called `OrderSatis` so that she could apply it three times.

```
# order variables function
OrderSatis <- function(x){
  return(ordered(x, levels = c("Very dissatisfied",
                                "Somewhat dissatisfied",
                                "Somewhat satisfied",
                                "Very satisfied")))
}
```

```
# use function to order 3 satisfaction variables
stem.samp.f.cleaned <- stem.samp.f %>%
    mutate(satis.advance = OrderSatis(x = satis.advance)) %>%
    mutate(satis.salary = OrderSatis(x = satis.salary)) %>%
    mutate(satis.contrib = OrderSatis(x = satis.contrib))

# check the data
summary(object = stem.samp.f.cleaned)
##       age                  job.cat            satis.advance
##  Min.   :23.00   CS, Math, Eng :149   Very dissatisfied    :178
##  1st Qu.:31.00   Other Sciences:162   Somewhat dissatisfied:241
##  Median :39.00   Nonscience    :689   Somewhat satisfied   :375
##  Mean   :41.58                        Very satisfied       :206
##  3rd Qu.:51.00
##  Max.   :75.00
##                 satis.salary            satis.contrib        sex
##  Very dissatisfied    :250   Very dissatisfied    : 52   Male  :   0
##  Somewhat dissatisfied:250   Somewhat dissatisfied:107   Female:1000
##  Somewhat satisfied   :250   Somewhat satisfied   :330
##  Very satisfied       :250   Very satisfied       :511
##
##
```

It looked good to the team, with the very satisfied category being the last category so that satisfaction gets more favorable as it increases from the first to the last category. While Leslie was admiring her function results, Nancy typed up the next set of tests.

```
# examine salary satisfaction by job type for females
sat.kw <- kruskal.test(formula = as.integer(x = satis.salary) ~ job.cat,
            data = stem.samp.f.cleaned)

sat.kw
##
## 	Kruskal-Wallis rank sum test
##
## data:  as.integer(satis.salary) by job.cat
## Kruskal-Wallis chi-squared = 25.973, df = 2, p-value = 2.291e-06
# examine salary satisfaction by age
sat.rho <- cor.test(formula = ~ as.integer(x = satis.salary) + age,
        method = "spearman",
        data = stem.samp.f.cleaned)
```

```
sat.rho

##

##   Spearman's rank correlation rho

##

## data: as.integer(satis.salary) and age

## S = 156712046, p-value = 0.05902

## alternative hypothesis: true rho is not equal to 0

## sample estimates:

##        rho

## 0.05972678
```

Leslie saw that satisfaction with salary was significantly associated with job type but not with age. Specifically, there was a statistically significant relationship between job type and satisfaction with salary ($\chi^2_{KW}(2) = 25.97; p < .001$). In addition, there was a non-significant and weak positive correlation between age and salary satisfaction ($r_s = 0.06; p = 0.06$).

11.7.3 ACHIEVEMENT 4: CHECK YOUR UNDERSTANDING

Create and interpret graphs and bivariate statistical tests to examine the relationship between each of the predictor variables (`job.cat`, `age`) and satisfaction with contribution to society.

11.8 Achievement 5: Estimating and interpreting an ordinal logistic regression model

For ordinal categorical variables, a model is needed that can account for the order of the outcome variable (Norris et al., 2006). Since she had already examined graphs and bivariate statistics about satisfaction with salary, Leslie decided to start by applying the ordinal regression model to the salary satisfaction variable.

11.8.1 NHST FOR THE ORDINAL REGRESSION MODEL

11.8.1.1 NHST STEP 1: WRITE THE NULL AND ALTERNATE HYPOTHESES

H0: Job type and age are not helpful in explaining satisfaction with salary for female college graduates.

HA: Job type and age are helpful in explaining satisfaction with salary for female college graduates.

11.8.1.2 NHST STEP 2: COMPUTE THE TEST STATISTIC

The ordinal regression model is estimated using the `polr()` function from the **MASS** package. Like all of the regression model functions so far, the `polr()` function options include the regression formula and the data source. In this case, the formula is `satis.salary ~ age + job.cat` to explain satisfaction with salary based on age and job type.

```
# ordinal logistic regression for salary satisfaction
library(package = "MASS")

# model salary satisfaction based on job type and age
salary.mod <- polr(formula = satis.salary ~ job.cat + age,
                   data = stem.samp.f.cleaned)

summary(object = salary.mod)
## Call:
## polr(formula = satis.salary ~ job.cat + age, data = stem.samp.f.cleaned)
##
## Coefficients:
##                         Value Std.  Error  t value
## job.catOther Sciences -0.636236  0.204817  -3.106
## job.catNonscience     -0.835247  0.162788  -5.131
## age                    0.008173  0.004517   1.809
##
## Intercepts:
##                                                Value   Std. Error  t value
## Very dissatisfied|Somewhat dissatisfied       -1.4595  0.2358      -6.1908
## Somewhat dissatisfied|Somewhat satisfied      -0.3400  0.2314      -1.4696
## Somewhat satisfied|Very satisfied              0.7827  0.2332       3.3558
##
## Residual Deviance: 2743.702
## AIC: 2755.702
```

Similar to the multinomial model, the model summary includes the residual deviance but not the null deviance to compute the model chi-squared. Following the strategy used for the multinomial model, Leslie computed the null deviance by estimating a model with no predictors and computing the chi-squared using the deviance values from the two models.

```
# estimate null model
salary.mod.null <- polr(formula = satis.salary ~ 1,
                   data = stem.samp.f.cleaned)

# job model chi-squared
salary.chisq <- salary.mod.null$deviance - salary.mod$deviance

# degrees of freedom for chi-squared
salary.df <- length(x = salary.mod$coefficients) - length(x = salary.mod.
null$coefficients)

# pvalue for chi-squared
salary.p <- pchisq(q = salary.chisq, df = salary.df, lower.tail = FALSE)
```

```
# put together and print
modelsig.salary <- round(x = c(salary.chisq, salary.df, salary.p), 3)
names(x = modelsig.salary) <- c("Chi-squared", "d.f.", "p")
modelsig.salary
## Chi-squared         d.f.              p
##      28.887        3.000          0.000
```

The model chi-squared is 28.89 with 3 degrees of freedom.

11.8.1.3 NHST STEP 3: CALCULATE THE PROBABILITY THAT YOUR TEST STATISTIC IS AT LEAST AS BIG AS IT IS IF THERE IS NO RELATIONSHIP (I.E., THE NULL IS TRUE)

The p-value for $\chi^2(3) = 28.89$ is less than .001.

11.8.1.4 NHST STEPS 4 AND 5: INTERPRET THE PROBABILITY AND WRITE A CONCLUSION

Leslie rejected the null hypothesis. Job type and age statistically significantly help to predict satisfaction with salary for female college graduates [$\chi^2(3) = 28.89$; $p < .001$].

11.8.2 ORDINAL LOGISTIC REGRESSION MODEL FIT

Next, Leslie examined model fit, using the same strategy as with the multinomial outcome. She looked through the model object in the Environment tab for a few minutes before she found the observed values of satis.salary (see Figure 11.16).

After reviewing the model object a little more, she made the tables of observed and predicted values to see about fit.

```
# observed vs. predicted category for each observation
fit.n.soc <- table(observed = salary.mod$model$satis.salary,
                   predicted = predict(object = salary.mod))
fit.n.soc
##                         predicted
## observed                Very dissatisfied Somewhat dissatisfied
##    Very dissatisfied                   148                    37
##    Somewhat dissatisfied               149                    30
##    Somewhat satisfied                  136                    34
##    Very satisfied                      104                    45
##                         predicted
## observed                Somewhat satisfied Very satisfied
##    Very dissatisfied                    36             29
```

```
##    Somewhat dissatisfied              24              47
##    Somewhat satisfied                 17              63
##    Very satisfied                     29              72
```

```
# observed vs. predicted category for each observation
fit.perc <- prop.table(x = table(observed = salary.mod$model$satis.salary,
                    predicted = predict(object = salary.mod)),
                    margin = 1)
```

```
fit.perc
##                              predicted
## observed               Very dissatisfied Somewhat dissatisfied
##    Very dissatisfied           0.592                 0.148
##    Somewhat dissatisfied       0.596                 0.120
##    Somewhat satisfied          0.544                 0.136
##    Very satisfied              0.416                 0.180
##                              predicted
## observed               Somewhat satisfied Very satisfied
##    Very dissatisfied           0.144                 0.116
##    Somewhat dissatisfied       0.096                 0.188
##    Somewhat satisfied          0.068                 0.252
##    Very satisfied              0.116                 0.288
```

The model was pretty good at predicting very dissatisfied, with 59.2% correctly predicted, and very satisfied, with 28.8% correctly predicted, but was not as good at predicting somewhat dissatisfied, at 12% correct, or somewhat satisfied, at 6.8% correct. In looking at the columns for these middle categories, it appears that the model expected 59.6% of those in the somewhat dissatisfied category to be in the very dissatisfied group. Likewise, 25.2% of those in the somewhat satisfied category were predicted into the very satisfied category. It seems that the model was best at classifying people into the very dissatisfied category and worst at classifying people into somewhat disagree and somewhat agree.

11.8.3 ORDINAL REGRESSION PREDICTOR SIGNIFICANCE AND INTERPRETATION

To examine significance and to interpret the relationships, Kiara suggested using the same strategy as for the multinomial model and computing odds ratios and their 95% confidence intervals. Fortunately, this was a little easier for ordinal models than for multinomial models. Nancy wrote some code while Leslie followed along.

FIGURE 11.16 Screenshot of model object from Environment pane

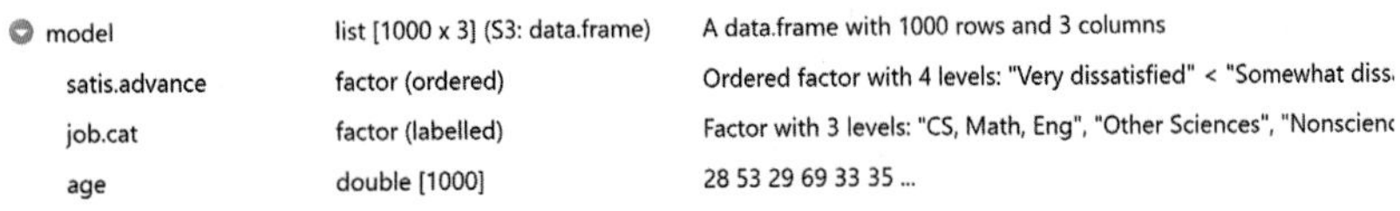

model	list [1000 x 3] (S3: data.frame)	A data.frame with 1000 rows and 3 columns
satis.advance	factor (ordered)	Ordered factor with 4 levels: "Very dissatisfied" < "Somewhat diss.
job.cat	factor (labelled)	Factor with 3 levels: "CS, Math, Eng", "Other Sciences", "Nonscienc
age	double [1000]	28 53 29 69 33 35 ...

```
# odds ratios and confidence intervals
or.sal <- data.frame(OR = exp(x = salary.mod$coefficients),
                     CI = exp(x = confint(object = salary.mod)))
or.sal
##                             OR  CI.2.5.. CI.97.5..
## job.catOther Sciences 0.5292810 0.3538288 0.7900786
## job.catNonscience     0.4337674 0.3146893 0.5959697
## age                   1.0082061 0.9993314 1.0171889
```

Kiara explained that, for ordinal models, the odds ratios are called *proportional odds ratios* and are the increases or decreases in odds of being in a higher group or groups versus all the lower groups for each one-unit increase in the predictor. This was super confusing to Leslie. Kiara tried to explain further using the other sciences predictor:

- Compared to females with computer science, math, or engineering jobs, females with other science jobs have 47% lower odds of being very satisfied compared to the other satisfaction categories (OR = 0.53; 95% CI: 0.35–0.79).

- Compared to females with computer science, math, or engineering jobs, females with other science jobs have 47% lower odds of being very or somewhat satisfied compared to the other satisfaction categories (OR = 0.53; 95% CI: 0.35–0.79).

- Compared to females with computer science, math, or engineering jobs, females with other jobs have 47% lower odds of being very or somewhat satisfied or somewhat dissatisfied compared to very dissatisfied (OR = 0.53; 95% CI: 0.35–0.79).

Wow. Leslie thought this was a lot of odds ratios for one predictor! She tried it for herself with the non-science job category:

- Compared to females with computer science, math, or engineering jobs, females with non-science jobs have 57% lower odds of being very satisfied compared to the other satisfaction categories (OR = 0.43; 95% CI: 0.31–0.60).

- Compared to females with computer science, math, or engineering jobs, females with non-science jobs have 57% lower odds of being very or somewhat satisfied compared to the other satisfaction categories (OR = 0.43; 95% CI: 0.31–0.60).

- Compared to females with computer science, math, or engineering jobs, females with non-science jobs have 57% lower odds of being very or somewhat satisfied or somewhat dissatisfied compared to very dissatisfied (OR = 0.43; 95% CI: 0.31–0.60).

Kiara approved. She said it might be worth having a summary sentence that basically stated that females are no more likely to be satisfied with their salary as they get older and that females who go into computer science, math, or engineering are more satisfied with their salary than females in other science or nonscience jobs.

11.8.4 ACHIEVEMENT 5: CHECK YOUR UNDERSTANDING

Build the ordinal regression model for satisfaction with contribution to society predicted by job type and age. Determine whether the model is statistically significantly better than the baseline at explaining satisfaction with contribution to society.

11.9 Achievement 6: Checking assumptions for ordinal logistic regression

11.9.1 ASSUMPTION OF INDEPENDENT OBSERVATIONS

The independence of observations assumption requires that the observations in the data be independent of each other. Data sets that include spouses, siblings, neighbors, or multiple observations on the same people would not meet this assumption. Since these data are from a random sample of college graduates, this assumption is met.

11.9.2 ASSUMPTION OF PROPORTIONAL ODDS

The proportional odds assumption requires that the odds for every shift from category to category of the outcome are the same for each level of the predictors. For example, say the odds of someone being in the very dissatisfied group compared to the somewhat dissatisfied group were 2.5 times higher in the nonscience group compared to the computer science, math, or engineering group. The proportional odds assumption would require that the odds of someone being in the somewhat dissatisfied group compared to the somewhat satisfied group would also need to be 2.5 times higher in the nonscience compared to computer science, math, and engineering group.

In the **ordinal** package, the `nominal_test()` function tests the proportional odds assumption. The null hypothesis for this is that the proportional odds assumption is met; the alternate hypothesis is that the proportional odds assumption is not met. The assumption is checked for each predictor in the model. Unfortunately, `nominal_test()` does not like `polr()` objects, so the model has to be re-estimated using `clm()` from the **ordinal** package. Although this is a little extra work, Nancy explained, the `nominal_test()` is the best way she knew of in R to test the proportional odds assumption.

Leslie tried using `nominal_test()` with `clm()` nested inside.

```
# check proportional odds assumption
library(package = "ordinal")
nominal_test(object = clm(formula = satis.salary ~ job.cat + age,
                          data = stem.samp.f.cleaned))
## Tests of nominal effects
##
## formula: satis.salary ~ job.cat + age
##          Df  logLik   AIC    LRT   Pr(>Chi)
## <none>       -1371.8  2755.7
## job.cat  4  -1369.8  2759.5  4.1760  0.3827
## age      2  -1369.8  2755.7  4.0489  0.1321
## ---
## Signif. codes:  0 '***' 0.001 '**' 0.01 '*' 0.05 '.' 0.1 ' ' 1
```

The *p*-values are .38 and .13, so the null hypothesis is retained for the job type predictor and for the age predictor. The proportional odds assumption is met for this model.

11.9.3 FULL INTERPRETATION OF MODEL RESULTS

An ordinal logistic regression using job type and age was better at predicting satisfaction with salary among female college graduates than a baseline model including no predictors [$\chi^2(3) =$ 28.89; $p < .001$]. The model met its assumptions and correctly predicted 267 of the 1,000 (26.7%) observations. Female college graduates in nonscience careers have 57% lower odds than those in computer science, math, or engineering of being very satisfied with their salary compared to being in another satisfaction group. Likewise, female college graduates in other sciences had 47% lower odds than those in computer science, math, or engineering of being very satisfied with their salary compared to being in another satisfaction group. There was no significant relationship between age and salary satisfaction.

Leslie was excited about what she had learned about STEM careers from the multinomial and ordinal logistic regression models. She had learned that female college graduates do not go into computer science, math, or engineering jobs at high rates; however, a higher percentage of those who did reported being somewhat or very satisfied with their salary compared with those in the other fields of science. In addition, female college graduates who go into computer science, math, or engineering jobs have significantly higher odds of being very satisfied with their salary compared to female college graduates who are employed in other sciences or a nonscience field. Leslie thought that later she would check out models of contribution to society and advancement satisfaction, but she was done for now.

The most important result of the day was that Leslie's mind was made up! After several months of statistics and coding with the R-Team and reviewing this initial evidence of job satisfaction among women in the STEM fields, she had determined that she wanted to pursue a career in data science. Kiara and Nancy were happy to hear her decision.

"Yes! Another brilliant woman in the field. Welcome!" said Kiara.

"We've got a little something for you," Nancy said, handing her an envelope.

Inside was a hexagonal **tidyverse** sticker (Figure 1.9). "Thanks! Can't wait to put this on my laptop!" Leslie exclaimed.

Nancy suggested they might celebrate the success of the R-Team sometime soon at the pub.

"Sure," said Leslie. "I've got to try a Guinness in honor of William Sealy Gosset [Box 6.2] of course. And I will definitely see you both at the next R-Ladies gathering [Box 1.1]." Then she thanked them again for their guidance through statistics and R.

As they packed up for the day, Kiara reminded Leslie that she could always call them to collaborate or for advice. And Nancy sang the *A-Team* theme song again: "If you have a problem, if no one else can help . . ."

11.9.4 ACHIEVEMENT 6: CHECK YOUR UNDERSTANDING

Check the proportional odds assumption for the contribution to society satisfaction model created in Check Your Understanding for Achievement 5.

11.10.1 Achievements unlocked in this chapter: Recap

Congratulations! Like Leslie, you've learned and practiced the following in this chapter.

11.10.1.1 Achievement 1 recap: Using exploratory data analysis for multinomial logistic regression

Prior to developing a multinomial model, use graphs and bivariate descriptive and inferential statistics to explore the relationship between the outcome variable and each of the predictors. Use bar graphs to visualize the relationship between the outcome and a categorical predictor, and use boxplots to aid in understanding the relationship between the outcome and continuous predictors. Chi-squared is useful to determine if a categorical predictor has a significant association with the outcome, while ANOVA or Kruskal-Wallis might be used to test associations between the outcome and a continuous predictor depending on whether or not it is normally distributed.

11.10.1.2 Achievement 2 recap: Estimating and interpreting a multinomial logistic regression model

The `multinom()` function from the **nnet** package can be used to estimate a multinomial model that includes a nominal outcome variable with three or more categories and continuous or categorical predictors. After estimating the model, compute model fit (percent correctly predicted), model significance (chi-squared with p-value), and the value and significance of the relationships between each predictor and the outcome (odds ratios and confidence intervals).

11.10.1.3 Achievement 3 recap: Checking assumptions for multinomial logistic regression

Multinomial logistic regression has two assumptions: independent observations and independence of irrelevant alternatives (IIA). The independent observations assumption requires that the observations in the data set be unrelated to each other. Data with related observations such as family members, spouses, co-workers, or multiple observations on individuals would not meet this assumption. The IIA assumption requires that the categories of the outcome be independent of one another. For example, the relative probability of choosing a job in the computer science, math, or engineering field compared to the other sciences field cannot depend on the existence of nonscience jobs. The test used for this assumption is the Hausman-McFadden test.

11.10.1.4 Achievement 4 recap: Using exploratory data analysis for ordinal logistic regression

Ordinal variables are categorical but with categories that have a specific logical order. The underlying idea of an ordinal variable is that its values lie along a continuum, so exploratory analyses may use visualization and statistics often used with more traditionally continuous variables. The relationship between the outcome and a categorical predictor can be shown with a bar graph that uses color strategically to emphasize the distribution of the ordinal variable within each category. For continuous predictors, boxplots that show the underlying data can be useful to see patterns. Bivariate statistics used for nonnormal continuous variables, such as Mann-Whitney U, Kruskal-Wallis, and Spearman's rho, are good for examining associations between predictor variables and the ordinal outcome.

11.10.1.5 Achievement 5 recap: Estimating and interpreting an ordinal logistic regression model

The `polr()` function from the **ordinal** package can be used to estimate an ordinal logistic regression model that includes an ordinal outcome variable with three or more categories and continuous or categorical predictors. After estimating the model, compute model fit (percent correctly predicted), model significance (chi-squared with p-value), and the value and significance of the relationships between each predictor and the outcome (odds ratios and confidence intervals).

11.10.1.6 Achievement 6 recap: Checking assumptions for ordinal logistic regression

The assumptions for ordinal regression include the independence of observations and the proportional odds assumption. The independence of observations requires observations to be independent of one another. The proportional odds assumption requires the relationship between the predictors and the outcome to be consistent at each level of the outcome. This assumption can be tested using the `nominal_test()` function, which conducts a likelihood ratio test of the proportional odds assumption.

11.10.2 Chapter exercises

The coder and hacker exercises are an opportunity to apply the skills from this chapter to a new scenario or a new data set. The coder edition evaluates the application of the concepts and functions learned in this R-Team meeting to scenarios similar to those in the meeting. The hacker edition evaluates the use of the concepts and functions from this R-Team meeting in new scenarios, often going a step beyond what was explicitly explained.

The coder edition might be best for those who found some or all of the Check Your Understanding activities to be challenging or if they needed review before picking the correct responses to the multiple-choice questions. The hacker edition might be best if the Check Your Understanding activities were not too challenging and the multiple-choice questions were a breeze.

The multiple-choice questions and materials for the exercises are online at **edge.sagepub.com/harris1e**.

Q1: Multinomial logistic regression is used when

   a. the outcome variable is nominal with three or more categories.

   b. the outcome variable is ordinal with three or more categories.

   c. at least one predictor is nominal with three or more categories.

   d. at least one predictor is ordinal with three or more categories.

Q2: The model significance tests for multinomial and ordinal regression use which of the following test statistics?

   a. Odds ratios with 95% confidence intervals

   b. *F*-statistics

   c. Chi-squared statistics

   d. Percent correctly predicted

Q3: One way to examine model fit for multinomial and ordinal regression is to compute

   a. odds ratios with 95% confidence intervals.

   b. *F*-statistics.

   c. chi-squared statistics.

   d. percent correctly predicted.

Q4: The assumptions for multinomial regression include

   a. the proportional odds assumption.

   b. a normally distributed outcome variable.

   c. equal group variances.

   d. independence of irrelevant alternatives.

Q5: The assumptions for ordinal regression include

   a. the proportional odds assumption.

   b. a normally distributed outcome variable.

   c. equal group variances.

   d. independence of irrelevant alternatives.

11.10.2.1 Chapter exercises: Coder edition

Depending on your score on the knowledge check, choose either the coder or hacker edition of the chapter exercises. Use the data from this chapter and the appropriate tests to examine additional predictors of job type and job satisfaction.

1) Import the data from this chapter.

2) Create a small STEM data frame containing variables for job type, sex, age, race-ethnicity, and the three satisfaction variables from the chapter.

3) Clean the variables in the small data frame. Use the strategies shown in this chapter for job type, sex, age, and the satisfaction variables. Write new code to clean the race-ethnicity variable.

4) Use the functions in the chapter to take a random sample of 500 participants in each job category.

5) Create a graph and a table examining the relationship between race-ethnicity and job type (Achievement 1).

6) Use `multinom()` to run a multinomial model predicting job type by age and race-ethnicity. Compute model significance, model fit, and odds ratios with confidence intervals (Achievement 2).

7) Discuss model significance and model fit (Achievement 2).

8) Interpret the model odds ratios and confidence intervals (Achievement 2).

9) Check model assumptions and interpret the results (Achievement 3).

10) Run the functions in the chapter to take a sample of 250 participants in each category of advancement satisfaction.

11) Create graphs and a table to examine the relationships between advancement satisfaction and the two predictors of age and job type (Achievement 4).

12) Use `polr()` to develop an ordinal logistic regression. Compute and interpret model significance, model fit, and odds ratios with confidence intervals (Achievement 5).

13) Check model assumptions and interpret the results (Achievement 6).

11.10.2.2 Chapter exercises: Hacker edition

Complete the coder edition with two modifications to the models:

14) For the multinomial model computed in #6, include the sex variable in addition to age and race-ethnicity. Add at least one interaction term (Achievements 2 and 3).

15) For the ordinal model computed in #12, add sex and an interaction term between age and sex (Achievements 5 and 6).

11.10.2.3 Instructor note

Solutions to exercises can be found on the website for this book, along with ideas for gamification for those who want to take it further.

Visit **edge.sagepub.com/harris1e** to download the datasets, complete the chapter exercises, and watch R tutorial videos.

adjusted count R^2: a measure of model fit for binary logistic regression that adjusts the percent correctly predicted (or count R^2) by the model for the number of people in the largest outcome category,

$$R^2_{count.adj} = \frac{n_{correct} - n_{most.common.outcome}}{n_{total} - n_{most.common.outcome}}$$

adjusted R-squared: a measure of model fit for ordinary least squares linear regression that penalizes the R-squared, or percentage of variance explained, for the number of variables in the model

aesthetics: part of the *grammar of graphics* used in ggplot to change visual components of a graph such as the colors, shapes, or types of lines

alpha: the threshold for the upper limit for statistical significance set prior to analyses that limits the probability of a Type I error; an alpha of .05 would result in *p*-values below .05 being considered statistically significant

alternate hypothesis: a claim that there is a difference or relationship among things; the alternate hypothesis is paired with the null hypothesis that typcially states there is no relationship or no difference between things

amfAR: the Foundation for AIDS Research, which was originally the American Foundation for AIDS Research (https://www.amfar.org/)

analysis of variance: a statistical method used to compare means across groups to determine whether there is a statistically significant difference among the means; typically used when there are three or more means to compare

annotation: statements included in code but not analyzed; in R, annotation is denoted by a hashtag (#) and is often used to clarify the code or analytic choices

arcsine transformation: a data transformation technique often recommended to normalize percent or proportion data; the arcsine transformation uses the inverse of the sine function and the square root of the variable to transform

area under the curve: in a density plot, the probability of a single observation or a range of observations

argument: information input into a function that controls how the function behaves

ASCII: an acronym for American Standard Code for Information Interchange, which are the characters used to represent letters and punctuation

assigning: assigning a name to an object is done by using an arrow, `<-`, with the arrow separating the name of the object on the left from the object itself on the right: `name <- object`

assumptions: characteristics of the data required for a statistical test to work as intended; for example, the outcome variable is required to be normally distributed in linear regression

B index: one measure of variability or spread for a nominal variable that indicates how spread out observations are among categories; the B index ranges from 0 to 1, where 0 is no variability and 1 is perfectly distributed across all available categories

bar chart: a visual display of data often used to examine similarities and differences across categories of things; bars can represent frequencies, percentages, means, or other statistics

bimodal: a distribution that has two modes

binomial random variable: a variable measured the same way *n* times with only two possible values, independent observations, and the same probability of success for each observation; the random variable is the number of successes in *n* measurements

Bonferroni post hoc test: a pairwise test used after a statistically significant ANOVA that conducts a *t*-test for each pair of means but adjusts the threshold for statistical significance to ensure that there is a small enough risk of Type I error; it is generally considered a very conservative post hoc test that only identifies the largest differences between means as statistically significant

boxplot: a visual representation of data that shows central tendency (usually the median) and spread (usually the interquartile range) of a numeric variable for one or more groups; boxplots are often used to compare the distribution of a continuous variable across several groups

breaks: the lower and upper limits of each category of values

Breusch-Pagan test: a statistical test for determining whether variance is constant, which is used to test the assumption of homoscedasticity; Breusch-Pagan relies on the chi-squared distribution and is used during assumption checking for linear regression

broom: an R package for cleaning and using the results in objects from statistical models

Brown-Forsythe: alternate *F*-statistic used for analysis of variance when the assumption of homogeneity of variance is not met; the Brown-Forsythe *F*-statistic is computed after transforming the values of the outcome to represent the distance from the median

BSDA: an R package containing functions and data from the book *Basic Statistics and Data Analysis* by Larry J. Kitchens

camel case: capitalizing the first letter of each word in an object name, with the exception of the first word (the capital letters kind of look like camel humps 🐪🐪)

car: an R package with functions that go with the book *An R Companion to Applied Regression* by John Fox

categorical: variables measured in categories; there are two types of categorical variables: ordinal variables have categories with a logical order (e.g., Likert scales), while nominal variables have categories with no logical order (e.g., religious affiliation)

ceiling effect: when many observations are at the highest possible value for a variable

Central Limit Theorem: a foundational idea in inferential statistics that shows the mean of a sampling distribution of a variable will be a close approximation to the mean of the variable in the population, regardless of whether the variable is normally distributed; the Central Limit Theorem demonstrates why samples can be used to infer information about the population

central tendency: a measure of the center, or typical value, of a variable; the mean, median, and mode are the three common measures of central tendency

character: a data type in R that comprises things that cannot be used in mathematical operations; often, character variables are names, addresses, zip codes, or other similar values

chi-squared: the test statistic following the chi-squared probability distribution; the chi-squared test statistic is used in inferential tests, including examining the association between two categorical variables and determining statistical significance for a logistic regression model

chi-squared goodness-of-fit: chi-squared analysis comparing the distribution of people across categories for a single categorical variable to the distribution of people in the same categories in a population or hypothesized group

Cochran's Q-test: an alternative to the chi-squared test of independence for when observations are not independent; for example, comparing groups before and after an intervention would fail the independent observations assumption

code monkey: a person who writes code, often for software that is designed by someone else; see Jonathan Coulton

coefficient of determination: the percentage of variance in one variable that is accounted for by another variable or by a group of variables; often referred to as R-squared and used to determine model fit for linear models

Cohen's d: an effect size to determine the strength of a relationship for a t-test

commenting: using short statements in statistical code to explain something; comments are ignored by the software but can be valuable for humans reading and working with the code

confidence interval: a range of values around a statistic that suggests where the true or population value of the statistic likely lies with some level of certainty; for example, a 95% confidence interval around a mean suggests that the true or population value of the mean will likely fall within the bounds of this confidence interval for about 95 out of every 100 samples

continuous: a variable that can take any value over a range of values

contrasts: sets of numbers used in planned contrasts to specify which means or groups of means to compare to each other, usually to identify statistically significant differences among means after a statistically significant analysis of variance

contributed packages: R packages that have been submitted to the Comprehensive R Archive Network (CRAN)

Cook's distance: a diagnostic measure used to find influential values following a linear regression by re-estimating the model without each observation and comparing it to the original model

co-pilot: a person who can write the code with you or run the code you have written and let you know if it worked

correlation: a statistical relationship between two things

correlation coefficient: a standardized measure of how two variables are related, or co-vary; commonly used correlation coefficients include Pearson's r, which is

computed $r_{xy} = \dfrac{cov_{xy}}{s_x s_y}$, and Spearman's rho

count R^2: a measure of model fit for logistic regression that is the proportion of observations with the outcome value correctly predicted by the regression model out of all observations modeled,

or $R^2_{count} = \dfrac{n_{correct}}{n_{total}}$

covariance: a descriptive statistic quantifying whether two variables vary together (e.g., as one goes up, the other goes up), which is computed as

$cov_{xy} = \dfrac{\sum_{i=1}^{n}\left(x_i - m_x\right)\left(y_i - m_y\right)}{n-1}$, where x_i

and y_i are the observed values for each observation, m_x and m_y are the mean values for each variable, i represents an individual observation, and n represents the sample size

coxcomb (rose) diagram: a visual display of data used to display parts of a whole, similar to a pie chart but with multiple layers

Cramér's V: an effect size to determine the strength of the relationship between two categorical variables; often reported with the results of a chi-squared test

and computed $V = \sqrt{\dfrac{\chi^2}{n(k-1)}}$ where n

is the sample size and k is the number of categories in the variable with the fewest categories

CRAN: the Comprehensive R Archive Network that stores R packages

critical region: region of the distribution of a test statistic that is outside the threshold set by alpha; test statistics that are in the rejection region have small p-values that support rejecting the null hypothesis

csv: a file extension indicating that the file contains comma separated values

cumulative distribution function: a function that determines the probability that some variable has a value less than or equal to some specified number,

$f\left(x,n,p\right) = \sum_{x=0}^{x_{floor}} \binom{n}{x} p^x \left(1-p\right)^{(n-x)}$

custom function: an R function written by the coder to perform specific tasks

data frame: an object type in R that holds data with values in rows and columns with rows treated as observations and columns treated as variables

data management: the procedures used to prepare the data for analysis; data management often includes recoding variables, ensuring that missing values are treated properly, checking and fixing data types, and other data-cleaning procedures

data types: in R, these include numeric, character, factor, logical, string, and others; the data type suggests how a variable was measured and recorded or recoded, and different analytic strategies are used to manage and analyze different variable types

data visualization: using visual tools to examine or communicate about characteristics of data; graphs are visual displays of data

data.table: an R package for aggregating and managing large data files quickly

degrees of freedom: the number of pieces of information that are allowed to vary in computing a statistic before the remaining pieces of information are known; degrees of freedom are often used as parameters for distributions (e.g., chi-squared, *F*)

denominator: the bottom of a fraction, below the line

density plot: used for examining the distribution of a variable measured along a continuum; density plots are similar to histograms but are smoothed and may not show existing gaps in data

dependent-samples *t*-test: a statistical test that compares the means of two related groups using the *t*-statistic, computed $t = \dfrac{m_d - 0}{\sqrt{\dfrac{s_d^2}{n_d}}}$, where m_d is the mean of the differences between the two groups, s_d is the standard deviation of the differences, and n_d is the sample size; for example, the mean time spent exercising per week of a group of people before and after an intervention to increase exercise duration would be tested using the dependent-samples *t*-test

dependent variable: the variable being predicted or explained by a statistical model; also called an outcome variable

descr: an R package for computing descriptive statistics

descriptive statistics: statistics used to describe a sample without making any inference about the population that was sampled; descriptive statistics vary by data type and include measures of central tendency, spread, frequencies, and percentages

deterministic: a model that perfectly predicts values of the outcome

deviance: in logistic regression, finding the differences between observed values (0s and 1s) and the predicted values (percentages), squaring each difference, and adding up all the squared differences from each person in the data set; the deviance measures how well the model fits the data

deviation scores: scores that show the difference from some value like the mean; for example, *z*-scores show the deviation from the mean in standard deviation units

devtools: an R package that includes functions to support development of other R packages

df-betas: one of the diagnostic tests to identify influential observations following a regression analysis; df-betas are calculated by removing each observation

from the data frame, re-estimating the model, and comparing the model with all observations to the model without the observation

diagnostics: in linear and logistic regression, a set of tests to identify outliers and influential values among the observations

discrete: a variable that can take only certain values; all categorical variables are discrete, while some numeric variables are also discrete

distribution: most distributions show the values of a variable and the frequency or probability of each value, either in the form of a table or a graph

dot case: using a dot to separate words in a variable name, like this: dot.case

dplyr: an R package for data management that includes selecting variables, filtering cases, and changing variables

dunn.test: an R package for conducting a Dunn's post hoc test following a statistically significant Kruskal-Wallis test

Dunn's post hoc test: pairwise comparisons to determine which groups are statistically significantly different from one another following a significant Kruskal-Wallis test

Durbin-Watson: a statistical test that is used to test the assumption of independent residuals in linear regression; a Durbin-Watson statistic of 2 indicates that the residuals are independent

effect size: a measure of the strength of a relationship; effect sizes are important in inferential statistics in order to determine and communicate whether a statistically significant result has practical importance

Environment pane: part of the RStudio window that shows what objects are currently open and available in R

eta-squared: an effect size interpreted as the proportion of variability in the continuous outcome variable that is explained by groups in an analysis of variance; recent research suggests that eta-squared is biased and that omega-squared may be a less biased alternative following analysis of variance

expected value: the value that should occur given certain conditions; for example, in a chi-squared analysis, the null hypothesis suggests that a table showing the categories of one of the variables as the rows and the other as the

columns would have (row × column) / total observations expected in each cell

explained variance: variation in an outcome that is explained by a model; explained and unexplained variance are used in ANOVA and linear regression to compute model fit and model significance statistics

exploratory data analysis: analytic and graphic techniques for examining data to learn about the variables and observations

exponentiating: to raise a value to some power; in the context of exponentiating the coefficients in logistic regression, the exponentiation is taking the constant *e* to the power of the coefficient, like this: e^{coeff}

exposure: a characteristic, behavior, or other factor that may be associated with an outcome

factor: a data type used for constants and variables that are made up of data elements that fall into categories

familywise error: the alpha or Type I error rate when conducting multiple statistical tests that is computed $\alpha_f = 1 - (1 - \alpha_i)^c$, where *c* is the number of statistical tests and α_i is the alpha for each test; a large familywise alpha is one of the reasons that analysis of variance is preferable to conducting multiple *t*-tests when comparing means across more than two groups

***F*-distribution:** the probability distribution underlying the *F*-statistic, which is used to determine statistical significance for ANOVA and linear regression

Fisher's exact test: an alternative to the chi-squared test for use with small samples

floor effect: when a variable has many observations that take the lowest value of the variable, which can indicate that the range of values was insufficient to capture the true variability of the data

fmsb: an R package containing functions for the medical statistics book *Practices of Medical and Health Data Analysis Using R* by Minako Nakazawa

for loop: a way of doing the same thing multiple times, or doing something iteratively; a for loop can be read as "for each item in (things you want to iterate over), do something"

forest plot: a data visualization that includes a measure and its confidence interval; forest plots are often used to show odds ratios and confidence intervals but could also be used to show means and confidence intervals or other measures

frequency: the number of times a particular value of a variable occurs

frequency distribution: the set of frequencies of each value of a variable

F-statistic: a test statistic comparing explained and unexplained variance in ANOVA and linear regression

function: a set of machine-readable instructions to perform a task in R; often, the task is to conduct some sort of data management or analysis, but there are also functions that exist just for fun, like pupR, which is a function that shows you a picture of a dog (https://github.com/melissanjohnson/pupR)

General Social Survey: a large survey of a sample of people in the United States conducted regularly since 1972; the General Social Survey is abbreviated GSS and is conducted by the National Opinion Research Center at the University of Chicago

generalized linear model: a linear regression model that has been generalized to handle a different situation; the binary logistic regression model is one example of a generalized linear model

generalized variance inflation factor: a generalized version of the variance inflation factor (VIF) that is used to identify problems with multicollinearity; the GVIF is used in binary logistic regression

geometry: part of the *grammar of graphics* used in `ggplot` to specify the type of graph to be created

`ggmosaic`: an R package to add a layer that makes a mosaic plot within `ggplot()`

`ggplot2`: the grammar of graphics R package used to make data visualizations

`ggrepel`: an R package for fixing overlapping labels on plots

Grammy's pancakes: mix one teaspoon baking soda in one cup sour cream, add this mixture to one well-beaten egg, stir in one cup flour that has been sifted with one teaspoon baking powder and one-half teaspoon salt, thin the mixture with milk; cook on non-stick or greased griddle and serve with maple syrup

grand mean: the overall mean of a continuous variable that is used to determine distances from the mean for individuals and groups in ANOVA

`gridExtra`: an R package that facilitates printing more than one ggplot in columns or rows

grouped bar chart: a data visualization that shows two categorical variables in a bar chart where one group is shown along the *x*-axis for vertical bars or *y*-axis for horizontal bars and the other grouping is shown as separate bars within each of the first grouping variable categories; the bars are often different colors to distinguish the groups

`haven`: an R package that facilitates importing data from the statistical software programs of SPSS, Stata, and SAS

histogram: a visual display of data used to examine the distribution of a numeric variable

History pane: part of the RStudio window that keeps a running list of the commands you have used so far

`Hmisc`: an R package that contains data management, graphics, and table-making functions

homogeneity of variance: equal variances among groups; homogeneity of variance is one of the assumptions tested for independent and dependent *t*-tests and analysis of variance

homoscedasticity: an assumption of correlation and linear regression that requires that the variance of *y* be constant across all the values of *x*; visually, this assumption would show points along a fit line between *x* and *y* being evenly spread on either side of the line for the full range of the relationship

`httr`: an R package for working with URLs when importing data or accessing other online information

independence of irrelevant alternatives: an assumption of multinomial logistic regression that requires the categories of the outcome to be independent of one another; for a three-category outcome variable with Categories A, B, and C, the probability of being in Category A compared to Category B cannot change because Category C exists

independent: observations that are unrelated to each other

independent-samples *t*-test: a statistical test that compares the means of some numeric variable across two unrelated groups; the test statistic is *t* and is

computed $t = \dfrac{m_1 - m_2}{\sqrt{\dfrac{s_1^2}{n_1} + \dfrac{s_2^2}{n_2}}}$, where m_1 and m_2

are the group means, s_1 and s_2 are the group standard deviations, and n_1 and n_2 are the group sample sizes

independent variable: a variable used to explain or predict some outcome or dependent variable

index of qualitative variation: a type of statistic used to measure variation for nominal variables, which is often computed by examining how spread out observations are among the groups

individual level: at the level of a person; data that are at the individual level include characteristics of individual humans

inferential statistics: statistical approaches that infer population characteristics based on sample data

influential observation: an observation that changes the slope of a regression line

integer: a similar data type to numeric, but containing only whole numbers

interquartile range: the upper and lower boundaries around the middle 50% of the data in a numeric variable or the difference between the upper and lower boundaries around the middle 50% of the data in a numeric variable

iterative: a way of doing the same thing multiple times

`kableExtra`: an R package for making well-formatted tables

`knitr`: an R package that controls the format of R output so that well-formatted reports can be generated without extensive complex coding

Kolmogorov-Smirnov test: used when the assumption of equal variances (homogeneity of variances) fails for the independent-samples *t*-test; the test compares the distributions of the groups rather than their means

Kruskal-Wallis test: used to compare ranks across three or more groups when the normal distribution assumption fails for analysis of variance (ANOVA)

kurtosis: a measure of how many observations are in the tails of a distribution; distributions that look bell-shaped, but have a lot of observations in the tails (platykurtic) or very few observations in the tails (leptokurtic), are computed as follows:

$$kurtosis_x = \frac{1}{n} \sum_{i=1}^{n} \left(\frac{x_i - m_x}{s_x} \right)^4$$

`labelled`: an R package used to access and work with variable labels

labels: attributes of an object that further explain some characteristic of the data;

two commonly used labels in R are labels for what is in a category of a factor variable and labels for a longer description of what is contained in a vector or variable

layer: in `ggplot`, a function used to specify a data source, a statistical procedure, or a visual option for a graph

left-skewed: a distribution that has extreme values in the left-hand-side tail, toward the negative numbers on the number line; left skew is also known as negative skew because the extreme variables are in the left-hand side of the distribution

leptokurtic: the distribution of a numeric variable that has many values clustered around the middle of the distribution; leptokurtic distributions often appear tall and pointy compared to mesokurtic or platykurtic distributions

Levene's test: a statistical test to determine whether observed data meet the homogeneity of variances assumption; Levene's test is used to test this assumption for t-tests and analysis of variance

leverage: a statistic used to identify influential observations when using regression; the average leverage is $\frac{p}{n}$, with p being how many parameters are in the model and n being the sample size; observations with two or three times the mean leverage are often considered influential

likelihood ratio test: a test that compares two nested binary logistic regression models to determine which is a better fit to the data; the difference between two log-likelihoods follows a chi-squared distribution with a significant result indicating the larger model is a better fitting model

Likert scale: a symmetric ordinal scale usually used to measure agreement; Likert scales tend to have *strongly agree* and *strongly disagree* as the anchoring values and the middle value is *neutral*, like this: *strongly agree, agree, neutral, disagree, strongly disagree*

line graph: a visual display of data often used to examine the relationship between two continuous variables or for something measured over time

linear transformation: transformations that keep existing linear relationships between variables, often by multiplying or dividing one or both of the variables by some amount

linearity: assumption of some statistical models that requires the outcome, or transformed outcome, to have a linear relationship with numeric predictors, where linear relationships are relationships that are evenly distributed around a line

`lmtest`: an R package with tests for checking diagnostics for linear regression models

Loess curve: a graph curve that shows the relationship between two variables without constraining the line to be straight; it can be compared to a linear fit line to determine whether the relationship is close to linear or not

logical: a data type in R that includes the values of TRUE and FALSE

logit transformation: a transformation that takes the log value of $\frac{p}{1-p}$; this transformation is often used to normalize percentage data and is used in the logistic model to transform the outcome

`lsr`: an R package that goes with the book *Learning Statistics With R: A Tutorial for Psychology Students and Other Beginners* by Danielle Navarro

main effect: the relationship between only one of the independent variables and the dependent variable, ignoring the impact of any additional independent variables or interaction effects

Mann-Whitney U test: an alternative for comparing a numeric or ordinal variable across two groups when the independent-samples t-test assumption of normality is not met

matrix: information, or data elements, stored in a rectangular format with rows and columns

McNemar's test: an alternative to the chi-squared test of independence for when observations are not independent and both variables are binary; for example, McNemar's test could be used to compare proportions in two groups before and after an intervention

mean: a summary statistic denoted as μ in the population and m_x or $\bar{x}$ in a sample that shows the middle or typical value for that variable computed by finding the sum of the values of a variable divided by the number of values, $m_x = \frac{\sum_{i=1}^{n} x_i}{n}$; the mean is influenced by extreme values and is not a good metric to represent the middle in skewed distributions

mean square: the mean of the squared differences between two values; mean squares are used to compute the F-statistic in analysis of variance and linear regression

means plot: a visual display of data that shows mean values connected by lines (see Figure 7.20)

median: the middle value, or the mean of the two middle values, for a variable

mesokurtic: distributions that are neither platykurtic nor leptokurtic are mesokurtic; a normal distribution is a common example of a mesokurtic distribution

mode: the most common value of a variable

model fit: how well the model captures the relationship in the observed data

monotonic: a statistical relationship that, when visualized, goes up or down, but not both

mosaic plot: a visual representation of data to show the relationship between two categorical variables; useful primarily when both variables have few categories

multiple regression: a regression analysis where more than one independent variable is on the right-hand side of the equal sign and is used to predict or explain the dependent variable

NA: the R placeholder for missing values, often translated as "not available."

names: the characteristic of an object in R that is used to refer to the object; there is also a function in R called names that allows printing or changing the name of an object

namespace: a characteristic of packages that manages the names of functions in the package and the names of functions used by a package; occasionally, two packages have the same function name and this can result in a namespace conflict

National Health and Nutrition Examination Survey: a regularly conducted survey of adults and children in the United States in order to have information on demographic and health-related behaviors and conditions

negative correlation: a statistical relationship where two things move in opposite directions; as one goes up, the other goes down, and vice versa

negatively skewed: a distribution that has extreme values in the left-hand-side tail, toward the negative numbers on the number line; negative skew is also known as left skew

nesting: refers to functions that are used inside other functions

nominal: variables containing categories that have no logical order; religious affiliation and marital status are examples of nominal variable types because there is no logical order to these characteristics (e.g., Methodist is not inherently greater or less than Catholic)

nonlinear transformation: a transformation that increases (or decreases) the linear relationship between two variables by applying an exponent (i.e., power transformation) or other function to one or both of the variables

normal distribution: a distribution that is symmetric around its mean, median, and mode without excessive observations in the middle or either tail

normality: normality is the characteristic of being normally distributed; it is an assumption of the mean and of continuous variables in several inferential statistical tests, including the *t*-test, ANOVA, and linear regression

normally distributed: the distribution of a numeric variable that is symmetric around its mean, median, and mode without excessive observations in the middle or either tail; it is shaped like a bell and is sometimes referred to as a bell-shaped curve

null hypothesis: a statement of no difference or no association that is used to guide statistical inference testing

Null Hypothesis Significance Testing: a process for organizing inferential statistical tests

numerator: the top portion of a fraction, above the line

numeric: the default data type that R assigns to constants and variables that contain only numbers; the numeric data type can be whole numbers and numbers with decimal places, so it is the most appropriate data type for variables measured along a continuum, or continuous variables

object: information stored by R; data analysis and data management are then performed on these stored objects; before an object can be used in data management or analysis in R, it has to be stored in the R environment

observation: a single row of data in a data frame that usually represents one person or other entity

odds ratio: the odds of some event or outcome occurring given a particular

exposure compared to the odds of it happening without that exposure

`odds.n.ends`: an R package for computing model significance, odds ratios, and model fit following a logistic regression

omega-squared: an effect size for determining the strength of a relationship following an analysis of variance (ANOVA) statistical test, computed

$$\omega^2 = \frac{F-1}{F + \frac{n-k+1}{k-1}}$$, where F is the test

statistic from ANOVA, n is the sample size, and k is the number of groups

omnibus: a statistical test that identifies that there is some relationship going on between two categorical variables, but not what that relationship is

one-sample *t*-test: an inferential statistical test comparing the mean of a numeric variable to a population or hypothesized mean; the test statistic

is computed $t = \frac{m_x - \mu_x}{\frac{s_x}{\sqrt{n_x}}}$ where m_x is

the sample mean, μ_x is the population or hypothesized mean, s_x is the sample standard deviation, and n_x is the sample size

open source: software, data, or other tools and materials that are made freely available to be accessed and used by anyone

order of operations: the order in which mathematical operations should be performed when solving an equation: parentheses, exponents, multiplication, division, addition, and subtraction (PEMDAS)

ordinal: ordinal variables containing categories that have some logical order; for example, categories of age can logically be put in order from younger to older: 18–25, 26–39, 40–59, 60+

ordinary least squares: a method of estimating a linear regression model that finds the regression line by minimizing the squared differences between each data point and the regression line

outcome: the variable being explained or predicted by a model; in linear and logistic regression, the outcome variable is on the left-hand side of the equal sign

outlier: an observation with unusual values

output: when running code, the result that is displayed is the output

package: a collection of code and data for use in R that usually has a specific purpose, such as conducting a chi-squared analysis or conducting data management tasks

paired-samples *t*-test: an inferential test comparing two related means; another name for the dependent-samples *t*-test

pairwise comparison: comparisons between every pair of groups to identify which are statistically significantly different from one another following a statistically significant result in an analysis of variance (ANOVA) or other multigroup analysis

panes: the different parts of the main window in RStudio

parameter: a number that is a defining characteristic of some population or a feature of a population

partial correlation: a standardized measure of the amount of variance two variables share after accounting for variance they both share with a third variable

Partial-*F* test: a statistical test to see if two nested linear regression models are statistically significantly different from each other; this test is usually used to determine if a larger model accounts for enough additional variance to justify the complexity in interpretation that comes with including more variables in a model

Pascal case: a variation of the camel case object-naming format that capitalizes each word in an object name including the first word (also called "upper camel case"); for example, a function that squares a number and subtracts two could be SquareMinusTwo in Pascal case

Pearson's *r*: a statistic that indicates the strength and direction of the relationship between two numeric variables that meet certain assumptions

PEMDAS: an acronym for remembering the order of operations when solving mathematical formulas: parentheses, exponents, multiplication, division, addition, and subtraction

percent correctly predicted: a measure of model fit for a logistic regression model that is the proportion of the outcome values that were correctly predicted out of all observations modeled; this fit measure is sometimes referred to as the count R^2

and is computed $R^2_{count} = \frac{n_{correct}}{n_{total}}$

phi coefficient: an effect size to determine the strength of the relationship between two binary variables; often reported with the results of a chi-squared test and computed $\phi = \sqrt{\dfrac{\chi^2}{n}}$, where n is the sample size

pie chart: used to show parts of a whole; pie charts get their name from looking like a pie with pieces representing different groups, and they are not recommended for most situations because they can be difficult to interpret; pies, on the other hand, are recommended for dessert because they are delicious

planned comparisons: a statistical strategy for comparing different groups, often used after a statistically significant analysis of variance to test hypotheses about which group means are statistically significantly different from one another

platykurtic: a distribution of a numeric variable that has more observations in the tails than a normal distribution would have; platykurtic distributions often look flatter than a normal distribution

point chart: a chart that shows a summary value for a numeric variable, typically across groups; for example, a point chart could be used in place of a bar graph to show mean or median across groups

pooled variance: the assumption that the variances in two groups are equal, so it combines them

population: all the observations that fit some criterion; for example, all of the people currently living in the country of Bhutan or all of the people in the world currently eating strawberry ice cream

positive correlation: a statistical relationship where two things move together in the same direction; as one goes up, the other also goes up, or as one goes down, the other also goes down

positively skewed: a distribution with some extreme large positive values relative to the rest of the values in the distribution, making the tail of the distribution extend to the right or in the direction of larger positive numbers; this type of skew is also known as right skew

power transformation: transformation of a measure using an exponent like squaring or cubing or taking the square root or cube root; power transformations are nonlinear transformations

ppcor: an R package for conducting partial correlation analyses

predicted values: values of the outcome variable that were determined by substituting data for the independent variables into a regression model and computing the predicted value of the outcome

predictor: an independent variable on the right-hand side of the equal sign in a regression model; predictors are used to explain or predict the values of the outcome or dependent variable

probability density function: a probability distribution used to determine the probability of a numeric variable falling within a specified range of values

probability distribution: the numeric or visual representation of the set of probabilities that each value or range of values of a variable occurs

probability mass function: a function that computes the probability that an exact number of successes happens for a discrete random variable x, given the sample size (n) and probability of success (p), $f\left(x,n,p\right) = \binom{n}{x} p^x \left(1-p\right)^{n-x}$

product-moment: a term referring to the mean, or "moment," of some products (i.e., results of multiplication)

prolog: a set of comments at the top of a code file that provides information about what is in the file; it includes some or all of the following: Project name, Project purpose, Name(s) of data set(s) used in the project, Location(s) of data set(s) used in the project, Code author name, Date code created, Date last time code was edited

proportional odds ratios: odds ratios resulting from ordinal regression that represent the odds of being in a higher group or groups compared to being in all the lower groups with each one-unit increase in the predictor

p-value: the probability that the test statistic is at least as big as it is under the null hypothesis

Q-Q plot: a visualization of data using probabilities to show how closely a variable follows a normal distribution

qualvar: an R package for computing indices of qualitative variation which determine the extent to which observations are spread out among categories for nominal variables

questionable research practice: a research practice that introduces bias, usually in pursuit of statistical significance; an example of such practices might be

dropping or recoding values or variables solely to improve a model fit statistic

R package: a collection of code and data for use in R that usually has a specific purpose, such as conducting a chi-squared analysis or conducting data management tasks

range: the highest and lowest values of a variable, showing the full spread of values; the range can also be reported as a single number computed by taking the difference between the highest and lowest values of the variable

rcompanion: an R package that includes functions and data to go with *An R Companion for the Handbook of Biological Statistics* by Salvatore Mangiafico

readxl: an R package used to read files saved in Microsoft Excel formats with file extensions like xls and xlsx

recode: assigning a different value or label to one or more values of a variable; for example, a variable coded as 1 for alive and 2 for dead could be recoded as 1 for alive and 0 for dead

regression outlier: an observation that has an unusual value for the outcome given its value(s) of predictor(s)

rejection region: the area under the curve of a sampling distribution where the probability of obtaining a value is very small, often below 5%; the rejection region is in the end of the tail or tails of the distribution

representative sample: a sample of observations that has the characteristics of the population sampled

reproducible: given the same data and instructions or code for analysis, the results of analysis would be the same

residual: the difference between the observed value and the predicted value

RGB: stands for red-green-blue; RGB codes are six-character codes for specifying colors

right-skewed: a distribution of a numeric variable that has extreme large values in the right-hand-side tail of the distribution

R-Ladies: a global organization with the mission of increasing gender diversity in the R community (www.rladies.org)

RNHANES: an R package for directly accessing the online data files from the National Health and Nutrition Evaluation Survey (NHANES) conducted by the Centers for Disease Control and Prevention (CDC)

r-squared: the percent of variance in a numeric variable that is explained by one or more other variables; the r-squared (R^2) is also known as the coefficient of determination and is used as a measure of model fit in linear regression and an effect size in correlation analyses

sample: a subset of observations from some population that is often analyzed to learn about the population sampled

sample with replacement: taking a sample where each observation is returned to the pool of data being sampled after it is selected

sample without replacement: taking a sample where each observation is kept out of the pool of data being sampled after it is selected

sampling distribution: the distribution of summary statistics, like means, from repeated samples taken from a population

sav: the file extension for a data file saved in a format for the Statistical Package for Social Sciences (SPSS) statistical software

scales: an R package that can be used to change the scale of the axes in graphs so that they show percentages or other values

scatterplot: a graph that shows one dot for each observation in the data set

scientific notation: a way to display very large or very small numbers by multiplying the number by the value of 10 to some power to move the decimal to the left or right; for example, 1,430,000,000 could be displayed as 1.43×10^9 in scientific notation

Script file: a text file in R similar to something written in the Notepad text editor on a Windows computer or the TextEdit text editor on a Mac computer; it is saved with a .R file extension

semTools: an R package that supports the statistical activities related to structural equation modeling (SEM)

sensitivity: the percentage of "yes" values or 1s a logistic regression model got right

Shapiro-Wilk: a statistical test to determine or confirm whether a variable has a normal distribution; it is sensitive to small deviations from normality and not useful for sample sizes above 5,000 because it will nearly always find non-normality

sign test: a statistical test that compares the median of a variable to a hypothesized or population value; used in lieu of

the one-sample t-test when the t-test assumptions are not met

simple linear regression: a statistical model used to predict or explain a continuous outcome by a single predictor

skewed: distribution of a numeric variable that has more extreme values in one of the two tails of the distribution

skewness: the extent to which a variable has extreme values in one of the two tails of its distribution, computed as follows:

$$skewness_x = \frac{1}{n} \Sigma_{i=1}^{n} \left(\frac{x_i - m_x}{s_x} \right)^3$$

slope: the amount that y changes for every one-unit change in x in a linear regression model; visually, it is the steepness of a line representing the relationship between two variables

Source pane: the section of the RStudio window used for writing R commands

Spearman's rho: a statistical test used to examine the strength, direction, and significance of the relationship between two numeric variables when they do not meet the assumptions for Pearson's r

special variables: statistics computed from a data set; they are added to code using ..variable.. formatting

specificity: the percentage of "no" values or 0s a logistic regression model predicted correctly

spread: measures that indicate how much variation there is for a variable; different measures of spread are appropriate depending on the type of variable and its distribution

SPSS: Statistical Package for the Social Sciences, which is a statistical software program used to conduct statistical analysis

stacked bar chart: a data visualization that shows parts of a whole in a bar chart format; this type of chart can be used to examine two categorical variables together by showing the categories of one variable as the bars and the categories of the other variable as different colors within each bar

standard deviation: a measure of spread for numeric variables that approximates how far from the mean a typical value is; the standard deviation is the square root of the variance and is represented by σ in the population and s for a sample:

$$s_x = \sqrt{\frac{\Sigma_{i=1}^{n}(x_i - m_x)^2}{n-1}}$$

standard error: a measure of variability that estimates how much variability there

is in a population based on the variability in the sample and the size of the sample; the formula is $se = \frac{s}{\sqrt{n}}$ for numeric variables and $se_p = \sqrt{\frac{p(1-p)}{n}}$ for binary variables

standardized: transforming a measure so it is on a standard scale and can be compared to other measures or to some threshold value

standardized residuals: the standardized difference between observed and expected values in a chi-squared analysis; a large standardized residual indicates that the observed and expected values were very different

statistical inference: used to infer from the sample to the population; it is often impossible to collect information on every single person or organization, so scientists use samples of people or organizations to understand the population

statistical power: the probability that the results of a test are not a Type II error; it is the probability of finding a relationship when there is a relationship

statistically significant: the result of a statistical test that indicates the test statistic is unlikely to have been as large as it was if the null hypothesis were true

STEM: science, technology, engineering, and math, which is a set of disciplines often grouped together

stochastic: data that cannot be precisely predicted due to random variability

Student's t-test: an inferential statistical test for comparing the means of two groups when the variances are equal

summary statistics: used to provide an overview of the characteristics of a sample; this typically includes measures of central tendency and spread for numeric variables and the frequencies and percentages of factor variables

tableone: an R package for creating a table of descriptive or inferential statistics

tail: the values to the far right and far left of a distribution

tidyverse: a set of R packages for managing, exploring, and visualizing data

transform: adding, multiplying, or performing some other mathematical operation to change the values of a variable, often to normalize the distribution of the variable

trend line: a line that follows the relationship between variables in a graph, sometimes called the line of best fit

Tukey's Honestly Significant Difference: a post hoc test to determine which means are statistically significantly different from each other following a significant ANOVA result; Tukey's HSD compares each pair of means and so is considered a pairwise test, but it is less conservative than the Bonferroni post hoc test

two-way ANOVA: analysis of variance (ANOVA) with the means of a numeric variable compared across the categories of two categorical predictors

Type I error: rejecting the null hypothesis when it should be retained; also called alpha and used as the threshold to determine statistical significance

Type II error: retaining the null hypothesis when it should be rejected; also called beta

unexplained variance: variability in the outcome that is not explained by the predictor(s); the unexplained variability and explained variability are used in calculations for model significance and model fit

uniform distribution: a distribution of a numeric variable that has a constant value; the uniform distribution is sometimes called the rectangle distribution because it looks like a rectangle

variable: a measured characteristic of some entity (e.g., income, years of education, sex, height, blood pressure, smoking status, etc.); in data frames in R, the columns are variables that contain information about the observations (rows)

variance: a measure of spread for numeric variables that is essentially the average of the squared differences between each observation value on some variable and the mean for that variable with population variance represented by σ^2 and sample variance represented by s^2,

computed as follows: $s_x^2 = \dfrac{\sum_{i=1}^{n}\left(x_i - m_x\right)^2}{n-1}$

variance inflation factor: a statistic for determining whether there is problematic multicollinearity in a linear regression model

vector: a set of data elements saved as the same type (numeric, logical, etc.); each entry in a vector is called a member or component of the vector

Venn diagram: a visual display of data that shows overlap among groups

violin plot: a visual display of data that combines features of density plots and boxplots to show the distribution of numeric variables, often across groups

waffle: an R package for making waffle charts

waffle chart: a visual display of data that shows the parts of a whole similar to a pie chart; waffle charts are generally preferred over pie charts, but the author believes both actual pie and actual waffles are equally delicious

Wald test: the statistical test for comparing the value of the coefficient in linear or logistic regression to the hypothesized value of zero; the form is similar to a one-sample t-test, although some Wald tests use a t-statistic and others use a z-statistic as the test statistic

Welch's F-statistic: an alternate F-statistic used in analysis of variance when the assumption of homogeneity of variance is not met; the calculations for the Welch's

F-statistic use weights to calculate the group means and the grand mean

Welch's t-test: a variation on the Student's t-test that does not assume equal variances in groups

Wilcoxon rank sum test: synonym for the Mann-Whitney U test; an inferential test used to compare two groups when the normality assumption for a t-test is failed

Wilcoxon signed-ranks test: an alternative to the dependent-samples t-test when the continuous variable is not normally distributed; it uses ranks to determine whether the values of a numeric variable are different across two related groups

x-axis: the horizontal axis of a graph

xpt: a file extension indicating that the file is a transport file from the SAS (Statistical Analysis System) statistical software program

Yates continuity correction: a correction for chi-squared that subtracts .5 from the difference between observed and expected in each cell, making the chi-squared value smaller and statistical significance harder to reach; it is often used when there are few observations in one or more of the cells

y-axis: the vertical axis of a graph

y-intercept: the value of y when $x = 0$; the y-intercept is part of the linear regression model

z-score: the number of standard deviations an observation is away from the mean on some numeric variable, $z_i = \dfrac{x_i - m_x}{s_x}$, where x_i is the value of the variable x for person i, m_x is the mean of x, and s_x is the standard deviation of x

Altman, N., & Krzywinski, M. (2016). Analyzing outliers: Influential or nuisance? *Nature Methods, 13*, 281–282.

Anderson, C. J., Bahnik, S., Barnett-Cowan, M., Bosco, F. A., Chandler, J., Chartier, C. R., Cheung, F., et al. (2016). Response to comment on "estimating the reproducibility of psychological science." *Science, 351*(6277), 1037. https://doi .org/10.1126/science.aad9163

Andreason, S., Bozarth, A., DeRenzis, B., Johnson, M., Hirsch, R., & Pack, A. (2018). Building a skilled workforce for a stronger Southern economy. Retrieved from https://www.stlouisfed.org/~/media/files/ pdfs/community-development/southern_ states_report.pdf?la=en

Angell, T. (2019, January 28). Trump attorney general pick puts marijuana enforcement pledge in writing. Retrieved from https://www.forbes .com/sites/tomangell/2019/01/28/ trump-attorney-general-pick-puts- marijuana-enforcement-pledge-in- writing/#600f7a0b5435

Available CRAN packages by name. (n.d.). Retrieved from https://cran.r-project.org/ web/packages/available_packages_by_ name.html

Banks, G. C., Rogelberg, S. G., Woznyj, H. M., Landis, R. S., & Rupp, D. E. (2016). Editorial: Evidence on questionable research practices: The good, the bad, and the ugly. *Journal of Business and Psychology, 31*(3), 323–338.

Baral, S. D., Poteat, T., Strömdahl, S., Wirtz, A. L., Guadamuz, T. E., & Beyrer, C. (2013). Worldwide burden of HIV in transgender women: A systematic review and meta- analysis. *The Lancet Infectious Diseases, 13*(3), 214–222.

Barkley, J. E., & Lepp, A. (2016). Mobile phone use among college students is a sedentary leisure behavior which may interfere with exercise. *Computers in Human Behavior, 56*, 29–33.

Bazzi, A. R., Whorms, D. S., King, D. S., & Potter, J. (2015). Adherence to mammography screening guidelines among transgender persons and sexual minority women.

American Journal of Public Health, 105(11), 2356–2358.

Benotsch, E. G., Zimmerman, R., Cathers, L., McNulty, S., Pierce, J., Heck, T., . . . Snipes, D. (2013). Non-medical use of prescription drugs, polysubstance use, and mental health in transgender adults. *Drug and Alcohol Dependence, 132*(1–2), 391–394.

Best, D. J., & Roberts, D. E. (1975). The upper tail probabilities of Spearman's rho. *Journal of the Royal Statistical Society, Series C (Applied Statistics), 24*(3), 377–379.

Bjornsen, C. A., & Archer, K. J. (2015). Relations between college students' cell phone use during class and grades. *Scholarship of Teaching and Learning in Psychology, 1*(4), 326–336.

Blickenstaff, J. C. (2005). Women and science careers: Leaky pipeline or gender filter? *Gender and Education, 17*(4), 369–386.

Boehmer, U., Bowen, D. J., & Bauer, G. R. (2007). Overweight and obesity in sexual-minority women: Evidence from population-based data. *American Journal of Public Health, 97*(6), 1134–1140.

Bowler, S., Brunell, T., Donovan, T., & Gronke, P. (2015). Election administration and perceptions of fair elections. *Electoral Studies, 38*, 1–9.

Box, G. E. P., & Cox, D. R. (1964). An analysis of transformations. *Journal of the Royal Statistical Society: Series B (Methodological), 26*(2), 211–243.

Box, J. F. (1987). Guinness, Gosset, Fisher, and small samples. *Statistical Science, 2*(1), 45–52.

Bradford, J., Reisner, S. L., Honnold, J. A., & Xavier, J. (2013). Experiences of transgender-related discrimination and implications for health: Results from the Virginia Transgender Health Initiative Study. *American Journal of Public Health, 103*(10), 1820–1829.

Brasseur, L. (2005). Florence Nightingale's visual rhetoric in the rose diagrams. *Technical Communication Quarterly, 14*(2), 161–182.

C. (2010, July 29). Pie charts in ggplot2 [Blog post]. Retrieved from

https://www.r-bloggers.com/ pie-charts-in-ggplot2/

Cahir, J., & Lloyd, J. (2015). "People just don't care": Practices of text messaging in the presence of others. *Media, Culture & Society, 37*(5), 703–719.

Cals, J., & Winkens, B. (2018). The Student t-test is a beer test. *Nederlands Tijdschrift Voor Geneeskunde, 162*.

Camerer, C. F., Dreber, A., Forsell, E., Ho, T. H., Huber, J., Johannesson, M., Kirchler, M., et al. (2016). Evaluating replicability of laboratory experiments in economics. *Science, 351*(6280), 1433–1436. https:// doi.org/10.1126/science.aaf0918

Canary, L., Hariri, S., Campbell, C., Young, R., Whitcomb, J., Kaufman, H., & Vellozzi, C. (2017). Geographic disparities in access to syringe services programs among young persons with Hepatitis C virus infection in the United States. *Clinical Infectious Diseases, 65*(3), 514–517.

Centers for Disease Control and Prevention. (2015). Behavioral Risk Factor Surveillance System 2014 codebook report: Land-line and cell-phone data. Retrieved from https://www .cdc.gov/brfss/annual_data/2014/pdf/ CODEBOOK14_LLCP.pdf

Centers for Disease Control and Prevention. (2017). NHANES 2015–2016: Data documentation, codebook, and frequencies. Retrieved from https:// wwwn.cdc.gov/Nchs/Nhanes/2015-2016/ BPX_I.htm

Centers for Disease Control and Prevention. (n.d.). Transgender persons. Retrieved from https://www.cdc.gov/lgbthealth/ transgender.htm

Christensen, Rune Haubo Bojesen. 2019. "Ordinal Package." June 28, 2019. https://www.rdocumentation.org/ packages/ordinal/versions/2019.4-25

Cohen, B. H. (2008). *Explaining psychological statistics* (3rd ed.). Hoboken, NJ: Wiley.

Connelly, L. M. (2011). *t*-tests. *Medsurg Nursing, 20*(6), 341.

Connery, H. S. (2015). Medication-assisted treatment of opioid use disorder: Review of the evidence and future directions. *Harvard Review of Psychiatry*, *23*(2), 63–75.

CRAN Repository Policy. (n.d.). Retrieved from https://cran.r-project.org/web/packages/policies.html

Cribari-Neto, F., & Zeileis, A. (2010). Beta regression in R. *Journal of Statistical Software*, *34*(2), 1–24.

Daish, A., Frick, H., LeDell, E., de Queiroz, G., & Vitolo, C. (2019). R-Ladies Global. Retrieved from https://rladies.org/

Daniel, H., & Butkus, R. (2015). Lesbian, gay, bisexual, and transgender health disparities: Executive summary of a policy position paper from the American College of Physicians. *Annals of Internal Medicine*, *163*(2), 135–137.

Dasgupta, N., & Stout, J. G. (2014). Girls and women in science, technology, engineering, and mathematics: STEMing the tide and broadening participation in STEM careers. *Policy Insights From the Behavioral and Brain Sciences*, *1*(1), 21–29.

David, F. N. (1938). Tables of the correlation coefficient. In *Tables of the ordinates and probability integral of the distribution of the correlation coefficient in small samples (Biometrika Trust)* (pp. 44–59). Cambridge, UK: Cambridge University Press.

DeCarlo, L. T. (1997). On the meaning and use of kurtosis. *Psychological Methods*, *2*(3), 292–307.

Delacre, M., Lakens, D., & Leys, C. (2017). Why psychologists should by default use Welch's *t*-test instead of Student's *t*-test. *International Review of Social Psychology*, *30*(1), 92–101. doi: http://doi.org/10.5334/irsp.82

Devnarain, B., & Matthias, C. R. (2011). Poor access to water and sanitation: Consequences for girls at a rural school. *Agenda*, *25*(2), 27–34.

Digital divide in the United States. (n.d.). Retrieved from https://en.wikipedia.org/wiki/Digital_divide_in_the_United_States

Dowle, M., & Srinivasan, S. (2019, April 7). Data.table package documentation. Retrieved from https://cran.r-project.org/web/packages/data.table/data.table.pdf

Edelman, E. J., Gordon, K. S., Crothers, K., Akgün, K., Bryant, K. J., Becker, W. C., . . . Fiellin, D. A. (2019). Association of prescribed opioids with increased risk of community-acquired pneumonia among patients with and without HIV. *JAMA Internal Medicine*, *179*(3), 297–304.

Falk, R., & Well, A. D. (1997). Many faces of the correlation coefficient. *Journal of Statistics Education*, *5*(3). Retrieved from https://www.tandfonline.com/doi/full/10.1080/10691898.1997.11910597

Feir-Walsh, B. J., & Toothaker, L. E. (1974). An empirical comparison of the ANOVA *F*-test, normal scores test and Kruskal-Wallis test under violation of assumptions. *Educational and Psychological Measurement*, *34*(4), 789–799.

Ferrari, S., & Cribari-Neto, F. (2004). Beta regression for modelling rates and proportions. *Journal of Applied Statistics*, *31*(7), 799–815.

Field, A. (2013). *Discovering statistics using IBM SPSS statistics* (4th ed.). London: Sage.

Frisone, C. (2017, May 27). WASH in schools: Female hygiene management—Bahati School, Temeke District, Dar Es Salaam. Retrieved from https://www.unicef.org/tanzania/stories/wash-schools

Fritz, C. O., & Morris, P. E. (2018). Effect size. In B. B. Frey (Ed.), *Encyclopedia of educational research, measurement, and evaluation* (pp. 576–578). Thousand Oaks, CA: Sage.

Fritz, C. O., Morris, P. E., & Richler, J. J. (2012). Effect size estimates: Current use, calculations, and interpretation. *Journal of Experimental Psychology: General*, *141*(1), 2–18.

García-Berthou, E., & Alcaraz, C. (2004). Incongruence between test statistics and *p* values in medical papers. *BMC Medical Research Methodology*, *4*(13). Retrieved from https://bmcmedresmethodol.biomedcentral.com/articles/10.1186/1471-2288-4-13

Garner, R. (2010). *The joy of stats: A short guide to introductory statistics in the social sciences*. Toronto: University of Toronto Press.

Giffords Law Center. (n.d.). Statistics on gun deaths & injuries. Retrieved from https://lawcenter.giffords.org/gun-deaths-and-injuries-statistics/

Golden, M. R., Lechtenberg, R., Glick, S. N., Dombrowski, J., Duchin, J., Reuer, J. R., . . . Buskin, S. E. (2019, April 19). Outbreak of human immunodeficiency virus infection among heterosexual persons who are living homeless and inject drugs—Seattle, Washington, 2018. *Morbidity and Mortality Weekly Report*, *68*(15), 344–349.

Goodlatte, R., Armey, R., & Tiahrt, T. (1999). Send the right message to our children: Just say NO to free needles for drug addicts [Letter to the U.S. Congress]. Washington, DC: Congress of the United States of America.

Google's R style guide. (n.d.). Retrieved from https://google.github.io/styleguide/Rguide.xml

Gosselin, R.-D. (n.d.). Open letter to scientific journals. Retrieved from http://en.biotelligences.com/open-letter.html

Gravetter, F. J., & Wallnau, L. B. (2009). *Statistics for behavioral sciences* (8th ed.). Belmont, CA: Wadsworth.

Haegerich, T. M., Paulozzi, L. J., Manns, B. J., & Jones, C. M. (2014). What we know, and don't know, about the impact of state policy and systems-level interventions on prescription drug overdose. *Drug and Alcohol Dependence*, *145*, 34–47. https://doi.org/10.1016/j.drugalcdep.2014.10.001

Hardin, J. W., & Hilbe, J. M. (2007). *Generalized linear models and extensions*. College Station, TX: Stata Press.

Harris, J., Johnson, K., Carothers, B., Wang, X., Coombs, T., & Luke, D. (2019, January 25). Module 1. Retrieved from https://coding2share.github.io/ReproducibilityToolkit/

Harris, J. K., Wondmeneh, S. B., Zhao, Y., & Leider, J. P. (2019). Examining the reproducibility of 6 published studies in public health services and systems research. *Journal of Public Health Management Practices*, *25*(2), 128–136.

Hartung, D. M., Kim, H., Ahmed, S. M., Middleton, L., Keast, S., Deyo, R. A., . . . McConnell, K. J. (2018). Effect of a high dosage opioid prior authorization policy on prescription opioid use, misuse, and overdose outcomes. *Substance Abuse*, *39*(2), 239–246.

Harwell, M. R., & Serlin, R. C. (1994). A Monte Carlo study of the Friedman test and some competitors in the single factor, repeated measures design with unequal covariances. *Computational Statistics & Data Analysis*, *17*(1), 35–49.

Herrmann, S. D., Adelman, R. M., Bodford, J. E., Graudejus, O., Okun, M. A., & Kwan, V.S.Y. (2016). The effects of a female role model on academic performance and persistence of women in STEM courses. *Basic and Applied Social Psychology*, *38*(5), 258–268.

Horrigan, J. B. (2016). Libraries 2016. Retrieved from https://www.pewinternet.org/wp-content/uploads/sites/9/2016/09/PI_2016.09.09_Libraries-2016_FINAL.pdf

Institute of Medicine. (2001). *Clearing the smoke: Assessing the science base for tobacco harm reduction*. Washington, DC: National Academies Press.

Jackson, S. (2016, August 23). Visualising residuals [Blog post]. Retrieved from https://drsimonj.svbtle.com/visualising-residuals

Jaeger, P. T., Bertot, J. C., McClure, C. R., & Langa, L. A. (2006). The policy implications of Internet connectivity in public libraries. *Government Information Quarterly*, *23*(1), 123–141.

Johnson, D. R. (2011). Women of color in science, technology, engineering, and mathematics (STEM). *New Directions for Institutional Research*, *2011*(152), 75–85.

Kahn, S., & Ginther, D. (2017). Women and STEM. NBER Working Paper No. w23525. Retrieved from https://papers.ssrn.com/sol3/papers.cfm?abstract_id=2988746

Kane, J. V. (2017). Why can't we agree on ID? Partisanship, perceptions of fraud, and public support for voter identification laws. *Public Opinion Quarterly*, *81*(4), 943–955.

Keller, J. (2007). Stereotype threat in classroom settings: The interactive effect of domain identification, task difficulty and stereotype threat on female students' maths performance. *British Journal of Educational Psychology*, *77*(2), 323–338.

Kellermann, A. L., & Rivara, F. P. (2013). Silencing the science on gun research. *JAMA*, *309*(6), 549–550.

Khan, N., & Carson, C. (2012, August 12). Comprehensive database of U.S. voter fraud uncovers no evidence that photo ID is needed. Retrieved from https://votingrights.news21.com/article/election-fraud/

Kim, H.-Y. (2013). Statistical notes for clinical researchers: Assessing normal distribution (2) using skewness and kurtosis. *Restorative Dentistry & Endodontics*, *38*(1), 52–54.

Kim, H.-Y. (2017). Statistical notes for clinical researchers: Chi-squared test and Fisher's exact test. *Restorative Dentistry & Endodontics*, *42*(2), 152–155.

Krishnaswamy, G., & Marinova, D. (2012). FOSS in education: IT@School project, Kerala, India. *Journal of Free Software & Free Knowledge*, *1*(1). Retrieved from https://pdfs.semanticscholar.org/5c66/f4703de485f6d9bc877090c5f37909da4fba.pdf

Lane, D., Beevers, M., Barnes, N., Bourne, J., John, A., Malins, S., & Beevers, D. G. (2002). Inter-arm differences in blood pressure: When are they clinically significant? *Journal of Hypertension*, *20*(6), 1089–1095.

Lepp, A., Barkley, J. E., & Karpinski, A. C. (2014). The relationship between cell phone use, academic performance, anxiety, and satisfaction with life in college students. *Computers in Human Behavior*, *31*, 343–350.

Lepp, A., Barkley, J. E., & Karpinski, A. C. (2015). The relationship between cell phone use and academic performance

in a sample of U.S. college students. *SAGE Open*, *5*(1). Retrieved from https://journals.sagepub.com/doi/full/10.1177/2158244015573169

Levitt, J. (2014, August 6). A comprehensive investigation of voter impersonation finds 31 credible incidents out of one billion ballots cast. *Washington Post*. Retrieved from http://www.washingtonpost.com/blogs/wonkblog/wp/2014/08/06/a-comprehensive-investigation-of-voter-impersonation-finds-31-credible-incidents-out-of-one-billion-ballots-cast/

Lix, L. M., Keselman, J. C., & Keselman, H. J. (1996). Consequences of assumption violations revisited: A quantitative review of alternatives to the one-way analysis of variance *F* test. *Review of Educational Research*, *66*(4), 579–619.

Lombardi, E. (2010). Transgender health: A review and guidance for future research—Proceedings from the Summer Institute at the Center for Research on Health and Sexual Orientation, University of Pittsburgh. *International Journal of Transgenderism*, *12*(4), 211–229.

MacFarland, T. W., & Yates, J. M. 2016. Friedman twoway analysis of variance (ANOVA) by ranks. In *Introduction to nonparametric statistics for the biological sciences using R* (pp. 213–247). New York: Springer.

Manikandan, S. (2010). Data transformation. *Journal of Pharmacology and Pharmacotherapeutics*, *1*(2), 126–127.

Mayer, K. H., Bradford, J. B., Makadon, H. J., Stall, R., Goldhammer, H., & Landers, S. (2008). Sexual and gender minority health: What we know and what needs to be done. *American Journal of Public Health*, *98*(6), 989–995.

Mays, M. Z., & Melnyk, B. M. (2009). A call for the reporting of effect sizes in research reports to enhance critical appraisal and evidence-based practice. *Worldviews on Evidence-Based Nursing*, *6*(3), 125–129.

McCrum-Gardner, E. (2008). Which is the correct statistical test to use? *British Journal of Oral and Maxillofacial Surgery*, *46*(1), 38–41.

McHugh, M. L. (2013). The chi-square test of independence. *Biochemia Medica*, *23*(2), 143–149.

Meyer, I. H., Brown, T. N. T., Herman, J. L., Reisner, S. L., & Bockting, W. O. (2017). Demographic characteristics and health status of transgender adults in select U.S. regions: Behavioral Risk Factor Surveillance System, 2014. *American Journal of Public Health*, *107*(4), 582–589.

Minnite, L. C. (2017). *The myth of voter fraud*. Ithaca, NY: Cornell University Press.

Muenchen, R. A. (2019). The popularity of data science software. Retrieved from http://r4stats.com/articles/popularity/

Mukaka, M. M. (2012). A guide to appropriate use of correlation coefficient in medical research. *Malawi Medical Journal*, *24*(3), 69–71.

Narayan, A., Lebron-Zapata, L., & Morris, E. (2017). Breast cancer screening in transgender patients: Findings from the 2014 BRFSS survey. *Breast Cancer Research and Treatment*, *166*(3), 875–879.

National Opinion Research Center. (2019). *General Social Surveys, 1972–2018 cumulative codebook*. Retrieved from http://gss.norc.org/documents/codebook/GSS_Codebook.pdf

New voting restrictions in America. (n.d.). Retrieved from https://www.brennancenter.org/new-voting-restrictions-america

Norris, C. M., Ghali, W. A., Saunders, L. D., Brant, R., Galbraith, D., Faris, P., & Knudtson, M. L. (2006). Ordinal regression model and the linear regression model were superior to the logistic regression models. *Journal of Clinical Epidemiology*, *59*(5), 448–456.

Nuijten, M. B., Hartgerink, C. H. J., Assen, M. A. L. M., Epskamp, S., & Wicherts, J. M. (2015). The prevalence of statistical reporting errors in psychology (1985–2013). *Behavior Research Methods*, *48*(4), 1205–1226.

Omnibus Consolidated Appropriations Act of 1997, Pub. L. 104-208. 110 Stat. 3009. Retrieved from https://www.govinfo.gov/content/pkg/PLAW-104publ208/pdf/PLAW-104publ208.pdf

Open Science Collaboration. (2015). Estimating the reproducibility of psychological science. *Science*, *349*(6251), aac4716. https://doi.org/10.1126/science.aac4716

Osborne, J. (2002). Notes on the use of data transformations. *Practical Assessment, Research & Evaluation*, *8*(6). Retrieved from https://pareonline.net/getvn.asp?v=8&n=6

Peng, C.Y.J., Kuk, L. L., & Ingersoll, G. M. (2002). An introduction to logistic regression analysis and reporting. *Journal of Educational Research*, *96*(1), 3–14.

Peters, P. J., Pontones, P., Hoover, K. W., Patel, M. R., Galang, R. R., Shields, J., . . . Duwve, J. M. 2016. HIV infection linked to injection use of oxymorphone in Indiana, 2014–2015. *New England Journal of Medicine*, *375*(3), 229–239.

Prinz, F., Schlange, T., & Asadullah, K. (2011). Believe it or not: How much can we rely on published data on potential drug targets? *Nature Reviews Drug Discovery, 10*(9), 712.

Public supports aim of making it "easy" for all citizens to vote. (2017, June 28). Retrieved from https://www.people-press .org/2017/06/28/public-supports-aim-of-making-it-easy-for-all-citizens-to-vote/

Puth, M.-T., Neuhäuser, M., & Ruxton, G. D. (2014). Effective use of Pearson's product–moment correlation coefficient. *Animal Behaviour, 93*, 183–189.

Reisner, S. L., Poteat, T., Keatley, J., Cabral, M., Mothopeng, T., Dunham, E., . . . Baral, S. D. (2016). Global health burden and needs of transgender populations: A review. *The Lancet, 388*(10042), 412–436.

Rogers, D. E., & Osborn, J. E. (1993). AIDS policy: Two divisive issues. *JAMA, 270*(4), 494–495.

Rosen, L., Carrier, L. M., Miller, A., Rokkum, J., & Ruiz, A. (2016). Sleeping with technology: Cognitive, affective, and technology usage predictors of sleep problems among college students. *Sleep Health, 2*(1), 49–56.

Rubin, R. (2016). Tale of 2 agencies: CDC avoids gun violence research but NIH funds it. *JAMA, 315*(16), 1689–1692.

Safer, J. D., Coleman, E., Feldman, J., Garofalo, R., Hembree, W., Radix, A., & Sevelius, J. (2016). Barriers to health care for transgender individuals. *Current Opinion in Endocrinology, Diabetes, and Obesity, 23*(2), 168–171.

Salkind, N. J. (Ed.). (2010). *Encyclopedia of research design* (Vol. 3). Thousand Oaks, CA: Sage.

Santos, G.-M., Rapues, J., Wilson, E. C., Macias, O., Packer, T., Colfax, G., & Raymond, H. F. (2014). Alcohol and substance use among transgender women in San Francisco: Prevalence and association with human immunodeficiency virus infection. *Drug and Alcohol Review, 33*(3), 287–295.

Scales, A. (2018, April 5). CDC joins Department of Public Health in investigating HIV cluster among people who inject drugs [Press release]. Retrieved from https://www.mass.gov/news/cdc-joins-department-of-public-health-in-investigating-hiv-cluster-among-people-who-inject

Schechter, M. T., Strathdee, S. A., Cornelisse, P. G., Currie, S., Patrick, D. M., Rekart, M. L., & O'Shaughnessy, M. V. (1999). Do needle exchange programmes increase the spread of HIV among injection drug users? An investigation of the Vancouver outbreak. *AIDS, 13*(6), F45–F51.

Schmid, M., Wickler, F., Maloney, K. O., Mitchell, R., Fenske, N., & Mayr, A. (2013). Boosted beta regression. *PloS ONE, 8*(4), e61623.

Schranz, A. J., Fleischauer, A., Chu, V. H., Wu, L.-T., & Rosen, D. L. (2019). Trends in drug use-associated infective endocarditis and heart valve surgery, 2007 to 2017: A study of statewide discharge data. *Annals of Internal Medicine, 170*(1), 31–40.

Sin, S.-C. J. (2011). Neighborhood disparities in access to information resources: Measuring and mapping U.S. public libraries' funding and service landscapes. *Library & Information Science Research, 33*(1), 41–53.

Skidmore, S. T., & Thompson, B. (2013). Bias and precision of some classical ANOVA effect sizes when assumptions are violated. *Behavior Research Methods, 45*(2), 536–546.

Smith, A. (2015). Searching for work in the digital era. Retrieved from https://www .pewresearch.org/wp-content/uploads/ sites/9/2015/11/PI_2015-11-19-Internet-and-Job-Seeking_FINAL.pdf

Smith, V. K., Gifford, K., Ellis, E., Edwards, B., Rudowitz, R., Hinton, E., . . . Valentine, A. (2016). Implementing coverage and payment initiatives: Results from a 50-state Medicaid budget survey for state fiscal years 2016 and 2017. Retrieved from https://www.kff.org/report-section/ implementing-coverage-and-payment-initiatives-benefits-and-pharmacy/

Smith, V. M., Siegel, M., Xuan, Z., Ross, C. S., Galea, S., Kalesan, B., . . . Goss, K. A. (2017). Broadening the perspective on gun violence: An examination of the firearms industry, 1990–2015. *American Journal of Preventive Medicine, 53*(5), 584–591.

Sommer, M. (2010). Where the education system and women's bodies collide: The social and health impact of girls' experiences of menstruation and schooling in Tanzania. *Journal of Adolescence, 33*(4), 521–529.

Spencer, S. J., Steele, C. M., & Quinn, D. M. (1999). Stereotype threat and women's math performance. *Journal of Experimental Social Psychology, 35*(1), 4–28.

Stanton, J. M. (2001). Galton, Pearson, and the peas: A brief history of linear regression for statistics instructors. *Journal of Statistics Education, 9*(3). Retrieved from https://doi.org/10.1080/10691898.2001 .11910537

Stark, D. E., & Shah, N. H. (2017). Funding and publication of research on gun violence and other leading causes of death. *JAMA, 317*(1), 84–85.

Steen, R. G., Casadevall, A., & Fang, F. C. (2013). Why has the number of scientific retractions increased? *PloS One, 8*(7), e68397.

Stewart, C., III, Ansolabehere, S., & Persily, N. (2016). Revisiting public opinion on voter identification and voter fraud in an era of increasing partisan polarization. *Stanford Law Review, 68*(6), 1455–1489.

Stoltzfus, J. C. (2011). Logistic regression: A brief primer. *Academic Emergency Medicine, 18*(10), 1099–1104.

Sullivan, G. M., & Feinn, R. (2012). Using effect size—or why the *p* value is not enough. *Journal of Graduate Medical Education, 4*(3), 279–282.

Sullivan, J. L. (2011). Free, open source software advocacy as a social justice movement: The expansion of F/OSS movement discourse in the 21st century. *Journal of Information Technology & Politics, 8*(3), 223–239.

Susmann, H. (2016). Introduction to RNHANES. Retrieved from https://cran.r-project .org/web/packages/RNHANES/vignettes/ introduction.html

Szumilas, M. (2010). Explaining odds ratios. *Journal of the Canadian Academy of Child and Adolescent Psychiatry, 19*(3), 227–229.

Teshale, E. H., Asher, A., Aslam, M. V., Augustine, R., Duncan, E., Rose-Wood, A., . . . Dietz, P. M. (2019). Estimated cost of comprehensive syringe service program in the United States. *PloS ONE, 14*(4), e0216205.

Thomée, S., Härenstam, A., & Hagberg, M. (2011). Mobile phone use and stress, sleep disturbances, and symptoms of depression among young adults—a prospective cohort study. *BMC Public Health, 11*. Retrieved from https:// bmcpublichealth.biomedcentral.com/ articles/10.1186/1471-2458-11-66

Thompson, J. A., Folifac, F., & Gaskin, S. J. (2011). Fetching water in the unholy hours of the night: The impacts of a water crisis on girls' sexual health in semi-urban Cameroon. *Girlhood Studies, 4*(2), 111–129.

Timeline of cannabis laws in the United States. (n.d.). Retrieved from https://en.wikipedia .org/wiki/Timeline_of_cannabis_laws_in_ the_United_States

Tookes, H. E., Kral, A. H., Wenger, L. D., Cardenas, G. A., Martinez, A. N., Sherman, R. L., . . . Metsch, L. R. (2012). A comparison of syringe disposal practices among injection drug users in a city with versus a city without needle and syringe programs. *Drug and Alcohol Dependence, 123*(1–3), 255–259.

Tukey, J. W. (1977). *Exploratory data analysis.* Reading, MA: Addison-Wesley.

UNESCO Institute for Statistics. (n.d.). Education: Out-of-school children of primary school age, both sexes (number)—2015. Retrieved from http://data.uis.unesco.org/Index.aspx?DataSetCode=edulit_ds

Upton, G., & Cook, I. (2014). *A dictionary of statistics* (3rd ed.). Oxford, UK: Oxford University Press.

Van Hecke, T. (2012). Power study of ANOVA versus Kruskal-Wallis test. *Journal of Statistics and Management Systems*, *15*(2–3), 241–247.

Virupaksha, H. G., Muralidhar, D., & Ramakrishna, J. (2016). Suicide and suicidal behavior among transgender persons. *Indian Journal of Psychological Medicine*, *38*(6), 505–509.

Volkow, N. D., Frieden, T. R., Hyde, P. S., & Cha, S. S. (2014). Medication-assisted therapies—Tackling the opioid-overdose epidemic. *New England Journal of Medicine*, *370*(22), 2063–2066.

von Hippel, P. T. (2005). Mean, median, and skew: Correcting a textbook rule. *Journal of Statistics Education*, *13*(2). Retrieved from http://jse.amstat.org/v13n2/vonhippel.html

Warrington, M., & Kiragu, S. (2012). "It makes more sense to educate a boy": Girls "against the odds" in Kajiado, Kenya. *International Journal of Educational Development*, *32*(2), 301–309.

Warton, D. I., & Hui, F.K.C. (2011). The arcsine is asinine: The analysis of proportions in ecology. *Ecology*, *92*(1), 3–10.

Westfall, P. H. (2004). Kurtosis as peakedness, 1905–2014. R.I.P. *American Statistician*, *68*(3), 191–195.

World Health Organization. (2019). Gender. Retrieved from https://www.who.int/gender-equity-rights/understanding/gender-definition/en/

World Health Organization. (n.d.). Global Health Observatory data repository. Retrieved from http://apps.who.int/gho/data/?theme=main

Wickham, H., Chang, W., Henry, L., Pedersen, T. L., Takahashi, K., Wilke, C., . . . Yutani, H. (n.d.). Sequential, diverging and qualitative colour scales from colorbrewer.org. Retrieved from https://ggplot2.tidyverse.org/reference/scale_brewer.html#palettes

Wilcoxon, F. (1945). Individual comparisons by ranking methods. *Biometrics Bulletin*, *1*(6), 80–83.

Wilke, C. O. (2019). *Fundamentals of data visualization: A primer on making informative and compelling figures*. Retrieved from https://serialmentor.com/dataviz/

Wilson, D. C., & Brewer, P. R. (2013). The foundations of public opinion on voter ID laws: Political predispositions, racial resentment, and information effects. *Public Opinion Quarterly*, *77*(4), 962–984.

Wilson, R. (2018, January 22). Vermont governor signs marijuana legalization bill. Retrieved from https://thehill.com/homenews/state-watch/370139-vermont-governor-signs-marijuana-legalization-bill

Wolak, J. (2014). How campaigns promote the legitimacy of elections. *Electoral Studies*, *34*, 205–215.

Wood, E., Kerr, T., Small, W., Li, K., Marsh, D. C., Montaner, J.S.G., & Tyndall, M. W. (2004). Changes in public order after the opening of a medically supervised safer injecting facility for illicit injection drug users. *Canadian Medical Association Journal*, *171*(7), 731–734.

Xiao, N., & Li, M. (2019). Scientific journal and sci-fi themed color palettes for ggplot2. Retrieved from https://nanx.me/ggsci/articles/ggsci.html

Yoshida, K. (n.d.). What is tableone? Retrieved from https://cran.r-project.org/web/packages/tableone/vignettes/introduction.html

Zhao, L., Chen, Y., & Schaffner, D. W. (2001). Comparison of logistic regression and linear regression in modeling percentage data. *Applied and Environmental Microbiology*, *67*(5), 2129–2135.

Zimmerman, D. W., & Zumbo, B. D. (1993). Relative power of the Wilcoxon test, the Friedman test, and repeated-measures ANOVA on ranks. *Journal of Experimental Education*, *62*(1), 75–86.

Zou, K. H., Tuncali, K., & Silverman, S. G. (2003). Correlation and simple linear regression. *Radiology*, *227*(3), 617–622.